BRITISH • HIT
ALBUMS

THE GUINNESS BOOK OF

BRITISH • HIT ALBUMS

PAUL GAMBACCINI • TIM RICE • JO RICE

Acknowledgements: Cover Artwork: Julia King and Peter Harper. (Our thanks to those record companies who supplied reference for the following artists' albums: Grateful Dead, Stevie Wonder, The Beatles, Fleetwood Mac, Elvis Costello, U2, Genesis, Dire Straits and Virgin's *Now That's What I Call Music* collection.)
    Also, our thanks to the many record company press officers for their patient help; Syndication International, London Features International and Popperfoto for photographs; *Melody Maker* and *Music Week*, and John English for his editorial help.

Editor: Honor Head
Art Editor: David Roberts
Picture Editor: Alex Goldberg
GRR Editorial Associate: Tony Brown

First edition 1983, reprinted once
Second edition 1986
Third edition 1988

Published in Great Britain by Guinness Publishing Ltd,
33 London Road, Enfield, Middlesex

Typeset in Bembo by Ace Filmsetting Ltd, Frome, Somerset
Printed and bound in Great Britain by Adlard & Son Ltd, Letchworth, Herts.

'Guinness' is a registered trade mark of Guinness Superlatives Ltd

British Library Cataloguing in Publication Data
Gambaccini, Paul
    The Guinness book of British hit albums.—3rd ed.
    1. Pop music. Long playing sound discs, to 1987– Discographies
    I. Title   II. Rice, Tim   III. Rice, Jo   IV. Guinness British hit albums
    016.7899′12
    ISBN 0-85112-888-2

THE AUTHORS

When **PAUL GAMBACCINI** enrolled at Dartmouth College in New Hampshire the number one album was *Revolver*. When he first came to Britain *Bridge Over Troubled Water* was chart champ. *Goat's Head's Soup* led the list when he first appeared on Radio One while an Oxford student, and *Diamond Dogs* was the best seller when he reached his exams. When *The Guinness Book of British Hit Singles* first reached number one *The Official BBC Album of the Royal Wedding* topped the table. The Beatles, Simon and Garfunkel, the Rolling Stones, David Bowie, Charles and Diana . . . these are among his favourite album artists.

JO RICE lost two windows and half his roof (and gained a tree horizontally from next door) in the storm of 16 October 1987, but fortunately his album collection was untouched. Repairs have progressed slowly over the subsequent months, partly because there is a serious shortage of glass and tiles in East Kent, and partly because the roofers and glaziers seem to take longer tea breaks when listening to gems of his collection like *Savage*, *Graceland* and *Tango In The Night*, not to mention old favourites like *A Date With Elvis* and *Tea For The Tillerman*. It's an ill wind that blows no good.

TIM RICE first ventured into the world of 33 r.p.m. when he purchased *Elvis' Golden Records* (the original release that contained an 8-page colour booklet) and Duane Eddy's *Have Twangy Guitar Will Travel* in late 1959, for personal reasons. He now purchases with total lack of discrimination every album that hits the UK Top 100 for historical reasons. He plays most of them and enjoys about half of what he hears. In his opinion the quality of the UK singles chart in the first months of 1988 makes this edition of the album survey the most essential purchase yet.

INTRODUCTION

The Guinness Book of British Hit Albums is now three, and how this younger sibling of *Hit Singles* is growing! The first and very obvious way is that this third edition follows the second by only two years, whereas the second arrived at booksellers three years after the original. The shorter interval is due to the support of fine readers like yourself, who have demanded a biennial frequency to fill the years between editions of *Hit Singles*.

The second and equally evident way this title is growing is in its sheer size. When we issued the first volume in 1983 British album charts had only been going for a quarter of a century. The five years since represent a full 20% more charts to cover. There is an even more substantial increase in the percentage of albums in the charts during this period, since the Top 100 is far longer than the Top 10s, 20s and 40s printed in earlier years. If it seems to you there are more entries in this book from the 1980s than the 1960s, you are not hallucinating.

The third and perhaps most portentous way in which this book is growing is in its significance. During the two years since our last meeting the record market in the UK, as in the other major markets of the world, has been characterized by rises in LP purchases and falls in singles sales. The new technologies of the Eighties have all favoured the long player: cassette sales have increased and compact disc purchases have soared. The introduction of Digital Audio Tape, whenever and however it arrives, can only encourage listeners further to buy longer works.

It is not that singles cannot be issued on CD or cassette. Many labels have tried this approach as a sales stimulus, but at least at time of publication these efforts have merely had the minor impact that coloured vinyl and picture discs did in the late 1970s. The last technical innovation that greatly benefited singles revenue was the 12-inch single.

Our past reports indicated how cassette and CD were making inroads into black vinyl's traditional majority share of the LP market. In the period October 1986 to September 1987 cassettes accounted for 51.7% of unit sales. CDs had gone above 10% to 10.7% and black vinyl had fallen to 37.6%. With their higher price CDs were taking 22.1% of LP revenue. Total unit sales were up 19% at a new record high of 140.9 million.

The popularity of the CD increased not only as more consumers became convinced of its finer fidelity but as they actually purchased their own systems. The introduction of back catalogue items onto CD caused a phenomenon unseen since stereo joined mono in the marketplace: listeners literally replaced perfectly good pieces in their collection with the new versions, a boon for record companies searching for a saleable product. In some cases this trend has affected our listings. Classic albums have extended their already lengthy stays on the chart. Long-awaited CD issues of the Beatles' works brought many of them back after an absence of two decades, and the twentieth anniversary of *Sergeant Pepper's Lonely Hearts Club Band* resulted in a sentimental journey back to the top three.

Record company marketing philosophy has also made the album more important. Lost in the haze of antiquity is the time when hit singles preceded the albums that collected them. Gone, at least temporarily, are the more recent days when only two or three singles were taken off successful albums. After Michael Jackson lifted six hit singles off *Thriller* (seven in the US), bosses realized there was gold in them thar grooves. Hit LPs have recently been mined to the extent of five or more singles.

Airplay for a single off an album is free advertising for the LP as well as a boon for the song in question. Companies have been loath to pass up that free exposure until the singles start faltering. Consequently Genesis, who began their existence as the virtual antithesis of a singles act, found themselves with five releases off *Invisible Touch*. The constant publicity kept the album in the chart longer than any of their previous works. So it is with many of the leading acts of the Eighties. You will find in their individual tables that recent albums, their lives prolonged by lengthy singles programmes, are their longest runners.

The rich get richer, and in the last few years this has proved true in the UK album charts. The young adult consumer who buys albums rather than singles, often on CD and frequently for background rather than foreground listening, recently received a good deal of attention. This buyer was not a media invention but a demographic target at which the music industry aimed. Almost unprecedented television campaigns promoted albums that were already months and in some cases over a year old. Labels knew these discs had proved themselves with this substantial market and that with a little reminding other members of the population group, who do not rush out and buy records immediately upon release, would purchase in still larger numbers. Copies of *Brothers In Arms* and *Graceland*, for example, became the audio analogue of coffee table books. Their great musical virtues aside, they became cultural icons of the young and well-off, and their sales boomed accordingly.

Albums in this latter category proved the current importance of the LP. Not since the Sixties, when new LPs by luminaries like the Beatles, Rolling Stones and Bob Dylan were awaited like messages from mission control, have albums been so predominant in the popular consciousness. 'Have you heard the new Whitney Houston?' means 'Have you heard *Whitney*?', not 'Have you heard *Didn't We Almost Have It All?*'. An allusion to 'the new Michael Jackson' refers to *Bad* the album, not the single. Although the prime memory marker for individuals, and the chief source of exposure for artists, will continue to be the single song, in whatever configuration it is sold, the LP is both the main moneymaker for record companies and a cultural event for consumers. This is a healthy environment in which *Hit Albums* will grow.

Happy reading and good listening. If you've read this far without buying the book, you've missed your train.

THE CHARTS

If ever a week went by without a chart being compiled, the previous week's chart was used again for the purposes of all the statistics and information in this book. The dates used throughout correspond to the Saturday ending the week in which the chart was published.

The charts used in compiling this book are:

8 Nov 58 First album chart published by *Melody Maker*. It is a Top 10.

27 Jun 59 Newspaper strike. No chart published until 8 August, so the 20 Jun chart is repeated throughout.

26 Mar 60 First *Record Retailer* chart published, a Top 20. We have taken our information from the *Record Retailer* from this date onward, although the *Melody Maker* chart continued.

14 Apr 66 Chart becomes a Top 30.

8 Dec 66 Chart becomes a Top 40.

12 Feb 69 Chart drops back to a Top 15.

8 Mar 69 Incorrect chart published. Correct chart calculated by backtracking from the following week's listings.

11 Jun 69 Chart becomes a Top 20 again.

25 Jun 69 Chart becomes a Top 40 again.

9 Aug 69 Chart is a Top 32 (!) for this one week only.

11 Oct 69 Chart drops back to a Top 25.

8 Nov 69 Chart varies from a Top 20 to a Top 24 until 24 Jan '70.

31 Jan 70 Chart lists between 47 and 77 albums each week until 9 Jan '71.

9 Jan 71 *Record Retailer* became *Record And Tape Retailer*.

16 Jan 71 Chart stabilizes as a Top 50.

6 Feb 71 Postal strike means no chart published until 3 Apr '71. 30 Jan chart repeated throughout.

7 Aug 71 *Record And Tape Retailer* combine their Full Price chart (the one we've been using) with their previously separate Budget chart. This means there is a sudden influx of budget label albums into the chart.

8 Jan 72 The chart reverts to Full Price albums only, so the budget albums disappear as quickly as they appeared.

18 Mar 72 *Record and Tape Retailer* becomes *Music Week*.

13 Jan 73 Chart is a Top 24 for this week only.

5 Jan 74 Chart is a Top 42 for this week only.

5 Jul 75 Chart becomes a Top 60.

14 Jan 78 Chart is a Top 30 for this week only.

2 Dec 78 Chart becomes a Top 75.

13 Oct 79 Two consecutive weeks' charts published simultaneously as a result of a speedy new chart compilation system which enabled *Music Week* to catch up a week. Until this date, the publication of the chart had been more than a week after the survey period. Both charts of this date are included in our calculations.

8 Aug 81 Chart becomes a Top 100.

HIT ALBUMS ALPHABETICALLY BY ARTIST

The information given in this part of the book is as follows:

DATE the album first hit the chart, the album **TITLE**, **LABEL**, **CATALOGUE NUMBER**, the **HIGHEST POSITION** it reached on the chart, and the **TOTAL WEEKS** it remained on the chart. Number One albums are highlighted with a **STAR** ★ and Top 10 albums with a **DOT** ●. A **DAGGER** † indicates the album is still on the charts on 26 December 1987, the final chart included in our calculations for this edition.

For the purposes of this book, an album is considered a re-issue if it hits the chart for a second time with a new catalogue number. From the time when albums began to be produced in both mono and stereo versions (around 1966), we list only the stereo catalogue number. Cassette sales, and since the mid-Eighties CD sales, have become rapidly more significant in the compilation of the albums charts, but we have for consistency's sake listed only the 33⅓ rpm record catalogue number.

Describing a recording act in one sentence is often fraught with danger, but we have attempted to do so above each act's list of hits. Although we are aware that many of the 'vocalists' thus described also play an instrument, we have only mentioned this fact where the artist's instrumental skills were an important factor in the album's success.

A

AARONSON – *See HAGAR, SCHON, AARONSON, SHRIEVE*

ABBA
Sweden/Norway, male/female vocal/instrumental group   *499 wks*

8 Jun 74	**WATERLOO** *Epic EPC 80179*	28	2 wks
31 Jan 76	**ABBA** *Epic EPC 80835*	13	10 wks
10 Apr 76	★ **GREATEST HITS** *Epic EPC 69218*	1	130 wks
27 Nov 76	★ **ARRIVAL** *Epic EPC 86108*	1	92 wks
4 Feb 78	★ **THE ALBUM** *Epic EPC 86052*	1	61 wks
19 May 79	★ **VOULEZ-VOUS** *Epic EPC 86086*	1	43 wks
10 Nov 79	★ **GREATEST HITS VOL.2** *Epic EPC 10017*	1	63 wks
22 Nov 80	★ **SUPER TROUPER** *Epic EPC 10022*	1	43 wks
19 Dec 81	★ **THE VISITORS** *Epic EPC 10032*	1	21 wks
20 Nov 82	★ **THE SINGLES-THE FIRST TEN YEARS** *Epic ABBA 10*	1	22 wks
19 Nov 83	**THANK YOU FOR THE MUSIC** *Epic EPC 10043*	17	12 wks

Russ ABBOT *UK, male vocalist*   *16 wks*

5 Nov 83	**RUSS ABBOT'S MADHOUSE** *Ronco RTL 2096*	41	7 wks
23 Nov 85	**I LOVE A PARTY** *K-Tel ONE 1313*	12	9 wks

Gregory ABBOTT *US, male vocalist*   *5 wks*

10 Jan 87	**SHAKE YOU DOWN** *CBS 450061-1*	53	5 wks

ABC *UK, male vocal/instrumental group*   *75 wks*

3 Jul 82	★ **THE LEXICON OF LOVE** *Neutron NTRS 1*	1	50 wks
26 Nov 83	**BEAUTY STAB** *Neutron NTRL 2*	12	13 wks
26 Oct 85	**HOW TO BE A ZILLIONAIRE** *Neutron NTRH 3*	28	3 wks
24 Oct 87	● **ALPHABET CITY** *Neutron NTRH 4*	7	9 wks

Father ABRAHAM and the SMURFS
Holland, male vocalist as himself and Smurfs   *11 wks*

25 Nov 78	**FATHER ABRAHAM IN SMURFLAND** *Decca SMURF 1*	19	11 wks

A.B.'s *Japan, instrumental group*   *2 wks*

14 Apr 84	**DEJA VU** *Street Sounds XKHAN 503*	80	2 wks

ACADEMY of ANCIENT MUSIC conducted by Christopher HOGWOOD *UK, male conductor/instrumentalist – harpsichord, UK chamber orchestra*   *2 wks*

16 Mar 85	**THE FOUR SEASONS (VIVALDI)** *L'Oiseau Lyre 4101261*	85	2 wks

ACADEMY OF ST MARTIN IN THE FIELDS – *See Neville MARRINER and the ACADEMY OF ST MARTIN IN THE FIELDS*

ACCEPT *Germany, male vocal/instrumental group*   *5 wks*

7 May 83	**RESTLESS AND WILD** *Heavy Metal Worldwide HMILP 6*	98	2 wks
30 Mar 85	**METAL HEART** *Portrait PRT 26358*	50	1 wk
15 Feb 86	**KAIZOKU-BAN** *Portrait PRT 5916*	91	1 wk
3 May 86	**RUSSIAN ROULETTE** *Portrait PRT 26893*	80	1 wk

Only the Beatles and Rolling Stones had more number ones than ABBA.

AC/DC *Australia/UK, male vocal/instrumental group* 204 wks

Date	Title	Label	Pos	Weeks
5 Nov 77	LET THERE BE ROCK *Atlantic K 50366*		17	5 wks
20 May 78	POWERAGE *Atlantic K 50483*		26	9 wks
28 Oct 78	IF YOU WANT BLOOD YOU'VE GOT IT *Atlantic K 50532*		13	58 wks
18 Aug 79 ●	HIGHWAY TO HELL *Atlantic K 50628*		8	32 wks
9 Aug 80 ★	BACK IN BLACK *Atlantic K 50735*		1	40 wks
5 Dec 81 ●	FOR THOSE ABOUT TO ROCK *Atlantic K 50851*		3	29 wks
3 Sep 83 ●	FLICK OF THE SWITCH *Atlantic 78-0100-1*		4	9 wks
13 Jul 85 ●	FLY ON THE WALL *Atlantic 781263*		7	10 wks
7 Jun 86	WHO MADE WHO *Atlantic WX 57*		11	12 wks

Bryan ADAMS
Canada, male vocalist/instrumentalist – guitar 128 wks

Date	Title	Pos	Weeks
2 Mar 85 ●	RECKLESS *A & M AMA 5013*	7	96 wks
24 Aug 85	YOU WANT IT, YOU GOT IT *A & M AMLH 64854*	78	5 wks
15 Mar 86	CUTS LIKE A KNIFE *A & M AMLH 64919*	30	6 wks
11 Apr 87 ●	INTO THE FIRE *A & M AMA 3907*	10	21 wks

Cliff ADAMS SINGERS
UK, male/female vocal group 20 wks

Date	Title	Pos	Weeks
16 Apr 60	SING SOMETHING SIMPLE *Pye MPL 28013*	15	4 wks
24 Nov 62	SING SOMETHING SIMPLE *Pye Golden Guinea GGL 0150*	15	2 wks
20 Nov 76	SING SOMETHING SIMPLE '76 *Warwick WW 5016/17*	23	8 wks
25 Dec 82	SING SOMETHING SIMPLE *Ronco RTD 2087*	39	6 wks

All the identically titled albums are different.

King Sunny ADE and his AFRICAN BEATS
Nigeria, male vocalist and male vocal/instrumental group 1 wk

Date	Title	Pos	Weeks
9 Jul 83	SYNCHRO SYSTEM *Island ILPS 9737*	93	1 wk

ADICTS *UK, male vocal/instrumental group* 1 wk

Date	Title	Pos	Weeks
4 Dec 82	SOUND OF MUSIC *Razor RAZ 2*	99	1 wk

ADVERTS *UK, male/female vocal/instrumental group* 1 wk

Date	Title	Pos	Weeks
11 Mar 78	CROSSING THE RED SEA WITH THE ADVERTS *Bright BRL 201*	38	1 wk

AEROSMITH *US, male vocal/instrumental group* 8 wks

Date	Title	Pos	Weeks
5 Sep 87	PERMANENT VACATION *Geffen WX 126*	37	8 wks

AFTER THE FIRE *UK, male vocal/instrumental group* 4 wks

Date	Title	Pos	Weeks
13 Oct 79	LASER LOVE *CBS 83795*	57	1 wk
1 Nov 80	80F *Epic EPC 84545*	69	1 wk
3 Apr 82	BATTERIES NOT INCLUDED *CBS 85566*	82	2 wks

AFRICAN BEATS – *See King Sunny ADE and his AFRICAN BEATS*

A-HA *Norway, male vocal/instrumental group* 106 wks

Date	Title	Pos	Weeks
9 Nov 85 ●	HUNTING HIGH AND LOW *Warner Bros. WX 30*	2	77 wks
18 Oct 86 ●	SCOUNDREL DAYS *Warner Bros. WX 62*	2	29 wks

ALARM *UK, male vocal/instrumental group* 21 wks

Date	Title	Pos	Weeks
25 Feb 84 ●	DECLARATION *IRS IRSA 7044*	6	11 wks
26 Oct 85	STRENGTH *IRS MIRF 1004*	18	6 wks
14 Nov 87	EYE OF THE HURRICANE *IRS MIRG 1023*	23	4 wks

ALEXANDER BROTHERS *UK, male vocal duo* 1 wk

Date	Title	Pos	Weeks
10 Dec 66	THESE ARE MY MOUNTAINS *Pye GGL 0375*	29	1 wk

ALLEN – *See FOSTER and ALLEN*

ALIEN SEX FIEND
UK, male/female vocal/instrumental group 1 wk

Date	Title	Pos	Weeks
12 Oct 85	MAXIMUM SECURITY *Anagram GRAM 24*	100	1 wk

Mose ALLISON *US, male vocalist/instrumentalist – piano* 1 wk

Date	Title	Pos	Weeks
4 Jun 66	MOSE ALIVE *Atlantic 587-007*	30	1 wk

ALLMAN BROTHERS BAND
US, male vocal/instrumental group 4 wks

Date	Title	Pos	Weeks
6 Oct 73	BROTHERS AND SISTERS *Warner Bros. K 47507*	42	3 wks
6 Mar 76	THE ROAD GOES ON FOREVER *Capricorn 2637 101*	54	1 wk

Marc ALMOND *UK, male vocalist* 7 wks

Date	Title	Pos	Weeks
10 Nov 84	VERMIN IN ERMINE *Some Bizzare BIZL 8*	36	2 wks
5 Oct 85	STORIES OF JOHNNY *Some Bizzare FAITH 1*	22	3 wks
18 Apr 87	MOTHER FIST AND HER FIVE DAUGHTERS *Some Bizzare FAITH 2*	41	2 wks

Vermin In Ermine and Mother Fist and Her Five Daughters credited to Marc Almond and the Willing Sinners – UK, male/female vocal/instrumental group. See also Marc and the Mambas.

Herb ALPERT and the TIJUANA BRASS
US, male band leader/instrumentalist – trumpet 309 wks

Date	Title	Pos	Weeks
29 Jan 66 ●	GOING PLACES *Pye NPL 28065*	4	138 wks
23 Apr 66 ●	WHIPPED CREAM AND OTHER DELIGHTS *Pye NPL 28058*	2	42 wks
28 May 66	WHAT NOW MY LOVE *Pye NPL 28077*	18	17 wks
11 Feb 67 ●	S.R.O. *Pye NSPL 28088*	5	26 wks
15 Jul 67	SOUNDS LIKE *A&M AMLS 900*	21	10 wks
3 Feb 68	NINTH *A&M AMLS 905*	26	9 wks
29 Jun 68 ●	BEAT OF THE BRASS *A&M AMLS 916*	4	21 wks
9 Aug 69	WARM *A&M AMLS 937*	30	4 wks
14 Mar 70	THE BRASS ARE COMIN' *A&M AMLS 962*	40	1 wk
30 May 70 ●	GREATEST HITS *A&M AMLS 980*	8	27 wks
27 Jun 70	DOWN MEXICO WAY *A&M AMLS 974*	64	1 wk
13 Nov 71	AMERICA *A&M AMLB 1000*	45	1 wk
12 Nov 77	40 GREATEST *K-Tel NE 1005*	45	2 wks
17 Nov 79	RISE *A&M AMLH 64790*	37	7 wks
4 Apr 87	KEEP YOUR EYE ON ME *Breakout AMA 5125*	79	3 wks

Last two hits credit only Herb Alpert. On 29 Jun 67 Going Places and What Now My Love changed labels and numbers to A&M AMLS 965 and AMLS 977 respectively.

ALTERED IMAGES
UK, male/female vocal/instrumental group 40 wks

Date	Title	Pos	Weeks
19 Sep 81 ●	HAPPY BIRTHDAY *Epic EPC 84893*	26	21 wks
15 May 82	PINKY BLUE *Epic EPC 85665*	12	10 wks
25 Jun 83	BITE *Epic EPC 25413*	16	9 wks

AMAZULU
UK, female vocal group — 1 wk

6 Dec 86	**AMAZULU**	*Island ILPS 9851*	97	1 wk

AMEN CORNER
UK, male vocal/instrumental group — 8 wks

30 Mar 68	**ROUND AMEN CORNER**	*Deram SML 1021*	26	7 wks
1 Nov 69	**EXPLOSIVE COMPANY**	*Immediate IMSP 023*	19	1 wk

AMERICA
US, male vocal/instrumental group — 22 wks

22 Jan 72	**AMERICA**	*Warner Bros. K 46093*	14	13 wks
9 Dec 72	**HOMECOMING**	*Warner Bros. K 46180*	21	5 wks
10 Nov 73	**HAT TRICK**	*Warner Bros. K 56016*	41	3 wks
7 Feb 76	**HISTORY – AMERICA'S GREATEST HITS**		60	1 wk
	Warner Bros. K 56169			

Ian ANDERSON
UK, male vocalist/instrumentalist – flute — 1 wk

26 Nov 83	**WALK INTO LIGHT**	*Chrysalis CDL 1443*	78	1 wk

Jon ANDERSON
UK, male vocalist — 19 wks

24 Jul 76	● **OLIAS OF SUNHILLOW**	*Atlantic K 50261*	8	10 wks
15 Nov 80	**SONG OF SEVEN**	*Atlantic K 50756*	38	3 wks
5 Jun 82	**ANIMATION**	*Polydor POLD 5044*	43	6 wks

See also Jon and Vangelis.

Laurie ANDERSON
US, female vocalist/multi-instrumentalist — 8 wks

1 May 82	**BIG SCIENCE**	*Warner Bros. K 57002*	29	6 wks
10 Mar 84	**MISTER HEARTBREAK**	*Warner Bros. 92–5077–1* ...	93	2 wks

Lynn ANDERSON
US, female vocalist — 1 wk

17 Apr 71	**ROSE GARDEN**	*CBS 64333*	45	1 wk

Moira ANDERSON
UK, female vocalist — 1 wk

20 Jun 70	**THESE ARE MY SONGS**	*Decca SKL 5016*	50	1 wk

See also Harry Secombe and Moira Anderson.

Julie ANDREWS
UK, female vocalist — 5 wks

16 Jul 83	**LOVE ME TENDER**	*Peach River JULIE 1*	63	5 wks

ANGELIC UPSTARTS
UK, male vocal/instrumental group — 20 wks

18 Aug 79	**TEENAGE WARNING**	*Warner Bros. K 50634*	29	7 wks
12 Apr 80	**WE'VE GOTTA GET OUT OF THIS PLACE**		54	3 wks
	Warner Bros. K 56806			
7 Jun 81	**2,000,000 VOICES**	*Zonophone ZONO 104*	32	3 wks
26 Sep 81	**ANGELIC UPSTARTS**	*Zonophone ZEM 102*	27	7 wks

ANIMAL NIGHTLIFE
UK, male vocal/instrumental group — 6 wks

24 Aug 85	**SHANGRI-LA**	*Island ILPS 9830*	36	6 wks

ANIMALS
UK, male vocal/instrumental group — 86 wks

14 Nov 64	● **THE ANIMALS**	*Columbia 33SX 1669*	6	20 wks
22 May 65	● **ANIMAL TRACKS**	*Columbia 33SX 1708*	6	26 wks
16 Apr 66	● **MOST OF THE ANIMALS**	*Columbia 33SX 6035* ...	4	20 wks
28 May 66	● **ANIMALISMS**	*Decca LK 4797*	4	17 wks
25 Sep 71	**MOST OF THE ANIMALS**	*MFP 5218*	18	3 wks

Adam ANT
UK, male vocalist — 139 wks

15 Nov 80	★ **KINGS OF THE WILD FRONTIER**	*CBS 84549* ..	1	66 wks
17 Jan 81	**DIRK WEARS WHITE SOX**	*Do It RIDE 3*	16	29 wks
14 Nov 81	● **PRINCE CHARMING**	*CBS 85268*	2	21 wks
23 Oct 82	● **FRIEND OR FOE**	*CBS 25040*	5	12 wks
19 Nov 83	**STRIP**	*CBS 25705*	20	8 wks
14 Sep 85	**VIVE LE ROCK**	*CBS 26583*	42	3 wks

All the albums up to and including Prince Charming credited to Adam and the Ants – UK, male vocal/instrumental group.

ANTHRAX
US, male vocal/instrumental group — 5 wks

18 Apr 87	**AMONG THE LIVING**	*Island ILPS 9865*	18	5 wks

ANTI-NOWHERE LEAGUE
UK, male vocal/instrumental group — 12 wks

22 May 82	**WE ARE…THE LEAGUE**	*WXYZ LMNOP 1* ...	24	11 wks
5 Nov 83	**LIVE IN YUGOSLAVIA**	*I.D. NOSE 3*	88	1 wk

ANTI-PASTI
UK, male vocal/instrumental group — 7 wks

15 Aug 81	**THE LAST CALL**	*Rondelet ABOUT 5*	31	7 wks

ANTS – See Adam ANT

Carmine APPICE – See Jeff BECK, Tim BOGERT and Carmine APPICE

APRIL WINE
Canada, male vocal/instrumental group — 8 wks

15 Mar 80	**HARDER…FASTER**	*Capitol EST 12013*	34	5 wks
24 Jan 81	**THE NATURE OF THE BEAST**	*Capitol EST 12125*	48	3 wks

ARCADIA
UK, male vocal/instrumental group — 10 wks

7 Dec 85	**SO RED THE ROSE**	*Parlophone Odeon PCSD 101* ...	30	10 wks

ARGENT
UK, male vocal/instrumental group — 9 wks

29 Apr 72	**ALL TOGETHER NOW**	*Epic EPC 64962*	13	8 wks
31 Mar 73	**IN DEEP**	*Epic EPC 65475*	49	1 wk

Joan ARMATRADING
UK, female vocalist — 164 wks

4 Sep 76	**JOAN ARMATRADING**	*A & M AMLH 64588*	12	27 wks
1 Oct 77	● **SHOW SOME EMOTION**	*A & M AMLH 68433* ...	6	11 wks
14 Oct 78	**TO THE LIMIT**	*A & M AMLH 64732*	13	10 wks
24 May 80	● **ME MYSELF I**	*A & M AMLH 64809*	5	23 wks
12 Sep 81	● **WALK UNDER LADDERS**	*A & M AMLH 64876* ..	6	29 wks
12 Mar 83	● **THE KEY**	*A & M AMLX 64912*	10	14 wks
26 Nov 83	**TRACK RECORD**	*A & M JA 2001*	18	32 wks
16 Feb 85	**SECRET SECRETS**	*A & M AMA 5040*	14	12 wks
24 May 86	**SLEIGHT OF HAND**	*A & M AMA 5130*	34	6 wks

ARMOURY SHOW
UK, male vocal/instrumental group — 1 wk

21 Sep 85	**WAITING FOR THE FLOODS**	*Parlophone ARM 1*	57	1 wk

(Above) The ADVERTS had a seven day sea crossing and then disappeared. Andy Fairweather-Low (front, second from left) is shown in the company of AMEN CORNER.

(Left) AMERICA were the first chart group to be more or less named after a country, unless one counts the England World Cup Football Squad 1970.

Louis ARMSTRONG
US, male band leader vocalist/instrumentalist – trumpet　　　　*14 wks*

28 Oct 61	**JAZZ CLASSICS** *Ace of Hearts AH 7*	20	1 wk
22 Oct 60	**SATCHMO PLAYS KING OLIVER**		
	Audio Fidelity AFLP 1930	20	1 wk
27 Jun 64	**HELLO DOLLY** *London HAR 8190*	11	6 wks
16 Nov 68	**WHAT A WONDERFUL WORLD**		
	Stateside SSL 10247	37	3 wks
20 Feb 82	**THE VERY BEST OF LOUIS ARMSTRONG**		
	Warwick WW 5112	30	3 wks

Steve ARRINGTON
US, male vocalist　　　　*11 wks*

13 Apr 85	**DANCIN' IN THE KEY OF LIFE** *Atlantic 781245* ...	41	11 wks

Davey ARTHUR – *See FUREYS and DAVEY ARTHUR*

ART OF NOISE
UK, male/female studio group with producer Trevor Horn　　　　*34 wks*

3 Nov 84	**(WHO'S AFRAID OF) THE ART OF NOISE**		
	ZTT ZTTIQ 2	27	17 wks
26 Apr 86	**IN VISIBLE SILENCE** *Chrysalis WOL 2*	18	15 wks
10 Oct 87	**IN NO SENSE/NONSENSE** *China WOL 4*	55	2 wks

ASHFORD and SIMPSON
US, male/female vocal duo　　　　*6 wks*

16 Feb 85	**SOLID** *Capitol SASH 1*	42	6 wks

ASIA
UK, male vocal/instrumental group　　　　*50 wks*

10 Apr 82	**ASIA** *Geffen GEF 85577*	11	38 wks
20 Aug 83	● **ALPHA** *Geffen GRF 25508*	5	11 wks
14 Dec 85	**ASTRA** *Geffen GEF 26413*	68	1 wk

ASSOCIATES
UK, male vocal/instrumental group　　　　*27 wks*

22 May 82	● **SULK** *Associates ASCL 1*	10	20 wks
16 Feb 85	**PERHAPS** *WEA WX 9*	23	7 wks

Duo for the first album.

Rick ASTLEY
UK, male vocalist　　　　*5 wks*

28 Nov 87	★ **WHENEVER YOU NEED SOMEBODY**		
	RCA PL 71529	1†	5 wks

ASWAD
UK, male vocal/instrumental group　　　　*27 wks*

24 Jul 82	**NOT SATISFIED** *CBS 85666*	50	6 wks
10 Dec 83	**LIVE AND DIRECT** *Island IMA 6*	57	16 wks
3 Nov 84	**REBEL SOULS** *Island ILPS 9780*	48	2 wks
28 Jun 86	**TO THE TOP** *Simba SIMBALP 2*	71	3 wks

ATHLETICO SPIZZ 80
UK, male vocal/instrumental group　　　　*5 wks*

26 Jul 80	**DO A RUNNER** *A & M AMLE 68514*	27	5 wks

Chet ATKINS
US, male instrumentalist – guitar　　　　*5 wks*

18 Mar 61	**THE OTHER CHET ATKINS** *RCA RD 27194*	20	1 wk
17 Jun 61	**CHET ATKINS' WORKSHOP** *RCA RD 27214* .	19	1 wk
30 Feb 63	**CARIBBEAN GUITAR** *RCA RD 7519*	17	3 wks

Rowan ATKINSON
UK, male comedian　　　　*9 wks*

7 Feb 81	**LIVE IN BELFAST** *Arista SPART 1150*	44	9 wks

ATLANTIC STARR
US, male/female vocal/instrumental group　　　　*15 wks*

15 Jun 85	**AS THE BAND TURNS** *A & M AMA 5019*	64	3 wks
11 Jul 87	**ALL IN THE NAME OF LOVE** *WEA WX 115*	48	12 wks

ATOMIC ROOSTER
UK, male vocal/instrumental group　　　　*13 wks*

13 Jun 70	**ATOMIC ROOSTER** *B & C CAS 1010*	49	1 wk
16 Jan 71	**DEATH WALKS BEHIND YOU**		
	Charisma CAS 1026	12	8 wks
21 Aug 71	**IN HEARING OF ATOMIC ROOSTER**		
	Pegasus PEG 1	18	4 wks

ATTRACTIONS – *See Elvis COSTELLO and the ATTRACTIONS*

AU PAIRS
UK, female/male vocal/instrumental group　　　　*10 wks*

6 Jun 81	**PLAYING WITH A DIFFERENT SEX**		
	Human HUMAN 1	33	7 wks
4 Sep 82	**SENSE AND SENSUALITY** *Kamera KAM 010* ...	79	3 wks

Brian AUGER TRINITY – *See Julie DRISCOLL and the Brian AUGER TRINITY*

Patti AUSTIN
US, female vocalist　　　　*1 wk*

26 Sep 81	**EVERY HOME SHOULD HAVE ONE**		
	Quest K 56931	99	1 wk

AVERAGE WHITE BAND
UK, male vocal/instrumental group　　　　*47 wks*

1 Mar 75	● **AVERAGE WHITE BAND** *Atlantic K 50058*	6	14 wks
5 Jul 75	**CUT THE CAKE** *Atlantic K 50146*	28	4 wks
31 Jul 76	**SOUL SEARCHING TIME** *Atlantic K 50272*	60	1 wk
10 Mar 79	**I FEEL NO FRET** *RCA XL 13063*	15	15 wks
31 May 80	**SHINE** *RCA XL 13123*	14	13 wks

Roy AYERS
US, male vocalist/instrumentalist – vibraphone　　　　*2 wks*

26 Oct 85	**YOU MIGHT BE SURPRISED** *CBS 26653*	91	2 wks

Pam AYRES
UK, female vocalist　　　　*29 wks*

27 Mar 76	**SOME OF ME POEMS AND SONGS**		
	Galaxy GAL 6003	13	23 wks
11 Dec 76	**SOME MORE OF ME POEMS AND SONGS**		
	Galaxy GAL 6010	23	6 wks

Charles AZNAVOUR
France, male vocalist　　　　*21 wks*

29 Jun 74	**AZNAVOUR SINGS AZNAVOUR VOL. 3**		
	Barclay 80472	23	7 wks
7 Sep 74	● **A TAPESTRY OF DREAMS** *Barclay 90003*	9	13 wks
2 Aug 80	**HIS GREATEST LOVE SONGS** *K-Tel NE 1078* ..	73	1 wk

(Right) The man ARGENT were named after, Rod Argent, is at the rear; Russ Ballard is in front.
(Below) LAURIE ANDERSON is one of New York's leading 'performance artists'.

AZTEC CAMERA *UK, male vocal/instrumental group* *26 wks*

23 Apr 83	**HIGH LAND HARD RAIN** *Rough Trade ROUGH 47*		22	18 wks
29 Sep 84	**KNIFE** *WEA WX 8*		14	6 wks
21 Nov 87	**LOVE** *WEA WX 128*		49	2 wks

B

Eric B. and RAKIM *US, male vocal/instrumental duo* *2 wks*

12 Sep 87	**PAID IN FULL** *Fourth & Broadway BRLP 514*		89	2 wks

BACCARA *Spain, female vocal duo* *6 wks*

4 Mar 78	**BACCARA** *RCA PL 28316*		26	6 wks

Burt BACHARACH *US, orchestra and chorus* *43 wks*

22 May 65	● **HIT MAKER – BURT BACHARACH**			
	London HAR 8233		3	18 wks
28 Nov 70	**REACH OUT** *A & M AMLS 908*		52	3 wks
3 Apr 71	● **PORTRAIT IN MUSIC** *A & M AMLS 2010*		5	22 wks

BACHELORS *Ireland, male vocal group* *103 wks*

27 Jun 64	● **THE BACHELORS AND 16 GREAT SONGS**			
	Decca LK 4614		2	44 wks
9 Oct 65	**MORE GREAT SONG HITS FROM THE**			
	BACHELORS *Decca LK 4721*		15	6 wks
9 Jul 66	**HITS OF THE SIXTIES** *Decca TXL 102*		12	9 wks
5 Nov 66	**BACHELORS' GIRLS** *Decca LK 4827*		24	8 wks
1 Jul 67	**GOLDEN ALL TIME HITS** *Decca SKL 4849*		19	7 wks
14 Jun 69	● **WORLD OF THE BACHELORS** *Decca SPA 2* ...		8	18 wks
23 Aug 69	**WORLD OF THE BACHELORS VOL. 2**			
	Decca SPA 22		11	7 wks
22 Dec 79	**25 GOLDEN GREATS** *Warwick WW 5068*		38	4 wks

BACHMAN-TURNER OVERDRIVE
Canada, male vocal/instrumental group *13 wks*

14 Dec 74	**NOT FRAGILE** *Mercury 9100 007*		12	13 wks

BAD COMPANY *UK, male vocal/instrumental group* *87 wks*

15 Jun 74	● **BAD COMPANY** *Island ILPS 9279*		3	25 wks
12 Apr 75	● **STRAIGHT SHOOTER** *Island ILPS 9304*		3	27 wks
21 Feb 76	● **RUN WITH THE PACK** *Island ILPS 9346*		4	12 wks
19 Mar 77	**BURNIN' SKY** *Island ILPS 9441*		17	8 wks
17 Mar 79	● **DESOLATION ANGELS** *Swansong SSK 59408* ...		10	9 wks
28 Aug 82	**ROUGH DIAMONDS** *Swansong SSK 59419*		15	6 wks

BAD MANNERS *UK, male vocal/instrumental group* *44 wks*

26 Apr 80	**SKA 'N' B** *Magnet MAG 5033*		34	13 wks
29 Nov 80	**LOONEE TUNES** *Magnet MAG 5038*		36	12 wks
24 Oct 81	**GOSH IT'S BAD MANNERS** *Magnet MAGL 5043* .		18	12 wks
27 Nov 82	**FORGING AHEAD** *Magnet MAGL 5050*		78	1 wk
7 May 83	**THE HEIGHT OF BAD MANNERS**			
	Telstar STAR 2229		23	6 wks

BAD NEWS *UK, male vocal group* *1 wk*

24 Oct 87	**BAD NEWS** *EMI EMC 3535*		69	1 wk

BAD SEEDS – *See Nick CAVE featuring the BAD SEEDS*

Joan BAEZ *US, female vocalist* *88 wks*

18 Jul 64	● **JOAN BAEZ IN CONCERT VOL. 2**			
	Fontana TFL 6033		8	19 wks
15 May 65	● **JOAN BAEZ NO. 5** *Fontana TFL 6043*		3	27 wks
19 Jun 65	● **JOAN BAEZ** *Fontana TFL 6002*		9	13 wks
27 Nov 65	● **FAREWELL ANGELINA** *Fontana TFL 6058*		5	23 wks
19 Jul 69	**JOAN BAEZ ON VANGUARD** *Vanguard SVXL 100*		15	5 wks
3 Apr 71	**FIRST TEN YEARS** *Vanguard 6635 003*		41	1 wk

Philip BAILEY *US, male vocalist* *17 wks*

30 Mar 85	**CHINESE WALL** *CBS 26161*		29	17 wks

Anita BAKER *US, female vocalist* *47 wks*

3 May 86	**RAPTURE** *Elektra EKT 37*		13	47 wks

BAKER-GURVITZ ARMY
UK, male vocal/instrumental group *5 wks*

22 Feb 75	**BAKER-GURVITZ ARMY** *Vertigo 9103 201*		22	5 wks

See also Ginger Baker's Air Force.

Ginger BAKER'S AIR FORCE
UK, male vocal/instrumental group *1 wk*

13 Jun 70	**GINGER BAKER'S AIR FORCE** *Polydor 2662-001* .		37	1 wk

See also Baker-Gurvitz Army.

BALAAM AND THE ANGEL
UK, male vocal/instrumental group *2 wks*

16 Aug 86	**THE GREATEST STORY EVER TOLD**			
	Virgin V 2377		67	2 wks

Kenny BALL
UK, male vocalist/instrumentalist – trumpet *26 wks*

7 Sep 63	● **KENNY BALL'S GOLDEN HITS**			
	Pye Golden Guinea GGL 0209		4	26 wks

See also Kenny Ball, Chris Barber and Acker Bilk.

Kenny BALL, Chris BARBER and Acker BILK
UK, male jazz band leaders/vocalists/instrumentalists –
trumpet, trombone and clarinet respectively *24 wks*

25 Aug 62	★ **BEST OF BALL, BARBER AND BILK**			
	Pye Golden Guinea GGL 0131		1	24 wks

See also Kenny Ball; Chris Barber; Mr Acker Bilk; Chris Barber and Acker Bilk.

BANANARAMA *UK, female vocal group* *39 wks*

19 Mar 83	● **DEEP SEA SKIVING** *London RAMA 1*		7	16 wks
28 Apr 84	**BANANARAMA** *London RAMA 2*		16	11 wks
19 Jul 86	**TRUE CONFESSIONS** *London RAMA 3*		46	5 wks
19 Sep 87	**WOW!** *London RAMA 4*		59	7 wks

BAND *Canada, male vocal/instrumental group* *18 wks*

31 Jan 70	**THE BAND** *Capitol EST 132*		25	11 wks
3 Oct 70	**STAGE FRIGHT** *Capitol EA SW 425*		15	6 wks

Even at the latter end of his career LOUIS ARMSTRONG managed several chart appearances.

ROWAN ATKINSON tests the lines of sight of his live audience.

(Right) The BACHELORS finally found a woman to make their tea.

(Below) Of course BANANARAMA play their own instruments!

27 Nov 71	**CAHOOTS** Capitol EA-ST 651		41	1 wk

See film soundtracks for The Last Waltz.

BANGLES *US, female vocal/instrumental group*   *48 wks*

16 Mar 85	**ALL OVER THE PLACE** CBS 26015		86	1 wk
15 Mar 86	● **DIFFERENT LIGHT** CBS 26659		3	47 wks

Tony BANKS *UK, male instrumentalist – keyboards*   *7 wks*

20 Oct 79	**A CURIOUS FEELING** Charisma CAS 1148		21	5 wks
25 Jun 83	**THE FUGITIVE** Charisma TBLP 1		50	2 wks

BANSHEES – *See SIOUXSIE and the BANSHEES*

Chris BARBER

UK, male vocalist/instrumentalist – trombone   *3 wks*

24 Sep 60	**CHRIS BARBER BAND BOX NO. 2**			
	Columbia 33SCX 3277		17	1 wk
5 Nov 60	**ELITE SYNCOPATIONS** Columbia 33SX 1245 .		18	1 wk
12 Nov 60	**BEST OF CHRIS BARBER** Ace Of Clubs ACL 1037 .		17	1 wk

See also Kenny Ball, Chris Barber and Acker Bilk; Chris Barber and Acker Bilk.

Chris BARBER and Acker BILK *UK, male band*

leaders/vocalists/instrumentalists – trombone and clarinet   *61 wks*

27 May 61	● **BEST OF BARBER AND BILK VOL. 1**			
	Pye GGL 0075		4	43 wks
11 Nov 61	● **BEST OF BARBER AND BILK VOL. 2**			
	Pye GGL 0096		8	18 wks

See also Kenny Ball, Chris Barber and Acker Bilk; Chris Barber; Mr Acker Bilk.

BARCLAY JAMES HARVEST

UK, male vocal/instrumental group   *42 wks*

14 Dec 74	**BARCLAY JAMES HARVEST LIVE**			
	Polydor 2683 052		40	2 wks
18 Oct 75	**TIME HONOURED GHOST** Polydor 2383 361 .		32	3 wks
23 Oct 76	**OCTOBERON** Polydor 2442 144		19	4 wks
1 Oct 77	**GONE TO EARTH** Polydor 2442 148		30	7 wks
21 Oct 78	**BARCLAY JAMES HARVEST XII**			
	Polydor POLD 5006		31	2 wks
23 May 81	**TURN OF THE TIDE** Polydor POLD 5040		55	2 wks
24 Jul 82	**A CONCERT FOR THE PEOPLE (BERLIN)**			
	Polydor POLD 5052		15	11 wks
28 May 83	**RING OF CHANGES** Polydor POLH 3		36	4 wks
14 Apr 84	**VICTIMS OF CIRCUMSTANCE**			
	Polydor POLD 5135		33	6 wks
14 Feb 87	**FACE TO FACE** Polydor POLD 5209		65	1 wk

Daniel BARENBOIM – *See John WILLIAMS and Daniel BARENBOIM*

Syd BARRETT *UK, male vocalist/instrumentalist – guitar*   *1 wk*

7 Feb 70	**MADCAP LAUGHS** Harvest SHVL 765		40	1 wk

Wild Willy BARRETT – *See John OTWAY and Wild Willy BARRETT*

BARRON KNIGHTS

UK, male vocal/instrumental group   *22 wks*

2 Dec 78	**NIGHT GALLERY** Epic EPC 83221		15	13 wks
1 Dec 79	**TEACH THE WORLD TO LAUGH**			
	Epic EPC 83891		51	4 wks
13 Dec 80	**JUST A GIGGLE** Epic EPC 84550		62	5 wks

John BARRY *UK, male arranger/conductor*   *9 wks*

29 Jan 72	**THE PERSUADERS** CBS 64816		18	9 wks

Count BASIE

US, male orchestra leader/instrumentalist – piano   *1 wk*

16 Apr 60	**CHAIRMAN OF THE BOARD**			
	Columbia 33SX 1209		17	1 wk

See also Frank Sinatra and Count Basie.

Toni BASIL *US, female vocalist*   *16 wks*

6 Feb 82	**WORD OF MOUTH** Radialchoice BASIL 1		15	16 wks

Shirley BASSEY *UK, female vocalist*   *259 wks*

28 Jan 61	**FABULOUS SHIRLEY BASSEY**			
	Columbia 33SX 1178		12	2 wks
25 Feb 61	● **SHIRLEY** Columbia 33SX 1286		9	10 wks
17 Feb 62	**SHIRLEY BASSEY** Columbia 33SX 1382		14	11 wks
15 Dec 62	**LET'S FACE THE MUSIC** Columbia 33SX 1454		12	7 wks
4 Dec 65	**SHIRLEY BASSEY AT THE PIGALLE**			
	Columbia 33SX 1787		16	7 wks
27 Aug 66	**I'VE GOT A SONG FOR YOU**			
	United Artists ULP 1142		26	1 wk
17 Feb 68	**TWELVE OF THOSE SONGS**			
	Columbia SCX 6204		38	3 wks
7 Dec 68	**GOLDEN HITS OF SHIRLEY BASSEY**			
	Columbia SCX 6294		28	40 wks
11 Jul 70	**LIVE AT THE TALK OF THE TOWN**			
	United Artists UAS 29095		38	6 wks
29 Aug 70	● **SOMETHING** United Artists UAS 29100		5	28 wks
15 May 71	● **SOMETHING ELSE** United Artists UAG 29149 ...		7	9 wks
2 Oct 71	**BIG SPENDER** Sunset SLS 50262		27	8 wks
30 Oct 71	**IT'S MAGIC** Starline SRS 5082		32	1 wk
6 Nov 71	**THE FABULOUS SHIRLEY BASSEY** MFP 1398 .		48	1 wk
4 Dec 71	**WHAT NOW MY LOVE** MFP 5230		17	5 wks
8 Jan 72	**THE SHIRLEY BASSEY COLLECTION**			
	United Artists UAD 60013/4		37	1 wk
19 Feb 72	**I CAPRICORN** United Artists UAS 29246		13	11 wks
29 Nov 72	**AND I LOVE YOU SO** United Artists UAS 29385		24	9 wks
2 Jun 73	● **NEVER NEVER NEVER**			
	United Artists UAG 29471		10	10 wks
15 Mar 75	● **THE SHIRLEY BASSEY SINGLES ALBUM**			
	United Artists UAS 29728		2	23 wks
1 Nov 75	**GOOD, BAD BUT BEAUTIFUL**			
	United Artists UAS 29881		13	7 wks
15 May 76	**LOVE, LIFE AND FEELINGS**			
	United Artists UAS 29944		13	5 wks
4 Dec 76	**THOUGHTS OF LOVE** United Artists UAS 30011		15	9 wks
25 Jun 77	**YOU TAKE MY HEART AWAY**			
	United Artists UAS 30037		34	5 wks
4 Nov 78	● **25TH ANNIVERSARY ALBUM**			
	United Artists SBTV 601 4748		3	12 wks
12 May 79	**THE MAGIC IS YOU** United Artists UATV 30230		40	5 wks
17 Jul 82	**LOVE SONGS** Applause APKL 1163		48	5 wks
20 Oct 84	**I AM WHAT I AM** Towerbell TOWLP 7		25	18 wks

Let's Face The Music has credit 'with The Nelson Riddle Orchestra'.

BAUHAUS *UK, male vocal/instrumental group*   *24 wks*

15 Nov 80	**IN THE FLAT FIELD** 4AD CAD 13		72	1 wk
24 Oct 81	**MASK** Beggars Banquet BEGA 29		30	5 wks
30 Oct 82	● **THE SKY'S GONE OUT** Beggars Banquet BEGA 42 ·		4	6 wks
23 Jul 83	**BURNING FROM THE INSIDE**			
	Beggars Banquet BEGA 45		13	10 wks
30 Nov 85	**1979–1983** Beggars Banquet BEGA 64		36	2 wks

BAY CITY ROLLERS

UK, male vocal/instrumental group   *127 wks*

12 Oct 74	★ **ROLLIN'** Bell BELLS 244		1	62 wks

(Right) The young SHIRLEY BASSEY managed to get her name in almost every album title.

(Below) CILLA BLACK seems disturbed that her *Best Of* collection has broken her Top Ten string.

3 May 75	★ **ONCE UPON A STAR** *Bell SYBEL 8001*	1	37 wks
13 Dec 75	● **WOULDN'T YOU LIKE IT** *Bell SYBEL 8002*	3	12 wks
25 Sep 76	● **DEDICATION** *Bell SYBEL 8005*	4	12 wks
13 Aug 77	**IT'S A GAME** *Arista SPARTY 1009*	18	4 wks

B BOYS *US, male vocal/instrumental group*   *1 wk*

28 Jan 84	**CUTTIN' HERBIE** *Streetwave X KHAN 501*	90	1 wk

BBC SYMPHONY ORCHESTRA, SINGERS and CHORUS *UK, orchestra/choir and audience*   *6 wks*

4 Oct 69	**LAST NIGHT OF THE PROMS** *Philips SFM 23033*	36	1 wk
11 Dec 82	**HIGHLIGHTS – LAST NIGHT OF THE PROMS '82** *K-Tel NE 1198*	69	5 wks

Last Night Of The Proms *was conducted by Colin Davis and* Highlights – Last Night Of The Proms '82 *by James Loughran.*

BBC WELSH CHORUS – *See Aled JONES with the BBC WELSH CHORUS*

BEACH BOYS *US, male vocal/instrumental group*   *524 wks*

25 Sep 65	**SURFIN' USA** *Capitol T 1890*	17	7 wks
19 Feb 66	● **BEACH BOYS PARTY** *Capitol T 2398*	3	14 wks
16 Apr 66	● **BEACH BOYS TODAY** *Capitol T 2269*	6	25 wks
9 Jul 66	● **PET SOUNDS** *Capitol T 2458*	2	39 wks
16 Jul 66	● **SUMMER DAYS** *Capitol T 2354*	4	22 wks
12 Nov 66	● **BEST OF THE BEACH BOYS** *Capitol T 20865*	2	142 wks
11 Mar 67	**SURFER GIRL** *Capitol T 1981*	13	14 wks
21 Oct 67	● **BEST OF THE BEACH BOYS VOL. 2** *Capitol ST 20956*	3	39 wks
18 Nov 67	● **SMILEY SMILE** *Capitol ST 9001*	9	8 wks
16 Mar 68	● **WILD HONEY** *Capitol ST 2859*	7	15 wks
21 Sep 68	**FRIENDS** *Capitol ST 2895*	13	8 wks
23 Nov 68	● **BEST OF THE BEACH BOYS VOL. 3** *Capitol ST 21142*	9	12 wks
29 Mar 69	● **20/20** *Capitol EST 133*	3	10 wks
19 Sep 70	● **GREATEST HITS** *Capitol ST 21628*	5	30 wks
5 Dec 70	**SUNFLOWER** *Stateside SSL 8251*	29	6 wks
27 Nov 71	**SURF'S UP** *Stateside SLS 10313*	15	7 wks
24 Jun 72	**CARL AND THE PASSIONS/SO TOUGH** *Reprise K 44184*	25	1 wk
17 Feb 73	**HOLLAND** *Reprise K 54008*	20	7 wks
10 Jul 76	★ **20 GOLDEN GREATS** *Capitol EMTV 1*	1	86 wks
24 Jul 76	**15 BIG ONES** *Reprise K 54079*	31	3 wks
7 May 77	**THE BEACH BOYS LOVE YOU** *Brother/Reprise K 54087*	28	1 wk
21 Apr 79	**LA (LIGHT ALBUM)** *Caribou CRB 86081*	32	6 wks
12 Apr 80	**KEEPING THE SUMMER ALIVE** *Caribou CRB 86109*	54	3 wks
30 Jul 83	★ **THE VERY BEST OF THE BEACH BOYS** *Capitol BBTV 1867193*	1	17 wks
22 Jun 85	**THE BEACH BOYS** *Caribou CRB 26378*	60	2 wks

BEAKY – *See Dave DEE, DOZY, BEAKY, MICK and TICH*

BEASTIE BOYS *US, male vocal group*   *40 weeks*

31 Jan 87	● **LICENCE TO ILL** *Def Jam 450062*	7	40 wks

BEAT *UK, male vocal/instrumental group*   *69 wks*

31 May 80	● **JUST CAN'T STOP IT** *Go-Feet BEAT 001*	3	32 wks
16 May 81	● **WHA'PPEN** *Go-Feet BEAT 3*	3	18 wks
9 Oct 82	● **SPECIAL BEAT SERVICE** *Go-Feet BEAT 5*	21	6 wks
11 Jun 83	● **WHAT IS BEAT? (THE BEST OF THE BEAT)** *Go-Feet BEAT 6*	10	13 wks

BEATLES *UK, male vocal/instrumental group*   *1081 wks*

6 Apr 63	★ **PLEASE PLEASE ME** *Parlophone PMC 1202*	1	70 wks
30 Nov 63	★ **WITH THE BEATLES** *Parlophone PMC 1206*	1	51 wks
18 Jul 64	★ **A HARD DAY'S NIGHT** *Parlophone PMC 1230*	1	38 wks
12 Dec 64	★ **BEATLES FOR SALE** *Parlophone PMC 1240*	1	46 wks
14 Aug 65	★ **HELP** *Parlophone PMC 1255*	1	37 wks
11 Dec 65	★ **RUBBER SOUL** *Parlophone PMC 1267*	1	42 wks
13 Aug 66	★ **REVOLVER** *Parlophone PMC 7009*	1	34 wks
10 Dec 66	● **A COLLECTION OF BEATLES OLDIES** *Parlophone PMC 7016*	7	34 wks
3 Jun 67	★ **SERGEANT PEPPER'S LONELY HEARTS CLUB BAND** *Parlophone PCS 7027*	1	148 wks
13 Jan 68	**MAGICAL MYSTERY TOUR (import)** *Capitol SMAL 2835*	31	2 wks
7 Dec 68	★ **THE BEATLES** *Apple PCS 7067/8*	1	22 wks
1 Feb 69	● **YELLOW SUBMARINE** *Apple PCS 7070*	3	10 wks
4 Oct 69	★ **ABBEY ROAD** *Apple PCS 7088*	1	81 wks
23 May 70	★ **LET IT BE** *Apple PXS 1*	1	59 wks
16 Jan 71	**A HARD DAY'S NIGHT (re-issue)** *Parlophone PCS 3058*	30	1 wk
24 Jul 71	**HELP (re-issue)** *Parlophone PCS 3071*	33	2 wks
5 May 73	● **THE BEATLES 1967–1970** *Apple PCSP 718*	2	113 wks
5 May 73	● **THE BEATLES 1962–1966** *Apple PCSP 717*	3	148 wks
25 Jun 76	**ROCK 'N' ROLL MUSIC** *Parlophone PCSP 719*	11	15 wks
21 Aug 76	**THE BEATLES TAPES** *Polydor 2683 068*	45	1 wk
21 May 77	★ **THE BEATLES AT THE HOLLYWOOD BOWL** *Parlophone EMTV 4*	1	17 wks
17 Dec 77	● **LOVE SONGS** *Parlophone PCSP 721*	7	17 wks
3 Nov 79	**RARITIES** *Parlophone PCM 1001*	71	1 wk
15 Nov 80	**BEATLES BALLADS** *Parlophone PCS 7214*	17	16 wks
30 Oct 82	● **20 GREATEST HITS** *Parlophone PCTC 260*	10	30 wks
7 Mar 87	**PLEASE PLEASE ME (re-issue)** *Parlophone CDP 746 435-2*	32	4 wks
7 Mar 87	**WITH THE BEATLES (re-issue)** *Parlophone CDP 746 436-2*	40	2 wks
7 Mar 87	**A HARD DAY'S NIGHT (second re-issue)** *Parlophone CDP 746 437-2*	30	4 wks
7 Mar 87	**BEATLES FOR SALE (re-issue)** *Parlophone CDP 746 438-2*	45	2 wks
9 May 87	**HELP (second re-issue)** *Parlophone CDP 746 439-2*	61	3 wks
9 May 87	**RUBBER SOUL (re-issue)** *Parlophone CDP 746 440-2*	60	3 wks
9 May 87	**REVOLVER (re-issue)** *Parlophone CDP 746 441-2*	55	5 wks
6 Jun 87	● **SERGEANT PEPPER'S LONELY HEARTS CLUB BAND** *Parlophone CDP 746 442-2*	3	16 wks
5 Sep 87	**THE BEATLES (re-issue)** *Parlophone CDS 746 443-9*	18	2 wks
5 Sep 87	**YELLOW SUBMARINE (re-issue)** *Parlophone CDP 746 445-2*	60	1 wk
3 Oct 87	**MAGICAL MYSTERY TOUR** *Parlophone PCTC 255*	52	1 wk
31 Oct 87	**ABBEY ROAD (re-issue)** *Parlophone CDP 746 446-2*	30	2 wks
31 Oct 87	**LET IT BE (re-issue)** *Parlophone CDP 746 447-2*	50	1 wk

Yellow Submarine *featured several tracks by the George Martin Orchestra. The albums that recharted in 1987 are compact discs. The label numbers are the CD catalogue numbers of these re-issues.*

BE-BOP DELUXE
UK, male vocal/instrumental group   *28 wks*

31 Jan 76	**SUNBURST FINISH** *Harvest SHSP 4053*	17	12 wks
25 Sep 76	**MODERN MUSIC** *Harvest SHSP 4058*	12	6 wks
6 Aug 77	● **LIVE! IN THE AIR AGE** *Harvest SHVL 816*	10	5 wks
25 Feb 78	**DRASTIC PLASTIC** *Harvest SHSP 4091*	22	5 wks

Jeff BECK *UK, male vocalist/instrumentalist – guitar*   *11 wks*

13 Sep 69	**BECK-OLA** *Columbia SCX 6351*	39	1 wk
24 Jul 76	**WIRED** *CBS 86012*	38	5 wks
19 Jul 80	**THERE AND BACK** *Epic EPC 83288*	38	4 wks
17 Aug 85	**FLASH** *Epic EPC 26112*	83	1 wk

See also Jeff Beck, Tim Bogert and Carmine Appice.

CHUCK BERRY does his trademark
duck walk.

Jeff BECK, Tim BOGERT and Carmine APPICE
UK/US, male vocal/instrumental group   *3 wks*

| 28 Apr 73 | JEFF BECK, TIM BOGERT & CARMINE APPICE Epic EPC 65455 | 28 | 3 wks |

See also Jeff Beck.

BEE GEES *UK/Australia, male vocal/instrumental group*   *163 wks*

12 Aug 67	●	BEE GEES FIRST *Polydor 583–012*	8	26 wks
24 Feb 68		HORIZONTAL *Polydor 582–020*	16	15 wks
28 Sep 68	●	IDEA *Polydor 583–036*	4	18 wks
5 Apr 69	●	ODESSA *Polydor 583–049/50*	10	1 wk
8 Nov 69	●	BEST OF THE BEE GEES *Polydor 583–063*	7	22 wks
9 May 70		CUCUMBER CASTLE *Polydor 2383–010*	57	2 wks
17 Feb 79	★	SPIRITS HAVING FLOWN *RSO RSBG 001*	1	33 wks
10 Nov 79	●	BEE GEES GREATEST *RSO RSDX 001*	6	25 wks
7 Nov 81		LIVING EYES *RSO RSBG 002*	73	8 wks
3 Oct 87		E.S.P. *Warner Bros. WX 83*	5†	13 wks

All albums from Cucumber Castle onwards group were UK only.

Sir Thomas BEECHAM *UK, conductor*   *2 wks*

| 26 Mar 60 | CARMEN *HMV ALP 1762/4* | 18 | 2 wks |

Full credit on sleeve reads 'Orchestre National de la Radio Diffusion Francaise, conducted by Sir Thomas Beecham'.

Captain BEEFHEART and his MAGIC BAND
US, male vocal/instrumental group   *16 wks*

6 Dec 69	TROUT MASK REPLICA *Straight STS 1053*	21	1 wk
23 Jan 71	LICK MY DECALS OFF BABY *Straight STS 1063*	20	10 wks
29 May 71	MIRROR MAN *Buddah 2365 002*	49	1 wk
19 Feb 72	THE SPOTLIGHT KID *Reprise K 44162*	44	2 wks
18 Sep 82	ICE CREAM FOR CROW *Virgin V 2337*	90	2 wks

BELLAMY BROTHERS *US, male vocal duo*   *6 wks*

| 19 Jun 76 | BELLAMY BROTHERS *Warner Bros. K 56242* | 21 | 6 wks |

Regina BELLE *US, female vocalist*   *4 wks*

| 1 Aug 87 | ALL BY MYSELF *CBS 450 998–1* | 53 | 4 wks |

BELLE STARS *UK, female vocal/instrumental group*   *12 wks*

| 5 Feb 83 | THE BELLE STARS *Stiff SEEZ 45* | 15 | 12 wks |

Pierre BELMONDE
France, male instrumentalist – panpipes   *10 wks*

| 7 Jun 80 | THEMES FOR DREAMS *K-Tel ONE 1077* | 13 | 10 wks |

BELMONTS – *See DION and the BELMONTS*

Pat BENATAR *US, female vocalist*   *56 wks*

25 Jul 81		PRECIOUS TIME *Chrysalis CHR 1346*	30	7 wks
13 Nov 82		GET NERVOUS *Chrysalis CHR 1396*	73	6 wks
15 Oct 83		LIVE FROM EARTH *Chrysalis CHR 1451*	60	5 wks
17 Nov 84		TROPICO *Chrysalis CHR 1471*	31	25 wks
24 Aug 85		IN THE HEAT OF THE NIGHT *Chrysalis CHR 1236*	98	1 wk
7 Dec 85		SEVEN THE HARD WAY *Chrysalis CHR 1507*	69	4 wks
7 Nov 87	●	BEST SHOTS *Chrysalis PATV 1*	6	8 wks

Cliff BENNETT and the REBEL ROUSERS
UK, male vocal/instrumental group   *3 wks*

| 22 Oct 66 | DRIVIN' ME WILD *MFP 1121* | 25 | 3 wks |

Tony BENNETT *US, male vocalist*   *63 wks*

29 May 65		I LEFT MY HEART IN SAN FRANCISCO *CBS BPG 62201*	13	14 wks
19 Feb 66	●	A STRING OF TONY'S HITS *CBS DP 66010*	9	13 wks
10 Jun 67		TONY'S GREATEST HITS *CBS SBPG 62821*	14	24 wks
23 Sep 67		TONY MAKES IT HAPPEN *CBS SBPG 63055*	31	3 wks
23 Mar 68		FOR ONCE IN MY LIFE *CBS SBPG 63166*	29	5 wks
26 Feb 77		THE VERY BEST OF TONY BENNETT – 20 GREATEST HITS *Warwick PA 5021*	23	4 wks

George BENSON
US, male vocalist/instrumentalist – guitar   *239 wks*

19 Mar 77		IN FLIGHT *Warner Bros. K 56237*	19	23 wks
18 Feb 78		WEEKEND IN L.A. *Warner Bros. K 66074*	47	1 wk
24 Mar 79		LIVING INSIDE YOUR LOVE *Warner Bros. K 66085*	24	14 wks
26 Jul 80	●	GIVE ME THE NIGHT *Warner Bros. K 56823*	3	40 wks
14 Nov 81		GEORGE BENSON COLLECTION *Warner Bros. K 66107*	19	35 wks
11 Jun 83	●	IN YOUR EYES *Warner Bros. 92-3744-1*	3	53 wks
26 Jan 85	●	20/20 *Warner Bros. 92-5178-1*	9	19 wks
19 Oct 85	★	THE LOVE SONGS *K-Tel NE 1308*	1	27 wks
6 Sep 86		WHILE THE CITY SLEEPS … *Warner Bros. WX 55*	13	27 wks

See also George Benson and Earl Klugh.

George BENSON and Earl KLUGH
US, male instrumental duo   *6 wks*

| 11 Jul 87 | COLLABORATION *Warner Bros. WX 91* | 47 | 6 wks |

See also George Benson.

BERLIN *US, male/female vocal/instrumental group*   *11 wks*

| 17 Jan 87 | COUNT THREE AND PRAY *Mercury MER 101* | 32 | 11 wks |

BERLIN PHILHARMONIC ORCHESTRA conducted by HERBERT VON KARAJAN
Germany, orchestra   *2 wks*

| 26 Sep 70 | BEETHOVEN TRIPLE CONCERTO *HMV ASD 2582* | 51 | 2 wks |

Soloists: David Oistrakh (violin), Mstislav Rostropovich (cello) and Sviatoslav Richter (piano).

LEONARD BERNSTEIN'S WEST SIDE STORY – *See Studio Cast Recordings*

Shelley BERMAN *US, male vocalist – comedian*   *4 wks*

| 19 Nov 60 | INSIDE SHELLEY BERMAN *Capitol CLP 1300* | 12 | 4 wks |

Chuck BERRY
US, male vocalist/instrumentalist – guitar   *53 wks*

25 May 63		CHUCK BERRY *Pye International NPL 28024*	12	16 wks
5 Oct 63	●	CHUCK BERRY ON STAGE *Pye International NPL 28027*	6	11 wks
7 Dec 63	●	MORE CHUCK BERRY *Pye International NPL 28028*	9	8 wks

30 May 64 ●	HIS LATEST AND GREATEST *Pye NPL 28037* ..	8	7 wks
3 Oct 64	YOU NEVER CAN TELL *Pye NPL 29039*	18	2 wks
12 Feb 77 ●	MOTORVATIN' *Chess 9288 690*	7	9 wks

Mike BERRY *UK, male vocalist* *3 wks*

24 Jan 81	THE SUNSHINE OF YOUR SMILE		
	Polydor 2383 592	63	3 wks

Nick BERRY *UK, male vocalist* *1 wk*

20 Dec 86	NICK BERRY *BBC REB 618*	99	1 wk

BEVERLEY-PHILLIPS ORCHESTRA
UK, orchestra *9 wks*

9 Oct 76	GOLD ON SILVER *Warwick WW 5018*	22	9 wks

Frankie BEVERLY – *See MAZE featuring Frankie BEVERLY*

B52s *US, male/female vocal/instrumental group* *33 wks*

4 Aug 79	B-52s *Island ILPS 9580*	22	12 wks
13 Sep 80	WILD PLANET *Island ILPS 9622*	18	4 wks
11 Jul 81	THE PARTY MIX ALBUM *Island IPM 1001*	36	5 wks
27 Feb 82	MESOPOTAMIA *EMI ISSP 4006*	18	6 wks
21 May 83	WHAMMY! *Island ILPS 9759*	33	4 wks
8 Aug 87	BOUNCING OFF THE SATELLITES		
	Island ILPS 9871	74	2 wks

BIG AUDIO DYNAMITE
UK, male vocal/instrumental group *35 wks*

16 Nov 85	THIS IS BIG AUDIO DYNAMITE *CBS 26714*	27	27 wks
8 Nov 86	No. 10 UPPING STREET *CBS 450 137-1*	11	8 wks

BIG BEN BANJO BAND
UK, male instrumental group *1 wk*

17 Dec 60	MORE MINSTREL MELODIES		
	Columbia 33SX 1254	20	1 wk

BIG COUNTRY *UK, male vocal/instrumental group* *117 wks*

6 Aug 83 ●	THE CROSSING *Mercury MERS 27*	3	80 wks
27 Oct 84 ★	STEELTOWN *Mercury MERH 49*	1	21 wks
12 Jul 86	THE SEER *Mercury MERH 87*	2	16 wks

BIG DISH *UK, male vocal/instrumental group* *1 wk*

11 Oct 86	SWIMMER *Virgin V 2374*	85	1 wk

BIG ROLL BAND – *See Zoot MONEY and the BIG ROLL BAND*

BIG SOUND – *See Simon DUPREE and the BIG SOUND*

Mr. Acker BILK
UK, male band leader, vocalist/instrumentalist – clarinet *76 wks*

19 Mar 60 ●	SEVEN AGES OF ACKER *Columbia 33SX 1205* ...	6	6 wks
9 Apr 60	ACKER BILK'S OMNIBUS *Pye NJL 22*	14	3 wks
4 Mar 61	ACKER *Columbia 33SX 1248*	17	1 wk
1 Apr 61	GOLDEN TREASURY OF BILK		
	Columbia 33SX 1304	11	6 wks
26 May 62 ●	STRANGER ON THE SHORE		
	Columbia 33SX 1407	6	28 wks
4 May 63	A TASTE OF HONEY *Columbia 33SX 1493*	17	4 wks
9 Oct 76	THE ONE FOR ME *Pye NSPX 41052*	38	6 wks

4 Jun 77 ●	SHEER MAGIC *Warwick WW 5028*	5	8 wks
11 Nov 78	EVERGREEN *Warwick PW 5045*	17	14 wks

See also Kenny Ball, Chris Barber and Acker Bilk; Chris Barber and Acker Bilk.

BIRTHDAY PARTY
Australia, male vocal/instrumental group *3 wks*

24 Jul 82	JUNKYARD *4AD CAD 207*	73	3 wks

Stephen BISHOP *US, male instrumentalist – piano* *3 wks*

1 Apr 72	GREIG AND SCHUMANN PIANO CONCERTOS		
	Philips 6500 166	34	3 wks

BLACK *UK, male vocalist/instrumentalist*
Colin Vearncombe under an assumed group name *13 wks*

26 Sep 87 ●	WONDERFUL LIFE *A & M AMA 5165*	3†	13 wks

Cilla BLACK *UK, female vocalist* *61 wks*

13 Feb 65 ●	CILLA *Parlophone PMC 1243*	5	11 wks
14 May 66 ●	CILLA SINGS A RAINBOW *Parlophone PMC 7004*	4	15 wks
13 Apr 68 ●	SHER-OO *Parlophone PCS 7041*	7	11 wks
30 Nov 68	BEST OF CILLA BLACK *Parlophone PCS 7065*	21	11 wks
25 Jul 70	SWEET INSPIRATION *Parlophone PCS 7103*	42	4 wks
29 Jan 83	THE VERY BEST OF CILLA BLACK		
	Parlophone EMTV 38	20	9 wks

BLACK LACE *UK, male vocal/instrumental group* *26 wks*

8 Dec 84 ●	PARTY PARTY – 16 GREAT PARTY		
	ICEBREAKERS *Telstar STAR 2250*	4	14 wks
7 Dec 85	PARTY PARTY 2 *Telstar STAR 2266*	18	6 wks
6 Dec 86	PARTY CRAZY *Telstar STAR 2288*	58	6 wks

BLACKHEARTS – *See Joan JETT and the BLACKHEARTS*

BLACK SABBATH
UK/US, male vocal/instrumental group *204 wks*

7 Mar 70 ●	BLACK SABBATH *Vertigo VO 6*	8	42 wks
26 Sep 70 ★	PARANOID *Vertigo 6360 011*	1	27 wks
21 Aug 71 ●	MASTER OF REALITY *Vertigo 6360 050*	5	13 wks
30 Sep 72 ●	BLACK SABBATH VOL. 4 *Vertigo 6360 071*	8	10 wks
8 Dec 73 ●	SABBATH BLOODY SABBATH		
	WWA WWA 005	4	11 wks
27 Sep 75 ●	SABOTAGE *NEMS 9119 001*	7	7 wks
7 Feb 76	WE SOLD OUR SOUL FOR ROCK 'N' ROLL		
	NEMS 6641 335	35	5 wks
6 Nov 76	TECHNICAL ECSTASY *Vertigo 9102 750*	13	6 wks
14 Oct 78	NEVER SAY DIE *Vertigo 9102 751*	12	6 wks
26 Apr 80 ●	HEAVEN AND HELL *Vertigo 9102 752*	9	22 wks
5 Jul 80 ●	BLACK SABBATH LIVE AT LAST *NEMS BS 001*	5	15 wks
27 Sep 80	PARANOID (re-issue) *NEMS NEL 6003*	54	2 wks
14 Nov 81	MOB RULES *Mercury 6V02119*	12	14 wks
22 Jan 83	LIVE EVIL *Vertigo SAB 10*	13	11 wks
24 Sep 83 ●	BORN AGAIN *Vertigo VERL 8*	4	7 wks
1 Mar 86	SEVENTH STAR *Vertigo VERH 29*	27	5 wks
28 Nov 87	THE ETERNAL IDOL *Vertigo VERH 51*	66	1 wk

Seventh Star credits Black Sabbath featuring Tony Iommi.

BLACK UHURU
Jamaica, male/female vocal/instrumental group *22 wks*

13 Jun 81	RED *Island ILPS 9625*	28	13 wks
22 Aug 81	BLACK UHURU *Virgin VX 1004*	81	2 wks
19 Jun 82	CHILL OUT *Island ILPS 9701*	38	6 wks
25 Aug 84	ANTHEM *Island ILPS 0773*	90	1 wk

Band of the BLACK WATCH *UK, military band*   *13 wks*

7 Feb 76	**SCOTCH ON THE ROCKS** *Spark SRLM 503*	11	13 wks

BLACK WIDOW *UK, male vocal/instrumental group*   *2 wks*

4 Apr 70	**SACRIFICE** *CBS 63948*	32	2 wks

BLACKFOOT *US, male vocal/instrumental group*   *22 wks*

18 Jul 81	**MARAUDER** *Atco K 50799*	38	12 wks
11 Sep 82	**HIGHWAY SONG-BLACKFOOT LIVE** *Atco K 50910*	14	6 wks
21 May 83	**SIOGO** *Atco 79-0080-1*	28	3 wks
29 Sep 84	**VERTICAL SMILES** *Atco 790218* ...	82	1 wk

Ritchie BLACKMORE'S RAINBOW – *See RAINBOW*

Howard BLAKE conducting the SINFONIA OF LONDON *UK, conductor and orchestra*   *11 wks*

22 Dec 84	**THE SNOWMAN** *CBS 71116*	54†	11 wks

Narration by Bernard Cribbins.

BLANCMANGE *UK, male vocal/instrumental duo*   *57 wks*

9 Oct 82	**HAPPY FAMILIES** *London SH 8552*	30	38 wks
26 May 84	● **MANGE TOUT** *London SH 8554*	8	17 wks
26 Oct 85	**BELIEVE YOU ME** *London LONLP 10*	54	2 wks

BLIND FAITH *UK, male vocal/instrumental group*   *10 wks*

13 Sep 69	★ **BLIND FAITH** *Polydor 583-059*	1	10 wks

BLITZ *UK, male vocal/instrumental group*   *3 wks*

6 Nov 82	**VOICE OF A GENERATION** *No Future PUNK 1* .	27	3 wks

BLIZZARD OF OZ – *See Ozzy OSBOURNE*

BLOCKHEADS – *See Ian DURY and the BLOCKHEADS*

BLODWYN PIG *UK, male vocal/instrumental group*   *11 wks*

16 Aug 69	● **AHEAD RINGS OUT** *Island ILPS 9101*	9	4 wks
23 Apr 70	● **GETTING TO THIS** *Island ILPS 9122*	8	7 wks

BLONDIE
US/UK, female/male vocal/instrumental group   *264 wks*

4 Mar 78	● **PLASTIC LETTERS** *Chrysalis CHR 1166*	10	54 wks
23 Sep 78	★ **PARALLEL LINES** *Chrysalis CDL 1992*	1	105 wks
10 Mar 79	**BLONDIE** *Chrysalis CHR 1165*	75	1 wk
13 Oct 79	★ **EAT TO THE BEAT** *Chrysalis CDL 1225*	1	38 wks
29 Nov 80	● **AUTOAMERICAN** *Chrysalis CDL 1290*	3	16 wks
31 Oct 81	● **BEST OF BLONDIE** *Chrysalis CDLTV 1*	4	38 wks
5 Jun 82	● **THE HUNTER** *Chrysalis CDL 1384*	9	12 wks

BLOOD SWEAT AND TEARS
US/Canada, male vocal/instrumental group   *21 wks*

13 Jul 68	**CHILD IS FATHER TO THE MAN** *CBS 63296* ...	40	1 wk
12 Apr 69	**BLOOD SWEAT AND TEARS** *CBS 63504*	15	8 wks
8 Aug 70	**BLOOD SWEAT AND TEARS 3** *CBS 64024*	14	12 wks

BLOW MONKEYS
UK, male vocal/instrumental group   *16 wks*

19 Apr 86	**ANIMAL MAGIC** *RCA PL 70910*	21	8 wks
25 Apr 87	**SHE WAS ONLY A GROCER'S DAUGHTER** *RCA PL 71245*	20	8 wks

BLUE NILE *UK, male vocal/instrumental group*   *2 wks*

19 May 84	**A WALK ACROSS THE ROOFTOPS** *Linn LKH 1*	80	2 wks

BLUE OYSTER CULT
US, male vocal/instrumental group   *40 wks*

3 Jul 76	**AGENTS OF FORTUNE** *CBS 81385*	26	10 wks
4 Feb 78	**SPECTRES** *CBS 86050*	60	1 wk
28 Oct 78	**SOME ENCHANTED EVENING** *CBS 86074*	18	4 wks
18 Aug 79	**MIRRORS** *CBS 86087*	46	5 wks
19 Jul 80	**CULTOSAURUS ERECTUS** *CBS 86120*	12	7 wks
25 Jul 81	**FIRE OF UNKNOWN ORIGIN** *CBS 85137*	29	7 wks
22 May 82	**EXTRATERRESTRIAL LIVE** *CBS 22203*	39	5 wks
19 Nov 83	**THE REVOLUTION BY NIGHT** *CBS 25686*	95	1 wk

BLUE RONDO A LA TURK
UK, male vocal/instrumental group   *2 wks*

6 Nov 82	**CHEWING THE FAT** *Diable Noir V 2240*	80	2 wks

BLUES BAND *UK, male vocal/instrumental group*   *18 wks*

8 Mar 80	**OFFICIAL BOOTLEG ALBUM** *Arista BBBP 101*	40	9 wks
18 Oct 80	**READY** *Arista BB 2*	36	6 wks
17 Oct 81	**ITCHY FEET** *Arista BB 3*	60	3 wks

BLUEBELLS *UK, male vocal/instrumental group*   *10 wks*

11 Aug 84	**SISTERS** *London LONLP 1*	22	10 wks

Marc BOLAN – *See T.REX*

BODINES *UK, male vocal/instrumental group*   *1 wk*

29 Aug 87	**PLAYED** *Pop BODL 2001*	94	1 wk

Tim BOGERT – *See Jeff BECK, Tim BOGERT and Carmine APPICE*

BOLSHOI *UK, male vocal/instrumental group*   *1 wk*

3 Oct 87	**LINDY'S PARTY** *Beggars Banquet BEGA 86*	100	1 wk

Graham BOND
UK, male vocalist/instrumentalist – keyboards   *2 wks*

20 Jun 70	**SOLID BOND** *Warner Bros. WS 3001*	40	2 wks

Gary U.S. BONDS *US, male vocalist*   *8 wks*

22 Aug 81	**DEDICATION** *EMI America AML 3017*	43	3 wks
10 Jul 82	**ON THE LINE** *EMI America AML 3022*	55	5 wks

BONEY M
Various West Indian islands, male/female vocal group   *130 wks*

23 Apr 77	**TAKE THE HEAT OFF ME** *Atlantic K 50314*	40	15 wks

BLOOD SWEAT AND TEARS (lead singer David Clayton-Thomas middle row, second from left) are shown just before the release of their historic second album (*You've Made Me So Very Happy, Spinning Wheel, And When I Die*).

6 Aug 77		LOVE FOR SALE	Atlantic K 50385	....	60	1 wk
29 Jul 78	★	NIGHT FLIGHT TO VENUS			1	65 wks
		Atlantic/Hansa K 50498				
29 Sep 79	★	OCEANS OF FANTASY	Atlantic/Hansa K 50610		1	18 wks
12 Apr 80	★	THE MAGIC OF BONEY M			1	26 wks
		Atlantic/Hansa BMTV 1				
6 Sep 86		THE BEST OF 10 YEARS	Stylus SMR 621	....	38	5 wks

BON JOVI US, male vocal/instrumental group   75 wks

28 Apr 84		BON JOVI	Vertigo VERL 14	....	71	3 wks
11 May 85		7800° FAHRENHEIT	Vertigo VERL 24	......	28	12 wks
20 Sep 86	●	SLIPPERY WHEN WET	Vertigo VERH 38	.....	6	60 wks

Graham BONNET UK, male vocalist   3 wks

| 7 Nov 81 | | LINE UP | Mercury 6302151 | .... | 62 | 3 wks |

BONNIE – *See DELANEY and BONNIE and FRIENDS*

BONZO DOG DOO-DAH BAND
UK, male vocal/instrumental group   4 wks

18 Jan 69		DOUGHNUT IN GRANNY'S GREENHOUSE				
		Liberty LBS 83158		......	40	1 wk
30 Aug 69		TADPOLES	Liberty LBS 83257	....	36	1 wk
22 Jun 74		THE HISTORY OF THE BONZOS				
		United Artists UAD 60071		....	41	2 wks

BOOKER T. and the MG'S
US, male instrumental group   5 wks

| 25 Jul 64 | | GREEN ONIONS | London HAK 8182 | .... | 11 | 4 wks |
| 11 Jul 70 | | McLEMORE AVENUE | Stax SXATS 1031 | ...... | 70 | 1 wk |

BOOMTOWN RATS
Ireland, male vocal/instrumental group   93 wks

17 Sep 77		BOOMTOWN RATS	Ensign ENVY 1	....	18	11 wks
8 Jul 78	●	TONIC FOR THE TROOPS	Ensign ENVY 3	....	8	44 wks
3 Nov 79	●	THE FINE ART OF SURFACING				
		Ensign ENROX 11		....	7	26 wks
24 Jan 81	●	MONDO BONGO	Mercury 6359 042	....	6	7 wks
3 Apr 82		V DEEP	Mercury 6359 082	....	64	5 wks

Pat BOONE US, male vocalist   12 wks

22 Nov 58	●	STARDUST	London HAD 2127	....	10	1 wk
28 May 60		HYMNS WE HAVE LOVED	London HAD 2228	..	12	2 wks
25 Jun 60		HYMNS WE LOVE	London HAD 2092	....	14	1 wk
24 Apr 76		PAT BOONE ORIGINALS	ABC ABSD 301	.....	16	8 wks

BOSTON US, male vocal/instrumental group   43 wks

5 Feb 77		BOSTON	Epic EPC 81611	....	11	20 wks
9 Sep 78	●	DON'T LOOK BACK	Epic EPC 86057	......	9	10 wks
4 Apr 81		BOSTON	Epic EPC 32038	....	58	2 wks
18 Oct 86		THIRD STAGE	MCA MCG 6017	....	37	11 wks

Judy BOUCHER UK, female vocalist   1 wk

| 25 Apr 87 | | CAN'T BE WITH YOU TONIGHT | | | | |
| | | Orbitone OLP 024 | | .... | 95 | 1 wk |

BOW WOW WOW
UK, female/male vocal/instrumental group   13 wks

| 24 Oct 81 | | SEE JUNGLE! SEE JUNGLE! GO JOIN YOUR GANG YEAH CITY ALL OVER! GO APE CRAZY! | RCA RCALP 0027 3000 | .... | 26 | 7 wks |

| 7 Aug 82 | | I WANT CANDY | EMI EMC 3416 | .... | 26 | 6 wks |

David BOWIE UK, male vocalist   829 wks

1 Jul 72	●	THE RISE AND FALL OF ZIGGY STARDUST AND THE SPIDERS FROM MARS				
		RCA Victor SF 8287		....	5	106 wks
23 Sep 72	●	HUNKY DORY	RCA Victor SF 8244	....	3	69 wks
29 Nov 72		SPACE ODDITY	RCA Victor LSP 4813	....	17	37 wks
29 Nov 72		THE MAN WHO SOLD THE WORLD				
		RCA Victor LSP 4816		....	26	22 wks
5 May 73	★	ALADDIN SANE	RCA Victor RS 1001	....	1	47 wks
3 Nov 73	●	PIN-UPS	RCA Victor RS 1003	....	1	21 wks
8 Jun 74	★	DIAMOND DOGS	RCA Victor APLI 0576	...	1	17 wks
16 Nov 74	●	DAVID LIVE	RCA Victor APL 2 0771	......	2	12 wks
5 Apr 75	●	YOUNG AMERICANS	RCA Victor RS 1006	...	2	12 wks
7 Feb 76	●	STATION TO STATION	RCA Victor APLI 1327	..	5	16 wks
12 Jun 76	●	CHANGESONEBOWIE	RCA Victor RS 1055	..	2	28 wks
29 Jan 77	●	LOW	RCA Victor PL 12030	....	2	18 wks
29 Oct 77	●	HEROES	RCA Victor PL 12522	....	3	18 wks
14 Oct 78	●	STAGE	RCA Victor PL 02913	....	5	10 wks
9 Jun 79	●	LODGER	RCA Bow LP1	....	4	17 wks
27 Sep 80	★	SCARY MONSTERS AND SUPER CREEPS				
		RCA Bow LP2		....	1	32 wks
10 Jan 81	●	VERY BEST OF DAVID BOWIE	K-Tel NE 1111	.	3	20 wks
17 Jan 81		HUNKY DORY (re-issue)				
		RCA International INTS 5064		....	32	51 wks
31 Jan 81		THE RISE AND FALL OF ZIGGY STARDUST AND THE SPIDERS FROM MARS (re-issue)				
		RCA International INTS 5063		....	33	62 wks
28 Nov 81		CHANGESTWOBOWIE	RCA BOW LP3	....	24	17 wks
6 Mar 82		ALADDIN SANE (re-issue)				
		RCA International INTS 5067		....	49	24 wks
14 Jan 83		RARE	RCA PL 45406	....	34	11 wks
23 Apr 83	★	LETS DANCE	EMI America AML 3029	.....	1	56 wks
30 Apr 83		PIN-UPS (re-issue)	RCA International INTS 5236		57	15 wks
30 Apr 83		THE MAN WHO SOLD THE WORLD (re-issue)				
		RCA International INTS 5237		....	64	8 wks
14 May 83		DIAMOND DOGS (re-issue)				
		RCA International INTS 5068		....	60	14 wks
11 Jun 83		HEROES (re-issue)	RCA International INTS 5066		75	8 wks
11 Jun 83		LOW (re-issue)	RCA International INTS 5065	...	85	5 wks
20 Aug 83		GOLDEN YEARS	RCA BOWLP 4	....	33	5 wks
5 Nov 83		ZIGGY STARDUST – THE MOTION PICTURE				
		RCA PL 84862		....	17	6 wks
28 Apr 84		FAME AND FASHION (ALL TIME GREATEST HITS)	RCA PL 84919		40	6 wks
19 May 84		LOVE YOU TILL TUESDAY	Deram BOWIE 1	...	53	4 wks
6 Oct 84	★	TONIGHT	EMI America DB 1	....	1	19 wks
2 May 87	●	NEVER LET ME DOWN	EMI America AMLS 3117		6	16 wks

BOXCAR WILLIE US, male vocalist   12 wks

| 31 May 80 | ● | KING OF THE ROAD | Warwick WW 5084 | .... | 5 | 12 wks |

Max BOYCE UK, male vocalist/comedian   105 wks

5 Jul 75		LIVE AT TREORCHY	One Up OU 2033	....	21	32 wks
1 Nov 75	★	WE ALL HAD DOCTORS' PAPERS				
		EMI MB 101		....	1	17 wks
20 Nov 76	●	THE INCREDIBLE PLAN	EMI MB 102	......	9	12 wks
7 Jan 78		THE ROAD AND THE MILES	EMI MB 103	...	50	3 wks
11 Mar 78		LIVE AT TREORCHY (re-issue)				
		One Up OU 54043		....	42	6 wks
27 May 78	●	I KNOW COS I WAS THERE	EMI MAX 1001	..	6	14 wks
13 Oct 79		NOT THAT I'M BIASED	EMI MAX 1002	....	27	13 wks
15 Nov 80		ME AND BILLY WILLIAMS	EMI MAX 1003	....	37	8 wks

BOY GEORGE UK, male vocalist   6 wks

| 27 Jun 87 | | SOLD | Virgin V 2430 | .... | 29 | 6 wks |

BOYS UK, male vocal/instrumental group   1 wk

1 Oct 77	THE BOYS *NEMS NEL 6001*	50	1 wk

Billy BRAGG UK, male vocalist   63 wks

21 Jan 84	LIFE'S A RIOT WITH SPY VS SPY		
	Go! Discs UTILITY UTIL 1	30	30 wks
20 Oct 84	BREWING UP WITH BILLY BRAGG		
	Go! Discs AGOLP 4	16	21 wks
4 Oct 86	TALKING WITH THE TAXMAN ABOUT POETRY		
	Go! Discs AGOLP 6	8	8 wks
13 Jun 87	BACK TO BASICS *Go! Discs AGOLP 8*	37	4 wks

Wilfred BRAMBELL and Harry H. CORBETT
UK, male comic duo   34 wks

23 Mar 63	● STEPTOE AND SON *Pye NPL 18081*	4	28 wks
11 Mar 64	STEPTOE & SON *Pye GGL 0217*	14	5 wks
14 Mar 64	MORE JUNK *Pye NPL 18090*	19	1 wk

BRAND X UK, male vocal/instrumental group   6 wks

| 21 May 77 | MOROCCAN ROLL *Charisma CAS 1126* .... | 37 | 5 wks |
| 11 Sep 82 | IS THERE ANYTHING ABOUT? *CBS 85967* .... | 93 | 1 wk |

Laura BRANIGAN US, female vocalist   18 wks

| 18 Aug 84 | SELF CONTROL *Atlantic 780147* .... | 16 | 14 wks |
| 24 Aug 85 | HOLD ME *Atlantic 78-1265-1* .... | 64 | 4 wks |

BRASS CONSTRUCTION
US, male vocal/instrumental group   12 wks

20 Mar 76	● BRASS CONSTRUCTION		
	United Artists UAS 29923	9	11 wks
30 Jun 84	RENEGADES *Capitol EJ 24 0160*	94	1 wk

BREAD US, male vocal/instrumental group   179 wks

26 Sep 70	ON THE WATERS *Elektra 2469-005*	34	5 wks
18 Mar 72	● BABY I'M A WANT-YOU *Elektra K 42100*	9	19 wks
28 Oct 72	● BEST OF BREAD *Elektra K 42115*	7	100 wks
27 Jul 74	THE BEST OF BREAD VOL. 2 *Elektra K 42161* ...	48	1 wk
29 Jan 77	LOST WITHOUT YOUR LOVE *Elektra K 52044* ..	17	6 wks
5 Nov 77	★ THE SOUND OF BREAD *Elektra K 52062*	1	46 wks
28 Nov 87	THE VERY BEST OF BREAD *Telstar STAR 2303*	84	2 wks

BREAK MACHINE US, male vocal/dance group   16 wks

| 9 Jun 84 | BREAK MACHINE *Record Shack SOHO LP 3* ..... | 17 | 16 wks |

Adrian BRETT UK, male instrumentalist – flute   11 wks

| 10 Nov 79 | ECHOES OF GOLD *Warwick WW 5062* .... | 19 | 11 wks |

Paul BRETT UK, male instrumentalist – guitar   7 wks

| 19 Jul 80 | ROMANTIC GUITAR *K-Tel ONE 1079* .... | 24 | 7 wks |

BRIGHOUSE AND RASTRICK BRASS BAND
UK, male brass band   11 wks

| 28 Jan 78 | ● FLORAL DANCE *Logo 1001* .... | 10 | 11 wks |

BRILLIANT UK, male/female vocal/instrumental group   1 wk

| 20 Sep 86 | KISS THE LIPS OF LIFE *Food BRILL 1* .... | 83 | 1 wk |

Johnny BRISTOL US, male vocalist   7 wks

| 5 Oct 74 | HANG ON IN THERE BABY *MGM 2315 303* .... | 12 | 7 wks |

June BRONHILL and Thomas ROUND
Australia/UK, female/male vocal duo   1 wk

| 18 Jun 60 | LILAC TIME *HMV CLP 1248* .... | 17 | 1 wk |

BRONSKI BEAT UK, male vocal/instrumental group   65 wks

20 Oct 84	● THE AGE OF CONSENT *Forbidden Fruit BITLP 1*	4	53 wks
21 Sep 85	HUNDREDS AND THOUSANDS		
	Forbidden Fruit BITLP 2	24	6 wks
10 May 86	TRUTHDARE DOUBLEDARE		
	Forbidden Fruit BITLP 3	18	6 wks

Elkie BROOKS UK, female vocalist   202 wks

18 Jun 77	TWO DAYS AWAY *A & M AMLH 68409*	16	20 wks
13 May 78	SHOOTING STAR *A & M AMLH 64695*	20	13 wks
13 Oct 79	LIVE AND LEARN *A & M AMLH 68509*	34	6 wks
14 Nov 81	● PEARLS *A & M ELK 1981*	2	79 wks
13 Nov 82	● PEARLS II *A & M ELK 1982*	5	25 wks
14 Jul 84	MINUTES *A & M AML 68565*	35	7 wks
8 Dec 84	SCREEN GEMS *EMI SCREEN 1*	35	11 wks
6 Dec 86	NO MORE THE FOOL *Legend LMA 1*	5	23 wks
27 Dec 86	● THE VERY BEST OF ELKIE BROOKS		
	Telstar STAR 2284	10	18 wks

Nigel BROOKS SINGERS
UK, male/female vocal choir   17 wks

29 Nov 75	● SONGS OF JOY *K-Tel NE 706*	5	16 wks
5 Jun 76	20 ALL TIME EUROVISION FAVOURITES		
	K-Tel NE 712	44	1 wk

BROTHERHOOD OF MAN
UK, male/female vocal group   40 wks

24 Apr 76	LOVE AND KISSES FROM *Pye NSPL 18490*	20	8 wks
12 Aug 78	B FOR BROTHERHOOD *Pye NSPL 18567*	18	9 wks
7 Oct 78	● BROTHERHOOD OF MAN *K-Tel BML 7980*	6	15 wks
29 Nov 80	SING 20 NUMBER ONE HITS *Warwick WW 5087* .	14	8 wks

BROTHERS JOHNSON
US, male vocal/instrumental duo   22 wks

19 Aug 78	BLAM!! *A & M AMLH 64714*	48	8 wks
23 Feb 80	LIGHT UP THE NIGHT *A & M AMLK 63716*	22	12 wks
18 Jul 81	WINNERS *A & M AMLK 63724*	42	2 wks

Edgar BROUGHTON BAND
UK, male vocal/instrumental group   6 wks

20 Jun 70	SING BROTHER SING *Harvest SHVL 772*	18	4 wks
5 Jun 71	THE EDGAR BROUGHTON BAND		
	Harvest SHVL 791	28	2 wks

(Right) ELKIE BROOKS demands everyone realize she's had more weeks on chart than former Vinegar Joe partner Robert Palmer. (Below) BLACK SABBATH model quintessential seventies fashions.

Crazy World Of Arthur BROWN
UK, male vocal/instrumental group   *16 wks*

6 Jul 68	● CRAZY WORLD OF ARTHUR BROWN		
	Track 612005	2	16 wks

Dennis BROWN *Jamaica, male vocalist*   *6 wks*

26 Jun 82	LOVE HAS FOUND ITS WAY		
	A & M AMLH 64886	72	6 wks

James BROWN *US, male vocalist*   *15 wks*

18 Oct 86	GRAVITY *Scotti Bros.* SCT 57108	85	3 wks
10 Oct 87	THE BEST OF JAMES BROWN *K-Tel* NE 1376 ..	17†	12 wks

Joe BROWN *UK, male vocalist/instrumentalist – guitar*   *47 wks*

1 Sep 62	● A PICTURE OF YOU *Pye Golden Guinea* GGL 0146	3	39 wks
25 May 63	JOE BROWN – LIVE *Piccadilly* NPL 38006	14	8 wks

Jackson BROWNE *US, male vocalist*   *31 wks*

4 Dec 76	THE PRETENDER *Asylum* K 53048	26	5 wks
21 Jan 78	RUNNING ON EMPTY *Asylum* K 53070	28	7 wks
12 Jul 80	HOLD OUT *Asylum* K 52226	44	5 wks
13 Aug 83	LAWYERS IN LOVE *Asylum* 96–0268–1	37	7 wks
8 Mar 86	LIVES IN THE BALANCE *Asylum* EKT 31	36	7 wks

Dave BRUBECK QUARTET
US, male instrumental group   *17 wks*

25 Jun 60	TIME OUT *Fontana* TFL 5085	11	1 wk
7 Apr 62	TIME FURTHER OUT *Fontana* TFL 5161	12	16 wks

Second album just credited to Dave Brubeck.

Jack BRUCE
UK, male vocalist/instrumentalist – bass   *9 wks*

27 Sep 69	● SONGS FOR A TAILOR *Polydor* 583–058	6	9 wks

Peabo BRYSON and Roberta FLACK
US, male/female vocal duo   *10 wks*

17 Sep 83	BORN TO LOVE *Capitol* EST 7122841	15	10 wks

See also Roberta Flack; Roberta Flack and Donny Hathaway.

BUCKS FIZZ *UK, male/female vocal group*   *80 wks*

8 Aug 81	BUCKS FIZZ *RCA* RCALP 5050	14	28 wks
18 May 82	● ARE YOU READY? *RCA* RCALP 8000	10	23 wks
19 Mar 83	HAND CUT *RCA* RCALP 6100	17	13 wks
3 Dec 83	GREATEST HITS *RCA* RCA PL 70022	25	13 wks
24 Nov 84	I HEAR TALK *RCA* PL 70397	66	2 wks
13 Dec 86	THE WRITING ON THE WALL *Polydor* POHL 30	89	1 wk

Harold BUDD/Liz FRASER/Robin GUTHRIE/ Simon RAYMOND
UK, male/female vocal/instrumental group   *2 wks*

22 Nov 86	THE MOON AND THE MELODIES *4AD* CAD 611	46	2 wks

BUDGIE *UK, male vocal/instrumental group*   *10 wks*

8 Jun 74	IN FOR THE KILL *MCA* MCF 2546	29	3 wks
27 Sep 75	BANDOLIER *MCA* MCF 2723	36	4 wks
31 Oct 81	NIGHT FLIGHT *RCA* RCALP 6003	68	2 wks
23 Oct 82	DELIVER US FROM EVIL *RCA* RCALP 6054 ...	62	1 wk

BUGGLES *UK, male vocal/instrumental duo*   *6 wks*

16 Feb 80	THE AGE OF PLASTIC *Island* ILPS 9585	27	6 wks

BUNNYMEN – *See ECHO and the BUNNYMEN*

Eric BURDON and WAR
UK, male vocalist and US, male vocal/instrumental group   *2 wks*

3 Oct 70	ERIC BURDON DECLARES WAR		
	Polydor 2310–041	50	2 wks

Jean-Jacques BURNEL
UK, male vocalist/instrumentalist – bass guitar   *5 wks*

21 Apr 79	EUROMAN COMETH *United Artists* UAG 30214 ..	40	5 wks

See also Dave Greenfield and Jean-Jacques Burnel.

Kate BUSH *UK, female vocalist*   *234 wks*

11 Mar 78	● THE KICK INSIDE *EMI* EMC 3223	3	70 wks
25 Nov 78	● LIONHEART *EMI* EMA 787	6	36 wks
20 Sep 80	★ NEVER FOR EVER *EMI* EMA 796	1	23 wks
25 Sep 82	● THE DREAMING *EMI* EMC 3419	3	10 wks
28 Sep 85	★ HOUNDS OF LOVE *EMI* KAB 1	1	51 wks
22 Nov 86	★ THE WHOLE STORY *EMI* KBTV 1	1	44 wks

Jonathan BUTLER
South Africa, male vocalist/instrumentalist – guitar   *11 wks*

12 Sep 87	JONATHAN BUTLER *Jive* HIP 46	12	11 wks

BUZZCOCKS *UK, male vocal/instrumental group*   *23 wks*

25 Mar 78	ANOTHER MUSIC IN A DIFFERENT KITCHEN		
	United Artists UAG 30159	15	11 wks
7 Oct 78	LOVE BITES *United Artists* UAG 30184	13	9 wks
6 Oct 79	A DIFFERENT KIND OF TENSION		
	United Artists UAG 30260	26	3 wks

Max BYGRAVES *UK, male vocalist*   *151 wks*

23 Sep 72	● SING ALONG WITH MAX *Pye* NSPL 18361	4	44 wks
2 Dec 72	SING ALONG WITH MAX VOL. 2		
	Pye NSPL 18383	11	23 wks
5 May 73	● SINGALONGAMAX VOL. 3 *Pye* NSPL 18401	5	30 wks
29 Sep 73	● SINGALONGAMAX VOL. 4 *Pye* NSPL 18410	7	12 wks
15 Dec 73	SINGALONGPARTY SONG *Pye* NSPL 18419	15	6 wks
12 Oct 74	YOU MAKE ME FEEL LIKE SINGING A SONG		
	Pye NSPL 18436	39	3 wks
7 Dec 74	SINGALONGAXMAS *Pye* NSPL 18439	21	6 wks
13 Nov 76	● 100 GOLDEN GREATS *Ronco* RTDX 2019	3	21 wks
28 Oct 78	LINGALONGAMAX *Ronco* RPL 2033	39	5 wks
16 Dec 78	THE SONG AND DANCE MEN *Pye* NSPL 18574 .	67	1 wk

Charlie BYRD – *See Stan GETZ and Charlie BYRD*

Donald BYRD
US, male vocalist/instrumentalist – trumpet — *3 wks*

10 Oct 81	**LOVE BYRD** *Elektra K 52301*	70	3 wks

BYRDS *US, male vocal/instrumental group* — *42 wks*

28 Aug 65 ●	**MR. TAMBOURINE MAN** *CBS BPG 62571*	7	12 wks
9 Apr 66	**TURN, TURN, TURN** *CBS BPG 62652*	11	5 wks
1 Oct 66	**5TH DIMENSION** *CBS BPG 62783*	27	2 wks
22 Apr 67	**YOUNGER THAN YESTERDAY** *CBS SBPG 62988*	37	4 wks
4 May 68	**THE NOTORIOUS BYRD BROTHERS** *CBS 63169*	12	11 wks
24 May 69	**DR. BYRDS AND MR. HYDE** *CBS 63545*	15	1 wk
14 Feb 70	**BALLAD OF EASY RIDER** *CBS 63795*	41	1 wk
28 Nov 70	**UNTITLED** *CBS 66253*	11	4 wks
14 Apr 73	**BYRDS** *Asylum SYLA 8754*	31	1 wk
19 May 73	**HISTORY OF THE BYRDS** *CBS 68242*	47	1 wk

David BYRNE – *See Brian ENO and David BYRNE*

C

CABARET VOLTAIRE
UK, male vocal/instrumental group — *11 wks*

26 Jun 82	**2 X 45** *Rough Trade ROUGH 42*	98	1 wk
13 Aug 83	**THE CRACKDOWN** *Some Bizzare CV 1* ...	31	5 wks
10 Nov 84	**MICRO-PHONIES** *Some Bizzare CV 2*	69	1 wk
3 Aug 85	**DRINKING GASOLINE** *Some Bizzare CVM 1*	71	2 wks
26 Oct 85	**THE COVENANT, THE SWORD AND THE ARM OF THE LORD** *Some Bizzare CV 3* ...	57	2 wks

CACTUS WORLD NEWS
Ireland, male vocal/instrumental group — *2 wks*

24 May 86	**URBAN BEACHES** *MCA MCG 6005*	56	2 wks

J.J. CALE *US, male vocalist/instrumentalist – guitar* — *22 wks*

2 Oct 76	**TROUBADOUR** *Island ISA 5011*	53	1 wk
25 Aug 79	**5** *Shelter ISA 5018*	40	6 wks
21 Feb 81	**SHADES** *Shelter ISA 5021*	44	7 wks
20 Mar 82	**GRASSHOPPER** *Shelter IFA 5022*	36	5 wks
24 Sep 83	**#8** *Mercury MERL 22*	47	3 wks

Maria CALLAS *Greece, female vocalist* — *7 wks*

20 Jun 87	**THE MARIA CALLAS COLLECTION** *Stylus SMR 732*	50	7 wks

CAMEL *UK, male vocal/instrumental group* — *47 wks*

24 May 75	**THE SNOW GOOSE** *Decca SKL 5207*	22	13 wks
17 Apr 76	**MOON MADNESS** *Decca TXS 115*	15	6 wks
17 Sep 77	**RAIN DANCES** *Decca TXS 124*	20	8 wks
14 Oct 78	**BREATHLESS** *Decca TXS 132*	26	1 wk
27 Oct 79	**I CAN SEE YOUR HOUSE FROM HERE** *Decca TXS 137*	45	3 wks
31 Jan 81	**NUDE** *Decca SKL 5323*	34	7 wks
15 May 82	**THE SINGLE FACTOR** *Decca FKL 5328*	57	5 wks
21 Apr 84	**STATIONARY TRAVELLER** *Decca SKL 5334* ..	57	4 wks

CAMEO *US, male vocal/instrumental group* — *46 wks*

10 Aug 85	**SINGLE LIFE** *Club JABH 11*	66	12 wks
18 Oct 86 ●	**WORD UP** *Club JABH 19*	7	34 wks

Glen CAMPBELL *US, male vocalist* — *179 wks*

31 Jan 70	**GLEN CAMPBELL LIVE** *Capitol SB 21444*	16	14 wks
30 May 70	**TRY A LITTLE KINDNESS** *Capitol ESW 389*	37	10 wks
12 Dec 70	**THE GLEN CAMPBELL ALBUM** *Capitol ST 22493*	16	5 wks
27 Nov 71 ●	**GREATEST HITS** *Capitol ST 21885*	8	113 wks
25 Oct 75	**RHINESTONE COWBOY** *Capitol E-SW 11430*	38	9 wks
20 Nov 76 ★	**20 GOLDEN GREATS** *Capitol EMTV 2*	1	27 wks
23 Apr 77	**SOUTHERN NIGHTS** *Capitol E-ST 11601*	51	1 wk

See also Bobbie Gentry and Glen Campbell.

CANNED HEAT *US, vocal/instrumental group* — *40 wks*

29 Jun 68 ●	**BOOGIE WITH CANNED HEAT** *Liberty LBL 83103*	5	21 wks
14 Feb 70 ●	**CANNED HEAT COOKBOOK** *Liberty LBS 83303*	8	12 wks
4 Jul 70	**CANNED HEAT '70 CONCERT** *Liberty LBS 83333*	15	3 wks
10 Oct 70	**FUTURE BLUES** *Liberty LBS 83364*	27	4 wks

Freddy CANNON *US, male vocalist* — *11 wks*

27 Feb 60 ★	**THE EXPLOSIVE FREDDY CANNON** *Top Rank 25/108*	1	11 wks

CAPTAIN and TENNILLE
US, male instrumentalist – keyboards and female vocalist — *6 wks*

22 Mar 80	**MAKE YOUR MOVE** *Casablanca CAL 2060*	33	6 wks

CARAVAN *UK, male vocal/instrumental group* — *2 wks*

30 Aug 75	**CUNNING STUNTS** *Decca SKL 5210*	50	1 wk
15 May 76	**BLIND DOG AT ST. DUNSTAN'S** *BTM BTM 1007*	53	1 wk

CARMEL *UK, female/male vocal/instrumental group* — *11 wks*

1 Oct 83	**CARMEL** *Red Flame RFM 9*	94	2 wks
24 Mar 84	**THE DRUM IS EVERYTHING** *London SH 8555* ..	19	8 wks
27 Sep 86	**THE FALLING** *London LONLP 17*	88	1 wk

Eric CARMEN *US, male vocalist* — *1 wk*

15 May 76	**ERIC CARMEN** *Arista ARTY 120*	58	1 wk

Kim CARNES *US, female vocalist* — *16 wks*

20 Jun 81	**MISTAKEN IDENTITY** *EMI America AML 3018* ..	26	16 wks

CARPENTERS
US, male/female vocal/instrumental duo — *473 wks*

23 Jan 71	**CLOSE TO YOU** *A & M AMLS 998*	23	82 wks
30 Oct 71	**THE CARPENTERS** *A & M AMLS 63502*	12	36 wks
15 Apr 72	**TICKET TO RIDE** *A & M AMLS 64342*	20	3 wks
23 Sep 72	**A SONG FOR YOU** *A & M AMLS 63511*	13	37 wks
7 Jul 73 ●	**NOW AND THEN** *A & M AMLH 63519*	2	65 wks
26 Jan 74 ★	**THE SINGLES 1969–1973** *A & M AMLH 63601* ..	1	116 wks
28 Jun 75 ★	**HORIZON** *A & M AMLK 64530*	1	27 wks

23 Aug 75	TICKET TO RIDE (re-issue) *Hamlet AMLP 8001*	35	2 wks
3 Jul 76	● A KIND OF HUSH *A & M AMLK 64581*	3	15 wks
8 Jan 77	LIVE AT THE PALLADIUM *A & M AMLS 68403*	28	3 wks
8 Oct 77	PASSAGE *A & M AMLK 64703*	12	12 wks
2 Dec 78	● SINGLES 1974–78 *A & M AMLT 19748*	2	20 wks
27 Jun 81	MADE IN AMERICA *A & M AMLK 63723*	12	10 wks
15 Oct 83	● VOICE OF THE HEART *A & M AMLX 64954*	6	19 wks
20 Oct 84	● YESTERDAY ONCE MORE *EMI/A & M SING 1*	10	26 wks

Vikki CARR *US, female vocalist* 12 wks

22 Jul 67	WAY OF TODAY *Liberty SLBY 1331*	31	2 wks
12 Aug 67	IT MUST BE HIM *Liberty LBS 83037*	12	10 wks

Jasper CARROTT *UK, male comedian* 66 wks

18 Oct 75	● RABBITS ON AND ON *DJM DJLPS 462*	10	7 wks
6 Nov 76	CARROTT IN NOTTS *DJM DJF 20482*	56	1 wk
25 Nov 78	THE BEST OF JASPER CARROTT *DJM DJF 20549*	38	13 wks
20 Oct 79	THE UNRECORDED JASPER CARROTT *DJM DJF 20560*	19	15 wks
19 Sep 81	BEAT THE CARROTT *DJM DJF 20575*	13	16 wks
25 Dec 82	CARROTT'S LIB *DJM DJF 20580*	80	3 wks
19 Nov 83	THE STUN (CARROTT TELLS ALL) *DJF 20582*	57	8 wks
7 Feb 87	COSMIC CARROTT *Portrait LAUGH 1*	66	3 wks

CARS *US, male vocal/instrumental group* 72 wks

2 Dec 78	CARS *Elektra K 52088*	29	15 wks
7 Jul 79	CANDY-O *Elektra K 52148*	30	6 wks
6 Oct 84	HEARTBEAT CITY *Elektra 960296*	25	30 wks
9 Nov 85	THE CARS GREATEST HITS *Elektra EKT 25*	27	19 wks
5 Sep 87	DOOR TO DOOR *Elektra EKT 42*	72	2 wks

Johnny CASH *US, male vocalist* 285 wks

23 Jul 66	EVERYBODY LOVES A NUT *CBS BPG 62717*	28	1 wk
4 May 68	FROM SEA TO SHINING SEA *CBS 62972*	40	1 wk
6 Jul 68	OLD GOLDEN THROAT *CBS 63316*	37	2 wks
24 Aug 68	● FOLSOM PRISON *CBS 63308*	8	53 wks
23 Aug 69	● JOHNNY CASH AT SAN QUENTIN *CBS 63629*	2	114 wks
4 Oct 69	GREATEST HITS VOL. 1 *CBS 63062*	23	25 wks
7 Mar 70	● HELLO I'M JOHNNY CASH *CBS 63796*	6	16 wks
15 Aug 70	● WORLD OF JOHNNY CASH *CBS 66237*	5	31 wks
12 Dec 70	THE JOHNNY CASH SHOW *CBS 64089*	18	6 wks
18 Sep 71	MAN IN BLACK *CBS 64331*	18	7 wks
13 Nov 71	JOHNNY CASH *Hallmark SHM 739*	43	2 wks
20 May 72	● A THING CALLED LOVE *CBS 64898*	8	11 wks
14 Oct 72	STAR PORTRAIT *CBS 67201*	16	7 wks
10 Jul 76	ONE PIECE AT A TIME *CBS 81416*	49	3 wks
9 Oct 76	THE BEST OF JOHNNY CASH *CBS 10000*	48	2 wks
2 Sep 78	ITCHY FEET *CBS 10009*	36	4 wks

CASHFLOW *US, male vocal/instrumental group* 3 wks

28 Jun 86	CASHFLOW *Club JABH 17*	33	3 wks

CASHMERE *US, male vocal/instrumental group* 5 wks

2 Mar 85	CASHMERE *Fourth & Broadway BRLP 503*	63	5 wks

David CASSIDY *US, male vocalist* 94 wks

20 May 72	● CHERISH *Bell BELLS 210*	2	43 wks
24 Feb 73	● ROCK ME BABY *Bell BELLS 218*	2	20 wks
24 Nov 73	★ DREAMS ARE NOTHIN' MORE THAN WISHES *Bell BELLS 231*	1	13 wks
3 Aug 74	● CASSIDY LIVE *Bell BELLS 243*	9	7 wks

9 Aug 75	THE HIGHER THEY CLIMB *RCA Victor RS 1012*	22	5 wks
8 Jun 85	ROMANCE *Arista 206 983*	20	6 wks

Nick CAVE featuring the BAD SEEDS
Australia, male vocalist with male vocal/instrumental group 5 wks

2 Jun 84	FROM HER TO ETERNITY *Mute STUMM 17*	40	3 wks
15 Jun 85	THE FIRST BORN IS DEAD *Mute STUMM 21*	53	1 wk
30 Aug 86	KICKING AGAINST THE PRICKS *Mute STUMM 28*	89	1 wk

C.C.S. *UK, male vocal/instrumental group* 5 wks

8 Apr 72	C.C.S. *RAK SRAK 503*	23	5 wks

CENTRAL LINE *UK, male vocal/instrumental group* 5 wks

13 Feb 82	BREAKING POINT *Mercury MERA 001*	64	5 wks

CERRONE *France, male producer and multi-instrumentalist* 1 wk

30 Sep 78	SUPERNATURE *Atlantic K 50431*	60	1 wk

A CERTAIN RATIO
UK, male vocal/instrumental group 3 wks

30 Jan 82	SEXTET *Factory FACT 55*	53	3 wks

Peter CETERA *US, male vocalist* 4 wks

13 Sep 86	SOLITUDE/SOLITAIRE *Full Moon 925474–1*	56	4 wks

Richard CHAMBERLAIN *US, male vocalist* 8 wks

16 Mar 63	● RICHARD CHAMBERLAIN SINGS *MGM C 923*	8	8 wks

CHAMELEONS *UK, male vocal/instrumental group* 4 wks

25 May 85	WHAT DOES ANYTHING MEAN? BASICALLY *Statik STAT LP 22*	60	2 wks
20 Sep 86	STRANGE TIMES *Geffen 924 119–1*	44	2 wks

CHAMPAIGN *US, male/female vocal/instrumental group* 4 wks

27 Jun 81	HOW 'BOUT US *CBS 84927*	38	4 wks

CHANGE *US, male/female vocal/instrumental group* 23 wks

19 May 84	CHANGE OF HEART *WEA WX 5*	34	17 wks
27 Apr 85	TURN ON THE RADIO *Cooltempo CHR 1504*	39	6 wks

Michael CHAPMAN *UK, male vocalist* 1 wk

21 Mar 70	FULLY QUALIFIED SURVIVOR *Harvest SHVL 764*	45	1 wk

(Below) JASPER CARROTT is nonplussed to find a Trafalgar Square tourist crowd more interested in taking pictures of pigeons than hearing jokes.

(Above) DAVID CASSIDY displays the smouldering look that ignited album charts of the early seventies.

(Right) The great NAT KING COLE died of lung cancer in 1965 at the age of 48. He's seen smoking even in this carefully conceived publicity photo.

CHAQUITO ORCHESTRA
UK, orchestra arranged and conducted by Johnny Gregory   *2 wks*

24 Feb 68	**THIS CHAQUITO** *Fontana SFXL 50*	**36**	1 wk
4 Mar 72	**THRILLER THEMES** *Philips 6308 087*	**48**	1 wk

First album credited to Chaquito and Quedo Brass.

CHARGE GBH *UK, male vocal/instrumental group*   *6 wks*

14 Aug 82	**CITY BABY ATTACKED BY RATS** *Clay CLAYLP 4*	**17**	6 wks

CHARLENE *US, female vocalist*   *4 wks*

17 Jul 82	**I'VE NEVER BEEN TO ME** *Motown STML 12171*	**43**	4 wks

Ray CHARLES
US, male vocalist/instrumentalist – piano   *39 wks*

28 Jul 62	● **MODERN SOUNDS IN COUNTRY & WESTERN MUSIC** *HMV CLP 1580*	**6**	16 wks
23 Feb 63	**MODERN SOUNDS IN COUNTRY AND WESTERN MUSIC VOL. 2** *HMV CLP 1613* . . .	**15**	5 wks
20 Jul 63	**GREATEST HITS** *HMV CLP 1626*	**16**	5 wks
5 Oct 68	**GREATEST HITS VOL. 2** *Stateside SSL 10241* . . .	**24**	8 wks
19 Jul 80	**HEART TO HEART – 20 HOT HITS** *London RAY TV 1*	**29**	5 wks

Tina CHARLES *UK, female vocalist*   *7 wks*

3 Dec 77	**HEART 'N' SOUL** *CBS 82180*	**35**	7 wks

CHAS and DAVE *UK, male vocal/instrumental duo*   *96 wks*

5 Dec 81	**CHAS AND DAVE'S CHRISTMAS JAMBOREE BAG** *Warwick WW 5166*	**25**	15 wks
17 Apr 82	**MUSTN'T GRUMBLE** *Rockney 909*	**35**	11 wks
8 Jan 83	**JOB LOT** *Rockney ROC 910*	**59**	15 wks
15 Oct 83	● **CHAS & DAVE'S KNEES UP – JAMBOREE BAG NO 2** *Rockney ROC 911*	**7**	17 wks
11 Aug 84	**WELL PLEASED** *Rockney ROC 912*	**27**	10 wks
17 Nov 84	**CHAS & DAVE'S GREATEST HITS** *Rockney ROC 913*	**16**	10 wks
15 Dec 84	**CHAS & DAVE'S CHRISTMAS JAMBOREE BAG (re-issue)** *Rockney ROCM 001*	**87**	1 wk
9 Nov 85	**JAMBOREE BAG NUMBER 3** *Rockney ROC 914* . .	**15**	13 wks
13 Dec 86	**CHAS & DAVE'S CHRISTMAS CAROL ALBUM** *Telstar STAR 2293*	**37**	4 wks

CHEAP TRICK *US, male vocal/instrumental group*   *15 wks*

24 Feb 79	**CHEAP TRICK AT BUDOKAN** *Epic EPC 86083* .	**29**	9 wks
6 Oct 79	**DREAM POLICE** *Epic EPC 83522*	**41**	5 wks
5 Jun 82	**ONE ON ONE** *Epic EPC 85740*	**95**	1 wk

Chubby CHECKER *US, male vocalist*   *7 wks*

27 Jan 62	**TWIST WITH CHUBBY CHECKER** *Columbia 33SX 1315*	**13**	4 wks
3 Mar 62	**FOR TWISTERS ONLY** *Columbia 33SX 1341*	**17**	3 wks

CHER *US, female vocalist*   *20 wks*

2 Oct 65	● **ALL I REALLY WANT TO DO** *Liberty LBY 3058* .	**7**	9 wks
7 May 66	**SONNY SIDE OF CHER** *Liberty LBY 3072*	**11**	11 wks

See also Sonny and Cher.

CHERELLE *US, female vocalist*   *9 wks*

25 Jan 86	**HIGH PRIORITY** *Tabu TBU 26699*	**17**	9 wks

CHIC *US, male/female vocal/instrumental group*   *44 wks*

3 Feb 79	● **C'EST CHIC** *Atlantic K 50565*	**2**	24 wks
18 Aug 79	**RISQUE** *Atlantic K 50634*	**29**	12 wks
15 Dec 79	**THE BEST OF CHIC** *Atlantic K 50686*	**30**	8 wks

See also Chic and Sister Sledge.

CHIC and SISTER SLEDGE *US, male/female*
vocal/instrumental group and female vocal group   *3 wks*

5 Dec 87	**FREAK OUT** *Telstar STAR 2319*	**72**	3 wks

See also Chic; Sister Sledge.

CHICAGO *US, male vocal/instrumental group*   *92 wks*

27 Sep 69	● **CHICAGO TRANSIT AUTHORITY** *CBS 66221* .	**9**	14 wks
4 Apr 70	● **CHICAGO** *CBS 66233*	**6**	27 wks
3 Apr 71	**CHICAGO 3** *CBS 66260*	**31**	1 wk
30 Sep 72	**CHICAGO 5** *CBS 69108*	**24**	2 wks
23 Oct 76	**CHICAGO X** *CBS 86010*	**21**	11 wks
2 Oct 82	**CHICAGO 16** *Full Moon K 99235*	**44**	9 wks
4 Dec 82	**LOVE SONGS** *TV Records TVA 6*	**42**	8 wks
1 Dec 84	**CHICAGO 17** *Full Moon 925060*	**24**	20 wks

First album credited to Chicago Transit Authority.

CHICKEN SHACK
UK, male/female vocal/instrumental group   *9 wks*

22 Jul 68	**40 BLUE FINGERS FRESHLY PACKED** *Blue Horizon 7–63203*	**12**	8 wks
15 Feb 69	● **OK KEN?** *Blue Horizon 7–63209*	**9**	1 wk

CHIEFTAINS – See James GALWAY and the CHIEFTAINS

CHINA CRISIS *UK, male vocal/instrumental group*   *62 wks*

20 Nov 82	**DIFFICULT SHAPES AND PASSIVE RHYTHMS** *Virgin V 2243*	**21**	18 wks
12 Nov 83	**WORKING WITH FIRE AND STEEL – POSSIBLE POP SONGS VOL 2** *Virgin V 2286*	**20**	16 wks
11 May 85	● **FLAUNT THE IMPERFECTION** *Virgin V 2342* . .	**9**	22 wks
6 Dec 86	**WHAT PRICE PARADISE** *Virgin V 2410*	**63**	6 wks

CHORDS *UK, male vocal/instrumental group*   *3 wks*

24 May 80	**SO FAR AWAY** *Polydor POLS 1019*	**30**	3 wks

CHRISTIANS *UK, male vocal/instrumental group*   *9 wks*

31 Oct 87	● **THE CHRISTIANS** *Island ILPS 9876*	**2**	9 wks

Tony CHRISTIE *UK, male vocalist*   *10 wks*

24 Jul 71	**I DID WHAT I DID FOR MARIA** *MCA MKPS 2016*	**37**	1 wk
17 Feb 73	**WITH LOVING FEELING** *MCA MUPS 468* . . .	**19**	2 wks
31 May 75	**TONY CHRISTIE – LIVE** *MCA MCF 2703* . .	**33**	3 wks
6 Nov 76	**BEST OF TONY CHRISTIE** *MCA MCF 2769* . . .	**28**	4 wks

CHRON GEN UK, male vocal/instrumental group *3 wks*

| 3 Apr 82 | CHRONIC GENERATION Secret SEC 3 .... | 53 | 3 wks |

Sir Winston CHURCHILL UK, male statesman *8 wks*

| 13 Feb 65 ● | THE VOICE OF CHURCHILL Decca LXT 6200 .. | 6 | 8 wks |

CITY BEAT BAND – *See PRINCE CHARLES and the CITY BEAT BAND*

CLANCY BROTHERS and Tommy MAKEM
Ireland, male vocal/instrumental group and male vocalist *5 wks*

| 16 Apr 66 | ISN'T IT GRAND BOYS CBS BPG 62674 .... | 22 | 5 wks |

CLANNAD *Ireland, male/female vocal/instrumental group* *90 wks*

2 Apr 83	MAGICAL RING RCA RCALP 6072	26	21 wks
12 May 84	LEGEND (MUSIC FROM ROBIN OF SHERWOOD) RCA PL 70188	15	40 wks
2 Jun 84	MAGICAL RING (re-issue) RCA PL 70003	91	1 wk
26 Oct 85	MACALLA RCA PL 70894	33	24 wks
7 Nov 87	SIRIUS RCA PL 71513	34	4 wks

Eric CLAPTON
UK, male vocalist/instrumentalist – guitar *200 wks*

5 Sep 70	ERIC CLAPTON Polydor 2383–021	17	8 wks
26 Aug 72	HISTORY OF ERIC CLAPTON Polydor 2659 2478 027	20	6 wks
24 Aug 74 ●	461 OCEAN BOULEVARD RSO 2479 118 ...	3	19 wks
12 Apr 75	THERE'S ONE IN EVERY CROWD RSO 2479 132	15	8 wks
13 Sep 75	E.C. WAS HERE RSO 2394 160	14	6 wks
11 Sep 76 ●	NO REASON TO CRY RSO 2479 179	8	7 wks
26 Nov 77	SLOWHAND RSO 2479 201	23	13 wks
9 Dec 78	BACKLESS RSO RSD 5001	18	12 wks
10 May 80 ●	JUST ONE NIGHT RSO RSDX 2	3	12 wks
7 Mar 81	ANOTHER TICKET RSO RSD 5008	18	8 wks
24 Apr 82	TIME PIECES – THE BEST OF ERIC CLAPTON RSO RSD 5010	20	13 wks
19 Feb 83	MONEY & CIGARETTES Duck W 3773 ...	13	17 wks
9 Jun 84	BACKTRACKIN' Starblend ERIC 1	29	16 wks
23 Mar 85 ●	BEHIND THE SUN Duck 92–5166–1 ...	8	14 wks
6 Dec 86 ●	AUGUST Duck WX 71	3†	41 wks

See also Eric Clapton and Cream; John Mayall and Eric Clapton.

Eric CLAPTON and CREAM UK, male vocalist/
instrumentalist – guitar and male vocal/instrumental group *14 wks*

| 26 Sep 87 ● | THE CREAM OF ERIC CLAPTON Polydor ECTV 1 .... | 9† | 14 wks |

See also Eric Clapton; Cream; John Mayall and Eric Clapton.

Petula CLARK UK, female vocalist *43 wks*

30 Jul 66	I COULDN'T LIVE WITHOUT YOUR LOVE Pye NPL 18148	11	10 wks
4 Feb 67	HIT PARADE Pye NPL 18159	18	13 wks
18 Feb 67	COLOUR MY WORLD Pye NSPL 18171	16	9 wks
7 Oct 67	THESE ARE MY SONGS Pye NSPL 18197	38	3 wks
6 Apr 68	THE OTHER MAN'S GRASS IS ALWAYS GREENER Pye NSPL 18211	37	1 wk
5 Feb 77	20 ALL TIME GREATEST K-Tel NE 945	18	7 wks

Dave CLARK FIVE
UK, male vocal/instrumental group *26 wks*

18 Apr 64 ●	A SESSION WITH THE DAVE CLARK FIVE Columbia 33SX 1598	3	8 wks
14 Aug 65 ●	CATCH US IF YOU CAN Columbia 33SX 1756	8	8 wks
4 Mar 78 ●	25 THUMPING GREAT HITS Polydor POLTV 7 ..	7	10 wks

Louis CLARK/ROYAL PHILHARMONIC ORCHESTRA
Australia, conductor/arranger and UK, orchestra *90 wks*

19 Sep 81 ●	HOOKED ON CLASSICS K-Tel ONE 1146	4	43 wks
31 Jul 82	CAN'T STOP THE CLASSICS – HOOKED ON CLASSICS 2 K-Tel ONE 1173	13	26 wks
9 Apr 83	JOURNEY THROUGH THE CLASSICS – HOOKED ON CLASSICS 3 K-Tel ONE 1226 ..	19	15 wks
10 Dec 83	THE BEST OF HOOKED ON CLASSICS K-Tel ONE 1266	51	6 wks

See also Royal Philharmonic Orchestra; Juan Martin and the Royal Philharmonic Orchestra.

John Cooper CLARKE UK, male vocalist *9 wks*

| 19 Apr 80 | SNAP CRACKLE AND BOP Epic EPC 84083 ... | 26 | 7 wks |
| 5 Jun 82 | ZIP STYLE METHOD Epic EPC 85667 .... | 97 | 2 wks |

Stanley CLARKE
US, male vocalist/instrumentalist – bass *2 wks*

| 12 Jul 80 | ROCKS PEBBLES AND SAND Epic EPC 84342 .. | 42 | 2 wks |

CLASH UK, male vocal/instrumental group *85 wks*

30 Apr 77	CLASH CBS 82000	12	16 wks
25 Nov 78 ●	GIVE 'EM ENOUGH ROPE CBS 82431	2	14 wks
22 Dec 79 ●	LONDON CALLING CBS CLASH 3	9	20 wks
20 Dec 80	SANDINISTA CBS FSLN 1	19	9 wks
22 May 82 ●	COMBAT ROCK CBS FMLN 2	2	23 wks
16 Nov 85	CUT THE CRAP CBS 26601	16	3 wks

CLASSIX NOUVEAUX
UK, male vocal/instrumental group *6 wks*

| 30 May 81 | NIGHT PEOPLE Liberty LBG 30325 ...... | 66 | 2 wks |
| 24 Apr 82 | LA VERITE Liberty LBG 30346 .... | 44 | 4 wks |

Richard CLAYDERMAN
France, male instrumentalist – piano *150 wks*

13 Nov 82 ●	RICHARD CLAYDERMAN Decca SKL 5329	2	64 wks
8 Oct 83	THE MUSIC OF RICHARD CLAYDERMAN Decca SKL 5333	21	28 wks
24 Nov 84	THE MUSIC OF LOVE Decca SKL 5340	28	21 wks
1 Dec 84	RICHARD CLAYDERMAN – CHRISTMAS Decca SKL 5337	53	5 wks
23 Nov 85	THE CLASSIC TOUCH Decca SKL 5343	17	18 wks
22 Nov 86	HOLLYWOOD AND BROADWAY Decca SKL 5344	28	9 wks
28 Nov 87	SONGS OF LOVE Decca SKL 5345	19†	5 wks

The Classic Touch is credited to Richard Clayderman with the Royal Philharmonic Orchestra.

John CLEESE UK, male comedian *7 wks*

| 7 Feb 81 | FAWLTY TOWERS VOL. 2 BBC REB 405 ...... | 26 | 7 wks |

Album also features Prunella Scales, Andrew Sachs and Connie Booth.

CLIMAX BLUES BAND
UK, male vocal/instrumental group   *1 wk*

13 Nov 76	**GOLD PLATED** *BTM 1009*	**56**	1 wk

Eddie COCHRAN
US, male vocalist/instrumentalist – guitar   *44 wks*

30 Jul 60	**SINGING TO MY BABY** *London HAU 2093*	**19**	1 wk
1 Oct 60 ●	**EDDIE COCHRAN MEMORIAL ALBUM**		
	London HAG 2267	**9**	12 wks
12 Jan 63	**CHERISHED MEMORIES** *Liberty LBY 1109*	**15**	3 wks
20 Apr 63	**EDDIE COCHRAN MEMORIAL ALBUM**		
	(re-issue) *Liberty LBY 1127*	**11**	18 wks
19 Oct 63	**SINGING TO MY BABY** **(re-issue)**		
	Liberty LBY 1158	**20**	1 wk
9 May 70	**VERY BEST OF EDDIE COCHRAN**		
	Liberty LBS 83337	**34**	3 wks
18 Aug 79	**THE EDDIE COCHRAN SINGLES ALBUM**		
	United Artists UAK 30244	**39**	6 wks

Joe COCKER *UK, male vocalist*   *13 wks*

26 Sep 70	**MAD DOGS AND ENGLISHMEN**		
	A & M AMLS 6002	**16**	8 wks
6 May 72	**JOE COCKER/WITH A LITTLE HELP FROM MY**		
	FRIENDS *Double Back TOOFA 1/2*	**29**	4 wks
30 Jun 84	**A CIVILISED MAN** *Capitol EJ 24 0139 1*	**100**	1 wk

COCKNEY REBEL – *See Steve HARLEY and COCKNEY REBEL*

COCKNEY REJECTS
UK, male vocal/instrumental group   *17 wks*

15 Mar 80	**GREATEST HITS VOL. 1** *Zonophone ZONO 101*	**22**	11 wks
25 Oct 80	**GREATEST HITS VOL. 2** *Zonophone ZONO 102*	**23**	3 wks
18 Apr 81	**GREATEST HITS VOL. 3 (LIVE AND LOUD)**		
	Zonophone ZEM 101	**27**	3 wks

COCONUTS – *See Kid CREOLE and the COCONUTS*

COCTEAU TWINS *UK, male/female vocal group*   *30 wks*

29 Oct 83	**HEAD OVER HEELS** *4AD CAD 313*	**51**	15 wks
24 Nov 84	**TREASURE** *4AD CAD 412*	**29**	8 wks
26 Apr 86	**VICTORIALAND** *4AD CAD 602*	**10**	7 wks

Leonard COHEN *Canada, male vocalist*   *129 wks*

31 Aug 68	**SONGS OF LEONARD COHEN** *CBS 63241* ...	**13**	71 wks
3 May 69 ●	**SONGS FROM A ROOM** *CBS 63587*	**2**	26 wks
24 Apr 71 ●	**SONGS OF LOVE AND HATE** *CBS 69004*	**4**	18 wks
28 Sep 74	**NEW SKIN FOR THE OLD CEREMONY**		
	CBS 69087	**24**	3 wks
10 Dec 77	**DEATH OF A LADIES' MAN** *CBS 86042*	**35**	5 wks
16 Feb 85	**VARIOUS POSITIONS** *CBS 26222*	**52**	6 wks

Lloyd COLE and the COMMOTIONS
UK, male vocalist and male vocal/instrumental group *55 wks*

20 Oct 84	**RATTLESNAKES** *Polydor LCLP 1*	**13**	30 wks
30 Nov 85 ●	**EASY PIECES** *Polydor LCLP 2*	**5**	18 wks
7 Nov 87 ●	**MAINSTREAM** *Polydor LCLP 3*	**9**	7 wks

Nat King COLE *US, male vocalist*   *95 wks*

19 Aug 61	**STRING ALONG WITH NAT KING COLE**		
	Encore ENC 102	**12**	9 wks

27 Mar 65	**UNFORGETTABLE NAT KING COLE**			
	Capitol W 20664		**19**	8 wks
7 Dec 68 ●	**BEST OF NAT KING COLE** *Capitol ST 21139*		**5**	18 wks
5 Dec 70	**BEST OF NAT KING COLE VOL. 2**			
	Capitol ST 21687		**39**	2 wks
8 Apr 78 ★	**20 GOLDEN GREATS** *Capitol EMTV 9*		**1†**	32 wks
20 Nov 82 ●	**GREATEST LOVE SONGS** *Capitol EMTV 35*		**7**	26 wks

See also Nat King Cole and Dean Martin; Nat King Cole and the George Shearing Quintet.

Nat King COLE and Dean MARTIN
US, male vocalists   *1 wk*

27 Nov 71	**WHITE CHRISTMAS** *MFP 5224*	**45**	1 wk

See also Nat King Cole; Nat King Cole and the George Shearing Quintet; Dean Martin.

Nat King COLE and the George SHEARING QUINTET
US, male vocalist and UK/US instrumental group   *7 wks*

20 Oct 62 ●	**NAT KING COLE SINGS AND THE GEORGE**		
	SHEARING QUINTET PLAYS *Capitol W 1675* .	**8**	7 wks

See also Nat King Cole; Nat King Cole and Dean Martin; Peggy Lee and George Shearing.

Dave and Ansil COLLINS *Jamaica, male vocal duo*   *2 wks*

7 Aug 71	**DOUBLE BARREL** *Trojan TBL 162*	**41**	2 wks

Joan COLLINS – *See Anthony NEWLEY, Peter SELLERS, Joan COLLINS*

Judy COLLINS *US, female vocalist*   *18 wks*

10 Apr 71	**WHALES AND NIGHTINGALES**		
	Elektra EKS 75010	**37**	2 wks
31 May 75 ●	**JUDITH** *Elektra K 52019*	**7**	12 wks
14 Dec 85	**AMAZING GRACE** *Telstar STAR 2265*	**34**	4 wks

Phil COLLINS
UK, male vocalist/instrumentalist – drums   *519 wks*

21 Feb 81 ★	**FACE VALUE** *Virgin V 2185*	**1**	247 wks
13 Nov 82 ●	**HELLO I MUST BE GOING** *Virgin V 2252*	**2**	135 wks
2 Mar 85 ★	**NO JACKET REQUIRED** *Virgin V 2345*	**1**	137 wks

Willie COLLINS *US, male vocalist*   *1 wk*

14 Jun 86	**WHERE YOU GONNA BE TONIGHT?**		
	Capitol EST 2012	**97**	1 wk

COLOSSEUM *UK, male vocal/instrumental group*   *14 wks*

17 May 69	**COLOSSEUM** *Fontana S 5510*	**15**	1 wk
22 Nov 69	**VALENTYNE SUITE** *Vertigo VO 1*	**15**	2 wks
5 Dec 70	**DAUGHTER OF TIME** *Vertigo 6360 017*	**23**	5 wks
26 Jun 71	**COLOSSEUM LIVE** *Bronze ICD 1*	**17**	6 wks

COLOURBOX *UK, male vocal/instrumental group*   *2 wks*

24 Aug 85	**COLOURBOX** *4AD CAD 508*	**67**	2 wks

COLOUR FIELD *UK, male vocal/instrumental group*   *8 wks*

4 May 85	**VIRGINS & PHILISTINES** *Chrysalis CHR 1480* ...	**12**	7 wks
4 Apr 87	**DECEPTION** *Chrysalis CDL 1546*	**95**	1 wk

Alice COLTRANE – *See Carlos SANTANA and Alice COLTRANE*

COMETS – *See Bill HALEY and his COMETS*

COMIC RELIEF *UK, charity ensemble of comedians* 8 wks

10 May 86	●	UTTERLY UTTERLY LIVE! *WEA WX 51*	10	8 wks

COMMODORES
US/UK, male vocal/instrumental group 126 wks

13 May 78		LIVE *Motown TMSP 6007*	60	1 wk
10 Jun 78	●	NATURAL HIGH *Motown STML 12087*	8	23 wks
2 Dec 78		GREATEST HITS *Motown STML 12100*	19	16 wks
18 Aug 79		MIDNIGHT MAGIC *Motown STMA 8032* ...	15	25 wks
28 Jun 80		HEROES *Motown STMA 8034*	50	5 wks
18 Jul 81		IN THE POCKET *Motown STML 12156*	69	5 wks
14 Aug 82	●	LOVE SONGS *K-Tel NE 1171*	5	28 wks
23 Feb 85		NIGHTSHIFT *Motown ZL 72343*	13	10 wks
9 Nov 85		THE VERY BEST OF THE COMMODORES *Telstar STAR 2249*	25	13 wks

Group were US only for first seven albums.

COMMOTIONS – *See Lloyd COLE and the COMMOTIONS*

COMMUNARDS *UK, male vocal/instrumental duo* 56 wks

2 Aug 86	●	COMMUNARDS *London LONLP 18*	7	45 wks
17 Oct 87	●	RED *London LONDLP 39*	4†	11 wks

Perry COMO *US, male vocalist* 191 wks

8 Nov 58	●	DEAR PERRY *RCA RD 27078*	6	5 wks
31 Jan 59	●	COMO'S GOLDEN RECORDS *RCA RD 27100* ..	4	5 wks
10 Apr 71		IT'S IMPOSSIBLE *RCA Victor SF 8175*	13	13 wks
7 Jul 73	★	AND I LOVE YOU SO *RCA Victor SF 8360*	1	109 wks
24 Aug 74		PERRY *RCA Victor APLI 0585*	26	3 wks
19 Apr 75		MEMORIES ARE MADE OF HITS *RCA Victor RS 1005*	14	16 wks
25 Oct 75	★	40 GREATEST HITS *K-Tel NE 700*	1	34 wks
3 Dec 83		FOR THE GOOD TIMES *Telstar STAR 2235*	41	6 wks

COMPILATION ALBUMS – *See VARIOUS ARTISTS*

COMSAT ANGELS
UK, male vocal/instrumental group 9 wks

5 Sep 81		SLEEP NO MORE *Polydor POLS 1038*	51	5 wks
18 Sep 82		FICTION *Polydor POLS 1075*	94	2 wks
8 Oct 83		LAND *Jive HIP 8*	91	2 wks

Ray CONNIFF *US, male orchestra leader* 96 wks

28 May 60		IT'S THE TALK OF THE TOWN *Philips BBL 7354*	15	1 wk
25 Jun 60		S'AWFUL NICE *Philips BBL 7281*	13	1 wk
26 Nov 60	●	HI-FI COMPANION ALBUM *Philips BET 101* ..	3	44 wks
20 May 61		MEMORIES ARE MADE OF THIS *Philips BBL 7439*	14	4 wks
29 Dec 62		WE WISH YOU A MERRY CHRISTMAS *CBS BPG 62092*	12	1 wk
29 Dec 62		'S WONDERFUL 'S MARVELLOUS *CBS DPG 66001*	18	3 wks
16 Apr 66		HI-FI COMPANION (re-issue) *CBS DP 66011* ...	24	4 wks
9 Sep 67		SOMEWHERE MY LOVE *CBS SBPG 62740*	34	3 wks
21 Jun 69	★	HIS ORCHESTRA, HIS CHORUS, HIS SINGERS, HIS SOUND *CBS SPR 27*	1	16 wks
23 May 70		BRIDGE OVER TROUBLED WATER *CBS 64020*	30	14 wks
12 Jun 71		LOVE STORY *CBS 64294*	34	1 wk
19 Feb 72		I'D LIKE TO TEACH THE WORLD TO SING *CBS 64449*	17	4 wks

Billy CONNOLLY *UK, male vocalist* 108 wks

20 Jul 74	●	SOLO CONCERT *Transatlantic TRA 279*	8	33 wks
18 Jan 75	●	COP YER WHACK OF THIS *Polydor 2383 310* ...	10	29 wks
20 Sep 75		WORDS AND MUSIC *Transatlantic TRA SAM 32*	34	10 wks
6 Dec 75	●	GET RIGHT INTAE HIM *Polydor 2383 368* ...	6	14 wks
11 Dec 76		ATLANTIC BRIDGE *Polydor 2383 419* ...	20	9 wks
28 Jan 78		RAW MEAT FOR THE BALCONY *Polydor 2383 463*	57	3 wks
5 Dec 81		PICK OF BILLY CONNOLLY *Polydor POLTV 15*	23	8 wks
5 Dec 87		BILLY AND ALBERT *10 DIX 65*	81	2 wks

Russ CONWAY *UK, male instrumentalist – piano* 69 wks

22 Nov 58	●	PACK UP YOUR TROUBLES *Columbia 33SX 1120*	9	5 wks
2 May 59	●	SONGS TO SING IN YOUR BATH *Columbia 33SX 1149*	8	10 wks
19 Sep 59	●	FAMILY FAVOURITES *Columbia 33SX 1169*	3	16 wks
19 Dec 59	●	TIME TO CELEBRATE *Columbia 33SX 1197*	3	7 wks
26 Mar 60	●	MY CONCERTO FOR YOU *Columbia 33SX 1214*	5	17 wks
17 Dec 60	●	PARTY TIME *Columbia 33SX 1279* ...	7	11 wks
23 Apr 77		RUSS CONWAY PRESENTS 24 PIANO GREATS *Ronco RTL 2022*	25	3 wks

Ry COODER *US, male vocalist/instrumentalist – guitar* 29 wks

11 Aug 79		BOP TILL YOU DROP *Warner Bros. K 56691*	36	9 wks
18 Oct 80		BORDER LINE *Warner Bros. K 56864*	35	6 wks
24 Apr 82		THE SLIDE AREA *Warner Bros. K 56976*	18	12 wks
14 Nov 87		GET RHYTHM *Warner Bros. WX 121*	75	2 wks

Peter COOK and Dudley MOORE
UK, male comedy duo 34 wks

21 May 66		ONCE MOORE WITH COOK *Decca LK 4785*	25	1 wk
18 Sep 76		DEREK AND CLIVE LIVE *Island ILPS 9434*	12	25 wks
24 Dec 77		COME AGAIN *Virgin V 2094*	18	8 wks

See also Dudley Moore.

Sam COOKE *US, male vocalist* 27 wks

26 Apr 86	●	THE MAN AND HIS MUSIC *RCA PL 87127*	8	27 wks

Rita COOLIDGE *US, female vocalist* 40 wks

6 Aug 77	●	ANYTIME ANYWHERE *A & M AMLH 64616* ...	6	28 wks
8 Jul 78		LOVE ME AGAIN *A & M AMLH 64699*	51	1 wk
14 Mar 81	●	VERY BEST OF *A & M AMLH 68520*	6	11 wks

See also Kris Kristofferson and Rita Coolidge.

COOL NOTES
UK, male/female vocal/instrumental group 2 wks

9 Nov 85		HAVE A GOOD FOREVER *Abstract Dance ADLP 1*	66	2 wks

Alice COOPER *US, male vocalist* 102 wks

5 Feb 72		KILLER *Warner Bros. K 56005*	27	18 wks
22 Jul 72	●	SCHOOL'S OUT *Warner Bros. K 56007*	4	20 wks
9 Sep 72		LOVE IT TO DEATH *Warner Bros. K 46177*	28	7 wks
24 Mar 73	★	BILLION DOLLAR BABIES *Warner Bros. K 56013*	1	23 wks
12 Jan 74		MUSCLE OF LOVE *Warner Bros. K 56018* ...	34	4 wks
15 Mar 75		WELCOME TO MY NIGHTMARE *Anchor ANCL 2011*	19	8 wks
24 Jul 76		ALICE COOPER GOES TO HELL *Warner Bros. K 56171*	23	7 wks
28 May 77		LACE AND WHISKY *Warner Bros. K 56365*	33	3 wks
23 Dec 78		FROM THE INSIDE *Warner Bros. K 56577*	68	3 wks
17 May 80		FLUSH THE FASHION *Warner Bros. K 56805* ...	56	3 wks

12 Sep 81	SPECIAL FORCES	Warner Bros. K 56927	96	1 wk
12 Nov 83	DADA	Warner Bros. 92–3969–1	93	1 wk
1 Nov 86	CONSTRICTOR	MCA MCF 3341	41	2 wks
7 Nov 87	RAISE YOUR FIST AND YELL	MCA MCF 3392	48	2 wks

Julian COPE *UK, male vocalist* *15 wks*

3 Mar 84	WORLD SHUT YOUR MOUTH			
	Mercury MERL 37	40	4 wks
24 Nov 84	FRIED *Mercury MERL 48*	87	1 wk
14 Mar 87	SAINT JULIAN *Island ILPS 9861*	11	10 wks

Harry H. CORBETT – *See Wilfred BRAMBELL and Harry H. CORBETT*

CORRIES *UK, male vocal/instrumental duo* *5 wks*

| 9 May 70 | SCOTTISH LOVE SONGS *Fontana 6309–004* | 46 | 4 wks |
| 16 Sep 72 | SOUND OF PIBROCH *Columbia SCX 6511* | 39 | 1 wk |

Elvis COSTELLO and the ATTRACTIONS
UK, male vocalist and male vocal/instrumental group *150 wks*

6 Aug 77	MY AIM IS TRUE *Stiff SEEZ 3*	14	12 wks
1 Apr 78	● THIS YEAR'S MODEL *Radar RAD 3*	4	14 wks
20 Jan 79	● ARMED FORCES *Radar RAD 14*	2	28 wks
23 Feb 80	● GET HAPPY *F-Beat XXLP 1*	2	14 wks
31 Jan 81	● TRUST *F-Beat XXLP 11*	9	7 wks
31 Oct 81	● ALMOST BLUE *F-Beat XXLP 13*	7	18 wks
10 Jul 82	● IMPERIAL BEDROOM *F-Beat XXLP 17*	6	12 wks
6 Aug 83	● PUNCH THE CLOCK *F-Beat XXLP 19*	3	13 wks
7 Jul 84	● GOODBYE CRUEL WORLD *F-Beat ZL 70317*	10	10 wks
20 Apr 85	● THE BEST OF ELVIS COSTELLO – THE MAN		
	Telstar STAR 2247	8	17 wks
27 Sep 86	BLOOD AND CHOCOLATE		
	Imp XFIEND 80	16	5 wks

My Aim Is True, This Year's Model, Trust *and* The Best of Elvis Costello – The Man *are credited to Elvis Costello only. See also Costello Show.*

COSTELLO SHOW
UK/US, male vocal/instrumental group *9 wks*

| 1 Mar 86 | KING OF AMERICA *F-Beat ZL 70946* | 11 | 9 wks |

See also Elvis Costello and the Attractions.

Phil COULTER
Ireland, male orchestra leader/instrumentalist – piano *15 wks*

| 13 Oct 84 | SEA OF TRANQUILITY *K-Tel Ireland KLP 185* | 46 | 14 wks |
| 18 May 85 | PHIL COULTER'S IRELAND *K-Tel ONE 1296* | 86 | 1 wk |

David COVERDALE *UK, male vocalist* *1 wk*

| 27 Feb 82 | NORTHWINDS *Purple TTS 3513* | 78 | 1 wk |

CRAMPS *US, male/female vocal/instrumental group* *12 wks*

25 Jun 83	OFF THE BONE *Illegal ILP 012*	44	4 wks
26 Nov 83	SMELL OF FEMALE *Big Beat NED 6*	74	2 wks
1 Mar 86	A DATE WITH ELVIS *Big Beat WIKA 46*	34	6 wks

CRASS *UK, male vocal/instrumental group* *2 wks*

| 28 Aug 82 | CHRIST THE ALBUM *Crass BOLLOX 2U2* | 26 | 2 wks |

Michael CRAWFORD and LONDON SYMPHONY ORCHESTRA
UK, male vocalist with orchestra *5 wks*

| 28 Nov 87 | SONGS FROM THE STAGE AND SCREEN | | |
| | *Telstar STAR 2308* | 12† | 5 wks |

See also the London Symphony Orchestra; Cyril Ornadel/London Symphony Orchestra; Kimera; Julian Lloyd Webber, both with the London Symphony Orchestra; Spike Milligan.

Randy CRAWFORD *US, female vocalist* *136 wks*

28 Jun 80	● NOW WE MAY BEGIN *Warner Bros. K 56791*	10	16 wks
16 May 81	● SECRET COMBINATION *Warner Bros. K 56904*	2	60 wks
12 Jun 82	● WINDSONG *Warner Bros. K 57011*	7	17 wks
22 Oct 83	NIGHTLINE *Warner Bros. 92–3976–1*	37	4 wks
13 Oct 84	● MISS RANDY CRAWFORD – THE GREATEST		
	HITS *K-Tel NE 1281*	10	17 wks
28 Jun 86	ABSTRACT EMOTIONS *Warner Bros. WX 46*	14	10 wks
10 Oct 87	THE LOVE SONGS *Telstar STAR 2299*	27†	12 wks

Robert CRAY BAND
US, male vocal/instrumental group *29 wks*

| 12 Oct 85 | FALSE ACCUSATIONS *Demon FIEND 43* | 68 | 1 wk |
| 15 Nov 86 | STRONG PERSUADER *Mercury MERH 97* | 34 | 28 wks |

CRAZY HORSE – *See Neil YOUNG*

CRAZY WORLD – *See Crazy World of Arthur BROWN*

CREAM *UK, male vocal/instrumental group* *182 wks*

24 Dec 66	● FRESH CREAM *Reaction 593–001*	6	17 wks
18 Nov 67	● DISRAELI GEARS *Reaction 594–003*	5	42 wks
17 Aug 68	● WHEELS OF FIRE (double) *Polydor 583–031/2*	3	26 wks
17 Aug 68	● WHEELS OF FIRE (single) *Polydor 583–033*	7	13 wks
8 Feb 69	● FRESH CREAM (re-issue) *Reaction 594–001*	7	2 wks
15 Mar 69	★ GOODBYE *Polydor 583–053*	1	28 wks
8 Nov 69	● BEST OF CREAM *Polydor 583–060*	6	34 wks
4 Jul 70	● LIVE CREAM *Polydor 2383–016*	4	15 wks
24 Jun 72	LIVE CREAM VOL. 2 *Polydor 2383 119*	15	5 wks

See Eric Clapton and Cream.

CREATURES *UK, male/female vocal/instrumental duo* *9 wks*

| 28 May 83 | FEAST *Wonderland SHELP 1* | 17 | 9 wks |

CREEDENCE CLEARWATER REVIVAL
US, male vocal/instrumental group *65 wks*

24 Jan 70	GREEN RIVER *Liberty LBS 83273*	20	6 wks
28 Mar 70	● WILLY AND THE POOR BOYS *Liberty LBS 83338*	10	24 wks
2 May 70	BAYOU COUNTRY *Liberty LBS 83261*	62	1 wk
12 Sep 70	★ COSMO'S FACTORY *Liberty LBS 83388*	1	15 wks
23 Jan 71	PENDULUM *Liberty LBG 83400*	23	12 wks
30 Jun 79	GREATEST HITS *Fantasy FT 558*	35	5 wks
19 Oct 85	THE CREEDENCE COLLECTION		
	Impression IMDP	68	2 wks

CREME – *See GODLEY and CREME*

Kid CREOLE and the COCONUTS
US, male/female vocal/instrumental group *54 wks*

22 May 82	● TROPICAL GANGSTERS *Ze ILPS 7016*	3	40 wks
26 Jun 82	FRESH FRUIT IN FOREIGN PLACES		
	Ze ILPS 7014	99	1 wk
17 Sep 83	DOPPELGANGER *Island ILPS 9743*	21	6 wks
15 Sep 84	CRE-OLE *Island IMA 13*	21	7 wks

(Above) ALICE COOPER listens to
some real golden oldies.

(Right) RANDY CRAWFORD has never
hit the Top Ten in her native America,
but she's done so frequently in Britain.

CRICKETS US, male vocal/instrumental group   7 wks

25 Mar 61	**IN STYLE WITH THE CRICKETS**			
	Coral LVA 9142		13	7 wks

See also Buddy Holly and the Crickets; Bobby Vee and the Crickets.

Bing CROSBY US, male vocalist   39 wks

8 Oct 60	● **JOIN BING AND SING ALONG**			
	Warner Brothers WM 4021		7	11 wks
21 Dec 74	**WHITE CHRISTMAS** MCA MCF 2568		45	3 wks
20 Sep 75	**THAT'S WHAT LIFE IS ALL ABOUT**			
	United Artists UAG 2973		28	6 wks
5 Nov 77	**THE BEST OF BING** MCA MCF 2540		41	7 wks
5 Nov 77	● **LIVE AT THE LONDON PALLADIUM**			
	K-Tel NE 951		9	2 wks
17 Dec 77	**SEASONS** Polydor 2442 151		25	7 wks
5 May 79	**SONGS OF A LIFETIME** Philips 6641 923		29	3 wks

Dave CROSBY US, male vocalist   7 wks

24 Apr 71	**IF ONLY I COULD REMEMBER MY NAME**			
	Atlantic 2401-005		12	7 wks

See also Crosby, Stills and Nash; Crosby, Stills, Nash and Young; Graham Nash and David Crosby.

CROSBY, STILLS and NASH
US/UK, male vocal/instrumental group   14 wks

23 Aug 69	**CROSBY STILLS AND NASH** Atlantic 588-189 ...		25	5 wks
9 Jul 77	**CSN** Atlantic K 50369		23	9 wks

See also Dave Crosby; Crosby, Stills, Nash and Young; Graham Nash; Graham Nash and David Crosby; Stephen Stills; Stills-Young Band; Stephen Stills' Manassas.

CROSBY, STILLS, NASH and YOUNG
US/UK/Canada, male vocal/instrumental group   79 wks

30 May 70	● **DEJA VU** Atlantic 2401-001		5	61 wks
22 May 71	● **FOUR-WAY STREET** Atlantic 2956 004		5	12 wks
21 Sep 74	**SO FAR** Atlantic K 50023		25	6 wks

See also Dave Crosby; Crosby, Stills and Nash; Graham Nash; Graham Nash and David Crosby; Stephen Stills; Stills-Young Band; Stephen Stills' Manassas; Neil Young.

Christopher CROSS US, male vocalist   93 wks

21 Feb 81	**CHRISTOPHER CROSS** Warner Bros. K 56789 ...		14	77 wks
19 Feb 83	● **ANOTHER PAGE** Warner Bros. W 3757		4	16 wks

CROWN HEIGHTS AFFAIR
US, male vocal/instrumental group   3 wks

23 Sep 78	**DREAM WORLD** Philips 6372 754		40	3 wks

CRUSADERS US, male vocal/instrumental group   30 wks

21 Jul 79	● **STREET LIFE** MCA MCF 3008		10	16 wks
19 Jul 80	**RHAPSODY AND BLUE** MCA MCG 4010		40	5 wks
12 Sep 81	**STANDING TALL** MCA MCF 3122		47	5 wks
7 Apr 84	**GHETTO BLASTER** MCA MCF 3176		46	4 wks

Bobby CRUSH UK, male instrumentalist – piano   12 wks

29 Nov 72	**BOBBY CRUSH** Philips 6308 135		15	7 wks
18 Dec 82	**THE BOBBY CRUSH INCREDIBLE DOUBLE**			
	DECKER PARTY Warwick WW 5126/7		53	5 wks

CUDDLES – *See Keith HARRIS, ORVILLE and CUDDLES*

CULT UK, male vocal/instrumental group   60 wks

18 Jun 83	**SOUTHERN DEATH CULT**			
	Beggars Banquet BEGA 46		43	3 wks
8 Sep 84	**DREAMTIME** Beggars Banquet BEGA 57		21	8 wks
26 Oct 85	● **LOVE** Beggars Banquet BEGA 65		4	22 wks
18 Apr 87	**ELECTRIC** Beggars Banquet BEGA 80		4	27 wks

First album credited to Southern Death Cult.

CULT JAM – *See LISA LISA and CULT JAM with FULL FORCE*

CULTURE Jamaica, male vocal/instrumental group   1 wk

1 Apr 78	**TWO SEVENS CLASH** Lightning LIP 1		60	1 wk

CULTURE CLUB
UK, male vocal/instrumental group   144 wks

16 Oct 82	● **KISSING TO BE CLEVER** Virgin V 2232		5	59 wks
22 Oct 83	★ **COLOUR BY NUMBERS** Virgin V 2285		1	56 wks
3 Nov 84	● **WAKING UP WITH THE HOUSE ON FIRE**			
	Virgin V 2330		2	13 wks
12 Apr 86	● **FROM LUXURY TO HEARTACHE** Virgin V 2380		10	6 wks
18 Apr 87	● **THIS TIME** Virgin VTV 1		8	10 wks

CURE UK, male vocal/instrumental group   127 wks

2 Jun 79	**THREE IMAGINARY BOYS** Fiction FIX 001		44	3 wks
3 May 80	**17 SECONDS** Fiction FIX 004		20	10 wks
25 Apr 81	**FAITH** Fiction FIX 6		14	8 wks
15 May 82	● **PORNOGRAPHY** Fiction FIX D7		8	9 wks
3 Sep 83	**BOYS DON'T CRY** Fiction SPELP 26		93	3 wks
24 Dec 83	**JAPANESE WHISPERS** Fiction FIXM 8		26	14 wks
3 Mar 84	**BOYS DON'T CRY** Fiction SPELP 26		71	4 wks
12 May 84	● **THE TOP** Fiction FIXS 9		10	10 wks
3 Nov 84	**CONCERT – THE CURE LIVE** Fiction FIXH 10		26	4 wks
7 Sep 85	● **THE HEAD ON THE DOOR** Fiction FIXH 11		7	13 wks
31 May 86	● **STANDING ON A BEACH – THE SINGLES**			
	Fiction FIXH 12		4	34 wks
6 Jun 87	● **KISS ME KISS ME KISS ME** Fiction FIXH 13 ...		6	15 wks

The compact disc version of FIXH 12 was titled Staring At The Sea.

CURIOSITY KILLED THE CAT
UK, male vocal/instrumental group   24 wks

9 May 87	★ **KEEP YOUR DISTANCE** Mercury CATLP 1		1	24 wks

CURVED AIR
UK, male/female vocal/instrumental group   32 wks

5 Dec 70	● **AIR CONDITIONING** Warner Bros. WSX 3012		8	21 wks
9 Oct 71	**CURVED AIR** Warner Bros. K 46092		11	6 wks
13 May 72	**PHANTASMAGORIA** Reprise K 46158		20	5 wks

Adge CUTLER and the WURZELS
UK, male vocal/instrumental group   4 wks

11 Mar 67	**ADGE CUTLER AND THE WURZELS**			
	Columbia SX 6126		38	4 wks

See also the Wurzels.

CUTTING CREW UK, male vocal/instrumental group   5 wks

29 Nov 86	**BROADCAST** Siren SIRENLP 7		41	5 wks

D

DAINTEES – *See Martin STEPHENSON and the DAINTEES*

DAKOTAS – *See Billy J. KRAMER and the DAKOTAS*

DALEK I *UK, male vocal/instrumental group* **2 wks**

9 Aug 80	**COMPASS KUMPAS**	*Backdoor OPEN 1*	....	**54**	2 wks

DALI'S CAR *UK, male vocal/instrumental duo* **1 wk**

1 Dec 84	**THE WAKING HOUR**	*Paradox DOXLP 1*	....	**84**	1 wk

Roger DALTREY *UK, male vocalist* **24 wks**

26 Jul 75	**RIDE A ROCK HORSE**	*Polydor 2660 111*	....	**14**	10 wks
4 Jul 77	**ONE OF THE BOYS**	*Polydor 2442 146*	....	**45**	1 wk
23 Aug 80	**McVICAR (film soundtrack)**	*Polydor POLD 5034*	..	**39**	11 wks
2 Nov 85	**UNDER A RAGING MOON**	*10 DIX 17*	....	**52**	2 wks

Glen DALY *UK, male vocalist* **2 wks**

20 Nov 71	**GLASGOW NIGHT OUT**	*Golden Guinea GGL 0479*	**28**	2 wks

DAMNED *UK, male vocal/instrumental group* **54 wks**

12 Mar 77	**DAMNED DAMNED DAMNED**	*Stiff SEEZ 1*	...	**36**	10 wks
17 Nov 79	**MACHINE GUN ETIQUETTE** *Chiswick CWK 3011*	....		**31**	5 wks
29 Nov 80	**THE BLACK ALBUM**	*Chiswick CWK 3015*	....	**29**	3 wks
28 Nov 81	**BEST OF**	*Chiswick DAM 1*	....	**43**	12 wks
23 Oct 82	**STRAWBERRIES**	*Bronze BRON 542*	.....	**15**	4 wks
27 July 85	**PHANTASMAGORIA**	*MCA MCF 3275*	......	**11**	17 wks
13 Dec 86	**ANYTHING**	*MCA MCG 6015*	....	**40**	2 wks
12 Dec 87	**LIGHT AT THE END OF THE TUNNEL** *MCA MCSP 312*	....		**94**	1 wk

Vic DAMONE *US, male vocalist* **4 wks**

25 Apr 81	**NOW!**	*RCA INTS 5080*	....	**44**	3 wks
2 Apr 83	**VIC DAMONE SINGS THE GREAT SONGS** *CBS 32261*	....		**87**	1 wk

Suzanne DANDO *UK, female exercise instructor* **1 wk**

17 Mar 84	**SHAPE UP AND DANCE WITH SUZANNE DANDO** *Lifestyle LEG 21*	....	**87**	1 wk

Charlie DANIELS BAND
US, male vocal/instrumental group **1 wk**

10 Nov 79	**MILLION MILE REFLECTIONS**	*Epic EPC 83446*		**74**	1 wk

Terence Trent D'ARBY *US, male vocalist* **23 wks**

25 Jul 87	★ **INTRODUCING THE HARDLINE ACCORDING TO TERENCE TRENT D'ARBY**	*CBS 450 911-1*	..	**1†**	23 wks

Bobby DARIN *US, male vocalist* **15 wks**

19 Mar 60	● **THIS IS DARIN**	*London HA 2235*	....	**4**	8 wks

9 Apr 60	**THAT'S ALL**	*London HAE 2172*	....	**15**	1 wk
5 Oct 85	**THE LEGEND OF BOBBY DARIN – HIS GREATEST HITS**	*Atlantic SMR 8504*	....	**39**	6 wks

DARTS *UK, male/female vocal/instrumental group* **57 wks**

3 Dec 77	● **DARTS**	*Magnet MAG 5020*	....	**9**	22 wks
3 Jun 78	**EVERYONE PLAYS DARTS**	*Magnet MAG 5022*	.	**12**	18 wks
18 Nov 78	● **AMAZING DARTS**	*K-Tel/Magnet DLP 7981*	......	**8**	13 wks
6 Oct 79	**DART ATTACK**	*Magnet MAG 5030*	....	**38**	4 wks

DANSE SOCIETY
UK, male vocal/instrumental group **4 wks**

11 Feb 84	**HEAVEN IS WAITING**	*Society 205 972*	....	**39**	4 wks

DAVE – *See CHAS and DAVE*

DAVE – *See SAM and DAVE*

F.R. DAVID *France, male vocalist* **6 wks**

7 May 83	**WORDS**	*Carrere CAL 145*	....	**46**	6 wks

Windsor DAVIES – *See Don ESTELLE and Windsor DAVIES*

Miles DAVIS *US, male instrumentalist – trumpet* **4 wks**

11 Jul 70	**BITCHES BREW**	*CBS 66236*	....	**71**	1 wk
15 Jun 85	**YOU'RE UNDER ARREST**	*CBS 26447*	....	**88**	1 wk
18 Oct 86	**TUTU**	*Warner Bros. WX 62*	....	**74**	2 wks

Spencer DAVIS GROUP
UK, male vocal/instrumental group **47 wks**

8 Jan 66	● **THEIR 1ST LP**	*Fontana TL 5242*	....	**6**	9 wks
22 Jan 66	● **THE 2ND LP**	*Fontana TL 5295*	....	**3**	18 wks
11 Sep 66	● **AUTUMN '66**	*Fontana TL 5359*	....	**4**	20 wks

Sammy DAVIS JR. *US, male vocalist* **1 wk**

13 Apr 63	**SAMMY DAVIS JR. AT THE COCONUT GROVE** *Reprise R 6063/2*	....		**19**	1 wk

DAWN *US, male/female vocal group* **2 wks**

4 May 74	**GOLDEN RIBBONS**	*Bell BELLS 236*	....	**46**	2 wks

Doris DAY *US, female vocalist* **11 wks**

6 Jan 79	**20 GOLDEN GREATS**	*Warwick PR 5053*	....	**12**	11 wks

Chris DE BURGH *Ireland, male vocalist* **161 wks**

12 Sep 81	**BEST MOVES**	*A & M AMLH 68532*	....	**65**	4 wks
9 Oct 82	**THE GETAWAY**	*A & M AMLH 68549*	....	**30**	16 wks
19 May 84	**MAN ON THE LINE**	*A & M AMLX 65002*	......	**11**	24 wks
29 Dec 84	◗ **THE VERY BEST OF CHRIS DE BURGH** *Telstar STAR 2248*	....		**6**	55 wks
24 Aug 85	**SPANISH TRAIN & OTHER STORIES** *A & M AMLH 68343*	....		**78**	3 wks
7 Jun 86	● **INTO THE LIGHT**	*A & M AM 5121*	....	**2**	58 wks
4 Oct 86	**CRUSADER**	*A & M AMLH 64746*	....	**72**	1 wk

(Right) DEPECHE MODE earned some great reward every time they released an album.

(Below) BOBBY DARIN, born Walden Robert Cassotto in the Bronx, died of heart disease at the age of 37.

(Above) This DRIFTERS line-up includes Ben E. King (second from left), who sang lead on several of their greatest hits, most notably *Save The Last Dance For Me*.

(Right) DR. HOOK were fronted by Ray Sawyer (with the eye patch) and Dennis Locorriere (third from right).

Waldo DE LOS RIOS *Argentina, orchestra*　　26 wks

1 May 71 ● SYMPHONIES FOR THE SEVENTIES
A & M AMLS 2014 .... **6** 26 wks

Manitas DE PLATA
Spanish, male instrumentalist – guitar　　1 wk

29 Jul 67　FLAMENCO GUITAR　*Philips SBL 7786* .... **40** 1 wk

DEACON BLUE
UK, male/female vocal/instrumental group　　2 wks

6 Jun 87　RAINTOWN　*CBS 450 549–1* .... **82** 2 wks

DEAD KENNEDYS
US, male vocal/instrumental group　　8 wks

13 Sep 80　FRESH FRUIT FOR ROTTING VEGETABLES
Cherry Red BRED 10 .... **33** 6 wks
4 Jul 87　GIVE ME CONVENIENCE
Alternative Tentacles VIRUS 5 .... **84** 2 wks

DEAD OR ALIVE *UK, male vocal/instrumental group*　　22 wks

28 Apr 84　SOPHISTICATED BOOM BOOM
Epic EPC 25835 .... **29** 3 wks
25 May 85 ● YOUTHQUAKE　*Epic EPC 26420* ...... **9** 15 wks
14 Feb 87　MAD, BAD AND DANGEROUS TO KNOW
Epic 450 257–1 .... **27** 4 wks

DeBARGE *US, male/female vocal group*　　2 wks

25 May 85　RHYTHM OF THE NIGHT　*Gordy ZL 72340* ..... **94** 2 wks

DEAN – *See JAN and DEAN*

Kiki DEE *UK, female vocalist*　　9 wks

26 Mar 77　KIKI DEE　*Rocket ROLA 3* .... **24** 5 wks
18 Jul 81　PERFECT TIMING　*Ariola ARL 5050* ..... **47** 4 wks

Dave DEE, DOZY, BEAKY, MICK and TICH
UK, male vocal/instrumental group　　15 wks

2 Jul 66　DAVE DEE, DOZY, BEAKY, MICK AND TICH
Fontana STL 5350 .... **11** 10 wks
7 Jan 67　IF MUSIC BE THE FOOD OF LOVE . . . PREPARE
FOR INDIGESTION　*Fontana STL 5388* .... **27** 5 wks

DEEP PURPLE *UK, male vocal/instrumental group*　　267 wks

24 Jan 70　CONCERTO FOR GROUP AND ORCHESTRA
Harvest SHVL 767 .... **26** 4 wks
20 Jun 70 ● DEEP PURPLE IN ROCK　*Harvest SHVL 777* .... **4** 68 wks
18 Sep 71 ★ FIREBALL　*Harvest SHVL 793* ... **1** 25 wks
15 Apr 72 ★ MACHINE HEAD　*Purple TPSA 7504* ... **1** 24 wks
6 Jan 73　MADE IN JAPAN　*Purple TPSP 351* ... **16** 14 wks
17 Feb 73 ● WHO DO WE THINK WE ARE
Purple TPSA 7508 ... **4** 11 wks
2 Mar 74 ● BURN　*Purple TPA 3505* ... **3** 21 wks
23 Nov 74 ● STORM BRINGER　*Purple TPS 3508* ... **6** 12 wks
5 Jul 75　24 CARAT PURPLE　*Purple TPSM 2002* ... **14** 17 wks
22 Nov 75　COME TASTE THE BAND　*Purple TPSA 7515* ... **19** 4 wks
27 Nov 76　DEEP PURPLE LIVE　*Purple TPSA 7517* ... **12** 6 wks

21 Apr 79　THE MARK II PURPLE SINGLES
Purple TPS 3514 .... **24** 6 wks
19 Jul 80 ★ DEEPEST PURPLE　*Harvest EMTV 25* .... **1** 15 wks
13 Dec 80　IN CONCERT　*Harvest SHDW 4121/4122* .... **30** 8 wks
4 Sep 82　DEEP PURPLE LIVE IN LONDON
Harvest SHSP 4124 .... **23** 5 wks
10 Nov 84 ● PERFECT STRANGERS　*Polydor POLH 16* ... **5** 15 wks
29 Jun 85　THE ANTHOLOGY　*Harvest PUR 1* ... **50** 3 wks
24 Jan 87　THE HOUSE OF BLUE LIGHT　*Polydor POLH 32* . **10** 9 wks

DEF LEPPARD *UK, male vocal/instrumental group*　　42 wks

22 Mar 80　ON THROUGH THE NIGHT　*Vertigo 9102 040* ... **15** 8 wks
25 Jul 81　HIGH 'N' DRY　*Vertigo 6359 045* ... **26** 8 wks
12 Mar 83　PYROMANIA　*Vertigo VERS 2* ... **18** 8 wks
29 Aug 87 ★ HYSTERIA　*Bludgeon Riffola HYSLP 1* ... **1†** 18 wks

Desmond DEKKER *Jamaica, male vocalist*　　4 wks

5 Jul 69　THIS IS DESMOND DEKKER　*Trojan TTL 4* ..... **27** 4 wks

DELANEY and BONNIE and FRIENDS
US/UK, male/female vocal/instrumental group　　3 wks

6 Jun 70　ON TOUR　*Atlantic 2400–013* .... **39** 3 wks

DEMON *UK, male vocal/instrumental group*　　5 wks

14 Aug 82　THE UNEXPECTED GUEST　*Carrere CAL 139* ... **47** 3 wks
2 Jul 83　THE PLAGUE　*Clay CLAY LP 6* .... **73** 2 wks

Sandy DENNY *UK, female vocalist*　　2 wks

2 Oct 71　THE NORTH STAR GRASSMAN AND THE
RAVENS　*Island ILPS 9165* .... **31** 2 wks

John DENVER *US, male vocalist*　　204 wks

2 Jun 73　POEMS, PRAYERS AND PROMISES
RCA SF 8219 .... **19** 5 wks
23 Jun 73　RHYMES AND REASONS　*RCA Victor SF 8348* . **21** 5 wks
30 Mar 74 ● THE BEST OF JOHN DENVER
RCA Victor APLI 0374 .... **7** 69 wks
7 Sep 74 ● BACK HOME AGAIN　*RCA Victor APLI 0548* ..... **3** 29 wks
22 Mar 75　AN EVENING WITH JOHN DENVER
RCA Victor LSA 32211/12 .... **31** 4 wks
11 Oct 75　WIND SONG　*RCA Victor APLI 1183* ... **14** 21 wks
15 May 76 ● LIVE IN LONDON　*RCA Victor RS 1050* ... **2** 29 wks
4 Sep 76　SPIRIT　*RCA Victor APLI 1694* ... **9** 11 wks
19 Mar 77 ● BEST OF JOHN DENVER VOL. 2
RCA Victor PL 42120 ... **9** 9 wks
11 Feb 78　I WANT TO LIVE　*RCA PL 12561* ... **25** 5 wks
21 Apr 79　JOHN DENVER　*RCA Victor PL 13075* ... **68** 1 wk
22 Oct 83　IT'S ABOUT TIME　*RCA RCALP 6087* ... **90** 2 wks
1 Dec 84　JOHN DENVER COLLECTION
Telstar STAR 2253 ... **20** 11 wks
23 Aug 86　ONE WORLD　*RCA PL 85811* ... **91** 3 wks

See also Placido Domingo and John Denver.

Karl DENVER *UK, male vocalist*　　27 wks

23 Dec 61 ● WIMOWEH　*Ace Of Clubs ACL 1098* .... **7** 27 wks

DEPECHE MODE
UK, male vocal/instrumental group　　105 wks

14 Nov 81 ● SPEAK AND SPELL　*Mute STUMM 5* .... **10** 33 wks
9 Oct 82 ● A BROKEN FRAME　*Mute STUMM 9* .... **8** 11 wks

3 Sep 83 ● **CONSTRUCTION TIME AGAIN** *Mute STUMM 13* .... **6** 12 wks
6 Sep 84 ● **SOME GREAT REWARD** *Mute STUMM 19* ... **5** 12 wks
26 Oct 85 ● **THE SINGLES 81–85** *Mute MUTEL 1* **6** 22 wks
29 Mar 86 ● **BLACK CELEBRATION** *Mute STUMM 26* ..... **4** 11 wks
10 Oct 87 ● **MUSIC FOR THE MASSES** *Mute STUMM 47* .... **10** 4 wks

DEREK AND CLIVE – *See Peter COOK and Dudley MOORE*

DEREK and the DOMINOES
UK/US, male vocal/instrumental group   *1 wk*

24 Mar 73 **IN CONCERT** *RSO 2659 020* .... **36** 1 wk

DESTROYERS – *See George THOROGOOD and the DESTROYERS*

DETROIT SPINNERS *US, male vocal group*   *3 wks*

14 May 77 **DETROIT SPINNERS' SMASH HITS**
Atlantic K 50363 .... **37** 3 wks

Sidney DEVINE *UK, male vocalist*   *11 wks*

10 Apr 76 **DOUBLE DEVINE** *Philips 6625 019* .... **14** 10 wks
11 Dec 76 **DEVINE TIME** *Philips 6308 283* .... **49** 1 wk

DEVO *US, male vocal/instrumental group*   *22 wks*

16 Sep 78 **Q: ARE WE NOT MEN? A: NO WE ARE DEVO!**
Virgin V 2106 .... **12** 7 wks
23 Jun 79 **DUTY NOW FOR THE FUTURE** *Virgin V 2125* **49** 6 wks
24 May 80 **FREEDOM OF CHOICE** *Virgin V 2162* . **47** 5 wks
5 Sep 81 **NEW TRADITIONALISTS** *Virgin V 2191* .... **50** 4 wks

Howard DEVOTO *UK, male vocalist*   *2 wks*

6 Aug 83 **JERKY VERSIONS OF THE DREAM**
Virgin V 2272 .... **57** 2 wks

DEXY'S MIDNIGHT RUNNERS
UK, male/female vocal/instrumental group   *64 wks*

26 Jul 80 ● **SEARCHING FOR THE YOUNG SOUL REBELS**
Parlophone PCS 7213 .... **6** 10 wks
7 Aug 82 ● **TOO-RYE-AY** *Mercury MERS 5* .... **2** 46 wks
26 Mar 83 **GENO** *EMI EMS 1007* .... **79** 2 wks
21 Sep 85 **DON'T STAND ME DOWN** *Mercury MERH 56* ... **22** 6 wks

Group were all male for first album.

Neil DIAMOND *US, male vocalist*   *466 wks*

3 Apr 71 **TAP ROOT MANUSCRIPT** *Uni UNLS 117* ..... **19** 12 wks
3 Apr 71 **GOLD** *Uni UNLS 116* .... **23** 11 wks
11 Dec 71 **STONES** *Uni UNLS 121* .... **18** 14 wks
5 Aug 72 ● **MOODS** *Uni UNLS 128* .... **7** 19 wks
12 Jan 74 **HOT AUGUST NIGHT** *Uni ULD 1* .... **32** 2 wks
16 Feb 74 **JONATHAN LIVINGSTON SEAGULL**
CBS 69047 .... **35** 1 wk
9 Mar 74 **RAINBOW** *MCA MCF 2529* .... **39** 5 wks
29 Jul 74 **HIS 12 GREATEST HITS** *MCA MCF 2550* ... **13** 78 wks
9 Nov 74 **SERENADE** *CBS 69067* .... **11** 14 wks
10 Jul 76 ● **BEAUTIFUL NOISE** *CBS 86004* .... **10** 26 wks
12 Mar 77 ● **LOVE AT THE GREEK** *CBS 95001* ... **3** 32 wks
6 Aug 77 **HOT AUGUST NIGHT (re-issue)** *MCA MCSP 255* **60** 1 wk
17 Dec 77 **I'M GLAD YOU'RE HERE WITH ME TONIGHT**
CBS 86044 .... **16** 12 wks
25 Nov 78 ● **20 GOLDEN GREATS** *MCA EMTV 14* ... **2** 26 wks
6 Jan 79 **YOU DON'T BRING ME FLOWERS** *CBS 86077* . **15** 23 wks
19 Jan 80 **SEPTEMBER MORN** *CBS 86096* .... **14** 11 wks

22 Nov 80 **THE JAZZ SINGER** *Capitol EAST 12120* .... **14** 109 wks
28 Feb 81 **LOVE SONGS** *MCA MCF 3092* .... **43** 6 wks
5 Dec 81 **THE WAY TO THE SKY** *CBS 85343* .... **39** 13 wks
19 Jun 82 **12 GREATEST HITS VOL 2** *CBS 85844* .... **32** 8 wks
13 Nov 82 **HEARTLIGHT** *CBS 25073* .... **43** 10 wks
10 Dec 83 **THE VERY BEST OF NEIL DIAMOND**
K-Tel NE 1265 .... **33** 11 wks
28 Jul 84 ● **PRIMITIVE** *CBS 86306* .... **7** 10 wks
24 May 86 **HEADED FOR THE FUTURE** *CBS 26952* .... **36** 8 wks
28 Nov 87 **HOT AUGUST NIGHT 2** *CBS 460 408-1* .... **74** 4 wks

DIAMOND HEAD *UK, male vocal/instrumental group*   *9 wks*

23 Oct 82 **BORROWED TIME** *MCA DH 1001* .... **24** 5 wks
24 Sep 83 **CANTERBURY** *MCA DH 1002* .... **32** 4 wks

DICKIES *US, male vocal/instrumental group*   *19 wks*

17 Feb 79 **THE INCREDIBLE SHRINKING DICKIES**
A & M AMLE 64742 .... **18** 17 wks
24 Nov 79 **DAWN OF THE DICKIES** *A & M AMLE 68510* ... **60** 2 wks

Barbara DICKSON *UK, female vocalist*   *119 wks*

18 Jun 77 ● **MORNING COMES QUICKLY** *RSO 2394 188* ... **58** 1 wk
12 Apr 80 ● **THE BARBARA DICKSON ALBUM**
Epic EPC 84088 .... **7** 12 wks
16 May 81 **YOU KNOW IT'S ME** *Epic EPC 84551* .... **39** 6 wks
6 Feb 82 ● **ALL FOR A SONG** *Epic 10030* .... **3** 38 wks
24 Sep 83 **TELL ME IT'S NOT TRUE** *Legacy LLM 101* .... **100** 1 wk
23 Jun 84 **HEARTBEATS** *Epic EPC 25706* .... **21** 8 wks
12 Jan 85 ● **THE BARBARA DICKSON SONGBOOK**
K-Tel NE 1287 .... **5** 19 wks
23 Nov 85 **GOLD** *K-Tel ONE 1312* .... **11** 18 wks
15 Nov 86 **THE VERY BEST OF BARBARA DICKSON**
Telstar STAR 2276 .... **80** 8 wks
29 Nov 86 **THE RIGHT MOMENT** *K-Tel ONE 1335* .... **39** 8 wks

Tell Me It's Not True is a mini-album featuring songs from the musical Blood Brothers.

Bo DIDDLEY
US, male vocalist/instrumentalist – guitar   *16 wks*

5 Oct 63 **BO DIDDLEY** *Pye International NPL 28026* .... **11** 8 wks
9 Oct 63 **BO DIDDLEY IS A GUNSLINGER** *Pye NJL 33* .. **20** 1 wk
30 Nov 63 **BO DIDDLEY RIDES AGAIN**
Pye International NPL 28029 .... **19** 1 wk
15 Feb 64 **BO DIDDLEY'S BEACH PARTY** *Pye NPL 28032* . **13** 6 wks

DIFFORD and TILBROOK
UK, male vocal/instrumental duo   *3 wks*

14 Jul 84 **DIFFORD AND TILBROOK** *A & M AMLX 64985* ... **47** 3 wks

Richard DIMBLEBY *UK, male broadcaster*   *5 wks*

4 Jun 66 **VOICE OF RICHARD DIMBLEBY** *MFP 1087* ... **14** 5 wks

DIO *UK/US, male vocal/instrumental group*   *45 wks*

11 Jun 83 **HOLY DIVER** *Vertigo VERS 5* .... **13** 15 wks
21 Jul 84 ● **THE LAST IN LINE** *Vertigo VERL 16* .... **4** 14 wks
7 Sep 85 ● **SACRED HEART** *Vertigo VERH 30* .... **4** 6 wks
5 Jul 86 **INTERMISSION** *Vertigo VERB 40* .... **22** 5 wks
22 Aug 87 ● **DREAM EVIL** *Vertigo VERH 46* .... **8** 5 wks

DION and the BELMONTS *US, male vocal group*   *5 wks*

12 Apr 80 **20 GOLDEN GREATS** *K-Tel NE 1057* .... **31** 5 wks

DIRE STRAITS *UK, male vocal/instrumental group* 900 wks

22 Jul	78	● DIRE STRAITS *Vertigo 9102 021*		5	129 wks
23 Jun	79	● COMMUNIQUE *Vertigo 9102 031*		5	32 wks
25 Oct	80	● MAKIN' MOVIES *Vertigo 6359 034*		4	247 wks
2 Oct	82	★ LOVE OVER GOLD *Vertigo 6359 109*		1	197 wks
24 Mar	84	● ALCHEMY – DIRE STRAITS LIVE			
		Vertigo VERY 11		3	159 wks
25 May	85	★ BROTHERS IN ARMS *Vertigo VERH 25*		1†	136 wks

DISCHARGE *UK, male vocal/instrumental group* 5 wks

15 May	82	HEAR NOTHING, SEE NOTHING, SAY NOTHING *Clay CLAYLP 3*		40	5 wks

DISCIPLES OF SOUL – *See LITTLE STEVEN*

Sacha DISTEL *France, male vocalist* 14 wks

2 May	70	SACHA DISTEL *Warner Bros. WS 3003*		21	14 wks

DJ JAZZY JEFF and FRESH PRINCE
US, male rap duo 1 wk

28 Feb	87	ROCK THE HOUSE *Champion CHAMP 1004*		97	1 wk

DOCTOR and the MEDICS
UK, male/female vocal/instrumental group 3 wks

21 Jun	86	LAUGHING AT THE PIECES *MCA MIRG 1010*		25	3 wks

DR. FEELGOOD *UK, male vocal/instrumental group* 33 wks

18 Oct	75	MALPRACTICE *United Artists UAS 29880*		17	6 wks
2 Oct	76	★ STUPIDITY *United Artists UAS 29990*		1	9 wks
4 Jun	77	● SNEAKIN' SUSPICION *United Artists UAS*		10	6 wks
8 Oct	77	BE SEEING YOU *United Artists UAS 30123*		55	3 wks
7 Oct	78	PRIVATE PRACTICE *United Artists UAG 30184*		41	5 wks
2 Jun	79	AS IT HAPPENS *United Artists UAK 30239*		42	4 wks

DR. HOOK *US, male vocal/instrumental group* 130 wks

25 Jun	76	● A LITTLE BIT MORE *Capitol E-ST 23795*		5	42 wks
29 Oct	77	MAKING LOVE AND MUSIC *Capitol EST 11632*		39	4 wks
27 Oct	79	PLEASURE AND PAIN *Capitol EAST 11859*		47	6 wks
17 Nov	79	SOMETIMES YOU WIN *Capitol EST 12018*		14	44 wks
29 Nov	80	RISING *Mercury 6302 076*		44	5 wks
6 Dec	80	● DR. HOOK'S GREATEST HITS			
		Capitol EST 26037		2	28 wks
14 Nov	81	DR. HOOK LIVE IN THE UK *Capitol EST 26706*		90	1 wk

Ken DODD *UK, male vocalist* 36 wks

25 Dec	65	● TEARS OF HAPPINESS *Columbia 33SX 1793*		6	12 wks
23 Jul	66	HITS FOR NOW AND ALWAYS			
		Columbia SX 6060		14	11 wks
14 Jan	67	FOR SOMEONE SPECIAL *Columbia SCX 6224*		40	1 wk
29 Nov	80	● 20 GOLDEN GREATS OF KEN DODD			
		Warwick WW 5098		10	12 wks

DOKKEN *US, male vocal/instrumental group* 1 wk

21 Nov	87	BACK FOR THE ATTACK *Elektra EKT 43*		96	1 wk

Thomas DOLBY
UK, male vocalist/instrumentalist – keyboards 24 wks

22 May	82	THE GOLDEN AGE OF WIRELESS			
		Venice In Peril VIP 1001		65	10 wks
18 Feb	84	THE FLAT EARTH			
		Parlophone ODEON PCS 2400341		14	14 wks

DOLLAR *UK, male/female vocal duo* 28 wks

15 Sep	79	SHOOTING STARS *Carrere CAL 111*		36	8 wks
24 Apr	82	THE VERY BEST OF DOLLAR			
		Carrere CAL 3001		31	9 wks
30 Oct	82	THE DOLLAR ALBUM *WEA DTV 1*		18	11 wks

Placido DOMINGO *Spain, male vocalist* 22 wks

21 May	83	MY LIFE FOR A SONG *CBS 73683*		31	8 wks
27 Dec	86	PLACIDO DOMINGO COLLECTION			
		Stylus SMR 625		30	14 wks

See also Placido Domingo and John Denver; Andrew Lloyd Webber.

Placido DOMINGO and John DENVER
Spain/US, male vocal duo 21 wks

28 Nov	81	PERHAPS LOVE *CBS 73592*		26	21 wks

See also Placido Domingo; John Denver; Andrew Lloyd Webber.

Fats DOMINO *US, male vocalist/instrumentalist – piano* 1 wk

16 May	70	VERY BEST OF FATS DOMINO			
		Liberty LBS 83331		56	1 wk

DOMINOES – *See DEREK and the DOMINOES*

Lonnie DONEGAN *UK, male vocalist* 29 wks

1 Sep	62	● GOLDEN AGE OF DONEGAN			
		Pye Golden Guinea GGL 0135		3	23 wks
9 Feb	63	GOLDEN AGE OF DONEGAN VOL. 2			
		Pye Golden Guinea GGL 0170		15	3 wks
25 Feb	78	PUTTING ON THE STYLE *Chrysalis CHR 1158*		51	3 wks

DONOVAN *UK, male vocalist* 73 wks

5 Jun	65	● WHAT'S BIN DID AND WHAT'S BIN HID			
		Pye NPL 18117		3	16 wks
6 Nov	65	FAIRY TALE *Pye NPL 18128*		20	2 wks
8 Jul	67	SUNSHINE SUPERMAN *Pye NPL 18181*		25	7 wks
14 Oct	67	● UNIVERSAL SOLDIER *Marble Arch MAL 718*		5	18 wks
11 May	68	A GIFT FROM A FLOWER TO A GARDEN			
		Pye NSPL 20000		13	14 wks
12 Sep	70	OPEN ROAD *Dawn DNLS 3009*		30	4 wks
24 Mar	73	COSMIC WHEELS *Epic EPC 65450*		15	12 wks

DOOBIE BROTHERS
US, male vocal/instrumental group 30 wks

30 Mar	74	WHAT WERE ONCE VICES ARE NOW HABITS			
		Warner Bros. K 56206		19	10 wks
17 May	75	STAMPEDE *Warner Bros. K 56094*		14	11 wks
10 Apr	76	TAKIN' IT TO THE STREETS			
		Warner Bros. K 56196		42	2 wks
17 Sep	77	LIVING ON THE FAULT LINE			
		Warner Bros. K 56383		25	5 wks
11 Oct	80	ONE STEP CLOSER *Warner Bros. K 56824*		53	2 wks

DOOLEYS UK, male/female vocal/instrumental group — 27 wks

30 Jun 79	● THE BEST OF THE DOOLEYS GTO GTTV 038	6	21 wks
3 Nov 79	THE CHOSEN FEW GTO GTLP 040	56	4 wks
25 Oct 80	FULL HOUSE GTO GTTV 050	54	2 wks

Val DOONICAN Ireland, male vocalist — 164 wks

12 Dec 64	● LUCKY 13 SHADES OF VAL DOONICAN Decca LK 4648	2	27 wks
3 Dec 66	● GENTLE SHADES OF VAL DOONICAN Decca LK 4831	5	52 wks
2 Dec 67	★ VAL DOONICAN ROCKS BUT GENTLY Pye NSPL 18204	1	23 wks
30 Nov 68	● VAL Pye NSPL 18236	6	11 wks
14 Jun 69	● WORLD OF VAL DOONICAN Decca SPA 3	2	31 wks
13 Dec 69	SOUNDS GENTLE Pye NSPL 18321	22	9 wks
19 Dec 70	THE MAGIC OF VAL DOONICAN Philips 6642 003	34	3 wks
27 Nov 71	THIS IS VAL DOONICAN Philips 6382 017	40	1 wk
22 Feb 75	I LOVE COUNTRY MUSIC Philips 9299261	37	2 wks
21 May 77	SOME OF MY BEST FRIENDS ARE SONGS Philips 6641 607	29	5 wks

DOORS US, male vocal/instrumental group — 31 wks

28 Sep 68	WAITING FOR THE SUN Elektra EKS7 4024	16	10 wks
11 Apr 70	MORRISON HOTEL Elektra EKS 75007	12	8 wks
26 Sep 70	ABSOLUTELY LIVE Elektra 2665 002	69	1 wk
31 Jul 71	L.A. WOMAN Elektra K42090	28	3 wks
1 Apr 72	WEIRD SCENES INSIDE THE GOLD MINE Elektra K 62009	50	1 wk
29 Oct 83	ALIVE, SHE CRIED Elektra 96-0269-1	36	5 wks
4 Jul 87	LIVE AT THE HOLLYWOOD BOWL Elektra EKT 40	51	3 wks

Lee DORSEY US, male vocalist — 4 wks

17 Dec 66	NEW LEE DORSEY Stateside SSL 10192	34	4 wks

DOUBLE Switzerland, male vocal/instrumental duo — 4 wks

8 Mar 86	BLUE Polydor POLD 5187	69	4 wks

Craig DOUGLAS UK, male vocalist — 2 wks

6 Aug 60	CRAIG DOUGLAS Top Rank BUY 049	17	2 wks

DREAM ACADEMY
UK, male/female vocal/instrumental group — 2 wks

12 Oct 85	THE DREAM ACADEMY blanco y negro BYN 6	58	2 wks

DOZY – See Dave DEE, DOZY, BEAKY, MICK and TICH

DREAMERS – See FREDDIE and the DREAMERS

DRIFTERS US, male vocal group — 65 wks

18 May 68	GOLDEN HITS Atlantic 588-103	27	7 wks
10 Jun 72	GOLDEN HITS Atlantic K 40018	26	8 wks
8 Nov 75	● 24 ORIGINAL HITS Atlantic K 60106	2	34 wks
13 Dec 75	LOVE GAMES Bell BELLS 246	51	1 wk
18 Oct 86	THE VERY BEST OF THE DRIFTERS Telstar STAR 2280	24	15 wks

See also Ben E. King; Cliff Richard.

Julie DRISCOLL and the Brian AUGER TRINITY UK, female vocalist/male instrumental group — 13 wks

8 Jun 68	OPEN Marmalade 608-002	12	13 wks

D-TRAIN US, male vocalist/multi-instrumentalist — 4 wks

8 May 82	D-TRAIN Epic EPC 85683	72	4 wks

D-Train is a pseudonym for Hubert Eaves.

DUBLINERS Ireland, male vocal/instrumental group — 88 wks

13 May 67	● A DROP OF THE HARD STUFF Major Minor MMLP 3	5	41 wks
9 Sep 67	BEST OF THE DUBLINERS Transatlantic TRA 158	25	11 wks
7 Oct 67	● MORE OF THE HARD STUFF Major Minor MMLP 5	8	23 wks
2 Mar 68	DRINKIN' AND COURTIN' Major Minor SMLP 14	31	3 wks
25 Apr 87	THE DUBLINERS 25 YEARS CELEBRATION Stylus SMR 731	43	10 wks

Stephen 'Tin Tin' DUFFY UK, male vocalist — 7 wks

20 Apr 85	THE UPS AND DOWNS 10 DIX 5	35	7 wks

George DUKE
US, male vocalist/instrumentalist – keyboards — 4 wks

26 Jul 80	BRAZILIAN LOVE AFFAIR Epic EPC 84311	33	4 wks

Simon DUPREE and the BIG SOUND
UK, male vocal/instrumental group — 1 wk

13 Aug 67	WITHOUT RESERVATIONS Parlophone PCS 7029	39	1 wk

DURAN DURAN
UK, male vocal/instrumental group — 321 wks

27 Jun 81	● DURAN DURAN EMI EMC 3372	3	118 wks
22 May 82	● RIO EMI EMC 3411	2	109 wks
3 Dec 83	★ SEVEN AND THE RAGGED TIGER EMC 1654541	1	47 wks
24 Nov 84	● ARENA Parlophone DD 2	6	31 wks
6 Dec 86	NOTORIOUS EMI DDN 331	16	16 wks

Deanna DURBIN US, female vocalist — 4 wks

30 Jan 82	THE BEST OF DEANNA DURBIN MCA International MCL 1634	84	4 wks

Ian DURY and the BLOCKHEADS
UK, male vocal/instrumental group — 118 wks

22 Oct 77	● NEW BOOTS AND PANTIES!! Stiff SEEZ 4	5	90 wks
2 Jun 79	● DO IT YOURSELF Stiff SEEZ 14	2	18 wks
6 Dec 80	LAUGHTER Stiff SEEZ 30	48	4 wks
10 Oct 81	LORD UPMINSTER Polydor POLD 5042	53	4 wks
4 Feb 84	4,000 WEEKS HOLIDAY Polydor POLD 5112	54	2 wks

4,000 Weeks Holiday credits the Music Students – UK, male vocal/instrumental group.

(Left) *John Wesley Harding* was the longest-running of six BOB DYLAN number ones.

(Below) IAN DURY was in the chart for all of 1978 with *New Boots and Panties!!*

Bob DYLAN *US, male vocalist* 541 wks

23 May 64	★ THE FREEWHEELIN' BOB DYLAN *CBS BPG 62193*		1	49 wks
11 Jul 64	● THE TIMES THEY ARE A-CHANGIN' *CBS BPG 62251*		4	20 wks
21 Nov 64	● ANOTHER SIDE OF BOB DYLAN *CBS BPG 62429*		8	19 wks
8 May 65	BOB DYLAN *CBS BPG 62022*		13	6 wks
15 May 65	★ BRINGING IT ALL BACK HOME *CBS BPG 62515*		1	29 wks
9 Oct 65	● HIGHWAY 61 REVISITED *CBS BPG 62572*		4	15 wks
20 Aug 66	● BLONDE ON BLONDE *CBS DDP 66012*		3	15 wks
14 Jan 67	● GREATEST HITS *CBS SBPG 62847*		6	82 wks
2 Mar 68	★ JOHN WESLEY HARDING *CBS SBPG 63252*		1	29 wks
17 May 69	● NASHVILLE SKYLINE *CBS 63601*		1	42 wks
11 Jul 70	★ SELF PORTRAIT *CBS 66250*		1	15 wks
28 Nov 70	★ NEW MORNING *CBS 69001*		1	18 wks
25 Dec 71	MORE BOB DYLAN GREATEST HITS *CBS 67238/9*		12	15 wks
29 Sep 73	PAT GARRETT & BILLY THE KID (film soundtrack) *CBS 69042*		29	11 wks
23 Feb 74	● PLANET WAVES *Island ILPS 9261*		7	8 wks
13 Jul 74	● BEFORE THE FLOOD *Asylum IDBD 1*		8	7 wks
15 Feb 75	● BLOOD ON THE TRACKS *CBS 69097*		4	16 wks
26 Jul 75	● THE BASEMENT TAPES *CBS 88147*		8	10 wks
31 Jan 76	● DESIRE *CBS 86003*		3	35 wks
9 Oct 76	● HARD RAIN *CBS 86016*		3	7 wks
1 Jul 78	● STREET LEGAL *CBS 86067*		2	20 wks
26 May 79	● BOB DYLAN AT BUDOKAN *CBS 96004*		4	19 wks
8 Sep 79	● SLOW TRAIN COMING *CBS 86095*		2	13 wks
28 Jun 80	● SAVED *CBS 86113*		3	8 wks
29 Aug 81	● SHOT OF LOVE *CBS 85178*		6	8 wks
12 Nov 83	● INFIDELS *CBS 25539*		9	12 wks
15 Dec 84	REAL LIVE *CBS 26334*		54	2 wks
22 Jun 85	● EMPIRE BURLESQUE *CBS 86313*		11	6 wks
2 Aug 86	KNOCKED OUT LOADED *CBS 86236*		35	5 wks

E

E STREET BAND – *See Bruce SPRINGSTEEN*

EAGLES *US, male vocal/instrumental group* 241 wks

27 Apr 74	ON THE BORDER *Asylum SYL 9016*		28	9 wks
12 Jul 75	● ONE OF THESE NIGHTS *Asylum SYLA 8759*		8	40 wks
12 Jul 75	DESPERADO *Asylum SYLL 9011*		39	9 wks
6 Mar 76	● THEIR GREATEST HITS 1971–1975 *Asylum K 53017*		2	77 wks
25 Dec 76	● HOTEL CALIFORNIA *Asylum K 53051*		2	62 wks
13 Oct 79	● THE LONG RUN *Asylum K 52181*		4	16 wks
22 May 80	LIVE *Asylum K 62032*		24	4 wks
18 May 85	● BEST OF THE EAGLES *Asylum EKT 5*		10	24 wks

Steve EARLE *US, male vocalist/instrumentalist – guitar* 2 wks

4 Jul 87	EXIT 0 *MCA MCF 3379*		77	2 wks

EARTH WIND AND FIRE
US, male vocal/instrumental group 154 wks

21 Jan 78	ALL 'N' ALL *CBS 86051*		13	23 wks
16 Dec 78	● THE BEST OF EARTH WIND AND FIRE VOL. 1 *CBS 83284*		6	42 wks
23 Jun 79	● I AM *CBS 86084*		5	41 wks
1 Nov 80	● FACES *CBS 88498*		10	6 wks
14 Nov 81	RAISE *CBS 85272*		14	22 wks
19 Feb 83	POWERLIGHT *CBS 25120*		22	7 wks
10 May 86	● THE COLLECTION *K-Tel NE 1322*		5	13 wks

EASTERHOUSE *UK, male vocal/instrumental group* 1 wk

28 Jun 86	CONTENDERS *Rough Trade ROUGH 94*		91	1 wk

EAST OF EDEN *UK, male vocal/instrumental group* 2 wks

14 Mar 70	SNAFU *Deram SML 1050*		29	2 wks

Sheena EASTON *UK, female vocalist* 20 wks

31 Jan 81	TAKE MY TIME *EMI EMC 3354*		17	9 wks
3 Oct 81	YOU COULD HAVE BEEN WITH ME *EMI EMC 3378*		33	6 wks
25 Sep 82	MADNESS, MONEY AND MUSIC *EMI EMC 3414*		44	4 wks
15 Oct 83	BEST KEPT SECRET *EMI EMC 1077951*		99	1 wk

Clint EASTWOOD and General SAINT
Jamaica, male vocal duo 3 wks

6 Feb 82	TWO BAD DJ *Greensleeves GREL 24*		99	2 wks
28 May 83	STOP THAT TRAIN *Greensleeves GREL 53*		98	1 wk

ECHO and the BUNNYMEN
UK, male vocal/instrumental group 89 wks

26 Jul 80	CROCODILES *Korova KODE 1*		17	6 wks
6 Jun 81	● HEAVEN UP HERE *Korova KODE 3*		10	16 wks
12 Feb 83	● PORCUPINE *Korova KODE 6*		2	17 wks
12 May 84	● OCEAN RAIN *Korova KODE 8*		4	26 wks
23 Nov 85	● SONGS TO LEARN & SING *Korova KODE 13*		6	15 wks
18 Jul 87	● ECHO AND THE BUNNYMEN *WEA WX 108*		4	9 wks

Hubert EAVES – *See D-TRAIN*

EDDIE and the HOT RODS
UK, male vocal/instrumental group 5 wks

18 Dec 76	TEENAGE DEPRESSION *Island ILPS 9457*		43	1 wk
3 Dec 77	LIFE ON THE LINE *Island ILPS 9509*		27	3 wks
24 Mar 79	THRILLER *Island ILPS 9563*		50	1 wk

Duane EDDY *US, male instrumentalist – guitar* 88 wks

6 Jun 59	● HAVE TWANGY GUITAR WILL TRAVEL *London HAW 2160*		6	3 wks
31 Oct 59	● SPECIALLY FOR YOU *London HAW 2191*		6	8 wks
19 Mar 60	● THE TWANG'S THE THANG *London HAW 2236*		2	25 wks
26 Nov 60	SONGS OF OUR HERITAGE *London HAW 2285*		13	5 wks
1 Apr 61	● A MILLION DOLLARS' WORTH OF TWANG *London HAW 2325*		5	19 wks
9 Jun 62	A MILLION DOLLARS' WORTH OF TWANG VOL. 2 *London HAW 2435*		18	1 wk
21 Jul 62	● TWISTIN' & TWANGIN' *RCA RD 27264*		8	12 wks
8 Dec 62	TWANGY GUITAR – SILKY STRINGS *RCA RD 7510*		13	11 wks
16 Mar 63	DANCE WITH THE GUITAR MAN *RCA RD 7545*		14	4 wks

Dave EDMUNDS
UK, male vocalist/instrumentalist – guitar 21 wks

23 Jun 79	REPEAT WHEN NECESSARY *Swansong SSK 59409*		39	12 wks
18 Apr 81	TWANGIN' *Swansong SSK 59411*		37	4 wks
3 Apr 82	DE7 *Arista SPART 1184*		60	3 wks
30 Apr 83	INFORMATION *Arista 205 348*		92	2 wks

ECHO AND THE BUNNYMEN perform atop an HMV
Oxford Street store already advertising the work of
another Liverpudlian group.

(Right) DUANE EDDY (left) was the album chart's first guitar hero.

(Far right) DAVID ESSEX reads a 1963 *New Musical Express* in a scene from his 1973 film *That'll Be the Day*.

(Below) Members of the ELECTRIC LIGHT ORCHESTRA realize they're not in Birmingham any more.

Dennis EDWARDS *US, male vocalist*   *1 wk*

14 Apr 84	**DON'T LOOK ANY FURTHER** *Gordy ZL 72148* .	91	1 wk

EEK-A-MOUSE *Jamaica, male vocalist*   *3 wks*

14 Aug 82	**SKIDIP** *Greensleeves GREL 41*	61	3 wks

801 *UK, male vocal/instrumental group*   *2 wks*

20 Nov 76	**801 LIVE** *Island ILPS 9444*	52	2 wks

ELECTRIC LIGHT ORCHESTRA
UK, male vocal/instrumental group   *345 wks*

12 Aug 72	**ELECTRIC LIGHT ORCHESTRA** *Harvest SHVL 797*	32	4 wks
31 Mar 73	**ELO 2** *Harvest SHVL 806*	35	1 wk
11 Dec 76	● **A NEW WORLD RECORD** *United Artists UAG 30017*	6	100 wks
12 Nov 77	● **OUT OF THE BLUE** *United Artists UAR 100*	4	108 wks
6 Jan 79	**THREE LIGHT YEARS** *Jet JET BX 1*	38	9 wks
16 Jun 79	★ **DISCOVERY** *Jet JET LX 500*	1	46 wks
1 Dec 79	**ELO'S GREATEST HITS** *Jet JET LX 525*	7	18 wks
8 Aug 81	★ **TIME** *Jet LP 236*	1	32 wks
2 Jul 83	● **SECRET MESSAGES** *Jet JETLX 527*	4	15 wks
15 Mar 86	● **BALANCE OF POWER** *Epic EPC 26467*	9	12 wks

A New World Record changed to JET LP 200 and Out Of The Blue changed label number to JET DP 400 during their chart runs.

ELECTRIC WIND ENSEMBLE
UK, male instrumental group   *9 wks*

18 Feb 84	**HAUNTING MELODIES** *Nouveau Music NML1007*	28	9 wks

Duke ELLINGTON *US, orchestra*   *2 wks*

8 Apr 61	**NUT CRACKER SUITE** *Philips BBL 7418*	11	2 wks

Ben ELTON *UK, male comedian*   *2 wks*

14 Nov 87	**MOTORMOUTH** *Mercury BENLP 1*	86	2 wks

EMERSON, LAKE and PALMER
UK, male instrumental group   *135 wks*

5 Dec 70	● **EMERSON, LAKE AND PALMER** *Island ILPS 9132*	4	28 wks
19 Jun 71	★ **TARKUS** *Island ILPS 9155*	1	17 wks
4 Dec 71	● **PICTURES AT AN EXHIBITION** *Island HELP 1* .	3	5 wks
8 Jul 72	● **TRILOGY** *Island ILPS 9186*	2	29 wks
22 Dec 73	● **BRAIN SALAD SURGERY** *Manticore K 53501* . . .	2	17 wks
24 Aug 74	● **WELCOME BACK MY FRIENDS TO THE SHOW THAT NEVER ENDS – LADIES AND GENTLEMEN: EMERSON, LAKE AND PALMER** *Manticore K 63500*	5	5 wks
9 Apr 77	● **WORKS** *Atlantic K 80009*	9	25 wks
10 Dec 77	**WORKS VOL. 2** *Atlantic K 50422*	20	5 wks
9 Dec 78	**LOVE BEACH** *Atlantic K 50552*	48	4 wks

See also Greg Lake; Emerson, Lake and Powell.

EMERSON, LAKE and POWELL
UK, male vocal/instrumental group   *5 wks*

14 Jun 86	**EMERSON, LAKE AND POWELL** *Polydor POLD 5191*	35	5 wks

See also Greg Lake; Cozy Powell; Emerson, Lake and Palmer.

ENGLAND FOOTBALL WORLD CUP SQUAD 1970 *UK, male football team vocalists*   *8 wks*

16 May 70	● **THE WORLD BEATERS SING THE WORLD BEATERS** *Pye NSPL 18337*	4	8 wks

ENGLAND FOOTBALL WORLD CUP SQUAD 1982 *UK, male football team vocalists*   *10 wks*

15 May 82	**THIS TIME** *K-Tel NE 1169*	37	10 wks

ENGLISH CHAMBER ORCHESTRA – *See John WILLIAMS with the ENGLISH CHAMBER ORCHESTRA*

ENIGMA *UK, male vocal/instrumental group*   *3 wks*

5 Sep 81	**AIN'T NO STOPPIN'** *Creole CRX 1*	80	3 wks

Brian ENO *UK, male instrumentalist – keyboards*   *3 wks*

9 Mar 74	**HERE COME THE WARM JETS** *Island ILPS 9268*	26	2 wks
21 Oct 78	**MUSIC FOR FILMS** *Polydor 2310 623*	55	1 wk

See also Brian Eno and David Byrne.

Brian ENO and David BYRNE
UK, male instrumentalist – keyboards and US, male vocalist   *8 wks*

21 Feb 81	**MY LIFE IN THE BUSH OF GHOSTS** *Polydor EGLP 48*	29	8 wks

See also Brian Eno.

ENYA *Ireland, female vocalist*   *4 wks*

6 Jun 87	**ENYA** *BBC REB 605*	71	4 wks

EQUALS *UK, male vocal/instrumental group*   *10 wks*

18 Nov 67	● **UNEQUALLED EQUALS** *President PTL 1006*	10	9 wks
9 Mar 68	**EQUALS EXPLOSION** *President PTLS 1015*	32	1 wk

ERASURE *UK, male vocal/instrumental duo*   *41 wks*

14 Jun 86	**WONDERLAND** *Mute STUMM 25*	71	3 wks
11 Apr 87	● **THE CIRCUS** *Mute STUMM 35*	6†	38 wks

David ESSEX *UK, male vocalist*   *137 wks*

24 Nov 73	● **ROCK ON** *CBS 65823*	7	22 wks
19 Oct 74	● **DAVID ESSEX** *CBS 69088*	2	24 wks
27 Sep 75	● **ALL THE FUN OF THE FAIR** *CBS 69160*	3	20 wks
5 Jun 76	**ON TOUR** *CBS 95000*	51	1 wk
30 Oct 76	**OUT ON THE STREET** *CBS 86017*	31	9 wks
8 Oct 77	**GOLD AND IVORY** *CBS 86038*	29	4 wks
6 Jan 79	**DAVID ESSEX ALBUM** *CBS 10011*	29	7 wks
31 Mar 79	**IMPERIAL WIZARD** *Mercury 9109 616*	12	9 wks
12 Jun 80	**HOT LOVE** *Mercury 6359 017*	75	1 wk
19 Jun 82	**STAGE-STRUCK** *Mercury MERS 4*	31	15 wks

27 Nov 82	**THE VERY BEST OF DAVID ESSEX**		
	TV Records TVA 4	37	11 wks
15 Oct 83	**MUTINY** *Mercury MERH 30*	39	4 wks
17 Dec 83	**THE WHISPER** *Mercury MERH 34*	67	6 wks
6 Dec 86	**CENTRE STAGE** *K-Tel ONE 1333*	82	4 wks

Mutiny is a studio recording of a musical that was not staged until 1985. Both this album and the eventual stage production starred David Essex and Frank Finlay.

Don ESTELLE and Windsor DAVIES
UK, male vocal duo   *8 wks*

| 10 Jan 76 | ● **SING LOFTY** *EMI EMC 3102* | 10 | 8 wks |

EUROPE *Sweden, male vocal/instrumental group*   *37 wks*

| 22 Nov 86 | ● **THE FINAL COUNTDOWN** *Epic EPC 26808* | 9 | 37 wks |

EUROPEANS *UK, male vocal/instrumental group*   *1 wk*

| 11 Feb 84 | **LIVE** *A & M SCOT 1* | 100 | 1 wk |

EURYTHMICS
UK, female/male vocal/instrumental group   *267 wks*

12 Feb 83	● **SWEET DREAMS (ARE MADE OF THIS)**		
	RCA RCALP 6063	3	59 wks
26 Nov 83	★ **TOUCH** *RCA PL 70109*	1	48 wks
9 Jun 84	**TOUCH DANCE** *RCA PG 70354*	31	5 wks
24 Nov 84	**1984 (FOR THE LOVE OF BIG BROTHER)**		
	Virgin V 1984	23	17 wks
11 May 85	● **BE YOURSELF TONIGHT** *RCA PL 70711*	3	80 wks
12 Jul 86	● **REVENGE** *RCA PL 71050*	3	52 wks
21 Nov 87	● **SAVAGE** *RCA PL 71555*	7†	6 wks

Phil EVERLY *US, male vocalist*   *1 wk*

| 7 May 83 | **PHIL EVERLY** *Capitol EST 27670* | 61 | 1 wk |

See also the Everly Brothers.

EVERLY BROTHERS *US, male vocal duo*   *118 wks*

2 Jul 60	● **IT'S EVERLY TIME** *Warner Bros. WM 4006*	2	23 wks
15 Oct 60	● **FABULOUS STYLE OF THE EVERLY BROTHERS** *London HAA 2266*	4	11 wks
4 Mar 61	● **A DATE WITH THE EVERLY BROTHERS**		
	Warner Bros. WM 4028	3	14 wks
21 Jul 62	**INSTANT PARTY** *Warner Bros. WM 4061*	20	1 wk
12 Sep 70	● **ORIGINAL GREATEST HITS** *CBS 66255*	7	16 wks
8 Jun 74	**THE VERY BEST OF THE EVERLY BROTHERS**		
	Warner Bros. K 46008	43	1 wk
29 Nov 75	● **WALK RIGHT BACK WITH THE EVERLYS**		
	Warner Bros. K 56118	10	10 wks
9 Apr 77	**LIVING LEGENDS** *Warwick WW 5027*	12	10 wks
18 Dec 82	**LOVE HURTS** *K-Tel NE 1197*	31	22 wks
7 Jan 84	**EVERLY BROTHERS REUNION CONCERT**		
	Impression IMDP 1	47	6 wks
3 Nov 84	**THE EVERLY BROTHERS** *Mercury MERH 44*	36	4 wks

See also Phil Everly.

EVERYTHING BUT THE GIRL
UK, male/female vocal/instrumental group   *40 wks*

16 Jun 84	● **EDEN** *blanco y negro BYN 2*	14	22 wks
27 Apr 85	● **LOVE NOT MONEY** *blanco y negro BYN 3*	10	9 wks
6 Sep 86	**BABY THE STARS SHINE BRIGHT**		
	blanco y negro WEA BYN 9	22	9 wks

EXPLOITED *UK, male vocal/instrumental group*   *26 wks*

16 May 81	**PUNK'S NOT DEAD** *Secret SEC 1*	20	11 wks
14 Nov 81	**EXPLOITED LIVE** *Superville EXPLP 2001*	52	3 wks
19 Jun 82	**TROOPS OF TOMORROW** *Secret SEC 8*	17	12 wks

F

FACES *UK, male vocal/instrumental group*   *56 wks*

4 Apr 70	**FIRST STEP** *Warner Bros. WS 3000*	45	1 wk
8 May 71	**LONG PLAYER** *Warner Bros. W 3011*	31	7 wks
25 Dec 71	● **A NOD'S AS GOOD AS A WINK . . . TO A BLIND HORSE** *Warner Bros. K 56006*	2	22 wks
21 Apr 73	★ **OOH-LA-LA** *Warner Bros. K 56011*	1	13 wks
26 Jan 74	● **OVERTURE AND BEGINNERS**		
	Mercury 9100 001	3	7 wks
21 May 77	**THE BEST OF THE FACES** *Riva RVLP 3*	24	6 wks

Overture And Beginners credited to Rod Stewart and the Faces. See also Rod Stewart.

Donald FAGEN *US, male vocalist*   *16 wks*

| 20 Oct 82 | **THE NIGHTFLY** *Warner Bros. 923696* | 44 | 16 wks |

FAIRPORT CONVENTION
UK, male/female vocal/instrumental group   *40 wks*

2 Aug 69	**UNHALFBRICKING** *Island ILPS 9102*	12	8 wks
17 Jan 70	**LIEGE AND LIEF** *Island ILPS 9115*	17	15 wks
18 Jul 70	**FULL HOUSE** *Island ILPS 9130*	13	11 wks
3 Jul 71	● **ANGEL DELIGHT** *Island ILPS 9162*	8	5 wks
12 Jul 75	**RISING FOR THE MOON** *Island ILPS 9313*	52	1 wk

FAITH BROTHERS
UK, male vocal/instrumental group   *1 wk*

| 9 Nov 85 | **EVENTIDE** *Siren SIRENLP 1* | 66 | 1 wk |

Adam FAITH *UK, male vocalist*   *44 wks*

19 Nov 60	● **ADAM** *Parlophone PMC 1128*	6	36 wks
11 Feb 61	**BEAT GIRL (film soundtrack)**		
	Columbia 33SX 1225	11	3 wks
24 Mar 62	**ADAM FAITH** *Parlophone PMC 1162*	20	1 wk
25 Sep 65	**FAITH ALIVE** *Parlophone PMC 1249*	19	1 wk
19 Dec 81	**20 GOLDEN GREATS** *Warwick WW 5113*	61	3 wks

Marianne FAITHFULL *UK, female vocalist*   *19 wks*

5 Jun 65	**COME MY WAY** *Decca LK 4688*	12	7 wks
5 Jun 65	**MARIANNE FAITHFULL** *Decca LK 4689*	15	2 wks
24 Nov 79	**BROKEN ENGLISH** *Island M1*	57	3 wks
17 Oct 81	**DANGEROUS ACQUAINTANCES**		
	Island ILPS 9648	45	4 wks
26 Mar 83	**A CHILD'S ADVENTURE** *Island ILPS 9734*	99	1 wk
8 Aug 87	**STRANGE WEATHER** *Island ILPS 9874*	78	2 wks

FALCO *Austria, male vocalist*   *15 wks*

| 26 Apr 86 | **FALCO 3** *A & M AMA 5105* | 32 | 15 wks |

FALL *UK, male vocal/instrumental group*   *10 wks*

| 20 Mar 82 | **HEX ENDUCTION HOUR** *Kamera KAM 005* | 71 | 3 wks |

20 Oct 84	**THE WONDERFUL AND FRIGHTENING WORLD OF . . .** *Beggars Banquet BEGA 58*	62	2 wks
5 Oct 85	**THE NATION'S SAVING GRACE** *Beggars Banquet BEGA 67*	54	2 wks
11 Oct 86	**BEND SINISTER** *Beggars Banquet BEGA 75*	36	3 wks

Agnetha FALTSKOG *Sweden, female vocalist*   *16 wks*

11 Jun 83	**WRAP YOUR ARMS AROUND ME** *Epic EPC 25505*	18	13 wks
4 May 85	**EYES OF A WOMAN** *Epic EPC 26646*	38	3 wks

Georgie FAME *UK, male vocalist*   *72 wks*

17 Oct 64	**FAME AT LAST** *Columbia 33SX 1638*	15	8 wks
14 May 66	● **SWEET THINGS** *Columbia SX 6043*	6	22 wks
15 Oct 66	● **SOUND VENTURE** *Columbia SX 6076*	9	9 wks
11 Mar 67	**HALL OF FAME** *Columbia SX 6120*	12	18 wks
1 Jul 67	**TWO FACES OF FAME** *CBS SBPG 63018*	22	15 wks

FAMILY *UK, male vocal/instrumental group*   *41 wks*

10 Aug 68	**MUSIC IN THE DOLLS HOUSE** *Reprise RLP 6312*	35	3 wks
22 Mar 69	● **FAMILY ENTERTAINMENT** *Reprise RSLP 6340* .	6	3 wks
7 Feb 70	● **A SONG FOR ME** *Reprise RSLP 9001*	4	13 wks
28 Nov 70	● **ANYWAY** *Reprise RSX 9005*	7	7 wks
20 Nov 71	**FEARLESS** *Reprise K 54003*	14	2 wks
30 Sep 72	**BANDSTAND** *Reprise K 54006*	15	10 wks
29 Sep 73	**IT'S ONLY A MOVIE** *Raft RA 58501*	30	3 wks

FAMILY STONE – *See SLY and the FAMILY STONE*

Chris FARLOWE *UK, male vocalist*   *3 wks*

2 Apr 66	**14 THINGS TO THINK ABOUT** *Immediate IMLP 005*	19	1 wk
10 Dec 66	**THE ART OF CHRIS FARLOWE** *Immediate IMLP 006*	37	2 wks

FARMERS BOYS *UK, male vocal/instrumental group*   *1 wk*

29 Oct 83	**GET OUT AND WALK** *EMI EMC 1077991*	49	1 wk

John FARNHAM *Australia, male vocalist*   *9 wks*

11 Jul 87	**WHISPERING JACK** *RCA PL 71224*	35	9 wks

FARRAR – *See MARVIN, WELCH and FARRAR*

FASHION *UK, male vocal/instrumental group*   *17 wks*

3 Jul 82	● **FABRIQUE** *Arista SPART 1185*	10	16 wks
16 Jun 84	**TWILIGHT OF IDOLS** *De Stijl EPC 25909* . . .	69	1 wk

FASTWAY *UK, male vocal/instrumental group*   *2 wks*

30 Apr 83	**FASTWAY** *CBS 25359*	43	2 wks

FAT LARRY'S BAND
US, male vocal/instrumental group   *4 wks*

9 Oct 82	**BREAKIN' OUT** *Virgin V 2229*	58	4 wks

FATBACK BAND *US, male vocal/instrumental group*   *7 wks*

6 Mar 76	**RAISING HELL** *Polydor 2391 203*	19	6 wks
4 Jul 87	**FATBACK LIVE** *Start STL 12*	80	1 wk

FAT BOYS *US, male rap group*   *4 wks*

3 Oct 87	**CRUSHIN'** *Urban URBLP 3*	49	4 wks

FATHER – *See Steven SMITH and FATHER*

Phil FEARON and GALAXY
UK, male/female vocal/instrumental group   *9 wks*

25 Aug 84	● **PHIL FEARON AND GALAXY** *Ensign ENCL 2* . .	8	8 wks
14 Feb 85	**THIS KIND OF LOVE** *Ensign ENCL 4*	98	1 wk

Jose FELICIANO
US, male vocalist/instrumentalist – guitar   *40 wks*

2 Nov 68	● **FELICIANO** *RCA Victor SF 7946*	6	36 wks
29 Nov 69	**JOSE FELICIANO** *RCA Victor SF 8044*	29	2 wks
14 Feb 70	**10 TO 23** *RCA SF 7946*	38	1 wk
22 Aug 70	**FIREWORKS** *RCA SF 8124*	65	1 wk

Wilton FELDER *US, male instrumentalist – tenor sax*   *3 wks*

23 Feb 85	**SECRETS** *MCA MCF 3237*	77	3 wks

Also featuring Bobby Womack and introducing Alltrinna Grayson.

Julie FELIX *US, female vocalist*   *4 wks*

11 Sep 66	**CHANGES** *Fontana TL 5368*	27	4 wks

Bryan FERRY *UK, male vocalist*   *145 wks*

3 Nov 73	● **THESE FOOLISH THINGS** *Island ILPS 9249*	5	42 wks
20 Jul 74	● **ANOTHER TIME, ANOTHER PLACE** *Island ILPS 9284*	4	25 wks
2 Oct 76	**LET'S STICK TOGETHER** *Island ILPSX 1*	19	5 wks
5 Mar 77	● **IN YOUR MIND** *Polydor 2302 055*	5	17 wks
30 Sep 78	**THE BRIDE STRIPPED BARE** *Polydor POLD 5003*	13	5 wks
15 Jun 85	★ **BOYS AND GIRLS** *EG EGLP 62*	1	44 wks
14 Nov 87	● **BETE NOIRE** *Virgin V 2474*	9†	7 wks

See also Bryan Ferry and Roxy Music.

Bryan FERRY and ROXY MUSIC
UK, male vocal/instrumental group   *65 wks*

26 Apr 86	★ **STREET LIFE – 20 GREAT HITS** *EG EGTV 1* . . .	1	65 wks

See also Bryan Ferry; Roxy Music.

Gracie FIELDS *UK, female vocalist*   *3 wks*

20 Dec 75	**THE GOLDEN YEARS** *Warwick WW 5007*	48	3 wks

FIELDS OF NEPHILIM
UK, male vocal/instrumental group   *2 wks*

30 May 87	**DAWNRAZOR** *Situation 2 SITUP 18*	62	2 wks

52ND STREET
UK, male/female vocal/instrumental group   *1 wk*

19 Apr 86	**CHILDREN OF THE NIGHT** *10 DIX 25*	71	1 wk

FINE YOUNG CANNIBALS

UK, male vocal/instrumental group   *25 wks*

21 Dec 85	**FINE YOUNG CANNIBALS**	*London LONLP 16*	..	**11**	25 wks

FIRM *UK, male vocal/instrumental group*   *8 wks*

2 Mar 85	**THE FIRM**	*Atlantic 78–1239–1*	....	**15**	5 wks
5 Apr 86	**MEAN BUSINESS**	*Atlantic WX 35*	....	**46**	3 wks

FIRST CIRCLE *US, male vocal/instrumental group*   *2 wks*

2 May 87	**BOYS' NIGHT OUT**	*EMI America AML 3118*	.....	**70**	2 wks

FISCHER-Z *UK, male vocal/instrumental group*   *1 wk*

23 Jun 79	**WORD SALAD**	*United Artists UAG 30232*	....	**66**	1 wk

Ella FITZGERALD *US, female vocalist*   *13 wks*

11 Jun 60	**ELLA SINGS GERSHWIN**	*Brunswick LA 8648*	....	**13**	3 wks
18 Jun 60	**ELLA AT THE OPERA HOUSE**				
	Columbia 3SX 10126			**16**	1 wk
23 Jul 60	**ELLA SINGS GERSHWIN VOL. 5**				
	HMV CLP 1353	....		**18**	2 wks
10 May 80	**THE INCOMPARABLE ELLA**	*Polydor POLTV 9*	..	**40**	7 wks

FIVE PENNY PIECE

UK, male/female vocal/instrumental group   *6 wks*

24 Mar 73	**MAKING TRACKS**	*Columbia SCX 6536*	....	**37**	1 wk
3 Jul 76	● **KING COTTON**	*EMI EMC 3129*	....	**9**	5 wks

FIVE STAR *UK, male/female vocal group*   *141 wks*

3 Aug 85	**LUXURY OF LIFE**	*Tent PL 70735*	....	**12**	70 wks
30 Aug 86	★ **SILK AND STEEL**	*Tent PL 71100*	....	**1**	57 wks
26 Sep 87	● **BETWEEN THE LINES**	*Tent PL 71505*	....	**7†**	14 wks

FIXX *UK, male vocal/instrumental group*   *7 wks*

22 May 82	**SHUTTERED ROOM**	*MCA FX 1001*	....	**54**	6 wks
21 May 83	**REACH THE BEACH**	*MCA FX 1002*	....	**91**	1 wk

Roberta FLACK *US, female vocalist*   *18 wks*

15 Jul 72	**FIRST TAKE**	*Atlantic K 40040*	....	**47**	2 wks
13 Oct 73	**KILLING ME SOFTLY**	*Atlantic K 50021*	......	**40**	2 wks
31 Mar 84	**GREATEST HITS**	*K-Tel NE 1269*	....	**35**	14 wks

See also Roberta Flack and Donny Hathaway; Peabo Bryson and Roberta Flack.

Roberta FLACK and Donny HATHAWAY

US, female/male vocal duo   *7 wks*

7 Jun 80	**ROBERTA FLACK AND DONNY HATHAWAY**				
	Atlantic K 50696	....		**31**	7 wks

See also Roberta Flack; Peabo Bryson and Roberta Flack.

FLASH AND THE PAN

Australia, male vocal/instrumental group   *2 wks*

16 Jul 83	**PAN-ORAMA**	*East Beat EASLP 100*	....	**69**	2 wks

FLEETWOOD MAC

UK/US, male/female vocal/instrumental group   *600 wks*

2 Mar 68	● **FLEETWOOD MAC**	*Blue Horizon BPG 7–63200*	..	**4**	37 wks
7 Sep 68	● **MR. WONDERFUL**	*Blue Horizon 7–63205*	....	**10**	11 wks
30 Aug 69	**PIOUS BIRD OF GOOD OMEN**				
	Blue Horizon 7–63215			**18**	4 wks
4 Oct 69	● **THEN PLAY ON**	*Reprise RSLP 9000*	......	**6**	11 wks
10 Oct 70	**KILN HOUSE**	*Reprise RSLP 9004*	....	**39**	2 wks
19 Feb 72	**GREATEST HITS**	*CBS 6901*	....	**36**	11 wks
6 Nov 76	**FLEETWOOD MAC**	*Reprise K 54043*	....	**23**	19 wks
26 Feb 77	★ **RUMOURS**	*Warner Bros. K 56344*	......	**1**	402 wks
27 Oct 79	★ **TUSK**	*Warner Bros. K 66088*	......	**1**	23 wks
13 Dec 80	**FLEETWOOD MAC LIVE**	*Warner Bros. K 66097*	..	**31**	9 wks
10 Jul 82	● **MIRAGE**	*Warner Bros. K 56592*	......	**5**	35 wks
25 Apr 87	★ **TANGO IN THE NIGHT**	*Warner Bros. WX 65*	....	**1†**	36 wks

Group were UK and male only for first 6 albums.

Berni FLINT *UK, male vocalist*   *6 wks*

2 Jul 77	**I DON'T WANT TO PUT A HOLD ON YOU**				
	EMI EMC 3184	....		**37**	6 wks

FLOATERS *US, male vocal/instrumental group*   *8 wks*

20 Aug 77	**FLOATERS**	*ABC ABCL 5229*	....	**17**	8 wks

FLOCK *UK, male vocal/instrumental group*   *2 wks*

2 May 70	**FLOCK**	*CBS 63733*	....	**59**	2 wks

A FLOCK OF SEAGULLS

UK, male vocal/instrumental group   *59 wks*

17 Apr 82	**A FLOCK OF SEAGULLS**	*Jive HOP 201*	....	**32**	44 wks
7 May 83	**LISTEN**	*Jive HIP 4*	....	**16**	10 wks
1 Sep 84	**THE STORY OF A YOUNG HEART**				
	Jive HIP 14	....		**30**	5 wks

Eddie FLOYD *US, male vocalist*   *5 wks*

29 Apr 67	**KNOCK ON WOOD**	*Stax 589–006*	....	**36**	5 wks

A FLUX OF PINK INDIANS

UK, male vocal/instrumental group   *2 wks*

5 Feb 83	**STRIVE TO SURVIVE CAUSING LEAST**				
	SUFFERING POSSIBLE *Spiderleg SDL 8*	......		**79**	2 wks

FLYING LIZARDS

UK, male/female vocal/instrumental group   *3 wks*

16 Feb 80	**FLYING LIZARDS**	*Virgin V 2150*	....	**60**	3 wks

FLYING PICKETS *UK, male vocal group*   *22 wks*

17 Dec 83	**LIVE AT THE ALBANY EMPIRE**				
	AVM AVMLP 0001	....		**48**	11 wks
9 Jun 84	**LOST BOYS**	*10 DIX 4*	....	**11**	11 wks

FM *UK, male vocal/instrumental group*   *1 wk*

20 Sep 86	**INDISCREET**	*Portrait PRT 26827*	....	**76**	1 wk

FOCUS *Holland, male instrumental group* 65 wks

11 Nov 72	● MOVING WAVES *Polydor 2931 002*	2	34 wks
2 Dec 72	● FOCUS 3 *Polydor 2383 016*	6	15 wks
20 Oct 73	FOCUS AT THE RAINBOW *Polydor 2442 118*	23	5 wks
25 May 74	HAMBURGER CONCERTO *Polydor 2442 124* ...	20	5 wks
9 Aug 75	FOCUS *Polydor 2384 070*	23	6 wks

Dan FOGELBERG *US, male vocalist* 3 wks

29 Mar 80	PHOENIX *Epic EPC 83317*	42	3 wks

John FOGERTY
US, male vocalist/instrumentalist – guitar 11 wks

16 Feb 85	CENTERFIELD *Warner Bros. 92–5203–1*	48	11 wks

Ellen FOLEY *US, female vocalist* 3 wks

17 Nov 79	NIGHT OUT *Epic EPC 83718*	68	1 wk
4 Apr 81	SPIRIT OF ST. LOUIS *Epic EPC 84809*	57	2 wks

Jane FONDA *US, female exercise instructor* 51 wks

29 Jan 83	● JANE FONDA'S WORKOUT RECORD *CBS 88581*	7	47 wks
22 Sep 84	JANE FONDA'S WORKOUT RECORD: NEW AND IMPROVED *CBS 88640*	60	4 wks

Wayne FONTANA and the MINDBENDERS
UK, male vocalist and male vocal/instrumental group 1 wk

20 Feb 65	WAYNE FONTANA AND THE MINDBENDERS *Fontana TL 5230*	18	1 wk

See also the Mindbenders.

Steve FORBERT *US, male vocalist* 3 wks

9 Jun 79	ALIVE ON ARRIVAL *Epic EPC 83308*	56	1 wk
24 Nov 79	JACK RABBIT SLIM *Epic EPC 83879*	54	2 wks

Clinton FORD *UK, male vocalist* 4 wks

26 May 62	CLINTON FORD *Oriole PS 40021*	16	4 wks

Lita FORD *UK, female vocalist* 1 wk

26 May 84	DANCIN' ON THE EDGE *Vertigo VERL 13*	96	1 wk

FOREIGNER
UK/US, male vocal/instrumental group 112 wks

26 Aug 78	DOUBLE VISION *Atlantic K 50476*	32	5 wks
25 Jul 81	● 4 *Atlantic K 50796*	5	62 wks
18 Dec 82	RECORDS *Atlantic A 0999*	58	11 wks
22 Dec 84	★ AGENT PROVOCATEUR *Atlantic 78–1999–1*	1	32 wks
19 Dec 87	INSIDE INFORMATION *Atlantic WX 143*	64†	2 wks

FOSTER and ALLEN *Ireland, male vocal duo* 60 wks

14 May 83	MAGGIE *Ritz RITZLP 0012*	72	6 wks
5 Nov 83	I WILL LOVE YOU ALL OF MY LIFE *Ritz RITZLP 0015*	71	6 wks
17 Nov 84	THE VERY BEST OF FOSTER AND ALLEN *Ritz RITZ LP TV 1*	18	18 wks
29 Mar 86	AFTER ALL THESE YEARS *Ritz RITZLP 0032* ..	82	2 wks
25 Oct 86	REMINISCING *Stylus SMR 623*	11	15 wks
27 Jun 87	LOVE SONGS – THE VERY BEST OF FOSTER AND ALLEN VOL 2 *Ritz RITZLP 0036*	92	1 wk
10 Oct 87	REFLECTIONS *Stylus SMR 739*	16†	12 wks

FOTHERINGAY
UK, male/female vocal/instrumental group 6 wks

11 Jul 70	FOTHERINGAY *Island ILPS 9125*	18	6 wks

FOUR PENNIES *UK, male vocal/instrumental group* 5 wks

7 Nov 64	TWO SIDES OF FOUR PENNIES *Philips BL 7642*	13	5 wks

FOUR SEASONS *US, male vocal group* 40 wks

6 Jul 63	SHERRY *Stateside SL 10033*	20	1 wk
10 Apr 71	EDIZIONE D'ORO *Philips 6640–002*	11	7 wks
20 Nov 71	THE BIG ONES *Philips 6336–208*	37	1 wk
6 Mar 76	THE FOUR SEASONS STORY *Private Stock DAPS 1001*	20	8 wks
6 Mar 76	WHO LOVES YOU *Warner Bros. K 56179*	12	17 wks
20 Nov 76	● GREATEST HITS *K-Tel NE 942*	4	6 wks

Greatest Hits album credited to Frankie Valli and the Four Seasons. It contains some solo Valli items.

4-SKINS *UK, male vocal/instrumental group* 4 wks

17 Apr 82	THE GOOD, THE BAD AND THE 4-SKINS *Secret SEC 4*	80	4 wks

FOUR TOPS *US, male vocal group* 233 wks

19 Nov 66	● FOUR TOPS ON TOP *Tamla Motown TML 11037* ..	9	23 wks
11 Feb 67	● FOUR TOPS LIVE! *Tamla Motown STML 11041* ...	4	72 wks
25 Nov 67	● REACH OUT *Tamla Motown STML 11056*	4	34 wks
20 Jan 68	★ GREATEST HITS *Tamla Motown STML 11061* ..	1	67 wks
8 Feb 69	YESTERDAY'S DREAMS *Tamla Motown STML 11087*	37	1 wk
27 Jun 70	STILL WATERS RUN DEEP *Tamla Motown STML 11149*	29	8 wks
27 Nov 71	FOUR TOPS' GREATEST HITS VOL. 2 *Tamla Motown STML 11195*	25	10 wks
10 Nov 73	THE FOUR TOPS STORY 1964–72 *Tamla Motown TMSP 11241/2*	35	5 wks
13 Feb 82	THE BEST OF THE FOUR TOPS *K-Tel NE 1160*	13	13 wks

See also Supremes and Four Tops.

FOX *UK, male/female vocal instrumental group* 8 wks

17 May 75	● FOX *GTO GTLP 001*	7	8 wks

Samantha FOX *UK, female vocalist* 16 wks

26 Jul 86	TOUCH ME *Jive HIP 39*	17	10 wks
1 Aug 87	SAMANTHA FOX *Jive HIP 48*	22	6 wks

Bruce FOXTON *UK, male vocalist* 4 wks

12 May 84	TOUCH SENSITIVE *Arista 206 251*	68	4 wks

John FOXX *UK, male vocalist* 17 wks

2 Feb 80	METAMATIX *Metalbeat V 2146*	18	7 wks

3 Oct 81	**THE GARDEN** *Virgin V 2194*	**24**	6 wks
8 Oct 83	**THE GOLDEN SECTION** *Virgin V 2233*	**27**	3 wks
5 Oct 85	**IN MYSTERIOUS WAYS** *Virgin V 2355*	**85**	1 wk

FRAGGLES *UK/US puppets*   *4 wks*

21 Apr 84	**FRAGGLE ROCK** *RCA PL 70221*	**38**	4 wks

Peter FRAMPTON *UK, male vocalist*   *49 wks*

22 May 76	● **FRAMPTON COMES ALIVE**		
	A & M AMLM 63703	**6**	39 wks
18 Jun 77	**I'M IN YOU** *A & M AMLK 64039*	**19**	10 wks

Connie FRANCIS *US, female vocalist*   *26 wks*

26 Mar 60	**ROCK 'N' ROLL MILLION SELLERS**		
	MGM C 804	**12**	1 wk
11 Feb 61	**CONNIE'S GREATEST HITS** *MGM C 831*	**16**	3 wks
18 Jun 77	★ **20 ALL TIME GREATS** *Polydor 2391 290*	**1**	22 wks

FRANKIE GOES TO HOLLYWOOD
UK, male vocal/instrumental group   *71 wks*

10 Nov 84	★ **WELCOME TO THE PLEASUREDOME**		
	ZTT ZTTIQ 1	**1**	58 wks
1 Nov 86	● **LIVERPOOL** *ZTT ZTTIQ 8*	**5**	13 wks

Aretha FRANKLIN *US, female vocalist*   *57 wks*

12 Aug 67	**I NEVER LOVED A MAN** *Atlantic 587-006*	**36**	2 wks
13 Apr 68	**LADY SOUL** *Atlantic 588-099*	**25**	18 wks
14 Sep 68	● **ARETHA NOW** *Atlantic 588-114*	**6**	11 wks
18 Jan 86	**WHO'S ZOOMIN' WHO?** *Arista 2072 02*	**49**	12 wks
24 May 86	**THE FIRST LADY OF SOUL** *Stylus SMR 8506* . .	**89**	1 wk
8 Nov 86	**ARETHA** *Arista 208 020*	**51**	13 wks

Rodney FRANKLIN
US, male instrumentalist – piano   *2 wks*

24 May 80	**YOU'LL NEVER KNOW** *CBS 83812*	**64**	2 wks

Liz FRASER – *See Harold BUDD/Liz FRASER/Robin GUTHRIE/Simon RAYMOND*

FREDDIE and the DREAMERS
UK, male vocal/instrumental group   *26 wks*

9 Nov 63	● **FREDDIE AND THE DREAMERS**		
	Columbia 33SX 1577	**5**	26 wks

FREDERICK – *See NINA and FREDERICK*

FREE *UK, male vocal/instrumental group*   *62 wks*

11 Jul 70	● **FIRE AND WATER** *Island ILPS 9120*	**2**	18 wks
23 Jan 71	**HIGHWAY** *Island ILPS 9138*	**41**	10 wks
26 Jun 71	● **FREE LIVE!** *Island ILPS 9160*	**4**	12 wks
17 Jun 72	● **FREE AT LAST** *Island ILPS 9192*	**9**	9 wks
3 Feb 73	● **HEARTBREAKER** *Island ILPS 9217*	**9**	7 wks
16 Mar 74	● **THE FREE STORY** *Island ISLD 4*	**2**	6 wks

FREEEZ *UK, male vocal/instrumental group*   *18 wks*

7 Feb 81	**SOUTHERN FREEEZ** *Beggars Banquet BEGA 22* . .	**17**	15 wks
22 Oct 83	**GONNA GET YOU** *Beggars Banquet BEGA 48*	**46**	3 wks

FRESH PRINCE – *See DJ JAZZY JEFF and FRESH PRINCE*

Glenn FREY *US, male vocalist*   *9 wks*

6 Jul 85	**THE ALLNIGHTER** *MCA MCF 3277*	**31**	9 wks

FRIDA *Norway, female vocalist*   *8 wks*

18 Sep 82	**SOMETHING'S GOING ON** *Epic EPC 85966*	**18**	7 wks
20 Oct 84	**SHINE** *Epic EPC 26178*	**67**	1 wk

Dean FRIEDMAN *US, male vocalist*   *14 wks*

21 Oct 78	**WELL, WELL, SAID THE ROCKING CHAIR**		
	Lifesong LSLP 6019	**21**	14 wks

FRIENDS – *See DELANEY and BONNIE and FRIENDS*

FRIENDS – *See Brian MAY and FRIENDS*

Robert FRIPP *UK, male vocalist/instrumentalist – guitar*   *1 wk*

12 May 79	**EXPOSURE** *Polydor EGLP 101*	**71**	1 wk

FULL FORCE – *See LISA LISA and CULT JAM with FULL FORCE*

FUNBOY THREE
UK, male vocal/instrumental group   *40 wks*

20 Mar 82	● **FUNBOY THREE** *Chrysalis CHR 1383*	**7**	20 wks
19 Feb 83	**WAITING** *Chrysalis CHR 1417*	**14**	20 wks

FUNK FEDERATION – *See Arlene PHILLIPS*

FUNKADELIC *US, male vocal/instrumental group*   *5 wks*

23 Dec 78	**ONE NATION UNDER A GROOVE**		
	Warner Bros. K 56539	**56**	5 wks

FUREYS and DAVEY ARTHUR
Ireland/UK, male vocal/instrumental group   *37 wks*

8 May 82	**WHEN YOU WERE SWEET SIXTEEN**		
	Ritz RITZLP 0004	**99**	1 wk
10 Nov 84	**GOLDEN DAYS** *K-Tel ONE 1283*	**17**	19 wks
26 Oct 85	**AT THE END OF THE DAY** *K-Tel ONE 1310* . .	**35**	11 wks
21 Nov 87	**FUREYS FINEST** *Telstar HSTAR 2311*	**65†**	6 wks

FURIOUS FIVE – *See GRANDMASTER FLASH and the FURIOUS FIVE*

Billy FURY *UK, male vocalist*   *51 wks*

4 Jun 60	**THE SOUND OF FURY** *Decca LF 1329*	**18**	2 wks
23 Sep 61	● **HALFWAY TO PARADISE**		
	Ace Of Clubs ACL 1083	**5**	9 wks
11 May 63	● **BILLY** *Decca LK 4533*	**6**	21 wks
26 Oct 63	**WE WANT BILLY** *Decca LK 4548*	**14**	2 wks
19 Feb 83	**HIT PARADE** *Decca TAB 37*	**44**	15 wks
26 Mar 83	**THE ONE AND ONLY** *Polydor POLD 5069*	**54**	2 wks

G

Kenny G *US, male instrumentalist – saxophone*   *10 wks*

17 Mar 84	**G FORCE** *Arista 296 168*	**56**	5 wks
8 Aug 87	**DUOTONES** *Arista 207 792*	**28**	5 wks

(Left) GEORGIE FAME punned on his name for three hit titles.

(Below) Holly and Paul of FRANKIE GOES TO HOLLYWOOD lit up the chart in late 1984.

(Above) The original FREE: (left to right) Paul Rodgers, Paul Kossoff, Simon Kirke and Andy Fraser.

(Left) CONNIE FRANCIS got her number one album nineteen years after her number one singles.

PETER GABRIEL sitting pretty with the
distinction of most hit albums named
after the artist.

Peter GABRIEL *UK, male vocalist* *148 wks*

12 Mar 77	● **PETER GABRIEL** *Charisma CDS 4006*	7	19 wks
17 Jun 78	● **PETER GABRIEL** *Charisma CDS 4013*	10	8 wks
7 Jun 80	★ **PETER GABRIEL** *Charisma CDS 4019*	1	18 wks
18 Sep 82	● **PETER GABRIEL** *Charisma PG 4*	6	16 wks
18 Jun 83	● **PETER GABRIEL PLAYS LIVE**		
	Charisma PGDL 1	8	9 wks
30 Apr 85	**BIRDY – MUSIC FROM THE FILM**		
	Charisma CAS 1167	51	3 wks
31 May 86	★ **SO** *Virgin PG 5*	1	75 wks

First four albums are different.

GALAXY – See Phil FEARON and GALAXY

GALLAGHER and LYLE
UK, male vocal/instrumental duo *44 wks*

28 Feb 76	● **BREAKAWAY** *A & M AMLH 68348*	6	35 wks
29 Jan 77	**LOVE ON THE AIRWAYS**		
	A & M AMLH 64620	19	9 wks

Rory GALLAGHER
UK, male vocalist/instrumentalist – guitar *43 wks*

29 May 71	**RORY GALLAGHER** *Polydor 2383-044*	32	2 wks
4 Dec 71	**DEUCE** *Polydor 2383-076*	39	1 wk
20 May 72	● **LIVE IN EUROPE** *Polydor 2383 112*	9	15 wks
24 Feb 73	**BLUE PRINT** *Polydor 2383 189*	12	7 wks
17 Nov 73	**TATTOO** *Polydor 2383 230*	32	3 wks
27 Jul 74	**IRISH TOUR '74** *Polydor 2659 031*	36	2 wks
30 Oct 76	**CALLING CARD** *Chrysalis CHR 1124*	32	1 wk
22 Sep 79	**TOP PRIORITY** *Chrysalis CHR 1235*	56	4 wks
8 Nov 80	**STAGE STRUCK** *Chrysalis CHR 1280*	40	3 wks
8 May 82	**JINX** *Chrysalis CHR 1359*	68	5 wks

James GALWAY *UK, male instrumentalist – flute* *63 wks*

27 May 78	**THE MAGIC FLUTE OF JAMES GALWAY**		
	RCA Red Seal LRL1 5131	43	6 wks
1 Jul 78	**THE MAN WITH THE GOLDEN FLUTE**		
	RCA Red Seal LRL1 5127	52	3 wks
9 Sep 78	● **JAMES GALWAY PLAYS SONGS FOR ANNIE**		
	RCA Red Seal RL 25163	7	40 wks
15 Dec 79	**SONGS OF THE SEASHORE** *Solar RL 25253*	39	6 wks
18 Dec 82	**THE JAMES GALWAY COLLECTION**		
	Telstar STAR 2224	41	8 wks

See also James Galway and the Chieftains; James Galway and Henry Mancini; Cleo Laine and James Galway.

James GALWAY and Henry MANCINI with NATIONAL PHILHARMONIC ORCHESTRA
UK, male instrumentalist – flute,
US, conductor with UK, orchestra *6 wks*

8 Dec 84	**IN THE PINK** *RCA Red Seal RL 85315*	62	6 wks

See also James Galway; James Galway and the Chieftains; Cleo Laine and James Galway; Henry Mancini; Johnny Mathis and Henry Mancini; Luciano Pavarotti with the Henry Mancini Orchestra.

James GALWAY and the CHIEFTAINS
UK, male instrumentalist – flute with Ireland, male instrumental group *5 wks*

28 Mar 87	**JAMES GALWAY AND THE CHIEFTAINS IN**		
	IRELAND *Red Seal RL 85798*	32	5 wks

See also James Galway; James Galway and Henry Mancini; Cleo Laine and James Galway.

GANG OF FOUR *UK, male vocal/instrumental group* *9 wks*

13 Oct 79	**ENTERTAINMENT** *EMI EMC 3313*	45	3 wks
21 Mar 81	**SOLID GOLD** *EMI EMC 3364*	52	2 wks
29 May 82	**SONGS OF THE FREE** *EMI EMC 3412*	61	4 wks

GAP BAND *US, male vocal/instrumental group* *3 wks*

7 Feb 87	**GAP BAND 8** *Total Experience FL 89992*	47	3 wks

Art GARFUNKEL *US, male vocalist* *58 wks*

13 Oct 73	**ANGEL CLARE** *CBS 69021*	14	7 wks
1 Nov 75	● **BREAKAWAY** *CBS 86002*	7	10 wks
18 Mar 78	**WATER MARK** *CBS 86054*	25	5 wks
21 Apr 79	● **FATE FOR BREAKFAST** *CBS 86082*	2	20 wks
19 Sep 81	**SCISSORS CUT** *CBS 85259*	51	3 wks
17 Nov 84	**THE ART GARFUNKEL ALBUM** *CBS 10046*	12	13 wks

See also Simon and Garfunkel.

Judy GARLAND *US, female vocalist* *3 wks*

3 Mar 62	**JUDY AT CARNEGIE HALL** *Capitol W 1569*	13	3 wks

Errol GARNER *US, male instrumentalist – piano* *1 wk*

14 Jul 62	**CLOSE UP IN SWING** *Philips BBL 7579*	20	1 wk

David GATES *US, male vocalist* *4 wks*

31 May 75	**NEVER LET HER GO** *Elektra K 52012*	32	1 wk
29 Jul 78	**GOODBYE GIRL** *Elektra K 52091*	28	3 wks

Marvin GAYE *US, male vocalist* *93 wks*

16 Mar 68	**GREATEST HITS** *Tamla Motown STML 11065*	40	1 wk
10 Nov 73	**LET'S GET IT ON** *Tamla Motown STMA 8013*	39	1 wk
15 May 76	**I WANT YOU** *Tamla Motown STML 12025*	22	5 wks
30 Oct 76	**THE BEST OF MARVIN GAYE**		
	Tamla Motown STML 12042	56	1 wk
28 Feb 81	**IN OUR LIFETIME** *Motown STML 12149*	48	4 wks
20 Nov 82	● **MIDNIGHT LOVE** *CBS 85977*	10	16 wks
12 Nov 83	**GREATEST HITS** *Telstar STAR 2234*	13	61 wks
15 Jun 85	**DREAM OF A LIFETIME** *CBS 26239*	46	4 wks

See also Marvin Gaye and Tammi Terrell; Diana Ross and Marvin Gaye.

Marvin GAYE and Tammi TERRELL
US male/female vocal duo *4 wks*

22 Aug 70	**GREATEST HITS** *Tamla Motown STML 11153*	60	4 wks

See also Marvin Gaye; Diana Ross and Marvin Gaye.

GAYE BYKERS ON ACID
UK, male vocal/instrumental group *1 wk*

14 Nov 87	**DRILL YOUR OWN HOLE** *Virgin V 2478*	95	1 wk

Crystal GAYLE *US, female vocalist* *25 wks*

21 Jan 78	**WE MUST BELIEVE IN MAGIC**		
	United Artists UAG 30108	15	7 wks
23 Sep 78	**WHEN I DREAM** *United Artists UAG 30169*	25	8 wks
22 Mar 80	● **THE CRYSTAL GAYLE SINGLES ALBUM**		
	United Artists UAG 30287	7	10 wks

Gloria GAYNOR *US, female vocalist*   17 wks

8 Mar 75	NEVER CAN SAY GOODBYE *MGM 2315 321* ..	32	8 wks
24 Mar 79	LOVE TRACKS *Polydor 2391 385*	31	7 wks
16 Aug 86	THE POWER OF GLORIA GAYNOR		
	Stylus SMR 618	81	2 wks

J. GEILS BAND *US, male vocal/instrumental group*   15 wks

| 27 Feb 82 | FREEZE FRAME *EMI America AML 3020* .... | 12 | 15 wks |

Bob GELDOF *Ireland, male vocalist*   1 wk

| 6 Dec 86 | DEEP IN THE HEART OF NOWHERE | | |
| | *Mercury BOBLP 1* .... | 79 | 1 wk |

GENE LOVES JEZEBEL
UK, male vocal/instrumental group   5 wks

| 19 Jul 87 | DISCOVER *Beggars Banquet BEGA 73* .... | 32 | 4 wks |
| 24 Oct 87 | HOUSE OF DOLLS *Beggars Banquet BEGA 87* ... | 81 | 1 wk |

GENERATION X *UK, male vocal/instrumental group*   9 wks

| 8 Apr 78 | GENERATION X *Chrysalis CHR 1169* .... | 29 | 4 wks |
| 17 Feb 79 | VALLEY OF THE DOLLS *Chrysalis CHR 1193* ... | 51 | 5 wks |

GENESIS *UK, male vocal/instrumental group*   363 wks

14 Oct 72	FOXTROT *Charisma CAS 1058*	12	7 wks
11 Aug 73	● GENESIS LIVE *Charisma CLASS 1*	9	10 wks
20 Oct 73	● SELLING ENGLAND BY THE POUND		
	Charisma CAS 1074	3	21 wks
11 May 74	NURSERY CRYME *Charisma CAS 1052*	39	1 wk
7 Dec 74	● THE LAMB LIES DOWN ON BROADWAY		
	Charisma CGS 101	10	6 wks
28 Feb 76	● A TRICK OF THE TAIL *Charisma CDS 4001* ..	3	39 wks
15 Jan 77	● WIND AND WUTHERING *Charisma CDS 4005* ..	7	22 wks
29 Oct 77	● SECONDS OUT *Charisma GE 2001*	4	17 wks
15 Apr 78	● AND THEN THERE WERE THREE		
	Charisma CDS 4010	3	32 wks
5 Apr 80	★ DUKE *Charisma CBR 101*	1	30 wks
26 Sep 81	★ ABACAB *Charisma CBR 102*	1	27 wks
12 Jun 82	● 3 SIDES LIVE *Charisma GE 2002*	2	19 wks
15 Oct 83	★ GENESIS *Charisma GENLP 1*	1	45 wks
31 Mar 84	NURSERY CRYME (re-issue)		
	Charisma CHC 22	68	1 wk
21 Apr 84	TRESPASS *Charisma CHC 12*	98	1 wk
21 Jun 86	★ INVISIBLE TOUCH *Charisma GENLP 2* ...	1	79 wks
11 Jul 87	GENESIS (re-issue) *EMI GENLP 1*	57	6 wks

Jackie GENOVA *UK, female exercise instructor*   2 wks

| 21 May 83 | WORK THAT BODY *Island ILPS 9732* .... | 74 | 2 wks |

Bobbie GENTRY *US, female vocalist*   1 wk

| 25 Oct 69 | TOUCH 'EM WITH LOVE *Capitol EST 155* ...... | 21 | 1 wk |

See also Bobbie Gentry and Glen Campbell.

Bobbie GENTRY and Glen CAMPBELL
US, female/male vocal duo   1 wk

| 28 Feb 70 | BOBBIE GENTRY AND GLEN CAMPBELL | | |
| | *Capitol ST 2928* .... | 50 | 1 wk |

See also Bobbie Gentry; Glen Campbell.

Lowell GEORGE
US, male vocalist/instrumentalist – guitar   1 wk

| 21 Apr 79 | THANKS BUT I'LL EAT IT HERE | | |
| | *Warner Bros. K 56487* .... | 71 | 1 wk |

Robin GEORGE
UK, male vocalist/instrumentalist – guitar   3 wks

| 2 Mar 85 | DANGEROUS MUSIC *Bronze BRON 554* .... | 65 | 3 wks |

GEORGIA SATELLITES
US, male vocal/instrumental group   7 wks

| 7 Feb 87 | GEORGIA SATELLITES *Elektra 980 496–1* ...... | 52 | 7 wks |

GERRY and the PACEMAKERS
UK, male vocal/instrumental group   29 wks

26 Oct 63	● HOW DO YOU LIKE IT? *Columbia 33SX 1546*	2	28 wks
6 Feb 65	FERRY CROSS THE MERSEY		
	Columbia 33SX 1676	19	1 wk

Stan GETZ and Charlie BYRD
US, male instrumental duo – saxophone and guitar   7 wks

| 23 Feb 63 | JAZZ SAMBA *Verve SULP 9013* .... | 15 | 7 wks |

Andy GIBB *UK, male vocalist*   9 wks

| 19 Aug 78 | SHADOW DANCING *RSO RSS 0001* .... | 15 | 9 wks |

Barry GIBB *UK, male vocalist*   2 wks

| 20 Oct 84 | NOW VOYAGER *Polydor POLH 14* .... | 85 | 2 wks |

Steve GIBBONS BAND
UK, male vocal/instrumental group   3 wks

| 22 Oct 77 | CAUGHT IN THE ACT *Polydor 2478 112* .... | 22 | 3 wks |

Don GIBSON *US, male vocalist*   10 wks

| 22 Mar 80 | COUNTRY NUMBER ONE *Warwick WW 5079* .. | 13 | 10 wks |

GIBSON BROTHERS
Martinique, male vocal/instrumental group   3 wks

| 30 Aug 80 | ON THE RIVIERA *Island ILPS 9620* .... | 50 | 3 wks |

GILLAN *UK, male vocal/instrumental group*   53 wks

17 Jul 76	CHILD IN TIME *Polydor 2490 136*	55	1 wk
20 Oct 79	MR. UNIVERSE *Acrobat ACRO 3*	11	6 wks
16 Aug 80	● GLORY ROAD *Virgin V 2171*	3	12 wks
25 Apr 81	● FUTURE SHOCK *Virgin VK 2196*	2	13 wks
7 Nov 81	DOUBLE TROUBLE *Virgin VGD 3506*	12	15 wks
2 Oct 82	MAGIC *Virgin V 2238*	17	6 wks

Child In Time credited to Ian Gillan Band.

(Left) GARY GLITTER said goodbye to the chart in 1976.

(Below) How can you comment on the musical prowess of a group like the GOODIES when they have already done so themselves in a photo like this?

(Right) The GROUNDHOGS are shown in January, 1973, the year they took a break from the chart.

David GILMOUR
UK, male instrumentalist – guitar 18 wks

10 Jun 78	**DAVID GILMOUR** *Harvest SHVL 817*	17	9 wks
17 Mar 84	**ABOUT FACE** *Harvest SHSP 2400791*	21	9 wks

Gordon GILTRAP *UK, male instrumentalist – guitar* 7 wks

18 Feb 78	**PERILOUS JOURNEY** *Electric TRIX 4*	29	7 wks

GIRL *UK, male vocal/instrumental group* 6 wks

9 Feb 80	**SHEER GREED** *Jet JETLP 224*	33	5 wks
23 Jan 82	**WASTED YOUTH** *Jet JETLP 238*	92	1 wk

GIRLS AT OUR BEST
UK, male/female vocal/instrumental group 3 wks

7 Nov 81	**PLEASURE** *Happy Birthday RVLP 1*	60	3 wks

GIRLSCHOOL *UK, female vocal/instrumental group* 23 wks

5 Jul 80	**DEMOLITION** *Bronze BRON 525*	28	10 wks
25 Apr 81	● **HIT 'N' RUN** *Bronze BRON 534*	5	6 wks
12 Jun 82	**SCREAMING BLUE MURDER** *Bronze BRON 541*	27	6 wks
12 Nov 83	**PLAY DIRTY** *Bronze BRON 548*	66	1 wk

Gary GLITTER *UK, male vocalist* 92 wks

21 Oct 72	● **GLITTER** *Bell BELLS 216*	8	40 wks
16 Jun 73	● **TOUCH ME** *Bell BELLS 222*	2	33 wks
29 Jun 74	● **REMEMBER ME THIS WAY** *Bell BELLS 237*	5	14 wks
27 Mar 76	**GARRY GLITTER'S GREATEST HITS** *Bell BELLS 262*	33	5 wks

GLITTER BAND *UK, male vocal/instrumental group* 17 wks

14 Sep 74	**HEY** *Bell BELLS 241*	13	12 wks
3 May 75	**ROCK 'N' ROLL DUDES** *Bell BELLS 253*	17	4 wks
19 Jun 76	**GREATEST HITS** *Bell BELLS 264*	52	1 wk

GLOVE *UK, male vocal/instrumental group* 3 wks

17 Sep 83	**BLUE SUNSHINE** *Wonderland SHELP 2*	35	3 wks

GO-BETWEENS
Australia, male/female vocal/instrumental group 1 wk

13 Jun 87	**TALLULAH** *Beggars Banquet BEGA 81*	91	1 wk

GODLEY and CREME
UK, male vocal/instrumental duo 16 wks

19 Nov 77	**CONSEQUENCES** *Mercury CONS 017*	52	1 wk
9 Sep 78	**L** *Mercury 9109 611*	47	2 wks
17 Oct 81	**ISMISM** *Polydor POLD 5043*	29	13 wks

Consequences *credited to Kevin Godley and Lol Creme. See also 10 C.C. and Godley and Creme.*

GO-GOs *US, female vocal/instrumental group* 3 wks

21 Aug 82	**VACATION** *IRS/A & M SP 70031*	75	3 wks

Andrew GOLD
US, male vocalist/instrumentalist – piano 7 wks

15 Apr 78	**ALL THIS AND HEAVEN TOO** *Asylum K 53072* .	31	7 wks

GOLDEN EARRING
Holland, male vocal/instrumental group 4 wks

2 Feb 74	**MOONTAN** *Track 2406 112*	24	4 wks

GOODIES *UK, male vocal group* 11 wks

8 Nov 75	**THE NEW GOODIES LP** *Bradley's BRADL 1010* ..	25	11 wks

Benny GOODMAN
US, male instrumentalist – clarinet 1 wk

3 Apr 71	**BENNY GOODMAN TODAY** *Decca DDS 3*	49	1 wk

Ron GOODWIN *UK, orchestra* 1 wk

2 May 70	**LEGEND OF THE GLASS MOUNTAIN** *Studio two TWO 220*	49	1 wk

GOOMBAY DANCE BAND
Germany, male/female vocal group 9 wks

10 Apr 82	**SEVEN TEARS** *Epic EPC 85702*	16	9 wks

GOONS *UK, male comic group* 31 wks

28 Nov 59	● **BEST OF THE GOON SHOWS** *Parlophone PMC 1108*	8	14 wks
17 Dec 60	**BEST OF THE GOON SHOWS VOL. 2** *Parlophone PMC 1129*	12	6 wks
4 Nov 72	● **LAST GOON SHOW OF ALL** *BBC Radio Enterprises REB 142*	8	11 wks

GORDON – *See PETER and GORDON*

GO WEST *UK, male vocal/instrumental group* 88 wks

13 Apr 85	● **GO WEST/BANGS AND CRASHES** *Chrysalis CHR 1495*	8	83 wks
6 Jun 87	**DANCING ON THE COUCH** *Chrysalis CDL 1550* .	19	5 wks

Bangs and Crashes *is an album of remixed versions of Go West tracks and some new material. From 31 May 1986 both records were available together as a double album.*

Jaki GRAHAM *UK, female vocalist* 10 wks

14 Sep 85	**HEAVEN KNOWS** *EMI JK 1*	48	5 wks
20 Sep 86	**BREAKING AWAY** *EMI EMC 3514*	25	5 wks

GRANDMASTER FLASH and the FURIOUS FIVE *US, male vocalist and male vocal group* 20 wks

23 Oct 82	**THE MESSAGE** *Sugar Hill SHLP 1007*	77	3 wks
23 Jun 84	**GREATEST MESSAGES** *Sugar Hill SHLP 5552* ...	41	16 wks
23 Feb 85	**THEY SAID IT COULDN'T BE DONE** *Elektra 9–60389–1*	95	1 wk

GRANDMASTER MELLE MEL
US, male vocalist   *5 wks*

| 20 Oct 84 | **WORK PARTY** *Sugar Hill SHLP 5553* .... | 45 | 5 wks |

GRAND PRIX *UK, male vocal/instrumental group*   *2 wks*

| 18 Jun 83 | **SAMURAI** *Chrysalis CHR 1430* .... | 65 | 2 wks |

David GRANT *UK, male vocalist*   *7 wks*

| 5 Nov 83 | **DAVID GRANT** *Chrysalis CHR 1448* .... | 32 | 6 wks |
| 18 May 85 | **HOPES & DREAMS** *Chrysalis CHR 1483* .... | 96 | 1 wk |

Eddy GRANT
Guyana, male vocalist/multi-instrumentalist   *39 wks*

30 May 81	**CAN'T GET ENOUGH** *Ice ICEL 21*	39	6 wks
27 Nov 82	● **KILLER ON THE RAMPAGE** *Ice ICELP 3023* ...	7	23 wks
17 Nov 84	**ALL THE HITS** *K-Tel NE 1284*	23	10 wks

GRATEFUL DEAD
US, male vocal/instrumental group   *9 wks*

19 Sep 70	**WORKINGMAN'S DEAD** *Warner Bros. WS 1869* .	69	2 wks
3 Aug 74	**GRATEFUL DEAD FROM THE MARS HOTEL**		
	Atlantic K 59302	47	1 wk
1 Nov 75	**BLUES FOR ALLAH** *United Artists UAS 29895*	45	1 wk
4 Sep 76	**STEAL YOUR FACE** *United Artists UAS 60131/2*	42	1 wk
20 Aug 77	**TERRAPIN STATION** *Arista SPARTY 1016*	30	1 wk
19 Sep 87	**IN THE DARK** *Arista 208 564*	57	3 wks

David GRAY and Tommy TYCHO
UK, male arrangers   *6 wks*

| 16 Oct 76 | **ARMCHAIR MELODIES** *K-Tel NE 927* .... | 21 | 6 wks |

Alltrina GRAYSON – *See Wilton FELDER*

Al GREEN *US, male vocalist*   *16 wks*

| 26 Apr 75 | **AL GREEN'S GREATEST HITS** | | |
| | *London SHU 8481* .... | 18 | 16 wks |

Peter GREEN
UK, male vocalist/instrumentalist – guitar   *17 wks*

| 9 Jul 79 | **IN THE SKIES** *Creole PULS 101* .... | 32 | 13 wks |
| 24 May 80 | **LITTLE DREAMER** *PUK PULS 102* .... | 34 | 4 wks |

Dave GREENFIELD and Jean-Jacques BURNEL
UK, male vocal/instrumental duo   *1 wk*

| 3 Dec 83 | **FIRE AND WATER** *Epic EPC 25707* .... | 94 | 1 wk |

See also Jean-Jacques Burnel.

GREEN ON RED *US, male vocal/instrumental group*   *1 wk*

| 26 Oct 85 | **NO FREE LUNCH** *Mercury MERM 78* .... | 99 | 1 wk |

GREENSLADE *UK, male vocal/instrumental group*   *3 wks*

| 14 Sep 74 | **SPYGLASS GUEST** *Warner Bros. K 56055* .... | 34 | 3 wks |

Christina GREGG
UK, female exercise instructor   *1 wk*

| 27 May 78 | **MUSIC 'N' MOTION** *Warwick WW 5041* .... | 51 | 1 wk |

GROUNDHOGS *UK, male vocal/instrumental group*   *50 wks*

6 Jun 70	● **THANK CHRIST FOR THE BOMB**		
	Liberty LBS 83295	9	13 wks
3 Apr 71	● **SPLIT** *Liberty LBG 83401*	5	27 wks
18 Mar 72	● **WHO WILL SAVE THE WORLD**		
	United Artists UAG 29237	8	9 wks
13 Jul 74	**SOLID** *WWA WWA 004*	31	1 wk

GTR *UK, male vocal/instrumental group*   *4 wks*

| 19 Jul 86 | **GTR** *Arista 207 716* .... | 41 | 4 wks |

GUILDFORD CATHEDRAL CHOIR
UK, choir   *4 wks*

| 10 Dec 66 | **CHRISTMAS CAROLS FROM GUILDFORD** | | |
| | **CATHEDRAL** *MFP 1104* .... | 24 | 4 wks |

Record credits Barry Rose as conductor.

David GUNSON *US, male comedian*   *2 wks*

| 25 Dec 82 | **WHAT GOES UP MIGHT COME DOWN** | | |
| | *Big Ben BB0012* .... | 92 | 2 wks |

GUNS N' ROSES *US, male vocal/instrumental group*   *3 wks*

| 1 Aug 87 | **APPETITE FOR DESTRUCTION** *Geffen WX 125* | 68 | 3 wks |

G.U.S. (FOOTWEAR) BAND and the MORRISTOWN ORPHEUS CHOIR
UK, male instrumental group and male/female vocal group   *1 wk*

| 3 Oct 70 | **LAND OF HOPE AND GLORY** | | |
| | *Columbia SCX 6406* .... | 54 | 1 wk |

Arlo GUTHRIE *US, male vocalist*   *1 wk*

| 7 Mar 70 | **ALICE'S RESTAURANT** *Reprise RSLP 6267* ..... | 44 | 1 wk |

Gwen GUTHRIE *US, female vocalist*   *14 wks*

| 23 Aug 86 | **GOOD TO GO LOVER** *Boiling Point POLD 5201* . | 42 | 14 wks |

Robin GUTHRIE – *See Harold BUDD/Liz FRASER/Robin GUTHRIE/Simon RAYMOND*

GUYS 'N' DOLLS *UK, male/female vocal group*   *1 wk*

| 31 May 75 | **GUYS 'N' DOLLS** *Magnet MAG 5005* .... | 43 | 1 wk |

GWENT CHORALE – *See Byn YEMM*

Looking at STEVE HACKETT's chart placings makes one realize he should never have got the Lamborghini.

(Above) STEVE HARLEY was not the kind of performer afraid to make eye contact with members of his audience.

H

Steve HACKETT
UK, male vocalist/instrumentalist – guitar   *38 wks*

1 Nov 75	**VOYAGE OF THE ACOLYTE**			
	Charisma CAS 1111	26	4 wks
6 May 78	**PLEASE DON'T TOUCH** *Charisma CDS 4012*	38	5 wks
26 May 79	**SPECTRAL MORNINGS** *Charisma CDS 4017* ..	22	11 wks
21 Jun 80 ●	**DEFECTOR** *Charisma CDS 4018*	9	7 wks
29 Aug 81	**CURED** *Charisma CDS 4021*	15	5 wks
30 Apr 83	**HIGHLY STRUNG** *Charisma HACK 1*	16	3 wks
19 Nov 83	**BAY OF KINGS** *Lamborghini LMGLP 3000*	70	1 wk
22 Sep 84	**TILL WE HAVE FACES**			
	Lamborghini LMGLP 4000	54	2 wks

Sammy HAGAR
US, male vocalist/instrumentalist – guitar   *19 wks*

29 Sep 79	**STREET MACHINE** *Capitol EST 11983* ...	38	4 wks
22 Mar 80	**LOUD AND CLEAR** *Capitol EST 25330* ...	12	8 wks
7 Jun 80	**DANGER ZONE** *Capitol EST 12069*	25	3 wks
13 Feb 82	**STANDING HAMPTON** *Geffen GEF 85456*	84	2 wks
4 Jul 87	**SAMMY HAGAR** *Geffen WX 114*	86	2 wks

See also Hagar, Schon, Aaronson and Shrieve.

HAGAR, SCHON, AARONSON, SHRIEVE
US, male vocal/instrumental group   *1 wk*

19 May 84	**THROUGH THE FIRE** *Geffen GEF 25893*	92	1 wk

See also Sammy Hagar.

Paul HAIG   *UK, male vocalist*   *2 wks*

22 Oct 83	**RHYTHM OF LIFE** *Crepuscule ILPS 9742*	82	2 wks

HAIRCUT 100   *UK, male vocal/instrumental group*   *34 wks*

6 Mar 82 ●	**PELICAN WEST** *Arista HCC 100*	2	34 wks

Bill HALEY and his COMETS
US, male vocalist/guitarist, male vocal/instrumental backing group   *5 wks*

18 May 68	**ROCK AROUND THE CLOCK**			
	Ace Of Hearts AH 13	34	5 wks

HALF MAN HALF BISCUIT
UK, male vocal/instrumental group   *14 wks*

8 Feb 86	**BACK IN THE DHSS** *Probe Plus PROBE 4*	59	14 wks

Daryl HALL   *US, male vocalist*   *5 wks*

23 Aug 86	**THREE HEARTS IN THE HAPPY ENDING**			
	MACHINE *RCA PL 87196*	26	5 wks

See also Daryl Hall and John Oates.

Daryl HALL and John OATES
US, male vocal duo   *129 wks*

3 Jul 76	**HALL AND OATES** *RCA Victor APL1 1144*	56	1 wk
18 Sep 76	**BIGGER THAN BOTH OF US**			
	RCA Victor APL1 1467	25	7 wks
15 Oct 77	**BEAUTY ON A BACK STREET** *RCA PL 12300* ..	40	2 wks
6 Feb 82 ●	**PRIVATE EYES** *RCA RCALP 6001*	8	21 wks
23 Oct 82	**H2O** *RCA RCALP 6056*	24	35 wks
29 Oct 83	**ROCK 'N' SOUL (PART 1)** *RCA PL 84858*	16	45 wks
27 Oct 84	**BIG BAM BOOM** *RCA 85309*	28	13 wks
28 Sep 85	**LIVE AT THE APOLLO WITH DAVID RUFFIN**			
	& EDDIE KENDRICK *RCA PL 87035*	32	5 wks

See also Daryl Hall.

HAMBURG STUDENTS' CHOIR
Germany, male vocal group   *6 wks*

17 Dec 60	**HARK THE HERALD ANGELS SING**			
	Pye GGL 0023	11	6 wks

George HAMILTON IV   *US, male vocalist*   *11 wks*

10 Apr 71	**CANADIAN PACIFIC** *RCA SF 8062*	45	1 wk
10 Feb 79	**REFLECTIONS** *Lotus WH 5008*	25	9 wks
13 Nov 82	**SONGS FOR A WINTER'S NIGHT**			
	Ronco RTL 2082	94	1 wk

Jan HAMMER
Czechoslovakia, male instrumentalist – keyboards   *6 wks*

14 Nov 87	**ESCAPE FROM TV** *MCA MCF 3407*	34	6 wks

Herbie HANCOCK
US, male vocalist/instrumentalist – keyboards   *24 wks*

9 Sep 78	**SUNLIGHT** *CBS 82240*	27	6 wks
24 Feb 79	**FEETS DON'T FAIL ME NOW** *CBS 83491*	28	8 wks
27 Aug 83	**FUTURE SHOCK** *CBS 25540*	27	10 wks

Tony HANCOCK   *UK, male comedian*   *42 wks*

9 Apr 60 ●	**THIS IS HANCOCK** *Pye NPL 10845*	2	22 wks
12 Nov 60	**PIECES OF HANCOCK** *Pye NPL 18054* ...	17	2 wks
3 Mar 62	**HANCOCK** *Pye NPL 18068*	12	14 wks
14 Sep 63	**THIS IS HANCOCK (re-issue)**			
	Pye Golden Guinea GGL 0206	16	4 wks

HANOI ROCKS
Finland/UK, male vocal/instrumental group   *4 wks*

11 Jun 83	**BACK TO MYSTERY CITY** *Lick LICLP 1*	87	1 wk
20 Oct 84	**TWO STEPS FROM THE MOVE** *CBS 26066*	28	3 wks

Bo HANNSON   *Sweden, multi-instrumentalist*   *2 wks*

18 Nov 72	**LORD OF THE RINGS** *Charisma CAS 1059*	34	2 wks

John HANSON   *UK, male vocalist*   *12 wks*

23 Apr 60	**THE STUDENT PRINCE** *Pye NPL 18046*	17	1 wk
2 Sep 61 ●	**THE STUDENT PRINCE/VAGABOND KING**			
	Pye GGL 0086	9	7 wks
10 Dec 77	**JOHN HANSON SINGS 20 SHOWTIME GREATS**			
	K-Tel NE 1002	16	4 wks

Paul HARDCASTLE
UK, male producer/instrumentalist – synthesizer   *5 wks*

30 Nov 85	**PAUL HARDCASTLE** *Chrysalis CHR 1517*	53	5 wks

Mike HARDING *UK, male comedian*   *24 wks*

30 Aug 75	MRS 'ARDIN'S KID *Rubber RUB 011*	24	6 wks
10 Jul 76	ONE MAN SHOW *Philips 6625 022*	19	10 wks
11 Jun 77	OLD FOUR EYES IS BACK *Philips 6308 290*	31	6 wks
24 Jun 78	CAPTAIN PARALYTIC AND THE BROWN ALE COWBOY *Philips 6641 798*	60	2 wks

HARDY – *See LAUREL and HARDY*

Steve HARLEY and COCKNEY REBEL
UK, male vocalist and male vocal/instrumental group   *52 wks*

22 Jun 74	● THE PSYCHOMODO *EMI EMC 3033*	8	20 wks
22 Mar 75	● THE BEST YEARS OF OUR LIVES *EMI EMC 3068*	4	19 wks
14 Feb 76	TIMELESS FLIGHT *EMI EMA 775*	18	6 wks
27 Nov 76	LOVE'S A PRIMA DONNA *EMI EMC 3156*	28	3 wks
30 Jul 77	FACE TO FACE – A LIVE RECORDING *EMI EMSP 320*	40	4 wks

First album credited to Cockney Rebel.

Roy HARPER
UK, male vocalist/instrumentalist – guitar   *5 wks*

9 Mar 74	VALENTINE *Harvest SHSP 4027*	27	1 wk
21 Jun 75	H.Q. *Harvest SHSP 4046*	31	2 wks
12 Mar 77	BULLINAMINGVASE *Harvest SHSP 4060*	25	2 wks

See also Roy Harper and Jimmy Page.

Roy HARPER and Jimmy PAGE
UK, male vocal/instrumental duo   *4 wks*

| 16 Mar 85 | WHATEVER HAPPENED TO JUGULA? *Second Sight/Beggars Banquet BEGA 60* .... | 44 | 4 wks |

See also Roy Harper; Jimmy Page.

Anita HARRIS *UK, female vocalist*   *5 wks*

| 27 Jan 68 | JUST LOVING YOU *CBS SBPG 63182* .... | 29 | 5 wks |

Emmylou HARRIS *US, female vocalist*   *29 wks*

14 Feb 76	ELITE HOTEL *Reprise K 54060*	17	11 wks
29 Jan 77	LUXURY LINER *Warner Bros. K 56344*	17	6 wks
4 Feb 78	QUARTER MOON IN A TEN CENT TOWN *Warner Bros. K 56433*	40	5 wks
29 Mar 80	HER BEST SONGS *K-Tel NE 1058*	36	3 wks
14 Feb 81	EVANGELINE *Warner Bros. K 56880*	53	4 wks

See Dolly Parton/Linda Ronstadt/Emmylou Harris.

Keith HARRIS, ORVILLE and CUDDLES
UK, male ventriloquist vocalist with feathered dummies   *1 wk*

| 4 Jun 83 | AT THE END OF THE RAINBOW *BBC REH 465* .... | 92 | 1 wk |

George HARRISON
UK, male vocalist/instrumentalist – guitar   *60 wks*

26 Dec 70	● ALL THINGS MUST PASS *Apple STCH 639*	4	24 wks
7 Jul 73	● LIVING IN THE MATERIAL WORLD *Apple PAS 10006*	2	12 wks
18 Oct 75	EXTRA TEXTURE (READ ALL ABOUT IT) *Apple PAS 10009*	16	4 wks

18 Dec 76	THIRTY THREE AND A THIRD *Dark Horse K 56319*	35	4 wks
17 Mar 79	GEORGE HARRISON *Dark Horse K 56562*	39	5 wks
13 Jun 81	SOMEWHERE IN ENGLAND *Dark Horse K 56870*	13	4 wks
14 Nov 87	● CLOUD NINE *Dark Horse WX 123*	10†	7 wks

Debbie HARRY *US, female vocalist*   *18 wks*

| 8 Aug 81 | ● KOO KOO *Chrysalis CHR 1347* .... | 6 | 7 wks |
| 29 Nov 86 | ROCKBIRD *Chrysalis CHR 1540* .... | 31 | 11 wks |

Keef HARTLEY BAND
UK, male vocal/instrumental group   *3 wks*

| 5 Sep 70 | THE TIME IS NEAR *Deram SML 1071* .... | 41 | 3 wks |

HATFIELD AND THE NORTH
UK, male/female vocal/instrumental group   *1 wk*

| 29 Mar 75 | ROTTERS CLUB *Virgin V 2030* .... | 43 | 1 wk |

Donny HATHAWAY – *See Roberta FLACK and Donny HATHAWAY*

Ted HAWKINS
US, male vocalist/instrumentalist – guitar   *1 wk*

| 18 Apr 87 | HAPPY HOUR *Windows On The World WOLP 2* ... | 82 | 1 wk |

HAWKWIND *UK, male vocal/instrumental group*   *96 wks*

6 Nov 71	IN SEARCH OF SPACE *United Artists UAS 29202* .	18	19 wks
23 Dec 72	DOREMI FASOL LATIDO *United Artists UAS 29364*	14	5 wks
2 Jun 73	● SPACE RITUAL ALIVE *United Artists UAD 60037/8*	9	5 wks
21 Sep 74	HALL OF THE MOUNTAIN GRILL *United Artists UAG 29672*	16	5 wks
31 May 75	WARRIOR ON THE EDGE OF TIME *United Artists UAG 29766*	13	7 wks
24 Apr 76	ROAD HAWKS *United Artists UAK 29919*	34	4 wks
18 Sep 76	ASTONISHING SOUNDS, AMAZING MUSIC *Charisma CDS 4004*	33	5 wks
9 Jul 77	QUARK STRANGENESS AND CHARM *Charisma CDS 4008*	30	6 wks
21 Oct 78	25 YEARS ON *Charisma CD 4014*	48	3 wks
30 Jun 79	PXR 5 *Charisma CDS 4016*	59	5 wks
9 Aug 80	LIVE 1979 *Bronze BRON 527*	15	7 wks
8 Nov 80	LEVITATION *Bronze BRON 530*	21	4 wks
24 Oct 81	SONIC ATTACK *RCA RCALP 5004*	19	5 wks
22 May 82	CHURCH OF HAWKWIND *RCA RCALP 9004*	26	6 wks
23 Oct 82	CHOOSE YOUR MASQUES *RCA RCALP 6055* .	29	5 wks
5 Nov 83	ZONES *Flicknife SHARP 014*	57	2 wks
25 Feb 84	HAWKWIND *Liberty SLS 1972921*	75	1 wk
16 Nov 85	CHRONICLE OF THE BLACK SWORD *Flicknife SHARP 033*	65	2 wks

25 Years On credited to Hawklords, a pseudonym for Hawkwind.

Isaac HAYES *US, male vocalist/multi-instrumentalist*   *14 wks*

| 18 Dec 71 | SHAFT *Polydor 2659 007* .... | 17 | 13 wks |
| 12 Feb 72 | BLACK MOSES *Stax 2628 004* .... | 38 | 1 wk |

HAYSI FANTAYZEE *UK, male/female vocal duo*   *5 wks*

| 26 Feb 83 | BATTLE HYMNS FOR CHILDREN SINGING *Regard RGLP 6000* .... | 53 | 5 wks |

Justin HAYWARD *UK, male vocalist* *10 wks*

5 Mar 77	**SONGWRITER**	*Deram SDL 15*	....	28	5 wks
19 Jul 80	**NIGHT FLIGHT**	*Decca TXS 138*	....	41	4 wks
19 Oct 85	**MOVING MOUNTAINS**	*Towerbell TOWLP 15*	....	78	1 wk

See also Justin Hayward and John Lodge.

Justin HAYWARD and John LODGE
UK, male vocal/instrumental duo *18 wks*

29 Mar 75	● **BLUE JAYS**	*Threshold THS 12*	....	4	18 wks

See also Justin Hayward; John Lodge.

Lee HAZELWOOD – *See Nancy SINATRA and Lee HAZELWOOD*

HEART *US, female/male vocal/instrumental group* *60 wks*

22 Jan 77	**DREAMBOAT ANNIE**	*Arista ARTY 139*	....	36	8 wks
23 Jul 77	**LITTLE QUEEN**	*Portrait PRT 82075*		34	4 wks
19 Jun 82	**PRIVATE AUDITION**	*Epic EPC 85792*	..	77	2 wks
26 Oct 85	**HEART**	*Capitol EJ 24–0372–1*		50	17 wks
6 Jun 87	● **BAD ANIMALS**	*Capitol ESTU 2032*	....	7†	29 wks

Heart changed label number during its chart run to Capitol LOVE 1.

HEARTBREAKERS
US, male vocal/instrumental group *1 wk*

5 Nov 77	**L.A.M.F.**	*Track 2409 218*	....	55	1 wk

Ted HEATH AND HIS MUSIC
UK, conductor and orchestra *5 wks*

21 Apr 62	**BIG BAND PERCUSSION**	*Decca PFM 24004*	.....	17	5 wks

HEATWAVE *UK/US, male vocal/instrumental group* *26 wks*

11 Jun 77	**TOO HOT TO HANDLE**	*GTO GTLP 013*	.....	46	2 wks
6 May 78	**CENTRAL HEATING**	*GTO GTLP 027*	..	26	15 wks
14 Feb 81	**CANDLES**	*GTO GTLP 047*	..	29	9 wks

HEAVEN 17 *UK, male vocal/instrumental group* *126 wks*

26 Sep 81	**PENTHOUSE AND PAVEMENT**	*Virgin V 2208*	..	14	76 wks
7 May 83	● **THE LUXURY GAP**	*Virgin V 2253*		4	36 wks
6 Oct 84	**HOW MEN ARE**	*B.E.F. V 2326*		12	11 wks
12 Jul 86	**ENDLESS**	*Virgin TCVB/CDV 2383*		70	2 wks
29 Nov 86	**PLEASURE ONE**	*Virgin V 2400*		78	1 wk

Endless was available only on cassette and CD.

HEAVY PETTIN' *UK, male vocal/instrumental group* *4 wks*

29 Oct 83	**LETTIN' LOOSE**	*Polydor HEPLP 1*	.....	55	2 wks
13 Jul 85	**ROCK AIN'T DEAD**	*Polydor HEPLP 2*	....	81	2 wks

Jimi HENDRIX
US, male vocalist/instrumentalist – guitar *187 wks*

27 May 67	● **ARE YOU EXPERIENCED**	*Track 612–001*	......	2	33 wks
16 Dec 67	● **AXIS: BOLD AS LOVE**	*Track 613–003*	...	5	16 wks
27 Apr 68	● **SMASH HITS**	*Track 613–004*	...	4	25 wks
16 Nov 68	● **ELECTRIC LADYLAND**	*Track 613–008/9*	..	6	12 wks
4 Jul 70	● **BAND OF GYPSIES**	*Track 2406–001*	.....	6	30 wks
3 Apr 71	● **CRY OF LOVE**	*Track 2408–101*	....	2	14 wks

28 Aug 71	● **EXPERIENCE**	*Ember NR 5057*	....	9	6 wks
20 Nov 71	**JIMI HENDRIX AT THE ISLE OF WIGHT**				
		Track 2302 016	....	17	2 wks
4 Dec 71	**RAINBOW BRIDGE**	*Reprise K 44159*	.....	16	8 wks
5 Feb 72	● **HENDRIX IN THE WEST**	*Polydor 2302 018*	..	7	14 wks
11 Dec 72	**WAR HEROES**	*Polydor 2302 020*		23	3 wks
21 Jul 73	**SOUNDTRACK RECORDINGS FROM THE FILM**				
	'JIMI HENDRIX'	*Warner Bros. K 64017*	....	37	1 wk
29 Mar 75	**JIMI HENDRIX**	*Polydor 2343 080*		35	4 wks
30 Aug 75	**CRASH LANDING**	*Polydor 2310 398*		35	3 wks
29 Nov 75	**MIDNIGHT LIGHTNING**	*Polydor 2310 415*		46	1 wk
14 Aug 82	**THE JIMI HENDRIX CONCERTS**	*CBS 88592*	..	16	11 wks
19 Feb 83	**THE SINGLES ALBUM**	*Polydor PODV 6*		77	4 wks

See also Jimi Hendrix and Curtis Knight. Act billed as Jimi Hendrix Experience, US/UK, male vocal/instrumental group, for first four hits.

Jimi HENDRIX and Curtis KNIGHT
US, male vocal/instrumental duo *2 wks*

18 May 68	**GET THAT FEELING**	*London HA 8349*	....	39	2 wks

See also Jimi Hendrix.

Don HENLEY *US, male vocalist* *11 wks*

9 Mar 85	**BUILDING THE PERFECT BEAST**				
		Geffen GEF 25939	....	14	11 wks

Band and Chorus of HER MAJESTY'S
GUARDS DIVISION *UK, military band* *4 wks*

22 Nov 75	**30 SMASH HITS OF THE WAR YEARS**				
		Warwick WW 5006	....	38	4 wks

HERD *UK, male vocal/instrumental group* *1 wk*

24 Feb 68	**PARADISE LOST**	*Fontana STL 5458*	....	38	1 wk

HERMAN'S HERMITS
UK, male vocal/instrumental group *11 wks*

18 Sep 65	**HERMAN'S HERMITS**	*Columbia 33SX 1727*	.....	16	2 wks
25 Sep 71	**THE MOST OF HERMAN'S HERMITS**				
		MFP 5216	....	14	5 wks
8 Oct 77	**GREATEST HITS**	*K-Tel NE 1001*	....	37	4 wks

Nick HEYWARD *UK, male vocalist* *13 wks*

29 Oct 83	● **NORTH OF A MIRACLE**	*Arista NORTH 1*	......	10	13 wks

HI TENSION *UK, male vocal/instrumental group* *4 wks*

6 Jan 79	**HI TENSION**	*Island ILPS 9564*	....	74	4 wks

Benny HILL *UK, male vocalist* *8 wks*

11 Dec 71	● **WORDS AND MUSIC**	*Columbia SCX 6479*	....	9	8 wks

Vince HILL *UK, male vocalist* *10 wks*

20 May 67	**EDELWEISS**	*Columbia SCX 6141*	......	23	9 wks
29 Apr 78	**THAT LOVING FEELING**	*K-Tel NE 1017*	.....	51	1 wk

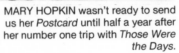

MARY HOPKIN wasn't ready to send
us her *Postcard* until half a year after
her number one trip with *Those Were
the Days*.

Do not adjust your set, it's merely a
typical HAWKWIND gig.

HEAVEN 17 appear to
have filled the luxury gap

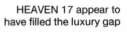

Steve HILLAGE
UK, male vocalist/instrumentalist – guitar   *41 wks*

3 May 75	**FISH RISING** *Virgin V 2031*	33	3 wks
16 Oct 76	● **L** *Virgin V 2066*	10	12 wks
22 Oct 77	**MOTIVATION RADIO** *Virgin V 2777*	28	5 wks
29 Apr 78	**GREEN VIRGIN** *V 2098*	30	8 wks
17 Feb 79	**LIVE HERALD** *Virgin VGD 3502*	54	5 wks
5 May 79	**RAINBOW DOME MUSIC** *Virgin VR 1* . . .	52	5 wks
27 Oct 79	**OPEN** *Virgin V 2135*	71	1 wk
5 Mar 83	**FOR TO NEXT** *Virgin V 2244*	48	2 wks

HIPSWAY *UK, male vocal/instrumental group*   *23 wks*

19 Apr 86	**HIPSWAY** *Mercury MERH 85*	42	23 wks

Roger HODGSON *UK, male vocalist*   *4 wks*

20 Oct 84	**IN THE EYE OF THE STORM**		
	A & M AMA 5004	70	4 wks

Gerrard HOFFNUNG *UK, male comedian*   *19 wks*

3 Sep 60	● **AT THE OXFORD UNION** *Decca LF 1330*	4	19 wks

Billie HOLIDAY *US, female vocalist*   *10 wks*

16 Nov 85	**THE LEGEND OF BILLIE HOLIDAY**		
	MCA BHTV 1	60	10 wks

HOLLIES *UK, male vocal/instrumental group*   *133 wks*

15 Feb 64	● **STAY WITH THE HOLLIES**		
	Parlophone PMC 1220	2	25 wks
2 Oct 65	● **HOLLIES** *Parlophone PMC 1261*	8	14 wks
16 Jul 66	**WOULD YOU BELIEVE** *Parlophone PMC 7008* .	16	8 wks
17 Dec 66	**FOR CERTAIN BECAUSE** *Parlophone PCS 17011* .	23	7 wks
17 Jun 67	**EVOLUTION** *Parlophone PCS 7022*	13	10 wks
17 Aug 68	★ **GREATEST HITS** *Parlophone PCS 7057*	1	27 wks
17 May 69	● **HOLLIES SING DYLAN** *Parlophone PCS 7078* .	3	7 wks
28 Nov 70	**CONFESSIONS OF THE MIND**		
	Parlophone PCS 7117	30	5 wks
16 Mar 74	**HOLLIES** *Polydor 2383 262*	38	3 wks
19 Mar 77	● **HOLLIES LIVE HITS** *Polydor 2383 428*	4	12 wks
22 Jul 78	● **20 GOLDEN GREATS** *EMI EMTV 11*	2	15 wks

Buddy HOLLY and the CRICKETS
US, male vocalist, male vocal/instrumental group   *308 wks*

2 May 59	● **BUDDY HOLLY STORY** *Coral No. LVA 9105*	2	156 wks
15 Oct 60	● **BUDDY HOLLY STORY VOL. 2**		
	Coral LVA 9127	7	14 wks
21 Oct 61	● **THAT'LL BE THE DAY** *Ace Of Hearts AH 3*	5	14 wks
6 Apr 63	● **REMINISCING** *Coral LVA 9212*	2	31 wks
13 Jun 64	● **BUDDY HOLLY SHOWCASE** *Coral LVA 9222* . .	3	16 wks
26 Jun 65	**HOLLY IN THE HILLS** *Coral LVA 9227*	13	6 wks
15 Jul 67	● **BUDDY HOLLY'S GREATEST HITS**		
	Ace Of Hearts AH 148	9	40 wks
12 Apr 69	**GIANT** *MCA MUPS 371*	13	1 wk
21 Aug 71	**BUDDY HOLLY'S GREATEST HITS (re-issue)**		
	Coral CP 8	32	6 wks
12 Jul 75	**BUDDY HOLLY'S GREATEST HITS (2nd re-issue)**		
	Coral CDLM 8007	42	3 wks
11 Mar 78	★ **20 GOLDEN GREATS** *MCA EMTV 8*	1	20 wks
8 Sep 84	**GREATEST HITS (3rd re-issue)** *MCA MCL 1618* .	100	1 wk

See also The Crickets; Bobby Vee and the Crickets. Most albums feature the Crickets on at least some tracks.

John HOLT *Jamaica, male vocalist*   *2 wks*

1 Feb 75	**A THOUSAND VOLTS OF HOLT**		
	Trojan TRLS 75	42	2 wks

HOME *UK, male vocal/instrumental group*   *1 wk*

11 Nov 72	**DREAMER** *CBS 67522*	41	1 wk

HONEYDRIPPERS
UK/US, male vocal/instrumental group   *10 wks*

1 Dec 84	**THE HONEYDRIPPERS VOLUME 1**		
	Es Paranza 790220	56	10 wks

John Lee HOOKER *US, male vocalist*   *2 wks*

4 Feb 67	**HOUSE OF THE BLUES** *Marble Arch MAL 663* . . .	34	2 wks

Mary HOPKIN *UK, female vocalist*   *9 wks*

1 Mar 69	● **POSTCARD** *Apple SAPCOR 5*	3	9 wks

Bruce HORNSBY and the RANGE
US, male vocal/instrumental group   *26 wks*

13 Sep 86	**THE WAY IT IS** *RCA PL 88901*	16	26 wks

HORSLIPS *Ireland, male vocal/instrumental group*   *3 wks*

30 Apr 77	**THE BOOK OF INVASIONS – A CELTIC**		
	SYMPHONY *DJM DJF 20498*	39	3 wks

HOT CHOCOLATE
UK, male vocal/instrumental group   *111 wks*

15 Nov 75	**HOT CHOCOLATE** *RAK SRAK 516*	34	7 wks
7 Aug 76	**MAN TO MAN** *RAK SRAK 522*	32	7 wks
20 Nov 76	● **GREATEST HITS** *RAK SRAK 524*	6	35 wks
8 Apr 78	**EVERY 1'S A WINNER** *RAK SRAK 531*	30	8 wks
15 Dec 79	● **20 HOTTEST HITS** *RAK EMTV 22*	3	19 wks
25 Sep 82	**MYSTERY** *RAK SRAK 549*	24	7 wks
21 Feb 87	● **THE VERY BEST OF HOT CHOCOLATE**		
	RAK EMTV 42	3	28 wks

HOT RODS – *See EDDIE and the HOT RODS*

HOUSEMARTINS
UK, male vocal/instrumental group   *55 wks*

5 Jul 86	● **LONDON 0 HULL 4** *Go! Discs AGOLP 7*	3	41 wks
27 Dec 86	**HOUSEMARTINS' CHRISTMAS SINGLES BOX**		
	Go! Discs GOD 816	84	1 wk
3 Oct 87	● **THE PEOPLE WHO GRINNED THEMSELVES TO**		
	DEATH *Go! Discs AGOLP 9*	9†	13 wks

Whitney HOUSTON *US, female vocalist*   *130 wks*

14 Dec 85	● **WHITNEY HOUSTON** *Arista 206 978*	2	101 wks
13 Jun 87	★ **WHITNEY** *Arista 208 142*	1†	29 wks

Steve HOWE
UK, male vocalist/instrumentalist – guitar — *6 wks*

15 Nov 75	**BEGINNINGS** *Atlantic K 50151*	**22**	4 wks
24 Nov 79	**STEVE HOWE ALBUM** *Atlantic K 50621*	**68**	2 wks

HUDDERSFIELD CHORAL SOCIETY
UK, choir — *14 wks*

15 Mar 86	● **THE HYMNS ALBUM** *HMV EMTV 40*	**8**	10 wks
13 Dec 86	**THE CAROLS ALBUM** *EMI EMTV 43*	**29**	4 wks

HUE AND CRY *UK, male vocal/instrumental duo* — *4 wks*

7 Nov 87	**SEDUCED AND ABANDONED** *Circa CIRCA 2* .	**22**	4 wks

Alan HULL *UK, male vocalist* — *3 wks*

28 Jul 73	**PIPEDREAM** *Charisma CAS 1069*	**29**	3 wks

HUMAN LEAGUE
UK, male/female vocal/instrumental group — *160 wks*

31 May 80	**TRAVELOGUE** *Virgin V 2160*	**16**	42 wks
22 Aug 81	**REPRODUCTION** *Virgin V 2133*	**49**	23 wks
24 Oct 81	★ **DARE** *Virgin V 2192*	**1**	71 wks
19 May 84	● **HYSTERIA** *Virgin V 2315*	**3**	18 wks
20 Sept 86	● **CRASH** *Virgin V 2391*	**7**	6 wks

HUMBLE PIE *UK, male vocal/instrumental group* — *10 wks*

6 Sep 69	**AS SAFE AS YESTERDAY IS** *Immediate IMSP 025*	**32**	1 wk
22 Jan 72	**ROCKING AT THE FILLMORE** *A & M AMLH 63506*	**32**	2 wks
15 Apr 72	**SMOKIN'** *A & M AMLS 64342*	**28**	5 wks
7 Apr 73	**EAT IT** *A & M AMLS 6004*	**34**	2 wks

Engelbert HUMPERDINCK
UK, male vocalist — *233 wks*

20 May 67	● **RELEASE ME** *Decca SKL 4868*	**6**	58 wks
25 Nov 67	● **THE LAST WALTZ** *Decca SKL 4901*	**3**	33 wks
3 Aug 68	● **A MAN WITHOUT LOVE** *Decca SKL 4939*	**3**	45 wks
1 Mar 69	● **ENGELBERT** *Decca SKL 4985*	**3**	8 wks
6 Dec 69	● **ENGELBERT HUMPERDINCK** *Decca SKL 5030* ..	**5**	23 wks
11 Jul 70	**WE MADE IT HAPPEN** *Decca SKL 5054*	**17**	11 wks
18 Sep 71	**ANOTHER TIME, ANOTHER PLACE** *Decca SKL 5097*	**48**	1 wk
26 Feb 72	**LIVE AT THE RIVIERA LAS VEGAS** *Decca TXS 105*	**45**	1 wk
21 Dec 74	★ **ENGELBERT HUMPERDINCK – HIS GREATEST HITS** *Decca SKL 5198*	**1**	34 wks
4 May 85	**GETTING SENTIMENTAL** *Telstar STAR 2254* ...	**35**	10 wks
4 Apr 87	**THE ENGELBERT HUMPERDINCK COLLECTION** *Telstar STAR 2294*	**35**	9 wks

Ian HUNTER *UK, male vocalist* — *26 wks*

12 Apr 75	**IAN HUNTER** *CBS 80710*	**21**	15 wks
29 May 76	**ALL AMERICAN ALIEN BOY** *CBS 81310*	**29**	4 wks
5 May 79	**YOU'RE NEVER ALONE WITH A SCHIZOPHRENIC** *Chrysalis CHR 1214*	**49**	3 wks
26 Apr 80	**WELCOME TO THE CLUB** *Chrysalis CJT 6*	**61**	2 wks
29 Aug 81	**SHORT BACK AND SIDES** *Chrysalis CHR 1326* ..	**79**	2 wks

HURRAH! *UK, male vocal/instrumental group* — *1 wk*

28 Feb 87	**TELL GOD I'M HERE** *Kitchenware 208 201*	**71**	1 wk

HURRICANES – *See JOHNNY and the HURRICANES*

HÜSKER DÜ *US, male vocal/instrumental group* — *1 wk*

14 Feb 87	**WAREHOUSE: SONGS AND STORIES** *Warner Bros. 925 544–1*	**72**	1 wk

Phyllis HYMAN *US, female vocalist* — *1 wk*

20 Sep 86	**LIVING ALL ALONE** *Philadelphia International PHIL 4001*	**97**	1 wk

I

ICEHOUSE *Australia, male vocal/instrumental group* — *6 wks*

5 Mar 83	**LOVE IN MOTION** *Chrysalis CHR 1390*	**64**	6 wks

ICICLE WORKS
UK, male vocal/instrumental group — *15 wks*

31 Mar 84	**THE ICICLE WORKS** *Beggars Banquet BEGA 50* ...	**24**	6 wks
28 Sep 85	**THE SMALL PRICE OF A BICYCLE** *Beggars Banquet BEGA 61*	**55**	3 wks
1 Mar 86	**SEVEN SINGLES DEEP** *Beggars Banquet BEGA 71*	**52**	2 wks
21 Mar 87	**IF YOU WANT TO DEFEAT YOUR ENEMY SING HIS SONG** *Beggars Banquet BEGA 78*	**28**	4 wks

Billy IDOL *UK, male vocalist* — *58 wks*

8 Jun 85	● **VITAL IDOL** *Chrysalis CUX 1502*	**7**	27 wks
28 Sep 85	**REBEL YELL** *Chrysalis CHR 1450*	**36**	11 wks
1 Nov 86	● **WHIPLASH SMILE** *Chrysalis CDL 1514*	**8**	20 wks

Frank IFIELD *UK, male vocalist* — *83 wks*

16 Feb 63	● **I'LL REMEMBER YOU** *Columbia 33SX 1467*	**3**	36 wks
21 Sep 63	● **BORN FREE** *Columbia 33SX 1462*	**3**	32 wks
28 Mar 64	● **BLUE SKIES** *Columbia 55SX 1588*	**10**	12 wks
19 Dec 64	● **GREATEST HITS** *Columbia 33SX 1633*	**9**	3 wks

Julio IGLESIAS *Spain, male vocalist* — *82 wks*

7 Nov 81	**DE NINA A MUJER** *CBS 85063*	**43**	5 wks
28 Nov 81	● **BEGIN THE BEGUINE** *CBS 85462*	**5**	28 wks
16 Oct 82	**AMOR** *CBS 25103*	**14**	14 wks
2 Jul 83	● **JULIO** *CBS 10038*	**5**	17 wks
1 Sep 84	**1100 BEL AIR PLACE** *CBS 86308*	**14**	14 wks
19 Oct 85	**LIBRA** *CBS 26623*	**61**	4 wks

I-LEVEL *UK, male vocal/instrumental group* — *4 wks*

9 Jul 83	**I-LEVEL** *Virgin V 2270*	**50**	4 wks

IMAGINATION *UK, male vocal group* — *68 wks*

24 Oct 81	**BODY TALK** *R & B RBLP 1001*	**22**	11 wks
11 Sep 82	● **IN THE HEAT OF THE NIGHT** *R & B RBLP 1002*	**7**	29 wks

(Right) FRANK IFIELD studies the sixties line-up of Radio Luxembourg.

(Below) IRON MAIDEN line up in 1980, when their eponymous album gave them their first top five hit.

(Left) The ISLEY BROTHERS are shown in vintage sixties form.

GRACE JONES moves well in *any* costume.

(Left) JERMAINE JACKSON remembers the golden year of 1980, when he had a new chart entry and brother Michael didn't.

(Below) The JACKSONS are shown on their *Victory* tour, which never reached Britain.

14 May 83 ●	NIGHT DUBBING *R & B RBDUB 1*	9	20 wks
12 Nov 83	SCANDALOUS *R & B RBLP 1004*	25	8 wks

IMMACULATE FOOLS
UK, male vocal/instrumental group   *2 wks*

11 May 85	HEARTS OF FORTUNE *A & M AMA 5030*	65	2 wks

INCANTATION *UK, male instrumental group*   *55 wks*

11 Dec 82 ●	CACHARPAYA (PANPIPES OF THE ANDES)		
	Beggars Banquet BEGA 39	9	26 wks
17 Dec 83	DANCE OF THE FLAMES		
	Beggars Banquet BEGA 49	61	10 wks
28 Dec 85	BEST OF INCANTATION – MUSIC FROM THE		
	ANDES *West Five CODA 19*	28	19 wks

INCOGNITO *France, male instrumental group*   *8 wks*

18 Apr 81	JAZZ FUNK *Ensign ENVY 504*	28	8 wks

INCREDIBLE STRING BAND
UK, male/female vocal/instrumental group   *36 wks*

21 Oct 67	5,000 SPIRITS OR THE LAYERS OF THE ONION		
	Elektra EUKS 257	26	4 wks
6 Apr 68 ●	HANGMAN'S BEAUTIFUL DAUGHTER		
	Elektra EVKS7 258	5	21 wks
20 Jul 68	INCREDIBLE STRING BAND *Elektra EKL 254* ..	34	3 wks
24 Jan 70	CHANGING HORSES *Elektra EKS 74057*	30	1 wk
9 May 70	I LOOKED UP *Elektra 2469–002*	30	4 wks
31 Oct 70	U *Elektra 2665–001*	34	2 wks
30 Oct 71	LIQUID ACROBAT AS REGARDS THE AIR		
	Island ILPS 9172	46	1 wk

INFA RIOT *UK, male vocal/instrumental group*   *4 wks*

7 Aug 82	STILL OUT OF ORDER *Secret SEC 7*	42	4 wks

James INGRAM *US, male vocalist*   *19 wks*

31 Mar 84	IT'S YOUR NIGHT *Qwest 9239701*	25	17 wks
30 Aug 86	NEVER FELT SO GOOD *Qwest WX 44*	72	2 wks

INSPIRATIONAL CHOIR *US, male/female choir*   *4 wks*

18 Jan 86	SWEET INSPIRATION *Portrait PRT 10048*	59	4 wks

INTI ILLIMANI-GUAMARY
Chile, male vocal/instrumental group – panpipes   *7 wks*

17 Dec 83	THE FLIGHT OF THE CONDOR – ORIGINAL		
	TV SOUNDTRACK *BBC REB 440*	62	7 wks

INVISIBLE GIRLS – *See Pauline MURRAY and the INVISIBLE GIRLS*

INXS *Australia, male vocal/instrumental group*   *18 wks*

8 Feb 86	LISTEN LIKE THIEVES *Mercury MERH 82*	48	15 wks
28 Nov 87	KICK *Mercury MERH 114*	37	3 wks

IQ *UK, male vocal/instrumental group*   *1 wk*

22 Jun 85	THE WAKE *Sahara SAH 136*	72	1 wk

IRON MAIDEN
UK, male vocal/instrumental group   *113 wks*

26 Apr 80 ●	IRON MAIDEN *EMI EMC 3330*	4	15 wks
28 Feb 81	KILLERS *EMI EMC 3357*	12	8 wks
10 Apr 82 ★	THE NUMBER OF THE BEAST *EMI EMC 3400* .	1	31 wks
28 May 83 ●	PIECE OF MIND *EMI EMA 800*	3	18 wks
15 Sep 84 ●	POWERSLAVE *EMI POWER 1*	2	13 wks
15 Jun 85	IRON MAIDEN (re-issue) *Fame FA 41–3121–1*	71	2 wks
26 Oct 85 ●	LIVE AFTER DEATH *EMI RIP 1*	2	14 wks
11 Oct 86 ●	SOMEWHERE IN TIME *EMI EMC 3512*	3	11 wks
20 Jun 87	THE NUMBER OF THE BEAST (re-issue)		
	Fame FA 3178	98	1 wk

Gregory ISAACS *Jamaica, male vocalist*   *6 wks*

12 Sep 81	MORE GREGORY *Charisma PREX 9*	93	1 wk
4 Sep 82	NIGHT NURSE *Island ILPS 9721*	32	5 wks

ISLEY BROTHERS
US, male vocal/instrumental group   *14 wks*

14 Dec 68	THIS OLD HEART OF MINE		
	Tamla Motown STML 11034	23	6 wks
14 Aug 76	HARVEST FOR THE WORLD *Epic EPC 81268* ..	50	5 wks
14 May 77	GO FOR YOUR GUNS *Epic EPC 86027*	46	2 wks
24 Jun 78	SHOWDOWN *Epic EPC 86039*	50	1 wk

IT BITES *UK, male vocal/instrumental group*   *5 wks*

6 Sep 86	THE BIG LAD IN THE WINDMILL *Virgin V 2378*	35	5 wks

IT'S A BEAUTIFUL DAY
US, male/female vocal/instrumental group   *3 wks*

23 May 70	IT'S A BEAUTIFUL DAY *CBS 63722*	58	1 wk
18 Jul 70	MARRYING MAIDEN *CBS 66236*	45	2 wks

IT'S IMMATERIAL
UK, male vocal/instrumental group   *3 wks*

27 Sep 86	LIFE'S HARD AND THEN YOU DIE		
	Siren SIRENLP 4	62	3 wks

J

Freddie JACKSON *US, male vocalist*   *30 wks*

18 May 85	ROCK ME TONIGHT *Capitol EJ 2440316–1*	27	22 wks
8 Nov 86	JUST LIKE THE FIRST TIME *Capitol EST 2023* ..	30	8 wks

Janet JACKSON *US, female vocalist*   *79 wks*

5 Apr 86 ●	CONTROL *A & M AMA 5016*	8	72 wks
14 Nov 87	CONTROL – THE REMIXES *Breakout MIXLP 1* ..	20†	7 wks

Jermaine JACKSON *US, male vocalist*   *12 wks*

31 May 80	LET'S GET SERIOUS *Motown STML 12127*	22	6 wks
12 May 84	DYNAMITE *Arista 206 317*	57	6 wks

See also Jacksons.

Joe JACKSON   *UK, male vocalist*   *90 wks*

17 Mar 79		LOOK SHARP *A & M AMLH 64743*		40	11 wks
13 Oct 79		I'M THE MAN *A & M AMLH 64794*		12	16 wks
18 Oct 80		BEAT CRAZY *A & M AMLH 64837*		42	3 wks
4 Jul 81		JUMPIN' JIVE *A & M AMLH 68530*		14	14 wks
3 Jul 82	●	NIGHT AND DAY *A & M AMLH 64906*		3	27 wks
7 Apr 84		BODY & SOUL *A & M AMLX 65000*		14	14 wks
5 Apr 86		BIG WORLD *A & M JWA 3*		41	5 wks

Jumpin' Jive credited to Joe Jackson's Jumpin' Jive.

Michael JACKSON   *US, male vocalist*   *373 wks*

3 Jun 72		GOT TO BE THERE *Tamla Motown STML 11205*		37	5 wks
13 Jan 73		BEN *Tamla Motown STML 11220*		17	7 wks
29 Sep 79	●	OFF THE WALL *Epic EPC 83468*		5	160 wks
20 Jul 81		BEST OF *Motown STMR 9009*		11	18 wks
18 Jul 81		ONE DAY IN YOUR LIFE *Motown STML 12158*		29	8 wks
11 Dec 82	★	THRILLER *Epic EPC 85930*		1	139 wks
12 Feb 83		E.T. THE EXTRA TERRESTRIAL *MCA 7000*		82	4 wks
3 Dec 83		MICHAEL JACKSON 9 SINGLE PACK *Epic MJ1*		66	3 wks
9 Jun 84	●	FAREWELL MY SUMMER LOVE *Motown ZL 72227*		9	14 wks
12 Sep 87	★	BAD *Epic EPC 450 291–1*		1†	16 wks
26 Dec 87		THE MICHAEL JACKSON MIX *Stylus SMR 745*		81†	1 wk

See also the Jacksons; Michael Jackson and Diana Ross; Diana Ross/Michael Jackson/Gladys Knight/Stevie Wonder.

Michael JACKSON and Diana ROSS
US, male/female vocal duo   *9 wks*

31 Oct 87		LOVE SONGS *Telstar STAR 2298*		13†	9 wks

See also Michael Jackson; Diana Ross; the Jacksons; Diana Ross and Marvin Gaye; Diana Ross/Michael Jackson/Gladys Knight/Stevie Wonder; Diana Ross and the Supremes with the Temptations.

Millie JACKSON   *US, female vocalist*   *7 wks*

18 Feb 84		E.S.P. *Sire 250382*		59	5 wks
6 Apr 85		LIVE & UNCENSORED *Important TADLP 001*		81	2 wks

JACKSONS   *US, male vocal group*   *134 wks*

21 Mar 70		DIANA ROSS PRESENTS THE JACKSON FIVE *Tamla Motown STML*		16	4 wks
15 Aug 70		ABC *Tamla Motown STML 11153*		22	6 wks
7 Oct 72		GREATEST HITS *Tamla Motown STML 11212*		26	14 wks
18 Nov 72		LOOKIN' THROUGH THE WINDOWS *Tamla Motown STML 11214*		16	8 wks
16 Jul 77		THE JACKSONS *Epic EPC 86009*		54	1 wk
3 Dec 77		GOIN' PLACES *Epic EPC 86035*		45	1 wk
5 May 79		DESTINY *Epic EPC 83200*		33	7 wks
11 Oct 80		TRIUMPH *Epic EPC 86112*		13	16 wks
12 Dec 81		THE JACKSONS *Epic EPC 88562*		53	9 wks
9 Jul 83	★	18 GREATEST HITS *Telstar STAR 2232*		1	55 wks
21 Jul 84	●	VICTORY *Epic EPC 86303*		3	13 wks

First four albums credited to Jackson Five. 18 Greatest Hits, credited to Michael Jackson plus the Jackson Five, contains hits by both acts. All other albums credited to the Jacksons. Jermaine Jackson appeared on the first four albums. See also Michael Jackson; Jermaine Jackson; Diana Ross/Michael Jackson/Gladys Knight/Stevie Wonder; Michael Jackson and Diana Ross.

Mick JAGGER   *UK, male vocalist*   *16 wks*

16 Mar 85	●	SHE'S THE BOSS *CBS 86310*		6	11 wks
26 Sep 87		PRIMITIVE COOL *CBS 460 123–1*		26	5 wks

JAM   *UK, male vocal/instrumental group*   *148 wks*

28 May 77		IN THE CITY *Polydor 2383 447*		20	18 wks
26 Nov 77		THIS IS THE MODERN WORLD *Polydor 2383 475*		22	5 wks
11 Nov 78	●	ALL MOD CONS *Polydor POLD 5008*		6	17 wks
24 Nov 79	●	SETTING SONS *Polydor POLD 5028*		4	19 wks
6 Dec 80	●	SOUND AFFECTS *Polydor POLD 5035*		2	19 wks
20 Mar 82	★	THE GIFT *Polydor POLD 5055*		1	24 wks
18 Dec 82	●	DIG THE NEW BREED *Polydor POLD 5075*		2	15 wks
27 Aug 83		IN THE CITY (re-issue) *Polydor SPELP 27*		100	1 wk
22 Oct 83	●	SNAP *Polydor SNAP 1*		2	30 wks

JAMES   *UK, male vocal/instrumental group*   *2 wks*

2 Aug 86		STUTTER *blanco y negro JIMLP 1*		68	2 wks

Rick JAMES   *US, male vocalist*   *2 wks*

24 Jul 82		THROWIN' DOWN *Motown STML 12167*		93	2 wks

JAN and DEAN   *US, male vocal duo*   *2 wks*

12 Jul 80		THE JAN AND DEAN STORY *K-Tel NE 1084*		67	2 wks

JAPAN   *UK, male vocal/instrumental group*   *136 wks*

9 Feb 80		QUIET LIFE *Ariola Hansa AHAL 8011*		53	8 wks
15 Nov 80		GENTLEMEN TAKE POLAROIDS *Virgin V 2180*		45	10 wks
26 Sep 81		ASSEMBLAGE *Hansa HANLP 1*		26	46 wks
28 Nov 81		TIN DRUM *Virgin V 2209*		12	50 wks
18 Jun 83	●	OIL ON CANVAS *Virgin VD 2513*		5	14 wks
8 Dec 84		EXORCISING GHOSTS *Virgin VGD 3510*		45	8 wks

Jeff JARRATT and Don REEDMAN
UK, male producers   *8 wks*

22 Nov 80		MASTERWORKS *K-Tel ONE 1093*		39	8 wks

Jean-Michel JARRE
France, male instrumentalist/producer   *176 wks*

20 Aug 77	●	OXYGENE *Polydor 2310 555*		2	24 wks
16 Dec 78		EQUINOXE *Polydor POLD 5007*		11	26 wks
6 Jun 81	●	MAGNETIC FIELDS *Polydor POLS 1033*		6	17 wks
15 May 82	●	THE CONCERTS IN CHINA *Polydor PODV 3*		6	17 wks
12 Nov 83		THE ESSENTIAL JEAN MICHEL JARRE *Polystar PROLP 3*		14	29 wks
24 Nov 84		ZOOLOOK *Dreyfus POLH 15*		47	14 wks
12 Apr 86	●	RENDEZ-VOUS *Dreyfus POLH 27*		9	37 wks
18 Jul 87		IN CONCERT LYON/HOUSTON *Dreyfus POLH 36*		18	12 wks

Al JARREAU   *US, male vocalist*   *37 wks*

5 Sep 81		BREAKING AWAY *Warner Bros. K 56917*		60	8 wks
30 Apr 83		JARREAU *WEA International U 0070*		39	18 wks
17 Nov 84		HIGH CRIME *WEA 250807*		81	1 wk
13 Sep 86		L IS FOR LOVER *WEA International 253 080–1*		45	10 wks

JEFFERSON AIRPLANE
US, female/male vocal/instrumental group   *10 wks*

28 Jun 69		BLESS ITS POINTED LITTLE HEAD *RCA SF 8019*		38	1 wk
7 Mar 70		VOLUNTEERS *RCA SF 8076*		34	7 wks
2 Oct 71		BARK *Grunt FTR 1001*		42	1 wk
2 Sep 72		LONG JOHN SILVER *Grunt FTR 1007*		30	1 wk

See also Jefferson Starship; Starship.

JEFFERSON STARSHIP
US, female/male vocal/instrumental group   *13 wks*

31 Jul 76	**SPITFIRE** *Grunt RFL 1557*	**30**	2 wks
9 Feb 80	**FREEDOM AT POINT ZERO** *Grunt FL 13452* ...	**22**	11 wks

See also Jefferson Airplane; Starship.

JELLYBEAN   *US, male instrumentalist – producer*   *7 wks*

31 Oct 87	**JUST VISITING THIS PLANET** *Chrysalis CHR 1569*	**58†**	7 wks

JESUS AND MARY CHAIN
UK, male vocal/instrumental group   *17 wks*

30 Nov 85	**PSYCHOCANDY** *blanco y negro BYN 7*	**31**	10 wks
12 Sep 87	● **DARKLANDS** *blanco y negro BYN 11*	**5**	7 wks

JETHRO TULL   *UK, male vocal/instrumental group*   *217 wks*

2 Nov 68	● **THIS WAS** *Island ILPS 9085*	**10**	22 wks
9 Aug 69	★ **STAND UP** *Island ILPS 9103*	**1**	29 wks
9 May 70	● **BENEFIT** *Island ILPS 9123*	**3**	13 wks
3 Apr 71	● **AQUALUNG** *Island ILPS 9145*	**4**	21 wks
18 Mar 72	● **THICK AS A BRICK** *Chrysalis CHR 1003*	**5**	14 wks
15 Jul 72	● **LIVING IN THE PAST** *Chrysalis CJT 1*	**8**	11 wks
28 Jul 73	**A PASSION PLAY** *Chrysalis CHR 1040*	**13**	8 wks
2 Nov 74	**WAR CHILD** *Chrysalis CHR 1067*	**14**	4 wks
27 Sep 75	**MINSTREL IN THE GALLERY** *Chrysalis CHR 1082*	**20**	6 wks
31 Jan 76	**M.U. THE BEST OF JETHRO TULL** *Chrysalis CHR 1078*	**44**	5 wks
15 May 76	**TOO OLD TO ROCK 'N' ROLL TOO YOUNG TO DIE** *Chrysalis CHR 1111*	**25**	10 wks
19 Feb 77	**SONGS FROM THE WOOD** *Chrysalis CHR 1132* .	**13**	12 wks
29 Apr 78	**HEAVY HORSES** *Chrysalis CHR 1175*	**20**	10 wks
14 Oct 78	**LIVE BURSTING OUT** *Chrysalis CJT 4*	**17**	8 wks
6 Oct 79	**STORMWATCH** *Chrysalis CDL 1238*	**27**	4 wks
6 Sep 80	**A** *Chrysalis CDL 1301*	**25**	5 wks
17 Apr 82	**BROADSWORD AND THE BEAST** *Chrysalis CDL 1380*	**27**	19 wks
15 Sep 84	**UNDER WRAPS** *Chrysalis CDL 1461*	**18**	5 wks
2 Nov 85	**ORIGINAL MASTERS** *Chrysalis JTTV 1*	**63**	3 wks
19 Sep 87	**CREST OF A KNAVE** *Chrysalis CDL 1590*	**19**	8 wks

JETS   *UK, male vocal/instrumental group*   *6 wks*

10 Apr 82	**100 PERCENT COTTON** *EMI EMC 3399*	**30**	6 wks

JETS   *US, male/female vocal/instrumental group*   *4 wks*

11 Apr 87	**CRUSH ON YOU** *MCA MCF 3312*	**57**	4 wks

Joan JETT and the BLACKHEARTS
US, female/male vocal/instrumental group   *7 wks*

8 May 82	**I LOVE ROCK 'N' ROLL** *Epic EPC 85686*	**25**	7 wks

JO BOXERS   *UK, male vocal/instrumental group*   *5 wks*

24 Sep 83	**LIKE GANGBUSTERS** *RCA BOXXLP 1*	**18**	5 wks

Billy JOEL   *US, male vocalist*   *264 wks*

25 Mar 78	**THE STRANGER** *CBS 82311*	**25**	40 wks
25 Nov 78	● **52ND STREET** *CBS 83181*	**10**	43 wks
22 Mar 80	● **GLASS HOUSES** *CBS 86108*	**9**	24 wks
10 Oct 81	**SONGS IN THE ATTIC** *CBS 85273*	**57**	3 wks
2 Oct 82	**NYLON CURTAIN** *CBS 85959*	**27**	8 wks
10 Sep 83	● **AN INNOCENT MAN** *CBS 25554*	**2**	94 wks
4 Feb 84	**COLD SPRING HARBOUR** *CBS 32400*	**95**	1 wk
23 Jun 84	**PIANO MAN** *CBS 32007*	**98**	1 wk
20 Jul 85	● **GREATEST HITS VOLUME I & VOLUME II** *CBS 88666*	**7**	39 wks
16 Aug 86	**THE BRIDGE** *CBS 86323*	**38**	10 wks
28 Nov 87	**KOHYEPT – LIVE IN LENINGRAD** *CBS 460 407-1*	**92**	1 wk

Elton JOHN
UK, male vocalist/instrumentalist – piano   *597 wks*

23 May 70	**ELTON JOHN** *DJM DJLPS 406*	**11**	14 wks
16 Jan 71	● **TUMBLEWEED CONNECTION** *DJM DJLPS 410*	**6**	20 wks
1 May 71	**THE ELTON JOHN LIVE ALBUM 17-11-70** *DJM DJLPS 414*	**20**	2 wks
20 May 72	**MADMAN ACROSS THE WATER** *DJM DJLPH 420*	**41**	2 wks
3 Jun 72	● **HONKY CHATEAU** *DJM DJLPH 423*	**2**	23 wks
10 Feb 73	★ **DON'T SHOOT ME I'M ONLY THE PIANO PLAYER** *DJM DJLPH 427*	**1**	42 wks
3 Nov 73	★ **GOODBYE YELLOW BRICK ROAD** *DJM DJLPO 1001*	**1**	84 wks
13 Jul 74	★ **CARIBOU** *DJM DJLPH 439*	**1**	18 wks
23 Nov 74	★ **ELTON JOHN'S GREATEST HITS** *DJM DJLPH 442*	**1**	84 wks
7 Jun 75	● **CAPTAIN FANTASTIC AND THE BROWN DIRT COWBOY** *DJM DJLPX 1*	**2**	24 wks
8 Nov 75	● **ROCK OF THE WESTIES** *DJM DJLPH 464*	**5**	12 wks
15 May 76	● **HERE AND THERE** *DJM DJLPH 473*	**6**	9 wks
6 Nov 76	● **BLUE MOVES** *Rocket ROSP 1*	**3**	15 wks
15 Oct 77	● **GREATEST HITS VOL. 2** *DJM DJH 20520* .	**6**	24 wks
4 Nov 78	● **A SINGLE MAN** *Rocket TRAIN 1*	**8**	26 wks
20 Oct 79	**VICTIM OF LOVE** *Rocket HISPD 125*	**41**	3 wks
8 Mar 80	**LADY SAMANTHA** *DJM 22085*	**56**	2 wks
31 May 80	**21 AT 33** *Rocket HISPD 126*	**12**	13 wks
25 Oct 80	**THE VERY BEST OF ELTON JOHN** *K-Tel NE 1094*	**24**	13 wks
30 May 81	**THE FOX** *Rocket TRAIN 16*	**12**	12 wks
17 Apr 82	**JUMP UP** *Rocket HISPD 127*	**13**	12 wks
6 Nov 82	**LOVE SONGS** *TV Records TVA 3*	**39**	13 wks
11 Jun 83	● **TOO LOW FOR ZERO** *Rocket HIS PD 24*	**7**	73 wks
30 Jun 84	● **BREAKING HEARTS** *Rocket HISPD 25*	**2**	23 wks
16 Nov 85	● **ICE ON FIRE** *Rocket HISPD 26*	**3**	23 wks
15 Nov 86	**LEATHER JACKETS** *Rocket EJLP 1*	**24**	9 wks
12 Sep 87	**LIVE IN AUSTRALIA** *Rocket EJBXL 1*	**70**	2 wks

Live In Australia credits Elton John and the Melbourne Symphony Orchestra.

JOHNNY and the HURRICANES
US, male instrumental group   *5 wks*

3 Dec 60	**STORMSVILLE** *London HAI 2269*	**18**	1 wk
1 Apr 61	**BIG SOUND OF JOHNNY AND THE HURRICANES** *London HAK 2322*	**14**	4 wks

Linton Kwesi JOHNSON   *Jamaica, male poet*   *8 wks*

30 Jun 79	**FORCE OF VICTORY** *Island ILPS 9566*	**66**	1 wk
31 Oct 80	**BASS CULTURE** *Island ILPS 9605*	**46**	5 wks
10 Mar 84	**MAKING HISTORY** *Island ILPS 9770*	**73**	2 wks

Paul JOHNSON *UK, male vocalist*   *2 wks*

4 Jul 87		**PAUL JOHNSON** *CBS 450 640–1*	63	2 wks

Al JOLSON *US, male vocalist*   *11 wks*

14 Mar 81		**20 GOLDEN GREATS** *MCA MCTV 4*	18	7 wks
17 Dec 83		**THE AL JOLSON COLLECTION**		
		Ronco RON LP 5	67	4 wks

JON and VANGELIS *UK, male vocalist and Greece,*
male instrumentalist – keyboards   *53 wks*

26 Jan 80	●	**SHORT STORIES** *Polydor POLD 5030*	4	11 wks
11 Jul 81	●	**THE FRIENDS OF MR. CAIRO**		
		Polydor POLD 5039	6	23 wks
2 Jul 83		**PRIVATE COLLECTION** *Polydor POLH 4*	22	10 wks
11 Aug 84		**THE BEST OF JON AND VANGELIS**		
		Polydor POLH 6	42	9 wks

See also Jon Anderson; Vangelis.

JONES – *See SMITH and JONES*

Aled JONES *UK, male chorister*   *43 wks*

22 Feb 86		**WHERE E'ER YOU WALK** *10 DIX 21*	36	6 wks
12 Jul 86		**PIE JESU** *10 AJ 2*	25	16 wks
29 Nov 86		**AN ALBUM OF HYMNS** *Telstar STAR 2272*	18	11 wks
14 Mar 87		**ALED (MUSIC FROM THE TV SERIES)** *10 AJ 3*	52	6 wks
5 Dec 87		**THE BEST OF ALED JONES** *10 AJ 5*	59	4 wks

See also Aled Jones with the BBC Welsh Chorus.

Aled JONES with the BBC WELSH CHORUS
UK, male chorister with chorus   *96 wks*

27 Apr 85	●	**VOICES FROM THE HOLY LAND**		
		BBC REC 564	6	43 wks
29 Jun 85	●	**ALL THROUGH THE NIGHT** *BBC REH 569* ...	3	43 wks
23 Nov 85		**ALED JONES WITH THE BBC WELSH CHORUS**		
		10/BBC AJ 1	11	10 wks

All Through The Night *credits the BBC Welsh Symphony Orchestra and was conducted by Robin Stapleton. Both other albums were conducted by John Hugh Thomas. See also Aled Jones.*

Glenn JONES *US, male vocalist*   *1 wk*

31 Oct 87		**GLENN JONES** *Jive HIP 51*	62	1 wk

Grace JONES *US, female vocalist*   *80 wks*

30 Aug 80		**WARM LEATHERETTE** *Island ILPS 9592*	45	2 wks
23 May 81		**NIGHTCLUBBING** *Island ILPS 9624*	35	16 wks
20 Nov 82		**LIVING MY LIFE** *Island ILPS 9722*	15	22 wks
9 Nov 85		**SLAVE TO THE RHYTHM**		
		ZTT/Island GRACE 1	12	8 wks
14 Dec 85	●	**ISLAND LIFE** *Island GJ 1*	4	30 wks
29 Nov 86		**INSIDE STORY** *Manhattan MTL 1007*	61	2 wks

Howard JONES *UK, male vocalist*   *119 wks*

17 Mar 84	★	**HUMAN'S LIB** *WEA WX 1*	1	57 wks
8 Dec 84		**THE 12″ ALBUM** *WEA WX 14*	15	33 wks
23 Mar 85	●	**DREAM INTO ACTION** *WEA WX 15*	2	25 wks
25 Oct 86	●	**ONE TO ONE** *WEA WX 68*	10	4 wks

Jack JONES *US, male vocalist*   *70 wks*

29 Apr 72	●	**A SONG FOR YOU** *RCA Victor SF 8228*	9	6 wks
3 Jun 72	●	**BREAD WINNERS** *RCA Victor SF 8280*	7	36 wks
7 Apr 73	●	**TOGETHER** *RCA Victor SF 8342*	8	10 wks
23 Feb 74	●	**HARBOUR** *RCA Victor APLI 0408*	10	5 wks
19 Feb 77		**THE FULL LIFE** *RCA Victor PL 12067*	41	5 wks
21 May 77		**ALL TO YOURSELF** *RCA TVL 2*	10	8 wks

Quincy JONES
US, male arranger/instrumentalist – keyboards   *29 wks*

18 Apr 81		**THE DUDE** *A & M AMLK 63721*	19	25 wks
20 Mar 82		**THE BEST** *A & M AMLH 68542*	41	4 wks

Rickie Lee JONES *US, female vocalist*   *37 wks*

16 Jun 79		**RICKIE LEE JONES** *Warner Bros. K 56628*	18	19 wks
8 Aug 81		**PIRATES** *Warner Bros. K 56816*	37	11 wks
2 Jul 83		**GIRL AT HER VOLCANO** *Warner Bros. 92–3805–1*	51	3 wks
13 Oct 84		**THE MAGAZINE** *Warner Bros. 925117*	40	4 wks

Tammy JONES *UK, female vocalist*   *5 wks*

12 Jul 75		**LET ME TRY AGAIN** *Epic EPC 80853*	38	5 wks

Tom JONES *UK, male vocalist*   *404 wks*

5 Jun 65		**ALONG CAME JONES** *Decca LK 6693*	11	5 wks
8 Oct 66		**FROM THE HEART** *Decca LK 4814*	23	8 wks
8 Apr 67	●	**GREEN GREEN GRASS OF HOME**		
		Decca SKL 4855	3	49 wks
24 Jun 67	●	**LIVE AT THE TALK OF THE TOWN**		
		Decca SKL 4874	6	90 wks
30 Dec 67	●	**13 SMASH HITS** *Decca SKL 4909*	5	49 wks
27 Jul 68	★	**DELILAH** *Decca SKL 4946*	1	29 wks
21 Dec 68	●	**HELP YOURSELF** *Decca SKL 4982*	4	9 wks
28 Jun 69	●	**THIS IS TOM JONES** *Decca SKL 5007*	2	20 wks
15 Nov 69	●	**TOM JONES LIVE IN LAS VEGAS**		
		Decca SKL 5032	3	45 wks
25 Apr 70	●	**TOM** *Decca SKL 5045*	4	18 wks
14 Nov 70	●	**I WHO HAVE NOTHING** *Decca SKL 5072*	10	10 wks
29 May 71	●	**SHE'S A LADY** *Decca SKL 5089*	9	7 wks
27 Nov 71		**LIVE AT CAESAR'S PALACE** *Decca 1/1–1/2* ...	27	5 wks
24 Jun 72		**CLOSE UP** *Decca SKL 5132*	17	4 wks
23 Jun 73		**THE BODY AND SOUL OF TOM JONES**		
		Decca SKL 5162	31	1 wk
5 Jan 74		**GREATEST HITS** *Decca SKL 5162*	15	13 wks
22 Mar 75	★	**20 GREATEST HITS** *Decca TJD 1/11/2*	1	21 wks
7 Oct 78		**I'M COMING HOME** *Lotus WH 5001*	12	9 wks
16 May 87		**THE GREATEST HITS** *Telstar STAR 2296*	16	12 wks

Janis JOPLIN *US, female vocalist*   *7 wks*

17 Apr 71		**PEARL** *CBS 64188*	50	1 wk
22 Jul 72		**JANIS JOPLIN IN CONCERT** *CBS 67241*	30	6 wks

JOURNEY *US, male vocal/instrumental group*   *30 wks*

20 Mar 82		**ESCAPE** *CBS 85138*	32	16 wks
19 Feb 83	●	**FRONTIERS** *CBS 25361*	6	8 wks
6 Aug 83		**EVOLUTION** *CBS 32342*	100	1 wk
24 May 86		**RAISED ON RADIO** *CBS 26902*	22	5 wks

JOY DIVISION *UK, male vocal/instrumental group*   *21 wks*

26 Jul 80	●	**CLOSER** *Factory FACT 25*	6	8 wks
30 Aug 80	●	**UNKNOWN PLEASURES** *Factory FACT 10*	71	1 wk
17 Oct 81	●	**STILL** *Factory FACT 40*	5	12 wks

JUDAS PRIEST *UK, male vocal/instrumental group* **70 wks**

14 May 77	**SIN AFTER SIN** *CBS 82008*	**23** 6 wks
25 Feb 78	**STAINED GLASS** *CBS 82430*	**27** 5 wks
11 Nov 78	**KILLING MACHINE** *CBS 83135*	**32** 9 wks
6 Oct 79	● **UNLEASHED IN THE EAST** *CBS 83852*	**10** 8 wks
19 Apr 80	● **BRITISH STEEL** *CBS 84160*	**4** 17 wks
7 Mar 81	**POINT OF ENTRY** *CBS 84834*	**14** 5 wks
17 Jul 82	**SCREAMING FOR VENGEANCE** *CBS 85941* ...	**11** 9 wks
28 Jan 84	**DEFENDERS OF THE FAITH** *CBS 25713*	**19** 5 wks
19 Apr 86	**TURBO** *CBS 26641*	**52** 4 wks
13 Jun 87	**PRIEST LIVE** *CBS 450 639-1*	**47** 2 wks

JUDGE DREAD *UK, male vocalist* **14 wks**

6 Dec 75	**BEDTIME STORIES** *Cactus CTLP 113*	**26** 12 wks
7 Mar 81	**40 BIG ONES** *Creole BIG 1*	**51** 2 wks

JUICY LUCY *UK, male vocal/instrumental group* **5 wks**

18 Apr 70	**JUICY LUCY** *Vertigo VO 2*	**41** 4 wks
21 Nov 70	**LIE BACK AND ENJOY IT** *Vertigo 6360 014*	**53** 1 wk

JULUKA
South Africa, male/female vocal/instrumental group **3 wks**

23 Jul 83	**SCATTERLINGS** *Safari SHAKA 1*	**50** 3 wks

JUNIOR *UK, male vocalist* **14 wks**

5 Jun 82	**JI** *Mercury/Phonogram MERS 3*	**28** 14 wks

K

Bert KAEMPFERT *Germany, orchestra* **104 wks**

5 Mar 66	● **BYE BYE BLUES** *Polydor BM 84086*	**4** 22 wks
16 Apr 66	**BEST OF BERT KAEMPFERT** *Polydor 84-012*	**27** 1 wk
28 May 66	**SWINGING SAFARI** *Polydor LPHM 46-384* ...	**20** 15 wks
30 Jul 66	**STRANGERS IN THE NIGHT** *Polydor LPHM 84-053*	**13** 26 wks
4 Feb 67	**RELAXING SOUND OF BERT KAEMPFERT** *Polydor 583-501*	**33** 3 wks
18 Feb 67	**BERT KAEMPFERT – BEST SELLER** *Polydor 583-551*	**25** 18 wks
29 Apr 67	**HOLD ME** *Polydor 184-072*	**36** 5 wks
26 Aug 67	**KAEMPFERT SPECIAL** *Polydor 236-207* ...	**24** 5 wks
19 Jun 71	**ORANGE COLOURED SKY** *Polydor 2310-091*	**49** 1 wk
5 Jul 80	**SOUNDS SENSATIONAL** *Polydor POLTB 10* ...	**17** 8 wks

KAJAGOOGOO *UK, male vocal/instrumental group* **23 wks**

30 Apr 83	● **WHITE FEATHERS** *EMI EMC 3433*	**5** 20 wks
26 May 84	**ISLANDS** *EMI KAJA 1*	**35** 3 wks

Nick KAMEN *UK, male vocalist* **7 wks**

18 Apr 87	**NICK KAMEN** *WEA WX 84*	**34** 7 wks

KANE GANG *UK, male vocal/instrumental group* **12 wks**

23 Feb 85	**THE BAD AND LOWDOWN WORLD OF THE KANE GANG** *Kitchenware KWLP 2*	**21** 8 wks
8 Aug 87	**MIRACLE** *Kitchenware KWLP 7*	**41** 4 wks

Mick KARN *UK, male vocalist/instrumentalist – bass* **4 wks**

20 Nov 82	**TITLES** *Virgin V 2249*	**74** 3 wks
28 Feb 87	**DREAMS OF REASON PRODUCE MONSTERS** *Virgin V 2389*	**89** 1 wk

KATRINA and the WAVES
UK/US, male/female vocal/instrumental group **7 wks**

8 Jun 85	**KATRINA AND THE WAVES** *Capitol KTW 1* ...	**28** 6 wks
10 May 86	**WAVES** *Capitol EST 2010*	**70** 1 wk

K.C. and the SUNSHINE BAND
US, male vocal/instrumental group **17 wks**

30 Aug 75	**K.C. AND THE SUNSHINE BAND** *Jayboy JSL 9* .	**26** 7 wks
1 Mar 80	● **GREATEST HITS** *TK TKR 83385*	**10** 6 wks
27 Aug 83	**ALL IN A NIGHT'S WORK** *Epic EPC 85847*	**46** 4 wks

KEEL *US, male vocal/instrumental group* **2 wks**

17 May 86	**THE FINAL FRONTIER** *Vertigo VERH 33*	**83** 2 wks

Howard KEEL *US, male vocalist* **31 wks**

14 Apr 84	● **AND I LOVE YOU SO** *Warwick WW 5137*	**6** 19 wks
9 Nov 85	**REMINISCING – THE HOWARD KEEL COLLECTION** *Telstar STAR 2259*	**20** 12 wks

Felicity KENDAL *UK, female exercise instructor* **47 wks**

19 Jun 82	**SHAPE UP AND DANCE (VOL 1) WITH FELICITY KENDAL** *Lifestyle LEG 1*	**29** 47 wks

Nigel KENNEDY/LONDON PHILHARMONIC ORCHESTRA *UK, male instrumentalist/orchestra* **1 wk**

1 Mar 86	**ELGAR VIOLIN CONCERTO** *EMI EMX 4120581*	**97** 1 wk

The orchestra was conducted by Vernon Handley. See also London Philharmonic Orchestra.

KENNY *UK, male vocal/instrumental group* **1 wk**

17 Jan 76	**THE SOUND OF SUPER K** *RAK SRAK 518*	**56** 1 wk

Gerard KENNY *US, male vocalist* **4 wks**

21 Jul 79	**MADE IT THROUGH THE RAIN** *RCA Victor PL 25218*	**19** 4 wks

Nik KERSHAW *UK, male vocalist* **100 wks**

10 Mar 84	● **HUMAN RACING** *MCA MCF 3197*	**5** 61 wks
1 Dec 84	● **THE RIDDLE** *RCA MCF 3245*	**8** 36 wks
8 Nov 86	**RADIO MUSICOLA** *MCA MCG 6016*	**47** 3 wks

Chaka KHAN *US, female vocalist* **24 wks**

20 Oct 84	**I FEEL FOR YOU** *Warner Bros. 925 162*	**15** 22 wks
9 Aug 86	**DESTINY** *Warner Bros. WX 45*	**77** 2 wks

See also Rufus and Chaka Khan.

Aram KHATCHATURIAN/VIENNA PHILMARMONIC ORCHESTRA
Russia, male conductor/Austria, orchestra **15 wks**

22 Jan 72	**SPARTACUS** *Decca SXL 6000*	**16** 15 wks

(Below) KATHY KIRBY based her hit on the TV show that launched her.

(Above) Lead singer James Taylor of KOOL AND THE GANG, who have now spent more weeks on chart than the solo artist James Taylor.

(Right) The KINKS scored four Top Ten LPs in two years at the height of the Mod era.

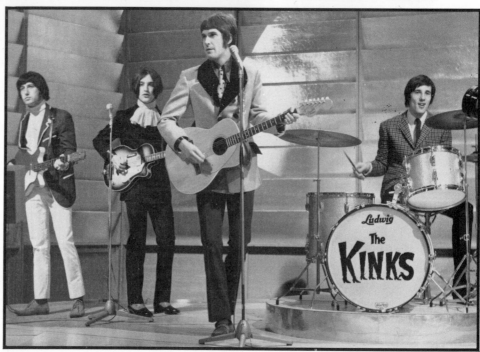

KIDS FROM FAME
US, male/female vocal/instrumental group — *117 wks*

24 Jul 82	★ KIDS FROM FAME *BBC REP 447*	**1**	45 wks
16 Oct 82	● KIDS FROM FAME AGAIN *RCA RCALP 6057* ...	**2**	21 wks
26 Feb 83	● THE KIDS FROM FAME LIVE *BBC KIDLP 003* ..	**8**	28 wks
14 May 83	THE KIDS FROM FAME SONGS *BBC KIDLP 004*	**14**	16 wks
20 Aug 83	SING FOR YOU *BBC KIDLP 005*	**28**	7 wks

KILLING JOKE
UK, male vocal/instrumental group — *29 wks*

25 Oct 80	KILLING JOKE *Polydor EGMD 545*	**39**	4 wks
20 Jun 81	WHAT'S THIS FOR *Malicious Damage EG MD 550*	**42**	4 wks
8 May 82	REVELATIONS *Malicious Damage EGMD 3*	**12**	6 wks
27 Nov 82	'HA' – KILLING JOKE LIVE *EG EGMDT 4*	**66**	2 wks
23 Jul 83	FIRE DANCES *EG EGMD 5*	**29**	3 wks
9 Mar 85	NIGHT TIME *EG EGLP 61*	**11**	9 wks
22 Nov 86	BRIGHTER THAN A THOUSAND SUNS *EG EGLP 66*	**54**	1 wk

KIM – *See MEL and KIM*

KIMERA with the LONDON SYMPHONY ORCHESTRA
Korea, female vocalist with UK, orchestra — *4 wks*

26 Oct 85	HITS ON OPERA *Stylus SMR 8505*	**38**	4 wks

See also London Symphony Orchestra; Michael Crawford; Julian Lloyd Webber; Cyril Ornadel, all with the London Symphony Orchestra; Spike Milligan.

KING
UK, male vocal/instrumental group — *32 wks*

9 Feb 85	● STEPS IN TIME *CBS 26095*	**6**	21 wks
23 Nov 85	BITTER SWEET *CBS 86320*	**16**	11 wks

B.B. KING
US, male vocalist/instrumentalist – guitar — *5 wks*

25 Aug 79	TAKE IT HOME *MCA MCF 3010*	**60**	5 wks

Ben E. KING
UK, male vocalist — *11 wks*

1 Jul 67	SPANISH HARLEM *Atlantic 590–001*	**30**	3 wks
14 Mar 87	STAND BY ME (THE ULTIMATE COLLECTION) *Atlantic WX 90*	**14**	8 wks

Stand By Me features tracks by the Drifters. See also the Drifters.

Carole KING
US, female vocalist/instrumentalist – piano — *102 wks*

24 Jul 71	● TAPESTRY *A & M AMLS 2025*	**4**	90 wks
15 Jan 72	MUSIC *A & M AMLH 67013*	**18**	10 wks
2 Dec 72	RHYMES AND REASONS *Ode 77016*	**40**	2 wks

Evelyn KING
US, female vocalist — *9 wks*

11 Sep 82	GET LOOSE *RCA RCALP 3093*	**35**	9 wks

Mark KING
UK, male vocalist/instrumentalist – bass — *2 wks*

21 Jul 84	INFLUENCES *Polydor MKLP 1*	**77**	2 wks

Solomon KING
US, male vocalist — *1 wk*

22 Jun 68	SHE WEARS MY RING *Columbia SCX 6250*	**40**	1 wk

KING CRIMSON
UK, male vocal/instrumental group — *53 wks*

1 Nov 69	● IN THE COURT OF THE CRIMSON KING *Island ILPS 9111*	**5**	18 wks
30 May 70	● IN THE WAKE OF POSEIDON *Island ILPS 9127* .	**4**	13 wks
16 Jan 71	LIZARD *Island ILPS 9141*	**30**	1 wk
8 Jan 72	ISLANDS *Island ILPS 9175*	**30**	1 wk
7 Apr 73	LARKS' TONGUES IN ASPIC *Island ILPS 9230*	**20**	4 wks
13 Apr 74	STARLESS AND BIBLE BLACK *Island ILPS 9275*	**28**	2 wks
26 Oct 74	RED *Island ILPS 9308*	**45**	1 wk
10 Oct 81	DISCIPLINE *EG EGLP 49*	**41**	4 wks
26 Jun 82	BEAT *EG EGLP 51*	**39**	5 wks
31 Mar 84	THREE OF A PERFECT PAIR *EG EGLP 55*	**30**	4 wks

KING KURT
UK, male vocal/instrumental group — *5 wks*

10 Dec 83	OOH WALLAH WALLAH *Stiff SEEZ 52*	**99**	1 wk
8 Mar 86	BIG COCK *Stiff SEEZ 62*	**50**	4 wks

The Choir of KING'S COLLEGE, CAMBRIDGE
UK, choir — *3 wks*

11 Dec 71	THE WORLD OF CHRISTMAS *Argo SPAA 104* .	**38**	3 wks

KINGS OF SWING ORCHESTRA
Australia, orchestra — *11 wks*

29 May 82	SWITCHED ON SWING *K-Tel ONE 1166*	**28**	11 wks

KINKS
UK, male vocal/instrumental group — *118 wks*

17 Oct 64	● KINKS *Pye NPL 18096*	**3**	25 wks
13 Mar 65	● KINDA KINKS *Pye NPL 18112*	**3**	15 wks
4 Dec 65	● KINKS KONTROVERSY *Pye NPL 18131*	**9**	12 wks
11 Sep 66	● WELL RESPECTED KINKS *Marble Arch MAL 612* .	**5**	31 wks
5 Nov 66	FACE TO FACE *Pye NPL 18149*	**12**	11 wks
14 Oct 67	SOMETHING ELSE *Pye NSPL 18193*	**35**	2 wks
2 Dec 67	● SUNNY AFTERNOON *Marble Arch MAL 716*	**9**	11 wks
23 Oct 71	GOLDEN HOUR OF THE KINKS *Golden Hour GH 501*	**21**	4 wks
14 Oct 78	20 GOLDEN GREATS *Ronco RPL 2031*	**19**	6 wks
5 Nov 83	KINKS GREATEST HITS – DEAD END STREET *PRT KINK 1*	**96**	1 wk

Kathy KIRBY
UK, female vocalist — *8 wks*

4 Jan 64	16 HITS FROM STARS AND GARTERS *Decca LK 5475*	**11**	8 wks

KISS
US, male vocal/instrumental group — *52 wks*

29 May 76	DESTROYER *Casablanca CBSP 4008*	**22**	5 wks
25 Jun 76	ALIVE! *Casablanca CBSP 401*	**49**	2 wks
17 Dec 77	ALIVE *Casablanca CALD 5004*	**60**	1 wk
7 Jul 79	DYNASTY *Casablanca CALH 2051*	**50**	6 wks
28 Jun 80	UNMASKED *Mercury 6302 032*	**48**	3 wks
5 Dec 81	THE ELDER *Casablanca 6302 163*	**51**	3 wks
26 Jun 82	KILLERS *Casablanca CANL 1*	**42**	6 wks
6 Nov 82	CREATURES OF THE NIGHT *Casablanca CANL 4*	**22**	4 wks
8 Oct 83	● LICK IT UP *Vertigo VERL 9*	**7**	7 wks
6 Oct 84	ANIMALISE *Vertigo VERL 18*	**11**	4 wks
5 Oct 85	ASYLUM *Vertigo VERH 32*	**12**	3 wks
7 Nov 87	● CRAZY NIGHTS *Vertigo VERH 49*	**4†**	8 wks

KISSING THE PINK
UK, male/female vocal/instrumental group — *5 wks*

4 Jun 83	NAKED *Magnet KTPL 1001*	**54**	5 wks

Eartha KITT *US, female vocalist*   *1 wk*

11 Feb 61	**REVISITED** *London HA 2296*	17	1 wk

KLEEER *US, male vocal/instrumental group*   *1 wk*

6 Jul 85	**SEEEKRET** *Atlantic 78–1254–1*	96	1 wk

Earl KLUGH – *See George BENSON and Earl KLUGH*

KNACK *US, male vocal/instrumental group*   *2 wks*

4 Aug 79	**GET THE KNACK** *Capitol EST 11948*	65	2 wks

Curtis KNIGHT – *See Jimi HENDRIX and Curtis KNIGHT*

Gladys KNIGHT and the PIPS
US, female vocalist/male vocal backing group   *94 wks*

31 May 75	**I FEEL A SONG** *Buddah BDLP 4030*	20	15 wks
28 Feb 76	● **THE BEST OF GLADYS KNIGHT & THE PIPS** *Buddah BDLH 5013*	6	43 wks
16 Jul 77	**STILL TOGETHER** *Buddah BDLH 5014*	42	3 wks
12 Nov 77	● **30 GREATEST** *K-Tel NE 1004*	3	22 wks
4 Oct 80	**A TOUCH OF LOVE** *K-Tel NE 1090*	16	6 wks
4 Feb 84	**THE COLLECTION – 20 GREATEST HITS** *Starblend NITE 1*	43	5 wks

See also Diana Ross/Michael Jackson/Gladys Knight/Stevie Wonder.

KNIGHTSBRIDGE STRINGS
UK, male orchestra   *1 wk*

25 Jun 60	**STRING SWAY** *Top Rank BUY 017*	20	1 wk

David KNOPFLER
UK, male vocalist/instrumentalist – guitar   *1 wk*

19 Nov 83	**RELEASE** *Peach River DAVID 1*	82	1 wk

Mark KNOPFLER
UK, male vocalist/instrumentalist – guitar   *14 wks*

16 Apr 83	**LOCAL HERO** *Vertigo VERL 4*	14	11 wks
20 Oct 84	**CAL – MUSIC FROM THE FILM** *Vertigo VERH 17*	65	3 wks

John KONGOS
South Africa, male vocalist/multi-instrumentalist   *2 wks*

15 Jan 72	**KONGOS** *Fly HIFLY 7*	29	2 wks

KOOL AND THE GANG
US, male vocal/instrumental group   *101 wks*

21 Nov 81	● **SOMETHING SPECIAL** *De-Lite DSR 001*	10	20 wks
2 Oct 82	**AS ONE** *De-Lite DSR 3*	49	10 wks
7 May 83	● **TWICE AS KOOL** *De-Lite PROLP 2*	4	23 wks
14 Jan 84	**IN THE HEART** *De-Lite DSR 4*	18	23 wks
15 Dec 84	**EMERGENCY** *De-Lite DSR 6*	47	25 wks

KORGIS *UK, male vocal/instrumental duo*   *4 wks*

26 Jul 80	**DUMB WAITERS** *Rialto TENOR 104*	40	4 wks

KRAFTWERK
Germany, male vocal/instrumental group   *65 wks*

17 May 75	● **AUTOBAHN** *Vertigo 6360 620*	4	18 wks
20 May 78	● **THE MAN-MACHINE** *Capitol EST 11728*	9	13 wks
23 May 81	**COMPUTER WORLD** *EMI EMC 3370*	15	22 wks
6 Feb 82	**TRANS-EUROPE EXPRESS** *Capitol EST 11603* .	49	7 wks
22 Jun 85	**AUTOBAHN (re-issue)** *Parlophone AUTO 1*	61	3 wks
15 Nov 86	**ELECTRIC CAFE** *EMI EMD 1001*	58	2 wks

Billy J. KRAMER and the DAKOTAS
UK, male vocalist, male instrumental backing group   *17 wks*

16 Nov 63	**LISTEN TO BILLY J. KRAMER** *Parlophone PMC 1209*	11	17 wks

Kris KRISTOFFERSON and Rita COOLIDGE
US, male/female vocal duo   *4 wks*

6 May 78	**NATURAL ACT** *A & M AMLH 64690*	35	4 wks

See also Rita Coolidge.

KROKUS
Switzerland/Malta, male vocal/instrumental group   *11 wks*

21 Feb 81	**HARDWARE** *Ariola ARL 5064*	44	4 wks
20 Feb 82	**ONE VICE AT A TIME** *Arista SPART 1189*	28	5 wks
16 Apr 83	**HEADHUNTER** *Arista 205 255*	74	2 wks

Charlie KUNZ *US, male instrumentalist – piano*   *11 wks*

14 Jun 69	● **THE WORLD OF CHARLIE KUNZ** *Decca SPA 15*	9	11 wks

L

Patti LaBELLE *US, female vocalist*   *17 wks*

24 May 86	**WINNER IN YOU** *MCA MCF 3319*	30	17 wks

LADYSMITH BLACK MAMBAZO
South Africa, male vocal group   *11 wks*

11 Apr 87	**SHAKA ZULU** *Warner Bros. WX 94*	36	11 wks

Cleo LAINE *UK, female vocalist*   *1 wk*

2 Dec 78	**CLEO** *Arcade ADEP 37*	68	1 wk

See also Cleo Laine and John Williams; Cleo Laine and James Galway.

Cleo LAINE and James GALWAY
UK, female vocalist and male instrumentalist – flute   *14 wks*

31 May 80	**SOMETIMES WHEN WE TOUCH** *RCA PL 25296*	15	14 wks

See also Cleo Laine; Cleo Laine and John Williams; James Galway; James Galway and the Chief-tains; James Galway and Henry Mancini.

(Left) Though the album charts began after FRANKIE LAINE's peak singles success, he still managed two Top Ten LPs.

(Below) MARIO LANZA's 1951 film *The Great Caruso* reportedly grossed five million dollars, a tremendous amount at the time.

(Left) Second only to Elvis Presley for Most Hit Albums, JAMES LAST is still active and charting in his later middle age.

Cleo LAINE and John WILLIAMS
UK, female vocalist/male instrumentalist – guitar   *22 wks*

7 Jan 78	**BEST OF FRIENDS** *RCA RS 1094*	**18**	22 wks

See also Cleo Laine; Cleo Laine and James Galway; John Williams; John Williams with the English Chamber Orchestra.

Frankie LAINE   *US, male vocalist*   *29 wks*

24 Jun 61	● **HELL BENT FOR LEATHER** *Philips BBL 7468* ..	**7**	23 wks
24 Sep 77	● **THE VERY BEST OF FRANKIE LAINE** *Warwick PR 5032*	**7**	6 wks

Greg LAKE   *UK, male vocalist*   *3 wks*

17 Oct 81	**GREG LAKE** *Chrysalis CHR 1357*	**62**	3 wks

See also Emerson, Lake and Palmer; Emerson, Lake and Powell.

Annabel LAMB   *UK, female vocalist*   *1 wk*

28 Apr 84	**THE FLAME** *A & M AMLX 68564*	**84**	1 wk

LAMBRETTAS   *UK, male vocal/instrumental group*   *8 wks*

5 Jul 80	**BEAT BOYS IN THE JET AGE** *Rocket TRAIN 10*	**28**	8 wks

LANDSCAPE   *UK, male vocal/instrumental group*   *12 wks*

21 Mar 81	**FROM THE TEAROOMS** *RCA RCALP 5003*	**16**	12 wks

Ronnie LANE and the Band SLIM CHANCE
UK, male vocal/instrumental group   *1 wk*

17 Aug 74	**ANYMORE FOR ANYMORE** *GM GML 1013* ...	**48**	1 wk

See also Pete Townshend and Ronnie Lane.

Mario LANZA   *US, male vocalist*   *55 wks*

6 Dec 58	● **THE STUDENT PRINCE/THE GREAT CARUSO** *RCA RB 16113*	**4**	21 wks
23 Jul 60	● **THE GREAT CARUSO** *RCA RB 16112*	**3**	15 wks
9 Jan 71	**HIS GREATEST HITS VOL. 1** *RCA LSB 4000* ...	**39**	1 wk
5 Sep 81	**THE LEGEND OF MARIO LANZA** *K-Tel NE 1110*	**29**	11 wks
14 Nov 87	**A PORTRAIT OF MARIO LANZA** *Stylus SMR 741* **49†**		7 wks

The Great Caruso side of the first album is a film soundtrack.

James LAST   *Germany, male orchestra leader*   *370 wks*

15 Apr 67	● **THIS IS JAMES LAST** *Polydor 104–678*	**6**	48 wks
22 Jul 67	**HAMMOND A-GO-GO** *Polydor 249–043*	**27**	10 wks
26 Aug 67	**NON-STOP DANCING** *Polydor 236–203*	**35**	1 wk
26 Aug 67	**LOVE THIS IS MY SONG** *Polydor 583–553*	**32**	2 wks
22 Jun 68	**JAMES LAST GOES POP** *Polydor 249–160*	**32**	3 wks
8 Feb 69	**DANCING '68 VOL. 1** *Polydor 249–216*	**40**	1 wk
31 May 69	**TRUMPET A-GO-GO** *Polydor 249–239*	**13**	1 wk
9 Aug 69	**NON-STOP DANCING '69** *Polydor 249–294*	**26**	1 wk
24 Jan 70	**NON-STOP DANCING '69/2** *Polydor 249/354*	**27**	3 wks
23 May 70	**NON-STOP EVERGREENS** *Polydor 249–370*	**26**	1 wk
11 Jul 70	**CLASSICS UP TO DATE** *Polydor 249–370*	**44**	1 wk
11 Jul 70	**NON-STOP DANCING '70** *Polydor 2371–04*	**67**	1 wk
24 Oct 70	**VERY BEST OF JAMES LAST** *Polydor 2371–054* ..	**45**	4 wks
8 May 71	**NON-STOP DANCING '71** *Polydor 2371–111*	**21**	4 wks
26 Jun 71	**SUMMER HAPPENING** *Polydor 2371–133*	**38**	1 wk
18 Sep 71	**BEACH PARTY 2** *Polydor 2371–211*	**47**	1 wk
2 Oct 71	**YESTERDAY'S MEMORIES** *Contour 2870–117* ...	**17**	14 wks
16 Oct 71	**NON-STOP DANCING 12** *Polydor 2371–141*	**30**	3 wks
19 Feb 72	**NON-STOP DANCING 13** *Polydor 2371–189*	**32**	2 wks
4 Mar 72	**POLKA PARTY** *Polydor 2371–190*	**22**	3 wks
29 Apr 72	**JAMES LAST IN CONCERT** *Polydor 2371–191* ...	**13**	6 wks
24 Jun 72	**VOODOO PARTY** *Polydor 2371–235*	**45**	1 wk
16 Sep 72	**CLASSICS UP TO DATE VOL. 2** *Polydor 184–061*	**49**	1 wk
30 Sep 72	**LOVE MUST BE THE REASON** *Polydor 2371–281* .	**32**	2 wks
27 Jan 73	**THE MUSIC OF JAMES LAST** *Polydor 2683 010* ..	**19**	12 wks
24 Feb 73	**JAMES LAST IN RUSSIA** *Polydor 2371 293*	**12**	9 wks
24 Feb 73	**NON-STOP DANCING VOL. 14** *Polydor 2371–319* ..	**27**	3 wks
28 Jul 73	**OLE** *Polydor 2371 384*	**24**	5 wks
1 Sep 73	**NON-STOP DANCING VOL. 15** *Polydor 2371–376* ..	**34**	2 wks
20 Apr 74	**NON-STOP DANCING VOL. 16** *Polydor 2371–444* ..	**43**	2 wks
29 Jun 74	**IN CONCERT VOL. 2** *Polydor 2371–320*	**49**	1 wk
23 Nov 74	**GOLDEN MEMORIES** *Polydor 2371–472*	**39**	2 wks
26 Jul 75	● **TEN YEARS NON-STOP JUBILEE** *Polydor 2660–111*	**5**	16 wks
2 Aug 75	**VIOLINS IN LOVE** *K-Tel /*	**60**	1 wk
22 Nov 75	● **MAKE THE PARTY LAST** *Polydor 2371–612*	**3**	19 wks
8 May 76	**CLASSICS UP TO DATE VOL. 3** *2371–538*	**54**	1 wk
6 May 78	**EAST TO WEST** *Polydor 2630–092*	**49**	4 wks
14 Apr 79	● **LAST THE WHOLE NIGHT LONG** *Polydor PTD 5008*	**2**	45 wks
23 Aug 80	**THE BEST FROM 150 GOLD** *Polydor 2681 211* ..	**56**	3 wks
1 Nov 80	**CLASSICS FOR DREAMING** *Polydor POLTV 11* ..	**12**	18 wks
14 Feb 81	**ROSES FROM THE SOUTH** *Polydor 2372 051* ..	**41**	5 wks
21 Nov 81	**HANSIMANIA** *Polydor POLTV 14*	**18**	13 wks
28 Nov 81	**LAST FOREVER** *Polydor 2630 135*	**88**	2 wks
5 Mar 83	**BLUEBIRD** *Polydor POLD 5072*	**57**	3 wks
30 Apr 83	**THE BEST OF MY GOLD RECORDS** *Polydor PODV 7*	**42**	5 wks
30 Apr 83	**NON-STOP DANCING '83 – PARTY POWER** *Polydor POLD 5094*	**56**	2 wks
3 Dec 83	**THE GREATEST SONGS OF THE BEATLES** *Polydor POLD 5119*	**52**	8 wks
13 Oct 84	**PARADISE** *Polydor POLD 5163*	**74**	2 wks
8 Dec 84	**JAMES LAST IN SCOTLAND** *Polydor POLD 5166*	**68**	9 wks
24 Mar 84	**THE ROSE OF TRALEE AND OTHER IRISH FAVOURITES** *Polydor POLD 5131*	**21**	11 wks
14 Sep 85	● **LEAVE THE BEST TO LAST** *Polydor PROLP 7* ..	**10**	41 wks
18 Apr 87	**BY REQUEST** *Polydor POLH 34*	**22**	11 wks

LATIN QUARTER
UK, male/female vocal/instrumental group   *3 wks*

1 Mar 86	**MODERN TIMES** *Rockin' Horse RHLP 1*	**91**	2 wks
6 Jun 87	**MICK AND CAROLINE** *Rockin' Horse 208 142*	**96**	1 wk

Cyndi LAUPER   *US, female vocalist*   *43 wks*

18 Feb 84	**SHE'S SO UNUSUAL** *Portrait PRT 25792*	**16**	31 wks
11 Oct 86	**TRUE COLORS** *Portrait PRT 26948*	**25**	12 wks

LAUREL and HARDY   *UK/US, male comic duo*   *4 wks*

6 Dec 75	**THE GOLDEN AGE OF HOLLYWOOD COMEDY** *United Artists UAG 29676*	**55**	4 wks

Syd LAWRENCE   *UK, orchestra*   *9 wks*

8 Aug 70	**MORE MILLER AND OTHER BIG BAND MAGIC** *Philips 6642 001*	**14**	4 wks
25 Dec 71	**SYD LAWRENCE WITH THE GLENN MILLER SOUND** *Fontana SFL 13178*	**31**	2 wks
25 Dec 71	**MUSIC OF GLENN MILLER IN SUPER STEREO** *Philips 6641–017*	**43**	2 wks
26 Feb 72	**SOMETHING OLD, SOMETHING NEW** *Philips 6308 090*	**34**	1 wk

LED ZEPPELIN are tied with Abba for most consecutive number ones. In this performance photo Jimmy Page is framed by Robert Plant.

JULIAN LENNON made his album chart debut twenty-one years after his father's Beatle breakthrough.

Ronnie LAWS
US, male vocalist/instrumentalist – saxophone   *1 wk*

17 Oct 81	**SOLID GROUND**	*Liberty LBG 30336*	**100**	1 wk

LEAGUE UNLIMITED ORCHESTRA
UK, male instrumental group   *52 wks*

17 Jul 82	● **LOVE AND DANCING**	*Virgin OVED 6*	**3**	52 wks

This album is an instrumental version of previously recorded Human League songs re-mixed by UK producer Martin Rushent.

LED ZEPPELIN
UK, male vocal/instrumental group   *411 wks*

12 Apr 69	● **LED ZEPPELIN** *Atlantic 588–171*		**6**	79 wks
8 Nov 69	★ **LED ZEPPELIN 2** *Atlantic 588–198*		**1**	138 wks
7 Nov 70	★ **LED ZEPPELIN 3** *Atlantic 2401–002*		**1**	40 wks
27 Nov 71	★ **FOUR SYMBOLS** *Atlantic 2401–012*		**1**	62 wks
14 Apr 73	★ **HOUSES OF THE HOLY** *Atlantic K 50014*		**1**	13 wks
15 Mar 75	★ **PHYSICAL GRAFFITI** *Swan Song SSK 89400*		**1**	27 wks
24 Apr 76	★ **PRESENCE** *Swan Song SSK 59402*		**1**	14 wks
6 Nov 76	★ **THE SONG REMAINS THE SAME**			
	Swan Song SSK 89402		**1**	15 wks
8 Sep 79	★ **IN THROUGH THE OUT DOOR**			
	Swan Song SSK 59410		**1**	16 wks
4 Dec 82	● **CODA** *Swan Song A 0051*		**4**	7 wks

Led Zeppelin 2 changed label/number to Atlantic K 40037, Four Symbols changed to Atlantic K 50008 during their runs. The fourth Led Zeppelin album appeared in the chart under various guises: The Fourth Led Zeppelin Album, Runes, The New Led Zeppelin Album, Led Zeppelin 4 and Four Symbols.

LEE – *See PETERS and LEE*

Brenda LEE   *US, female vocalist*   *57 wks*

24 Nov 62	**ALL THE WAY** *Brunswick LAT 8383*		**20**	2 wks
16 Feb 63	**BRENDA – THAT'S ALL** *Brunswick LAT 8516*		**13**	9 wks
13 Apr 63	● **ALL ALONE AM I** *Brunswick LAT 8530*		**8**	20 wks
16 Jul 66	**BYE BYE BLUES** *Brunswick LAT 8649*		**21**	2 wks
1 Nov 80	**LITTLE MISS DYNAMITE** *Warwick WW 5083*		**15**	11 wks
7 Jan 84	**25TH ANNIVERSARY** *MCA MALD 609*		**65**	4 wks
30 Mar 85	**THE VERY BEST OF BRENDA LEE**			
	MCA LETV 1		**16**	9 wks

Peggy LEE   *US, female vocalist*   *17 wks*

4 Jun 60	● **LATIN A LA LEE** *Capitol T 1290*		**8**	15 wks
20 May 61	**BEST OF PEGGY LEE VOL. 2**			
	Brunswick LAT 8355		**18**	1 wk
21 Oct 61	**BLACK COFFEE** *Ace of Hearts AH 5*		**20**	1 wk

See also Peggy Lee and George Shearing.

Peggy LEE and George SHEARING
US, female vocalist and UK, male instrumentalist – piano   *6 wks*

11 Jun 60	**BEAUTY AND THE BEAT** *Capitol T 1219*		**16**	6 wks

See also Peggy Lee; Nat King Cole and the George Shearing Quintet.

Raymond LEFEVRE   *France, orchestra*   *9 wks*

7 Oct 67	● **RAYMOND LEFEVRE** *Major Minor MMLP 4*		**10**	7 wks
17 Feb 68	**RAYMOND LEFEVRE VOL. 2**			
	Major Minor SMLP 13		**37**	2 wks

Tom LEHRER   *US, male comic vocalist*   *26 wks*

8 Nov 58	● **SONGS BY TOM LEHRER** *Decca LF 1311*		**7**	19 wks
25 Jun 60	● **AN EVENING WASTED WITH TOM LEHRER**			
	Decca LK 4332		**7**	7 wks

John LENNON   *UK, male vocalist*   *291 wks*

16 Jan 71	**JOHN LENNON AND THE PLASTIC ONO BAND**			
	Apple PCS 7124		**11**	11 wks
30 Oct 71	★ **IMAGINE** *Apple PAS 10004*		**1**	101 wks
14 Oct 72	**SOMETIME IN NEW YORK CITY**			
	Apple PCSP 716		**11**	6 wks
8 Dec 73	**MIND GAMES** *Apple PCS 7165*		**13**	12 wks
19 Oct 74	● **WALLS AND BRIDGES** *Apple PCTC 253*		**6**	10 wks
8 Mar 75	● **ROCK 'N' ROLL** *Apple PCS 7169*		**6**	28 wks
8 Nov 75	● **SHAVED FISH** *Apple PCS 7173*		**8**	29 wks
22 Nov 80	★ **DOUBLE FANTASY** *Geffen K 99131*		**1**	36 wks
20 Nov 82	★ **THE JOHN LENNON COLLECTION**			
	Parlophone EMTV 37		**1**	42 wks
4 Feb 84	● **MILK AND HONEY** *Polydor POLH 5*		**3**	13 wks
8 Mar 86	**LIVE IN NEW YORK CITY** *Parlophone PCS 7031*		**55**	3 wks

Imagine changed its label credit to Parlophone PAS 10004 between its initial chart run and later runs. John Lennon and the Plastic Ono Band is credited to John Lennon and the Plastic Ono Band. Imagine is credited to John Lennon and the Plastic Ono Band with the Flux Fiddlers. Sometime In New York City is credited to John and Yoko Lennon with the Plastic Ono Band and Elephant's Memory. Double Fantasy and Milk And Honey are credited to John Lennon and Yoko Ono. Shaved Fish and The John Lennon Collection are compilations and so have various credits. See also Yoko Ono.

Julian LENNON   *UK, male vocalist*   *16 wks*

3 Nov 84	**VALOTTE** *Charisma JLLP 1*		**20**	15 wks
5 Apr 86	**THE SECRET VALUE OF DAYDREAMING**			
	Charisma CAS 1171		**93**	1 wk

Deke LEONARD
UK, male vocalist/instrumentalist – guitar   *1 wk*

13 Apr 74	**KAMIKAZE** *United Artists UAG 29544*		**50**	1 wk

Paul LEONI   *UK, male instrumentalist – pan flute*   *19 wks*

24 Sep 83	**FLIGHTS OF FANCY** *Nouveau Music NML 1002*		**17**	19 wks

LEVEL 42   *UK, male vocal/instrumental group*   *178 wks*

29 Aug 81	**LEVEL 42** *Polydor POLS 1036*		**20**	18 wks
10 Apr 82	**THE EARLY TAPES JULY–AUGUST 1980**			
	Polydor POLS 1064		**46**	6 wks
18 Sep 82	**THE PURSUIT OF ACCIDENTS**			
	Polydor POLD 5067		**17**	16 wks
3 Sep 83	● **STANDING IN THE LIGHT** *Polydor POLD 5110*		**9**	13 wks
13 Oct 84	**TRUE COLOURS** *Polydor POLH 10*		**14**	8 wks
6 Jul 85	**A PHYSICAL PRESENCE** *Polydor POLH 23*		**28**	5 wks
26 Oct 85	● **WORLD MACHINE** *Polydor POLH 25*		**3**	72 wks
28 Mar 87	● **RUNNING IN THE FAMILY** *Polydor POLH 42*		**2†**	40 wks

LEVERT   *UK, male vocal group*   *1 wk*

29 Aug 87	**THE BIG THROWDOWN** *Atlantic 781773–1*		**86**	1 wk

Huey LEWIS and the NEWS
US, male vocal/instrumental group   *76 wks*

14 Sep 85	**SPORTS** *Chrysalis CHR 1412*		**23**	24 wks
20 Sep 86	**FORE!** *Chrysalis CDL 1534*		**8**	52 wks

Jerry Lee LEWIS
US, male vocalist/instrumentalist – piano   *6 wks*

| 2 Jun 62 | **JERRY LEE LEWIS VOL. 2** *London HA 2440* ..... | **14** | 6 wks |

Linda LEWIS   *UK, female vocalist*   *4 wks*

| 9 Aug 75 | **NOT A LITTLE GIRL ANYMORE** *Arista ARTY 109* .... | **40** | 4 wks |

Ramsey LEWIS TRIO
US, male vocal instrumental trio   *4 wks*

| 21 May 66 | **HANG ON RAMSEY** *Chess CRL 4520* .... | **20** | 4 wks |

LIGHT OF THE WORLD
UK, male vocal/instrumental group   *1 wk*

| 24 Jan 81 | **ROUND TRIP** *Ensign ENVY 14* .... | **73** | 1 wk |

Gordon LIGHTFOOT   *Canada, male vocalist*   *2 wks*

| 20 May 72 | **DON QUIXOTE** *Reprise K 44166* ...... | **44** | 1 wk |
| 17 Aug 74 | **SUNDOWN** *Reprise K 54020* .... | **45** | 1 wk |

LIMAHL   *UK, male vocalist*   *3 wks*

| 1 Dec 84 | **DON'T SUPPOSE** *EMI PLML 1* .... | **63** | 3 wks |

LINDISFARNE   *UK, male vocal/instrumental group*   *119 wks*

30 Oct 71	★ **FOG ON THE TYNE** *Charisma CAS 1050*	**1**	56 wks
15 Jan 72	● **NICELY OUT OF TUNE** *Charisma CAS 1025* ...	**8**	30 wks
30 Sep 72	● **DINGLY DELL** *Charisma CAS 1057*	**5**	10 wks
11 Aug 73	**LINDISFARNE LIVE** *Charisma CLASS 2*	**25**	6 wks
18 Oct 75	**FINEST HOUR** *Charisma CAS 1108*	**55**	1 wk
24 Jun 78	**BACK AND FOURTH** *Mercury 9109 609*	**22**	11 wks
9 Dec 78	**MAGIC IN THE AIR** *Mercury 6641 877*	**71**	1 wk
23 Oct 82	**SLEEPLESS NIGHT** *LMP GET 1*	**59**	4 wks

LINX   *UK, male vocal/instrumental group*   *23 wks*

| 28 Mar 81 | ● **INTUITION** *Chrysalis CHR 1332* .... | **8** | 19 wks |
| 31 Oct 81 | **GO AHEAD** *Chrysalis CHR 1358* .... | **35** | 4 wks |

LIQUID GOLD
UK, male/female vocal instrumental group   *3 wks*

| 16 Aug 80 | **LIQUID GOLD** *Polo POLP 101* .... | **34** | 3 wks |

LISA – *See WENDY and LISA*

LISA LISA and CULT JAM with FULL FORCE
US female vocalist with two US male vocal/instrumental groups   *1 wk*

| 21 Sep 85 | **LISA LISA AND CULT JAM WITH FULL FORCE** *CBS 26593* .... | **96** | 1 wk |

LITTLE FEAT   *US, male vocal/instrumental group*   *19 wks*

| 6 Dec 75 | **THE LAST RECORD ALBUM** *Warner Bros. K 56156* .... | **36** | 3 wks |

21 May 77	● **TIME LOVES A HERO** *Warner Bros. K 56349*	**8**	11 wks
11 Mar 78	**WAITING FOR COLUMBUS** *Warner Bros. K 66075*	**43**	1 wk
1 Dec 79	**DOWN ON THE FARM** *Warner Bros. K 56667*	**46**	3 wks
8 Aug 81	**HOY HOY** *Warner Bros. K 666100*	**76**	1 wk

LITTLE STEVEN
US, male vocalist/instrumentalist – guitar   *4 wks*

| 6 Nov 82 | **MEN WITHOUT WOMEN** *EMI America 3027* .... | **73** | 2 wks |
| 6 Jun 87 | **FREEDOM NO COMPROMISE** *Manhattan MTL 1010* .... | **52** | 2 wks |

First album credited to Little Steven and the Disciples of Soul.

LIVING IN A BOX   *UK, male vocal/instrumental group*   *19 wks*

| 9 May 87 | **LIVING IN A BOX** *Chrysalis CDL 1547* .... | **25** | 19 wks |

LL COOL J   *US, male rapper*   *20 wks*

| 15 Feb 86 | **RADIO** *Def Jam DEF 26745* .... | **71** | 1 wk |
| 13 Jun 87 | **BIGGER AND DEFFER** *Def Jam 450 515–1* ...... | **54** | 19 wks |

Andrew LLOYD WEBBER
UK, male composer/producer   *37 wks*

| 11 Feb 78 | ● **VARIATIONS** *MCA MCF 2824* .... | **2** | 19 wks |
| 23 Mar 85 | ● **REQUIEM** *HMV ALW 1* .... | **4** | 18 wks |

Variations features cellist Julian Lloyd Webber. Requiem credits Placido Domingo, Sarah Brightman, Paul Miles-Kingston, Winchester Cathedral Choir and the English Chamber Orchestra conducted by Lorin Maazel.

Julian LLOYD WEBBER and the LONDON SYMPHONY ORCHESTRA
UK, male instrumentalist – cello with UK, orchestra   *6 wks*

| 14 Sep 85 | **PIECES** *Polydor PROLP 6* .... | **59** | 5 wks |
| 21 Feb 87 | **ELGAR CELLO CONCERTO** *Philips 416 354–1* .. | **94** | 1 wk |

See also the London Symphony Orchestra; Michael Crawford; Kimera; Cyril Ornadel, all with the London Symphony Orchestra; Andrew Lloyd Webber; Spike Milligan.

Los LOBOS   *US, male vocal/instrumental group*   *9 wks*

| 6 Apr 85 | **HOW WILL THE WOLF SURVIVE?** *Slash SLMP 3* .... | **77** | 6 wks |
| 7 Feb 87 | **BY THE LIGHT OF THE MOON** *Slash/London SLAP 13* .... | **77** | 3 wks |

Josef LOCKE   *Ireland, male vocalist*   *1 wk*

| 28 Jun 69 | **THE WORLD OF JOSEF LOCKE TODAY** *Decca SPA 21* .... | **29** | 1 wk |

John LODGE
UK, male vocalist/instrumentalist – guitar   *2 wks*

| 19 Feb 77 | **NATURAL AVENUE** *Decca TXS 120* .... | **38** | 2 wks |

See also Justin Hayward and John Lodge.

Nils LOFGREN
US, male vocalist/instrumentalist – guitar   *29 wks*

| 17 Apr 76 | ● **CRY TOUGH** *A & M AMLH 64573* .... | **8** | 11 wks |
| 26 Mar 77 | **I CAME TO DANCE** *A & M AMLH 64628* | **30** | 4 wks |

5 Nov 77	**NIGHT AFTER NIGHT** *A & M AMLH AMLM*		38	2 wks
26 Sep 81	**NIGHT FADES AWAY** *Backstreet MCF 3121*		50	3 wks
1 May 82	**A RHYTHM ROMANCE** *A & M AMLH 68543*		100	1 wk
6 Jul 85	**FLIP** *Towerbell TOWLP 11*		36	7 wks
5 Apr 86	**CODE OF THE ROAD** *Towerbell TOWDLP 17*		86	1 wk

Johnny LOGAN *Australia, male vocalist* — 1 wk

22 Aug 87	**HOLD ME NOW** *CBS 451 073–1*		83	1 wk

LONDON PHILHARMONIC CHOIR
UK, choir — 17 wks

3 Dec 60	● **THE MESSIAH** *Pye Golden Guinea GGL 0062*		10	7 wks
13 Nov 76	● **SOUND OF GLORY** *Arcade ADEP 25*		10	10 wks

The Messiah credits the London Orchestra conducted by Walter Susskind. Sound Of Glory credits the National Philharmonic Orchestra and conductor John Aldiss.

LONDON PHILHARMONIC ORCHESTRA
UK, orchestra — 5 wks

23 Apr 60	**RAVEL'S BOLERO** *London HAV 2189*		15	4 wks
8 Apr 61	**VICTORY AT SEA** *Pye GGL 0073*		12	1 wk

See also Nigel Kennedy/London Philharmonic Orchestra; Ennio Morricone.

LONDON SYMPHONY ORCHESTRA
UK, orchestra — 137 wks

18 Mar 72	**TOP TV THEMES** *Studio Two STWO 372*		13	7 wks
5 Jul 75	**MUSIC FROM 'EDWARD VII'** *Polydor 2659 041*		52	1 wk
21 Jan 78	**STAR WARS (soundtrack)** *20th Century BTD 541*		21	12 wks
8 Jul 78	● **CLASSIC ROCK** *K-Tel ONE 1009*		3	39 wks
10 Feb 79	**CLASSIC ROCK – THE SECOND MOVEMENT** *K-Tel NE 1039*		26	8 wks
5 Jan 80	**RHAPSODY IN BLACK** *K-Tel ONE 1063*		34	5 wks
1 Aug 81	● **CLASSIC ROCK–ROCK CLASSICS** *K-Tel ONE 1123*		5	23 wks
27 Nov 82	**THE BEST OF CLASSIC ROCK** *K-Tel ONE 1080*		35	11 wks
27 Aug 83	**ROCK SYMPHONIES** *K-Tel ONE 1234*		40	9 wks
16 Nov 85	**THE POWER OF CLASSIC ROCK** *Portrait PRT 10049*		13	15 wks
14 Nov 87	**CLASSIC ROCK COUNTDOWN** *CBS MOOD 3*		32†	7 wks

See also Michael Crawford; Kimera; Julian Lloyd Webber; Cyril Ornadel, all with the London Symphony Orchestra; Spike Milligan.

LONDON WELSH MALE VOICE CHOIR
UK, male choir — 10 wks

5 Sep 81	**SONGS OF THE VALLEYS** *K-Tel NE 1117*		61	10 wks

LONE JUSTICE
US, male/female vocal/instrumental group — 5 wks

6 Jul 85	**LONE JUSTICE** *Geffen GEF 26288*		49	2 wks
8 Nov 86	**SHELTER** *Geffen WX 73*		86	3 wks

LONE STAR *UK, male vocal/instrumental group* — 7 wks

2 Oct 76	**LONE STAR** *Epic EPC 81545*		47	1 wk
17 Sep 77	**FIRING ON ALL SIX** *CBS 82213*		36	6 wks

LONG RYDERS *US, male vocal/instrumental group* — 1 wk

16 Nov 85	**STATE OF OUR UNION** *Island ILPS 9802*		66	1 wk

LOOSE ENDS
UK, male/female vocal/instrumental group — 30 wks

21 Apr 84	**A LITTLE SPICE** *Virgin V 2381*		46	9 wks
20 Apr 85	**SO WHERE ARE YOU?** *Virgin V 2340*		13	13 wks
18 Oct 86	**ZAGORA** *Virgin V 2384*		15	8 wks

Trini LOPEZ *US, male vocalist* — 42 wks

26 Oct 63	● **TRINI LOPEZ AT P.J.'S** *Reprise R 6093*		7	25 wks
25 Mar 67	● **TRINI LOPEZ IN LONDON** *Reprise RSLP 6238*		6	17 wks

Jeff LORBER
US, male vocalist/instrumentalist – keyboards — 2 wks

18 May 85	**STEP BY STEP** *Club JABH 9*		97	2 wks

Sophia LOREN – See Peter SELLERS and Sophia LOREN

Joe LOSS *UK, orchestra* — 10 wks

30 Oct 71	**ALL-TIME PARTY HITS** *MFP 5227*		24	10 wks

See also the George Mitchell Minstrels.

LOTUS EATERS *UK, male vocal/instrumental group* — 1 wk

16 Jun 84	**NO SENSE OF SIN** *Sylvan 206 263*		96	1 wk

Jacques LOUSSIER
France, male instrumentalist – piano — 3 wks

30 Mar 85	**THE BEST OF PLAY BACH** *Start STL 1*		58	3 wks

LOVE *US, male vocal/instrumental group* — 8 wks

24 Feb 68	**FOREVER CHANGES** *Elektra EKS7 4013*		24	6 wks
16 May 70	**OUT HERE** *Harvest Show 3/4*		29	2 wks

Geoff LOVE *UK, orchestra* — 28 wks

7 Aug 71	**BIG WAR MOVIE THEMES** *MFP 5171*		11	20 wks
21 Aug 71	**BIG WESTERN MOVIE THEMES** *MFP 5204*		38	3 wks
30 Oct 71	**BIG LOVE MOVIE THEMES** *MFP 5221*		28	5 wks

See also Manuel and his Music of the Mountains.

Lene LOVICH *US, female vocalist* — 17 wks

17 Mar 79	**STATELESS** *Stiff SEEZ 7*		35	11 wks
2 Feb 80	**FLEX** *Stiff SEEZ 19*		19	6 wks

LOVIN' SPOONFUL
US/Canada, male vocal/instrumental group — 11 wks

7 May 66	● **DAYDREAM** *Pye NPL 28078*		8	11 wks

Nick LOWE *UK, male vocalist* — 17 wks

11 Mar 78	**THE JESUS OF COOL** *Radar RAD 1*		22	9 wks
23 Jun 79	**LABOUR OF LUST** *Radar RAD 21*		43	6 wks
20 Feb 82	**NICK THE KNIFE** *F.Beat XXLP 14*		99	2 wks

LULU *UK, female vocalist*   *6 wks*

25 Sep 71	**THE MOST OF LULU** *MFP 5215*		**15**	6 wks

Bob LUMAN *US, male vocalist*   *1 wk*

14 Jan 61	**LET'S THINK ABOUT LIVING**			
	Warner Bros. WM 4025		**18**	1 wk

LURKERS *UK, male vocal/instrumental group*   *1 wk*

1 Jul 78	**FULHAM FALLOUT** *Beggars Banquet BEGA 2*		**57**	1 wk

LYLE – *See GALLAGHER and LYLE*

Vera LYNN *UK, female vocalist*   *12 wks*

21 Nov 81	**20 FAMILY FAVOURITES** *EMI EMTV 28*		**25**	12 wks

Philip LYNOTT *Ireland, male vocalist*   *6 wks*

26 Apr 80	**SOLO IN SOHO** *Vertigo 9102 038*		**28**	6 wks

See also Phil Lynott and Thin Lizzy; Thin Lizzy.

Phil LYNOTT and THIN LIZZY
Ireland/UK/US, male vocal/instrumental group   *7 wks*

14 Nov 87	**SOLDIER OF FORTUNE** – **THE BEST OF PHIL**			
	LYNOTT & THIN LIZZY *Telstar STAR 2300*		**55†**	7 wks

See also Philip Lynott; Thin Lizzy.

LYNYRD SKYNYRD
US, male vocal/instrumental group   *19 wks*

3 May 75	**NUTHIN' FANCY** *MCA MCF 2700*		**43**	1 wk
28 Feb 76	**GIMME BACK MY BULLETS** *MCA MCF 2744* ..		**34**	5 wks
6 Nov 76	**ONE MORE FOR THE ROAD** *MCA MCPS 279* .		**17**	4 wks
12 Nov 77	**STREET SURVIVORS** *MCA MCG 3525*		**13**	4 wks
4 Nov 78	**SKYNYRD'S FIRST AND LAST** *MCA MCG 3529*		**50**	1 wk
9 Feb 80	**GOLD AND PLATINUM** *MCA MCSP 308*		**49**	4 wks

M

Frankie McBRIDE *Ireland, male vocalist*   *3 wks*

17 Feb 68	**FRANKIE McBRIDE** *Emerald SLD 28*		**29**	3 wks

Paul McCARTNEY
UK, male vocalist/multi-instrumentalist   *467 wks*

2 May 70	● **McCARTNEY** *Apple PCS 7102*		**2**	32 wks
5 Jun 71	★ **RAM** *Apple PAS 10003*		**1**	24 wks
18 Dec 71	**WILD LIFE** *Apple PCS 7142*		**11**	9 wks
19 May 73	● **RED ROSE SPEEDWAY** *Apple PCTC 251* ...		**5**	16 wks
15 Dec 73	★ **BAND ON THE RUN** *Apple PAS 10007*		**1**	124 wks
21 Jun 75	★ **VENUS AND MARS** *Apple PCTC 254*		**1**	29 wks
17 Apr 76	● **WINGS AT THE SPEED OF SOUND**			
	Apple PAS 10010		**2**	35 wks
15 Jan 77	● **WINGS OVER AMERICA** *Parlophone PAS 720* .		**8**	22 wks
15 Apr 78	● **LONDON TOWN** *Parlophone PAS 10012*		**4**	23 wks
16 Dec 78	● **WINGS GREATEST HITS** *Parlophone PCTC 256*		**5**	32 wks
23 Jun 79	● **BACK TO THE EGG** *Parlophone PCTC 257*		**6**	15 wks
31 May 80	★ **McCARTNEY II** *Parlophone PCTC 258*		**1**	18 wks
7 Mar 81	**McCARTNEY INTERVIEW** *EMI CHAT 1*		**34**	4 wks
8 May 82	★ **TUG OF WAR** *Parlophone PCTC 259*		**1**	27 wks
12 Nov 83	● **PIPES OF PEACE** *Parlophone PCTC 1652301*		**4**	23 wks
3 Nov 84	★ **GIVE MY REGARDS TO BROAD STREET** –			
	ORIGINAL SOUNDTRACK *Parlophone PCTC 2*		**1**	21 wks
13 Sep 86	● **PRESS TO PLAY** *Parlophone PCSD 103*		**8**	6 wks
14 Nov 87	● **ALL THE BEST** *Parlophone PMTV 1*		**2†**	7 wks

Ram credited to Paul and Linda McCartney. Red Rose Speedway and Band On The Run credited to Paul McCartney and Wings. Wild Life and the five albums from Venus and Mars to Wings Greatest Hits inclusive credited to Wings. All other albums credited to Paul McCartney.

Van McCOY and the SOUL CITY SYMPHONY
US, orchestra   *11 wks*

5 Jul 75	**DISCO BABY** *Avco 9109 004*		**32**	11 wks

George McCRAE *US, male vocalist*   *29 wks*

3 Aug 74	**ROCK YOUR BABY** *Jayboy JSL 3*		**13**	28 wks
13 Sep 75	**GEORGE McCRAE** *Jayboy JSL 10*		**54**	1 wk

Michael McDONALD *US, male vocalist*   *35 wks*

22 Nov 86	● **SWEET FREEDOM: BEST OF MICHAEL McDONALD**			
	Warner Bros. WX 67		**6**	35 wks

Kate and Anna McGARRIGLE
Canada, female vocal duo   *4 wks*

26 Feb 77	**DANCER WITH BRUISED KNEES**			
	Warner Bros. K 56356		**35**	4 wks

Mary MacGREGOR *US, female vocalist*   *1 wk*

23 Apr 77	**TORN BETWEEN TWO LOVERS**			
	Ariola America AAS 1504		**59**	1 wk

McGUINNESS FLINT
UK, male vocal/instrumental group   *10 wks*

23 Jan 71	● **McGUINNESS FLINT** *Capitol EA-ST 22625*		**9**	10 wks

Kenneth McKELLAR *UK, male vocalist*   *10 wks*

28 Jun 69	**THE WORLD OF KENNETH McKELLAR**			
	Decca SPA 11		**27**	7 wks
31 Jan 70	**ECCO DI NAPOLI** *Decca SKL 5018*		**45**	3 wks

Malcolm McLAREN *UK, male vocalist*   *29 wks*

4 Jun 83	**DUCK ROCK** *Charisma MMLP 1*		**18**	17 wks
26 May 84	**WOULD YA LIKE MORE SCRATCHIN'**			
	Charisma CLAM 1		**44**	4 wks
29 Dec 84	**FANS** *Charisma MMDL 2*		**47**	8 wks

Would Ya Like More Scratchin' is credited to Malcolm McLaren and the World's Famous Supreme Team Show.

Don McLEAN *US, male vocalist*   *89 wks*

11 Mar 72	● **AMERICAN PIE** *United Artists UAS 29285*		**3**	54 wks
17 Jun 72	**TAPESTRY** *United Artists UAS 29350*		**16**	12 wks
24 Nov 73	**PLAYIN' FAVORITES** *United Artists UAG 29528* ..		**42**	2 wks
14 Jun 80	**CHAIN LIGHTNING** *EMI International INS 3025* ..		**19**	9 wks
27 Sep 80	● **THE VERY BEST OF DON McLEAN**			
	United Artists UAG 30314		**4**	12 wks

(Right) Paul Miles-Kingston's choirboy voice helped make ANDREW LLOYD WEBBER's *Requiem* the most successful classical religious work in chart history.

(Below) LINDISFARNE made themselves a hard act to follow, getting to number one with their first hit.

(Above) DON McLEAN's *Tapestry* had nothing to do with Carole King's and was actually his first album, recorded before *American Pie*.

(Left) LULU, shown at the age of 15 in 1964, only charted in the album lists with a compilation of her work with producer Mickie Most.

Ralph McTELL *UK, male vocalist*   17 wks

18 Nov 72	NOT TILL TOMORROW *Reprise K 44210*	36	1 wk
2 Mar 74	EASY *Reprise K 54013*	31	4 wks
15 Feb 75	STREETS *Warner Bros. K 56105*	13	12 wks

Christine McVIE *UK, female vocalist*   4 wks

| 11 Feb 84 | CHRISTINE McVIE *Warner Bros. 92 5059* | 58 | 4 wks |

David McWILLIAMS *UK, male vocalist*   9 wks

10 Jun 67	DAVID McWILLIAMS SINGS *Major Minor MMLP 2*	38	2 wks
4 Nov 67	DAVID McWILLIAMS VOL. 2 *Major Minor MMLP 10*	23	6 wks
9 Mar 68	DAVID McWILLIAMS VOL. 3 *Major Minor MMLP 11*	39	1 wk

MADNESS *UK, male vocal/instrumental group*   299 wks

3 Nov 79	● ONE STEP BEYOND *Stiff SEEZ 17*	2	78 wks
4 Oct 80	● ABSOLUTELY *Stiff SEEZ 29*	2	46 wks
10 Oct 81	● MADNESS 7 *Stiff SEEZ 39*	5	29 wks
1 May 82	★ COMPLETE MADNESS *Stiff HIT-TV 1*	1	88 wks
13 Nov 82	● THE RISE AND FALL *Stiff SEEZ 46*	10	22 wks
3 Mar 84	● KEEP MOVING *Stiff SEEZ 53*	6	19 wks
12 Oct 85	MAD NOT MAD *Zarjazz JZLP 1*	16	9 wks
6 Dec 86	UTTER MADNESS *Zarjazz JZLP 2*	29	8 wks

MADONNA *US, female vocalist*   355 wks

11 Feb 84	● MADONNA *Sire 923867*	6	123 wks
24 Nov 84	★ LIKE A VIRGIN *Sire 925157*	1	150 wks
12 Jul 86	★ TRUE BLUE *Sire WX 54*	1†	77 wks
28 Nov 87	● YOU CAN DANCE *Sire WX 76*	5†	5 wks

*From 22 Aug 85 Madonna was repackaged and was available as The First Album SIRE WX 22.
Like A Virgin changed label number during its chart run to SIRE WX 20.*

MAGAZINE *UK, male vocal/instrumental group*   24 wks

24 Jun 78	REAL LIFE *Virgin V 2100*	29	8 wks
14 Apr 79	SECONDHAND DAYLIGHT *Virgin V 2121*	38	8 wks
10 May 80	CORRECT USE OF SOAP *Virgin V 2156*	28	4 wks
13 Dec 80	PLAY *Virgin V 2184*	69	1 wk
27 Jun 81	MAGIC, MURDER AND THE WEATHER *Virgin V 2200*	39	3 wks

MAGIC BAND – *See Captain BEEFHEART and his MAGIC BAND*

MAGNA CARTA *UK, male vocal/instrumental group*   2 wks

| 8 Aug 70 | SEASONS *Vertigo 6360 003* | 55 | 2 wks |

MAGNUM *UK, male vocal/instrumental group*   29 wks

16 Sep 78	KINGDOM OF MADNESS *Jet JETLP 210*	58	1 wk
19 Apr 80	MARAUDER *Jet JETLP 230*	34	5 wks
6 Mar 82	CHASE THE DRAGON *Jet JETLP 235*	17	7 wks
21 May 83	THE ELEVENTH HOUR *Jet JETLP 240*	38	4 wks
25 May 85	ON A STORYTELLER'S NIGHT *FM WKFM LP 34*	24	7 wks
4 Oct 86	VIGILANTE *Polydor POLD 5198*	24	5 wks

MAHAVISHNU ORCHESTRA
UK/US, male instrumental group   5 wks

| 31 Mar 73 | BIRDS OF FIRE *CBS 65321* | 20 | 5 wks |

See also Carlos Santana and Mahavishnu John McLaughlin.

MAI TAI *Holland, female vocal group*   1 wk

| 6 Jul 85 | HISTORY *Virgin V 2359* | 91 | 1 wk |

MAJESTICS *UK, male vocal group*   4 wks

| 4 Apr 87 | TUTTI FRUTTI *BBC REN 629* | 64 | 4 wks |

Tommy MAKEM – *See CLANCY BROTHERS and Tommy MAKEM*

MAMA'S BOYS *Ireland, male vocal/instrumental group*   4 wks

| 6 Apr 85 | POWER & PASSION *Jive HIP 24* | 55 | 4 wks |

MAMAS and PAPAS *US, male/female vocal group*   61 wks

25 Jun 66	● THE MAMAS AND PAPAS *RCA Victor RD 7803*	3	18 wks
28 Jan 67	CASS, JOHN, MICHELLE, DENNY *RCA Victor SF 7639*	24	6 wks
24 Jun 67	● MAMAS AND PAPAS DELIVER *RCA Victor SF 7880*	4	22 wks
26 Apr 69	● HITS OF GOLD *Stateside S 5007*	7	2 wks
18 Jun 77	● THE BEST OF THE MAMAS AND PAPAS *Arcade ADEP 30*	6	13 wks

MAMBAS – *See MARC and the MAMBAS*

MAN *UK, male vocal/instrumental group*   11 wks

20 Oct 73	BACK INTO THE FUTURE *United Artists UAD 60053/4*	23	3 wks
25 May 74	RHINOS WINOS AND LUNATICS *United Artists UAG 29631*	24	4 wks
11 Oct 75	MAXIMUM DARKNESS *United Artists UAG 29872*	25	2 wks
17 Apr 76	WELSH CONNECTION *MCA MCF 2753*	40	2 wks

MANCHESTER BOYS CHOIR *UK, male choir*   2 wks

| 21 Dec 85 | THE NEW SOUND OF CHRISTMAS *K-Tel ONE 1314* | 80 | 2 wks |

Henry MANCINI *US, orchestra/chorus*   8 wks

| 16 Oct 76 | HENRY MANCINI *Arcade ADEP 24* | 26 | 8 wks |

See also James Galway and Henry Mancini; Johnny Mathis and Henry Mancini; Luciano Pavarotti with the Henry Mancini Orchestra.

MANFRED MANN
South Africa/UK, male vocal/instrumental group   72 wks

19 Sep 64	● FIVE FACES OF MANFRED MANN *HMV CLP 1731*	3	24 wks
23 Oct 65	● MANN MADE *HMV CLP 1911*	7	11 wks
17 Sep 66	MANN MADE HITS *HMV CLP 3559*	11	18 wks
29 Oct 66	AS IS *Fontana TL 5377*	22	4 wks
21 Jan 67	SOUL OF MANN *HMV CSD 3594*	40	1 wk
15 Sep 79	● SEMI-DETACHED SUBURBAN *EMI EMTV 19*	9	14 wks

See also Manfred Mann's Earth Band.

MANHATTAN TRANSFER
US, male/female vocal group   85 wks

12 Mar 77	COMING OUT *Atlantic K 50291*	12	20 wks
19 Mar 77	MANHATTAN TRANSFER *Atlantic K 50138*	49	7 wks
25 Feb 78	● PASTICHE *Atlantic K 50444*	10	34 wks

11 Nov 78 ●	**LIVE** *Atlantic K 50540*		4	17 wks
17 Nov 79	**EXTENSIONS** *Atlantic K 50674*		63	3 wks
18 Feb 84	**BODIES AND SOULS** *Atlantic 780104*		53	4 wks

MANHATTANS *US, male vocal group* *3 wks*

14 Aug 76	**MANHATTANS** *CBS 81513*		37	3 wks

Barry MANILOW *US, male vocalist* *303 wks*

23 Sep 78	**EVEN NOW** *Arista SPART 1047*		12	28 wks
3 Mar 79 ●	**MANILOW MAGIC** *Arista ARTV 2*		3	151 wks
20 Oct 79	**ONE VOICE** *Arista SPART 1106*		18	7 wks
29 Nov 80 ●	**BARRY** *Arista DLART 2*		5	34 wks
25 Apr 81	**GIFT SET** *Arista BOX 1*		62	1 wk
3 Oct 81 ●	**IF I SHOULD LOVE AGAIN** *Arista BMAN 1*		5	26 wks
1 May 82 ★	**BARRY LIVE IN BRITAIN** *Arista ARTV 4*		1	23 wks
27 Nov 82 ●	**I WANNA DO IT WITH YOU** *Arista BMAN 2*		7	9 wks
8 Oct 83 ●	**A TOUCH MORE MAGIC** *Arista BMAN 3*		10	12 wks
1 Dec 84	**2.00 AM PARADISE CAFE** *Arista 206 496*		28	6 wks
16 Nov 85	**MANILOW** *RCA PL 87044*		40	6 wks

Roberto MANN *UK, male orchestra leader* *9 wks*

9 Dec 67	**GREAT WALTZES** *Deram SML 1010*		19	9 wks

Shelley MANNE *US, male instrumentalist – drums* *1 wk*

18 Jun 60	**MY FAIR LADY** *Vogue LAC 12100*		20	1 wk

Manfred MANN'S EARTH BAND
South Africa/UK, male vocal/instrumental group *24 wks*

18 Sep 76 ●	**THE ROARING SILENCE** *Bronze ILPS 9357*		10	9 wks
17 Jun 78	**WATCH** *Bronze BRON 507*		33	6 wks
24 Mar 79	**ANGEL STATION** *Bronze BRON 516* ..		30	8 wks
26 Feb 83	**SOMEWHERE IN AFRICA** *Bronze BRON 543* ...		87	1 wk

See also Manfred Mann.

MANOWAR *US, male vocal/instrumental group* *3 wks*

18 Feb 84	**HAIL TO ENGLAND** *Music For Nations MFN 19* ...		83	2 wks
6 Oct 84	**SIGN OF THE HAMMER** *10 DIX 10*		73	1 wk

MANTOVANI *UK, orchestra* *151 wks*

21 Feb 59 ●	**CONTINENTAL ENCORES** *Decca LK 4298*		4	12 wks
18 Feb 61	**CONCERT SPECTACULAR** *Decca LK 4377* ...		16	2 wks
16 Apr 66 ●	**MANTOVANI MAGIC** *Decca LK 7949* ..		3	15 wks
15 Oct 66	**MR MUSIC – MANTOVANI** *Decca LK 4809*		24	3 wks
14 Jan 67 ●	**MANTOVANI'S GOLDEN HITS** *Decca SKL 4818*		10	43 wks
30 Sep 67	**HOLLYWOOD** *Decca SKL 4887*		37	1 wk
14 Jun 69 ●	**THE WORLD OF MANTOVANI** *Decca SPA 1*		6	31 wks
4 Oct 69 ●	**THE WORLD OF MANTOVANI VOL 2** *Decca SPA 36*		4	19 wks
16 May 70	**MANTOVANI TODAY** *Decca SKL 5003* ..		16	8 wks
26 Feb 72	**TO LOVERS EVERYWHERE** *Decca SKL 5112* ..		44	1 wk
3 Nov 79 ●	**20 GOLDEN GREATS** *Warwick WW 5067*		9	13 wks
16 Mar 85	**MANTOVANI MAGIC** *Telstar STAR 2237*		52	3 wks

Mantovani Magic on Telstar conducted by Roland Shaw.

MANTRONIX
Jamaica/US, male vocal/instrumental duo *6 wks*

29 Mar 86	**THE ALBUM** *10 DIX 37*		45	3 wks
13 Dec 86	**MUSIC MADNESS** *10 DIX 50*		66	3 wks

MANUEL and his MUSIC OF THE MOUNTAINS
UK, orchestra, leader Geoff Love *38 wks*

10 Sep 60	**MUSIC OF THE MOUNTAINS** *Columbia 33SX 1212*		17	1 wk
7 Aug 71	**THIS IS MANUEL** *Studio Two STWO 5*		18	19 wks
31 Jan 76 ●	**CARNIVAL** *Studio Two TWO 337*		3	18 wks

See also Geoff Love.

Phil MANZANERA
UK, male vocalist/instrumentalist – guitar *1 wk*

24 May 75	**DIAMOND HEAD** *Island ILPS 9315*		40	1 wk

MARC and the MAMBAS
UK, male/female vocal/instrumental group *9 wks*

16 Oct 82	**UNTITLED** *Some Bizzare/Phonogram BZA 13*		42	4 wks
20 Aug 83	**TORMENT AND TOREROS** *Some Bizzare BIZL 4*		28	5 wks

See also Marc Almond.

MARILLION *UK, male vocal/instrumental group* *128 wks*

26 Mar 83 ●	**SCRIPT FOR A JESTER'S TEARS** *EMI EMC 3429*		7	31 wks
24 Mar 84 ●	**FUGAZI** *EMI EMC 2400851*		5	20 wks
17 Nov 84 ●	**REAL TO REEL** *EMI JEST 1*		8	21 wks
29 Jun 85 ★	**MISPLACED CHILDHOOD** *EMI MRL 2*		1	41 wks
4 Jul 87 ●	**CLUTCHING AT STRAWS** *EMI EMD 1002*		2	15 wks

Yannis MARKOPOULOS *Greece, orchestra* *8 wks*

26 Aug 78	**WHO PAYS THE FERRYMAN** *BBC REB 315* ...		22	8 wks

Bob MARLEY and the WAILERS
Jamaica, male vocal/instrumental group *271 wks*

4 Oct 75	**NATTY DREAD** *Island ILPS 9281*		43	5 wks
20 Dec 75	**LIVE** *Island ILPS 9376*		38	11 wks
8 May 76	**RASTAMAN VIBRATION** *Island ILPS 9383*		15	13 wks
11 Jun 77 ●	**EXODUS** *Island ILPS 9498*		8	56 wks
1 Apr 78 ●	**KAYA** *Island ILPS 9517*		4	24 wks
16 Dec 78	**BABYLON BY BUS** *Island ISLD 11*		40	11 wks
13 Oct 79	**SURVIVAL** *Island ILPS 9542*		20	6 wks
28 Jun 80 ●	**UPRISING** *Island ILPS 9596*		6	17 wks
28 May 83 ●	**CONFRONTATION** *Island ILPS 9760*		5	19 wks
19 May 84 ★	**LEGEND** *Island BMW 1*		1	106 wks
28 Jul 86	**REBEL MUSIC** *Island ILPS 9843*		54	3 wks

Live Island ILPS 9376 returned to the chart in 1981 under the title Live At The Lyceum.

Neville MARRINER and the ACADEMY OF ST MARTIN IN THE FIELDS
UK, male conductor with chamber orchestra *6 wks*

6 Apr 85	**AMADEUS – ORIGINAL SOUNDTRACK** *London LONDP 6*		64	6 wks

Bernie MARSDEN
UK, male vocalist/instrumentalist – guitar *2 wks*

5 Sep 81	**LOOK AT ME NOW** *Parlophone PCF 7217*		71	2 wks

(Far left) MADONNA, the female chart champion of the mid-eighties.

(Left) The mid-eighties chart decline of BARRY MANILOW was no laughing matter.

(Below) The music business had to hand it to Fish (centre) and MARILLION for five consecutive Top Ten hits.

(Right) JOHN MAYALL, pioneer British bluesman, charted with an astonishing twelve albums in just over four years.

(Far right) MELANIE Safka was one of the favourite female stars of the singer-songwriter era of the early seventies.

(Below) MEN AT WORK shown not working.

Lena MARTELL   UK, female vocalist   71 wks

25 May 74	THAT WONDERFUL SOUND OF LENA MARTELL *Pye SPL 18427*	35	2 wks
8 Jan 77	THE BEST OF LENA MARTELL *Pye NSPL 18506*	13	16 wks
27 May 78	THE LENA MARTELL COLLECTION *Ronco RTL 2028*	12	19 wks
20 Oct 79	● LENA'S MUSIC ALBUM *Pye N 123*	5	18 wks
19 Apr 80	● BY REQUEST *Ronco RTL 2046*	9	9 wks
29 Nov 80	BEAUTIFUL SUNDAY *Ronco RTL 2052*	23	7 wks

MARTHA and the MUFFINS
Canada, male/female vocal instrumental group   6 wks

15 Mar 80	METRO MUSIC *DinDisc DID 1*	34	6 wks

Dean MARTIN   US, male vocalist   24 wks

13 May 61	THIS TIME I'M SWINGING *Capitol T 1442*	18	1 wk
25 Feb 67	AT EASE WITH DEAN *Reprise RSLP 6322*	35	1 wk
4 Nov 67	WELCOME TO MY WORLD *Philips DBL 001*	39	1 wk
12 Oct 68	GREATEST HITS VOL. 1 *Reprise RSLP 6301*	40	1 wk
22 Feb 69	● BEST OF DEAN MARTIN *Capitol ST 21194*	9	1 wk
22 Feb 69	● GENTLE ON MY MIND *Reprise RSLP 6330*	9	8 wks
13 Nov 76	● 20 ORIGINAL DEAN MARTIN HITS *Reprise K 54066*	7	11 wks

See also Nat King Cole and Dean Martin.

Juan MARTIN and the ROYAL PHILHARMONIC ORCHESTRA
Spain, male instrumentalist – guitar with UK, orchestra   9 wks

11 Feb 84	SERENADE *K-Tel NE 1267*	21	9 wks

See also Royal Philharmonic Orchestra; Louis Clark/Royal Philharmonic Orchestra.

John MARTYN
UK, male vocalist/instrumentalist – guitar   23 wks

4 Feb 78	ONE WORLD *Island ILPS 9492*	54	1 wk
1 Nov 80	GRACE AND DANGER *Island ILPS 9560*	54	2 wks
26 Sep 81	GLORIOUS FOOL *Geffen K 99178*	25	7 wks
4 Sep 82	WELL KEPT SECRET *WEA K 99255*	20	7 wks
17 Nov 84	SAPPHIRE *Island ILPS 9779*	57	2 wks
8 Mar 86	PIECE BY PIECE *Island ILPS 9807*	28	4 wks

Hank MARVIN
UK, male vocalist/instrumentalist – guitar   5 wks

22 Nov 69	HANK MARVIN *Columbia SCX 6352*	14	2 wks
20 Mar 82	WORDS AND MUSIC *Polydor POLD 5054*	66	3 wks

See also Marvin, Welch and Farrar.

MARVIN, WELCH and FARRAR
UK, male vocal/instrumental group   4 wks

3 Apr 71	MARVIN, WELCH AND FARRAR *Regal Zonophone SRZA 8502*	30	4 wks

See also Hank Marvin.

MARY JANE GIRLS   US, female vocal group   9 wks

28 May 83	MARY JANE GIRLS *Gordy STML 12189*	51	9 wks

MARY – See PETER, PAUL and MARY

MASSED WELSH CHOIRS   UK, male voice choir   7 wks

9 Aug 69	● CYMANSA GANN *BBC REC 53 M*	5	7 wks

MATCHBOX   UK, male vocal/instrumental group   14 wks

2 Feb 80	MATCHBOX *Magnet MAG 5031*	44	5 wks
11 Oct 80	MIDNITE DYNAMOS *Magnet MAG 5036*	23	9 wks

Mireille MATHIEU   France, female vocalist   1 wk

2 Mar 68	MIREILLE MATHIEU *Columbia SCX 6210*	39	1 wk

Johnny MATHIS   US, male vocalist   193 wks

8 Nov 58	● WARM *Fontana TBA TFL 5015*	6	2 wks
24 Jan 59	● SWING SOFTLY *Fontana TFL 5039*	10	1 wk
13 Feb 60	● RIDE ON A RAINBOW *Fontana TFL 5061*	10	2 wks
10 Dec 60	● RHYTHMS AND BALLADS OF BROADWAY *Fontana SET 101*	6	10 wks
17 Jun 61	I'LL BUY YOU A STAR *Fontana TFL 5143*	18	1 wk
16 May 70	RAINDROPS KEEP FALLING ON MY HEAD *CBS 63587*	23	10 wks
3 Apr 71	LOVE STORY *CBS 64334*	27	5 wks
9 Sep 72	FIRST TIME EVER I SAW YOUR FACE *CBS 64930*	40	3 wks
16 Dec 72	MAKE IT EASY ON YOURSELF *CBS 65161*	49	1 wk
8 Mar 75	I'M COMING HOME *CBS 65690*	18	11 wks
5 Apr 75	THE HEART OF A WOMAN *CBS 80533*	39	2 wks
26 Jul 75	WHEN WILL I SEE YOU AGAIN *CBS 80738*	13	10 wks
3 Jul 76	I ONLY HAVE EYES FOR YOU *CBS 81329*	14	12 wks
19 Feb 77	GREATEST HITS VOL. IV *CBS 86022*	31	5 wks
18 Jun 77	★ THE JOHNNY MATHIS COLLECTION *CBS 10003*	1	40 wks
17 Dec 77	SWEET SURRENDER *CBS 86036*	55	1 wk
29 Apr 78	● YOU LIGHT UP MY LIFE *CBS 86055*	3	19 wks
7 Apr 79	THE BEST DAYS OF MY LIFE *CBS 86080*	38	5 wks
3 Nov 79	MATHIS MAGIC *CBS 86103*	59	4 wks
8 Mar 80	★ TEARS AND LAUGHTER *CBS 10019*	1	15 wks
12 Jul 80	ALL FOR YOU *CBS 86115*	20	8 wks
19 Sep 81	● CELEBRATION *CBS 10028*	9	16 wks
15 May 82	FRIENDS IN LOVE *CBS 85652*	34	7 wks
15 Sep 84	A SPECIAL PART OF ME *CBS 25475*	45	3 wks

See also Johnny Mathis and Natalie Cole; Johnny Mathis and Henry Mancini; Johnny Mathis and Deniece Williams.

Johnny MATHIS and Deniece WILLIAMS
US, male/female vocal duo   11 wks

26 Aug 78	THAT'S WHAT FRIENDS ARE FOR *CBS 86068*	16	11 wks

See also Johnny Mathis; Deniece Williams; Johnny Mathis and Natalie Cole; Johnny Mathis and Henry Mancini.

Johnny MATHIS and Natalie COLE
US, male/female vocal duo   16 wks

17 Sep 83	● UNFORGETTABLE: A MUSICAL TRIBUTE TO NAT KING COLE *CBS 10042*	5	16 wks

See also Johnny Mathis; Johnny Mathis and Deniece Williams; Johnny Mathis and Henry Mancini.

Johnny MATHIS and Henry MANCINI
US, male vocalist with US, orchestra   8 wks

13 Dec 86	THE HOLLYWOOD MUSICALS *CBS 450 258–1*	52	8 wks

See also Johnny Mathis; Henry Mancini; Johnny Mathis and Deniece Williams; Johnny Mathis and Natalie Cole; James Galway and Henry Mancini; Luciano Pavarotti with the Henry Mancini Orchestra.

MATT BIANCO
UK/Poland male/female vocal/instrumental group — 52 wks

8 Sep 84	**WHOSE SIDE ARE YOU ON** *WEA WX 7* ……	35	39 wks
22 Mar 86	**MATT BIANCO** *WEA WX 35* ………………	26	13 wks

MATTHEWS' SOUTHERN COMFORT
UK, male vocal/instrumental group — 4 wks

25 Jul 70	**SECOND SPRING** *Uni UNLS 112* …………	52	4 wks

Brian MAY and FRIENDS
UK, male vocalist/instrumentalist – guitar, and UK/US male instrumental group — 4 wks

12 Nov 83	**STAR FLEET PROJECT** *EMI SFLT 1078061* ….	35	4 wks

Simon MAY ORCHESTRA *UK, orchestra* — 7 wks

27 Sep 86	**SIMON'S WAY** *BBC REB 594* ……………	59	7 wks

John MAYALL *UK, male vocalist* — 97 wks

4 Mar 67	● **A HARD ROAD** *Decca SKL 4853* …………	10	19 wks
23 Sep 67	● **CRUSADE** *Decca SKL 4890* …………	8	14 wks
25 Nov 67	**BLUES ALONE** *Ace Of Clubs SCL 1243* ……	24	5 wks
16 Mar 68	**DIARY OF A BAND VOL. 1** *Decca SKL 4918* …	27	9 wks
16 Mar 68	**DIARY OF A BAND VOL. 2** *Decca SKL 4919* …	28	5 wks
20 Jul 68	● **BARE WIRES** *Decca SKL 4945* …………	3	17 wks
18 Jan 69	**BLUES FROM LAUREL CANYON** *Decca SKL 4972*	33	3 wks
23 Aug 69	**LOOKING BACK** *Decca SKL 5010* ……	14	7 wks
15 Nov 69	**TURNING POINT** *Polydor 583–571* ……	11	7 wks
11 Apr 70	● **EMPTY ROOMS** *Polydor 583–580* ………	9	8 wks
12 Dec 70	**U.S.A. UNION** *Polydor 2425–020* ………	50	1 wk
26 Jun 71	**BACK TO THE ROOTS** *Polydor 2657–005* ……	31	2 wks

First four Decca albums credited to John Mayall's Bluesbreakers. See also John Mayall and Eric Clapton.

John MAYALL and Eric CLAPTON
UK, male instrumental duo — 17 wks

30 Jul 66	● **BLUES BREAKERS** *Decca LK 4804* …………	6	17 wks

See also John Mayall; Eric Clapton; Eric Clapton and Cream.

Curtis MAYFIELD *US, male vocalist* — 2 wks

31 Mar 73	**SUPER FLY** *Buddah 2318 065* …………	26	2 wks

MAZE featuring Frankie BEVERLY
US, male vocalist and male vocal/instrumental group — 20 wks

7 May 83	**WE ARE ONE** *Capitol EST 12262* …………	38	6 wks
9 Mar 85	**CAN'T STOP THE LOVE** *Capitol MAZE 1* ……	41	12 wks
27 Sep 86	**LIVE IN LOS ANGELES** *Capitol ESTSP 24* ……	70	2 wks

Vaughn MEADER *US, male comedian* — 8 wks

29 Dec 62	**THE FIRST FAMILY** *London HAA 8048* ………	12	8 wks

MEAT LOAF *US, male vocalist* — 521 wks

11 Mar 78	● **BAT OUT OF HELL** *Epic EPC 82419* …………	9	395 wks
12 Sep 81	★ **DEAD RINGER** *Epic EPC 83645* …………	1	46 wks
7 May 83	● **MIDNIGHT AT THE LOST AND FOUND** *Epic EPC 25243*	7	23 wks
10 Nov 84	● **BAD ATTITUDE** *Arista 206 619* …………	8	16 wks
26 Jan 85	● **HITS OUT OF HELL** *Epic EPC 26156* ……	2	33 wks
11 Oct 86	**BLIND BEFORE I STOP** *Arista 207 741* ………	28	6 wks
7 Nov 87	**LIVE AT WEMBLEY** *RCA 208599* …………	60	2 wks

MECHANICS – *See* MIKE and the MECHANICS

MEDICS – *See* DOCTOR and the MEDICS

MEL and KIM *UK, female vocal duo* — 25 wks

25 Apr 87	● **F.L.M.** *Supreme SU 2* …………………	3	25 wks

MELANIE *US, female vocalist* — 69 wks

19 Sep 70	● **CANDLES IN THE RAIN** *Buddah 2318–009* ……	5	27 wks
16 Jan 71	**LEFTOVER WINE** *Buddah 2318–011* …………	22	11 wks
29 May 71	● **GOOD BOOK** *Buddah 2322 001* …………	9	9 wks
8 Jan 72	**GATHER ME** *Buddah 2322 002* …………	14	14 wks
1 Apr 72	**GARDEN IN THE CITY** *Buddah 2318 054* ……	19	6 wks
7 Oct 72	**THE FOUR SIDES OF MELANIE** *Buddah 2659 013* ………………	23	2 wks

John Cougar MELLENCAMP *US, male vocalist* — 14 wks

6 Nov 82	**AMERICAN FOOL** *Riva RVLP 16* …………	37	6 wks
3 Mar 84	**UH-HUH** *Riva RIVL 1* …………………	92	1 wk
3 Oct 87	**THE LONESOME JUBILEE** *Mercury MERH 109* ..	31	7 wks

American Fool credited to John Cougar.

MEN AT WORK
Australia, male vocal/instrumental group — 71 wks

15 Jan 83	★ **BUSINESS AS USUAL** *Epic EPC 85669* ………	1	44 wks
30 Apr 83	● **CARGO** *Epic EPC 25372* …………………	8	27 wks

MEN THEY COULDN'T HANG
UK, male vocal/instrumental group — 4 wks

27 Jul 85	**NIGHT OF A THOUSAND CANDLES** *Imp FIEND 50* …………………	91	2 wks
8 Nov 86	**HOW GREEN IS THE VALLEY** *MCA MCF 3337*	68	2 wks

MEN WITHOUT HATS
Canada, male vocal/instrumental group — 1 wk

12 Nov 83	**RHYTHM OF YOUTH** *Statik STATLP 10* ……	96	1 wk

MEMBERS *UK, male vocal/instrumental group* — 5 wks

28 Apr 79	**AT THE CHELSEA NIGHTCLUB** *Virgin V 2120* .	45	5 wks

Freddie MERCURY *UK, male vocalist* — 23 wks

11 May 85	● **MR BAD GUY** *CBS 86312* …………………	6	23 wks

MERLE and ROY
UK, male/female vocal/instrumental duo — 4 wks

26 Sep 87	**REQUESTS** *Mynod Mawr RMBR 8713* ………	74	4 wks

MERSEYBEATS *UK, male vocal/instrumental group* 9 wks

20 Jun 64	**THE MERSEYBEATS** *Fontana TL 5210*	12	9 wks

METALLICA
US/Denmark, male vocal/instrumental group 6 wks

11 Aug 84	**RIDE THE LIGHTNING**		
	Music For Nations MFN 27	87	2 wks
15 Mar 86	**MASTER OF PUPPETS**		
	Music For Nations MFN 60	41	4 wks

METEORS *UK, male vocal/instrumental group* 3 wks

26 Feb 83	**WRECKIN' CREW** *I.D. NOSE 1*	53	3 wks

MEZZOFORTE *Iceland, male instrumental group* 10 wks

5 Mar 83	**SURPRISE SURPRISE** *Steinar STELP 02*	23	9 wks
2 Jul 83	**CATCHING UP WITH MEZZOFORTE**		
	Steinar STELP 03	95	1 wk

MG'S – *See Booker T. and the MG's*

George MICHAEL *UK, male vocalist* 7 wks

14 Nov 87	★ **FAITH** *Epic 460 000–1*	1†	7 wks

Keith MICHELL *Australia, male vocalist* 12 wks

| 9 Feb 80 | **CAPTAIN BEAKY AND HIS BAND** | | |
| | *Polydor 238 3462* | 28 | 12 wks |

MICK – *See Dave DEE, DOZY BEAKY, MICK and TICH*

MIDNIGHT STAR
US, male/female vocal/instrumental group 6 wks

| 2 Feb 85 | **PLANETARY INVASION** *Solar MCF 3251* | 85 | 2 wks |
| 5 Jul 86 | **HEADLINES** *Solar MCF 3322* | 42 | 4 wks |

MIGHTY LEMON DROPS
UK, male vocal/instrumental group 2 wks

4 Oct 86	**HAPPY HEAD** *Blue Guitar AZLP 1*	58	2 wks

MIGHTY WAH *UK, male vocal/instrumental group* 6 wks

| 4 Aug 84 | **A WORD TO THE WISE GUY** | | |
| | *Beggars Banquet BEGA 54* | 28 | 6 wks |

MIKE and the MECHANICS
UK, male vocal/instrumental group 3 wks

15 Mar 86	**MIKE AND THE MECHANICS** *WEA WX 49*	78	3 wks

See also Mike Rutherford.

Buddy MILES – *See Carlos SANTANA and Buddy MILES*

John MILES *UK, male vocalist/multi-instrumentalist* 25 wks

| 27 Mar 76 | ● **REBEL** *Decca SKL 5231* | 9 | 10 wks |
| 26 Feb 77 | **STRANGER IN THE CITY** *Decca TXS 118* | 37 | 3 wks |

1 Apr 78	**ZARAGON** *Decca TXS 126*	43	5 wks
21 Apr 79	**MORE MILES PER HOUR** *Decca TXS 135*	46	5 wks
29 Aug 81	**MILES HIGH** *EMI EMC 3374*	96	2 wks

PAUL MILES-KINGSTON – *See Andrew LLOYD WEBBER*

Frankie MILLER *UK, male vocalist* 1 wk

14 Apr 79	**FALLING IN LOVE** *Chrysalis CHR 1220*	54	1 wk

Glenn MILLER *US, orchestra* 68 wks

28 Jan 61	● **GLENN MILLER PLAYS SELECTIONS FROM 'THE GLENN MILLER STORY' AND OTHER HITS** *RCA RD 27068 0023*	10	18 wks
5 Jul 69	● **THE BEST OF GLENN MILLER** *RCA International 1002*	5	14 wks
6 Sep 69	**NEARNESS OF YOU** *RCA International INTS 1019*	30	2 wks
25 Apr 70	**A MEMORIAL 1944–1969** *RCA GM 1*	18	17 wks
25 Dec 71	**THE REAL GLENN MILLER AND HIS ORCHESTRA PLAY THE ORIGINAL MUSIC OF THE FILM 'THE GLENN MILLER STORY' AND OTHER HITS** *RCA International INTS 1157*	28	2 wks
14 Feb 76	**A LEGENDARY PERFORMER** *RCA Victor DPM 2065*	41	5 wks
14 Feb 76	**A LEGENDARY PERFORMER VOL 2** *RCA Victor CPL 11349*	53	2 wks
9 Apr 77	● **THE UNFORGETTABLE GLENN MILLER** *RCA Victor TVL 1*	4	8 wks

The Real Glenn Miller And His Orchestra Play . . . is a re-titled re-issue of the first album.

Steve MILLER BAND
US, male vocal/instrumental group 47 wks

12 Jun 76	**FLY LIKE AN EAGLE** *Mercury 9286 177*	11	17 wks
4 Jun 77	**BOOK OF DREAMS** *Mercury 9286 456*	12	12 wks
19 Jun 82	● **ABRACADABRA** *Mercury 6302 204*	10	16 wks
7 May 83	**STEVE MILLER BAND LIVE!** *Mercury MERL 18*	79	2 wks

MILLICAN and NESBIT *UK, male vocal duo* 24 wks

| 23 Mar 74 | ● **MILLICAN AND NESBIT** *Pye NSPL 18428* | 3 | 21 wks |
| 4 Jan 75 | **EVERYBODY KNOWS MILLICAN & NESBIT** *Pye NSPL 18446* | 23 | 3 wks |

Spike MILLIGAN *UK, male comedian* 5 wks

| 25 Nov 61 | **MILLIGAN PRESERVED** *Parlophone PMC 1152* | 11 | 4 wks |
| 18 Dec 76 | **THE SNOW GOOSE** *RCA RS 1088* | 49 | 1 wk |

Second album also credited the London Symphony Orchestra. See also Harry Secombe, Peter Sellers and Spike Milligan; London Symphony Orchestra; Michael Crawford; Kimera; Julian Lloyd Webber; Cyril Ornadel, all with the LSO.

Mrs. MILLS *UK, female instrumentalist – piano* 13 wks

10 Dec 66	**COME TO MY PARTY** *Parlophone PMC 7010*	17	7 wks
28 Dec 68	**MRS. MILLS' PARTY PIECES** *Parlophone PCS 7066*	32	3 wks
13 Dec 69	**LET'S HAVE ANOTHER PARTY** *Parlophone PCS 7035*	23	2 wks
6 Nov 71	**I'M MIGHTY GLAD** *MFP 5225*	49	1 wk

MINDBENDERS *UK, male vocal/instrumental group* 4 wks

25 Jun 66	**THE MINDBENDERS** *Fontana TL 5324*	28	4 wks

See also Wayne Fontana and the Mindbenders.

(Above) It only took MUD two years of hit singles to assemble their *Greatest Hits*.

(Near right) GARY MOORE went from label to label before finding his chart stride.

NEW ORDER evolved from Joy Division and have been the chart mainstay of Manchester-based Factory Records.

Liza MINELLI *US, female vocalist* — *16 wks*

7 Apr 73	● **LIZA WITH A 'Z'** *CBS 65212*	**9**	15 wks
16 Jun 73	**THE SINGER** *CBS 65555*	**45**	1 wk

MINIPOPS *UK, male/female vocal group* — *12 wks*

26 Dec 81	**MINIPOPS** *K-Tel NE 1102*	**63**	7 wks
19 Feb 83	**WE'RE THE MINIPOPS** *K-Tel ONE 1187*	**54**	5 wks

MIRAGE *UK, male/female vocal/instrumental group* — *1 wk*

26 Dec 87	**THE BEST OF MIRAGE JACK MIX '88**		
	Stylus SMR 746	**89†**	1 wk

MISSION *UK, male vocal/instrumental group* — *24 wks*

22 Nov 86	**GOD'S OWN MEDICINE** *Mercury MERH 102*	**14**	20 wks
4 Jul 87	**THE FIRST CHAPTER** *Mercury MISH 1*	**35**	4 wks

Joni MITCHELL *Canada, female vocalist* — *101 wks*

6 Jun 70	● **LADIES OF THE CANYON** *Reprise RSLP 6376* ...	**8**	25 wks
24 Jul 71	● **BLUE** *Reprise K 44128*	**3**	18 wks
16 Mar 74	**COURT AND SPARK** *Asylum SYLA 8756* ..	**14**	11 wks
1 Feb 75	**MILES OF AISLES** *Asylum SYSP 902* ..	**34**	4 wks
27 Dec 75	**THE HISSING OF SUMMER LAWNS**		
	Asylum SYLA 8763	**14**	10 wks
11 Dec 76	**HEJIRA** *Asylum K 53063*	**11**	5 wks
21 Jan 78	**DON JUAN'S RECKLESS DAUGHTER**		
	Asylum K 63003	**20**	7 wks
14 Jul 79	**MINGUS** *Asylum K 53091*	**24**	7 wks
4 Oct 80	**SHADOWS AND LIGHT** *Elektra K 62030* ..	**63**	3 wks
4 Dec 82	**WILD THINGS RUN FAST** *Geffen GEF 25102* ...	**32**	8 wks
30 Nov 85	**DOG EAT DOG** *Geffen GEF 26455* ...	**57**	3 wks

George MITCHELL MINSTRELS *UK, male/female vocal group* — *240 wks*

26 Nov 60	★ **THE BLACK AND WHITE MINSTREL SHOW**		
	HMV CLP 1399	**1**	90 wks
21 Oct 61	★ **ANOTHER BLACK AND WHITE MINSTREL**		
	SHOW *HMV CLP 1460*	**1**	64 wks
20 Oct 62	★ **ON STAGE WITH THE GEORGE MITCHELL**		
	MINSTRELS *HMV CLP 1599*	**1**	26 wks
2 Nov 63	● **ON TOUR WITH THE GEORGE MITCHELL**		
	MINSTRELS *HMV CLP 1667*	**6**	18 wks
12 Dec 64	● **SPOTLIGHT ON THE GEORGE MITCHELL**		
	MINSTRELS *HMV CLP 1803*	**6**	7 wks
4 Dec 65	● **MAGIC OF THE MINSTRELS** *HMV CLP 1917* ..	**9**	7 wks
26 Nov 66	**HERE COME THE MINSTRELS**		
	HMV CLP 3579	**11**	11 wks
16 Dec 67	**SHOWTIME** *HMV CSD 3642*	**26**	2 wks
14 Dec 68	**SING THE IRVING BERLIN SONGBOOK**		
	Columbia SCX 6267	**33**	1 wk
19 Dec 70	**THE MAGIC OF CHRISTMAS**		
	Columbia SCX 6431	**32**	4 wks
19 Nov 77	● **30 GOLDEN GREATS** *EMI EMTV 7*	**10**	10 wks

30 Golden Greats also credits the Joe Loss Orchestra.

MODERN EON *UK, male vocal/instrumental group* — *1 wk*

13 Jun 81	**FICTION TALES** *Dindisc DID 11*	**65**	1 wk

MODERN LOVERS – See Jonathan RICHMAN and the MODERN LOVERS

MODERN ROMANCE *UK, male vocal/instrumental group* — *13 wks*

16 Apr 83	**TRICK OF THE LIGHT** *WEA X 0127*	**53**	7 wks
3 Dec 83	**PARTY TONIGHT** *Ronco RON LP 3*	**45**	6 wks

MODERN TALKING *Germany, male vocal/instrumental group* — *3 wks*

11 Oct 86	**READY FOR ROMANCE** *RCA PL 71133*	**76**	3 wks

MOLLY HATCHET *US, male vocal/instrumental group* — *1 wk*

25 Jan 86	**DOUBLE TROUBLE – LIVE** *Epic EPC 88670*	**94**	1 wk

Zoot MONEY and the BIG ROLL BAND *UK, male vocalist and male instrumental backing group* — *3 wks*

15 Oct 66	**ZOOT** *Columbia SX 6075*	**23**	3 wks

MONKEES *US/UK, male vocal/instrumental group* — *92 wks*

28 Jan 67	★ **THE MONKEES** *RCA Victor SF 7844*	**1**	36 wks
15 Apr 67	★ **MORE OF THE MONKEES** *RCA Victor SF 7868* ..	**1**	25 wks
8 Jul 67	● **HEADQUARTERS** *RCA Victor SF 7886* ..	**2**	19 wks
13 Jan 68	● **PISCES, AQUARIUS, CAPRICORN & JONES**		
	LTD. *RCA Victor SF 7912*	**5**	11 wks
28 Nov 81	**THE MONKEES** *Arista DARTY 12*	**99**	1 wk

The two albums titled The Monkees are different.

MONOCHROME SET *UK, male vocal/instrumental group* — *4 wks*

3 May 80	**STRANGE BOUTIQUE** *Dindisc DID 4*	**62**	4 wks

Tony MONOPOLY *Australia, male vocalist* — *4 wks*

12 Jun 76	**TONY MONOPOLY** *BUK BULP 2000*	**25**	4 wks

Matt MONRO *UK, male vocalist* — *15 wks*

7 Aug 65	**I HAVE DREAMED** *Parlophone PMC 1250*	**20**	1 wk
17 Sep 66	**THIS IS THE LIFE** *Capitol T 2540*	**25**	2 wks
26 Aug 67	**INVITATION TO THE MOVIES** *Capitol ST 2730* .	**30**	1 wk
15 Mar 80	● **HEARTBREAKERS** *EMI EMTV 23*	**5**	11 wks

MONTROSE *US, male vocal/instrumental group* — *1 wk*

15 Jun 74	**MONTROSE** *Warner Bros. K 46276*	**43**	1 wk

MONTY PYTHON'S FLYING CIRCUS *UK, male comedy group* — *31 wks*

30 Oct 71	**ANOTHER MONTY PYTHON RECORD**		
	Charisma CAS 1049	**26**	3 wks
27 Jan 73	**MONTY PYTHON'S PREVIOUS ALBUM**		
	Charisma CAS 1063	**39**	3 wks
23 Feb 74	**MATCHING TIE AND HANDKERCHIEF**		
	Charisma CAS 1080	**49**	2 wks
27 Jul 74	**LIVE AT DRURY LANE** *Charisma CLASS 4*	**19**	8 wks
9 Aug 75	**MONTY PYTHON** *Charisma CAS 1003*	**45**	4 wks
24 Nov 79	**THE LIFE OF BRIAN** *Warner Bros. K 56751*	**63**	3 wks
18 Oct 80	**CONTRACTUAL OBLIGATION ALBUM**		
	Charisma CAS 1152	**13**	8 wks

MOODY BLUES *UK, male vocal/instrumental group* — *302 wks*

27 Jan 68	**DAYS OF FUTURE PASSED** *Deram SML 707* ...	**27**	16 wks
3 Aug 68	● **IN SEARCH OF THE LOST CHORD**		
	Deram SML 711	**5**	32 wks

3 May 69 ★	ON THE THRESHOLD OF A DREAM		
	Deram SML 1035	1	73 wks
6 Dec 69 ●	TO OUR CHILDREN'S CHILDREN'S CHILDREN		
	Threshold THS 1	2	44 wks
15 Aug 70 ★	A QUESTION OF BALANCE *Threshold THS 3* ...	1	19 wks
7 Aug 71 ★	EVERY GOOD BOY DESERVES FAVOUR		
	Threshold THS 5	1	21 wks
2 Dec 72 ●	SEVENTH SOJOURN *Threshold THS 7*	5	18 wks
16 Nov 74	THIS IS THE MOODY BLUES *Threshold MB 1/2* ..	14	18 wks
24 Jun 78 ●	OCTAVE *Decca TXS 129*	6	18 wks
10 Nov 79	OUT OF THIS WORLD *K-Tel NE 1051*	15	10 wks
23 May 81 ●	LONG DISTANCE VOYAGER		
	Threshold TXS 139	7	19 wks
10 Sep 83	THE PRESENT *Threshold TXS 140*	15	8 wks
10 May 86	THE OTHER SIDE OF LIFE *Threshold POLD 5190* .	24	6 wks

Dudley MOORE *UK, male instrumentalist – piano* *19 wks*

4 Dec 65	THE OTHER SIDE OF DUDLEY MOORE		
	Decca LK 4732	11	9 wks
11 Jun 66	GENUINE DUD *Decca LK 4788*	13	10 wks

Second album credited to the Dudley Moore Trio. See also Peter Cook and Dudley Moore.

Gary MOORE
UK, male vocalist/instrumentalist – guitar *40 wks*

3 Feb 79	BACK ON THE STREETS *MCA MCF 2853*	70	1 wk
16 Oct 82	CORRIDORS OF POWER *Virgin V 2245*	30	6 wks
18 Feb 84	VICTIMS OF THE FUTURE *10 DIX 2*	12	7 wks
13 Oct 84	WE WANT MOORE *10 GMDL 1*	32	3 wks
14 Sep 85	RUN FOR COVER *10 DIX 16*	12	8 wks
12 Jul 86	ROCKIN' EVERY NIGHT *10 XID 1*	99	1 wk
14 Mar 87 ●	WILD FRONTIER *10 DIX 56*	8	14 wks

Patrick MORAZ
Switzerland, male instrumentalist – keyboards *8 wks*

10 Apr 76	PATRICK MORAZ *Charisma CDS 4002*	28	7 wks
23 Jul 77	OUT IN THE SUN *Charisma CDS 4007*	44	1 wk

Georgio MORODER – *See Philip OAKEY and Georgio MORODER*

Ennio MORRICONE *Italy, orchestra* *15 wks*

2 May 81	THIS IS ENNIO MORRICONE *EMI THIS 33* ...	23	5 wks
9 May 81	CHI MAI *BBC REH 414*	29	6 wks
7 Mar 87	THE MISSION – ORIGINAL SOUNDTRACK		
	Virgin V 2402	73	4 wks

The Mission credits the London Philharmonic Orchestra. See also London Philharmonic Orchestra; Nigel Kennedy/London Philharmonic Orchestra.

Van MORRISON *UK, male vocalist* *71 wks*

18 Apr 70	MOONDANCE *Warner Bros. WS 1835*	32	2 wks
11 Aug 73	HARD NOSE THE HIGHWAY		
	Warner Bros. K 46242	22	3 wks
16 Nov 74	VEEDON FLEECE *Warner Bros. K 56068*	41	1 wk
7 May 77	A PERIOD OF TRANSITION		
	Warner Bros. K 56322	23	5 wks
21 Oct 78	WAVELENGTH *Warner Bros. K 56526*	27	6 wks
8 Sep 79	INTO THE MUSIC *Vertigo 9120 852*	21	9 wks
20 Sep 80	THE COMMON ONE *Mercury 6302 021*	53	3 wks
27 Feb 82	BEAUTIFUL VISION *Mercury 6302 122*	31	14 wks
26 Mar 83	INARTICULATE SPEECH OF THE HEART		
	Mercury MERL 16	14	8 wks
3 Mar 84	LIVE AT THE GRAND OPERA HOUSE		
	Mercury MERL 36	47	4 wks
9 Feb 85	A SENSE OF WONDER *Mercury MERH 54*	25	5 wks
2 Aug 86	NO GURU, NO METHOD, NO TEACHER		
	Mercury MERH 94	27	5 wks
19 Sep 87	POETIC CHAMPIONS COMPOSE		
	Mercury MERH 110	26	6 wks

MORRISSEY MULLEN
UK, male vocal/instrumental duo *11 wks*

18 Jul 81	BADNESS *Beggars Banquet BEGA 27*	43	5 wks
3 Apr 82	LIFE ON THE WIRE *Beggars Banquet BEGA 33*	47	5 wks
23 Apr 83	IT'S ABOUT TIME *Beggars Banquet BEGA 44*	95	1 wk

MORRISTOWN ORPHEUS CHOIR – *See G.U.S. (FOOTWEAR) BAND and the MORRISTOWN ORPHEUS CHOIR*

MOTHERS OF INVENTION
US, male vocal/instrumental group *12 wks*

29 Jun 68	WE'RE ONLY IN IT FOR THE MONEY		
	Verve SVLP 9199	32	5 wks
28 Mar 70	BURNT WEENY SANDWICH *Reprise RSLP 6370*	17	3 wks
3 Oct 70	WEASELS RIPPED MY FLESH *Reprise RSLP 2028*	28	4 wks

See also Frank Zappa.

MOTLEY CRUE *US, male vocal/instrumental group* *14 wks*

13 Jul 85	THEATRE OF PAIN *Elektra EKT 8*	36	3 wks
30 May 87	GIRLS GIRLS GIRLS *Elektra EKT 39*	14	11 wks

MOTORHEAD *UK, male vocal/instrumental group* *83 wks*

24 Sep 77	MOTORHEAD *Chiswick WIK 2*	43	5 wks
24 Mar 79	OVERKILL *Bronze BRON 515*	24	11 wks
8 Dec 79	ON PARADE *United Artists LBR 1004*	65	2 wks
8 Nov 80 ●	ACE OF SPADES *Bronze BRON 531*	4	16 wks
27 Jun 81 ★	NO SLEEP TILL HAMMERSMITH		
	Bronze BRON 535	1	21 wks
17 Apr 82 ●	IRONFIST *Bronze BRNA 539*	6	9 wks
26 Feb 83	WHAT'S WORDS WORTH *Big Beat NED 2*	71	2 wks
4 Jun 83	ANOTHER PERFECT DAY *Bronze BRON 546* ..	20	4 wks
15 Sep 84	NO REMORSE *Bronze PROTV MOTOR 1*	14	6 wks
9 Aug 86	ORGASMATRON *GWR GWLP 1*	21	4 wks
5 Sep 87	ROCK 'N' ROLL *GWR GWLP 14*	34	3 wks

MOTORS *UK, male vocal/instrumental group* *6 wks*

15 Oct 77	THE MOTORS *Virgin V 2089*	46	5 wks
3 Jun 78	APPROVED BY THE MOTORS *Virgin V 2101* ...	60	1 wk

MOTT THE HOOPLE
UK, male vocal/instrumental group *32 wks*

2 May 70	MOTT THE HOOPLE *Island ILPS 9108*	66	1 wk
17 Oct 70	MAD SHADOWS *Island ILPS 9119*	48	2 wks
17 Apr 71	WILD LIFE *Island ILPS 9144*	44	2 wks
23 Sep 72	ALL THE YOUNG DUDES *CBS 65184*	21	4 wks
11 Aug 73 ●	MOTT *CBS 69038*	7	15 wks
13 Apr 74	THE HOOPLE *CBS 69062*	11	5 wks
23 Nov 74	LIVE *CBS 69093*	32	2 wks
4 Oct 75	DRIVE ON *CBS 69154*	45	1 wk

MOUNTAIN *US/Canada, male vocal/instrumental group* *4 wks*

5 Jun 71	NANTUCKET SLEIGHRIDE *Island ILPS 9148* ..	43	1 wk
8 Jul 72	THE ROAD GOES EVER ON *Island ILPS 9199* .	21	3 wks

Nana MOUSKOURI *Greece, female vocalist* *200 wks*

7 Jun 69 ●	OVER AND OVER *Fontana S 5511*	10	105 wks
4 Apr 70 ●	THE EXQUISITE NANA MOUSKOURI		
	Fontana STL 5536	10	25 wks
10 Oct 70	RECITAL '70 *Fontana 6312 003*	68	1 wk

3 Apr 71	TURN ON THE SUN *Fontana 6312 008*	16	15 wks
29 Jul 72	BRITISH CONCERT *Fontana 6651 003*	29	11 wks
28 Apr 73	SONGS FROM HER TV SERIES		
	Fontana 6312 036	29	11 wks
28 Sep 74	SPOTLIGHT ON NANA MOUSKOURI		
	Fontana 6641 197	38	6 wks
10 Jul 76	● PASSPORT *Philips 9101 061*	3	16 wks
22 Feb 86	ALONE *Philips PHH 3*	19	10 wks

MOVE   *UK, male vocal/instrumental group*   *9 wks*

13 Apr 68	MOVE *Regal Zonophone SLPZ 1002*	15	9 wks

Alison MOYET   *UK, female vocalist*   *117 wks*

17 Nov 84	★ ALF *CBS 26229*	1	83 wks
18 Apr 87	● RAINDANCING *CBS 450 152–1*	2†	34 wks

MR. MISTER   *US, male vocal/instrumental group*   *24 wks*

15 Feb 86	● WELCOME TO THE REAL WORLD		
	RCA PL 89647	6	24 wks

MSG   *Germany/UK, male vocal/instrumental group*   *2 wks*

24 Oct 87	PERFECT TIMING *EMI EMC 3539*	65	2 wks

See also Michael Schenker Group.

MTUME   *US, male/female vocal/instrumental group*   *1 wk*

6 Oct 84	YOU, ME & HE *Epic EPC 26077*	85	1 wk

MUD   *UK, male vocal/instrumental group*   *58 wks*

28 Sep 74	● MUD ROCK *RAK SRAK 508*	8	35 wks
26 Jul 75	● MUD ROCK VOL 2 *RAK SRAK 513*	6	12 wks
1 Nov 75	MUD'S GREATEST HITS *RAK SRAK 6755*	25	6 wks
27 Dec 75	USE YOUR IMAGINATION		
	Private Stock PVLP 1003	33	5 wks

MUFFINS – *See MARTHA and the MUFFINS*

Gerry MULLIGAN and Ben WEBSTER
US, male instrumental duo – baritone and tenor sax   *1 wk*

24 Sep 60	GERRY MULLIGAN MEETS BEN WEBSTER		
	HMV CLP 1373	15	1 wk

MUNGO JERRY   *UK, male vocal/instrumental group*   *14 wks*

8 Aug 70	MUNGO JERRY *Dawn DNLS 3008*	13	6 wks
10 Apr 71	ELECTRONICALLY TESTED *Dawn DNLS 3020* ..	14	8 wks

MUPPETS   *US, puppets*   *45 wks*

11 Jun 77	★ THE MUPPET SHOW *Pye NSPH 19*	1	35 wks
25 Feb 78	THE MUPPET SHOW VOL. 2 *Pye NSPH 21*	16	10 wks

Peter MURPHY   *UK, male vocalist*   *1 wk*

26 Jul 86	SHOULD THE WORLD FAIL TO FALL APART		
	Beggars Banquet BEGA 69	82	1 wk

Anne MURRAY   *Canada, female vocalist*   *10 wks*

3 Oct 81	VERY BEST OF ANNE MURRAY		
	Capitol EMTV 31	14	10 wks

Pauline MURRAY and the INVISIBLE GIRLS
UK, female vocalist with male vocal/instrumental group   *4 wks*

11 Oct 80	PAULINE MURRAY AND THE INVISIBLE GIRLS		
	Elusive 2394 227	25	4 wks

MUSIC OF THE MOUNTAINS – *See MANUEL and his MUSIC OF THE MOUNTAINS*

MUSICAL YOUTH
UK, male vocal/instrumental group   *22 wks*

4 Dec 82	THE YOUTH OF TODAY *MCA YOULP 1*	24	22 wks

MUSIC STUDENTS – *See Ian DURY*

N

Graham NASH   *UK, male vocalist*   *8 wks*

26 Jun 71	SONGS FOR BEGINNERS *Atlantic 2401–011*	13	8 wks

See also Crosby, Stills and Nash; Crosby, Stills, Nash and Young; Graham Nash and David Crosby.

Graham NASH and David CROSBY
UK/US, male vocal duo   *5 wks*

13 May 72	GRAHAM NASH AND DAVID CROSBY		
	Atlantic K 50011	13	5 wks

See also Dave Crosby; Crosby, Stills and Nash; Crosby, Stills, Nash and Young; Graham Nash.

Johnny NASH   *US, male vocalist*   *17 wks*

5 Aug 72	I CAN SEE CLEARLY NOW *CBS 64860*	39	6 wks
10 Dec 77	JOHNNY NASH COLLECTION *Epic EPC 10008* .	18	11 wks

NASH THE SLASH
Canada, male vocalist/multi-instrumentalist   *1 wk*

21 Feb 81	CHILDREN OF THE NIGHT *DinDisc DID 9*	61	1 wk

NATASHA   *UK, female vocalist*   *3 wks*

9 Oct 82	CAPTURED *Towerbell TOWLP 2*	53	3 wks

NATIONAL BRASS BAND   *UK, orchestra*   *10 wks*

10 May 80	GOLDEN MEMORIES *K-Tel ONE 1075*	15	10 wks

NAZARETH   *UK, male vocal/instrumental group*   *51 wks*

26 May 73	RAZAMANAZ *Mooncrest CREST 1*	11	25 wks
24 Nov 73	● LOUD 'N' PROUD *Mooncrest CREST 4*	10	7 wks
18 May 74	RAMPANT *Mooncrest CREST 15*	13	3 wks
13 Dec 75	GREATEST HITS *Mountain TOPS 108*	54	1 wk
3 Feb 79	NO MEAN CITY *Mountain TOPS 123*	34	9 wks
28 Feb 81	THE FOOL CIRCLE *NEMS NEL 6019*	60	3 wks
3 Oct 81	NAZARETH LIVE *NEMS NELD 102*	78	3 wks

Bill NELSON   *UK, male vocalist/multi-instrumentalist*   *21 wks*

24 Feb 79	**SOUND ON SOUND** *Harvest SHSP 4095*	33	5 wks
23 May 81	● **QUIT DREAMING AND GET ON THE BEAM**		
	Mercury 6359 055	7	6 wks
3 Jul 82	**THE LOVE THAT WHIRLS (DIARY OF A**		
	THINKING HEART)		
	Mercury WHIRL 3	28	4 wks
14 May 83	**CHIMERA** *Mercury MERB 19*	30	5 wks
3 May 86	**GETTING THE HOLY GHOST ACROSS**		
	Portrait PRT 26602	91	1 wk

First album credited to Bill Nelson's Red Noise – UK male vocal/instrumental group.

Phyllis NELSON   *US, female vocalist*   *10 wks*

20 Apr 85	**MOVE CLOSER** *Carrere CAL 203*	29	10 wks

NENA   *Germany, female/male vocal/instrumental group*   *5 wks*

24 Mar 84	**NENA** *Epic EPC 25925*	31	5 wks

NESBIT – *See MILLICAN and NESBIT*

Robbie NEVIL   *US, male vocalist*   *1 wk*

13 Jun 87	**C'EST LA VIE** *Manhattan MTL 1006*	93	1 wk

NEW MODEL ARMY
UK, male vocal/instrumental group   *11 wks*

12 May 84	**VENGEANCE** *Abstract ABT 008*	73	5 wks
25 May 85	**NO REST FOR THE WICKED** *EMI NMAL 1* ...	22	3 wks
11 Oct 86	**THE GHOST OF CAIN** *EMI EMC 3516*	45	3 wks

NEW MUSIK   *UK, male vocal/instrumental group*   *11 wks*

17 May 80	**FROM A TO B** *GTO GTLP 041*	35	9 wks
14 Mar 81	**ANYWHERE** *GTO GTLP 044*	68	2 wks

NEW ORDER
UK, male/female vocal/instrumental group   *67 wks*

28 Nov 81	**MOVEMENT** *Factory FACT 50*	30	10 wks
14 May 83	● **POWER, CORRUPTION AND LIES**		
	Factory FACT 75	4	29 wks
25 May 85	● **LOW-LIFE** *Factory FACT 100*	7	10 wks
11 Oct 86	● **BROTHERHOOD** *Factory FACT 150*	9	5 wks
29 Aug 87	● **SUBSTANCE** *Factory FACT 200*	3	13 wks

NEW SEEKERS
UK, male/female vocal/instrumental group   *49 wks*

5 Feb 72	**NEW COLOURS** *Polydor 2383 066*	40	4 wks
1 Apr 72	● **WE'D LIKE TO TEACH THE WORLD TO SING**		
	Polydor 2883 103	2	25 wks
12 Aug 72	**NEVER ENDING SONG OF LOVE**		
	Polydor 2383 126	35	4 wks
14 Oct 72	**CIRCLES** *Polydor 2442 102*	23	5 wks
21 Apr 73	**NOW** *Polydor 2383 195*	47	2 wks
30 Mar 74	**TOGETHER** *Polydor 2383 264*	12	9 wks

NEW WORLD THEATRE ORCHESTRA
UK, orchestra   *1 wk*

24 Dec 60	**LET'S DANCE TO THE HITS OF THE 30'S AND**		
	40'S *Pye Golden Guinea GGL 0026*	20	1 wk

NEWCLEUS   *US, male vocal/instrumental group*   *2 wks*

25 Aug 84	**JAM ON REVENGE** *Sunnyview SVLP 6600*	84	2 wks

Bob NEWHART   *US, male comedian*   *37 wks*

1 Oct 60	● **BUTTON-DOWN MIND OF BOB NEWHART**		
	Warner Bros. WM 4010	2	37 wks

Anthony NEWLEY   *UK, male vocalist*   *14 wks*

14 May 60	**LOVE IS A NOW AND THEN THING**		
	Decca LK 4343	19	2 wks
8 Jul 61	● **TONY** *Decca LK 4406*	5	12 wks

See also Anthony Newley, Peter Sellers, Joan Collins.

Anthony NEWLEY, Peter SELLERS, Joan COLLINS   *UK, male/female vocalists*   *10 wks*

28 Sep 63	● **FOOL BRITANNIA** *Ember CEL 902*	10	10 wks

See also Anthony Newley; Peter Sellers; Harry Secombe, Peter Sellers and Spike Milligan; Peter Sellers and Sophia Loren.

NEWS – *See Huey LEWIS and the NEWS*

Olivia NEWTON-JOHN   *UK, female vocalist*   *93 wks*

2 Mar 74	**MUSIC MAKES MY DAY** *Pye NSPL 28186*	37	3 wks
29 Jun 74	**LONG LIVE LOVE** *EMI EMC 3028*	40	2 wks
26 Apr 75	**HAVE YOU NEVER BEEN MELLOW**		
	EMI EMC 3069	37	2 wks
29 May 76	**COME ON OVER** *EMI EMC 3124*	49	4 wks
27 Aug 77	**MAKING A GOOD THING BETTER**		
	EMI EMC 3192	60	1 wk
21 Jan 78	**GREATEST HITS** *EMI EMA 785*	19	9 wks
9 Dec 79	**TOTALLY HOT** *EMI EMA 789*	30	9 wks
31 Oct 81	**PHYSICAL** *EMI EMC 3386*	11	22 wks
23 Oct 82	● **GREATEST HITS** *EMI EMTV 36*	8	38 wks
8 Mar 86	**SOUL KISS** *Mercury MERH 77*	66	3 wks

NICE   *UK, male instrumental group*   *38 wks*

13 Sep 69	● **NICE** *Immediate IMSP 026*	3	6 wks
27 Jun 70	● **FIVE BRIDGES** *Charisma CAS 1014*	2	21 wks
17 Apr 71	● **ELEGY** *Charisma CAS 1030*	5	11 wks

Paul NICHOLAS   *UK, male vocalist*   *8 wks*

29 Nov 86	**JUST GOOD FRIENDS** *K-Tel ONE 1334*	30	8 wks

Stevie NICKS   *US, female vocalist*   *57 wks*

8 Aug 81	**BELLA DONNA** *WEA K 99169*	11	16 wks
2 Jul 83	**THE WILD HEART** *WEA 25-0071-1*	28	19 wks
14 Dec 85	**ROCK A LITTLE** *Modern PCS 7300*	30	22 wks

Hector NICOL   *UK, male vocalist*   *1 wk*

28 Apr 84	**BRAVO JULIET** *Klub KLP 42*	92	1 wk

NICOLE   *Germany, female vocalist*   *2 wks*

2 Oct 82	**A LITTLE PEACE** *CBS 85011*	85	2 wks

(Left) BILL NELSON enjoyed success with Be-Bop Deluxe in the seventies and as a solo artist in the eighties.

(Right) OLIVIA NEWTON JOHN's clothing reminds us that, although British-born, she grew up in Australia.

(Below) The statistics for *Living Ornaments 1979–80* by GARY NUMAN are not misprinted. This boxed set did reach number two yet was only on the chart for four weeks, the most spectacular in-and-out performance ever.

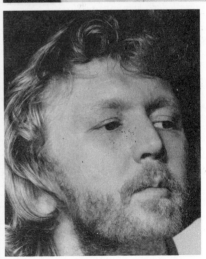

(Above) NILSSON had his greatest chart success with producer Richard Perry.

NILSSON *US, male vocalist* — *43 wks*

29 Jan 72	**THE POINT** *RCA Victor SF 8166*	46	1 wk
5 Feb 72	● **NILSSON SCHMILSSON** *RCA Victor SF 8242*	4	22 wks
19 Aug 72	**SON OF SCHMILSSON** *RCA Victor SF 8297*	41	1 wk
28 Jul 73	**A LITTLE TOUCH OF SCHMILSSON IN THE NIGHT** *RCA Victor SF 8371*	20	19 wks

NINA and FREDERICK
Denmark, male/female vocal duo — *6 wks*

13 Feb 60	● **NINA AND FREDERICK** *Pye NPT 19023*	9	2 wks
29 Apr 61	**NINA AND FREDERICK** *Columbia COL 1314*	11	4 wks

These two albums, although identically named, are different.

9 BELOW ZERO *UK, male vocal/instrumental group* — *12 wks*

14 Mar 81	**DON'T POINT YOUR FINGER** *A & M AMLH 68521*	56	6 wks
20 Mar 82	**THIRD DEGREE** *A & M AMLH 68537*	38	6 wks

999 *UK, male vocal/instrumental group* — *1 wk*

25 Mar 78	**999** *United Artists UAG 30199*	53	1 wk

NOLANS *Ireland, female vocal group* — *84 wks*

20 Jul 78	● **20 GIANT HITS** *Target TGS 502*	3	12 wks
19 Jan 80	**NOLANS** *Epic EPC 83892*	15	13 wks
25 Oct 80	**MAKING WAVES** *Epic EPC 10023*	11	33 wks
27 Mar 82	● **PORTRAIT** *Epic EPC 10033*	7	10 wks
20 Nov 82	**ALTOGETHER** *Epic EPC 10037*	52	8 wks
17 Nov 84	**GIRLS JUST WANNA HAVE FUN** *Towerbell TOWLP 10*	39	8 wks

First album credited to Nolan Sisters.

NOT THE 9 O'CLOCK NEWS CAST
UK, male/female TV cast — *51 wks*

8 Nov 80	● **NOT THE 9 O'CLOCK NEWS** *BBC REB 400*	5	23 wks
17 Oct 81	● **HEDGEHOG SANDWICH** *BBC REB 421*	5	24 wks
23 Oct 82	**THE MEMORY KINDA LINGERS** *BBC REF 453*	63	4 wks

NU SHOOZ *US, male/female vocal duo* — *8 wks*

14 Jun 86	**POOLSIDE** *Atlantic WX 60*	32	8 wks

NUCLEUS *UK, male instrumental group* — *1 wk*

11 Jul 70	**ELASTIC ROCK** *Vertigo 6360 006*	46	1 wk

Ted NUGENT
US, male vocalist/instrumentalist – guitar — *14 wks*

4 Sep 76	**TED NUGENT** *Epic EPC 81268*	56	1 wk
30 Oct 76	**FREE FOR ALL** *Epic EPC 81397*	33	2 wks
2 Jul 77	**CAT SCRATCH FEVER** *Epic EPC 82010*	28	5 wks
11 Mar 78	**DOUBLE LIVE GONZO** *Epic EPC 88282*	47	2 wks
14 Jun 80	**SCREAM DREAM** *Epic EPC 86111*	37	3 wks
25 Apr 81	**IN 10 CITIES** *Epic EPC 84917*	75	1 wk

Gary NUMAN *UK, male vocalist* — *132 wks*

9 Jun 79	★ **REPLICAS** *Beggars Banquet BEGA 7*	1	31 wks
25 Aug 79	**TUBEWAY ARMY** *Beggars Banquet BEGA 4*	14	10 wks
22 Sep 79	★ **THE PLEASURE PRINCIPLE** *Beggars Banquet BEGA 10*	1	21 wks
13 Sep 80	★ **TELEKON** *Beggars Banquet BEGA 19*	1	11 wks
2 May 81	● **LIVING ORNAMENTS 1979–1980** *Beggars Banquet BOX 1*	2	4 wks
2 May 81	**LIVING ORNAMENTS 1979** *Beggars Banquet BEGA 24*	47	3 wks
2 May 81	**LIVING ORNAMENTS 1980** *Beggars Banquet BEGA 25*	39	3 wks
12 Sep 81	● **DANCE** *Beggars Banquet BEGA 28*	3	8 wks
18 Sep 82	● **I, ASSASSIN** *Beggars Banquet BEGA 40*	8	6 wks
27 Nov 82	**NEW MAN NUMAN – THE BEST OF GARY NUMAN** *TV Records TVA 7*	45	7 wks
24 Sep 83	**WARRIORS** *Beggars Banquet BEGA 47*	12	6 wks
6 Oct 84	**THE PLAN** *Beggars Banquet BEGA 55*	29	4 wks
24 Nov 84	**BERSERKER** *Numa NUMA 1001*	45	3 wks
13 Apr 85	**WHITE NOISE-LIVE** *Numa NUMAD 1002*	29	5 wks
28 Sep 85	**THE FURY** *Numa NUMA 1003*	24	5 wks
8 Nov 86	**STRANGE CHARM** *Numa NUMA 1005*	59	2 wks
3 Oct 87	**EXHIBITION** *Beggars Banquet BEGA 88*	43	3 wks

First two albums credited to Tubeway Army. The Plan is credited to Tubeway Army and Gary Numan. All other albums are credited to Gary Numan. Living Ornaments 1979–1980 is a boxed set of Living Ornaments 1979 and Living Ornaments 1980.

O

Philip OAKEY and Georgio MORODER
UK/Italy male vocal/instrumental duo — *5 wks*

10 Aug 85	**PHILIP OAKEY AND GEORGIO MORODER** *Virgin V 2351*	52	5 wks

OASIS *UK, male/female vocal group* — *14 wks*

28 Apr 84	**OASIS** *WEA WX 3*	23	14 wks

OATES – *See Daryl HALL and John OATES*

Billy OCEAN *UK, male vocalist* — *91 wks*

24 Nov 84	● **SUDDENLY** *Jive JIP 12*	9	59 wks
17 May 86	● **LOVE ZONE** *Jive HIP 35*	2	32 wks

Des O'CONNOR *UK, male vocalist* — *41 wks*

7 Dec 68	● **I PRETEND** *Columbia SCX 6295*	8	10 wks
5 Dec 70	**WITH LOVE** *Columbia SCX 6417*	40	4 wks
2 Dec 72	**SING A FAVOURITE SONG** *Pye NSPL 18390*	25	6 wks
2 Feb 80	**JUST FOR YOU** *Warwick WW 5071*	17	7 wks
13 Oct 84	**DES O'CONNOR NOW** *Telstar STAR 2245*	24	14 wks

Hazel O'CONNOR *UK, female vocalist* — *45 wks*

9 Aug 80	● **BREAKING GLASS (film soundtrack)** *A & M AMLH 64820*	5	38 wks
12 Sep 81	**COVER PLUS** *Albion ALB 108*	32	7 wks

ODYSSEY *US, male/female vocal group* — *32 wks*

16 Aug 80	**HANG TOGETHER** *RCA PL 13526*	38	3 wks
4 Jul 81	**I'VE GOT THE MELODY** *RCA RCALP 5028*	29	7 wks
3 Jul 82	**HAPPY TOGETHER** *RCA RCALP 6036*	21	9 wks
20 Nov 82	**THE MAGIC TOUCH OF ODYSSEY** *Telstar STAR 2223*	69	5 wks
26 Sep 87	**THE GREATEST HITS** *Stylus SMR 735*	26	8 wks

Esther and Abi OFARIM
Israel, female/male vocal duo　　　　　*24 wks*

24 Feb 68	● **2 IN 3** *Philips SBL 7825*	6	20 wks
12 Jul 69	**OFARIM CONCERT – LIVE '69** *Philips XL 4*	29	4 wks

Mary O'HARA
UK, female vocalist/instrumentalist – harp　　　　　*12 wks*

8 Apr 78	**MARY O'HARA AT THE ROYAL FESTIVAL HALL** *Chrysalis CHR 1159*	37	3 wks
1 Dec 79	**TRANQUILLITY** *Warwick WW 5072*	12	9 wks

Mike OLDFIELD
UK, male multi-instrumentalist/vocalist　　　　　*466 wks*

14 Jul 73	★ **TUBULAR BELLS** *Virgin V 2001*	1	264 wks
14 Sep 74	★ **HERGEST RIDGE** *Virgin V 2013*	1	17 wks
8 Feb 75	**THE ORCHESTRAL TUBULAR BELLS (WITH THE ROYAL PHILHARMONIC ORCHESTRA)** *Virgin V 2026*	17	7 wks
15 Nov 75	● **OMMADAWN** *Virgin V 2043*	4	23 wks
20 Nov 76	**BOXED** *Virgin V BOX 1*	22	13 wks
9 Dec 78	**INCANTATIONS** *Virgin VDT 101*	14	17 wks
11 Aug 79	**EXPOSED** *Virgin VD 2511*	16	9 wks
8 Dec 79	**PLATINUM** *Virgin V 2141*	24	9 wks
8 Nov 80	**QE 2** *Virgin V 2181*	27	12 wks
27 Mar 82	● **FIVE MILES OUT** *Virgin V 2222*	7	27 wks
4 Jun 83	● **CRISES** *Virgin V 2262*	6	29 wks
7 Jul 84	**DISCOVERY** *Virgin V 2308*	15	16 wks
15 Dec 84	**THE KILLING FIELDS – ORIGINAL SOUNDTRACK** *Virgin V 2328*	97	1 wk
2 Nov 85	**THE COMPLETE MIKE OLDFIELD** *Virgin MOC 1*	36	17 wks
10 Oct 87	**ISLANDS** *Virgin V 2466*	29	5 wks

ONE HUNDRED & ONE STRINGS
Germany, orchestra　　　　　*35 wks*

26 Sep 59	● **GYPSY CAMPFIRES** *Pye GGL 0009*	9	7 wks
26 Mar 60	**SOUL OF SPAIN** *Pye GGL 0017*	17	1 wk
16 Apr 60	● **GRAND CANYON SUITE** *Pye GGL 0048*	10	1 wk
27 Aug 60	★ **DOWN DRURY LANE TO MEMORY LANE** *Pye GGL 0061*	1	21 wks
15 Oct 83	**MORNING, NOON & NIGHT** *Ronco RTL 2094* ...	32	5 wks

The orchestra was American based for last album.

Alexander O'NEAL　*US, male vocalist*　　　*39 wks*

1 Jun 85	**ALEXANDER O'NEAL** *Tabu TBU 26485*	19	18 wks
8 Aug 87	● **HEARSAY** *Tabu 450 936–1*	10†	21 wks

ONLY ONES　*UK, male vocal/instrumental group*　　*8 wks*

3 Jun 78	**THE ONLY ONES** *CBS 82830*	56	1 wk
31 Mar 79	**EVEN SERPENTS SHINE** *CBS 83451*	42	2 wks
3 May 80	**BABY'S GOT A GUN** *CBS 84089*	37	5 wks

Yoko ONO　*Japan, female vocalist*　　　*2 wks*

20 Jun 81	**SEASON OF GLASS** *Geffen K 99164*	47	2 wks

See also John Lennon.

ORANGE JUICE　*UK, male vocal/instrumental group*　*18 wks*

6 Mar 82	**YOU CAN'T HIDE YOUR LOVE FOREVER** *Polydor POLS 1057*	21	6 wks

20 Nov 82	**RIP IT UP** *Holden Caulfield Universal POLS 1076*	39	8 wks
10 Mar 84	**TEXAS FEVER** *Polydor OJMLP 1*	34	4 wks

Roy ORBISON　*US, male vocalist*　　　*144 wks*

8 Jun 63	**LONELY AND BLUE** *London HAU 2342*	15	8 wks
29 Jun 63	**CRYING** *London HAU 2437*	17	3 wks
30 Nov 63	● **IN DREAMS** *London HAU 8108*	6	57 wks
25 Jul 64	**EXCITING SOUNDS OF ROY ORBISON** *Ember NR 5013*	17	2 wks
5 Dec 64	● **OH PRETTY WOMAN** *London HAU 8207*	4	16 wks
25 Sep 65	● **THERE IS ONLY ONE ROY ORBISON** *London HAU 8252*	10	12 wks
26 Feb 66	**THE ORBISON WAY** *London HAU 8279*	11	10 wks
24 Sep 66	**THE CLASSIC ROY ORBISON** *London HAU 8297*	12	8 wks
22 Jul 67	**ORBISONGS** *Monument SMO 5004*	40	1 wk
30 Sep 67	**ROY ORBISON'S GREATEST HITS** *Monument SMO 5007*	40	1 wk
27 Jan 73	**ALL-TIME GREATEST HITS** *Monument MNT 67290*	39	3 wks
29 Nov 75	★ **THE BEST OF ROY ORBISON** *Arcade ADEP 19*	1	20 wks
18 Jul 81	**GOLDEN DAYS** *CBS 10026*	63	1 wk
4 Jul 87	**IN DREAMS: THE GREATEST HITS** *Virgin VGD 3514*	86	2 wks

ORCHESTRAL MANOEUVRES IN THE DARK
UK, male vocal/instrumental duo　　　　　*152 wks*

1 Mar 80	**ORCHESTRAL MANOEUVRES IN THE DARK** *DinDisc DID 2*	27	29 wks
1 Nov 80	● **ORGANISATION** *DinDisc DID 6*	6	25 wks
14 Nov 81	● **ARCHITECTURE AND MORALITY** *DinDisc DID 12*	3	39 wks
12 Mar 83	● **DAZZLE SHIPS** *Telegraph V 2261*	5	13 wks
12 May 84	● **JUNK CULTURE** *Virgin V 2310*	9	27 wks
29 Jun 85	**CRUSH** *Virgin V 2349*	13	12 wks
11 Oct 86	**THE PACIFIC AGE** *Virgin V 2398*	15	7 wks

L'ORCHESTRE ELECTRONIQUE
UK, male synthesized orchestra　　　　　*1 wk*

29 Oct 83	**SOUND WAVES** *Nouveau Musique NML 1005*	75	1 wk

Cyril ORNADEL/LONDON SYMPHONY ORCHESTRA　*UK, conductor and orchestra*　*21 wks*

16 Dec 72	● **THE STRAUSS FAMILY** *Polydor 2659 014*	2	21 wks

See also London Symphony Orchestra; Michael Crawford; Kimera; Julian Lloyd Webber, all with the London Symphony Orchestra; Spike Milligan.

ORVILLE – *See Keith HARRIS, ORVILLE and CUDDLES*

Jeffrey OSBORNE　*US, male vocalist*　　　*10 wks*

5 May 84	**STAY WITH ME TONIGHT** *A & M AMLX 64940*	56	7 wks
13 Oct 84	**DON'T STOP** *A & M AMA 5017*	59	3 wks

Ozzy OSBOURNE　*UK, male vocalist*　　　*49 wks*

20 Sep 80	● **OZZY OSBOURNE'S BLIZZARD OF OZ** *Jet JRTLP 234*	7	8 wks
7 Nov 81	**DIARY OF A MADMAN** *Jet JETLP 237*	14	12 wks
27 Nov 82	**TALK OF THE DEVIL** *Jet JETDP 401*	21	6 wks
10 Dec 83	**BARK AT THE MOON** *Epic EPC 25739*	24	7 wks
22 Feb 86	● **THE ULTIMATE SIN** *Epic EPC 26404*	8	10 wks
23 May 87	**TRIBUTE** *Epic 450 475–1*	13	6 wks

Ozzy Osbourne's Blizzard Of Oz are a UK/US male vocal/instrumental group.

Though his singles chart career was confined to the sixties, ROY ORBISON has subsequently charted with compilations of those hits.

(Left) HAZEL O'CONNOR is shown performing with saxophonist Wesley Magoogan, who backed her memorably on *Will You* from *Breaking Glass*.

(Below) GILBERT O'SULLIVAN is shown in the image he used to draw attention to *Himself*.

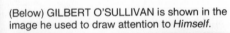

OSIBISA *Ghana/Nigeria, male vocal/instrumental group* 17 wks

22 May 71	OSIBISA	MCA MDKS 8001	....	11	10 wks
5 Feb 72	WOYAYA	MCA MDKS 8005	....	11	7 wks

Donny OSMOND *US, male vocalist* 104 wks

23 Sep 72	● PORTRAIT OF DONNY	MGM 2315 108	....	5	43 wks
16 Dec 72	● TOO YOUNG	MGM 2315 113	....	7	24 wks
26 May 73	● ALONE TOGETHER	MGM 2315 210	......	6	19 wks
15 Dec 73	● A TIME FOR US	MGM 2315 273	....	4	13 wks
8 Feb 75	DONNY	MGM 2315 314	....	16	4 wks
2 Oct 76	DISCOTRAIN	Polydor 2391 226	....	59	1 wk

See also Osmonds; Donny and Marie Osmond.

Donny and Marie OSMOND
US, male/female vocal duo 19 wks

2 Nov 74	I'M LEAVING IT ALL UP TO YOU			
	MGM 2315 307	....	13	15 wks
26 Jul 75	MAKE THE WORLD GO AWAY			
	MGM 2315 343	....	30	3 wks
5 Jun 76	DEEP PURPLE	Polydor 2391 220	... 48	1 wk

See also Osmonds; Donny Osmond; Marie Osmond.

Little Jimmy OSMOND *US, male vocalist* 12 wks

17 Feb 73	KILLER JOE	MGM 2315 157	....	20	12 wks

Marie OSMOND *US, female vocalist* 1 wk

9 Feb 74	PAPER ROSES	MGM 2315 262	....	46	1 wk

See also Donny and Marie Osmond.

OSMONDS *US, male vocal/instrumental group* 103 wks

18 Nov 72	OSMONDS LIVE	MGM 2315 117	....	13	22 wks
16 Dec 72	● CRAZY HORSES	MGM 2315 123	....	9	19 wks
25 Aug 73	● THE PLAN	MGM 2315 251	....	6	25 wks
17 Aug 74	● OUR BEST TO YOU	MGM 2315 300	....	5	20 wks
7 Dec 74	LOVE ME FOR A REASON	MGM 2315 312	.....	13	9 wks
14 Jun 75	I'M STILL GONNA NEED YOU	MGM 2315 342	.	19	7 wks
10 Jan 76	AROUND THE WORLD – LIVE IN CONCERT			
	MGM 2659 044	....	41	1 wk

See also Donny Osmond; Donny and Marie Osmond.

Gilbert O'SULLIVAN *UK, male vocalist* 191 wks

25 Sep 71	● HIMSELF	MAM 501	....	5	82 wks
18 Nov 72	★ BACK TO FRONT	MAM 502	....	1	64 wks
6 Oct 73	● I'M A WRITER NOT A FIGHTER	MAMS 505	...	2	25 wks
26 Oct 74	● STRANGER IN MY OWN BACK YARD			
	MAM MAMS 506		9	8 wks
18 Dec 76	GREATEST HITS	MAM MAMA 2003	....	13	11 wks
12 Sep 81	20 GOLDEN GREATS	K-Tel NE 1133	....	98	1 wk

John OTWAY and Wild Willy BARRETT
UK, male vocal/instrumental duo 1 wk

1 Jul 78	DEEP AND MEANINGLESS	Polydor 2382 501	...	44	1 wk

P

PACEMAKERS – *See GERRY and the PACEMAKERS*

Jimmy PAGE *UK, male instrumentalist – guitar* 4 wks

27 Feb 82	DEATHWISH II (film soundtrack)				
	Swansong SSK 59415	....	40	4 wks

See also Roy Harper with Jimmy Page.

Elaine PAIGE *UK, female vocalist* 109 wks

1 May 82	ELAINE PAIGE	WEA K 58385	....	56	6 wks
5 Nov 83	● STAGES	K-Tel NE 1262	....	2	48 wks
20 Oct 84	CINEMA	K-Tel NE 1282	....	12	25 wks
16 Nov 85	● LOVE HURTS	WEA WX 28	....	8	20 wks
29 Nov 86	CHRISTMAS	WEA WX 80	....	27	6 wks
5 Dec 87	MEMORIES – THE BEST OF ELAINE PAIGE			
	Telstar STAR 2313	....	14†	4 wks

PALE FOUNTAINS
UK, male vocal/instrumental group 3 wks

10 Mar 84	PACIFIC STREET	Virgin V 2274	....	85	2 wks
16 Feb 85	FROM ACROSS THE KITCHEN TABLE			
	Virgin V 2333	....	94	1 wk

PALLAS *UK, male vocal/instrumental group* 4 wks

25 Feb 84	SENTINEL	Harvest SHSP 2400121	....	41	3 wks
22 Feb 86	THE WEDGE	Harvest SHVL 850	....	70	1 wk

Robert PALMER *UK, male vocalist* 65 wks

6 Nov 76	SOME PEOPLE CAN DO WHAT THEY LIKE			
	Island ILPS 9420	....	46	1 wk
14 Jul 79	SECRETS	Island ILPS 9544	....	54	4 wks
6 Sep 80	CLUES	Island ILPS 9595	....	31	8 wks
3 Apr 82	MAYBE IT'S LIVE	Island ILPS 9665	....	32	6 wks
23 Apr 83	PRIDE	Island ILPS 9720	....	37	9 wks
16 Nov 85	● RIPTIDE	Island ILPS 9801	....	5	37 wks

PAPAS – *See MAMAS and PAPAS*

Graham PARKER and the RUMOUR
UK, male vocal/instrumental group 35 wks

27 Nov 76	HEAT TREATMENT	Vertigo 6360 137	....	52	2 wks
12 Nov 77	STICK TO ME	Vertigo 9102 017	....	19	4 wks
27 May 78	PARKERILLA	Vertigo 6641 797	....	14	5 wks
7 Apr 79	SQUEEZING OUT SPARKS	Vertigo 9102 030	....	18	8 wks
7 Jun 80	THE UP ESCALATOR	Stiff SEEZ 23	....	11	10 wks
27 Mar 82	ANOTHER GREY AREA	RCA RCALP 6029	...	40	6 wks

Another Grey Area credited to Graham Parker.

Ray PARKER Jr. *US, male vocalist* 7 wks

10 Oct 87	AFTER DARK	WEA WX 122	....	40	7 wks

John PARR *UK, male vocalist* 2 wks

2 Nov 85	JOHN PARR	London LONLP 12	....	60	2 wks

Alan PARSONS PROJECT
UK, male vocal/instrumental group **38 wks**

28 Aug 76	**TALES OF MYSTERY AND IMAGINATION** *Charisma CDS 4003*	56	1 wk
13 Aug 77	**I ROBOT** *Arista SPARTY 1016*	30	1 wk
10 Jun 78	**PYRAMID** *Arista SPART 1054*	49	4 wks
29 Sep 79	**EVE** *Arista SPARTY 1100*	74	1 wk
15 Nov 80	**THE TURN OF A FRIENDLY CARD** *Arista DLART 1*	38	4 wks
29 May 82	**EYE IN THE SKY** *Arista 204 666*	28	11 wks
26 Nov 83	**THE BEST OF THE ALAN PARSONS PROJECT** *Arista APP 1*	99	1 wk
3 Mar 84	**AMMONIA AVENUE** *Arista 206 100*	24	8 wks
23 Feb 85	**VULTURE CULTURE** *Arista 206 577*	40	5 wks
14 Feb 87	**GAUDI** *Arista 208 084*	66	2 wks

PARTISANS *UK, male vocal/instrumental group* **1 wk**

19 Feb 83	**THE PARTISANS** *No Future PUNK 4*	94	1 wk

Dolly PARTON *US, female vocalist* **13 wks**

25 Nov 78	**BOTH SIDES** *Lotus WH 5006*	45	12 wks
7 Sep 85	**GREATEST HITS** *RCA PL 84422*	74	1 wk

See also Dolly Parton/Linda Ronstadt/Emmylou Harris.

Dolly PARTON/Linda RONSTADT/Emmylou HARRIS *US, female vocal group* **4 wks**

14 Mar 87	**TRIO** *Warner Bros. 925 491–1*	60	4 wks

See also Dolly Parton; Linda Ronstadt; Emmylou Harris.

PARTRIDGE FAMILY
US, male/female vocal group **13 wks**

8 Jan 72	**UP TO DATE** *Bell SBLL 143*	46	2 wks
22 Apr 72	**THE PARTRIDGE FAMILY SOUND MAGAZINE** *Bell BELLS 206*	14	7 wks
30 Sep 72	**SHOPPING BAG** *Bell BELLS 212*	28	3 wks
9 Dec 72	**CHRISTMAS CARD** *Bell BELLS 214*	45	1 wk

PASSIONS *UK, male/female vocal/instrumental group* **1 wk**

3 Oct 81	**THIRTY THOUSAND FEET OVER CHINA** *Polydor POLS 1041*	92	1 wk

PAUL – *See PETER, PAUL and MARY*

Luciano PAVAROTTI *Italy, male vocalist* **34 wks**

15 May 82	**PAVAROTTI'S GREATEST HITS** *Decca D 2362*	95	1 wk
9 Aug 86	**THE PAVAROTTI COLLECTION** *Stylus SMR 8617*	12†	33 wks

See also Luciano Pavarotti with the Henry Mancini Orchestra.

Luciano PAVAROTTI with the Henry MANCINI ORCHESTRA
Italy, male vocalist with US, conductor/orchestra **1 wk**

30 Jun 84	**MAMMA** *Decca 411959*	96	1 wk

See also Luciano Pavarotti; Henry Mancini; James Galway and Henry Mancini; Johnny Mathis and Henry Mancini.

Tom PAXTON *US, male vocalist* **10 wks**

13 Jun 70	**NO. 6** *Elektra 2469–003*	23	5 wks
3 Apr 71	**THE COMPLEAT TOM PAXTON** *Elektra EKD 2003*	18	4 wks
1 Jul 72	**PEACE WILL COME** *Reprise K 44182*	47	1 wk

PEDDLERS *UK, male vocal/instrumental group* **16 wks**

16 Mar 68	**FREE WHEELERS** *CBS SBPG 63183*	27	13 wks
7 Feb 70	**BIRTHDAY** *CBS 63682*	16	3 wks

Kevin PEEK *UK, male instrumentalist – guitar* **2 wks**

21 Mar 81	**AWAKENING** *Ariola ARL 5065*	52	2 wks

See also Kevin Peek and Rick Wakeman.

Kevin PEEK and Rick WAKEMAN
UK, male instrumental duo – guitar and keyboards **6 wks**

13 Oct 84	**BEYOND THE PLANETS** *Woomera STAR 2244*	64	6 wks

Beyond the Planets also features Jeff Wayne with narration by Patrick Allen. See also Kevin Peek; Rick Wakeman; Jeff Wayne.

PENETRATION
UK, male/female vocal/instrumental group **8 wks**

28 Oct 78	**MOVING TARGETS** *Virgin V 2109*	22	4 wks
6 Oct 79	**COMING UP FOR AIR** *Virgin V 2131*	36	4 wks

PENGUIN CAFE ORCHESTRA
UK, male instrumental group **5 wks**

4 Apr 87	**SIGNS OF LIFE** *Edition EG EGED 50*	49	5 wks

PENTANGLE
UK, male/female vocal/instrumental group **39 wks**

15 Jun 68	**THE PENTANGLE** *Transatlantic TRA 162*	21	9 wks
1 Nov 69 ●	**BASKET OF LIGHT** *Transatlantic TRA 205*	5	28 wks
12 Dec 70	**CRUEL SISTER** *Transatlantic TRA 228*	51	2 wks

PEPSI and SHIRLIE *UK, female vocal duo* **2 wks**

7 Nov 87	**ALL RIGHT NOW** *Polydor POLH 38*	69	2 wks

Carl PERKINS *US, male vocalist* **3 wks**

15 Apr 78	**OL' BLUE SUEDES IS BACK** *Jet UATV 30146*	38	3 wks

Steve PERRY *US, male vocalist* **2 wks**

14 Jul 84	**STREET TALK** *CBS 25967*	59	2 wks

PESTALOZZI CHILDREN'S CHOIR
UK, male/female vocal group **2 wks**

26 Dec 81	**SONGS OF JOY** *K-Tel NE 1140*	65	2 wks

(Top) *Blue Gene* contained GENE PITNEY's immortal *Twenty Four Hours From Tulsa*.

(Below) DOLLY PARTON: *Both Sides* was her best-selling album.

To promote *Animals* PINK FLOYD floated a giant pig between the twin towers of Battersea Power Station. The porker got loose and became a menace to aviation.

PET SHOP BOYS UK, male vocal/instrumental duo 119 wks

5 Apr	86	● PLEASE Parlophone PSB 1	**3**	65 wks
29 Nov	86	DISCO EMI PRG 1001	**15**	39 wks
19 Sep	87	● PET SHOP BOYS ACTUALLY Parlophone PCSD 104	**2†**	15 wks

PETER and GORDON UK, male vocal duo 1 wk

20 Jun	64	PETER AND GORDON Columbia 33SX 1630	**18**	1 wk

PETER, PAUL and MARY
US, male/female vocal/instrumental group 26 wks

4 Jan	64	PETER PAUL & MARY Warner Bros. WM 4064 . . .	**18**	1 wk
21 Mar	64	IN THE WIND Warner Bros. WM 8142	**11**	19 wks
13 Feb	65	IN CONCERT VOL. 1 Warner Bros. WM 8158	**20**	2 wks
5 Sep	70	TEN YEARS TOGETHER Warner Bros. WS 2552 . . .	**60**	4 wks

PETERS and LEE UK, male/female vocal duo 166 wks

30 Jun	73	★ WE CAN MAKE IT Philips 6308 165	**1**	55 wks
22 Dec	73	● BY YOUR SIDE Philips 6308 192	**9**	48 wks
21 Sep	74	● RAINBOW Philips 6308 208	**6**	27 wks
4 Oct	75	● FAVOURITES Philips 9109 205	**2**	32 wks
18 Dec	76	INVITATION Philips 9101 027	**44**	4 wks

Tom PETTY and the HEARTBREAKERS
US, male vocal/instrumental group 38 wks

4 Jun	77	TOM PETTY AND THE HEARTBREAKERS Shelter ISA 5014	**24**	12 wks
1 Jul	78	YOU'RE GONNA GET IT Island ISA 5017	**34**	5 wks
17 Nov	79	DAMN THE TORPEDOES MCA MCF 3044	**57**	4 wks
23 May	81	HARD PROMISES MCA MCF 3098	**32**	5 wks
20 Nov	82	LONG AFTER DARK MCA MCF 3155	**45**	4 wks
20 Apr	85	SOUTHERN ACCENTS MCA MCF 3260	**23**	6 wks
2 May	87	LET ME UP (I'VE HAD ENOUGH) MCA MCG 6014	**59**	2 wks

PhD UK, male vocal/instrumental duo 8 wks

1 May	82	PhD WEA K 99150	**33**	8 wks

PHENOMENA UK, male vocal/instrumental group 2 wks

6 Jul	85	PHENOMENA Bronze PM 1	**63**	2 wks

Arlene PHILLIPS UK, female exercise instructor 24 wks

28 Aug	82	KEEP IN SHAPE SYSTEM Supershape SUP 01	**41**	23 wks
18 Feb	84	KEEP IN SHAPE SYSTEM VOL. 2 Supershape SUP 2	**100**	1 wk

Keep In Shape System features music by Funk Federation.

PHOTOS UK, female/male vocal/instrumental group 9 wks

21 Jun	80	● THE PHOTOS CBS PHOTO 5	**4**	9 wks

Edith PIAF France, female vocalist 5 wks

26 Sep	87	HEART AND SOUL Stylus SMR 736	**75**	5 wks

PIGBAG UK, male instrumental group 14 wks

13 Mar	82	DR HECKLE AND MR JIVE Y Y 17	**18**	14 wks

PILOT UK, male vocal/instrumental group 1 wk

31 May	75	SECOND FLIGHT EMI EMC 3075	**48**	1 wk

Courtney PINE UK, male instrumentalist – saxophone 11 wks

25 Oct	86	JOURNEY TO THE URGE WITHIN Island ILPS 9846	**39**	11 wks

PINK FAIRIES UK, male vocal/instrumental group 1 wk

29 Jul	72	WHAT A BUNCH OF SWEETIES Polydor 2383 132	**48**	1 wk

PINK FLOYD UK, male vocal/instrumental group 702 wks

19 Aug	67	● PIPER AT THE GATES OF DAWN Columbia SCX 6157	**6**	14 wks
13 Jul	68	● SAUCERFUL OF SECRETS Columbia SCX 6258 .	**9**	11 wks
28 Jun	69	● MORE (film soundtrack) Columbia SCX 6346 .	**9**	5 wks
15 Nov	69	● UMMAGUMMA Harvest SHDW 1/2	**5**	21 wks
24 Oct	70	★ ATOM HEART MOTHER Harvest SHVL 781	**1**	23 wks
7 Aug	71	RELICS Starline SRS 5071	**32**	6 wks
20 Nov	71	● MEDDLE Harvest SHVL 795	**3**	82 wks
17 Jun	72	● OBSCURED BY CLOUDS (film soundtrack) Harvest SHSP 4020	**6**	14 wks
31 Mar	73	● DARK SIDE OF THE MOON Harvest SHVL 804 . .	**2**	294 wks
19 Jan	74	A NICE PAIR (double re-issue) Harvest SHDW 403	**21**	20 wks
27 Sep	75	★ WISH YOU WERE HERE Harvest SHVL 814	**1**	83 wks
19 Feb	77	● ANIMALS Harvest SHVL 815	**2**	33 wks
8 Dec	79	● THE WALL Harvest SHDW 411	**3**	46 wks
5 Dec	81	A COLLECTION OF GREAT DANCE SONGS Harvest SHVL 822	**37**	10 wks
2 Apr	83	★ THE FINAL CUT Harvest SHPF 1983	**1**	25 wks
19 Sep	87	● A MOMENTARY LAPSE OF REASON EMI EMD 1003	**3†**	15 wks

A Nice Pair is a double re-issue of the first two albums.

PIPS – See Gladys KNIGHT and the PIPS

PIRANHAS UK, male vocal/instrumental group 3 wks

20 Sep	80	PIRANHAS Sire SRK 6098	**69**	3 wks

PIRATES UK, male vocal/instrumental group 3 wks

19 Nov	77	OUT OF THEIR SKULLS Warner Bros. K 56411 . . .	**57**	3 wks

Gene PITNEY US, male vocalist 66 wks

11 Apr	64	● BLUE GENE United Artists ULP 1061	**7**	11 wks
6 Feb	65	GENE PITNEY'S BIG 16 Stateside SL 10118	**12**	6 wks
20 Mar	65	I'M GONNA BE STRONG Stateside SL 10120	**15**	2 wks
20 Nov	65	LOOKIN' THRU THE EYES OF LOVE Stateside SL 10148	**15**	5 wks
17 Sep	66	NOBODY NEEDS YOUR LOVE Stateside SL 10183	**13**	17 wks
4 Mar	67	YOUNG WARM AND WONDERFUL Stateside SSL 10194	**39**	1 wk
22 Apr	67	GENE PITNEY'S BIG SIXTEEN Stateside SSL 10199	**40**	1 wk
20 Sep	69	● BEST OF GENE PITNEY Stateside SSL 10286 . .	**8**	9 wks
2 Oct	76	● HIS 20 GREATEST HITS Arcade ADEP 22	**6**	14 wks

Robert PLANT *UK, male vocalist*   *33 wks*

10 Jul	82	● PICTURES AT ELEVEN *Swansong SSK 59418* ...	2	15 wks
23 Jul	83	● THE PRINCIPLES OF MOMENTS *WEA 7901011*	7	14 wks
1 Jun	85	SHAKEN 'N' STIRRED *Es Paranza 79-0265-1*	19	4 wks

PLASMATICS *US, female/male vocal/instrumental group*   *3 wks*

11 Oct	80	NEW HOPE FOR THE WRETCHED *Stiff SEEZ 24*	55	3 wks

PLATTERS *US, male/female vocal group*   *13 wks*

8 Apr	78	● 20 CLASSIC HITS *Mercury 9100 049*	8	13 wks

PLAYERS ASSOCIATION
US, male/female vocal/instrumental group   *4 wks*

17 Mar	79	TURN THE MUSIC UP *Vanguard VSD 79421*	54	4 wks

PLAYN JAYN *UK, male vocal/instrumental group*   *1 wk*

1 Sep	84	FRIDAY THE 13TH (AT THE MARQUEE CLUB) *A&M JAYN 13*	93	1 wk

POGUES *Ireland, male vocal/instrumental group*   *14 wks*

3 Nov	84	RED ROSES FOR ME *Stiff SEEZ 55*	89	1 wk
17 Aug	85	RUM, SODOMY AND THE LASH *Stiff SEEZ 58*	13	13 wks

POINTER SISTERS *US, female vocal group*   *78 wks*

29 Aug	81	BLACK AND WHITE *Planet K 52300*	21	13 wks
5 May	84	● BREAK OUT *Planet FL 84705*	9	58 wks
27 Jul	85	CONTACT *Planet PL 85457*	34	7 wks

POLECATS *UK, male vocal/instrumental group*   *2 wks*

4 Jul	81	POLECATS *Vertigo 6359 057*	28	2 wks

POLICE *UK, male vocal/instrumental group*   *322 wks*

21 Apr	79	● OUTLANDOS D'AMOUR *A&M AMLH 68502* ..	6	96 wks
13 Oct	79	★ REGGATTA DE BLANC *A&M AMLH 64792* ...	1	74 wks
11 Oct	80	★ ZENYATTA MONDATTA *A&M AMLH 64831*	1	31 wks
10 Oct	81	★ GHOST IN THE MACHINE *A&M AMLK 63730*	1	27 wks
25 Jun	83	★ SYNCHRONICITY *A&M AMLX 63735* ..	1	48 wks
8 Nov	86	★ EVERY BREATH YOU TAKE – THE SINGLES *A&M EVERY 1*	1	46 wks

Su POLLARD *UK, female vocalist*   *3 wks*

22 Nov	86	SU *K-Tel NE 1327*	86	3 wks

Iggy POP *US, male vocalist*   *23 wks*

9 Apr	77	THE IDIOT *RCA Victor PL 12275*	30	3 wks
4 Jun	77	RAW POWER *Embassy 31464*	44	2 wks
1 Oct	77	LUST FOR LIFE *RCA PL 12488*	28	5 wks
19 May	79	NEW VALUES *Arista SPART 1092*	60	4 wks
16 Feb	80	SOLDIER *Arista SPART 1117*	62	2 wks
11 Oct	86	BLAH-BLAH-BLAH *A&M AMA 5145*	43	7 wks

Raw Power *credited to Iggy and the Stooges.*

Sandy POSEY *US, female vocalist*   *1 wk*

11 Mar	67	BORN A WOMAN *MGM MGMCS 8035*	39	1 wk

Frank POURCEL *France, male vocalist*   *7 wks*

20 Nov	71	● THIS IS POURCEL *Studio Two STWO 7*	8	7 wks

Cozy POWELL *UK, male instrumentalist – drums*   *8 wks*

26 Jan	80	OVER THE TOP *Ariola ARL 5038*	34	3 wks
19 Sep	81	TILT *Polydor POLD 5047*	58	4 wks
28 May	83	OCTOPUSS *Polydor POLD 5093*	86	1 wk

See also Emerson, Lake and Powell.

Peter POWELL *UK, male exercise instructor*   *13 wks*

20 Mar	82	● KEEP FIT AND DANCE *K-Tel NE 1167*	9	13 wks

POWER STATION
UK/US, male vocal/instrumental group   *23 wks*

6 Apr	85	THE POWER STATION *Parlophone POST 1* ...	12	23 wks

PRAYING MANTIS
UK, male vocal/instrumental group   *2 wks*

11 Apr	81	TIME TELLS NO LIES *Arista SPART 1153*	60	2 wks

PREFAB SPROUT
UK, male vocal/instrumental group   *42 wks*

17 Mar	84	SWOON *Kitchenware KWLP 1*	22	7 wks
22 Jun	85	STEVE McQUEEN *Kitchenware KWLP 3*	21	35 wks

Elvis PRESLEY *US, male vocalist*   *1018 wks*

8 Nov	58	● ELVIS' GOLDEN RECORDS *RCA RB 16069* ...	3	44 wks
8 Nov	58	● KING CREOLE (film soundtrack) *RCA RD 27086*	4	14 wks
4 Apr	59	● ELVIS (ROCK 'N' ROLL NO. 1) *HMV CLP 1093* .	4	9 wks
8 Aug	59	● A DATE WITH ELVIS *RCA RD 27128*	4	15 wks
18 Jun	60	★ ELVIS IS BACK *RCA RD 27171*	1	27 wks
18 Jun	60	● ELVIS' GOLDEN RECORDS VOL. 2 *RCA RD 27159*	4	20 wks
10 Dec	60	★ G.I. BLUES (film soundtrack) *RCA RD 27192* ...	1	55 wks
20 May	61	● HIS HAND IN MINE *RCA RD 27211*	3	25 wks
4 Nov	61	● SOMETHING FOR EVERYBODY *RCA RD 27224*	2	18 wks
9 Dec	61	★ BLUE HAWAII (film soundtrack) *RCA RD 27238*	1	65 wks
7 Jul	62	★ POT LUCK *RCA RD 27265*	1	25 wks
8 Dec	62	● ROCK 'N' ROLL NO. 2 *RCA RD 7528*	3	17 wks
26 Jan	63	● GIRLS! GIRLS! GIRLS! (film soundtrack) *RCA RD 7534*	2	21 wks
11 May	63	● IT HAPPENED AT THE WORLD'S FAIR (film soundtrack) *RCA RD 7565*	4	21 wks
28 Dec	63	● FUN IN ACAPULCO (film soundtrack) *RCA RD 7609*	9	14 wks
11 Apr	64	● ELVIS' GOLDEN RECORDS VOL. 3 *RCA RD 7630*	6	13 wks
4 Jul	64	● KISSIN' COUSINS (film soundtrack) *RCA RD 7645*	5	17 wks
9 Jan	65	ROUSTABOUT (film soundtrack) *RCA RD 7678*	12	4 wks
1 May	65	● GIRL HAPPY (film soundtrack) *RCA RD 7714* ..	8	18 wks
25 Sep	65	FLAMING STAR AND SUMMER KISSES *RCA RD 7723*	11	4 wks
4 Dec	65	● ELVIS FOR EVERYBODY *RCA RD 7782*	8	8 wks

15 Jan 66   **HAREM HOLIDAY** (film soundtrack)
    RCA RD 7767 .... **11**   5 wks

30 Apr 66   **FRANKIE AND JOHNNY** (film soundtrack)
    RCA RD 7793 .... **11**   5 wks

6 Aug 66 ● **PARADISE HAWAIIAN STYLE** (film soundtrack)
    RCA Victor RD 7810 .... **7**   9 wks

26 Nov 66   **CALIFORNIA HOLIDAY** (film soundtrack)
    RCA Victor RD 7820 .... **17**   6 wks

8 Apr 67   **HOW GREAT THOU ART**   *RCA Victor SF 7867* .. **11**   14 wks

2 Sep 67   **DOUBLE TROUBLE** (film soundtrack)
    RCA Victor SF 7892 .... **34**   1 wk

20 Apr 68   **CLAMBAKE** (film soundtrack)
    RCA Victor SD 7917 .... **39**   1 wk

3 May 69 ● **ELVIS – NBC TV SPECIAL**   *RCA RD 8011* ...... **2**   26 wks

5 Jul 69 ★ **FLAMING STAR**   *RCA International INTS 1012* ...... **2**   14 wks

23 Aug 69 ★ **FROM ELVIS IN MEMPHIS**   *RCA SF 8029* ...... **1**   13 wks

28 Feb 70   **PORTRAIT IN MUSIC** (import)   *RCA 558* ...... **36**   1 wk

14 Mar 70 ● **FROM MEMPHIS TO VEGAS – FROM VEGAS TO MEMPHIS**   *RCA SF 8080/1* ...... **3**   16 wks

1 Aug 70 ● **ON STAGE**   *RCA SF 8128* ...... **2**   18 wks

5 Dec 70   **ELVIS' GOLDEN RECORDS VOL. 1** (re-issue)
    RCA SF 8129 ...... **21**   11 wks

12 Dec 70   **WORLDWIDE 50 GOLD AWARD HITS VOL 1**
    RCA LPM 6401 ...... **49**   2 wks

30 Jan 71   **THAT'S THE WAY IT IS**   *RCA SF 8162* ...... **12**   41 wks

10 Apr 71 ● **ELVIS COUNTRY**   *RCA SF 8172* ...... **6**   9 wks

24 Jul 71 ● **LOVE LETTERS FROM ELVIS**   *RCA SF 8202* ... **7**   5 wks

7 Aug 71 ● **C'MON EVERYBODY**
    RCA International INTS 1286 ...... **5**   21 wks

7 Aug 71   **YOU'LL NEVER WALK ALONE**
    RCA Camden CDM 1088 ...... **20**   4 wks

25 Sep 71   **ALMOST IN LOVE**   *RCA International INTS 1206* .. **38**   2 wks

4 Dec 71 ● **ELVIS' CHRISTMAS ALBUM**
    RCA International INTS 1126 ...... **7**   5 wks

18 Dec 71   **I GOT LUCKY**   *RCA International INTS 1322* ...... **26**   3 wks

27 May 72   **ELVIS NOW**   *RCA Victor SF 8266* ...... **12**   8 wks

3 Jun 72   **ROCK AND ROLL** (re-issue of ROCK 'N' ROLL NO. 1)   *RCA Victor SF 8233* ...... **34**   4 wks

3 Jun 72   **ELVIS FOR EVERYONE**   *RCA Victor SF 8232* ...... **48**   1 wk

15 Jul 72 ● **ELVIS AT MADISON SQUARE GARDEN**
    RCA Victor SF 8296 ...... **3**   20 wks

12 Aug 72   **HE TOUCHED ME**   *RCA Victor SF 8275* ...... **38**   3 wks

24 Feb 73   **ALOHA FROM HAWAII VIA SATELLITE**
    RCA Victor DPS 2040 ...... **11**   10 wks

15 Sep 73   **ELVIS**   *RCA Victor SF 8378* ...... **16**   4 wks

2 Mar 74   **A LEGENDARY PERFORMER VOL. 1**
    RCA Victor CPLI 0341 ...... **20**   3 wks

25 May 74   **GOOD TIMES**   *RCA Victor APLI 0475* ...... **42**   1 wk

7 Sep 74   **ELVIS PRESLEY LIVE ON STAGE IN MEMPHIS**
    RCA Victor APLI 0606 ...... **44**   1 wk

22 Feb 75   **PROMISED LAND**   *RCA Victor APLI 0873* .... **21**   4 wks

14 Jun 75   **TODAY**   *RCA Victor RS 1011* ...... **48**   3 wks

5 Jul 75 ★ **40 GREATEST HITS**   *Arcade ADEP 12* ...... **1**   38 wks

6 Sep 75   **THE ELVIS PRESLEY SUN COLLECTION**
    RCA Starcall HY 1001 ...... **16**   13 wks

19 Jun 76   **FROM ELVIS PRESLEY BOULEVARD, MEMPHIS, TENNESSEE**   *RCA Victor RS 1060* ...... **29**   5 wks

19 Feb 77   **ELVIS IN DEMAND**   *RCA Victor PL 42003* ...... **12**   11 wks

27 Aug 77 ● **MOODY BLUE**   *RCA PL 12428* ...... **3**   15 wks

3 Sep 77   **WELCOME TO MY WORLD**   *RCA PL 12274* ...... **7**   9 wks

3 Sep 77   **G.I. BLUES** (re-issue)   *RCA SF 5078* ...... **14**   10 wks

10 Sep 77   **ELVIS GOLDEN RECORDS VOL. 2** (re-issue)
    RCA SF 8151 ...... **27**   4 wks

10 Sep 77   **HITS OF THE 70'S**   *RCA LPLI 7527* ...... **30**   4 wks

10 Sep 77   **BLUE HAWAII** (re-issue)   *RCA SF 8145* ...... **26**   6 wks

10 Sep 77   **ELVIS' GOLDEN RECORDS VOL 3** (re-issue)
    RCA SF 7630 ...... **49**   2 wks

10 Sep 77   **PICTURES OF ELVIS**   *RCA Starcall HY 1023* ...... **52**   1 wk

8 Oct 77   **THE SUN YEARS**   *Charly SUN 1001* ...... **31**   2 wks

15 Oct 77   **LOVING YOU**   *RCA PL 42358* ...... **24**   3 wks

19 Nov 77   **ELVIS IN CONCERT**   *RCA PL 02578* ...... **13**   11 wks

22 Apr 78   **HE WALKS BESIDE ME**   *RCA PL 12772* ...... **37**   1 wk

3 Jun 78   **THE '56 SESSIONS VOL 1**   *RCA PL 42101* ...... **47**   4 wks

2 Sep 78   **TV SPECIAL**   *RCA PL 42370* ...... **50**   2 wks

11 Nov 78   **40 GREATEST** (re-issue)   *RCA PL 42691* ...... **40**   14 wks

3 Feb 79   **A LEGENDARY PERFORMER VOL 3**
    RCA PL 13082 ...... **43**   3 wks

5 May 79   **OUR MEMORIES OF ELVIS**   *RCA PL 13279* .... **72**   1 wk

24 Nov 79 ● **LOVE SONGS**   *K-Tel NE 1062* ...... **4**   13 wks

21 Jun 80   **ELVIS PRESLEY SINGS LIEBER AND STOLLER**
    RCA International INTS 5031 ...... **32**   5 wks

23 Aug 80   **ELVIS ARON PRESLEY**   *RCA ELVIS 25* ...... **21**   4 wks

23 Aug 80   **PARADISE HAWAIIAN STYLE** (re-issue)
    RCA International INTS 5037 ...... **53**   2 wks

29 Nov 80 ● **INSPIRATION**   *K-Tel NE 1101* ...... **6**   8 wks

14 Mar 81   **GUITAR MAN**   *RCA RCALP 5010* ...... **33**   5 wks

9 May 81   **THIS IS ELVIS PRESLEY**   *RCA RCALP 5029* .... **47**   4 wks

28 Nov 81   **THE ULTIMATE PERFORMANCE**
    K-Tel NE 1141 ...... **45**   6 wks

13 Feb 82   **THE SOUND OF YOUR CRY**
    RCA RCALP 3060 ...... **31**   12 wks

6 Mar 82   **ELVIS PRESLEY EP PACK**   *RCA EPI* ...... **97**   1 wk

21 Aug 82   **ROMANTIC ELVIS/ROCKIN' ELVIS**
    RCA RCALP 1000/1 ...... **62**   5 wks

18 Dec 82   **IT WON'T SEEM LIKE CHRISTMAS WITHOUT YOU**   *RCA INTS 5235* ...... **80**   1 wk

30 Apr 83   **JAILHOUSE ROCK/LOVE IN LAS VEGAS**
    RCA RCALP 9020 ...... **40**   2 wks

20 Aug 83   **I WAS THE ONE**   *RCA RCALP 3105* ...... **83**   1 wk

3 Dec 83   **A LEGENDARY PERFORMER VOL. 4**
    RCA PL 84848 ...... **91**   1 wk

7 Apr 84   **I CAN HELP**   *RCA PL 89287* ...... **71**   3 wks

21 Jul 84   **THE FIRST LIVE RECORDINGS**
    RCA International PG 89387 ...... **69**   2 wks

26 Jan 85   **20 GREATEST HITS VOLUME 2**
    RCA International NL 89168 ...... **98**   1 wk

25 May 85   **RECONSIDER BABY**   *RCA PL 85418* ...... **92**   1 wk

12 Oct 85   **BALLADS**   *Telstar STAR 2264* ...... **23**   17 wks

29 Aug 87 ● **PRESLEY – THE ALL TIME GREATEST HITS**
    RCA PL 90100 ...... **4†**   17 wks

PRETENDERS
UK/US, male/female vocal/instrumental group   *114 wks*

19 Jan 80 ★ **PRETENDERS**   *Real RAL 3* ...... **1**   35 wks

15 Aug 81 ● **PRETENDERS II**   *Real SRK 3572* ...... **7**   27 wks

21 Jan 84   **LEARNING TO CRAWL**   *Real WX 2* ...... **11**   16 wks

1 Nov 86 ● **GET CLOSE**   *WEA WX 64* ...... **6**   28 wks

7 Nov 87 ● **THE SINGLES**   *WEA WX 135* ...... **6†**   8 wks

---

PRETTY THINGS
UK, male vocal/instrumental group   *13 wks*

27 Mar 65 ● **PRETTY THINGS**   *Fontana TL 5239* ...... **6**   10 wks

27 Jun 70   **PARACHUTE**   *Harvest SHVL 774* ...... **43**   3 wks

---

Alan PRICE
UK, male vocalist/instrumentalist – keyboards   *10 wks*

8 Jun 74 ● **BETWEEN TODAY AND YESTERDAY**
    Warner Bros. K 56032 ...... **9**   10 wks

Charley PRIDE   *US, male vocalist*   *17 wks*

10 Apr 71   **CHARLEY PRIDE SPECIAL**   *RCA SF 8171* ...... **29**   1 wk

28 May 77   **SHE'S JUST AN OLD LOVE TURNED MEMORY**
    RCA Victor PL 12261 ...... **34**   2 wks

3 Jun 78   **SOMEONE LOVES YOU HONEY**
    RCA PL 12478 ...... **48**   2 wks

26 Jan 80 ● **GOLDEN COLLECTION**   *K-Tel NE 1056* ...... **6**   12 wks

---

Maxi PRIEST   *UK, male vocalist*   *5 wks*

6 Dec 86   **INTENTIONS**   *10 DIX 32* ...... **96**   1 wk

5 Dec 87   **MAXI**   *10 DIX 64* ...... **48†**   4 wks

ELVIS PRESLEY makes a sixties scene with Nancy Sinatra. Between them they have had 1050 weeks on chart, 1018 of them his.

PRIMAL SCREAM
UK, male vocal/instrumental group   *1 wk*

17 Oct 87	**SONIC FLOWER GROOVE** *Elevation WLV 2*	62	1 wk

PRINCE and the REVOLUTION
US, male vocalist and male/female vocal/instrumental group   *159 wks*

21 Jul 84	● **PURPLE RAIN – MUSIC FROM THE MOTION PICTURE** *Warner Bros. 925110*	7	66 wks
8 Sep 84	**1999** *Warner Bros. 923720*	30	21 wks
4 May 85	● **AROUND THE WORLD IN A DAY** *Warner Bros. 92-5286-1*	5	20 wks
12 Apr 86	**PARADE – MUSIC FROM 'UNDER THE CHERRY MOON'** *Warner Bros. WX 39*	4	26 wks
11 Apr 87	● **SIGN 'O' THE TIMES** *Paisley Park WX 88*	4	26 wks

The albums 1999 and Sign 'O' The Times are credited simply to Prince.

PRINCE CHARLES and the CITY BEAT BAND
US, male vocalist with male vocal/instrumental group   *1 wk*

30 Apr 83	**STONE KILLERS** *Virgin V 2271*	84	1 wk

PRINCESS   *UK, female vocalist*   *14 wks*

17 May 86	**PRINCESS** *Supreme SU1*	15	14 wks

P.J. PROBY   *US, male vocalist*   *3 wks*

27 Feb 65	**I'M P.J. PROBY** *Liberty LBY 1235*	16	3 wks

PROCLAIMERS
UK, male vocal/instrumental duo   *9 wks*

9 May 87	**THIS IS THE STORY** *Chrysalis CHR 1602*	43†	9 wks

PROCOL HARUM
UK, male vocal/instrumental group   *11 wks*

19 Jul 69	**A SALTY DOG** *Regal Zonophone SLRZ 1009*	27	2 wks
27 Jun 70	**HOME** *Regal Zonophone SLRZ 1014*	49	1 wk
3 Jul 71	**BROKEN BARRICADES** *Island ILPS 9158*	42	1 wk
6 May 72	**A WHITER SHADE OF PALE/A SALTY DOG (double re-issue)** *Fly Double Back TOOFA 7/8*	26	4 wks
6 May 72	**PROCOL HARUM IN CONCERT WITH THE EDMONTON SYMPHONY ORCHESTRA** *Chrysalis CHR 1004*	48	1 wk
30 Aug 75	**PROCOL'S NINTH** *Chrysalis CHR 1080*	41	2 wks

A Whiter Shade Of Pale/A Salty Dog is a double re-issue although A Whiter Shade Of Pale was not previously a hit. The Edmonton Symphony Orchestra is a Canadian orchestra.

PROPAGANDA
Germany, male/female vocal/instrumental group   *14 wks*

13 Jul 85	**A SECRET WISH** *ZTT ZTTIQ 3*	16	12 wks
23 Nov 85	**WISHFUL THINKING** *ZTT ZTTIQ 20*	82	2 wks

Dorothy PROVINE   *US, female vocalist*   *49 wks*

2 Dec 61	● **THE ROARING TWENTIES – SONGS FROM THE TV SERIES** *Warner Bros. WM 4035*	3	42 wks
10 Feb 62	**VAMP OF THE ROARING TWENTIES** *Warner Bros. WM 4053*	9	7 wks

PSYCHEDELIC FURS
UK, male vocal/instrumental group   *34 wks*

15 Mar 80	**PSYCHEDELIC FURS** *CBS 84084*	18	6 wks
23 May 81	**TALK TALK TALK** *CBS 84892*	30	9 wks
2 Oct 82	**FOREVER NOW** *CBS 85909*	20	6 wks
19 May 84	**MIRROR MOVES** *CBS 25950*	15	9 wks
14 Feb 87	**MIDNIGHT TO MIDNIGHT** *CBS 450 256-1*	12	4 wks

PUBLIC IMAGE LTD.
UK, male vocal/instrumental group   *44 wks*

23 Dec 78	**PUBLIC IMAGE** *Virgin V 2114*	22	11 wks
8 Dec 79	**METAL BOX** *Virgin METAL 1*	18	8 wks
8 Mar 80	**SECOND EDITION OF PIL** *Virgin VD 2512*	46	2 wks
22 Nov 80	**PARIS IN THE SPRING** *Virgin V 2183*	61	2 wks
18 Apr 81	**FLOWERS OF ROMANCE** *Virgin V 2189*	11	5 wks
8 Oct 83	**LIVE IN TOKYO** *Virgin VGD 3508*	28	6 wks
21 Jul 84	**THIS IS WHAT YOU WANT . . . THIS IS WHAT YOU GET** *Virgin V 2309*	56	2 wks
15 Feb 86	**ALBUM/CASSETTE** *Virgin V 2366*	14	6 wks
26 Sep 87	**HAPPY?** *Virgin V 2455*	40	2 wks

Gary PUCKETT and the UNION GAP
US, male vocalist, male vocal/instrumental backing group   *4 wks*

29 Jun 68	**UNION GAP** *CBS 63342*	24	4 wks

Q

Q-TIPS   *UK, male vocal/instrumental group*   *1 wk*

30 Aug 80	**Q-TIPS** *CHR 1255*	50	1 wk

Suzi QUATRO
US, female vocalist/instrumentalist – guitar   *13 wks*

13 Oct 73	**SUZI QUATRO** *RAK SRAK 505*	32	4 wks
26 Apr 80	● **SUZI QUATRO'S GREATEST HITS** *RAK EMTV 24*	4	9 wks

QUEEN   *UK, male vocal/instrumental group*   *796 wks*

23 Mar 74	● **QUEEN 2** *EMI EMA 767*	5	29 wks
30 Mar 74	**QUEEN** *EMI EMC 3006*	24	18 wks
23 Nov 74	● **SHEER HEART ATTACK** *EMI EMC 3061*	2	42 wks
13 Dec 75	★ **A NIGHT AT THE OPERA** *EMI EMTC 103*	1	50 wks
25 Dec 76	★ **A DAY AT THE RACES** *EMI EMTC 104*	1	24 wks
12 Nov 77	● **NEWS OF THE WORLD** *EMI EMA 784*	4	20 wks
25 Nov 78	● **JAZZ** *EMI EMA 788*	2	27 wks
7 Jul 79	● **LIVE KILLERS** *EMI EMSP 330*	3	27 wks
12 Jul 80	★ **THE GAME** *EMI EMA 795*	1	18 wks
20 Dec 80	● **FLASH GORDON (film soundtrack)** *EMI EMC 3351*	10	15 wks
7 Nov 81	★ **GREATEST HITS** *EMI EMTV 30*	1†	312 wks
15 May 82	● **HOT SPACE** *EMI EMA 797*	4	19 wks
10 Mar 84	● **THE WORKS** *EMI EMC 240014*	2	93 wks
14 Jun 86	★ **A KIND OF MAGIC** *EMI EU 3509*	1	62 wks
13 Dec 86	● **LIVE MAGIC** *EMI EMC 3519*	3	40 wks

The Works changed label number during its run to EMI WORK 1.

PRINCE is shown as he outfitted
himself for *1999*.

(Top left) The original PRETENDERS had the first new number one album of the eighties.

(Bottom) The Q-TIPS only managed one week on the chart, but vocalist Paul Young (back row, left) went on to have 185 times that many.

(Top right) CHRIS REA took a long time to get his chart career off the ground but by the mid-eighties he was flying high.

QUEENSRHYCHE
UK, male vocal/instrumental group — 2 wks

| 29 Sep 84 | THE WARNING | EMI America EJ 2402201 | 100 | 1 wk |
| 26 Jul 86 | RAGE FOR ORDER | EMI America AML 3105 | 66 | 1 wk |

QUIET RIOT US, male vocal/instrumental group — 1 wk

| 4 Aug 84 | CONDITION CRITICAL | Epic EPC 26075 | 71 | 1 wk |

QUINTESSENCE
UK/Australia, male vocal/instrumental group — 6 wks

27 Jun 70	QUINTESSENCE	Island ILPS 9128	22	4 wks
3 Apr 71	DIVE DEEP	Island ILPS 9143	43	1 wk
27 May 72	SELF	RCA Victor SF 8273	50	1 wk

QUIVER – See SUTHERLAND BROTHERS and QUIVER

R

RACING CARS UK, male vocal/instrumental group — 6 wks

| 19 Feb 77 | DOWNTOWN TONIGHT | Chrysalis CHR 1099 | 39 | 6 wks |

Gerry RAFFERTY UK, male vocalist — 74 wks

25 Feb 78	● CITY TO CITY	United Artists UAS 30104	6	37 wks
2 Jun 79	● NIGHT OWL	United Artists UAK 30238	9	24 wks
26 Apr 80	SNAKES AND LADDERS	United Artists UAK 30298	15	9 wks
25 Sep 82	SLEEPWALKING	Liberty LBG 30352	39	4 wks

RAH BAND
UK, male/female group under control of Richard A. Hewson — 6 wks

| 6 Apr 85 | MYSTERY | RCA PL 70640 | 60 | 6 wks |

RAINBOW UK, male vocal/instrumental group — 163 wks

13 Sep 75	RITCHIE BLACKMORE'S RAINBOW	Oyster OYA 2001	11	6 wks
5 Jun 76	RAINBOW RISING	Polydor 2490 137	11	33 wks
30 Jul 77	● ON STAGE	Polydor 2657 016	7	10 wks
6 May 78	● LONG LIVE ROCK 'N' ROLL	Polydor POLD 5002	7	12 wks
18 Aug 79	● DOWN TO EARTH	Polydor POLD 5023	6	37 wks
21 Feb 81	● DIFFICULT TO CURE	Polydor POLD 5036	3	22 wks
8 Aug 81	RITCHIE BLACKMORE'S RAINBOW (re-issue)	Polydor 2490 141	91	2 wks
21 Nov 81	BEST OF RAINBOW	Polydor POLDV 2	14	17 wks
24 Apr 82	● STRAIGHT BETWEEN THE EYES	Polydor POLD 5056	5	14 wks
17 Sep 83	BENT OUT OF SHAPE	Polydor POLD 5116	11	6 wks
8 Mar 86	FINYL VINYL	Polydor PODV 8	31	4 wks

First two albums and re-issue of first album credited to Ritchie Blackmore's Rainbow.

RAIN PARADE US, male vocal/instrumental group — 1 wk

| 29 Jun 85 | BEYOND THE SUNSET | Island IMA 17 | 78 | 1 wk |

RAKIM – See Eric B. and RAKIM

RAMONES US, male vocal/instrumental group — 27 wks

23 Apr 77	LEAVE HOME	Philips 9103 254	45	1 wk
24 Dec 77	ROCKET TO RUSSIA	Sire 9103 255	60	2 wks
7 Oct 78	ROAD TO RUIN	Sire SRK 6063	32	2 wks
16 Jun 79	IT'S ALIVE	Sire SRK 26074	27	8 wks
19 Jan 80	END OF THE CENTURY	Sire SRK 6077	14	8 wks
26 Jan 85	TOO TOUGH TO DIE	Beggars Banquet BEGA 59	63	3 wks
31 May 86	ANIMAL BOY	Beggars Banquet BEGA 70	38	2 wks
10 Oct 87	HALFWAY TO SANITY	Beggars Banquet BEGA 89	78	1 wk

RANGE – See Bruce HORNSBY and the RANGE

RATT US, male vocal/instrumental group — 3 wks

| 13 Jul 85 | INVASION OF YOUR PRIVACY | Atlantic 78–1257–1 | 50 | 2 wks |
| 25 Oct 86 | DANCING UNDERCOVER | Atlantic 781 683–1 | 51 | 1 wk |

RAVEN UK, male vocal/instrumental group — 3 wks

| 17 Oct 81 | ROCK UNTIL YOU DROP | Neat NEAT 1001 | 63 | 3 wks |

Simon RAYMOND – See Harold BUDD/Liz FRASER/Robin GUTHRIE/Simon RAYMOND

Chris REA UK, male vocalist — 82 wks

28 Apr 79	DELTICS	Magnet MAG 5028	54	3 wks
12 Apr 80	TENNIS	Magnet MAG 5032	60	1 wk
3 Apr 82	CHRIS REA	Magnet MAGL 5040	52	4 wks
18 Jun 83	WATER SIGN	Magnet MAGL 5048	64	2 wks
21 Apr 84	WIRED TO THE MOON	Magnet MAGL 5057	35	7 wks
25 May 85	SHAMROCK DIARIES	Magnet MAGL 5062	15	14 wks
26 Apr 86	ON THE BEACH	Magnet MAGL 5069	11	37 wks
26 Sep 87	● DANCING WITH STRANGERS	Magnet MAGL 5071	2†	14 wks

REAL THING UK, male vocal/instrumental group — 17 wks

6 Nov 76	REAL THING	Pye NSPL 18507	34	3 wks
7 Apr 79	CAN YOU FEEL THE FORCE	Pye NSPH 18601	73	1 wk
10 May 80	20 GREATEST HITS	K-Tel NE 1073	56	2 wks
12 Jul 86	BEST OF THE REAL THING	West Five NRT 1	24	11 wks

REBEL ROUSERS – See Cliff BENNETT and the REBEL ROUSERS

RED BOX UK, male vocal/instrumental duo — 4 wks

| 6 Dec 86 | THE CIRCLE AND THE SQUARE | Sire WX 79 | 73 | 4 wks |

RED NOISE – See Bill NELSON

Sharon REDD US, female vocalist — 5 wks

| 23 Oct 82 | REDD HOTT | Prelude PRL 25056 | 59 | 5 wks |

Otis REDDING US, male vocalist — 192 wks

19 Feb 66	● OTIS BLUE	Atlantic ATL 5041	6	21 wks
23 Apr 66	SOUL BALLADS	Atlantic ATL 5029	30	1 wk
23 Jul 66	SOUL ALBUM	Atlantic 587–011	22	9 wks
21 Jan 67	OTIS REDDING'S DICTIONARY OF SOUL	Atlantic 588–050	23	16 wks
21 Jan 67	● OTIS BLUE (re-issue)	Atlantic 587–036	7	54 wks
29 Apr 67	PAIN IN MY HEART	Atlantic 587–042	28	9 wks
10 Feb 68	● HISTORY OF OTIS REDDING	Volt S 418	2	43 wks
30 Mar 68	OTIS REDDING IN EUROPE	Stax 589–016	14	16 wks
1 Jun 68	★ DOCK OF THE BAY	Stax 231–001	1	15 wks
12 Oct 68	IMMORTAL OTIS REDDING	Atlantic 588–113	19	8 wks

See also Otis Redding and Carla Thomas.

Otis REDDING and Carla THOMAS
US, male/female vocal duo   *17 wks*

1 Jul 67	KING AND QUEEN *Atlantic 589–007*	18	17 wks

See also Otis Redding.

Helen REDDY *Australia, female vocalist*   *27 wks*

8 Feb 75	FREE AND EASY *Capitol E-ST 11348*	17	9 wks
14 Feb 76	● THE BEST OF HELEN REDDY *Capitol E-ST 11467*	5	18 wks

REDSKINS *UK, male vocal/instrumental duo*   *4 wks*

22 Mar 86	NEITHER WASHINGTON, NOR MOSCOW *Decca FLP 1*	31	4 wks

Lou REED *US, male vocalist*   *36 wks*

21 Apr 73	TRANSFORMER *RCA Victor LSP 4807*	13	25 wks
20 Oct 73	● BERLIN *RCA Victor RS 1002*	7	5 wks
16 Mar 74	ROCK 'N' ROLL ANIMAL *RCA Victor APLI 0472*	26	1 wk
14 Feb 76	CONEY ISLAND BABY *RCA Victor RS 1035*	52	1 wk
3 Jul 82	TRANSFORMER (re-issue) *RCA INTS 5061*	91	2 wks
9 Jun 84	NEW SENSATIONS *RCA PL 84998*	92	1 wk
24 May 86	MISTRIAL *RCA PL 87190*	69	1 wk

Don REEDMAN – *See Jeff JARRATT and Don REEDMAN*

Jim REEVES *US, male vocalist*   *381 wks*

28 Mar 64	● GOOD 'N' COUNTRY *RCA Camden CDN 5114*	10	35 wks
9 May 64	● GENTLEMAN JIM *RCA RD 7541*	3	23 wks
15 Aug 64	● A TOUCH OF VELVET *RCA RD 7521*	8	9 wks
15 Aug 64	INTERNATIONAL JIM REEVES *RCA RD 7577*	11	15 wks
22 Aug 64	HE'LL HAVE TO GO *RCA RD 27176*	16	4 wks
29 Aug 64	THE INTIMATE JIM REEVES *RCA RD 27193*	12	4 wks
29 Aug 64	● GOD BE WITH YOU *RCA RD 7636*	10	10 wks
5 Sep 64	● MOONLIGHT AND ROSES *RCA RD 7639*	2	52 wks
19 Sep 64	COUNTRY SIDE OF JIM REEVES *RCA Camden CDN 5100*	12	5 wks
26 Sep 64	WE THANK THEE *RCA RD 7637*	17	3 wks
28 Nov 64	● TWELVE SONGS OF CHRISTMAS *RCA RD 7663*	3	17 wks
30 Jan 65	● BEST OF JIM REEVES *RCA RD 7666*	3	47 wks
10 Apr 65	HAVE I TOLD YOU LATELY THAT I LOVE YOU *RCA Camden CDN 5122*	12	5 wks
22 May 65	THE JIM REEVES WAY *RCA RD 7694*	16	4 wks
5 Nov 66	● DISTANT DRUMS *RCA Victor RD 7814*	2	34 wks
18 Jan 69	A TOUCH OF SADNESS *RCA SF 7978*	15	5 wks
5 Jul 69	★ ACCORDING TO MY HEART *RCA International INTS 1013*	1	14 wks
23 Aug 69	JIM REEVES AND SOME FRIENDS *RCA SF 8022*	24	4 wks
29 Nov 69	ON STAGE *RCA SF 8047*	13	4 wks
26 Dec 70	MY CATHEDRAL *RCA SF 8146*	48	2 wks
3 Jul 71	JIM REEVES WRITES YOU A RECORD *RCA SF 8176*	47	2 wks
7 Aug 71	● JIM REEVES' GOLDEN RECORDS *RCA International INTS 1070*	9	21 wks
14 Aug 71	● THE INTIMATE JIM REEVES (re-issue) *RCA International INTS 1256*	8	15 wks
21 Aug 71	GIRLS I HAVE KNOWN *RCA International INTS 1140*	35	5 wks
27 Nov 71	● TWELVE SONGS OF CHRISTMAS (re-issue) *RCA International INTS 1188*	3	6 wks
27 Nov 71	A TOUCH OF VELVET (re-issue) *RCA International INTS 1089*	49	2 wks
15 Apr 72	MY FRIEND *RCA SF 8258*	32	5 wks
20 Sep 75	★ 40 GOLDEN GREATS *Arcade ADEP 16*	1	25 wks
6 Sep 80	COUNTRY GENTLEMAN *K-Tel NE 1088*	53	4 wks

Neil REID *UK, male vocalist*   *18 wks*

5 Feb 72	★ NEIL REID *Decca SKL 5122*	1	16 wks
2 Sep 72	SMILE *Decca SKL 5136*	47	2 wks

R.E.M. *US, male vocal/instrumental group*   *14 wks*

28 Apr 84	RECKONING *IRS A 7045*	91	2 wks
29 Jun 85	FABLES OF THE RECONSTRUCTION *IRS MIRF 1003*	35	3 wks
6 Sep 86	LIFE'S RICH PAGEANT *IRS MIRG 1014*	43	4 wks
16 May 87	DEAD LETTER OFFICE *IRS SP 70054*	60	2 wks
26 Sep 87	DOCUMENT *MCA MIRG 1025*	28	3 wks

RENAISSANCE
UK, male/female vocal/instrumental group   *10 wks*

21 Feb 70	RENAISSANCE *Island ILPS 9114*	60	1 wk
19 Aug 78	A SONG FOR ALL SEASONS *Warner Bros. K 56460*	35	8 wks
2 Jun 79	AZUR D'OR *Warner Bros. K 56633*	73	1 wk

RENATO *Italy, male vocalist*   *14 wks*

25 Dec 82	SAVE YOUR LOVE *Lifestyle LEG 9*	26	14 wks

REO SPEEDWAGON
US, male vocal/instrumental group   *36 wks*

25 Apr 81	● HI INFIDELITY *Epic EPC 84700*	6	29 wks
17 Jul 82	GOOD TROUBLE *Epic EPC 85789*	29	7 wks

REVOLUTION – *See PRINCE and the REVOLUTION*

REZILLOS *UK, male/female vocal/instrumental group* *15 wks*

5 Aug 78	CAN'T STAND THE REZILLOS *Sire WEA K 56530*	16	10 wks
28 Apr 79	MISSION ACCOMPLISHED BUT THE BEAT GOES ON *Sire SRK 6069*	30	5 wks

Charlie RICH *US, male vocalist*   *28 wks*

23 Mar 74	● BEHIND CLOSED DOORS *Epic 65716*	4	26 wks
13 Jul 74	VERY SPECIAL LOVE SONGS *Epic 80031*	34	2 wks

RICH KIDS *UK, male vocal/instrumental group*   *1 wk*

7 Oct 78	GHOST OF PRINCES IN TOWERS *EMI EMC 3263*	51	1 wk

Cliff RICHARD *UK, male vocalist*   *638 wks*

18 Apr 59	● CLIFF *Columbia 33SX 1147*	4	31 wks
14 Nov 59	● CLIFF SINGS *Columbia 33SX 1192*	2	36 wks
15 Oct 60	● ME AND MY SHADOWS *Columbia 33SX 1261*	2	33 wks
22 Apr 61	● LISTEN TO CLIFF *Columbia 33SX 1320*	2	28 wks
21 Oct 61	★ 21 TODAY *Columbia 33SX 1368*	1	16 wks
23 Dec 61	★ THE YOUNG ONES (film soundtrack) *Columbia 33SX 1384*	1	42 wks
29 Sep 62	● 32 MINUTES AND 17 SECONDS *Columbia 33SX 1431*	3	21 wks
26 Jan 63	★ SUMMER HOLIDAY (film soundtrack) *Columbia 33SX 1472*	1	36 wks
13 Jul 63	● CLIFF'S HIT ALBUM *Columbia 33SX 1512*	2	19 wks
28 Sep 63	● WHEN IN SPAIN *Columbia 33SX 1541*	8	10 wks

11 Jul!	64	● WONDERFUL LIFE (film soundtrack) Columbia 33SX 1628		2	23 wks
9 Jan	65	ALADDIN (pantomime) Columbia 33SX 1676		13	5 wks
17 Apr	65	CLIFF RICHARD Columbia 33SX 1709		9	5 wks
14 Aug	65	MORE HITS BY CLIFF Columbia 33SX 1737		20	1 wk
8 Jan	66	LOVE IS FOREVER Columbia 33SX 1769		19	1 wk
21 May	66	● KINDA LATIN Columbia SX 6039		9	12 wks
17 Dec	66	● FINDERS KEEPERS (film soundtrack) Columbia SX 6079		6	18 wks
7 Jan	67	CINDERELLA (pantomime) Columbia 33SCX 6103		30	6 wks
15 Apr	67	DON'T STOP ME NOW ... Columbia SCX 6133		23	9 wks
11 Nov	67	GOOD NEWS Columbia SCX 6167		37	1 wk
1 Jun	68	CLIFF IN JAPAN Columbia SCX 6244		29	2 wks
16 Nov	68	ESTABLISHED 1958 Columbia SCX 6282		30	4 wks
12 Jul	69	● BEST OF CLIFF Columbia SCX 6343		5	17 wks
27 Sep	69	SINCERELY Columbia SCX 6357		24	3 wks
12 Dec	70	TRACKS 'N' GROOVES Columbia SCX 6435		37	2 wks
23 Dec	72	BEST OF CLIFF VOL. 2 Columbia SCX 6519		49	2 wks
19 Jan	74	TAKE ME HIGH (film soundtrack) EMI EMC 3016		41	4 wks
29 May	76	● I'M NEARLY FAMOUS EMI EMC 3122		5	21 wks
26 Mar	77	● EVERY FACE TELLS A STORY EMI EMC 3172		8	10 wks
22 Oct	77	★ 40 GOLDEN GREATS EMI EMTV 6		1	19 wks
4 Mar	78	SMALL CORNERS EMI EMC 3219		33	5 wks
21 Oct	78	GREEN LIGHT EMI EMC 3231		25	3 wks
17 Feb	79	● THANK YOU VERY MUCH – REUNION CONCERT AT THE LONDON PALLADIUM EMI EMTV 15		5	12 wks
15 Sep	79	● ROCK 'N' ROLL JUVENILE EMI EMC 3307		3	22 wks
13 Sep	80	● I'M NO HERO EMI EMA 796		4	11 wks
4 Jul	81	★ LOVE SONGS EMI EMTV 27		1	43 wks
26 Sep	81	● WIRED FOR SOUND EMI EMC 3377		4	25 wks
4 Sep	82	● NOW YOU SEE ME, NOW YOU DON'T EMI EMC 3415		4	14 wks
21 May	83	● DRESSED FOR THE OCCASION EMI EMC 3432		7	17 wks
15 Oct	83	● SILVER EMI EMC 1077871		7	24 wks
14 Jul	84	20 ORIGINAL GREATS EMI CRS 1		43	6 wks
1 Dec	84	THE ROCK CONNECTION EMI CLIF 2		43	5 wks
26 Sep	87	● ALWAYS GUARANTEED EMI EMD 1004		5†	14 wks

The Shadows featured on all or some of the tracks of all albums up to and including Aladdin and the following subsequent albums; More Hits By Cliff, Love Is Forever, Finders Keepers, Cinderella, Established 1958, Best Of Cliff, Best Of Cliff Vol. 2, 40 Golden Greats, Thank You Very Much, Love Songs and 20 Original Greats. Cliff credited to Cliff Richard and the Drifters. See also the Shadows; the Drifters.

Lionel RICHIE *US, male vocalist* 293 wks

27 Nov	82	● LIONEL RICHIE Motown STMA 8037		9	86 wks
29 Oct	83	★ CAN'T SLOW DOWN Motown STMA 8041		1	154 wks
23 Aug	86	● DANCING ON THE CEILING Motown ZL 72412		2	53 wks

Jonathan RICHMAN and the MODERN LOVERS *US, male vocal/instrumental group* 3 wks

27 Aug	77	ROCK 'N' ROLL WITH THE MODERN LOVERS Beserkeley BSERK 9		50	3 wks

RICHMOND STRINGS/MIKE SAMMES SINGERS *UK, orchestra/male/female vocal group* 7 wks

19 Jan	76	MUSIC OF AMERICA Ronco TRD 2016		18	7 wks

RIP RIG AND PANIC *UK, male/female vocal/instrumental group* 3 wks

26 Jun	82	I AM GOLD Virgin V 2228		67	3 wks

Minnie RIPERTON *US, female vocalist* 3 wks

17 May	75	PERFECT ANGEL Epic EPC 80426		33	3 wks

Angela RIPPON *UK, female exercise instructor* 26 wks

17 Apr	82	● SHAPE UP AND DANCE (VOL. II) Lifestyle LEG 2		8	26 wks

David ROACH
UK, male vocalist/instrumentalist – saxophone 1 wk

14 Apr	84	I LOVE SAX Nouveau Music NML 1006		73	1 wk

ROBBIE – *See SLY and ROBBIE*

Marty ROBBINS *US, male vocalist* 15 wks

13 Aug	60	GUNFIGHTER BALLADS Fontana TFL 5063		20	1 wk
10 Feb	79	● MARTY ROBBINS COLLECTION Lotus WH 5009		5	14 wks

Paddy ROBERTS *South Africa, male vocalist* 6 wks

26 Sep	59	● STRICTLY FOR GROWN-UPS Decca LF 1322		8	5 wks
17 Sep	60	PADDY ROBERTS TRIES AGAIN Decca LK 4358		16	1 wk

B.A. ROBERTSON *UK, male vocalist* 10 wks

29 Mar	80	INITIAL SUCCESS Asylum K 52216		32	8 wks
4 Apr	81	BULLY FOR YOU Asylum K 52275		61	2 wks

Robbie ROBERTSON *Canada, male vocalist* 3 wks

14 Nov	87	ROBBIE ROBERTSON Geffen WX 133		52	3 wks

Smokey ROBINSON *US, male vocalist* 10 wks

20 Jun	81	BEING WITH YOU Motown STML 12151		17	10 wks

Tom ROBINSON BAND
UK, male vocal/instrumental group 23 wks

3 Jun	78	● POWER IN THE DARKNESS EMI EMC 3226		4	12 wks
24 Mar	79	TRB2 EMI EMC 3296		18	6 wks
29 Sep	84	HOPE AND GLORY Castaway ZL 70483		21	5 wks

ROCK GODDESS
UK, female vocal/instrumental group 3 wks

12 Mar	83	ROCK GODDESS A&M AMLH 68554		65	2 wks
29 Oct	83	HELL HATH NO FURY A&M AMLX 68560		84	1 wk

ROCKIN' BERRIES
UK, male vocal/instrumental group 1 wk

19 Jun	65	IN TOWN Pye NPL 38013		15	1 wk

ROCKPILE *UK, male vocal/instrumental group* 5 wks

18 Oct	80	SECONDS OF PLEASURE F-Beat XXLP 7		34	5 wks

ROCKSTEADY CREW *US, male/female vocal group* 1 wk

16 Jun	84	READY FOR BATTLE Charisma RSC LP1		73	1 wk

(Left) TOM ROBINSON defies all known publicity convention by going to a launderette and keeping his clothes on.

(Below) DIANA ROSS and MARVIN GAYE were briefly re-united at the Motown 25th Anniversary celebration.

(Above) The re-formed ROXY MUSIC issued their *Manifesto* in 1979.

(Right) LINDA RONSTADT was more consistent in the UK as an album artist than a singles star.

ROCKWELL *US, male vocalist*   *5 wks*

| 25 Feb 84 | **SOMEBODY'S WATCHING ME** | | |
| | *Motown ZL 72147* .... | **52** | 5 wks |

Clodagh RODGERS *Ireland, female vocalist*   *1 wk*

| 13 Sep 69 | **CLODAGH RODGERS** *RCA SF 8033* .... | **27** | 1 wk |

RODS *US, male vocal/instrumental group*   *4 wks*

| 24 Jul 82 | **WILD DOGS** *Arista SPART 1196* .... | **75** | 4 wks |

Kenny ROGERS *US, male vocalist*   *93 wks*

18 Jun 77	**KENNY ROGERS** *United Artists UAS 30046*	**14**	7 wks
6 Oct 79	**THE KENNY ROGERS SINGLES ALBUM**		
	United Artists UAK 30263	**12**	22 wks
9 Feb 80	● **KENNY** *United Artists UAG 30273*	**7**	10 wks
31 Jan 81	**LADY** *Liberty LBG 30334*	**40**	5 wks
1 Oct 83	**EYES THAT SEE IN THE DARK**		
	RCA RCALP 6088	**53**	19 wks
27 Oct 84	**WHAT ABOUT ME?** *RCA PL 85043*	**97**	1 wk
27 Jul 85	● **THE KENNY ROGERS STORY**		
	Liberty EMTV 39	**4**	29 wks

ROLAND RAT SUPERSTAR
UK, male rat vocalist   *3 wks*

| 15 Dec 84 | **THE CASSETTE OF THE ALBUM** | | |
| | *Rodent RATL 1001* .... | **67** | 3 wks |

ROLLING STONES
UK, male vocal/instrumental group   *642 wks*

25 Apr 64	★ **ROLLING STONES** *Decca LK 4805* ...	**1**	51 wks
23 Jan 65	★ **ROLLING STONES NO. 2** *Decca LK 4661*	**1**	37 wks
2 Oct 65	● **OUT OF OUR HEADS** *Decca LK 4733* ..	**2**	24 wks
23 Apr 66	● **AFTERMATH** *Decca LK 4786* ..	**1**	28 wks
12 Nov 66	● **BIG HITS (HIGH TIDE AND GREEN GRASS)**		
	Decca TXS 101	**4**	43 wks
28 Jan 67	● **BETWEEN THE BUTTONS** *Decca SKL 4852*	**3**	22 wks
23 Dec 67	● **THEIR SATANIC MAJESTIES REQUEST**		
	Decca TXS 103	**3**	13 wks
21 Dec 68	● **BEGGARS BANQUET** *Decca SKL 4955*	**3**	12 wks
27 Sep 69	● **THROUGH THE PAST DARKLY (BIG HITS VOL. 2)** *Decca SKL 5019*	**2**	37 wks
20 Dec 69	★ **LET IT BLEED** *Decca SKL 5025* ...	**1**	29 wks
19 Sep 70	★ **GET YOUR YA-YAS OUT** *Decca SKL 5065* ...	**1**	15 wks
3 Apr 71	● **STONE AGE** *Decca SKL 5084*	**4**	7 wks
8 May 71	★ **STICKY FINGERS** *Rolling Stones COC 59100* ..	**1**	25 wks
18 Sep 71	**GIMME SHELTER** *Decca SKL 5101* ...	**19**	5 wks
11 Mar 72	**MILESTONES** *Decca SKL 5098* ...	**14**	8 wks
10 Jun 72	★ **EXILE ON MAIN STREET**		
	Rolling Stones COC 69100 ...	**1**	16 wks
11 Nov 72	**ROCK 'N' ROLLING STONES** *Decca SKL 5149* ..	**41**	1 wk
22 Sep 73	★ **GOAT'S HEAD SOUP** *Rolling Stones COC 59101* ..	**1**	14 wks
2 Nov 74	● **IT'S ONLY ROCK 'N' ROLL**		
	Rolling Stones COC 59103	**2**	9 wks
28 Jun 75	**MADE IN THE SHADE**		
	Rolling Stones COC 59104	**14**	12 wks
28 Jun 75	**METAMORPHOSIS** *Decca SKL 5212*	**45**	1 wk
29 Nov 75	● **ROLLED GOLD – THE VERY BEST OF THE ROLLING STONES** *Decca ROST 1/2* ...	**7**	50 wks
8 May 76	● **BLACK & BLUE** *Rolling Stones COC 59106* ..	**2**	14 wks
8 Oct 77	● **LOVE YOU LIVE** *Rolling Stones COC 89101* ...	**3**	8 wks
5 Nov 77	● **GET STONED** *Arcade ADEP 32* ..	**8**	15 wks
24 Jun 78	● **SOME GIRLS** *Rolling Stones COC 59108* ...	**2**	25 wks
5 Jul 80	★ **EMOTIONAL RESCUE** *Rolling Stones CUN 39111* ..	**1**	18 wks
12 Sep 81	● **TATTOO YOU** *Rolling Stones CUNS 39114*	**2**	29 wks
12 Jun 82	● **STILL LIFE (AMERICAN CONCERTS 1981)**		
	Rolling Stones CUN 39115	**4**	18 wks
31 Jul 82	**IN CONCERT (import)** *Decca (Holland) 6640 037*	**94**	3 wks
11 Dec 82	**STORY OF THE STONES** *K-Tel NE 1200*	**24**	12 wks
19 Nov 83	● **UNDERCOVER** *Rolling Stones CUN 1654361*	**3**	18 wks
7 Jul 84	**REWIND 1971–1984 (THE BEST OF THE ROLLING STONES)** *Rolling Stones CUN 1*	**23**	13 wks
5 Apr 86	● **DIRTY WORK** *Rolling Stones CUN 86321*	**4**	10 wks

ROMAN HOLIDAY
UK, male vocal/instrumental group   *3 wks*

| 22 Oct 83 | **COOKIN' ON THE ROOF** *Jive HIP 9* .... | **31** | 3 wks |

RONDO VENEZIANO
UK, male/female orchestral group   *26 wks*

| 5 Nov 83 | **VENICE IN PERIL** *Ferroway RON 1* .... | **39** | 13 wks |
| 10 Nov 84 | **THE GENIUS OF VENICE** *Ferroway RON 2* ..... | **60** | 13 wks |

Mick RONSON
UK, male vocalist/instrumentalist – guitar   *10 wks*

16 Mar 74	● **SLAUGHTER ON TENTH AVENUE**		
	RCA Victor APLI 0353	**9**	7 wks
8 Mar 75	**PLAY DON'T WORRY** *RCA Victor APL1 0681* ...	**29**	3 wks

Linda RONSTADT *US, female vocalist*   *31 wks*

4 Sep 76	**HASTEN DOWN THE WIND** *Asylum K 53045* ..	**32**	8 wks
25 Dec 76	**GREATEST HITS** *Asylum K 53055* ..	**37**	9 wks
1 Oct 77	**SIMPLE DREAMS** *Asylum K 53065* ..	**15**	5 wks
14 Oct 78	**LIVING IN THE USA** *Asylum K 53085* ..	**39**	2 wks
8 Mar 80	**MAD LOVE** *Asylum K 52210* ..	**65**	1 wk
28 Jan 84	**WHAT'S NEW** *Asylum 96 0260*	**31**	5 wks
19 Jan 85	**LUSH LIFE** *Asylum 96-0387-1*	**100**	1 wk

Last two albums credited to Linda Ronstadt with the Nelson Riddle Orchestra. See also Dolly Parton/Linda Ronstadt/Emmylou Harris.

ROSE MARIE *UK, female vocalist*   *23 wks*

13 Apr 85	**ROSE MARIE SINGS JUST FOR YOU**		
	A1 RMTV 1	**30**	13 wks
24 May 86	**SO LUCKY** *A1-Spartan RMLP 2* ..	**62**	3 wks
14 Nov 87	**SENTIMENTALLY YOURS** *Telstar STAR 2302* ..	**22†**	7 wks

ROSE ROYCE
US, male/female vocal/instrumental group   *62 wks*

22 Oct 77	**IN FULL BLOOM** *Warner Bros. K 56394*	**18**	13 wks
30 Sep 78	● **STRIKES AGAIN** *Whitfield K 56257* ..	**7**	11 wks
22 Sep 79	**RAINBOW CONNECTION IV** *Atlantic K 56714* ..	**72**	2 wks
1 Mar 80	★ **GREATEST HITS** *Whitfield K RRTV 1*	**1**	34 wks
13 Oct 84	**MUSIC MAGIC** *Streetwave MKL 2*	**69**	2 wks

ROSE TATTOO
Australia, male vocal/instrumental group   *4 wks*

| 26 Sep 81 | **ASSAULT AND BATTERY** *Carrere CAL 127* .... | **40** | 4 wks |

Diana ROSS *US, female vocalist*   *358 wks*

24 Oct 70	**DIANA ROSS** *Tamla Motown SFTML 11159*	**14**	5 wks
19 Jun 71	**EVERYTHING IS WAITING**		
	Tamla Motown STML 11178	**31**	3 wks
9 Oct 71	● **I'M STILL WAITING** *Tamla Motown STML 11193* ..	**10**	11 wks

9 Oct 71	**DIANA** *Tamla Motown STMA 8001*		43	1 wk
11 Nov 72	**GREATEST HITS** *Tamla Motown STMA 8006*		34	10 wks
1 Sep 73	● **TOUCH ME IN THE MORNING** *Tamla Motown STML 11239*		7	35 wks
27 Oct 73	**LADY SINGS THE BLUES** *Tamla Motown TMSP 1131*		50	1 wk
2 Mar 74	**LAST TIME I SAW HIM** *Tamla Motown STML 11255*		41	1 wk
8 Jun 74	**LIVE** *Tamla Motown STML 11248*		21	8 wks
27 Mar 76	● **DIANA ROSS** *Tamla Motown STML 12022*		4	26 wks
7 Aug 76	● **GREATEST HITS 2** *Tamla Motown STML 12036*		2	29 wks
19 Mar 77	**AN EVENING WITH DIANA ROSS** *Motown TMSP 6005*		52	1 wk
4 Aug 79	**THE BOSS** *Motown STML 12118*		52	2 wks
17 Nov 79	● **20 GOLDEN GREATS** *Motown EMTV 21*		2	29 wks
21 Jun 80	**DIANA** *Motown STMA 8033*		12	32 wks
28 Mar 81	**TO LOVE AGAIN** *Motown STML 12152*		26	10 wks
7 Nov 81	**WHY DO FOOLS FALL IN LOVE** *Capitol EST 26733*		17	24 wks
21 Nov 81	**ALL THE GREATEST HITS** *Motown STMA 8036*		21	31 wks
13 Feb 82	**DIANA ROSS** *Motown STML 12163*		43	6 wks
23 Oct 82	**SILK ELECTRIC** *Capitol EAST 27313*		33	12 wks
4 Dec 82	● **LOVE SONGS** *K-Tel NE 1200*		5	17 wks
19 Jul 83	**ROSS** *Capitol EST 1867051*		44	5 wks
24 Dec 83	● **PORTRAIT** *Telstar STAR 2238*		8	31 wks
6 Oct 84	**SWEPT AWAY** *Capitol ROSS 1*		40	5 wks
28 Sep 85	**EATEN ALIVE** *Capitol ROSS 2*		11	19 wks
30 May 87	**RED HOT RHYTHM 'N' BLUES** *EMI EMC 3532*		47	4 wks

See also Diana Ross and Marvin Gaye; Diana Ross and the Supremes with the Temptations; Michael Jackson and Diana Ross; Diana Ross/Michael Jackson/Gladys Knight/Stevie Wonder.

Diana ROSS and Marvin GAYE
US, female/male vocal duo — *45 wks*

19 Jan 74	● **DIANA AND MARVIN** *Tamla Motown STMA 8015*		6	43 wks
29 Aug 81	**DIANA AND MARVIN** (re-issue) *Motown STMS 5001*		78	2 wks

See also Marvin Gaye; Marvin Gaye and Tammi Terrell; Diana Ross; Diana Ross and the Supremes with the Temptations; Michael Jackson and Diana Ross; Diana Ross/Michael Jackson/Gladys Knight/ Stevie Wonder.

Diana ROSS/Michael JACKSON/Gladys KNIGHT/Stevie WONDER
US, female/male vocalists — *10 wks*

15 Nov 86	**DIANA ROSS. MICHAEL JACKSON. GLADYS KNIGHT. STEVIE WONDER. THEIR VERY BEST BACK TO BACK** *PrioriTyV PTVR 2*		21	10 wks

See also Diana Ross; Michael Jackson; Gladys Knight and the Pips; Stevie Wonder; Diana Ross and Marvin Gaye; Diana Ross and the Supremes with the Temptations; Michael Jackson and Diana Ross; Diana Ross/Michael Jackson/Gladys Knight/Stevie wonder; the Jacksons.

Diana ROSS and the SUPREMES with the TEMPTATIONS
US, male/female vocal group — *31 wks*

25 Jan 69	★ **DIANA ROSS AND THE SUPREMES JOIN THE TEMPTATIONS** *Tamla Motown STML 11096*		1	15 wks
28 Jun 69	**TCB** *Tamla Motown STML 11110*		11	12 wks
14 Feb 70	**TOGETHER** *Tamla Motown STML 11122*		28	4 wks

See also Supremes; Supremes and the Four Tops; Temptations; Diana Ross; Diana Ross and Marvin Gaye; Michael Jackson and Diana Ross; Diana Ross/Michael Jackson/Gladys Knight/Stevie wonder.

ROSTAL and SCHAEFER
UK, male instrumental duo — *2 wks*

14 Jul 79	**BEATLES CONCERTO** *Parlophone PAS 10014*		61	2 wks

David Lee ROTH
US, male vocalist — *11 wks*

2 Mar 85	**CRAZY FROM THE HEAT** *Warner Bros. 92–5222–1*		91	2 wks
19 Jul 86	**EAT 'EM AND SMILE** *Warner Bros. WX 56*		28	9 wks

Uli Jon ROTH
Germany, male vocalist — *2 wks*

23 Feb 85	**BEYOND THE ASTRAL SKIES** *EMI ROTH 1*		64	2 wks

The musicians and contributors to this album are collectively referred to as Electric Sun.

Thomas ROUND – *See June BRONHILL and Thomas ROUND*

Demis ROUSSOS
Greece, male vocalist — *143 wks*

22 Jun 74	● **FOREVER AND EVER** *Philips 6325 021*		2	68 wks
19 Apr 75	**SOUVENIRS** *Philips 6325 201*		25	18 wks
24 Apr 76	● **HAPPY TO BE** *Philips 9101 027*		4	34 wks
3 Jul 76	**MY ONLY FASCINATION** *Philips 6325 094*		39	6 wks
16 Apr 77	**THE MAGIC OF DEMIS ROUSSOS** *Philips 9101 131*		29	6 wks
28 Oct 78	**LIFE AND LOVE** *Philips 9199 873*		36	11 wks

ROY – *See MERLE and ROY*

ROXY MUSIC
UK, male vocal/instrumental group — *293 wks*

29 Jul 72	● **ROXY MUSIC** *Island ILPS 9200*		10	16 wks
7 Apr 73	● **FOR YOUR PLEASURE** *Island ILPS 9232*		4	27 wks
1 Dec 73	★ **STRANDED** *Island ILPS 9252*		1	17 wks
30 Nov 74	● **COUNTRY LIFE** *Island ILPS 9303*		3	10 wks
8 Nov 75	● **SIREN** *Island ILPS 9344*		4	17 wks
31 Jul 76	● **VIVA ROXY MUSIC** *Island ILPS 9400*		6	12 wks
19 Nov 77	**GREATEST HITS** *Polydor 2302 073*		20	11 wks
24 Mar 79	● **MANIFESTO** *Polydor POLH 001*		7	34 wks
31 May 80	★ **FLESH AND BLOOD** *Polydor POLH 002*		1	60 wks
5 Jun 82	★ **AVALON** *EG EGHP 50*		1	57 wks
19 Mar 83	**THE HIGH ROAD** *EG (Import) EGMLP 1*		26	7 wks
12 Nov 83	**ATLANTIC YEARS 1973–1980** *EG EGLP 54*		23	25 wks

See also Bryan Ferry and Roxy Music.

ROYAL PHILHARMONIC ORCHESTRA
UK, orchestra — *16 wks*

23 Dec 78	**CLASSIC GOLD VOL. 2** *Ronco RTD 42032*		31	4 wks
13 Jan 79	**CLASSICAL GOLD** *Ronco RTV 42020*		65	1 wk
8 Oct 83	**LOVE CLASSICS** *Nouveau Music NML 1003*		30	9 wks
26 May 84	**AS TIME GOES BY** *Telstar STAR 2240*		95	2 wks

Love Classics was conducted by Nick Portlock and As Time Goes By was conducted by Harry Rabinovitz. See also Louis Clark; Juan Martin; Andy Williams, all with the Royal Philharmonic Orchestra.

RUBETTES
UK, male vocal/instrumental group — *1 wk*

10 May 75	**WE CAN DO IT** *State ETAT 001*		41	1 wk

Jimmy RUFFIN
US, male vocalist — *10 wks*

13 May 67	**JIMMY RUFFIN WAY** *Tamla Motown STML 11048*		32	6 wks
1 Jun 74	**GREATEST HITS** *Tamla Motown STML 11259*		41	4 wks

RUFUS and Chaka KHAN
US, male instrumental group with female vocalist — *7 wks*

12 Apr 75	**RUFUSIZED** *ABC ABCL 5063*		48	2 wks
21 Apr 84	**STOMPIN' AT THE SAVOY** *Warner Bros. 923679*		64	5 wks

The first album gave Chaka Khan no separate billing. See also Chaka Khan.

RUMOUR – *See Graham PARKER and the RUMOUR*

Todd RUNDGREN *US, male vocalist* — *9 wks*

29 Jan 77	**RA** *Bearsville K 55514*	27	6 wks
6 May 78	**HERMIT OF MINK HOLLOW** *Bearsville K 55521* .	42	3 wks

RUN D.M.C. *US, male rap group* — *26 wks*

26 Jul 86	**RAISING HELL** *Profile LONLP 21*	41	26 wks

RUSH *Canada, male vocal/instrumental group* — *80 wks*

8 Oct 77	**FAREWELL TO KINGS** *Mercury 9100 042*	22	4 wks
25 Nov 78	**HEMISPHERES** *Mercury 9100 059*	14	6 wks
26 Jan 80	● **PERMANENT WAVES** *Mercury 9100 071*	3	16 wks
21 Feb 81	● **MOVING PICTURES** *Mercury 6337 160*	3	11 wks
7 Nov 81	● **EXIT STAGE LEFT** *Mercury 6619 053*	6	14 wks
18 Sep 82	● **SIGNALS** *Mercury 6337 243*	3	9 wks
28 Apr 84	● **GRACE UNDER PRESSURE** *Vertigo VERH 12* . .	5	12 wks
9 Nov 85	● **POWER WINDOWS** *Vertigo VERH 31*	9	4 wks
21 Nov 87	● **HOLD YOUR FIRE** *Vertigo VERH 47*	10	4 wks

Jennifer RUSH *US, female vocalist* — *43 wks*

16 Nov 85	● **JENNIFER RUSH** *CBS 26488*	7	35 wks
3 May 86	**MOVIN'** *CBS 26710*	32	5 wks
18 Apr 87	**HEART OVER MIND** *CBS 450 470–1*	48	3 wks

Patrice RUSHEN *US, female vocalist* — *17 wks*

1 May 82	**STRAIGHT FROM THE HEART** *Elektra K 52532*	24	14 wks
16 Jun 84	**NOW** *Elektra 9603060*	73	3 wks

Leon RUSSELL *US, male vocalist* — *1 wk*

3 Jul 71	**LEON RUSSELL AND THE SHELTER PEOPLE** *A & M AMLS 65003*	29	1 wk

Mike RUTHERFORD
UK, male vocalist/instrumentalist – guitar — *11 wks*

23 Feb 80	**SMALLCREEP'S DAY** *Charisma CAS 1149*	13	7 wks
18 Sep 82	**ACTING VERY STRANGE** *WEA K 99249*	23	4 wks

See also Mike and the Mechanics.

RUTLES *UK, male vocal/instrumental group* — *11 wks*

15 Apr 78	**THE RUTLES** *Warner Bros. K 56459*	12	11 wks

RUTS *UK, male vocal/instrumental group* — *10 wks*

13 Oct 79	**THE CRACK** *Virgin V 2132*	16	6 wks
18 Oct 80	**GRIN AND BEAR IT** *Virgin V 2188*	28	4 wks

Second album credited to Ruts D.C.

S

SAD CAFE *UK, male vocal/instrumental group* — *36 wks*

1 Oct 77	**FANX TA RA** *RCA PL 25101*	56	1 wk
29 Apr 78	**MISPLACED IDEALS** *RCA PL 25133*	50	1 wk

29 Sep 79	● **FACADES** *RCA PL 25249*	8	23 wks
25 Oct 80	**SAD CAFE** *RCA SADLP 4*	46	5 wks
21 Mar 81	**LIVE** *RCA SAD LP 5*	37	4 wks
24 Oct 81	**OLE** *Polydor POLD 5045*	72	2 wks

SADE *UK, female/male vocal/instrumental group* — *129 wks*

28 Jul 84	● **DIAMOND LIFE** *Epic EPC 26044*	2	98 wks
16 Nov 85	★ **PROMISE** *Epic EPC 86318*	1	31 wks

SAILOR *UK, male vocal/instrumental group* — *8 wks*

7 Feb 76	**TROUBLE** *Epic EPC 69192*	45	8 wks

General SAINT – *See Clint EASTWOOD and General SAINT*

ST. PAUL'S BOYS' CHOIR *UK, choir* — *8 wks*

29 Nov 80	**REJOICE** *K-Tel NE 1064*	36	8 wks

Ryuichi SAKAMOTO
Japan, male composer/multi-instrumentalist — *9 wks*

3 Sep 83	**MERRY CHRISTMAS MR LAWRENCE** (**film soundtrack**) *Virgin V 2276*	36	9 wks

SALVATION ARMY *UK, brass band* — *5 wks*

24 Dec 77	**BY REQUEST** *Warwick WW 5038*	16	5 wks

SAM and DAVE *US, male vocal duo* — *20 wks*

21 Jan 67	**HOLD ON I'M COMIN'** *Atlantic 588–045* . . .	35	7 wks
22 Apr 67	**DOUBLE DYNAMITE** *Stax 589–003*	28	5 wks
23 Mar 68	**SOUL MAN** *Stax 589–015*	32	8 wks

Mike SAMMES SINGERS – *See RICHMOND STRINGS/Mike SAMMES SINGERS*

SAMSON *UK, male vocal/instrumental group* — *6 wks*

26 Jul 80	**HEAD ON** *Gem GEMLP 108*	34	6 wks

David SANBORN *US, male instrumentalist – saxophone* — *1 wk*

14 Mar 87	**A CHANGE OF HEART** *Warner Bros. 925 479–1* . .	86	1 wk

SANTANA *US, male vocal/instrumental group* — *205 wks*

2 May 70	**SANTANA** *CBS 63815*	26	11 wks
28 Nov 70	● **ABRAXAS** *CBS 64807*	7	52 wks
13 Nov 71	● **SANTANA 3** *CBS 69015*	6	14 wks
29 Nov 72	● **CARAVANSERAI** *CBS 65299*	6	11 wks
8 Dec 73	● **WELCOME** *CBS 69040*	8	6 wks
21 Sep 74	**GREATEST HITS** *CBS 69081*	14	15 wks
30 Nov 74	**BARBOLETTA** *CBS 69084*	18	5 wks
10 Apr 76	**AMIGOS** *CBS 86005*	21	9 wks
8 Jan 77	**FESTIVAL** *CBS 86020*	27	3 wks
5 Nov 77	● **MOONFLOWER** *CBS 88272*	7	27 wks
11 Nov 78	**INNER SECRETS** *CBS 86075*	17	16 wks
24 Mar 79	**ONENESS – SILVER DREAMS GOLDEN REALITY** *CBS 86037*	55	4 wks
27 Oct 79	**MARATHON** *CBS 86098*	28	5 wks
20 Sep 80	**THE SWING OF DELIGHT** *CBS 22057*	74	2 wks
18 Apr 81	**ZE BOP** *CBS 84946*	33	4 wks
14 Aug 82	**SHANGO** *CBS 85914*	35	7 wks
30 Apr 83	**HAVANA MOON** *CBS 25350*	84	3 wks

| 23 Mar 85 | BEYOND APPEARANCES | CBS 86307 | .... | 58 | 3 wks |

15 Nov 86 **VIVA! SANTANA – THE VERY BEST**
K-Tel NE 1338 .... **50** 8 wks

Oneness-Silver Dreams Golden Reality, The Swing Of Delight and Havana Moon are all credited to Carlos Santana, US, male instrumentalist – guitar. See also Carlos Santana and Alice Coltrane; Carlos Santana and Mahavishnu John McLaughlin; Carlos Santana and Buddy Miles.

Carlos SANTANA and Alice COLTRANE
US, male/female instrumental duo   *1 wk*

| 2 Nov 74 | ILLUMINATIONS | CBS 69063 | .... | 40 | 1 wk |

See also Santana; Carlos Santana and Mahavishnu John McLaughlin; Carlos Santana and Buddy Miles.

Carlos SANTANA and Mahavishnu John McLAUGHLIN *US, male instrumental duo*   *9 wks*

| 28 Jul 73 | ● LOVE DEVOTION SURRENDER | CBS 69037 ... | 7 | 9 wks |

See also Mahavishnu Orchestra; Santana; Carlos Santana and Alice Coltrane; Carlos Santana and Buddy Miles.

Carlos SANTANA and Buddy MILES
US, male instrumental duo   *4 wks*

26 Aug 72 **CARLOS SANTANA AND BUDDY MILES LIVE**
CBS 65142 .... **29** 4 wks

See also Santana; Carlos Santana and Alice Coltrane; Carlos Santana and Mahavishnu John McLaughlin.

Peter SARSTEDT *UK, male vocalist*   *4 wks*

| 15 Mar 69 | ● PETER SARSTEDT | United Artists SULP 1219 | '.... | 8 | 4 wks |

Telly SAVALAS *US, male vocalist*   *10 wks*

| 22 Mar 75 | TELLY | MCA MCF 2699 | .... | 12 | 10 wks |

SAVOY BROWN *UK, male vocal/instrumental group*   *1 wk*

| 28 Nov 70 | LOOKIN' IN | Decca SKL 5066 | .... | 50 | 1 wk |

SAXON *UK, male vocal/instrumental group*   *74 wks*

12 Apr 80	● WHEELS OF STEEL	Carrere CAL 115	....	5	29 wks
15 Nov 80	STRONG ARM OF THE LAW	Carrere CAL 120	..	11	11 wks
3 Oct 81	DENIM AND LEATHER	Carrere CAL 128	....	9	11 wks
26 Mar 83	POWER AND THE GLORY	Carrere CAL 147	....	15	9 wks
11 Feb 84	CRUSADER	Carrere CAL 200	....	18	7 wks
14 Sep 85	INNOCENCE IS NO EXCUSE				
	Parlophone SAXON 2		....	36	4 wks
27 Sep 86	ROCK THE NATIONS	EMI EMC 3515	....	34	3 wks

Leo SAYER *UK, male vocalist*   *232 wks*

5 Jan 74	● SILVER BIRD	Chrysalis CHR 1050	.....	2	22 wks
26 Oct 74	● JUST A BOY	Chrysalis CHR 1068	....	4	14 wks
20 Sep 75	● ANOTHER YEAR	Chrysalis CHR 1087	....	8	9 wks
27 Nov 76	● ENDLESS FLIGHT	Chrysalis CHR 1125	....	4	66 wks
22 Oct 77	THUNDER IN MY HEART	Chrysalis CDL 1154	..	8	16 wks
2 Sep 78	LEO SAYER	Chrysalis CDL 1198	....	15	25 wks
31 Mar 79	★ THE VERY BEST OF LEO SAYER				
	Chrysalis CDL 1222		....	1	37 wks
13 Oct 79	HERE	Chrysalis CDL 1240	....	44	4 wks
23 Aug 80	LIVING IN A FANTASY	Chrysalis CDL 1297	.....	15	9 wks
8 May 82	WORLD RADIO	Chrysalis CDL 1345	....	30	12 wks
12 Nov 83	HAVE YOU EVER BEEN IN LOVE				
	Chrysalis LEOTV 1		....	15	18 wks

Alexei SAYLE *UK, male comedian*   *5 wks*

| 17 Mar 84 | THE FISH PEOPLE TAPES | Island IMA 9 | .... | 62 | 5 wks |

Boz SCAGGS *US, male vocalist*   *29 wks*

12 Mar 77	SILK DEGREES	CBS 81193	....	37	24 wks
17 Dec 77	DOWN TWO, THEN LEFT	CBS 86036	....	55	1 wk
3 May 80	MIDDLE MAN	CBS 86094	....	52	4 wks

SCARS *UK, male vocal/instrumental group*   *3 wks*

| 18 Apr 81 | AUTHOR AUTHOR | Pre PREX 5 | .... | 67 | 3 wks |

SCHAEFER – *See* ROSTAL *and* SCHAEFER

Michael SCHENKER GROUP
Germany/UK, male vocal/instrumental group   *42 wks*

6 Sep 80	● MICHAEL SCHENKER GROUP			
	Chrysalis CHR 1302	....	8	8 wks
19 Sep 81	MICHAEL SCHENKER GROUP (re-issue)			
	Chrysalis CHR 1336	....	14	8 wks
13 Mar 82	● ONE NIGHT AT BUDOKAN			
	Chrysalis CTY 1375	....	5	11 wks
23 Oct 82	ASSAULT ATTACK	Chrysalis CHR 1393	....	19	5 wks
10 Sep 83	BUILT TO DESTROY	Chrysalis CHR 1441	....	23	5 wks
23 Jun 84	ROCK WILL NEVER DIE	Chrysalis CUX 1470	...	24	5 wks

See also MSG.

SCHON – *See* HAGAR, SCHON, AARONSON, SHRIEVE

SCORPIONS *Germany, male vocal/instrumental group*   *42 wks*

21 Apr 79	LOVE DRIVE	Harvest SHSP 4097	....	36	11 wks
3 May 80	ANIMAL MAGNETISM	Harvest SHSP 4113	....	23	6 wks
10 Apr 82	BLACKOUT	Harvest SHVL 823	....	11	11 wks
24 Mar 84	LOVE AT FIRST STING	Harvest SHSP 2400071	....	17	6 wks
29 Jun 85	WORLD WIDE LIVE	Harvest SCORP 1	....	18	8 wks

SCOTLAND FOOTBALL WORLD CUP SQUAD 1974 *UK, male football team vocalists*   *9 wks*

| 25 May 74 | ● EASY EASY | Polydor 2383 282 | .... | 3 | 9 wks |

Band of the SCOTS GUARDS
UK, military band   *2 wks*

| 28 Jun 69 | BAND OF THE SCOTS GUARDS | | | |
| | Fontana SFXL 54 | .... | 25 | 2 wks |

Jack SCOTT *Canada, male vocalist*   *12 wks*

7 May 60	● I REMEMBER HANK WILLIAMS			
	Top Rank BUY 034	....	7	11 wks
3 Sep 60	WHAT IN THE WORLD'S COME OVER YOU			
	Top Rank 25/024	....	11	1 wk

SCREAMING BLUE MESSIAHS
UK, male vocal/instrumental group   *1 wk*

| 17 May 86 | GUN-SHY | WEA WX 41 | .... | 90 | 1 wk |

SCRITTI POLITTI
UK, male vocal/instrumental group — *26 wks*

11 Sep	82		**SONGS TO REMEMBER**	*Rough Trade ROUGH 20*	12	7 wks
22 Jun	85	●	**CUPID AND PSYCHE 85**	*Virgin V 2350*	5	19 wks

SEARCHERS *UK, male vocal/instrumental group* — *87 wks*

10 Aug	63	●	**MEET THE SEARCHERS**	*Pye NPL 18086*	2	44 wks
16 Nov	63	●	**SUGAR AND SPICE**	*Pye NPL 18089*	5	21 wks
30 May	64	●	**IT'S THE SEARCHERS**	*Pye NPL 18092*	4	17 wks
27 Mar	65	●	**SOUNDS LIKE THE SEARCHERS**	*Pye NPL 18111*	8	5 wks

Harry SECOMBE *UK, male vocalist* — *51 wks*

31 Mar	62		**SACRED SONGS**	*Philips RBL 7501*	16	1 wk
22 Apr	67	●	**SECOMBE'S PERSONAL CHOICE** *Philips BETS 707*		6	13 wks
7 Aug	71		**IF I RULED THE WORLD**	*Contour 6870 501*	17	20 wks
16 Dec	78	●	**20 SONGS OF JOY**	*Warwick WW 5052*	8	12 wks
13 Dec	86		**HIGHWAY OF LIFE**	*Telstar STAR 2289*	45	5 wks

See also Harry Secombe and Moira Anderson; Harry Secombe, Peter Sellers and Spike Milligan.

Harry SECOMBE and Moira ANDERSON
UK, male/female vocal duo — *5 wks*

5 Dec	81		**GOLDEN MEMORIES**	*Warwick WW 5107*	46	5 wks

See also Harry Secombe; Moira Anderson; Harry Secombe, Peter Sellers and Spike Milligan.

Harry SECOMBE, Peter SELLERS and Spike MILLIGAN *UK, male vocal group* — *1 wk*

18 Apr	64		**HOW TO WIN AN ELECTION**	*Philips AL 3464*	20	1 wk

See also Harry Secombe; Harry Secombe and Moira Anderson; Peter Sellers; Peter Sellers and Sophia Loren; Anthony Newley, Peter Sellers, Joan Collins; Spike Milligan.

SECOND IMAGE *UK, male vocal/instrumental group* — *1 wk*

30 Mar	85		**STRANGE REFLECTIONS**	*MCA MCF 3255*	100	1 wk

SECRET AFFAIR *UK, male vocal/instrumental group* — *15 wks*

1 Dec	79		**GLORY BOYS**	*I-Spy 1*	41	8 wks
20 Sep	80		**BEHIND CLOSED DOORS**	*I-Spy 2*	48	4 wks
13 Mar	82		**BUSINESS AS USUAL**	*I-Spy 3*	84	3 wks

Neil SEDAKA *US, male vocalist* — *52 wks*

1 Sep	73		**THE TRA-LA DAYS ARE OVER**	*MGM 2315 248*	13	10 wks
22 Jun	74		**LAUGHTER IN THE RAIN**	*Polydor 2383 265*	17	10 wks
23 Nov	74		**LIVE AT THE ROYAL FESTIVAL HALL** *Polydor 2383 299*		48	1 wk
1 Mar	75		**OVERNIGHT SUCCESS**	*Polydor 2442 131*	31	6 wks
10 Jul	76	●	**LAUGHTER AND TEARS – THE BEST OF NEIL SEDAKA TODAY**	*Polydor 2383 399*	2	25 wks

SEEKERS *Australia, male/female vocal group* — *268 wks*

3 Jul	65	●	**A WORLD OF OUR OWN**	*Columbia 33SX 1722*	5	36 wks
3 Jul	65		**THE SEEKERS**	*Decca LK 4694*	16	1 wk
19 Nov	66	●	**COME THE DAY**	*Columbia SX 6093*	3	67 wks
25 Nov	67		**SEEKERS – SEEN IN GREEN** *Columbia SCX 6193*		15	10 wks
14 Sep	68	●	**LIVE AT THE TALK OF THE TOWN** *Columbia SCX 6278*		2	29 wks
16 Nov	68	★	**BEST OF THE SEEKERS**	*Columbia SCX 6268*	1	125 wks

Bob SEGER and the SILVER BULLET BAND
US, male vocal/instrumental group — *38 wks*

3 Jun	78		**STRANGER IN TOWN**	*Capitol EAST 11698*	31	6 wks
15 Mar	80		**AGAINST THE WIND**	*Capitol EA-ST 12041*	26	6 wks
26 Sep	81		**NINE TONIGHT**	*Capitol ESTSP 23*	24	10 wks
8 Jan	83		**THE DISTANCE**	*Capitol EST 12254*	45	10 wks
26 Apr	86		**LIKE A ROCK**	*Capitol EST 2011*	35	6 wks

SELECTER *UK, male/female vocal/instrumental group* — *17 wks*

23 Feb	80	●	**TOO MUCH PRESSURE** *2-Tone CDL TT 5002*		5	13 wks
7 Mar	81		**CELEBRATE THE BULLET**	*Chrysalis CHR 1306*	41	4 wks

Peter SELLERS *UK, male vocalist* — *84 wks*

14 Feb	59	●	**THE BEST OF SELLERS**	*Parlophone PMD 1069*	3	47 wks
12 Dec	59	●	**SONGS FOR SWINGING SELLERS** *Parlophone PMC 1111*		3	37 wks

See also Peter Sellers and Sophia Loren; Harry Secombe, Peter Sellers and Spike Milligan; Anthony Newley, Peter Sellers, Joan Collins.

Peter SELLERS and Sophia LOREN
UK/Italy, male/female vocal duo — *18 wks*

3 Dec	60	●	**PETER AND SOPHIA**	*Parlophone PMC 1131*	5	18 wks

See also Peter Sellers; Harry Secombe, Peter Sellers and Spike Milligan; Anthony Newley, Peter Sellers, Joan Collins.

SENSATIONAL ALEX HARVEY BAND
UK, male vocal/instrumental group — *42 wks*

26 Oct	74		**THE IMPOSSIBLE DREAM**	*Vertigo 6360 112*	16	4 wks
10 May	75	●	**TOMORROW BELONGS TO ME** *Vertigo 9102 003*		9	10 wks
23 Aug	75		**NEXT**	*Vertigo 6360 103*	37	5 wks
27 Sep	75		**SENSATIONAL ALEX HARVEY BAND LIVE** *Vertigo 6360 122*		14	7 wks
10 Apr	76		**PENTHOUSE TAPES**	*Vertigo 9102 007*	14	7 wks
31 Jul	76		**SAHB STORIES**	*Mountain TOPS 112*	11	9 wks

Captain SENSIBLE *UK, male vocalist* — *3 wks*

11 Sep	82		**WOMEN AND CAPTAIN FIRST** *A&M AMLH 68548*		64	3 wks

SEX PISTOLS *UK, male vocal/instrumental group* — *97 wks*

12 Nov	77	★	**NEVER MIND THE BOLLOCKS HERE'S THE SEX PISTOLS**	*Virgin V 2086*	1	48 wks
10 Mar	79	●	**THE GREAT ROCK 'N' ROLL SWINDLE** *Virgin VD 2410*		7	33 wks
11 Aug	79	●	**SOME PRODUCT – CARRI ON SEX PISTOLS** *Virgin VR 2*		6	10 wks
16 Feb	80		**FLOGGING A DEAD HORSE**	*Virgin V 2142*	23	6 wks

SHADOWS *UK, male instrumental group* — *395 wks*

16 Sep	61	★	**THE SHADOWS**	*Columbia 33SX 1374*	1	57 wks
13 Oct	62	★	**OUT OF THE SHADOWS**	*Columbia 33SX 1458*	1	38 wks
22 Jun	63	●	**GREATEST HITS**	*Columbia 33SX 1522*	2	49 wks
9 May	64	●	**DANCE WITH THE SHADOWS** *Columbia 33SX 1619*		2	27 wks
17 Jul	65	●	**SOUND OF THE SHADOWS** *Columbia 33SX 1736*		4	17 wks
21 May	66	●	**SHADOW MUSIC**	*Columbia SX 6041*	5	17 wks

15 Jul	67	● **JIGSAW** Columbia SCX 6148	8	16 wks
24 Oct	70	**SHADES OF ROCK** Columbia SCX 6420	30	4 wks
13 Apr	74	**ROCKIN' WITH CURLY LEADS** EMI EMA 762	45	1 wk
11 May	74	**GREATEST HITS (re-issue)** Columbia SCX 1522	48	6 wks
29 Mar	75	**SPECS APPEAL** EMI EMC 3066	30	5 wks
12 Feb	77	★ **20 GOLDEN GREATS** EMI EMTV 3	1	38 wks
15 Sep	79	★ **STRING OF HITS** EMI EMC 3310	1	48 wks
26 Jul	80	**ANOTHER STRING OF HITS** EMI EMC 3339	16	8 wks
13 Sep	80	**CHANGE OF ADDRESS** Polydor 2442 179	17	6 wks
19 Sep	81	**HITS RIGHT UP YOUR STREET**		
		Polydor POLD 5046	15	16 wks
25 Sep	82	**LIFE IN THE JUNGLE/LIVE AT ABBEY ROAD**		
		Polydor SHADS 1	24	6 wks
22 Oct	83	**XXV** Polydor POLD 5120	34	6 wks
17 Nov	84	**GUARDIAN ANGEL** Polydor POLD 5169 ...	98	1 wk
24 May	86	● **MOONLIGHT SHADOWS** Polydor PROLP 8	6	19 wks
24 Oct	87	**SIMPLY SHADOWS** Polydor SHAD 1	11†	10 wks

See also Cliff Richard.

SHAKATAK
UK, male/female vocal/instrumental group   *72 wks*

30 Jan	82	**DRIVIN' HARD** Polydor POLS 1030	35	17 wks
15 May	82	● **NIGHT BIRDS** Polydor POLS 1059	4	28 wks
27 Nov	82	**INVITATIONS** Polydor POLD 5068	30	11 wks
22 Oct	83	**OUT OF THIS WORLD** Polydor POLD 5115 ...	30	4 wks
25 Aug	84	**DOWN ON THE STREET** Polydor POLD 5148 ..	17	9 wks
23 Feb	85	**LIVE!** Polydor POLH 21	82	3 wks

SHAKIN' PYRAMIDS
UK, male vocal/instrumental group   *4 wks*

| 4 Apr | 81 | **SKIN 'EM UP** Cuba/Libra V 2199 .... | 48 | 4 wks |

SHALAMAR
US, male/female vocal/instrumental group   *121 wks*

27 Mar	82	● **FRIENDS** Solar K 52345	6	72 wks
11 Sep	82	**GREATEST HITS** Solar SOLA 3001	71	5 wks
30 Jul	83	● **THE LOOK** Solar 960239	7	20 wks
12 Apr	86	● **THE GREATEST HITS** Stylus SMR 8615	5	24 wks

SHAM 69   *UK, male vocal/instrumental group*   *27 wks*

11 Mar	78	**TELL US THE TRUTH** Polydor 2383 491	25	8 wks
2 Dec	78	**THAT'S LIFE** Polydor POLD 5010	27	11 wks
29 Sep	79	● **THE ADVENTURES OF THE HERSHAM BOYS**		
		Polydor POLD 5025	8	8 wks

Jimmy SHAND, HIS BAND AND GUESTS
UK, male instrumentalist – accordian, with male/female
vocal/instrumental dance band   *2 wks*

| 24 Dec | 83 | **FIFTY YEARS ON WITH JIMMY SHAND** | | |
| | | Ross WGR 062 .... | 97 | 2 wks |

SHANNON   *US, female vocalist*   *12 wks*

| 10 Mar | 84 | **LET THE MUSIC PLAY** Club JABL 1 .... | 52 | 12 wks |

Del SHANNON   *US, male vocalist*   *23 wks*

11 May	63	● **HATS OFF TO DEL SHANNON**		
		London HAX 8071	9	17 wks
2 Nov	63	**LITTLE TOWN FLIRT** London HAX 8091	15	6 wks

Helen SHAPIRO   *UK, female vocalist*   *25 wks*

| 10 Mar | 62 | ● **TOPS WITH ME** Columbia 33SX 1397 .... | 2 | 25 wks |

Feargal SHARKEY   *UK, male vocalist*   *20 wks*

| 23 Nov | 85 | **FEARGAL SHARKEY** Virgin V 2360 .... | 12 | 20 wks |

Sandie SHAW   *UK, female vocalist*   *13 wks*

| 6 Mar | 65 | ● **SANDIE** Pye NPL 18110 .... | 3 | 13 wks |

George SHEARING QUINTET – *See Nat King COLE and the George SHEARING QUINTET; Peggy LEE and George SHEARING*

Pete SHELLEY   *UK, male vocalist*   *4 wks*

| 2 Jul | 83 | **XL-1** Genetic XL 1 .... | 42 | 4 wks |

SHERRICK   *US, male vocalist*   *6 wks*

| 29 Aug | 87 | **SHERRICK** Warner Bros. WX 118 .... | 27 | 6 wks |

Brendon SHINE   *Ireland, male vocalist*   *23 wks*

12 Nov	83	**THE BRENDON SHINE COLLECTION**		
		Play PLAYTV 1	51	12 wks
3 Nov	84	**WITH LOVE** Play PLAYTV 2	74	4 wks
16 Nov	85	**MEMORIES** Play PLAYTV 3	81	7 wks

SHIRLIE – *See PEPSI and SHIRLIE*

SHOP ASSISTANTS
UK, male/female vocal/instrumental group   *1 wk*

| 29 Nov | 86 | **SHOP ASSISTANTS** Blue Guitar AZLP 2 .... | 100 | 1 wk |

SHOWADDYWADDY
UK, male vocal/instrumental group   *126 wks*

7 Dec	74	● **SHOWADDYWADDY** Bell BELLS 248	9	19 wks
12 Jul	75	● **STEP TWO** Bell BELLS 256	7	17 wks
29 May	76	**TROCADERO** Bell SYBEL 8003	41	3 wks
25 Dec	76	● **GREATEST HITS** Arista ARTY 145	4	26 wks
3 Dec	77	**RED STAR** Arista SPARTY 1023	20	10 wks
9 Dec	78	★ **GREATEST HITS** Arista ARTV 1	1	17 wks
10 Nov	79	● **CREPES AND DRAPES** Arista ARTV 3	8	14 wks
20 Dec	80	**BRIGHT LIGHTS** Arista SPART 1142	54	8 wks
7 Nov	81	**THE VERY BEST OF** Arista SPART 1178	33	11 wks
5 Dec	87	**THE BEST STEPS TO HEAVEN** Tiger SHTV 1 ..	90	1 wk

SHRIEKBACK   *UK, male vocal/instrumental group*   *1 wk*

| 11 Aug | 84 | **JAM SCIENCE** Arista 206 416 .... | 85 | 1 wk |

SHRIEVE – *See HAGAR, SCHON, AARONSON, SHRIEVE*

SHY   *UK, male vocal/instrumental group*   *2 wks*

| 11 Apr | 87 | **EXCESS ALL AREAS** RCA PL 71221 .... | 74 | 2 wks |

Labi SIFFRE   *UK, male vocalist*   *2 wks*

24 Jul	71	**SINGER AND THE SONG** Pye NSPL 28147	47	1 wk
14 Oct	72	**CRYING, LAUGHING, LOVING, LYING**		
		Pye NSPL 28163	46	1 wk

SILVER BULLET BAND – *See Bob SEGER and the SILVER BULLET BAND*

(Left) SAXON, hitmakers with *Denim and Leather*, showing more of the finest in heavy metal clothes sense.

(Below) SEX PISTOLS '77: (left to right) Steve Jones, Paul Cook, Sid Vicious and Johnny Rotten.

(Above) LABI SIFFRE's fifteen year gap between hits is one of the longest ever.

(Right) SHOWADDYWADDY go through a routine on *Top of the Pops* with a few intruders looking completely clueless.

SIGUE SIGUE SPUTNIK
UK, male vocal/instrumental group   6 wks

9 Aug 86	●	**FLAUNT IT** *Parlophone PCS 7305*		**10**	6 wks

SILVER CONVENTION
Germany/US, female vocal group   3 wks

25 Jun 77	**SILVER CONVENTION: GREATEST HITS**			
	Magnet MAG 6001		**34**	3 wks

SIMON and GARFUNKEL
US, male vocal duo   1034 wks

16 Apr 66	**SOUNDS OF SILENCE** *CBS 62690*		**13**	104 wks
3 Aug 68	★ **BOOKENDS** *CBS 63101*		**1**	77 wks
31 Aug 68	**PARSLEY, SAGE, ROSEMARY & THYME**			
	CBS 62860		**13**	66 wks
26 Oct 68	● **THE GRADUATE (film soundtrack)** *CBS 70042* .		**3**	71 wks
9 Nov 68	**WEDNESDAY MORNING 3 A.M.** *CBS 63370* ...		**24**	6 wks
21 Feb 70	★ **BRIDGE OVER TROUBLED WATER** *CBS 63699*		**1**	303 wks
22 Jul 72	● **GREATEST HITS** *CBS 69003*		**2**	283 wks
4 Apr 81	**SOUNDS OF SILENCE (re-issue)** *CBS 32020*		**68**	1 wk
21 Nov 81	● **THE SIMON AND GARFUNKEL COLLECTION**			
	CBS 10029		**4**	80 wks
20 Mar 82	● **THE CONCERT IN CENTRAL PARK**			
	Geffen 96008		**6**	43 wks

See also Paul Simon; Art Garfunkel.

Carly SIMON *US, female vocalist*   54 wks

20 Jan 73	●	**NO SECRETS** *Elektra K 42127*		**3**	26 wks
16 Mar 74		**HOT CAKES** *Elektra K 52005*		**19**	9 wks
9 May 87		**COMING AROUND AGAIN** *Arista 208 140*		**25**	19 wks

Paul SIMON *US, male vocalist*   184 wks

26 Feb 72	★	**PAUL SIMON** *CBS 69007*		**1**	26 wks
2 Jun 73	●	**THERE GOES RHYMIN' SIMON** *CBS 69035*		**4**	22 wks
1 Nov 75	●	**STILL CRAZY AFTER ALL THESE YEARS**			
		CBS 86001		**6**	31 wks
3 Dec 77	●	**GREATEST HITS, ETC.** *CBS 10007*		**6**	15 wks
30 Aug 80		**ONE-TRICK PONY** *Warner Bros. K 56846* ...		**17**	12 wks
12 Nov 83		**HEARTS AND BONES** *Warner Bros. 92–3942–1* ...		**34**	8 wks
13 Sep 86	★	**GRACELAND** *Warner Bros. WX 52*		**1†**	68 wks
24 Jan 87		**GREATEST HITS, ETC. (re-issue)** *CBS 450 166–1*		**73**	2 wks

See also Simon and Garfunkel.

Nina SIMONE *US, female vocalist*   11 wks

24 Jul 65	**I PUT A SPELL ON YOU** *Philips BL 7671*		**18**	3 wks
15 Feb 69	**'NUFF SAID** *RCS SF 7979*		**11**	1 wk
14 Nov 87	**MY BABY JUST CARES FOR ME** *Charly CR 30217*		**56†**	7 wks

SIMPLE MINDS *UK, male vocal/instrumental group*   235 wks

5 May 79		**A LIFE IN THE DAY** *Zoom ZULP 1*		**30**	6 wks
27 Sep 80		**EMPIRES AND DANCE** *Arista SPART 1140*		**41**	3 wks
12 Sep 81		**SONS AND FASCINATIONS/SISTERS FEELINGS**			
		CALL *Virgin V 2207*		**11**	7 wks
27 Feb 82		**CELEBRATION** *Arista SPART 1183*		**45**	7 wks
25 Sep 82	●	**NEW GOLD DREAM (81, 82, 83, 84)** *Virgin V 2230*		**3**	52 wks
18 Feb 84	★	**SPARKLE IN THE RAIN** *Virgin V 2300*		**1**	57 wks
2 Nov 85	★	**ONCE UPON A TIME** *Virgin V 2364*		**1**	82 wks
6 Jun 87	★	**LIVE IN THE CITY OF LIGHT** *Virgin V SMDL 1*		**1**	21 wks

SIMPLY RED *UK, male vocal/instrumental group*   139 wks

26 Oct 85	●	**PICTURE BOOK** *Elektra EKT 27*		**2†**	100 wks
21 Mar 87	●	**MEN AND WOMEN** *WEA WX 85*		**2†**	39 wks

SIMPSON – *See ASHFORD and SIMPSON*

Frank SINATRA *US, male vocalist*   613 wks

8 Nov 58	●	**COME FLY WITH ME** *Capitol LCT 6154*		**2**	18 wks
15 Nov 58	●	**SONGS FOR SWINGING LOVERS**			
		Capitol LCT 6106		**8**	8 wks
29 Nov 58	●	**FRANK SINATRA STORY** *Fontana TFL 5030* ...		**8**	1 wk
13 Dec 58	●	**FRANK SINATRA SINGS FOR ONLY THE**			
		LONELY *Capitol LCT 6168*		**5**	13 wks
16 May 59	●	**COME DANCE WITH ME** *Capitol LCT 6179*		**2**	30 wks
22 Aug 59	●	**LOOK TO YOUR HEART** *Capitol LCT 6181*		**5**	8 wks
11 Jun 60	●	**COME BACK TO SORRENTO** *Fontana TFL 5082*		**6**	9 wks
29 Oct 60	●	**SWING EASY** *Capitol W 587*		**5**	17 wks
21 Jan 61	●	**NICE 'N EASY** *Capitol W 1417*		**4**	27 wks
15 Jul 61		**SINATRA SOUVENIR** *Fontana TFL 5138*		**18**	1 wk
19 Aug 61		**WHEN YOUR LOVER HAS GONE**			
		Encore ENC 101		**6**	10 wks
23 Sep 61		**SINATRA'S SWINGING SESSION**			
		Capitol W 1491		**6**	8 wks
28 Oct 61		**SINATRA SWINGS** *Reprise R 1002*		**8**	8 wks
25 Nov 61		**SINATRA PLUS** *Fontana SET 303*		**7**	9 wks
16 Dec 61	●	**RING-A-DING-DING** *Reprise R 1001*		**8**	9 wks
17 Feb 62		**COME SWING WITH ME** *Capitol W 1594*		**13**	4 wks
7 Apr 62		**I REMEMBER TOMMY** *Reprise R 1003*		**10**	12 wks
9 Jun 62		**SINATRA AND STRINGS** *Reprise R 1004*		**6**	20 wks
27 Oct 62		**GREAT SONGS FROM GREAT BRITAIN**			
		Reprise R 1006		**12**	9 wks
29 Dec 62		**SINATRA WITH SWINGING BRASS**			
		Reprise R 1005		**14**	11 wks
27 Jul 63	●	**CONCERT SINATRA** *Reprise R 1009*		**8**	18 wks
5 Oct 63	●	**SINATRA'S SINATRA** *Reprise R 1010*		**9**	24 wks
19 Sep 64		**IT MIGHT AS WELL BE SWING** *Reprise R 1012*		**17**	4 wks
20 Mar 65		**SOFTLY AS I LEAVE YOU** *Reprise R 1013*		**20**	1 wk
22 Jan 66	●	**A MAN AND HIS MUSIC** *Reprise R 1016*		**9**	19 wks
21 May 66		**MOONLIGHT SINATRA** *Reprise R 1018*		**18**	8 wks
2 Jul 66	●	**STRANGERS IN THE NIGHT** *Reprise R 1017*		**4**	18 wks
1 Oct 66	●	**SINATRA AT THE SANDS** *Reprise RLP 1019*		**7**	18 wks
3 Dec 66		**FRANK SINATRA SINGS SONGS FOR PLEASURE**			
		MFP 1120		**26**	2 wks
25 Feb 67		**THAT'S LIFE** *Reprise RSLP 1020*		**22**	12 wks
7 Oct 67		**FRANK SINATRA** *Reprise RSLP 1022*		**28**	5 wks
19 Oct 68	●	**GREATEST HITS** *Reprise RSLP 1025*		**8**	38 wks
7 Dec 68		**BEST OF FRANK SINATRA** *Capitol ST 21140* ...		**17**	10 wks
7 Jun 69	●	**MY WAY** *Reprise RSLP 1029*		**2**	59 wks
4 Oct 69		**A MAN ALONE** *Reprise RSLP 1030*		**18**	7 wks
9 May 70		**WATERTOWN** *Reprise RSLP 1031*		**14**	9 wks
12 Dec 70	●	**GREATEST HITS VOL. 2** *Reprise RSLP 1032* ...		**6**	40 wks
5 Jun 71	●	**SINATRA AND COMPANY** *Reprise RSLP 1033* ...		**9**	9 wks
27 Nov 71		**FRANK SINATRA SINGS RODGERS AND HART**			
		Starline SRS 5083		**35**	1 wk
8 Jan 72		**MY WAY (re-issue)** *Reprise K 44015*		**35**	1 wk
8 Jan 72		**GREATEST HITS VOL. 2** *Reprise K 44018*		**29**	3 wks
1 Dec 73		**OL' BLUE EYES IS BACK** *Warner Bros. K 44249* ..		**12**	13 wks
17 Aug 74		**SOME NICE THINGS I'VE MISSED**			
		Reprise K 54020		**35**	3 wks
15 Feb 75		**THE MAIN EVENT (TV soundtrack)**			
		Reprise K 54031		**30**	2 wks
14 Jun 75		**THE BEST OF OL' BLUE EYES** *Reprise K 54042* ..		**30**	3 wks
19 Mar 77	★	**PORTRAIT OF SINATRA** *Reprise K 64039*		**1**	18 wks
13 May 78	●	**20 GOLDEN GREATS** *Capitol EMTV 10*		**4**	11 wks
18 Aug 84		**L.A. IS MY LADY** *Qwest 925145*		**41**	8 wks
22 Mar 86		**NEW YORK NEW YORK (GREATEST HITS)**			
		Warner Bros. WX 32		**13**	12 wks
4 Oct 86		**THE FRANK SINATRA COLLECTION**			
		Capitol EMTV 41		**40**	5 wks

See also Frank Sinatra and Count Basie.

Frank SINATRA and Count BASIE US, male vocalist
and male orchestra leader/instrumentalist – piano
23 wks

23 Feb 63	● SINATRA – BASIE *Reprise R 1008*		2	23 wks

See also Count Basie; Frank Sinatra.

Nancy SINATRA US, female vocalist
15 wks

16 Apr 66	BOOTS *Reprise R 6202*		12	9 wks
18 Jun 66	HOW DOES THAT GRAB YOU *Reprise R 6207* ..		12	3 wks
10 Oct 70	NANCY'S GREATEST HITS *Reprise RSLP 6409* ..		39	3 wks

See also Nancy Sinatra and Lee Hazlewood.

Nancy SINATRA and Lee HAZELWOOD
US, female/male vocal duo
17 wks

29 Jun 68	NANCY AND LEE *Reprise RSLP 6273*		17	12 wks
25 Sep 71	NANCY AND LEE (re-issue) *Reprise K 44126*		42	1 wk
29 Jan 72	DID YOU EVER *RCA Victor SF 8240*		31	4 wks

See also Nancy Sinatra.

SINITTA US, female vocalist
1 wk

26 Dec 87	SINITTA! *Fanfare BOYLP 1*		85†	1 wk

SINFONIA OF LONDON – *See Howard BLAKE conducting the SINFONIA OF LONDON*

SIOUXSIE and the BANSHEES
UK, male/female vocal/instrumental group
106 wks

2 Dec 78	THE SCREAM *Polydor POLD 5009*		12	11 wks
22 Sep 79	JOIN HANDS *Polydor POLD 5024*		13	5 wks
16 Aug 80	● KALEIDOSCOPE *Polydor 2442 177*		5	6 wks
27 Jun 81	● JUJU *Polydor POLS 1034*		7	17 wks
12 Dec 81	ONCE UPON A TIME *Polydor POLS 1056*		21	26 wks
13 Nov 82	A KISS IN THE DREAMHOUSE *Polydor POLD 5064*		11	11 wks
3 Dec 83	NOCTURNE *Wonderland SHAH 1*		29	10 wks
16 Jun 84	HYENA *Wonderland SHEHP 3*		15	6 wks
26 Apr 86	TINDERBOX *Wonderland SHELP 3*		13	6 wks
14 Mar 87	THROUGH THE LOOKING GLASS *Wonderland SHELP 4*		15	8 wks

SISTER SLEDGE US, female vocal group
50 wks

12 May 79	● WE ARE FAMILY *Atlantic K 50587*		7	39 wks
22 Jun 85	WHEN THE BOYS MEET THE GIRLS *Atlantic 78–1255–1*		19	11 wks

See also Chic and Sister Sledge.

SISTERHOOD UK, male vocal/instrumental group
1 wk

26 Jul 86	GIFT *Merciful Release SIS 020*		90	1 wk

SISTERS OF MERCY
UK, male vocal/instrumental group
12 wks

23 Mar 85	FIRST AND LAST AND ALWAYS *Merciful Release MR 337 L*		14	8 wks
28 Nov 87	● FLOODLAND *Merciful Release MR 441 L*		9	4 wks

Peter SKELLERN UK, male vocalist
28 wks

9 Sep 78	SKELLERN *Mercury 9109 701*		48	3 wks
8 Dec 79	ASTAIRE *Mercury 9102 702*		23	20 wks
4 Dec 82	A STRING OF PEARLS *Mercury MERL 10*		67	5 wks

SKID ROW UK, male vocal/instrumental group
3 wks

17 Oct 70	SKID *CBS 63965*		30	3 wks

SKIDS UK, male vocal/instrumental group
20 wks

17 Mar 79	SCARED TO DANCE *Virgin V 2116*		19	10 wks
27 Oct 79	DAYS IN EUROPE *Virgin V 2138*		32	5 wks
27 Sep 80	● THE ABSOLUTE GAME *Virgin V 2174*		9	5 wks

SKY UK/Australia, male instrumental group
202 wks

2 Jun 79	● SKY *Ariola ARLH 5022*		9	56 wks
26 Apr 80	★ SKY 2 *Ariola ADSKY 2*		1	53 wks
28 Mar 81	● SKY 3 *Ariola ASKY 3*		3	23 wks
3 Apr 82	● SKY 4-FORTHCOMING *Ariola ASKY 4*		7	22 wks
22 Jan 83	SKY FIVE LIVE *Ariola 302 171*		14	14 wks
3 Dec 83	CADMIUM *Ariola 205 885*		44	10 wks
12 May 84	MASTERPIECES – THE VERY BEST OF SKY *Telstar STAR 2241*		15	18 wks
13 Apr 85	THE GREAT BALLOON RACE *Epic EPC 26419* .		63	6 wks

SKYY US, male vocal/instrumental group
1 wk

21 Jun 86	FROM THE LEFT SIDE *Capitol EST 2014*		85	1 wk

SLADE UK, male vocal/instrumental group
202 wks

8 Apr 72	● SLADE ALIVE *Polydor 2383 101*		2	58 wks
9 Dec 72	★ SLAYED? *Polydor 2383 163*		1	34 wks
6 Oct 73	★ SLADEST *Polydor 2442 119*		1	24 wks
23 Feb 74	★ OLD NEW BORROWED AND BLUE *Polydor 2383 261*		1	16 wks
14 Dec 74	● SLADE IN FLAME *Polydor 2442 126*		6	18 wks
27 Mar 76	NOBODY'S FOOL *Polydor 2383 377*		14	4 wks
22 Nov 80	SLADE SMASHES *Polydor POLTV 13*		21	15 wks
21 Mar 81	WE'LL BRING THE HOUSE DOWN *Cheapskate SKATE 1*		25	4 wks
28 Nov 81	TILL DEAF US DO PART *RCA RCALP 6021* ..		68	2 wks
18 Dec 82	SLADE ON STAGE *RCA RCALP 3107*		58	3 wks
24 Dec 83	THE AMAZING KAMIKAZE SYNDROME *RCA PL 70116*		49	13 wks
9 Jun 84	SLADE'S GREATS *Polydor SLAD 1*		89	1 wk
6 Apr 85	ROGUES GALLERY *RCA PL 70604*		60	2 wks
30 Nov 85	CRACKERS – THE SLADE CHRISTMAS PARTY ALBUM *Telstar STAR 2271*		34	7 wks
9 May 87	YOU BOYZ MAKE BIG NOIZE *RCA PL 71260* ..		98	1 wk

SLAYER US, male vocal/instrumental group
3 wks

2 May 87	REIGN IN BLOOD *Def Jam LONLP 34*		47	3 wks

Percy SLEDGE US, male vocalist
4 wks

14 Mar 87	WHEN A MAN LOVES A WOMAN (THE ULTIMATE COLLECTION) *Atlantic WX 89* ...		36	4 wks

SLEIGHRIDERS UK, male vocal/instrumental group
1 wk

17 Dec 83	A VERY MERRY DISCO *Warwick WW 5136*		100	1 wk

Grace SLICK US, female vocalist
6 wks

31 May 80	DREAMS *RCA PL 13544*		28	6 wks

SLIK UK, male vocal/instrumental group
1 wk

12 Jun 76	SLIK *Bell SYBEL 8004*		58	1 wk

SLIM CHANCE – *See Ronnie LANE and the Band SLIM CHANCE*

SLITS UK, female vocal/instrumental group — *5 wks*

22 Sep 79	**CUT** *Island ILPS 9573*	30	5 wks

SLY and ROBBIE *Jamaica, male vocal/instrumental duo* — *5 wks*

9 May 87	**RHYTHM KILLERS** *Fourth & Broadway BRLP 512* .	35	5 wks

SLY and the FAMILY STONE
US, male/female vocal/instrumental group — *2 wks*

5 Feb 72	**THERE'S A RIOT GOIN' ON** *Epic EPC 64613* ...	31	2 wks

SMALL FACES *UK, male vocal/instrumental group* — *66 wks*

14 May 66	● **SMALL FACES** *Decca LK 4790*	3	25 wks
17 Jun 67	**FROM THE BEGINNING** *Decca LK 4879*	17	5 wks
1 Jul 67	**SMALL FACES** *Immediate IMSP 008*	12	17 wks
15 Jun 68	★ **OGDEN'S NUT GONE FLAKE** *Immediate IMLP 012*	1	19 wks

Brian SMITH and his HAPPY PIANO
UK, male instrumentalist – piano — *1 wk*

19 Sep 81	**PLAY IT AGAIN** *Deram DS 047*	97	1 wk

Jimmy SMITH *US, male instrumentalist – organ* — *3 wks*

18 Jun 66	**GOT MY MOJO WORKING** *Verve VLP 912*	19	3 wks

Keely SMITH *US, female vocalist* — *9 wks*

16 Jan 65	**LENNON–McCARTNEY SONGBOOK** *Reprise R 6142*	12	9 wks

O.C. SMITH *US, male vocalist* — *1 wk*

17 Aug 68	**HICKORY HOLLER REVISITED** *CBS 63362* ...	40	1 wk

Steven SMITH and FATHER
UK, male instrumental duo — *3 wks*

13 May 72	**STEVEN SMITH AND FATHER AND 16 GREAT SONGS** *Decca SKL 5128*	17	3 wks

SMITH and JONES *UK, male comedy duo* — *8 wks*

15 Nov 86	**SCRATCH AND SNIFF** *10 DIX 51*	62	8 wks

Patti SMITH GROUP
US, female vocalist and male instrumental backing group — *20 wks*

1 Apr 78	**EASTER** *Arista SPART 1043*	16	14 wks
19 May 79	**WAVE** *Arista SPART 1086*	41	6 wks

SMITHS *UK, male vocal/instrumental group* — *146 wks*

3 Mar 84	● **THE SMITHS** *Rough Trade ROUGH 61*	2	33 wks
24 Nov 84	● **HATFUL OF HOLLOW** *Rough Trade ROUGH 76* ..	7	46 wks
23 Feb 85	★ **MEAT IS MURDER** *Rough Trade ROUGH 81*	1	13 wks
28 Jun 86	● **THE QUEEN IS DEAD** *Rough Trade ROUGH 96* ..	2	22 wks

---

7 Mar 87	● **THE WORLD WON'T LISTEN** *Rough Trade ROUGH 101*	2	15 wks
30 May 87	**LOUDER THAN BOMBS** *Rough Trade ROUGH 255*	38	5 wks
10 Oct 87	● **STRANGEWAYS HERE WE COME** *Rough Trade ROUGH 106*	2†	12 wks

SMOKIE *UK, male vocal/instrumental group* — *42 wks*

1 Nov 75	**SMOKIE/CHANGING ALL THE TIME** *RAK SRAK 517*	18	5 wks
30 Apr 77	● **GREATEST HITS** *RAK SRAK 526* ...	6	22 wks
4 Nov 78	**THE MONTREUX ALBUM** *RAK SRAK 6757*	52	2 wks
11 Oct 80	**SMOKIE'S HITS** *RAK SRAK 540*	23	13 wks

SMURFS – *See Father ABRAHAM and the SMURFS*

SOFT CELL *UK, male vocal/instrumental duo* — *87 wks*

5 Dec 81	● **NON-STOP EROTIC CABARET** *Some Bizzare BZLP 2*	5	46 wks
26 Jun 82	● **NON-STOP ECSTATIC DANCING** *Some Bizzare BZX 1012*	6	18 wks
22 Jan 83	● **THE ART OF FALLING APART** *Some Bizzare BIZL 3*	5	9 wks
31 Mar 84	**THE LAST NIGHT IN SODOM** *Some Bizzare BIZL 6*	12	5 wks
20 Dec 86	**THE SINGLES ALBUM** *Some Bizzare BZLP 3*	58	9 wks

SOFT MACHINE *UK, male vocal/instrumental group* — *8 wks*

4 Jul 70	**THIRD** *CBS 66246*	18	6 wks
3 Apr 71	**FOURTH** *CBS 64280*	32	2 wks

SOLID SENDERS
UK, male vocal/instrumental group — *3 wks*

23 Sep 78	**SOLID SENDERS** *Virgin V 2105*	42	3 wks

Diane SOLOMON *UK, female vocalist* — *6 wks*

9 Aug 75	**TAKE TWO** *Philips 6308 236*	26	6 wks

SONNY and CHER *US, male/female vocal duo* — *20 wks*

16 Oct 65	● **LOOK AT US** *Atlantic ATL 5036*	7	13 wks
14 May 66	**THE WONDROUS WORLD OF SONNY & CHER** *Atlantic 587–006*	15	7 wks

See also Cher.

S.O.S. BAND
US, male/female vocal/instrumental group — *19 wks*

1 Sep 84	**JUST THE WAY YOU LIKE IT** *Tabu TBU 26058* .	29	10 wks
17 May 86	**SANDS OF TIME** *Tabu TBU 26863*	15	9 wks

David SOUL *US, male vocalist* — *51 wks*

27 Nov 76	● **DAVID SOUL** *Private Stock PVLP 1012* ...	2	28 wks
17 Sep 77	● **PLAYING TO AN AUDIENCE OF ONE** *Private Stock PVLP 1026*	8	23 wks

SOUL CITY SYMPHONY – *See Van McCOY and the SOUL CITY SYMPHONY*

SOUNDS ORCHESTRAL *UK, orchestra* — *1 wk*

12 Jun 65	**CAST YOUR FATE TO THE WIND** *Piccadilly NPL 38041*	17	1 wk

(Top left) SIMPLE MINDS (lead singer Jim Kerr second from left) are shown in the days before they hit gold.

(Top right) The original SMALL FACES are seen during a photocall on 4 November 1965.

(Left) SPANDAU BALLET as they appeared in the early days of their journey to glory.

(Left) The SPECIALS were the top Two-Tone act on album.

SOUNDTRACKS (films, TV etc) – *See VARIOUS ARTISTS*

SOUTH BANK ORCHESTRA *UK, orchestra* — *6 wks*

2 Dec 78	**LILLIE** *Sounds MOR 516*	47	6 wks

This album was conducted by Joseph Morovitz and Laurie Holloway.

SOUTHERN DEATH CULT – *See the CULT*

SPACE *France, male instrumental group* — *9 wks*

17 Sep 77	**MAGIC FLY** *Pye NSPL 28232*	11	9 wks

SPANDAU BALLET
UK, male vocal/instrumental group — *244 wks*

14 Mar 81	● **JOURNEY TO GLORY** *Reformation CHR 1331*	5	29 wks
20 Mar 82	**DIAMOND** *Reformation CDL 1353*	15	18 wks
12 Mar 83	★ **TRUE** *Reformation CDL 1403*	1	90 wks
7 Jul 84	● **PARADE** *Reformation CDL 1473*	2	39 wks
16 Nov 85	● **THE SINGLES COLLECTION** *Chrysalis SBTV 1*	3	49 wks
29 Nov 86	**THROUGH THE BARRICADES** *Reformation CBS 450 259–1*	7	19 wks

SPARKS *US/UK, male vocal/instrumental group* — *42 wks*

1 Jun 74	● **KIMONO MY HOUSE** *Island ILPS 9272*	4	24 wks
23 Nov 74	● **PROPAGANDA** *Island ILPS 9312*	9	13 wks
18 Oct 75	**INDISCREET** *Island ILPS 9345*	18	4 wks
8 Sep 79	**NUMBER ONE IN HEAVEN** *Virgin V 2115*	73	1 wk

SPEAR OF DESTINY
UK, male vocal/instrumental group — *31 wks*

23 Apr 83	**GRAPES OF WRATH** *Epic EPC 25318*	62	2 wks
28 Apr 84	**ONE EYED JACKS** *Burning Rome EPC 25836*	22	7 wks
7 Sep 85	**WORLD SERVICE** *Burning Rome EPC 26514*	11	7 wks
2 May 87	**OUTLAND** *10 DIX 59*	16	12 wks
16 May 87	**S.O.D. – THE EPIC YEARS** *Epic 450 872–1*	53	3 wks

Billie Jo SPEARS *US, female vocalist* — *28 wks*

11 Sep 76	**WHAT I'VE GOT IN MIND** *United Artists UAS 29955*	47	2 wks
19 May 79	● **THE BILLIE JO SPEARS SINGLES ALBUM** *United Artists UAK 30231*	7	17 wks
21 Nov 81	**COUNTRY GIRL** *Warwick WW 5109*	17	9 wks

SPECIAL A.K.A.
UK, male/female vocal/instrumental group — *70 wks*

3 Nov 79	● **SPECIALS** *2-Tone CDL TT 5001*	4	45 wks
4 Oct 80	● **MORE SPECIALS** *2-Tone CHR TT 5003*	5	19 wks
23 Jun 84	**IN THE STUDIO** *2-Tone CHR TT 5008*	34	6 wks

Group were male only and billed simply as the Specials for the first two albums.

Phil SPECTOR *US, male producer* — *26 wks*

23 Dec 72	**PHIL SPECTOR'S CHRISTMAS ALBUM** *Apple SAPCOR 24*	21	3 wks
15 Oct 77	**PHIL SPECTOR'S ECHOES OF THE 60'S** *Phil Spector International 2307 013*	21	10 wks
25 Dec 82	**PHIL SPECTOR'S CHRISTMAS ALBUM (re-issue)** *Phil Spector International/Polydor 2307 005*	96	2 wks
10 Dec 83	**PHIL SPECTOR'S GREATEST HITS/PHIL SPECTOR'S CHRISTMAS ALBUM (2nd re-issue)** *Impression PSLP 1/2*	19	8 wks
12 Dec 87	**PHIL SPECTOR'S CHRISTMAS ALBUM (3rd re-issue)** *Chrysalis CDL 1625*	77†	3 wks

SPIDER *UK, male vocal/instrumental group* — *2 wks*

23 Oct 82	**ROCK 'N' ROLL GYPSIES** *RCA RCALP 3101*	75	1 wk
7 Apr 84	**ROUGH JUSTICE** *A & M AMLX 68563*	96	1 wk

SPINNERS *UK, male vocal group* — *24 wks*

5 Sep 70	**THE SPINNERS ARE IN TOWN** *Fontana 6309 014*	40	5 wks
7 Aug 71	**SPINNERS LIVE PERFORMANCE** *Contour 6870 502*	14	12 wks
13 Nov 71	**THE SWINGING CITY** *Philips 6382 002*	20	3 wks
8 Apr 72	**LOVE IS TEASING** *Columbia SCX 6493*	33	4 wks

SPIRIT *US, male vocal/instrumental duo* — *2 wks*

18 Apr 81	**POTATO LAND** *Beggars Banquet BEGA 23*	40	2 wks

SPITTING IMAGE *UK, puppets* — *3 wks*

18 Oct 86	**SPIT IN YOUR EAR** *Virgin V 2403*	55	3 wks

SPLIT ENZ
New Zealand/UK, male vocal/instrumental group — *9 wks*

30 Aug 80	**TRUE COLOURS** *A & M AMLH 64822*	42	8 wks
8 May 82	**TIME AND TIDE** *A & M AMLH 64894*	71	1 wk

SPOTNICKS *Sweden, male instrumental group* — *1 wk*

9 Feb 63	**OUT-A-SPACE** *Oriole PS 40036*	20	1 wk

Dusty SPRINGFIELD *UK, female vocalist* — *82 wks*

25 Apr 64	● **A GIRL CALLED DUSTY** *Philips BL 7594*	6	23 wks
23 Oct 65	● **EVERYTHING COMES UP DUSTY** *Philips RBL 1002*	6	12 wks
22 Oct 66	● **GOLDEN HITS** *Philips BL 7737*	2	36 wks
11 Nov 67	**WHERE AM I GOING** *Philips SBL 7820*	40	1 wk
21 Dec 68	**DUSTY...DEFINITELY** *Philips SBL 7864*	30	6 wks
2 May 70	**FROM DUSTY WITH LOVE** *Philips SBL 7927*	35	2 wks
4 Mar 78	**IT BEGINS AGAIN** *Mercury 9109 607*	41	2 wks

Rick SPRINGFIELD *Australia, male vocalist* — *7 wks*

11 Feb 84	**LIVING IN OZ** *RCA PL 84660*	41	4 wks
25 May 85	**TAO** *RCA PL 85370*	68	3 wks

Bruce SPRINGSTEEN *US, male vocalist* — *356 wks*

1 Nov 75	**BORN TO RUN** *CBS 69170*	17	50 wks
17 Jun 78	**DARKNESS ON THE EDGE OF TOWN** *CBS 86061*	16	40 wks
25 Oct 80	● **THE RIVER** *CBS 88510*	2	88 wks
2 Oct 82	● **NEBRASKA** *CBS 25100*	3	19 wks
16 Jun 84	★ **BORN IN THE USA** *CBS 86304*	1	117 wks
15 Jun 85	**THE WILD THE INNOCENT AND THE E STREET SHUFFLE** *CBS 32363*	33	12 wks
15 Jun 85	**GREETINGS FROM ASBURY PARK, N.J.** *CBS 32210*	41	10 wks
22 Nov 86	**LIVE 1975–1985** *CBS 450 227–1*	4	9 wks
17 Oct 87	★ **TUNNEL OF LOVE** *CBS 460 270–1*	1†	11 wks

Live 1975–1985 credits the E Street Band.

Only *The Sound of Music* soundtrack kept DUSTY SPRINGFIELD from being number one.

SPYRO GYRA US, male instrumental group — 22 wks

14 Jul 79	**MORNING DANCE** *Infinity INS 2003*		**11**	16 wks
23 Feb 80	**CATCHING THE SUN** *MCA MCG 4009*		**31**	6 wks

SQUEEZE UK, male vocal/instrumental group — 106 wks

28 Apr 79	**COOL FOR CATS** *A & M AMLH 68503*		**45**	11 wks
16 Feb 80	**ARGY BARGY** *A & M AMLH 64802*		**32**	15 wks
23 May 81	**EAST SIDE STORY** *A & M AMLH 64854*		**19**	26 wks
15 May 82	**SWEETS FROM A STRANGER** *A & M AMLH 64899*		**37**	10 wks
6 Nov 82	● **SINGLES–45'S AND UNDER** *A & M AMLH 68522*		**3**	29 wks
7 Sep 85	**COSI FAN TUTTI FRUTTI** *A & M AMA 5085*		**31**	7 wks
19 Sep 87	**BABYLON AND ON** *A & M AMA 5161*		**14**	8 wks

Chris SQUIRE UK, male vocalist/instrumentalist – bass — 7 wks

6 Dec 75	**FISH OUT OF WATER** *Atlantic K 50203*		**25**	7 wks

STAGE CAST RECORDINGS – See VARIOUS ARTISTS

Alvin STARDUST UK, male vocalist — 17 wks

16 Mar 74	● **THE UNTOUCHABLE** *Magnet MAG 5001*		**4**	12 wks
21 Dec 74	**ALVIN STARDUST** *Magnet MAG 5004*		**37**	3 wks
4 Oct 75	**ROCK WITH ALVIN** *Magnet MAG 5007*		**52**	2 wks

Kay STARR US, female vocalist — 1 wk

26 Mar 60	**MOVIN'** *Capitol T 1254*		**16**	1 wk

Ringo STARR UK, male vocalist — 28 wks

18 Apr 70	● **SENTIMENTAL JOURNEY** *Apple PCS 7101*		**7**	6 wks
8 Dec 73	● **RINGO** *Apple PCTC 252*		**7**	20 wks
7 Dec 74	**GOODNIGHT VIENNA** *Apple PMC 7168*		**30**	2 wks

STARSHIP US, male/female vocal/instrumental group — 5 wks

18 Jul 87	**NO PROTECTION** *Grunt FL 86413*		**26**	5 wks

See also Jefferson Airplane; Jefferson Starship.

STARSOUND Holland, disco aggregation — 28 wks

16 May 81	★ **STARS ON 45** *CBS 86132*		**1**	21 wks
19 Sep 81	**STARS ON 45 VOL. 2** *CBS 85181*		**18**	6 wks
3 Apr 82	**STARS MEDLEY** *CBS 85651*		**94**	1 wk

STARTRAX UK, disco aggregation — 7 wks

1 Aug 81	**STARTRAX CLUB DISCO** *Picksy KSYA 1001*		**26**	7 wks

Candi STATON US, female vocalist — 3 wks

24 Jul 76	**YOUNG HEARTS RUN FREE** *Warner Bros. K 56259*		**34**	3 wks

STATUS QUO UK, male vocal/instrumental group — 392 wks

20 Jan 73	● **PILEDRIVER** *Vertigo 6360 082*		**5**	37 wks
9 Jun 73	**THE BEST OF STATUS QUO** *Pye NSPL 18402*		**32**	7 wks
6 Oct 73	★ **HELLO** *Vertigo 6360 098*		**1**	28 wks
18 May 74	● **QUO** *Vertigo 9102 001*		**2**	16 wks
1 Mar 75	★ **ON THE LEVEL** *Vertigo 9102 002*		**1**	27 wks
8 Mar 75	**DOWN THE DUSTPIPE** *Golden Hour CH 604*		**20**	6 wks
20 Mar 76	★ **BLUE FOR YOU** *Vertigo 9102 006*		**1**	30 wks
12 Mar 77	● **LIVE** *Vertigo 6641 580*		**3**	14 wks
26 Nov 77	● **ROCKIN' ALL OVER THE WORLD** *Vertigo 9102 014*		**5**	15 wks
11 Nov 78	● **CAN'T STAND THE HEAT** *Vertigo 9102 027*		**3**	14 wks
20 Oct 79	● **WHATEVER YOU WANT** *Vertigo 9102 037*		**3**	14 wks
22 Mar 80	● **12 GOLD BARS** *Vertigo QUO TV 1*		**3**	48 wks
25 Oct 80	● **JUST SUPPOSIN'** *Vertigo 6302 057*		**4**	18 wks
28 Mar 81	● **NEVER TOO LATE** *Vertigo 6302 104*		**2**	13 wks
10 Oct 81	● **FRESH QUOTA** *PRT DOW 2*		**74**	1 wk
24 Apr 82	● **1982** *Vertigo 6302 169*		**1**	20 wks
13 Nov 82	● **FROM THE MAKERS OF . . .** *Vertigo PROLP 1*		**4**	18 wks
3 Dec 83	● **BACK TO BACK** *Vertigo VERH 10*		**9**	22 wks
4 Aug 84	**STATUS QUO LIVE AT THE NEC** *Vertigo (Holland) 8189 471*		**83**	3 wks
1 Dec 84	**12 GOLD BARS VOLUME 2 (AND 1)** *Vertigo QUO TV 2*		**12**	18 wks
6 Sep 86	● **IN THE ARMY NOW** *Vertigo VERH 36*		**7**	23 wks

STEEL PULSE UK, male vocal/instrumental group — 18 wks

5 Aug 78	● **HANDSWORTH REVOLUTION** *Island EMI ILPS 9502*		**9**	12 wks
14 Jul 79	**TRIBUTE TO MARTYRS** *Island ILPS 9568*		**42**	6 wks

STEELEYE SPAN
UK, male/female vocal instrumental group — 48 wks

10 Apr 71	**PLEASE TO SEE THE KING** *B & C CAS 1029*		**45**	2 wks
14 Oct 72	**BELOW THE SALT** *Chrysalis CHR 1008*		**43**	1 wk
28 Apr 73	**PARCEL OF ROGUES** *Chrysalis CHR 1046*		**26**	5 wks
23 Mar 74	**NOW WE ARE SIX** *Chrysalis CHR 1053*		**13**	13 wks
15 Feb 75	**COMMONER'S CROWN** *Chrysalis CHR 1071*		**21**	4 wks
25 Oct 75	● **ALL AROUND MY HAT** *Chrysalis CHR 1091*		**7**	20 wks
16 Oct 76	**ROCKET COTTAGE** *Chrysalis CHR 1123*		**41**	3 wks

STEELY DAN US, male vocal/instrumental group — 77 wks

30 Mar 74	**PRETZEL LOGIC** *Probe SPBA 6282*		**37**	2 wks
3 May 75	**KATY LIED** *ABC ABCL 5094*		**13**	6 wks
20 Sep 75	**CAN'T BUY A THRILL** *ABC ABCL 5024*		**38**	1 wk
22 May 76	**ROYAL SCAM** *ABC ABCL 5161*		**11**	13 wks
8 Oct 77	● **AJA** *ABC ABCL 5225*		**5**	10 wks
2 Dec 78	**GREATEST HITS** *ABC BLD 616*		**41**	18 wks
29 Nov 80	**GAUCHO** *MCA MCF 3090*		**27**	12 wks
3 Jul 82	**GOLD** *MCA MCF 3145*		**44**	6 wks
26 Oct 85	**REELIN' IN THE YEARS – THE VERY BEST OF STEELY DAN** *MCA DANTV 1*		**43**	5 wks
10 Oct 87	**DO IT AGAIN – THE VERY BEST OF STEELY DAN** *Telstar STAR 2297*		**64**	4 wks

Wout STEENHUIS
Holland, male instrumentalist – guitar — 7 wks

21 Nov 81	**HAWAIIAN PARADISE/CHRISTMAS** *Warwick WW 5106*		**28**	7 wks

Jim STEINMAN US, male vocalist — 24 wks

9 May 81	● **BAD FOR GOOD** *Epic EPC 84361*		**7**	24 wks

Martin STEPHENSON and the DAINTEES
UK, male vocal/instrumental group — 3 wks

17 May 86	**BOAT TO BOLIVIA** *Kitchenware KWLP 5*		**85**	3 wks

(Below) STEELY DAN became a duo of Donald Fagen (rear right) and Walter Becker (right front) after *Pretzel Logic. Can't Buy A Thrill*, the band's first album, enjoyed a subsequent one-week entry.

(Bottom) The IV in the title of the first STRANGLERS album was the number of group members, not an indication that this was their fourth album.

The American STRAY CATS had to stray all the way to London to make it. They subsequently became big stars at home, too.

STEPPENWOLF US, male vocal/instrumental group · 20 wks

28 Feb 70		MONSTER	Stateside SSL 5021	43	4 wks
25 Apr 70		STEPPENWOLF	Stateside SSL 5020	59	2 wks
4 Jul 70		STEPPENWOLF LIVE	Stateside SSL 5029	16	14 wks

Cat STEVENS UK, male vocalist · 243 wks

25 Mar 67	●	MATTHEW AND SON	Deram SML 1004	7	16 wks
11 Jul 70		MONA BONE JAKON	Island ILPS 9118	63	4 wks
28 Nov 70		TEA FOR THE TILLERMAN	Island ILPS 9135	20	39 wks
2 Oct 71	●	TEASER AND THE FIRECAT	Island ILPS 9154	3	93 wks
7 Oct 72	●	CATCH BULL AT FOUR	Island ILPS 9206	2	27 wks
21 Jul 73	●	FOREIGNER	Island ILPS 9240	3	10 wks
6 Apr 74	●	BUDDAH AND THE CHOCOLATE BOX Island ILPS 9274		3	15 wks
19 Jul 75	●	GREATEST HITS	Island ILPS 9310	2	24 wks
14 May 77		IZITSO	Island ILPS 9451	18	15 wks

Ray STEVENS US, male vocalist · 8 wks

26 Sep 70		EVERYTHING IS BEAUTIFUL	CBS 64074	62	1 wk
13 Sep 75		MISTY	Janus 9109 401	23	7 wks

Shakin' STEVENS UK, male vocalist · 144 wks

15 Mar 80		TAKE ONE	Epic EPC 83978	62	2 wks
4 Apr 81	●	THIS OLE HOUSE	Epic EPC 84985	2	28 wks
8 Aug 81		SHAKIN' STEVENS	Hallmark/Pickwick SHM 3065	34	5 wks
19 Sep 81	★	SHAKY	Epic EPC 10027	1	28 wks
9 Oct 82	●	GIVE ME YOUR HEART TONIGHT Epic EPC 10035		3	18 wks
26 Nov 83		THE BOP WON'T STOP	Epic EPC 86301	21	27 wks
17 Nov 84	●	GREATEST HITS	Epic EPC 10047	8	22 wks
16 Nov 85		LIPSTICK POWDER AND PAINT Epic EPC 26646		37	9 wks
31 Oct 87		LET'S BOOGIE	Epic 460 126–1	59	5 wks

Al STEWART UK, male vocalist · 20 wks

11 Apr 70		ZERO SHE FLIES	CBS 63848	40	4 wks
5 Feb 77		YEAR OF THE CAT	RCA RS 1082	38	7 wks
21 Oct 78		TIME PASSAGES	RCA PL 25173	39	1 wk
6 Sep 80		24 CARAT	RCA PL 25306	55	6 wks
9 Jun 84		RUSSIANS AND AMERICANS	RCA PL 70307	83	2 wks

Andy STEWART UK, male vocalist · 2 wks

3 Feb 62		ANDY STEWART	Top Rank 35–116	13	2 wks

Jermaine STEWART US, male vocalist · 4 wks

4 Oct 86		FRANTIC ROMANTIC	10 DIX 26	49	4 wks

Rod STEWART UK, male vocalist · 557 wks

3 Oct 70		GASOLINE ALLEY	Vertigo 6360 500	62	1 wk
24 Jul 71	★	EVERY PICTURE TELLS A STORY Mercury 6338 063		1	81 wks
5 Aug 72	★	NEVER A DULL MOMENT	Philips 6499 153	1	36 wks
25 Aug 73	★	SING IT AGAIN ROD	Mercury 6499 484	1	30 wks
19 Oct 74	★	SMILER	Mercury 9104 011	1	20 wks
30 Aug 75	★	ATLANTIC CROSSING	Warner Bros. K 56151	1	88 wks
3 Jul 76	★	A NIGHT ON THE TOWN	Riva RVLP 1	1	47 wks
16 Jul 77		BEST OF ROD STEWART	Mercury 6643 030	18	22 wks
19 Nov 77	●	FOOT LOOSE AND FANCY FREE Riva RVLP 5		3	26 wks
21 Jan 78		ATLANTIC CROSSING (re-issue)	Riva RVLP 4	60	1 wk
9 Dec 78	●	BLONDES HAVE MORE FUN	Riva RVLP 8	3	31 wks
10 Nov 79	★	GREATEST HITS	Riva ROD TV 1	1	74 wks
22 Nov 80	●	FOOLISH BEHAVIOUR	Riva RVLP 11	4	13 wks
14 Nov 81		TONIGHT I'M YOURS	Riva RVLP 14	8	21 wks
13 Nov 82		ABSOLUTELY LIVE	Riva RVLP 17	35	5 wks
18 Jun 83	●	BODY WISHES	Warner Bros. K 923 8771	5	27 wks
23 Jun 84	●	CAMOUFLAGE	Warner Bros. 925095	8	17 wks
5 Jul 86	●	EVERY BEAT OF MY HEART Warner Bros. WX 53		5	17 wks

See also Rod Stewart and the Faces. Greatest Hits changed label/number to Warner Bros. K 56744 during its chart run.

STIFF LITTLE FINGERS
UK, male vocal/instrumental group · 57 wks

3 Mar 79		INFLAMMABLE MATERIAL Rough Trade ROUGH 1		14	19 wks
15 Mar 80	●	NOBODY'S HEROES	Chrysalis CHR 1270	8	10 wks
20 Sep 80	●	HANX	Chrysalis CHR 1300	9	5 wks
25 Apr 81		GO FOR IT	Chrysalis CHX 1339	14	8 wks
2 Oct 82		NOW THEN	Chrysalis CHR 1400	24	6 wks
12 Feb 83		ALL THE BEST	Chrysalis CTY 1414	19	9 wks

Stephen STILLS US, male vocalist · 7 wks

19 Dec 70		STEPHEN STILLS	Atlantic 2401 004	30	1 wk
14 Aug 71		STEPHEN STILLS 2	Atlantic 2401 013	22	3 wks
26 Jul 75		STILLS	CBS 69146	31	1 wk
29 May 76		ILLEGAL STILLS	CBS 81330	54	2 wks

See also Crosby, Stills and Nash; Crosby, Stills, Nash and Young; Stills–Young Band; Stephen Stills' Manassas.

STILLS–YOUNG BAND
US/Canada male vocal/instrumental group · 5 wks

9 Oct 76		LONG MAY YOU RUN	Reprise K 54081	12	5 wks

See also Crosby, Stills and Nash; Crosby, Stills, Nash and Young; Stephen Stills; Stephen Stills' Manassas; Neil Young.

Stephen STILLS' MANASSAS
US, male vocal/instrumental group · 7 wks

20 May 72		MANASSAS	Atlantic K 60021	30	5 wks
19 May 73		DOWN THE ROAD	Atlantic K 40440	33	2 wks

See also Crosby, Stills and Nash; Crosby, Stills, Nash and Young; Stephen Stills; Stills–Young Band.

STING UK, male vocalist · 86 wks

29 Jun 85	●	THE DREAM OF THE BLUE TURTLES A & M DREAM 1		3	64 wks
28 Jun 86		BRING ON THE NIGHT	A & M BRING 1	16	12 wks
24 Oct 87	★	NOTHING LIKE THE SUN	A & M AMA 6402	1†	10 wks

STONE THE CROWS
UK, female/male vocal/instrumental group · 3 wks

7 Oct 72		ONTINUOUS PERFORMANCE	Polydor 2391 043	33	3 wks

STORYVILLE JAZZMEN – See Bob WALLIS and his STORYVILLE JAZZMEN

STRANGLERS UK, male vocal/instrumental group · 157 wks

30 Apr 77	●	STRANGLERS IV (RATTUS NORVEGICUS) United Artists UAG 30045		4	34 wks
8 Oct 77	●	NO MORE HEROES	United Artists UAG 30200	2	19 wks
3 Jun 78	●	BLACK AND WHITE	United Artists UAK 30222	2	18 wks
10 Mar 79	●	LIVE (X CERT)	United Artists UAG 30224	7	10 wks
6 Oct 79	●	THE RAVEN	United Artists UAG 30262	4	8 wks

(Above) DONNA SUMMER is seen as millions around the world saw her in a 1979 broadcast from the United Nations, serenading a child with a song donated to UNICEF.

(Right) SUPERTRAMP continue the food motif of their most successful album, *Breakfast in America*.

21 Feb 81	●	THE MEN IN BLACK Liberty LBG 30313		8	5 wks
21 Nov 81		LA FOLIE Liberty LBG 30342		11	18 wks
25 Sep 82		THE COLLECTION 1977–1982 Liberty LBS 30353		12	16 wks
22 Jan 83	●	FELINE Epic EPC 25237		4	11 wks
17 Nov 84		AURAL SCULPTURE Epic EPC 26220		14	10 wks
20 Sep 86		OFF THE BEATEN TRACK Liberty LBG 5001		80	2 wks
8 Nov 86		DREAMTIME Epic EPC 26648		16	6 wks

STRAWBERRY SWITCHBLADE
UK, female vocal duo　　　　　　　　　　　　　　　　*4 wks*

13 Apr 85	STRAWBERRY SWITCHBLADE *Korova KODE 11*		25	4 wks

STRAWBS *UK, male vocal/instrumental group*　　　　*31 wks*

21 Nov 70	JUST A COLLECTION OF ANTIQUES AND CURIOS *A & M AMLS 994*		27	2 wks
17 Jul 71	FROM THE WITCHWOOD *A & M AMLH 64304*		39	2 wks
26 Feb 72	GRAVE NEW WORLD *A & M AMLH 68078*		11	12 wks
24 Feb 73 ●	BURSTING AT THE SEAMS *A & M AMLH 68144*		2	12 wks
27 Apr 74	HERO AND HEROINE *A & M AMLH 63607*		35	3 wks

STRAY CATS *US, male vocal/instrumental group*　　*31 wks*

28 Feb 81 ●	STRAY CATS *Arista STRAY 1*		6	22 wks
21 Nov 81	GONNA BALL *Arista STRAY 2*		48	4 wks
3 Sep 83	RANT 'N' RAVE WITH THE STRAY CATS *Arista STRAY 3*		51	5 wks

STREETWALKERS
UK, male vocal/instrumental group　　　　　　　　*6 wks*

12 Jun 76	RED CARD *Vertigo 9102 010*		16	6 wks

Barbra STREISAND *US, female vocalist*　　　*361 wks*

22 Jan 66 ●	MY NAME IS BARBRA, TWO *CBS BPG 62603*		6	22 wks
4 Apr 70	GREATEST HITS *CBS 63921*		44	2 wks
17 Apr 71	STONEY END *CBS 64269*		28	2 wks
15 Jun 74	THE WAY WE WERE *CBS 69057*		49	1 wk
23 Jul 77	STREISAND SUPERMAN *CBS 86030*		32	9 wks
15 Jul 78	SONGBIRD *CBS 86060*		50	1 wk
17 Mar 79 ★	BARBRA STREISAND HITS VOL. 2 *CBS 10012*		1	30 wks
17 Nov 79	WET *CBS 86104*		25	13 wks
11 Oct 80 ★	GUILTY *CBS 86122*		1	82 wks
16 Jan 82 ★	LOVE SONGS *CBS 10031*		1	129 wks
19 Nov 83	YENTL (original soundtrack) *CBS 86302*		21	35 wks
27 Oct 84	EMOTION *CBS 86309*		15	12 wks
18 Jan 86 ●	THE BROADWAY ALBUM *CBS 86322*		3	16 wks
30 May 87	ONE VOICE *CBS 450 890-1*		27	7 wks

STRINGS FOR PLEASURE *UK, orchestra*　　*1 wk*

4 Dec 71	BEST OF BACHARACH *MFP 1334*		49	1 wk

STYLE COUNCIL *UK, male vocal/instrumental duo*　*75 wks*

24 Mar 84 ●	CAFE BLEU *Polydor TSCLP*		2	38 wks
8 Jun 85 ★	OUR FAVOURITE SHOP *Polydor TSCLP 2*		1	22 wks
17 May 86 ●	HOME AND ABROAD *Polydor TSCLP 3*		8	8 wks
14 Feb 87	THE COST OF LOVING *Polydor TSCLP 4*		2	7 wks

STYLISTICS *US, male vocal group*　　　　　*139 wks*

24 Aug 74	ROCKIN' ROLL BABY *Avco 6466 012*		42	3 wks
21 Sep 74	LET'S PUT IT ALL TOGETHER *Avco 6466 013*		26	14 wks
1 Mar 75	FROM THE MOUNTAIN *Avco 9109 002*		36	1 wk
5 Apr 75 ★	THE BEST OF THE STYLISTICS *Avco 9109 003*		1	63 wks
5 Jul 75	THANK YOU BABY *Avco 9109 005*		5	23 wks
6 Dec 75	YOU ARE BEAUTIFUL *Avco 9109 006*		26	9 wks
12 Jun 76	FABULOUS *Avco 9109 008*		21	5 wks
18 Sep 76 ★	BEST OF THE STYLISTICS VOL. 2 *H & L 9109 010*		1	21 wks

STYX *US, male vocal/instrumental group*　　　*24 wks*

3 Nov 79	CORNERSTONE *A & M AMLK 63711*		36	8 wks
24 Jan 81 ●	PARADISE THEATER *A & M AMLH 63719*		8	8 wks
12 Mar 83	KILROY WAS HERE *A & M AMLX 63734*		67	6 wks
5 May 84	CAUGHT IN THE ACT *A & M AMLM 66704*		44	2 wks

SUICIDAL TENDENCIES
UK, male vocal/instrumental group　　　　　　　　*1 wk*

9 May 87	JOIN THE ARMY *Virgin V 2424*		81	1 wk

Donna SUMMER *US, female vocalist*　　　*159 wks*

31 Jan 76	LOVE TO LOVE YOU BABY *GTO GTLP 008*		16	9 wks
22 May 76	A LOVE TRILOGY *GTO GTLP 010*		41	10 wks
25 Jun 77 ●	I REMEMBER YESTERDAY *GTO GTLP 025*		3	23 wks
26 Nov 77	ONCE UPON A TIME *Casablanca CALD 5003*		24	13 wks
7 Jan 78 ●	GREATEST HITS *GTO GTLP 028*		4	18 wks
21 Oct 78	LIVE AND MORE *Casablanca CALD 5006*		16	16 wks
2 Jun 79	BAD GIRLS *Casablanca CALD 5007*		23	23 wks
10 Nov 79	ON THE RADIO – GREATEST HITS VOLS. 1 & 2 *Casablanca CALD 5008*		24	22 wks
1 Nov 80	THE WANDERER *Geffen K 99124*		55	2 wks
31 Jul 82	DONNA SUMMER *Warner Bros. K 99163*		13	16 wks
16 Jul 83	SHE WORKS HARD FOR THE MONEY *Mercury MERL 21*		28	5 wks
15 Sep 84	CATS WITHOUT CLAWS *Warner Bros. 250806*		69	2 wks

SUNSHINE BAND – *See KC and the SUNSHINE BAND*

SUPERTRAMP
UK/US, male vocal/instrumental group　　　　　*170 wks*

23 Nov 74 ●	CRIME OF THE CENTURY *A & M AMLS 68258*		4	22 wks
6 Dec 75	CRISIS? WHAT CRISIS? *A & M AMLH 68347*		20	15 wks
23 Apr 77	EVEN IN THE QUIETEST MOMENTS *A & M AMLK 64634*		12	22 wks
31 Mar 79 ●	BREAKFAST IN AMERICA *A & M AMLK 63708*		3	53 wks
4 Oct 80 ●	PARIS *A & M AMLM 66702*		7	17 wks
6 Nov 82 ●	FAMOUS LAST WORDS *A & M AMLK 63732*		6	16 wks
25 May 85	BROTHER WHERE YOU BOUND *A & M AMA 5014*		20	5 wks
18 Oct 86 ●	THE AUTOBIOGRAPHY OF SUPERTRAMP *A & M TRAMP 1*		9	19 wks
31 Oct 87	FREE AS A BIRD *A & M AMA 5181*		93	1 wk

SUPREMES *US, female vocal group*　　　　*171 wks*

5 Dec 64 ●	MEET THE SUPREMES *Stateside SL 10109*		8	6 wks
17 Dec 66	SUPREMES A GO-GO *Tamla Motown STML 11039*		15	21 wks
13 May 67	SUPREMES SING MOTOWN *Tamla Motown STML 11047*		15	16 wks
30 Sep 67	SUPREMES SING RODGERS AND HART *Tamla Motown STML 11054*		25	7 wks
20 Jan 68 ★	GREATEST HITS *Tamla Motown STML 11063*		1	60 wks
30 Mar 68 ●	LIVE AT THE TALK OF THE TOWN *Tamla Motown STML 11070*		6	18 wks
20 Jul 68	REFLECTIONS *Tamla Motown STML 11073*		30	2 wks
1 Feb 69 ●	LOVE CHILD *Tamla Motown STML 11095*		8	6 wks

| 25 Sep 71 | **TOUCH** Tamla Motown STML 11189 .... | **40** | 1 wk |
| 17 Sep 77 | ★ **20 GOLDEN GREATS** Motown EMTV 5 .... | **1** | 34 wks |

See also Diana Ross and the Supremes with the Temptations; Supremes and the Four Tops. 20 Golden Greats is credited to Diana Ross and the Supremes.

SUPREMES and the FOUR TOPS
US, female and male vocal groups   *11 wks*

| 29 May 71 | ● **MAGNIFICENT SEVEN** | | |
| | Tamla Motown STML 11179 .... | **6** | 11 wks |

See also Diana Ross and the Supremes with the Temptations; Supremes; Four Tops.

SURVIVOR *US, male vocal/instrumental group*   *10 wks*

| 21 Aug 82 | **EYE OF THE TIGER** Scotti Bros SCT 85845 ...... | **12** | 10 wks |

SUTHERLAND BROTHERS and QUIVER
UK, male vocal/instrumental group   *11 wks*

| 15 May 76 | **REACH FOR THE SKY** CBS 69191 .... | **26** | 8 wks |
| 9 Oct 76 | **SLIPSTREAM** CBS 81593 .... | **49** | 3 wks |

SWANS WAY *UK, male/female vocal/instrumental group*   *1 wk*

| 3 Nov 84 | **THE FUGITIVE KIND** Balgier SWAN 1 .... | **88** | 1 wk |

SWEET *UK, male vocal/instrumental group*   *8 wks*

18 May 74	**SWEET FANNY ADAMS** RCA LPI 5038	**27**	2 wks
22 Sep 84	**SWEET 16 – IT'S . . . IT'S . . . SWEET'S HITS**		
	Anagram GRAM 16	**49**	6 wks

SWINGLE SINGERS
US/France, male/female vocal group   *18 wks*

| 1 Feb 64 | **JAZZ SEBASTIAN BACH** Philips BL 7572 .... | **13** | 18 wks |

SWING OUT SISTER
UK, male/female vocal/instrumental group   *20 wks*

| 23 May 87 | ★ **IT'S BETTER TO TRAVEL** Mercury OUTLP 1 ... | **1** | 20 wks |

SYBIL *US, female vocalist*   *1 wk*

| 5 Sep 87 | **LET YOURSELF GO** Champion CHAMP 1009 .... | **92** | 1 wk |

SYLVESTER *US, male vocalist*   *3 wks*

| 23 Jun 79 | **MIGHTY REAL** Fantasy FTA 3009 .... | **62** | 3 wks |

David SYLVIAN *UK, male vocalist*   *21 wks*

7 Jul 84	● **BRILLIANT TREES** Virgin V 2290	**4**	14 wks
13 Sep 86	**GONE TO EARTH** Virgin VDL 1	**24**	5 wks
7 Nov 87	**SECRETS OF THE BEEHIVE** Virgin V 2471	**37**	2 wks

SYNTHPHONIC VARIATIONS
Various session musicians   *1 wk*

| 1 Nov 86 | **SEASONS** CBS 450 149–1 .... | **84** | 1 wk |

T

TALK TALK *UK, male vocal/instrumental group*   *54 wks*

24 Jul 82	**THE PARTY'S OVER** EMI EMC 3431	**21**	25 wks
25 Feb 84	**IT'S MY LIFE** EMI EMC 2400021	**35**	8 wks
1 Mar 86	● **THE COLOUR OF SPRING** EMI EMC 3506	**8**	21 wks

TALKING HEADS
US, male/female vocal/instrumental group   *198 wks*

25 Feb 78	**TALKING HEADS '77** Sire 9103 328	**60**	1 wk
29 Jul 78	**MORE SONGS ABOUT FOOD AND BUILDINGS**		
	Sire K 56531	**21**	3 wks
15 Sep 79	**FEAR OF MUSIC** Sire SRK 6076	**33**	5 wks
1 Nov 80	**REMAIN IN LIGHT** Sire SRK 6095	**21**	17 wks
10 Apr 82	**THE NAME OF THIS BAND IS TALKING HEADS**		
	Sire SRK 23590	**22**	5 wks
18 Jun 83	**SPEAKING IN TONGUES** Sire K 923 8831	**21**	12 wks
27 Oct 84	**STOP MAKING SENSE** EMI TAH 1	**37**	81 wks
29 Jun 85	● **LITTLE CREATURES** EMI TAH 2	**10**	65 wks
27 Sep 86	● **TRUE STORIES** EMI EU 3511	**7**	9 wks

TANGERINE DREAM
Germany, male instrumental group   *77 wks*

20 Apr 74	**PHAEDRA** Virgin V 2010	**15**	15 wks
5 Apr 75	**RUBYCON** Virgin V 2025	**12**	14 wks
20 Dec 75	**RICOCHET** Virgin V 2044	**40**	2 wks
13 Nov 76	**STRATOSFEAR** Virgin V 2068	**39**	4 wks
23 Jul 77	**SORCERER (film soundtrack)** MCA MCF 2806 .	**25**	7 wks
19 Nov 77	**ENCORE** Virgin VD 2506	**55**	1 wk
1 Apr 78	**CYCLONE** Virgin V 2097	**37**	4 wks
17 Feb 79	**FORCE MAJEURE** Virgin V 2111	**26**	7 wks
7 Jun 80	**TANGRAM** Virgin V 2147	**36**	5 wks
18 Apr 81	**THIEF** Virgin V 2198	**43**	3 wks
19 Sep 81	**EXIT** Virgin V 2212	**43**	5 wks
10 Apr 82	**WHITE EAGLE** Virgin V 2226	**57**	5 wks
5 Nov 83	**HYPERBOREA** Virgin V 2292	**45**	2 wks
10 Nov 84	**POLAND** Jive Electro HIP 22	**90**	1 wk
26 Jul 86	**UNDERWATER SUNLIGHT** Jive Electro HIP 40 .	**97**	1 wk
27 Jun 87	**TYGER** Jive Electro HIP 47	**88**	1 wk

TANK *UK, male vocal/instrumental group*   *5 wks*

| 13 Mar 82 | **FILTH HOUNDS OF HADES** | | |
| | Kamaflage KAMLP 1 .... | **33** | 5 wks |

TASTE *Ireland, male vocal/instrumental group*   *12 wks*

7 Feb 70	**ON THE BOARDS** Polydor 583–083	**18**	11 wks
9 Sep 72	**TASTE LIVE AT THE ISLE OF WIGHT**		
	Polydor 2383 120	**41**	1 wk

TAVARES *US, male vocal group*   *15 wks*

| 21 Aug 76 | **SKY HIGH** Capitol EST 11533 .... | **22** | 13 wks |
| 1 Apr 78 | **THE BEST OF TAVARES** Capitol EST 11701 .... | **39** | 2 wks |

Andy TAYLOR
UK, male vocalist/instrumentalist – guitar   *1 wk*

| 30 May 87 | **THUNDER** MCA MCG 6018 .... | **61** | 1 wk |

(Above left) The longest title of a number one album belonged to TYRANNOSAURUS REX.

(Above right) The most successful line-up of the TEMPTATIONS, featuring David Ruffin on this lead vocal.

(Left) The original line-up of 10 C.C. (left to right, Lol Creme, Eric Stewart, Graham Gouldman and Kevin Godley) enjoyed four straight Top Ten hits.

James TAYLOR *US, male vocalist* — *111 wks*

21 Nov 70	● SWEET BABY JAMES *Warner Bros. ES 1843*	7	53 wks
29 May 71	● MUD SLIDE SLIM AND THE BLUE HORIZON *Warner Bros. WS 2561*	4	41 wks
8 Jan 72	SWEET BABY JAMES (re-issue) *Warner Bros. K 46043*	34	6 wks
18 Mar 72	MUD SLIDE SLIM AND THE BLUE HORIZON (re-issue) *Warner Bros. K 46085*	49	1 wk
9 Dec 72	ONE MAN DOG *Warner Bros. K 46185*	27	5 wks
4 Apr 87	CLASSIC SONGS *CBS/WEA JTV 1*	53	5 wks

Roger TAYLOR
UK, male vocalist/instrumentalist – drums — *9 wks*

18 Apr 81	FUN IN SPACE *EMI EMC 3369*	18	5 wks
7 Jul 84	STRANGE FRONTIER *EMI RTA 1*	30	4 wks

Kiri TE KANAWA *New Zealand, female vocalist* — *34 wks*

2 Apr 83	CHANTS D'AUVERGNE VOL. 1 *Decca SXDL 7604*	57	1 wk
26 Oct 85	BLUE SKIES *London KTKT 1*	40	29 wks
13 Dec 86	CHRISTMAS WITH KIRI *Decca PROLP 12*	47	4 wks

Chants d'Auvergne Vol. 1 *credits the English Chamber Orchestra. Blue Skies credits the Nelson Riddle Orchestra.*

TEARDROP EXPLODES
UK, male vocal/instrumental group — *41 wks*

18 Oct 80	KILIMANJARO *Mercury 6359 035*	24	35 wks
5 Dec 81	WILDER *Mercury 6359 056*	29	6 wks

TEARS FOR FEARS
UK, male vocal/instrumental duo — *145 wks*

19 Mar 83	★ THE HURTING *Mercury MERS 17*	1	65 wks
9 Mar 85	● SONGS FROM THE BIG CHAIR *Mercury MERH 58*	2	80 wks

TELEVISION *US, male vocal/instrumental group* — *17 wks*

26 Mar 77	MARQUEE MOON *Elektra K 52046*	28	13 wks
29 Apr 78	● ADVENTURE *Elektra K 52072*	7	4 wks

TEMPERANCE SEVEN
UK, male vocal/instrumental group — *10 wks*

13 May 61	TEMPERANCE SEVEN PLUS ONE *Argo RG 11* .	19	1 wk
25 Nov 61	TEMPERANCE SEVEN 1961 *Parlophone PMC 1152*	11	9 wks

TEMPLE CHURCH CHOIR
UK, male vocal/instrumental group — *3 wks*

16 Dec 61	● CHRISTMAS CAROLS *HMV CLP 1309*	8	3 wks

TEMPTATIONS *US, male vocal group* — *99 wks*

24 Dec 66	GETTING READY *Tamla Motown STML 11035* ...	40	2 wks
11 Feb 67	TEMPTATIONS GREATEST HITS *Tamla Motown STML 11042*	26	40 wks
22 Jul 67	TEMPTATIONS LIVE *Tamla Motown STML 11053*	20	4 wks
18 Nov 67	TEMPTATIONS WITH A LOT OF SOUL *Tamla Motown STML 11057*	19	18 wks
20 Sep 69	CLOUD NINE *Tamla Motown STML 11109*	32	1 wk
14 Feb 70	PUZZLE PEOPLE *Tamla Motown STML 11133*	20	4 wks
11 Jul 70	PSYCHEDELIC SHACK *Tamla Motown STML 11147*	56	1 wk
26 Dec 70	GREATEST HITS VOL. 2 *Tamla Motown STML 11170*	35	12 wks
29 Apr 72	SOLID ROCK *Tamla Motown STML 11202*	34	2 wks
20 Jan 73	ALL DIRECTIONS *Tamla Motown STML 11218* ...	19	7 wks
7 Jul 73	MASTERPIECE *Tamla Motown STML 11229* ...	28	3 wks
8 Dec 84	TRULY FOR YOU *Motown ZL 72342*	75	5 wks

See also Diana Ross and the Supremes with the Temptations.

10 C.C. *UK, male vocal/instrumental group* — *197 wks*

1 Sep 73	10 C.C. *UK UKAL 1005*	36	5 wks
15 Jun 74	● SHEET MUSIC *UK UKAL 1007*	9	24 wks
22 Mar 75	● THE ORIGINAL SOUNDTRACK *Mercury 9102 50Q*	4	40 wks
7 Jun 75	● GREATEST HITS OF 10 C.C. *Decca UKAL 1012*	9	18 wks
31 Jan 76	● HOW DARE YOU? *Mercury 9102 501*	5	31 wks
14 May 77	● DECEPTIVE BENDS *Mercury 9102 502*	3	21 wks
10 Dec 77	● LIVE AND LET LIVE *Mercury 6641 698*	14	15 wks
23 Sep 78	● BLOODY TOURISTS *Mercury 9102 503*	3	15 wks
6 Oct 79	● GREATEST HITS 1972–1978 *Mercury 9102 504* ..	5	21 wks
5 Apr 80	LOOK HERE *Mercury 9102 505* ...	35	5 wks
15 Oct 83	WINDOW IN THE JUNGLE *Mercury MERL 28* ..	70	2 wks

See also 10 C.C. and Godley and Creme.

10 C.C. and GODLEY AND CREME
UK, male vocal/instrumental group and instrumental duo — *18 wks*

29 Aug 87	● CHANGING FACES – THE VERY BEST OF 10 C.C. AND GODLEY & CREME *ProTV TGCLP 1*	4	18 wks

See also 10 C.C; Godley and Creme.

TEN POLE TUDOR
UK, male vocal/instrumental group — *8 wks*

9 May 81	● EDDIE, OLD BOB, DICK & GARRY *Stiff SEEZ 31*	4	8 wks

TEN YEARS AFTER
UK, male vocal/instrumental group — *73 wks*

21 Sep 68	UNDEAD *Deram SML 1023*	26	7 wks
22 Feb 69	● STONEDHENGE *Deram SML 1029*	6	5 wks
4 Oct 69	● SSSSH *Deram SML 1052*	4	18 wks
2 May 70	● CRICKLEWOOD GREEN *Deram SML 1065* ...	4	27 wks
9 Jan 71	● WATT *Deram SML 1078*	5	12 wks
13 Nov 71	SPACE IN TIME *Chrysalis CHR 1001*	36	1 wk
7 Oct 72	ROCK AND ROLL *Chrysalis CHR 1009*	27	1 wk
28 Jul 73	RECORDED LIVE *Chrysalis CHR 1049*	36	2 wks

TENNILLE – *See CAPTAIN and TENNILLE*

TERRAPLANE *UK, male vocal/instrumental group* — *1 wk*

25 Jan 86	BLACK AND WHITE *Epic EPC 26439*	74	1 wk

Tammi TERRELL – *See Marvin GAYE and Tammi TERRELL*

THAT PETROL EMOTION
UK, male vocal/instrumental group — *5 wks*

10 May 86	MANIC POP THRILL *Demon FIEND 70*	84	2 wks
23 May 87	BABBLE *Polydor TPELP 1*	30	3 wks

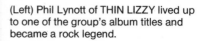

(Left) Phil Lynott of THIN LIZZY lived up to one of the group's album titles and became a rock legend.

(Below left) RONNIE LANE and PETE TOWNSHEND, both ex-Mods and devotees of Meher Baba, collaborated on a one-off project in 1977.

(Below right) A decade after she won the world's attention as a model, TWIGGY became an album chart artist.

The THE   *UK, male vocal/instrumental group*   *35 wks*

| 29 Oct 83 | **SOUL MINING** *Some Bizzare EPC 25525* .... | **27** | 5 wks |
| 29 Nov 86 | **INFECTED** *Some Bizzare EPC 26770* .... | **14** | 30 wks |

Matt Johnson leads The The which is an informal group of his studio guests and friends.

THEATRE OF HATE
UK, male vocal/instrumental group   *9 wks*

| 13 Mar 82 | **WESTWORLD** *Burning Rome ROME TOH 1* ..... | **17** | 6 wks |
| 18 Aug 84 | **REVOLUTION** *Burning Rome TOH 2* .... | **67** | 3 wks |

THEN JERICO   *UK, male vocal/instrumental group*   *7 wks*

| 3 Oct 87 | **FIRST (THE SOUND OF MUSIC)** *London LONLP 26* .... | **35** | 7 wks |

THIN LIZZY
Ireland/UK/US, male vocal/instrumental group   *212 wks*

27 Sep 75	**FIGHTING** *Vertigo 6360 121*	**60**	1 wk
10 Apr 76	● **JAILBREAK** *Vertigo 9102 008*	**10**	50 wks
6 Nov 76	● **JOHNNY THE FOX** *Vertigo 9102 012* ...	**11**	24 wks
1 Oct 77	● **BAD REPUTATION** *Vertigo 9102 016* ...	**4**	9 wks
17 Jun 78	● **LIVE AND DANGEROUS** *Vertigo 6641 807*	**2**	62 wks
5 May 79	● **BLACK ROSE (A ROCK LEGEND)** *Vertigo 9102 032*	**2**	21 wks
18 Oct 80	● **CHINA TOWN** *Vertigo 6359 030* ...	**7**	7 wks
11 Apr 81	● **ADVENTURES OF THIN LIZZY** *Vertigo LIZTV 1*	**6**	13 wks
5 Dec 81	● **RENEGADE** *Vertigo 6359 083*	**38**	8 wks
12 Mar 83	● **THUNDER AND LIGHTNING** *Vertigo VERL 3* ..	**4**	11 wks
26 Nov 83	**LIFE** *Vertigo VERD 6*	**29**	6 wks

See also Phil Lynott and Thin Lizzy.

THIRD EAR BAND   *UK, male instrumental group*   *2 wks*

| 27 Jun 70 | **AIR, EARTH, FIRE, WATER** *Harvest SHVL 773* . | **49** | 2 wks |

THIRD WORLD
Jamaica, male vocal/instrumental group   *18 wks*

21 Oct 78	**JOURNEY TO ADDIS** *Island ILPS 9554*	**30**	6 wks
11 Jul 81	**ROCKS THE WORLD** *CBS 85027*	**37**	9 wks
15 May 82	**YOU'VE GOT THE POWER** *CBS 85563*	**87**	3 wks

THIS MORTAL COIL
UK, male/female vocal/instrumental group   *7 wks*

| 20 Oct 84 | **IT'LL END IN TEARS** *4AD CAD 411* .... | **38** | 4 wks |
| 11 Oct 86 | **FILGREE AND SHADOW** *4AD DAD 609* ...... | **53** | 3 wks |

Carla THOMAS – *See Otis REDDING and Carla THOMAS*

Lillo THOMAS   *US, male vocalist*   *7 wks*

| 2 May 87 | **LILLO** *Capitol EST 2031* .... | **43** | 7 wks |

Ray THOMAS   *UK, male vocalist*   *3 wks*

| 26 Jul 75 | **FROM MIGHTY OAKS** *Threshold THS 16* ... | **23** | 3 wks |

Richard THOMPSON
UK, male vocalist/instrumentalist – guitar   *3 wks*

| 27 Apr 85 | **ACROSS A CROWDED ROOM** *Polydor POLD 5175* .... | **80** | 2 wks |
| 18 Oct 86 | **DARING ADVENTURES** *Polydor POLD 5202* ... | **92** | 1 wk |

THOMPSON TWINS
UK, male/female vocal/instrumental group   *120 wks*

13 Mar 82	**SET** *Tee TELP 2*	**48**	3 wks
26 Feb 83	● **QUICK STEP AND SIDE KICK** *Arista 204 924* ...	**2**	56 wks
25 Feb 84	★ **INTO THE GAP** *Arista 205 971*	**1**	51 wks
28 Sep 85	● **HERE'S TO FUTURE DAYS** *Arista 207 164* ...	**5**	9 wks
2 May 87	**CLOSE TO THE BONE** *Arista 208 143*	**90**	1 wk

George THOROGOOD and the DESTROYERS
US, male vocal/instrumental group   *1 wk*

| 2 Dec 78 | **GEORGE THOROGOOD AND THE DESTROYERS** *Sonet SNTF 781* .... | **67** | 1 wk |

THREE DEGREES   *US, female vocal group*   *91 wks*

10 Aug 74	**THREE DEGREES** *Philadelphia International 65858*	**12**	22 wks
17 May 75	● **TAKE GOOD CARE OF YOURSELF** *Philadelphia International PIR 69137*	**6**	16 wks
24 Feb 79	**NEW DIMENSIONS** *Ariola ARLH 5012* ...	**34**	13 wks
3 Mar 79	● **A COLLECTION OF THEIR 20 GREATEST HITS** *Epic EPC 10013*	**8**	18 wks
15 Dec 79	**3D** *Ariola 3D 1*	**61**	7 wks
27 Sep 80	● **GOLD** *Ariola 3D 2*	**9**	15 wks

TICH – *See Dave DEE, DOZY, BEAKY, MICK and TICH*

TIGHT FIT   *UK, male/female vocal group*   *6 wks*

| 26 Sep 81 | **BACK TO THE SIXTIES** *Jive HIP 1* .... | **38** | 4 wks |
| 4 Sep 82 | **TIGHT FIT** *Jive HIP 2* .... | **87** | 2 wks |

TIJUANA BRASS – *See Herb ALPERT and the TIJUANA BRASS*

TIK and TOK   *UK, male vocal/instrumental duo*   *2 wks*

| 4 Aug 84 | **INTOLERANCE** *Survival SUR LP 008* .... | **89** | 2 wks |

TILBROOK – *See DIFFORD and TILBROOK*

TIMBUK THREE
US, male/female vocal/instrumental duo   *4 wks*

| 14 Feb 87 | **GREETINGS FROM TIMBUK THREE** *IRS/MCA MIRF 1015* .... | **51** | 4 wks |

TOK – *See TIK and TOK*

TOM TOM CLUB
US, female/male vocal/instrumental group   *1 wk*

| 24 Oct 81 | **TOM TOM CLUB** *Island ILPS 9686* .... | **78** | 1 wk |

TOMITA   *Japan, male instrumentalist – synthesizer*   *33 wks*

| 7 Jun 75 | **SNOWFLAKES ARE DANCING** *RCA Red Seal ARL 1 0488* .... | **17** | 20 wks |

16 Aug 75	**PICTURES AT AN EXHIBITION**	
	RCA Red Seal ARL 1 0838	42	5 wks
7 May 77	**HOLST: THE PLANETS** *RCA Red Seal RL 11919*	41	6 wks
9 Feb 80	**TOMITA'S GREATEST HITS**	
	RCA Red Seal RL 43076	66	2 wks

TOPOL *Israel, male vocalist* — *1 wk*

11 May 85	**TOPOL'S ISRAEL** *BBC REH 529*	80	1 wk

Bernie TORME
UK, male vocalist/instrumentalist – guitar — *3 wks*

3 Jul 82	**TURN OUT THE LIGHTS** *Kamaflage KAMLP 2* . .	50	3 wks

Peter TOSH *Jamaica, male vocalist* — *1 wk*

25 Sep 76	**LEGALIZE IT** *Virgin V 2061*	54	1 wk

TOTAL CONTRAST
UK, male vocal/instrumental duo — *3 wks*

8 Mar 86	**TOTAL CONTRAST** *London LONLP 15*	66	3 wks

TOTO *US, male vocal/instrumental group* — *38 wks*

31 Mar 79	**TOTO** *CBS 83148*	37	5 wks
26 Feb 83	● **TOTO IV** *CBS 85529*	4	30 wks
17 Nov 84	**ISOLATION** *CBS 86305*	67	2 wks
20 Sep 86	**FAHRENHEIT** *CBS 57091*	99	1 wk

TOURISTS *UK, male/female vocal/instrumental group* — *18 wks*

14 Jul 79	**THE TOURISTS** *Logo GO 1018*	72	1 wk
3 Nov 79	**REALITY EFFECT** *Logo GO 1019*	23	16 wks
22 Nov 80	**LUMINOUS BASEMENT** *RCA RCALP 5001*	75	1 wk

Pete TOWNSHEND
UK, male vocalist/instrumentalist – guitar — *25 wks*

21 Oct 72	**WHO CAME FIRST** *Track 2408 201*	30	2 wks
3 May 80	**EMPTY GLASS** *Atco K 50699*	11	14 wks
3 Jul 82	**ALL THE BEST COWBOYS HAVE CHINESE EYES**	
	Atco K 50889	32	8 wks
30 Nov 85	**WHITE CITY** *Atco 25–2392–1*	70	1 wk

See also Pete Townshend and Ronnie Lane.

Pete TOWNSHEND and Ronnie LANE
UK, male vocal/instrumental duo — *3 wks*

15 Oct 77	**ROUGH MIX** *Polydor 2442 147*	44	3 wks

See also Pete Townshend; Ronnie Lane and the Band Slim Chance.

TOYAH *UK, female vocalist* — *97 wks*

14 Jun 80	**THE BLUE MEANING** *Safari IEYA 666*	40	4 wks
17 Jan 81	**TOYAH TOYAH TOYAH** *Safari LIVE 2*	22	14 wks
30 May 81	● **ANTHEM** *Safari VOOR 1*	2	46 wks
19 Jun 82	● **THE CHANGELING** *Safari VOOR 9*	6	12 wks
13 Nov 82	**WARRIOR ROCK – TOYAH ON TOUR**	
	Safari TNT 1	20	6 wks
5 Nov 83	**LOVE IS THE LAW** *Safari VOOR 10*	28	7 wks
25 Feb 84	**TOYAH! TOYAH! TOYAH!** *K-Tel NE 1268*	43	4 wks
3 Aug 85	**MINX** *Portrait PRT 26415*	24	4 wks

TOY DOLLS *UK, male vocal/instrumental group* — *1 wk*

25 May 85	**A FAR OUT DISC** *Volume VOLP 2*	71	1 wk

T'PAU *UK, female/male vocal/instrumental group* — *14 wks*

26 Sep 87	★ **BRIDGE OF SPIES** *Siren SIRENLP 8*	1†	14 wks

TRACIE *UK, female vocalist* — *2 wks*

30 Jun 84	**FAR FROM THE HURTING KIND**	
	Respond RRL 502	64	2 wks

TRAFFIC *UK, male vocal/instrumental group* — *37 wks*

30 Dec 67	● **MR. FANTASY** *Island ILP 9061*	8	16 wks
26 Oct 68	● **TRAFFIC** *Island ILPS 9081 T*	9	8 wks
8 Aug 70	**JOHN BARLEYCORN MUST DIE**	
	Island ILPS 9116	11	9 wks
24 Nov 73	**ON THE ROAD** *Island ISLD 2*	40	3 wks
28 Sep 74	**WHEN THE EAGLE FLIES** *Island ILPS 9273* . .	31	1 wk

Pat TRAVERS *US, male instrumentalist – guitar* — *3 wks*

2 Apr 77	**MAKIN' MAGIC** *Polydor 2383 436*	40	3 wks

John TRAVOLTA *US, male vocalist* — *6 wks*

23 Dec 78	**SANDY** *Polydor POLD 5014*	40	6 wks

TREMELOES *UK, male vocal/instrumental group* — *7 wks*

3 Jun 67	**HERE COME THE TREMELOES**	
	CBS SBPG 63017	15	7 wks

T. REX *UK, male vocal/instrumental group* — *200 wks*

13 Jul 68	**MY PEOPLE WERE FAIR AND HAD SKY IN THEIR HAIR BUT NOW THEY'RE CONTENT TO WEAR STARS ON THEIR BROWS**	
	Regal Zonophone SLRZ 1003	15	9 wks
7 Jun 69	**UNICORN** *Regal Zonophone S 1007*	12	3 wks
14 Mar 70	**A BEARD OF STARS**	
	Regal Zonophone SLRZ 1013	21	6 wks
16 Jan 71	**T. REX** *Fly HIFLY 2*	13	24 wks
7 Aug 71	**THE BEST OF T. REX** *Flyback TON 2*	21	7 wks
9 Oct 71	★ **ELECTRIC WARRIOR** *Fly HIFLY 6*	1	44 wks
29 Mar 72	★ **PROPHETS, SEERS AND SAGES THE ANGELS OF THE AGES/MY PEOPLE WERE FAIR . . .**	
	Fly Doubleback 0037 TOOFA 3/4	1	12 wks
20 May 72	★ **BOLAN BOOGIE** *Fly HIFLY 8*	1	19 wks
5 Aug 72	● **THE SLIDER** *EMI BLN 5001*	4	18 wks
9 Dec 72	**A BEARD OF STARS/UNICORN**	
	Cube TOOFA 9/10	44	2 wks
31 Mar 73	● **TANX** *EMI BLN 5002*	4	12 wks
10 Nov 73	**GREAT HITS** *EMI BLN 5003*	32	3 wks
16 Mar 74	**ZINC ALLOY AND THE HIDDEN RIDERS OF TOMORROW** *EMI BLNA 7751*	12	3 wks
21 Feb 76	**FUTURISTIC DRAGON** *EMI BLN 5004*	50	1 wk
9 Apr 77	**DANDY IN THE UNDERWORLD**	
	EMI BLN 5005	26	3 wks
30 Jun 79	**SOLID GOLD** *EMI NUT 5*	51	3 wks
12 Sep 81	**T. REX IN CONCERT** *Marc ABOLAN 1*	35	6 wks
7 Nov 81	**YOU SCARE ME TO DEATH**	
	Cherry Red ERED 20	88	1 wk
24 Sep 83	**DANCE IN THE MIDNIGHT**	
	Marc On Wax MARCL 501	83	3 wks

4 May 85 ● **BEST OF THE 20TH CENTURY BOY**
K-Tel NE 1297 . . . . **5** 21 wks

Prophets . . ./My People . . . is a double re-issue although Prophets had not previously been a hit. Beard Of Stars/Unicorn is a double re-issue. The first three albums and the two double re-issues are credited to Tyrannosaurus Rex. Zinc Alloy . . . and Best Of The 20th Century Boy are credited to Marc Bolan and T. Rex. You Scare Me To Death and Dance In The Midnight are credited to Marc Bolan.

TRIUMPH Canada, male vocal/instrumental group   8 wks

10 May 80	**PROGRESSIONS OF POWER** RCA PL 13524	. .	**61**	5 wks
3 Oct 81	**ALLIED FORCES** RCA RCALP 6002	. . . .	**64**	3 wks

TROGGS UK, male vocal/instrumental group   32 wks

30 Jul 66	● **FROM NOWHERE . . . THE TROGGS**			
	Fontana TL 5355		**6**	16 wks
25 Feb 67	● **TROGGLODYNAMITE** Page One POL 001	. . . . .	**10**	11 wks
5 Aug 67	**BEST OF THE TROGGS** Page One FOR 001	. . . . .	**24**	5 wks

TROUBADOURS DU ROI BAUDOUIN

Zaire, male/female vocal group   1 wk

22 May 76	**MISSA LUBA** Philips SBL 7952	. . . .	**59**	1 wk

TROUBLE FUNK US, male vocal/instrumental group   4 wks

8 Nov 86	**SAY WHAT!** Fourth & Broadway DCLP 101	. . . .	**75**	2 wks
5 Sep 87	**TROUBLE OVER HERE, TROUBLE OVER THERE**			
	Fourth & Broadway BRLP 513		**54**	2 wks

Robin TROWER UK, male instrumentalist – guitar   16 wks

1 Mar 75	**FOR EARTH BELOW** Chrysalis CHR 1073	. . . .	**26**	4 wks
13 Mar 76	**LIVE** Chrysalis CHR 1089	. . . .	**15**	6 wks
30 Oct 76	**LONG MISTY DAYS** Chrysalis CHR 1107	. . . . .	**31**	1 wk
29 Oct 77	**IN CITY DREAMS** Chrysalis CHR 1148	. . . . .	**58**	1 wk
16 Feb 80	**VICTIMS OF THE FURY** Chrysalis CHR 1215	. . . .	**61**	4 wks

TUBES US, male vocal/instrumental group   7 wks

4 Mar 78	**WHAT DO YOU WANT FROM LIFE**			
	A & M AMS 68460	. . . .	**38**	1 wk
2 Jun 79	**REMOTE CONTROL** A & M AMLH 64751	. . . . . .	**40**	5 wks
4 Jun 83	**OUTSIDE INSIDE** Capitol EST 12260	. . . .	**77**	1 wk

TUBEWAY ARMY – See Gary Numan

Ike and Tina TURNER

US, male instrumentalist – guitar and female vocalist   1 wk

1 Oct 66	**RIVER DEEP – MOUNTAIN HIGH**			
	London HAU 8298	. . . .	**27**	1 wk

See also Tina Turner.

Ruby TURNER UK, female vocalist   11 wks

18 Oct 86	**WOMEN HOLD UP HALF THE SKY**			
	Jive HIP 36	. . . .	**47**	11 wks

Tina TURNER US, female vocalist   195 wks

30 Jun 84	● **PRIVATE DANCER** Capitol TINA 1	. . . .	**2**	146 wks
20 Sep 86	● **BREAK EVERY RULE** Capitol EST 2018	. . . .	**2**	49 wks

See also Ike and Tina Turner.

TURTLES US, male vocal/instrumental group   9 wks

22 Jul 67	**HAPPY TOGETHER** London HAU 8330	. . . . . .	**18**	9 wks

TWELFTH NIGHT UK, male vocal/instrumental group   2 wks

27 Oct 84	**ART AND ILLUSION** Music For Nations MFN 36		**83**	2 wks

TWIGGY UK, female vocalist   11 wks

21 Aug 76	**TWIGGY** Mercury 9102 600	. . . .	**33**	8 wks
30 Apr 77	**PLEASE GET MY NAME RIGHT**			
	Mercury 9102 601	. . . .	**35**	3 wks

TWISTED SISTER US, male vocal/instrumental group   20 wks

25 Sep 82	**UNDER THE BLADE** Secret SECX 9	. . . .	**70**	3 wks
7 May 83	**YOU CAN'T STOP ROCK 'N' ROLL**			
	Atlantic A 0074		**14**	9 wks
16 Jun 84	**STAY HUNGRY** Atlantic 780156	. . . .	**34**	5 wks
14 Dec 85	**COME OUT AND PLAY** Atlantic 78–1275–1	. . . .	**95**	1 wk
25 Jul 87	**LOVE IS FOR SUCKERS** Atlantic WX 120	. . . . . .	**57**	2 wks

Tommy TYCHO – See David GRAY and Tommy TYCHO

TYGERS OF PAN TANG

UK, male vocal/instrumental group   20 wks

30 Aug 80	**WILD CAT** MCA MCF 3075	. . . .	**18**	5 wks
18 Apr 81	**SPELLBOUND** MCA MCF 3104	. . . .	**33**	4 wks
21 Nov 81	**CRAZY NIGHTS** MCA MCF 3123	. . . .	**51**	3 wks
28 Aug 82	**THE CAGE** MCA MCF 3150	. . . .	**13**	8 wks

Bonnie TYLER UK, female vocalist   70 wks

16 Apr 83	★ **FASTER THAN THE SPEED OF NIGHT**			
	CBS 25304	. . . .	**1**	45 wks
17 May 86	**SECRET DREAMS AND FORBIDDEN FIRE**			
	CBS 86319	. . . .	**24**	12 wks
29 Nov 86	**THE GREATEST HITS** Telstar STAR 2291	. . . . . .	**24**	13 wks

Judie TZUKE UK, female vocalist   60 wks

4 Aug 79	**WELCOME TO THE CRUISE** Rocket TRAIN 7	. . .	**14**	17 wks
10 May 80	● **SPORTS CAR** Rocket TRAIN 9	. . . .	**7**	11 wks
16 May 81	**I AM PHOENIX** Rocket TRAIN 15	. . . .	**17**	10 wks
17 Apr 82	**SHOOT THE MOON** Chrysalis CDL 1382	. . . . .	**19**	10 wks
30 Oct 82	**ROAD NOISE – THE OFFICIAL BOOTLEG**			
	Chrysalis CTY 1405	. . . .	**39**	4 wks
1 Oct 83	**RITMO** Chrysalis CDL 1442	. . . .	**26**	5 wks
15 Jun 85	**THE CAT IS OUT** Legacy LLP 102	. . . .	**35**	3 wks

U

UB 40 UK, male vocal/instrumental group   278 wks

6 Sep 80	● **SIGNING OFF** Graduate GRAD LP 2	. . . .	**2**	71 wks
6 Jun 81	● **PRESENT ARMS** DEP International LP DEP 1	. . . .	**2**	38 wks
10 Oct 81	**PRESENT ARMS IN DUB**			
	DEP International LPS DEP 2	. . . .	**38**	7 wks
28 Aug 82	**THE SINGLES ALBUM** Graduate GRADLSP 3	. . .	**17**	8 wks
9 Oct 82	● **UB 44** DEP International LP DEP 3	. . . .	**4**	8 wks
26 Feb 83	**UB 40 LIVE** DEP International LP DEP 4	. . . . . .	**44**	5 wks
24 Sep 83	★ **LABOUR OF LOVE** DEP International LP DEP 5	. .	**1**	76 wks

20 Oct 84	● GEFFREY MORGAN *DEP International DEP 6*		3	14 wks
14 Sep 85	BAGGARADDIM *DEP International LP DEP 10* ...		14	23 wks
9 Aug 86	RAT IN THE KITCHEN			
	DEP International LP DEP 11		8	20 wks
7 Nov 87	● THE BEST OF UB 40 VOL. 1			
	Virgin UBTV 1		3†	8 wks

UFO *UK, male vocal/instrumental group* 48 wks

4 Jun 77	LIGHTS OUT *Chrysalis CHR 1127*		54	2 wks
15 Jul 78	OBSESSION *Chrysalis CDL 1182*		26	7 wks
10 Feb 79	● STRANGERS IN THE NIGHT *Chrysalis CJT 5* ...		8	11 wks
19 Jan 80	NO PLACE TO RUN *Chrysalis CDL 1239*		11	7 wks
24 Jan 81	THE WILD THE WILLING AND THE			
	INNOCENT *Chrysalis CHR 1307*		19	5 wks
20 Feb 82	● MECHANIX *Chrysalis CHR 1360*		8	6 wks
12 Feb 83	MAKING CONTACT *Chrysalis CHR 1402* ..		32	4 wks
3 Sep 83	HEADSTONE – THE BEST OF UFO			
	Chrysalis CTY 1437		39	4 wks
16 Nov 85	MISDEMEANOUR *Chrysalis CHR 1518* ...		74	2 wks

U.K. *UK, male vocal/instrumental group* 3 wks

27 May 78	U.K. *Polydor 2302 080*		43	3 wks

U.K. SUBS *UK, male vocal/instrumental group* 26 wks

13 Oct 79	ANOTHER KIND OF BLUES *Gem GEMLP 100* ..		21	6 wks
19 Apr 80	BRAND NEW AGE *Gem GEMLP 106*		18	9 wks
27 Sep 80	● CRASH COURSE *Gem GEMLP 111*		8	6 wks
21 Feb 81	DIMINISHED RESPONSIBILITY			
	Gem GEMLP 112		18	5 wks

Tracey ULLMAN *UK, female vocalist* 22 wks

3 Dec 83	YOU BROKE MY HEART IN 17 PLACES			
	Stiff SEEZ 51		14	20 wks
8 Dec 84	YOU CAUGHT ME OUT *Stiff SEEZ 56*		92	2 wks

ULTRAVOX *UK, male vocal/instrumental group* 225 wks

19 Jul 80	● VIENNA *Chrysalis CHR 1296*		3	72 wks
19 Sep 81	● RAGE IN EDEN *Chrysalis CDL 1338*		4	23 wks
23 Oct 82	● QUARTET *Chrysalis CDL 1394*		6	30 wks
22 Oct 83	● MONUMENT – THE SOUNDTRACK			
	Chrysalis CUX 1452		9	15 wks
14 Apr 84	● LAMENT *Chrysalis CDL 1459*		8	26 wks
10 Nov 84	● THE COLLECTION *Chrysalis UTV 1*		2	53 wks
25 Oct 86	● U-VOX *Chrysalis CDL 1545*		9	6 wks

UNDERTONES *UK, male vocal/instrumental group* 47 wks

19 May 79	THE UNDERTONES *Sire SRK 6071*		13	21 wks
26 Apr 80	● HYPNOTISED *Sire SRK 6088*		6	10 wks
16 May 81	POSITIVE TOUCH *Ardeck ARD 103*		17	6 wks
19 Mar 83	THE SIN OF PRIDE *Ardeck ARD 104*		43	5 wks
10 Dec 83	ALL WRAPPED UP *Ardeck ARD 1654281/3*		67	4 wks
14 Jun 86	CHER O'BOWLIES: PICK OF UNDERTONES			
	Ardeck EMS 1172		96	1 wk

UNION GAP – *See Gary PUCKETT and the UNION GAP*

UNTOUCHABLES *US, male vocal/instrumental group* 7 wks

13 Jul 85	WILD CHILD *Stiff SEEZ 57*		51	7 wks

Midge URE *UK, male vocalist* 15 wks

19 Oct 85	● THE GIFT *Chrysalis CHR 1508*		2	15 wks

URIAH HEEP *UK, male vocal/instrumental group* 51 wks

13 Nov 71	LOOK AT YOURSELF *Island ILPS 9169*		39	1 wk
10 Jun 72	DEMONS AND WIZARDS *Bronze ILPS 9193* ...		20	11 wks
2 Dec 72	THE MAGICIAN'S BIRTHDAY			
	Bronze ILPS 9213		28	3 wks
19 May 73	LIVE *Island ISLD 1*		23	8 wks
29 Sep 73	SWEET FREEDOM *Island ILPS 9245*		18	3 wks
29 Jun 74	WONDERWORLD *Bronze ILPS 9280*		23	3 wks
5 Jul 75	● RETURN TO FANTASY *Bronze ILPS 9335* ...		7	6 wks
12 Jun 76	HIGH AND MIGHTY *Island ILPS 9384* ...		55	1 wk
22 Mar 80	CONQUEST *Bronze BRON 524*		37	3 wks
17 Apr 82	ABOMINOG *Bronze BRON 538*		34	6 wks
18 Jun 83	HEAD FIRST *Bronze BRON 545*		46	4 wks
6 Apr 85	EQUATOR *Portrait PRT 2614*		79	2 wks

USA FOR AFRICA
US, male/female vocal/instrumental group 5 wks

25 May 85	WE ARE THE WORLD *CBS USAID F1*		31	5 wks

This album contains tracks by various artists in addition to the title track.

U.T.F.O. *US, male vocal group* 1 wk

16 Mar 85	ROXANNE ROXANNE (6 track version)			
	Streetwave 6 TRACK X KHAN 506		72	1 wk

UTOPIA *UK, male vocal/instrumental group* 3 wks

1 Oct 77	OOPS SORRY WRONG PLANET			
	Bearsville K 53517		59	1 wk
16 Feb 80	ADVENTURES IN UTOPIA *Island ILPS 9602* ...		57	2 wks

U2 *Ireland, male vocal/instrumental group* 587 wks

29 Aug 81	BOY *Island ILPS 9646*		52	31 wks
24 Oct 81	OCTOBER *Island ILPS 9680*		11	41 wks
12 Mar 83	★ WAR *Island ILPS 9733*		1	143 wks
3 Dec 83	● U2 LIVE: UNDER A BLOOD RED SKY			
	Island IMA 3		2	192 wks
13 Oct 84	★ THE UNFORGETTABLE FIRE *Island U2 5*		1	123 wks
27 Jul 85	WIDE AWAKE IN AMERICA (import)			
	Island 902791A		11	16 wks
21 Mar 87	★ THE JOSHUA TREE *Island U2 6*		1†	41 wks

V

VAN DE GRAAFF GENERATOR
UK, male vocal/instrumental group 2 wks

25 Apr 70	THE LEAST WE CAN DO IS WAVE TO EACH			
	OTHER *Charisma CAS 1007*		47	2 wks

VAN HALEN
US/Holland, male vocal/instrumental group 75 wks

27 May 78	VAN HALEN *Warner Bros. K 56470*		34	11 wks
14 Apr 79	VAN HALEN II *Warner Bros. K 566116*		23	7 wks
5 Apr 80	WOMEN AND CHILDREN FIRST			
	Warner Bros. K 56793		15	7 wks
23 May 81	FAIR WARNING *Warner Bros. K 56899* ..		49	4 wks
1 May 82	DIVER DOWN *Warner Bros. K 57003* ...		36	5 wks
4 Feb 84	1984 *Warner Bros. 92–3985*		15	23 wks
5 Apr 86	5150 *Warner Bros. WS 5150*		16	18 wks

(Left) The UNDERTONES are shown on the doorstep of the agency that collects the reproduction fee for this photograph, London Features International.

(Below) URIAH HEEP (lead singer David Byron, now deceased, second from left) were one of the world's leading heavy bands of the early seventies.

Luther VANDROSS *US, male vocalist* *117 wks*

21 Jan 84		BUSY BODY *Epic EPC 25608*	42	8 wks
6 Apr 85		THE NIGHT I FELL IN LOVE *Epic EPC 26387* ...	19	10 wks
1 Nov 86	●	GIVE ME THE REASON *Epic EPC 450134–1*	9†	58 wks
21 Feb 87		NEVER TOO MUCH *Epic EPC 32807* ...	41	25 wks
4 Jul 87		FOREVER, FOR ALWAYS, FOR LOVE *Epic EPC 25013*	23	16 wks

VANGELIS *Greece, male instrumentalist – keyboards* *125 wks*

10 Jan 76		HEAVEN AND HELL *RCA Victor RS 1025*	31	7 wks
9 Oct 76		ALBEDO 0.39 *RCA Victor RS 1080* ...	18	6 wks
18 Apr 81	●	CHARIOTS OF FIRE (film soundtrack) *Polydor POLS 1026*	5	97 wks
5 May 84		CHARIOTS OF FIRE (re-issue) *Polydor POLD 5160*	39	9 wks
13 Oct 84		SOIL FESTIVITIES *Polydor POLH 11*	55	4 wks
30 Mar 85		MASK *Polydor POLH 19*	69	2 wks

See also Jon and Vangelis.

VANILLA FUDGE *US, male vocal/instrumental group* *3 wks*

4 Nov 67		VANILLA FUDGE *Atlantic 588–086*	31	3 wks

VAPORS *UK, male vocal/instrumental group* *6 wks*

7 Jun 80		NEW CLEAR DAYS *United Artists UAG 30300*	44	6 wks

VARDIS *UK, male vocal/instrumental group* *1 wk*

1 Nov 80		100 MPH *Logo MOGO 4012*	52	1 wk

Frankie VAUGHAN *UK, male vocalist* *20 wks*

5 Sep 59	●	FRANKIE VAUGHAN AT THE LONDON PALLADIUM *Philips BDL 7330*	6	2 wks
4 Nov 67		FRANKIE VAUGHAN SONGBOOK *Philips DBL 001*	40	1 wk
25 Nov 67		THERE MUST BE A WAY *Columbia SCX 6200* ...	22	8 wks
12 Nov 77		100 GOLDEN GREATS *Ronco RTDX 2021*	24	9 wks

Sarah VAUGHAN *US, female vocalist* *1 wk*

20 Mar 60		NO COUNT – SARAH *Mercury MMC 14021*	19	1 wk

Bobby VEE *US, male vocalist* *46 wks*

24 Feb 62	●	TAKE GOOD CARE OF MY BABY *London HAG 2428*	7	8 wks
31 Mar 62		HITS OF THE ROCKIN' 50'S *London HAG 2406* ..	20	1 wk
12 Jan 63	●	A BOBBY VEE RECORDING SESSION *Liberty LBY 1084*	10	11 wks
20 Apr 63	●	BOBBY VEE'S GOLDEN GREATS *Liberty LBY 1112*	10	14 wks
5 Oct 63		THE NIGHT HAS A THOUSAND EYES *Liberty LIB 1139*	15	2 wks
19 Apr 80	●	THE BOBBY VEE SINGLES ALBUM *United Artists UAG 30253*	5	10 wks

See also Bobby Vee and the Crickets.

Bobby VEE and the CRICKETS
US, male vocalist and male vocal/instrumental group *27 wks*

27 Oct 62	●	BOBBY VEE MEETS THE CRICKETS *Liberty LBY 1086*	2	27 wks

See also Bobby Vee; Crickets; Buddy Holly and the Crickets.

Suzanne VEGA *US, female vocalist* *103 wks*

19 Oct 85		SUZANNE VEGA *A & M AMA 5072*	11	71 wks
9 May 87	●	SOLITUDE STANDING *A & M SUZLP 2*	2†	32 wks

Rosie VELA *US, female vocalist* *11 wks*

31 Jan 87		ZAZU *A & M AMA 5016*	20	11 wks

VELVET UNDERGROUND
US, male/female vocal/instrumental group *4 wks*

23 Feb 85		V.U. *Polydor POLD 5167*	47	4 wks

VENOM *UK, male vocal/instrumental group* *2 wks*

21 Apr 84		AT WAR WITH SATAN *Neat NEAT 1015* ...	64	1 wk
13 Apr 85		POSSESSED *Neat NEAT 1024*	99	1 wk

Anthony VENTURA ORCHESTRA
Switzerland, orchestra *4 wks*

20 Jan 79		DREAM LOVER *Lotus WH 5007*	44	4 wks

Tom VERLAINE *US, male vocalist* *1 wk*

14 Mar 87		FLASH LIGHT *Fontana SFLP 1*	99	1 wk

VIBRATORS *UK, male vocal/instrumental group* *7 wks*

25 Jun 77		THE VIBRATORS *Epic EPC 82907*	49	5 wks
29 Apr 78		V2 *Epic EPC 82495*	33	2 wks

VICE SQUAD
UK, male/female vocal/instrumental group *10 wks*

24 Oct 81		NO CAUSE FOR CONCERN *Zonophone ZEM 103*	32	5 wks
22 May 82		STAND STRONG STAND PROUD *Zonophone ZEM 104*	47	5 wks

Sid VICIOUS *UK, male vocalist* *8 wks*

15 Dec 79		SID SINGS *Virgin V 2144*	30	8 wks

VIENNA PHILHARMONIC ORCHESTRA – *See Aram KHATCHATURIAN/ VIENNA PHILHARMONIC ORCHESTRA*

VIENNA SYMPHONY ORCHESTRA
Austria, orchestra *4 wks*

4 Apr 87		SYMPHONIC ROCK WITH THE VIENNA SYMPHONY ORCHESTRA *Stylus SMR 730* ..	43	4 wks

VILLAGE PEOPLE *US, male vocal group* *28 wks*

27 Jan 79		CRUISIN' *Mercury 9109 614*	24	9 wks
12 May 79		GO WEST *Mercury 9109 621*	14	19 wks

Gene VINCENT *US, male vocalist* *2 wks*

16 Jul 60		CRAZY TIMES *Capitol T 1342*	12	2 wks

VIOLENT FEMMES
US, male/female vocal/instrumental group — *1 wk*

1 Mar 86	**THE BLIND LEADING THE NAKED**		
	Slash SLAP 10	81	1 wk

VIOLINSKI *UK, male instrumental group* — *1 wk*

26 May 79	**NO CAUSE FOR ALARM** *Jet JETLU 219*	49	1 wk

VISAGE *UK, male vocal/instrumental group* — *49 wks*

24 Jan 81	**VISAGE** *Polydor 2490 157*	13	20 wks
3 Apr 82	● **THE ANVIL** *Polydor POLD 5050*	6	16 wks
19 Nov 83	**FADE TO GREY – THE SINGLES COLLECTION**		
	Polydor POLD 5117	38	11 wks
3 Nov 84	**BEAT BOY** *Polydor POLH 12*	79	2 wks

VOYAGE *UK/France, disco aggregation* — *1 wk*

9 Sep 78	**VOYAGE** *GTO GTLP 030*	59	1 wk

W

WAH! *UK, male vocal/instrumental group* — *5 wks*

18 Jul 81	**NAH-POO THE ART OF BLUFF**		
	Eternal CLASSIC 1	33	5 wks

John WAITE *UK, male vocalist* — *3 wks*

10 Nov 84	**NO BREAKS** *EMI America WAIT 1*	64	3 wks

TOM WAITS *US, male vocalist* — *13 wks*

8 Oct 83	**SWORDFISHTROMBONE** *Island ILPS 9762*	62	3 wks
19 Oct 85	**RAIN DOGS** *Island ILPS 9803*	29	5 wks
5 Sep 87	**FRANK'S WILD YEARS** *Island ITW 3*	20	5 wks

WAILERS – *See Bob MARLEY and the WAILERS*

Rick WAKEMAN
UK, male instrumentalist – keyboards — *123 wks*

24 Feb 73	● **THE SIX WIVES OF HENRY VIII**		
	A & M AMLH 64361	7	22 wks
18 May 74	★ **JOURNEY TO THE CENTRE OF THE EARTH**		
	A & M AMLH 63621	1	30 wks
12 Apr 75	● **THE MYTHS AND LEGENDS OF KING ARTHUR AND THE KNIGHTS OF THE ROUND TABLE** *A & M AMLH 64515 0022*	2	28 wks
24 Apr 76	● **NO EARTHLY CONNECTION**		
	A & M AMLK 64583	9	9 wks
12 Feb 77	**WHITE ROCK** *A & M AMLH 64614*	14	9 wks
3 Dec 77	**CRIMINAL RECORD** *A & M AMLK 64660*	25	5 wks
2 Jun 79	**RHAPSODIES** *A & M AMLX 68508*	25	10 wks
27 Jun 81	**1984** *Charisma CDS 4022*	24	9 wks
16 May 87	**THE GOSPELS** *Stylus SMR 729*	94	1 wk

See also Kevin Peek and Rick Wakeman.

Scott WALKER *US, male vocalist* — *44 wks*

16 Sep 67	● **SCOTT** *Philips SBL 7816*	3	17 wks
20 Apr 68	★ **SCOTT 2** *Philips SBL 7840*	1	18 wks
5 Apr 69	● **SCOTT 3** *Philips S 7882*	3	4 wks
5 Jul 69	● **SONGS FROM HIS TV SERIES** *Philips SBL 7900*	7	3 wks
31 Mar 84	**CLIMATE OF HUNTER** *Virgin V 2303*	60	2 wks

See also Walker Brothers.

WALKER BROTHERS *US, male vocal group* — *96 wks*

18 Dec 65	● **TAKE IT EASY** *Philips BL 7691*	3	36 wks
3 Sep 66	● **PORTRAIT** *Philips BL 7691*	3	23 wks
18 Mar 67	**IMAGES** *Philips SBL 7770*	6	15 wks
16 Sep 67	● **WALKER BROTHERS' STORY** *Philips DBL 002*	9	19 wks
21 Feb 76	**NO REGRETS** *GTO GTLP 007*	49	3 wks

See also Scott Walker.

Bob WALLIS and his STORYVILLE JAZZMEN
UK, male vocal/instrumental group — *1 wk*

11 Jun 60	**EVERYBODY LOVES SATURDAY NIGHT**		
	Top Rank BUY 023	20	1 wk

Joe WALSH *US, male vocalist* — *20 wks*

17 Apr 76	**YOU CAN'T ARGUE WITH A SICK MIND**		
	Anchor ABCL 5156	28	3 wks
10 Jan 78	**BUT SERIOUSLY FOLKS** *Asylum K 53081*	16	17 wks

WANG CHUNG *UK, male vocal/instrumental group* — *5 wks*

21 Apr 84	**POINTS ON THE CURVE** *Geffen GEF 25589*	34	5 wks

WAR – *See Eric BURDON and WAR*

Clifford T. WARD *UK, male vocalist* — *5 wks*

21 Jul 73	**HOME THOUGHTS** *Charisma CAS 1066*	40	3 wks
16 Feb 74	**MANTLE PIECES** *Charisma CAS 1077*	42	2 wks

Michael WARD *UK, male vocalist* — *3 wks*

5 Jan 74	**INTRODUCING MICHAEL WARD**		
	Philips 6308 189	26	3 wks

WARLOCK
Germany, male/female vocal/instrumental group — *2 wks*

14 Nov 87	**TRIUMPH AND AGONY** *Vertigo VERH 50*	54	2 wks

Jennifer WARNES *US, female vocalist* — *12 wks*

18 Jul 87	**FAMOUS BLUE RAINCOAT** *RCA PL 90048*	33	12 wks

Dionne WARWICK *US, female vocalist* — *131 wks*

23 May 64	**PRESENTING DIONNE WARWICK**		
	Pye NPL 28037	14	10 wks
7 May 66	● **BEST OF DIONNE WARWICK** *Pye NPL 28078*	8	11 wks
4 Feb 67	**HERE WHERE THERE IS LOVE** *Pye NPL 28096*	39	2 wks
18 May 68	● **VALLEY OF THE DOLLS** *Pye NSPL 28114*	10	13 wks
23 May 70	**GREATEST HITS VOL. 1** *Wand WNS 1*	31	26 wks
6 Jun 70	**GREATEST HITS VOL. 2** *Wand WNS 2*	28	14 wks
30 Oct 82	● **HEARTBREAKER** *Arista 204 974*	3	33 wks
21 May 83	**THE COLLECTION** *Arista DIONE 1*	11	17 wks
29 Oct 83	**SO AMAZING** *Arista 205 755*	60	3 wks
23 Feb 85	**WITHOUT YOUR LOVE** *Arista 206 571*	86	2 wks

See also Stevie Wonder.

Geno WASHINGTON   UK, male vocalist   51 wks

10 Dec 66 ●	HAND CLAPPIN' – FOOT STOMPIN' – FUNKY BUTT – LIVE! Piccadilly NPL 38026	5	38 wks
23 Sep 67 ●	HIPSTERS, FLIPSTERS, AND FINGER POPPIN' DADDIES Piccadilly NSPL 38032	8	13 wks

Grover WASHINGTON Jr
US, male instrumentalist – saxophone   10 wks

9 May 81	WINELIGHT Elektra K 52262	34	9 wks
19 Dec 81	COME MORNING Elektra K 52337	98	1 wk

W.A.S.P.   US, male vocal/instrumental group   10 wks

8 Sep 84	W.A.S.P. Capitol EJ 2401951	51	2 wks
9 Nov 85	THE LAST COMMAND Capitol WASP 2	48	1 wk
8 Nov 86	INSIDE THE ELECTRIC CIRCUS Capitol EST 2025	53	3 wks
26 Sep 87	LIVE IN THE RAW Capitol EST 2040	23	4 wks

WATERBOYS   UK, male vocal/instrumental group   18 wks

16 Jun 84	A PAGAN PLACE Ensign ENCL 3	100	1 wk
28 Sep 85	THIS IS THE SEA Ensign ENCL 5	37	17 wks

Roger WATERS
UK, male vocalist/instrumentalist – bass   17 wks

12 May 84	THE PROS AND CONS OF HITCH-HIKING Harvest SHVL 240105	13	11 wks
27 Jun 87	RADIO KAOS EMI KAOS 1	25	6 wks

Jody WATLEY   US, female vocalist   2 wks

5 Sep 87	JODY WATLEY MCA MCG 6024	62	2 wks

WAVES – See KATRINA and the WAVES

WAX   UK/US, male vocal/instrumental duo   3 wks

12 Sep 87	AMERICAN ENGLISH RCA PL 71430	59	3 wks

Jeff WAYNE   US/UK, orchestra and cast   226 wks

1 Jul 78 ●	WAR OF THE WORLDS CBS 96000	5	226 wks

This album featured various artists but is commonly credited to Jeff Wayne, its creator and producer.

WAYSTED   UK, male vocal/instrumental group   5 wks

8 Oct 83	VICES Chrysalis CHR 1438	78	3 wks
22 Sep 84	WAYSTED Music For Nations MFN 31	73	2 wks

WEATHER PROPHETS
UK, male vocal/instrumental group   2 wks

9 May 87	MAYFLOWER Elevation ELV 1	67	2 wks

WEATHER REPORT   US, male instrumental group   12 wks

23 Apr 77	HEAVY WEATHER CBS 81775	43	6 wks
11 Nov 78	MR. GONE CBS 82775	47	3 wks
27 Feb 82	WEATHER REPORT CBS 85326	88	2 wks
24 Mar 84	DOMINO THEORY CBS 25839	54	1 wk

Marti WEBB   UK, female vocalist   32 wks

16 Feb 80 ●	TELL ME ON A SUNDAY Polydor POLD 5031	2	23 wks
28 Sep 85	ENCORE Starblend BLEND 1	55	4 wks
6 Dec 86	ALWAYS THERE BBC REB 619	65	5 wks

Ben WEBSTER – See Gerry MULLIGAN and Ben WEBSTER

WEDDING PRESENT
UK, male vocal/instrumental group   2 wks

24 Oct 87	GEORGE BEST Reception LEEDS 001	47	2 wks

Bert WEEDON   UK, male instrumentalist – guitar   26 wks

16 Jul 60	KING SIZE GUITAR Top Rank BUY 026	18	1 wk
23 Oct 76 ★	22 GOLDEN GUITAR GREATS Warwick WW 5019	1	25 wks

WELCH – See MARVIN, WELCH and FARRAR

WENDY and LISA   US, female vocal duo   2 wks

10 Oct 87	WENDY AND LISA Virgin V 2444	84	2 wks

WESTWORLD
UK/US, male/female vocal/instrumental group   2 wks

5 Sep 87	WHERE THE ACTION IS RCA PL 71429	49	2 wks

WET WET WET   UK, male vocal/instrumental group   13 wks

3 Oct 87 ●	POPPED IN SOULED OUT Precious JWWWL 1 ..	2†	13 wks

WHAM!   UK, male/female vocal/instrumental group   233 wks

9 Jul 83 ★	FANTASTIC Inner Vision IVL 25328	1	116 wks
17 Nov 84 ★	MAKE IT BIG Epic EPC 86311	1	72 wks
19 Jul 86 ●	THE FINAL Epic EPC 88681	2	45 wks

WHISPERS   US, male vocal group   9 wks

14 Mar 81	IMAGINATION Solar SOLA 7	42	5 wks
6 Jun 87	JUST GETS BETTER WITH TIME Solar MCF 3381	63	4 wks

Alan WHITE   UK, male instrumentalist – drums   4 wks

13 Mar 76	RAMSHACKLED Atlantic K 50217	41	4 wks

Barry WHITE   US, male vocalist   120 wks

9 Mar 74	STONE GON' Pye NSPL 28186	18	17 wks
6 Apr 74	RHAPSODY IN WHITE Pye NSPL 28191	50	1 wk
2 Nov 74 ●	CAN'T GET ENOUGH 20th Century BT 444	4	34 wks
26 Apr 75	JUST ANOTHER WAY TO SAY I LOVE YOU 20th Century BT 466	12	15 wks
22 Nov 75	GREATEST HITS 20th Century BTH 8000	18	12 wks
21 Feb 76	LET THE MUSIC PLAY 20th Century BT 502	22	14 wks
9 Apr 77	BARRY WHITE'S GREATEST HITS VOL. 2 20th Century BTH 8001	17	7 wks
10 Feb 79	THE MAN 20th Century BT 571	46	4 wks
21 Dec 85	HEART AND SOUL K-Tel NE 1316	34	10 wks
17 Oct 87	THE RIGHT NIGHT AND BARRY WHITE Breakout AMA 5154	74	6 wks

(Top left) RICK WAKEMAN took the number one spot between chart-topping runs of The Carpenters.

(Middle left) SLIM WHITMAN was the first solo artist to benefit spectacularly from the television advertising of compilation albums.

The VICE SQUAD stood strong and proud in ten album charts of the early eighties.

(Bottom left) BOBBY WOMACK ponders why it took him two decades to become a UK chart star.

(Bottom middle) The VILLAGE PEOPLE spent twenty-eight weeks cruising the UK LP chart in 1979.

WISHBONE ASH prominently featured two lead guitarists.

Snowy WHITE
UK, male vocalist/instrumentalist – guitar   *5 wks*

| 11 Feb 84 | WHITE FLAMES | *Towerbell TOWLP 3* | 21 | 4 wks |
| 9 Feb 85 | SNOWY WHITE | *Towerbell TOWLP 8* | 88 | 1 wk |

Tony Joe WHITE *US, male vocalist*   *1 wk*

| 26 Sep 70 | TONY JOE | *CBS 63800* | 63 | 1 wk |

WHITESNAKE *UK, male vocal/instrumental group*   *116 wks*

18 Nov 78	TROUBLE *EMI International INS 3022*	50	2 wks
13 Oct 79	LOVE HUNTER *United Artists UAG 30264*	29	7 wks
7 Jun 80	● READY AND WILLING		
	United Artists UAG 30302	6	15 wks
8 Nov 80	● LIVE IN THE HEART OF THE CITY		
	United Artists SNAKE 1	5	15 wks
18 Apr 81	● COME AND GET IT *Liberty LBG 30327*	2	23 wks
27 Nov 82	● SAINTS 'N' SINNERS *Liberty LBG 30354*	9	9 wks
11 Feb 84	● SLIDE IT IN *Liberty LBG 2400001*	9	7 wks
11 Apr 87	● WHITESNAKE 1987 *EMI EMC 3258*	8†	38 wks

Slim WHITMAN *US, male vocalist*   *59 wks*

14 Dec 74	HAPPY ANNIVERSARY		
	United Artists UAS 29670	44	2 wks
31 Jan 76	★ THE VERY BEST OF SLIM WHITMAN		
	United Artists UAS 29898	1	17 wks
15 Jan 77	★ RED RIVER VALLEY *United Artists UAS 29993*	1	14 wks
15 Oct 77	● HOME ON THE RANGE		
	United Artists UATV 30102	2	13 wks
13 Jan 79	GHOST RIDERS IN THE SKY		
	United Artists UATV 30202	27	6 wks
22 Dec 79	SLIM WHITMAN'S 20 GREATEST LOVE SONGS		
	United Artists UAG 30270	18	7 wks

Roger WHITTAKER *Kenya, male vocalist*   *100 wks*

28 Jun 70	I DON'T BELIEVE IN IF ANYMORE		
	Columbia SCX 6404	23	1 wk
3 Apr 71	NEW WORLD IN THE MORNING		
	Columbia SCX 6456	45	2 wks
6 Sep 75	● THE VERY BEST OF ROGER WHITTAKER		
	Columbia SCX 6560	5	42 wks
15 May 76	THE SECOND ALBUM OF THE VERY BEST OF		
	ROGER WHITTAKER *EMI EMC 3117*	27	7 wks
9 Dec 78	ROGER WHITTAKER SINGS THE HITS		
	Columbia SCX 6601	52	5 wks
4 Aug 79	20 ALL TIME GREATS *Polydor POLTV 8*	24	9 wks
7 Feb 81	THE ROGER WHITTAKER ALBUM		
	K-Tel NE 1105	18	14 wks
27 Dec 86	SKYE BOAT SONG AND OTHER GREAT SONGS		
	Tembo TMB 113	89	1 wk
23 May 87	HIS FINEST COLLECTION *Tembo RWTV 1*	15	19 wks

WHO *UK, male vocal/instrumental group*   *187 wks*

25 Dec 65	● MY GENERATION *Brunswick LAT 8616*	5	11 wks
17 Dec 66	● A QUICK ONE *Reaction 593-002*	4	17 wks
13 Jan 68	THE WHO SELL-OUT *Track 613-002*	13	11 wks
7 Jun 69	● TOMMY *Track 613-013/4*	2	9 wks
6 Jun 70	● LIVE AT LEEDS *Track 2406-001*	3	21 wks
11 Sep 71	★ WHO'S NEXT *Track 2408-102*	1	13 wks
18 Dec 71	● MEATY, BEATY, BIG & BOUNCY *Track 2406-006*	9	8 wks
17 Nov 73	● QUADROPHENIA *Track 2647-013*	2	13 wks
26 Oct 74	● ODDS AND SODS *Track 2406-116*	10	4 wks
23 Aug 75	TOMMY (film soundtrack version)		
	Track 2657-007	30	2 wks
18 Oct 75	● THE WHO BY NUMBERS *Polydor 2490-129*	7	6 wks
9 Oct 76	● THE STORY OF THE WHO *Polydor 2683-069*	2	18 wks

9 Sep 78	● WHO ARE YOU *Polydor WHOD 5004*	6	9 wks
30 Jun 79	THE KIDS ARE ALRIGHT *Polydor 2675 174*	26	13 wks
25 Oct 80	MY GENERATION (re-issue) *Virgin V 2179*	20	7 wks
28 Mar 81	● FACE DANCES *Polydor WHOD 5037*	2	9 wks
11 Sep 82	IT'S HARD *Polydor WHOD 5066*	11	6 wks
17 Nov 85	WHO'S LAST *MCA WHO 1*	48	4 wks
12 Oct 85	THE WHO COLLECTION *Impression IMDP 4*	44	6 wks

WILD HORSES *UK, male vocal/instrumental group*   *4 wks*

| 26 Apr 80 | WILD HORSES *EMI EMC 3324* | 38 | 4 wks |

Eugene WILDE *US, male vocalist*   *4 wks*

| 8 Dec 84 | EUGENE WILDE *Fourth And Broadway BRLP 502* | 67 | 4 wks |

Kim WILDE *UK, female vocalist*   *37 wks*

11 Jul 81	● KIM WILDE *RAK SRAK 544*	3	14 wks
22 May 82	SELECT *RAK SRAK 548*	19	11 wks
26 Nov 83	CATCH AS CATCH CAN *RAK SRAK 165408*	90	1 wk
17 Nov 84	TEASES AND DARES *MCA MCF 3250*	66	2 wks
18 May 85	THE VERY BEST OF KIM WILDE *RAK WILDE 1*	78	4 wks
15 Nov 86	ANOTHER STEP *MCA MCF 3339*	73	5 wks

Another Step changed label number during its chart run to MCA KIML 1.

Andy WILLIAMS *US, male vocalist*   *439 wks*

26 Jun 65	● ALMOST THERE *CBS BPG 62533*	4	46 wks
7 Aug 65	CAN'T GET USED TO LOSING YOU		
	CBS BPG 62146	16	1 wk
19 Mar 66	MAY EACH DAY *CBS BPG 62658*	11	6 wks
30 Apr 66	GREAT SONGS FROM MY FAIR LADY		
	CBS BPG 62430	30	1 wk
23 Jul 66	SHADOW OF YOUR SMILE *CBS 62633*	24	4 wks
29 Jul 67	BORN FREE *CBS SBPG 63027*	22	11 wks
11 May 68	★ LOVE ANDY *CBS 63167*	1	22 wks
6 Jul 68	● HONEY *CBS 63311*	4	17 wks
26 Jul 69	HAPPY HEART *CBS 63614*	22	9 wks
27 Dec 69	GET TOGETHER WITH ANDY WILLIAMS		
	CBS 63800	13	12 wks
24 Jan 70	ANDY WILLIAMS' SOUND OF MUSIC *CBS 63920*	22	10 wks
11 Apr 70	★ GREATEST HITS *CBS 63920*	1	116 wks
20 Jun 70	● CAN'T HELP FALLING IN LOVE *CBS 64067*	7	48 wks
5 Dec 70	● ANDY WILLIAMS SHOW *CBS 64127*	10	6 wks
3 Apr 71	★ HOME LOVING MAN *CBS 64286*	1	25 wks
31 Jul 71	LOVE STORY *CBS 64467*	11	11 wks
29 Apr 72	THE IMPOSSIBLE DREAM *CBS 67236*	26	3 wks
29 Jul 72	LOVE THEME FROM 'THE GODFATHER'		
	CBS 64869	11	16 wks
16 Dec 72	GREATEST HITS VOL. 2 *CBS 65151*	23	10 wks
22 Dec 73	● SOLITAIRE *CBS 65638*	3	26 wks
15 Jun 74	● THE WAY WE WERE *CBS 80152*	7	11 wks
11 Oct 75	THE OTHER SIDE OF ME *CBS 69152*	60	1 wk
28 Jan 78	REFLECTIONS *CBS 10006*	2	17 wks
27 Oct 84	GREATEST LOVE CLASSICS *EMI ANDY 1*	22	10 wks

Greatest Love Classics also credits the Royal Philharmonic Orchestra. See also Royal Philharmonic Orchestra; Louis Clark; Juan Martin, both with RPO.

Deniece WILLIAMS *US, female vocalist*   *12 wks*

| 21 May 77 | THIS IS NIECEY *CBS 81869* | 31 | 12 wks |

See also Johnny Mathis and Deniece Williams.

Don WILLIAMS *US, male vocalist*   *136 wks*

10 Jul 76	GREATEST HITS VOL.1 *ABC ABCL 5147*	29	15 wks
19 Feb 77	VISIONS *ABC ABCL 5200*	13	20 wks
15 Oct 77	COUNTRY BOY *ABC ABCL 5233*	27	5 wks
5 Aug 78	● IMAGES *K-Tel NE 1033*	2	38 wks

5 Aug 78	YOU'RE MY BEST FRIEND *ABC ABCD 5127* ..	58	1 wk
4 Nov 78	EXPRESSIONS *ABC ABCL 5253*	28	8 wks
22 Sep 79	NEW HORIZONS *K-Tel NE 1048*	29	12 wks
15 Dec 79	PORTRAIT *MCA MCS 3045*	58	4 wks
6 Sep 80	I BELIEVE IN YOU *MCA MCF 3077*	36	5 wks
18 Jul 81	ESPECIALLY FOR YOU *MCA MCF 3114* ...	33	7 wks
17 Apr 82	LISTEN TO THE RADIO *MCA MCF 3135* ..	69	3 wks
23 Apr 83	YELLOW MOON *MCA MCF 3159*	52	1 wk
15 Oct 83	LOVE STORIES *K-Tel NE 1252*	22	13 wks
26 May 84	CAFE CAROLINA *MCA MCF 3225*	65	4 wks

Iris WILLIAMS *UK, female vocalist* `4 wks`

22 Dec 79	HE WAS BEAUTIFUL *Columbia SCX 6627*	69	4 wks

John WILLIAMS *UK, male instrumentalist – guitar* `31 wks`

3 Oct 70	PLAYS SPANISH MUSIC *CBS 72860*	46	1 wk
17 Jun 78	TRAVELLING *Cube HIFLY 27*	23	5 wks
30 Jun 79	● BRIDGES *Lotus WH 5015*	5	22 wks
4 Aug 79	CAVATINA *Cube HIFLY 32*	64	3 wks

See also John Williams with the English Chamber Orchestra conducted by Daniel Barenboim; Cleo Laine and John Williams.

John WILLIAMS *US, male conductor* `10 wks`

25 Dec 82	ET – THE EXTRATERRESTRIAL *MCA MCF 3160*	47	10 wks

John WILLIAMS with the ENGLISH CHAMBER ORCHESTRA conducted by Daniel BARENBOIM *UK, male instrumentalist – guitar, with orchestra and male conductor* `9 wks`

8 Feb 76	RODRIGO: CONCERTO DE ARANJUEZ *CBS 79369*	20	9 wks

See also John Williams (UK).

Wendy O. WILLIAMS *US, female vocalist* `1 wk`

30 Jun 84	W.O.W. *Music For Nations MFN 24*	100	1 wk

Ann WILLIAMSON *UK, female vocalist* `9 wks`

15 Feb 86	PRECIOUS MEMORIES *Emerald Gem ERTV 1* ...	16	9 wks

Sonny Boy WILLIAMSON
US, male vocalist/instrumentalist – guitar `1 wk`

20 Jun 64	DOWN AND OUT BLUES *Pye NPL 28036*	20	1 wk

Bruce WILLIS *US, male vocalist* `28 wks`

18 Apr 87	● THE RETURN OF BRUNO *Motown ZL 72571* ...	4	28 wks

Mari WILSON *UK, female vocalist* `9 wks`

26 Feb 83	SHOW PEOPLE *Compact COMP 2*	24	9 wks

Show People credits Mari Wilson with the Wilsations.

WIN *UK, male/female vocal/instrumental group* `1 wk`

25 Apr 87	UH! TEARS BABY *Swampland LONLP 31*	51	1 wk

WINDJAMMER *US, male vocal/instrumental group* `1 wk`

25 Aug 84	WINDJAMMER II *MCA MCF*	82	1 wk

WINGS – *See Paul McCartney*

Johnny WINTER *US, male/vocal instrumental group* `12 wks`

16 May 70	SECOND WINTER *CBS 66321*	59	2 wks
31 Oct 70	JOHNNY WINTER AND ... *CBS 64117* ...	29	4 wks
15 May 71	JOHNNY WINTER AND LIVE *CBS 64289*	20	6 wks

Ruby WINTERS *US, female vocalist* `16 wks`

10 Jun 78	RUBY WINTERS *Creole CRLP 512*	27	7 wks
23 Jun 79	SONGBIRD *K-Tel NE 1045*	31	9 wks

Steve WINWOOD *UK, male vocalist* `92 wks`

9 Jul 77	STEVE WINWOOD *Island ILPS 9494*	12	9 wks
10 Jan 81	ARC OF A DIVER *Island ILPS 9576*	13	20 wks
14 Aug 82	● TALKING BACK TO THE NIGHT *Island ILPS 9777*	6	13 wks
12 Jul 86	● BACK IN THE HIGH LIFE *Island ILPS 9844*	8	42 wks
7 Nov 87	CHRONICLES *Island SSW 1*	12†	8 wks

WIRE *UK, male vocal/instrumental group* `3 wks`

7 Oct 78	CHAIRS MISSING *Harvest SHSP 4093*	48	1 wk
13 Oct 79	154 *Harvest SHSP 4105*	39	1 wk
9 May 87	THE IDEAL COPY *Mute STUMM 42*	87	1 wk

WISHBONE ASH *UK, male vocal/instrumental group* `75 wks`

23 Jan 71	WISHBONE ASH *MCA MKPS 2014*	34	2 wks
9 Oct 71	PILGRIMAGE *MCA MDKS 8004*	14	9 wks
20 May 72	● ARGUS *MCA MDKS 8006*	3	20 wks
26 May 73	WISHBONE FOUR *MCA MDKS 8011* ...	12	10 wks
30 Nov 74	THERE'S THE RUB *MCA MCF 2585* ...	16	5 wks
3 Apr 76	LOCKED IN *MCA MCF 2750*	36	2 wks
27 Nov 76	NEW ENGLAND *MCA MCG 3523*	22	3 wks
29 Oct 77	FRONT PAGE NEWS *MCA MCG 3524* ...	31	4 wks
28 Oct 78	NO SMOKE WITHOUT FIRE *MCA MCG 3528* ..	43	4 wks
2 Feb 80	JUST TESTING *MCA MCF 3052*	41	4 wks
1 Nov 80	LIVE DATES II *MCA MCG 4012*	40	3 wks
25 Apr 81	NUMBER THE BRAVE *MCA MCF 3103* ...	61	5 wks
16 Oct 82	BOTH BARRELS BURNING *A&M ASH 1*	22	5 wks

Bill WITHERS *US, male vocalist* `6 wks`

11 Feb 78	MENAGERIE *CBS 82265*	27	5 wks
15 Jun 85	WATCHING YOU, WATCHING ME *CBS 26200* .	60	1 wk

WIZZARD *UK, male vocal/instrumental group* `11 wks`

19 May 73	WIZZARD BREW *Harvest SHSP 4025*	29	7 wks
17 Aug 74	INTRODUCING EDDY AND THE FALCONS *Warner Bros. K 52029*	19	4 wks

WOMACK and WOMACK
US, male/female vocal duo `15 wks`

21 Apr 84	LOVE WARS *Elektra 960293*	45	13 wks
22 Jun 85	RADIO M.U.S.C. MAN *Elektra EKT 6*	56	2 wks

Bobby WOMACK *US, male vocalist*   *15 wks*

| 28 Apr 84 | **THE POET II** *Motown ZL 72205* | 31 | 8 wks |
| 28 Sep 85 | **SO MANY RIVERS** *MCA MCF 3282* | 28 | 7 wks |

See also Wilton Felder.

WOMBLES *UK, male vocalist/arranger/producer, Mike Batt*
under group name   *55 wks*

2 Mar 74	**WOMBLING SONGS** *CBS 65803*	19	17 wks
13 Jul 74	**REMEMBER YOU'RE A WOMBLE** *CBS 80191*	18	31 wks
21 Dec 74	**KEEP ON WOMBLING** *CBS 80526*	17	6 wks
8 Jan 77	**20 WOMBLING GREATS** *Warwick PR 5022*	29	1 wk

Stevie WONDER
US, male vocalist/multi-instrumentalist   *325 wks*

7 Sep 68	**STEVIE WONDER'S GREATEST HITS** *Tamla Motown STML 11075*	25	10 wks
13 Dec 69	**MY CHERIE AMOUR** *Tamla Motown STML 11128*	17	2 wks
12 Feb 72	**GREATEST HITS VOL. 2** *Tamla Motown STML 11196*	30	4 wks
3 Feb 73	**TALKING BOOK** *Tamla Motown STMA 8007*	16	48 wks
1 Sep 73	● **INNERVISIONS** *Tamla Motown STMA 8011*	8	55 wks
17 Aug 74	● **FULFILLINGNESS' FIRST FINALE** *Tamla Motown STMA 8019*	5	16 wks
16 Oct 76	● **SONGS IN THE KEY OF LIFE** *Tamla Motown TMSP 6002*	2	54 wks
10 Nov 79	● **JOURNEY THROUGH THE SECRET LIFE OF PLANTS** *Motown TMSP 6009*	8	15 wks
8 Nov 80	● **HOTTER THAN JULY** *Motown STMA 8035*	2	55 wks
22 May 82	● **ORIGINAL MUSIQUARIUM 1** *Motown TMSP 6012*	8	17 wks
22 Sep 84	● **WOMAN IN RED – SELECTIONS FROM ORIGINAL MOTION PICTURE SOUNDTRACK** *Motown ZL 72285*	2	19 wks
24 Nov 84	**LOVE SONGS – 16 CLASSIC HITS** *Telstar STAR 2251*	20	10 wks
28 Sep 85	● **IN SQUARE CIRCLE** *Motown ZL 72005*	5	16 wks
28 Nov 87	**CHARACTERS** *RCA ZL 72001*	33	4 wks

The Woman In Red also features Dionne Warwick. See also Dionne Warwick.

Roy WOOD *UK, male vocalist/multi-instrumentalist*   *14 wks*

| 18 Aug 73 | **BOULDERS** *Harvest SHVL 803* | 15 | 8 wks |
| 24 Jul 82 | **THE SINGLES** *Speed SPEED 1000* | 37 | 6 wks |

WOODENTOPS *UK, male vocal/instrumental group*   *4 wks*

| 12 Jul 86 | **GIANT** *Rough Trade ROUGH 87* | 35 | 4 wks |

Edward WOODWARD *UK, male vocalist*   *12 wks*

| 6 Jun 70 | **THIS MAN ALONE** *DJM DJLPS 405* | 53 | 2 wks |
| 19 Aug 72 | **THE EDWARD WOODWARD ALBUM** *Jam JAL 103* | 20 | 10 wks |

WORKING WEEK
UK, male/female vocal/instrumental group   *10 wks*

| 6 Apr 85 | **WORKING NIGHTS** *Virgin V 2343* | 23 | 9 wks |
| 27 Sep 86 | **COMPANEROS** *Virgin V 2397* | 72 | 1 wk |

WORLD PARTY
Ireland/UK, male vocal/instrumental group   *4 wks*

| 21 Mar 87 | **PRIVATE REVOLUTION** *Chrysalis CHEN 4* | 56 | 4 wks |

WRECKLESS ERIC *UK, male vocalist*   *5 wks*

| 1 Apr 78 | **WRECKLESS ERIC** *Stiff SEEZ 6* | 46 | 1 wk |
| 8 Mar 80 | **BIG SMASH** *Stiff SEEZ 21* | 30 | 4 wks |

Klaus WUNDERLICH
Germany, male instrumentalist – organ   *19 wks*

30 Aug 75	**THE HIT WORLD OF KLAUS WUNDERLICH** *Decca SPA 434*	27	8 wks
20 May 78	**THE UNIQUE KLAUS WUNDERLICH SOUND** *Decca DBC 5/5*	28	4 wks
26 May 79	**THE FANTASTIC SOUND OF KLAUS WUNDERLICH** *Lotus LH 5013*	43	5 wks
17 Mar 84	**ON THE SUNNY SIDE OF THE STREET** *Polydor POLD 5133*	81	2 wks

WURZELS *UK, male vocal/instrumental group*   *25 wks*

| 3 Jul 76 | **COMBINE HARVESTER** *One-Up OU 2138* | 15 | 20 wks |
| 2 Apr 77 | **GOLDEN DELICIOUS** *EMI Note NTS 122* | 32 | 5 wks |

See also Adge Cutler and the Wurzels.

Bill WYMAN *UK, male vocalist/instrumentalist – bass*   *7 wks*

| 8 Jun 74 | **MONKEY GRIP** *Rolling Stones COC 59102* | 39 | 1 wk |
| 10 Apr 82 | **BILL WYMAN** *A & M AMLH 68540* | 55 | 6 wks |

Tammy WYNETTE *US, female vocalist*   *49 wks*

17 May 75	● **THE BEST OF TAMMY WYNETTE** *Epic EPC 63578*	4	23 wks
21 Jun 75	**STAND BY YOUR MAN** *Epic EPC 69141*	13	7 wks
17 Dec 77	**20 COUNTRY CLASSICS** *CBS PR 5040*	3	11 wks
4 Feb 78	**COUNTRY GIRL MEETS COUNTRY BOY** *Warwick PR 5039*	43	3 wks
6 Jun 87	**ANNIVERSARY – 20 YEARS OF HITS** *Epic 450 393–1*	45	5 wks

X

X MAL DEUTSCHLAND
UK/Germany, male/female vocal/instrumental group   *1 wk*

| 7 Jul 84 | **TOCSIN** *4AD CAD 407* | 86 | 1 wk |

X-RAY SPEX
UK, male/female vocal/instrumental group   *14 wks*

| 9 Dec 78 | **GERM FREE ADOLESCENTS** *EMI International INS 3023* | 30 | 14 wks |

XTC *UK, male vocal/instrumental group*   *42 wks*

11 Feb 78	**WHITE MUSIC** *Virgin V 2095*	38	4 wks
28 Oct 78	**GO 2** *Virgin V 2108*	21	3 wks
1 Sep 79	**DRUMS AND WIRES** *Virgin V 2129*	34	7 wks
20 Sep 80	**BLACK SEA** *Virgin V 2173*	16	7 wks
20 Feb 82	● **ENGLISH SETTLEMENT** *Virgin V 2223*	5	11 wks
13 Nov 82	**WAXWORKS – SOME SINGLES (1977–82)** *Virgin V 2251*	54	3 wks
10 Sep 83	**MUMMER** *Virgin V 2264*	51	4 wks
27 Oct 84	**THE BIG EXPRESS** *Virgin V 2325*	38	2 wks
8 Nov 86	**SKYLARKING** *Virgin V 2399*	90	1 wk

Y

YARDBIRDS *UK, male vocal/instrumental group* — *8 wks*

23 Jul 66	YARDBIRDS *Columbia SX 6063*	20	8 wks

YAZOO *UK, female/male vocal/instrumental duo* — *83 wks*

4 Sep 82	● UPSTAIRS AT ERIC'S *Mute STUMM 7*	2	63 wks
16 Jul 83	★ YOU AND ME BOTH *Mute STUMM 12*	1	20 wks

YELLO *Switzerland, male vocal/instrumental duo* — *6 wks*

21 May 83	YOU GOTTA SAY YES TO ANOTHER EXCESS *Stiff SEEZ 48*	65	2 wks
6 Apr 85	STELLA *Elektra EKT 1*	92	1 wk
4 Jul 87	ONE SECOND *Mercury MERH 100*	48	3 wks

Bryn YEMM *UK, male vocalist* — *14 wks*

9 Jun 84	HOW DO I LOVE THEE *Lifestyle LEG 17*	57	2 wks
7 Jul 84	HOW GREAT THOU ART *Lifestyle LEG 15*	67	8 wks
22 Dec 84	THE BRYN YEMM CHRISTMAS COLLECTION *Bay BAY 104*	95	2 wks
26 Oct 85	MY TRIBUTE – BRYN YEMM INSPIRATIONAL ALBUM *Word WSTR 9665*	85	2 wks

My Tribute . . . also credits the Gwent Chorale.

YES *UK, male vocal/instrumental group* — *200 wks*

1 Aug 70	TIME AND A WORD *Atlantic 2400–006*	45	3 wks
3 Apr 71	● THE YES ALBUM *Atlantic 2400–101*	7	29 wks
4 Dec 71	● FRAGILE *Atlantic 2409–019*	7	17 wks
23 Sep 72	● CLOSE TO THE EDGE *Atlantic K 50012*	4	13 wks
26 May 73	● YESSONGS *Atlantic K 60045*	7	13 wks
22 Dec 73	★ TALES FROM TOPOGRAPHIC OCEANS *Atlantic K 80001*	1	15 wks
21 Dec 74	● RELAYER *Atlantic K 50096*	4	11 wks
29 Mar 75	YESTERDAYS *Atlantic K 50048*	27	7 wks
30 Jul 77	★ GOING FOR THE ONE *Atlantic K 50379*	1	28 wks
7 Oct 78	● TORMATO *Atlantic K 50518*	8	11 wks
30 Aug 80	● DRAMA *Atlantic K 50736*	2	8 wks
10 Jan 81	YESSHOWS *Atlantic K 60142*	22	9 wks
26 Nov 83	90125 *Atco 790125*	16	28 wks
29 Mar 86	9012 LIVE: THE SOLOS *Atco 790 474–1*	44	3 wks
10 Oct 87	BIG GENERATOR *Atco WEX 70*	17	5 wks

Dwight YOAKAM *US, male vocalist/instrumentalist* — *3 wks*

9 May 87	HILLBILLY DELUXE *Reprise WX 106*	51	3 wks

Faron YOUNG *US, male vocalist* — *5 wks*

28 Oct 72	IT'S FOUR IN THE MORNING *Mercury 6338 095*	27	5 wks

Neil YOUNG *Canada, male vocalist* — *159 wks*

31 Oct 70	● AFTER THE GOLDRUSH *Reprise RSLP 6383*	7	68 wks
4 Mar 72	★ HARVEST *Reprise K 54005*	1	33 wks
27 Oct 73	TIME FADES AWAY *Warner Bros. K 54010*	20	2 wks
10 Aug 74	ON THE BEACH *Reprise K 54014*	42	2 wks
5 Jul 75	TONIGHT'S THE NIGHT *Reprise K 54040*	48	1 wk
27 Dec 75	ZUMA *Reprise K 54057*	44	2 wks
9 Jul 77	AMERICAN STARS'N' BARS *Reprise K 54088* ...	17	8 wks
17 Dec 77	DECADE *Reprise K 64037*	46	4 wks
28 Oct 78	COMES A TIME *Reprise K 54099*	42	3 wks
14 Jul 79	RUST NEVER SLEEPS *Reprise K 54105*	13	13 wks
1 Dec 79	LIVE RUST *Reprise K 64041*	55	3 wks
15 Nov 80	HAWKS AND DOVES *Reprise K 54109*	34	3 wks
14 Nov 81	RE-AC-TOR *Reprise K 54116*	69	3 wks
5 Feb 83	TRANS *Geffen GEF 25019*	29	5 wks
3 Sep 83	EVERYBODY'S ROCKIN' *Geffen GEF 25590* ...	50	3 wks
14 Sep 85	OLD WAYS *Geffen GEF 26377*	39	3 wks
2 Aug 86	LANDING ON WATER *Geffen 924 109–1*	52	2 wks
4 Jul 87	LIFE *Geffen WX 109*	71	1 wk

Rust Never Sleeps, Live Rust, Re-ac-tor and Life credited to Neil Young and Crazy Horse. Everybody's Rockin' credited to Neil Young and the Shocking Pinks. See also Stills-Young Band; Crosby, Stills, Nash and Young.

Paul YOUNG *UK, male vocalist* — *185 wks*

30 Jul 83	★ NO PARLEZ *CBS 25521*	1	119 wks
6 Apr 85	★ THE SECRET OF ASSOCIATION *CBS 26234* ...	1	49 wks
1 Nov 86	● BETWEEN TWO FIRES *CBS 450 150–1*	4	17 wks

Y&T *US, male vocal/instrumental group* — *15 wks*

11 Sep 82	BLACK TIGER *A&M AMLH 64910*	53	8 wks
10 Sep 83	MEAN STREAK *A&M AMLX 64960*	35	4 wks
18 Aug 84	IN ROCK WE TRUST *A&M AMLX 65007*	33	3 wks

Z

Frank ZAPPA *US, male vocalist/multi-instrumentalist* — *53 wks*

28 Feb 70	● HOT RATS *Reprise RSLP 6356*	9	27 wks
19 Dec 70	CHUNGA'S REVENGE *Reprise RSLP 2030*	43	1 wk
6 May 78	ZAPPA IN NEW YORK *Discreet K 69204*	55	1 wk
10 Mar 79	SHEIK YERBOUTI *CBS 88339*	32	7 wks
13 Oct 79	JOE'S GARAGE ACT 1 *CBS 86101*	62	3 wks
19 Jan 80	JOE'S GARAGE ACTS 2 & 3 *CBS 88475*	75	1 wk
16 May 81	TINSEL TOWN REBELLION *CBS 88516*	55	4 wks
24 Oct 81	YOU ARE WHAT YOU IS *CBS 88560*	51	2 wks
19 Jun 82	SHIP ARRIVING TOO LATE TO SAVE A DROWNING WITCH *CBS 85804*	61	4 wks
18 Jun 83	THE MAN FROM UTOPIA *CBS 25251*	87	1 wk
27 Oct 84	THEM OR US *EMI FZD 1*	53	2 wks

See also Mothers of Invention.

Lena ZAVARONI *UK, female vocalist* — *5 wks*

23 Mar 74	● MA *Philips 6308 201*	8	5 wks

Z.Z. TOP *US, male vocal/instrumental group* — *178 wks*

12 Jul 75	FANDANGO *London SHU 8482*	60	1 wk
8 Aug 81	EL LOCO *Warner Bros. K 56929*	88	2 wks
30 Apr 83	● ELIMINATOR *Warner Bros. W 3774*	3	135 wks
9 Nov 85	● AFTERBURNER *Warner Bros. WX 27*	2	40 wks

Vince Clarke and Alison Moyet of YAZOO pose on a rock in New York's Central Park.

Lead singer Jon Anderson (centre) seems to be enjoying the instrumental virtuosity of YES.

LENA ZAVARONI enjoyed the life of a child star in 1974.

Despite a mid-eighties surge by Lionel Richie, STEVIE WONDER is still the most successful Motown male album artist.

ANONYMOUS COVER VERSIONS

Date	Title	Catalogue	Pos	Weeks
29 Feb 64	BEATLEMANIA	Top Six TSL 1	19	1 wk
7 Aug 71	HOT HITS 5	MFP 5208	48	1 wk
7 Aug 71 ★	HOT HITS 6	MFP 5214	1	7 wks
7 Aug 71	TOP OF THE POPS VOL. 17	Hallmark SHM 740	16	3 wks
7 Aug 71 ★	TOP OF THE POPS VOL. 18	Hallmark SHM 745	1	12 wks
7 Aug 71	MILLION SELLER HITS	MFP 5203	46	2 wks
21 Aug 71	SMASH HIT SUPREMES STYLE	MFP 5184	36	3 wks
2 Oct 71 ●	TOP OF THE POPS VOL. 19	Hallmark SHM 750	3	9 wks
23 Oct 71 ●	HOT HITS 7	MFP 5236	3	9 wks
6 Nov 71	SMASH HITS COUNTRY STYLE	MFP 5228	38	1 wk
13 Nov 71 ★	TOP OF THE POPS VOL. 20	Hallmark SHM 739	1	8 wks
27 Nov 71	NON STOP 20 VOL. 4	Plexium PXMS 1006	35	2 wks
4 Dec 71	SMASH HITS 71	MFP 5229	21	3 wks
11 Dec 71 ●	HOT HITS 8	MFP 5243	2	4 wks
27 Sep 75	40 SINGALONG PUB SONGS	K-Tel NE 509	21	7 wks
6 Nov 76	FORTY MANIA	Ronco RDT 2018	21	6 wks

COMPILATIONS

Arcade

Date	Title	Catalogue	Pos	Weeks
29 Jul 72 ★	20 FANTASTIC HITS	Arcade 2891 001	1	24 wks
29 Nov 72 ●	20 FANTASTIC HITS VOL. 2	Arcade 2891 002	2	14 wks
7 Apr 73 ●	40 FANTASTIC HITS FROM THE 50'S AND 60'S	Arcade ADEP 3/4	2	15 wks
26 May 73	20 FANTASTIC HITS VOL. 3	Arcade ADEP 5	3	8 wks
15 Nov 75 ●	DISCO HITS '75	Arcade ADEP 18	5	11 wks
26 Mar 77	ROCK ON	Arcade ADEP 27	16	10 wks
2 Jun 77	RULE BRITANNIA	Arcade ADEP 29	56	1 wk
23 Feb 80	FIRST LOVE	Arcade ADEP 41	58	2 wks

Atlantic

Date	Title	Catalogue	Pos	Weeks
2 Apr 66	SOLID GOLD SOUL	Atlantic ATL 5048	12	27 wks
5 Nov 66	MIDNIGHT SOUL	Atlantic 587–021	22	19 wks
14 Jun 69	THIS IS SOUL	Atlantic 643–301	16	15 wks
25 Mar 72	THE NEW AGE OF ATLANTIC	Atlantic K 20024	25	1 wk
22 Jun 74	ATLANTIC BLACK GOLD	Atlantic K 40550	23	7 wks
3 Apr 76	BY INVITATION ONLY	Atlantic K 60112	17	6 wks
11 Apr 81	CONCERTS FOR THE PEOPLE OF KAMPUCHEA	Atlantic K 60153	39	2 wks
2 Feb 85	THIS IS SOUL	Atlantic SOUL 1	78	7 wks
6 Jun 87 ●	ATLANTIC SOUL CLASSICS	Atlantic WX 105	9	23 wks

CBS

Date	Title	Catalogue	Pos	Weeks
20 May 67	THRILL TO THE SENSATIONAL SOUNDS OF SUPER STEREO	CBS PR 5	20	30 wks
28 Jun 69	THE ROCK MACHINE TURNS YOU ON	CBS SPR 22	18	7 wks
28 Jun 69	ROCK MACHINE I LOVE YOU	CBS SPR 26	15	5 wks
20 May 72 ●	THE MUSIC PEOPLE	CBS 66315	10	9 wks
21 Oct 78 ●	SATIN CITY	CBS 10010	10	11 wks
2 Jun 79	THIS IS IT	CBS 10014	6	12 wks
19 Apr 80	FIRST LADIES OF COUNTRY	CBS 10018	37	6 wks
21 Jun 80	KILLER WATTS	CBS KW1	27	6 wks
4 Apr 81	BITTER SUITE	CBS 22082	55	3 wks
16 Oct 82 ●	REFLECTIONS	CBS 10034	4	91 wks
22 Oct 83	IMAGINATIONS	CBS 10044	15	21 wks
20 Apr 85	CLUB CLASSICS VOLUME 2	CBS VAULT 2	90	2 wks
14 Mar 87 ●	MOVE CLOSER	CBS MOOD 1	4	19 wks
27 Jun 87	THE HOLIDAY ALBUM	CBS MOOD 2	13	9 wks

Decca

Date	Title	Catalogue	Pos	Weeks
8 Feb 64	READY STEADY GO	Decca LK 4577	20	1 wk
16 May 64	OUT CAME THE BLUES	Ace Of Hearts AH 72	19	1 wk
28 Jun 69	THE WORLD OF BLUES POWER	Decca SPA 14	24	6 wks
5 Jul 69	THE WORLD OF BRASS BANDS	Decca SPA 20	13	11 wks
6 Sep 69 ●	THE WORLD OF HITS	Decca SPA 35	7	5 wks
20 Sep 69	THE WORLD OF PROGRESSIVE MUSIC (WOWIE ZOWIE)	Decca SPA 34	17	2 wks
20 Sep 69	THE WORLD OF PHASE 4 STEREO	Decca SPA 32	29	2 wks
7 Aug 71 ●	THE WORLD OF YOUR 100 BEST TUNES	Decca SPA 112	10	22 wks
9 Oct 71 ●	THE WORLD OF YOUR 100 BEST TUNES VOL. 2	Decca SPA 155	9	13 wks
27 Sep 75	THE WORLD OF YOUR 100 BEST TUNES VOL. 10	Decca SPA 400	41	4 wks
13 Dec 75	THE TOP 25 FROM YOUR 100 BEST TUNES	Decca HBT 1112	21	5 wks
26 Nov 83 ●	FORMULA 30	Decca PROLP 4	6	17 wks

EMI

Date	Title	Catalogue	Pos	Weeks
21 Jun 69	IMPACT	EMI STWO 2	15	14 wks
2 Jun 73 ★	PURE GOLD	EMI EMK 251	1	11 wks
18 Nov 78 ★	DON'T WALK BOOGIE	EMI EMTV 13	1	23 wks
21 Apr 79 ●	COUNTRY LIFE	EMI EMTV 16	2	14 wks
2 Jun 79	KNUCKLE SANDWICH	EMI International EMYV 18	19	6 wks
15 Dec 79	ALL ABOARD	EMI EMTX 101	13	8 wks
23 Feb 80	METAL FOR MUTHAS	EMI EMC 3318	16	7 wks
14 Jun 80	METAL FOR MUTHAS VOL. 2	EMI EMC 3337	58	1 wk
13 Mar 82	20 WITH A BULLET	EMI EMTV 32	11	8 wks
26 May 84 ●	THEN CAME ROCK 'N' ROLL	EMI THEN 1	5	15 wks

EMI/Virgin – see also Now!

Date	Title	Catalogue	Pos	Weeks
13 Jul 85	KERRANG! KOMPILATION	EMI/Virgin KER 1	84	2 wks

Epic

Date	Title	Catalogue	Pos	Weeks
2 Jul 83	DANCE MIX - DANCE HITS VOL. 1	Epic EPC 25564	85	2 wks
24 Sep 83	DANCE MIX - DANCE HITS VOL. 2	Epic DM 2	51	3 wks
3 Mar 84	DANCE MIX - DANCE HITS VOL. 3	Epic DM 3	70	1 wk
3 Mar 84	ELECTRO SHOCK VOLTAGE	Epic VOLT 1	73	1 wk
16 Jun 84 ●	AMERICAN HEARTBEAT	Epic EPC 10045	4	22 wks
16 Jun 84	DANCE MIX - DANCE HITS VOLUME 4	Epic DM 4	99	1 wk
8 Mar 86 ●	HITS FOR LOVERS	Epic EPC 10050	2	14 wks

Hits

Date	Title	Catalogue	Pos	Weeks
1 Dec 84 ★	THE HITS ALBUM	CBS/WEA HITS 1	1	36 wks
13 Apr 85 ★	HITS 2	CBS/WEA HITS 2	1	21 wks
7 Dec 85 ★	HITS 3	CBS/WEA HITS 3	2	21 wks
29 Mar 86 ★	HITS 4	CBS/WEA/RCA/Arista HITS 4	1	21 wks
22 Nov 86 ★	HITS 5	CBS/WEA/RCA/Arista HITS 5	1	25 wks
25 Jul 87 ★	HITS 6	CBS/WEA/BMG HITS 6	1	19 wks
5 Dec 87 ●	HITS 7	CBS/WEA/RCA/Arista HITS 7	2†	4 wks

Impression

Date	Title	Pos	Weeks
16 Oct 82	**BEST FRIENDS** *Impression LP IMP 1*	28	21 wks
3 Sep 83	**SUNNY AFTERNOON** *Impression LP IMP 2*	13	8 wks
26 Nov 83	**PRECIOUS MOMENTS** *Impression LP IMP 3*	77	5 wks
7 Apr 84	**ALWAYS AND FOREVER – THE COLLECTION** *Impression LP IMP 4*	24	12 wks
21 Jul 84	**WIPEOUT – 20 INSTRUMENTAL GREATS** *Impression LP IMP 5*	37	3 wks
28 Jul 84	**SUNNY AFTERNOON VOLUME TWO** *Impression LP IMP 7*	90	1 wk
22 Dec 84	**FRIENDS AGAIN** *Impression LP IMP 8*	91	1 wk

Island

Date	Title	Pos	Weeks
26 Aug 67	**CLUB SKA '67** *Island ILP 956*	37	19 wks
14 Jun 69	**YOU CAN ALL JOIN IN** *Island IWPS 2*	18	10 wks
29 Mar 80	**CLUB SKA '67 (re-issue)** *Island IRSP 4*	53	4 wks
16 Jun 84	**CREW CUTS** *Island IMA 11*	71	4 wks
27 Oct 84	**CREW CUTS – LESSON 2** *Island IMA 14*	95	2 wks
18 Jul 87	● **THE ISLAND STORY** *Island ISL 25*	9	10 wks

K-Tel

Date	Title	Pos	Weeks
10 Jun 72	★ **20 DYNAMIC HITS** *K-Tel TE 292*	1	28 wks
7 Oct 72	★ **20 ALL TIME HITS OF THE 50'S** *K-Tel NE 490*	1	22 wks
29 Nov 72	● **25 DYNAMIC HITS VOL. 2** *K-Tel TE 291*	2	12 wks
2 Dec 72	★ **25 ROCKIN' & ROLLIN' GREATS** *K-Tel NE 493*	1	18 wks
31 Mar 73	★ **20 FLASHBACK GREATS OF THE SIXTIES** *K-Tel NE 494*	1	11 wks
21 Apr 73	● **BELIEVE IN MUSIC** *K-Tel TE 294*	2	8 wks
8 Nov 75	**GOOFY GREATS** *K-Tel NE 707*	19	7 wks
13 Dec 75	● **40 SUPER GREATS** *K-Tel NE 708*	9	8 wks
31 Jan 76	● **MUSIC EXPRESS** *K-Tel TE 702*	3	10 wks
10 Apr 76	● **JUKE BOX JIVE** *K-Tel NE 709*	3	13 wks
17 Apr 76	**GREAT ITALIAN LOVE SONGS** *K-Tel NE 303*	17	14 wks
15 May 76	● **HIT MACHINE** *K-Tel TE 713*	4	10 wks
5 Jun 76	**EUROVISION FAVOURITES** *K-Tel NE 712*	44	1 wk
2 Oct 76	**SUMMER CRUISING** *K-Tel NE 918*	30	1 wk
16 Oct 76	● **COUNTRY COMFORT** *K-Tel NE 294*	8	12 wks
16 Oct 76	★ **SOUL MOTION** *K-Tel NE 930*	1	14 wks
4 Dec 76	● **DISCO ROCKET** *K-Tel NE 948*	3	14 wks
11 Dec 76	**44 SUPERSTARS** *K-Tel NE 939*	14	10 wks
12 Feb 77	● **HEARTBREAKERS** *K-Tel NE 954*	2	18 wks
19 Feb 77	● **DANCE TO THE MUSIC** *K-Tel NE 957*	5	9 wks
7 May 77	**HIT ACTION** *K-Tel NE 993*	15	9 wks
29 Oct 77	**SOUL CITY** *K-Tel NE 1003*	12	7 wks
12 Nov 77	● **FEELINGS** *K-Tel NE 1006*	3	24 wks
26 Nov 77	★ **DISCO FEVER** *K-Tel NE 1014*	1	20 wks
21 Jan 78	**40 NUMBER ONE HITS** *K-Tel NE 1008*	15	7 wks
4 Mar 78	● **DISCO STARS** *K-Tel NE 1022*	6	8 wks
10 Jun 78	● **DISCO DOUBLE** *K-Tel NE 1024*	10	6 wks
8 Jul 78	**ROCK RULES** *K-Tel RL 001*	12	11 wks
8 Jul 78	**THE WORLD'S WORST RECORD SHOW** *Yuk/K-Tel NE 1023*	47	2 wks
19 Aug 78	● **STAR PARTY** *K-Tel NE 1034*	4	9 wks
4 Nov 78	● **EMOTIONS** *K-Tel NE 1035*	2	17 wks
25 Nov 78	● **MIDNIGHT HUSTLE** *K-Tel NE 1037*	2	13 wks
20 Jan 79	● **ACTION REPLAY** *K-Tel NE 1040*	1	14 wks
7 Apr 79	**DISCO INFERNO** *K-Tel NE 1043*	11	9 wks
5 May 79	**HI ENERGY** *K-Tel NE 1044*	17	7 wks
22 Sep 79	**HOT TRACKS** *K-Tel NE 1049*	31	4 wks
24 Nov 79	● **NIGHT MOVES** *K-Tel NE 1065*	10	10 wks
24 Nov 79	**TOGETHER** *K-Tel NE 1053*	35	8 wks
12 Jan 80	● **VIDEO STARS** *K-Tel NE 1066*	5	10 wks
26 Jan 80	**THE SUMMIT** *K-Tel NE 1067*	17	5 wks
29 Mar 80	**STAR TRACKS** *K-Tel NE 1070*	6	8 wks
26 Apr 80	**GOOD MORNING AMERICA** *K-Tel NE 1072*	15	12 wks
17 May 80	**HAPPY DAYS** *K-Tel ONE 1076*	32	6 wks
17 May 80	● **MAGIC REGGAE** *K-Tel NE 1074*	9	17 wks
14 Jun 80	**HOT WAX** *K-Tel NE 1082*	3	10 wks
27 Sep 80	● **MOUNTING EXCITEMENT** *K-Tel NE 1091*	2	8 wks
11 Oct 80	● **THE LOVE ALBUM** *K-Tel NE 1062*	6	16 wks
25 Oct 80	**AXE ATTACK** *K-Tel NE 1100*	15	14 wks
15 Nov 80	● **CHART EXPLOSION** *K-Tel NE 1103*	6	17 wks
3 Jan 81	**NIGHTLIFE** *K-Tel NE 1107*	25	9 wks
14 Feb 81	**HIT MACHINE** *K-Tel NE 1113*	17	6 wks
21 Mar 81	**RHYTHM 'N' REGGAE** *K-Tel NE 1115*	42	4 wks
25 Apr 81	● **CHARTBUSTERS 81** *K-Tel NE 1118*	3	9 wks
2 May 81	**AXE ATTACK 2** *K-Tel NE 1120*	31	6 wks
23 May 81	**THEMES** *K-Tel NE 1122*	6	15 wks
29 Aug 81	**CALIFORNIA DREAMING** *K-Tel NE 1126*	27	11 wks
19 Sep 81	**DANCE DANCE DANCE** *K-Tel NE 1143*	29	4 wks
3 Oct 81	**THE PLATINUM ALBUM** *K-Tel NE 1134*	32	11 wks
10 Oct 81	**LOVE IS...** *K-Tel NE 1129*	10	15 wks
21 Nov 81	★ **CHART HITS 81** *K-Tel NE 1142*	1	17 wks
9 Jan 82	● **MODERN DANCE** *K-Tel NE 1156*	6	10 wks
6 Feb 82	● **DREAMING** *K-Tel NE 1159*	2	12 wks
6 Mar 82	● **ACTION TRAX** *K-Tel NE 1162*	2	12 wks
1 May 82	**MIDNIGHT HOUR** *K-Tel NE 1157*	98	1 wk
3 Jul 82	**TURBO TRAX** *K-Tel NE 1176*	17	7 wks
4 Sep 82	**THE NO 1 SOUNDS OF THE SEVENTIES** *K-Tel NE 1172*	83	1 wk
11 Sep 82	● **CHARTBEAT/CHARTHEAT** *K-Tel NE 1180*	2	14 wks
30 Oct 82	**THE LOVE SONGS ALBUM** *K-Tel NE 1179*	28	8 wks
6 Nov 82	**CHART HITS '82** *K-Tel NE 1195*	11	17 wks
6 Nov 82	**DISCO DANCER** *K-Tel NE 1190*	26	8 wks
18 Dec 82	**STREETSCENE** *K-Tel NE 1183*	42	6 wks
15 Jan 83	● **VISIONS** *K-Tel ONE 1199*	5	21 wks
12 Feb 83	**HEAVY** *K-Tel NE 1203*	46	12 wks
5 Mar 83	● **HOTLINE** *K-Tel NE 1207*	3	9 wks
11 Jun 83	● **CHART STARS** *K-Tel NE 1225*	7	9 wks
20 Aug 83	**COOL HEAT** *K-Tel NE 1231*	79	3 wks
10 Sep 83	● **HEADLINE HITS** *K-Tel NE 1253*	5	6 wks
8 Oct 83	● **THE TWO OF US** *K-Tel NE 1222*	3	16 wks
8 Oct 83	**IMAGES** *K-Tel NE 1254*	33	6 wks
12 Nov 83	**CHART HITS '83 VOLS 1 AND 2** *K-Tel NE 1256*	6	11 wks
24 Mar 84	**NIGHT MOVES** *K-Tel NE 1255*	15	11 wks
26 May 84	**HUNGRY FOR HITS** *K-Tel NE 1272*	4	11 wks
23 Jun 84	**THE THEMES ALBUM** *K-Tel ONE 1257*	43	3 wks
28 Jul 84	**BREAKDANCE, YOU CAN DO IT** *K-Tel ONE 1276*	18	12 wks
22 Sep 84	● **ALL BY MYSELF** *K-Tel NE 1273*	7	16 wks
1 Dec 84	**HOOKED ON NUMBER ONES – 100 NON-STOP HITS** *K-Tel ONE 1285*	25	15 wks
2 Feb 85	**FOUR STAR COUNTRY** *K-Tel NE 1278*	52	6 wks
2 Mar 85	**MODERN LOVE** *K-Tel NE 1286*	13	7 wks
5 Oct 85	**EXPRESSIONS** *K-Tel NE 1307*	11	8 wks
9 Nov 85	**ROCK ANTHEMS** *K-Tel NE 1309*	10	11 wks
9 Nov 85	**OVATION – THE BEST OF ANDREW LLOYD WEBBER** *K-Tel ONE 1311*	34	12 wks
12 Apr 86	● **HEART TO HEART** *K-Tel NE 1318*	8	15 wks
19 Apr 86	**ROCK ANTHEMS – VOLUME TWO** *K-Tel NE 1319*	43	9 wks
5 Jul 86	**RAP IT UP – RAP'S GREATEST HITS** *K-Tel NE 1324*	50	4 wks
19 Jul 86	**DRIVE TIME USA** *K-Tel NE 1321*	20	8 wks
18 Oct 86	**DANCE HITS '86** *K-Tel NE 1344*	35	7 wks
1 Nov 86	**TOGETHER** *K-Tel NE 1345*	20	10 wks
7 Feb 87	**IMPRESSIONS** *K-Tel NE 1346*	15	14 wks
21 Mar 87	**RHYTHM OF THE NIGHT** *K-Tel NE 1348*	36	7 wks
21 Mar 87	**HITS REVIVAL** *K-Tel (Holland) KTLP 2351*	63	1 wk
13 Jun 87	● **FRIENDS AND LOVERS** *K-Tel NE 1352*	10	10 wks
27 Jun 87	● **HITS REVIVAL** *K-Tel NE 1363*	10	9 wks
17 Oct 87	**TRUE LOVE** *K-Tel NE 1359*	38	5 wks
31 Oct 87	● **FROM MOTOWN WITH LOVE** *K-Tel NE 1381*	9	9 wks
14 Nov 87	**ALWAYS** *K-Tel NE 1377*	65	4 wks
19 Dec 87	**WOW WHAT A PARTY** *K-Tel NE 1388*	97	2 wks

Now! (EMI/Virgin/Polygram)

Date	Title	Pos	Weeks
10 Dec 83	★ **NOW THAT'S WHAT I CALL MUSIC** *EMI/Virgin NOW 1*	1	50 wks
7 Apr 84	★ **NOW THAT'S WHAT I CALL MUSIC 2** *EMI/Virgin NOW 2*	1	38 wks
11 Aug 84	★ **NOW THAT'S WHAT I CALL MUSIC 3** *EMI/Virgin NOW 3*	1	30 wks
8 Dec 84	● **NOW THAT'S WHAT I CALL MUSIC 4** *EMI/Virgin NOW 4*	2	43 wks
1 Jun 85	● **NOW DANCE** *EMI/Virgin NOD 1*	3	14 wks
17 Aug 85	★ **NOW THAT'S WHAT I CALL MUSIC 5** *EMI/Virgin NOW 5*	1	21 wks
30 Nov 85	★ **NOW – THE CHRISTMAS ALBUM** *EMI/Virgin NOX 1*	1	17 wks
7 Dec 85	★ **NOW THAT'S WHAT I CALL MUSIC 6** *EMI/Virgin NOW 6*	1	39 wks

19 Jul	86	● NOW – THE SUMMER ALBUM		
		EMI/Virgin SUMMER 1	7	9 wks
23 Aug	86	★ NOW THAT'S WHAT I CALL MUSIC 7		
		EMI/Virgin NOW 7	1	21 wks
8 Nov	86	● NOW DANCE '86 *EMI/Virgin NOD 2*	2	13 wks
29 Nov	86	NOW THAT'S WHAT I CALL MUSIC '86		
		EMI/Virgin CD NOW 86	65	4 wks
6 Dec	86	★ NOW THAT'S WHAT I CALL MUSIC 8		
		EMI/Virgin/Polygram NOW 8	1	23 wks
4 Apr	87	★ NOW THAT'S WHAT I CALL MUSIC 9		
		EMI/Virgin/Polygram NOW 9	1	26 wks
3 Oct	87	● NOW! SMASH HITS *EMI/Virgin/Polygram NOSH 1*	7	10 wks
5 Dec	87	★ NOW THAT'S WHAT I CALL MUSIC 10		
		EMI/Virgin/Polygram NOW 10	1†	4 wks

Polydor

10 Dec	66	STEREO MUSICALE SHOWCASE *Polydor 104–450*	26	2 wks
9 Oct	71	THE A–Z OF EASY LISTENING *Polydor 2661–005*	24	4 wks
24 Feb	79	20 OF ANOTHER KIND *Polydor POLS 1006*	45	3 wks
9 Feb	80	CAPTAIN BEAKY AND HIS BAND		
		Polydor 238 3462	28	12 wks
3 May	80	● CHAMPAGNE AND ROSES *Polydor ROSTV 1*	7	14 wks
30 Aug	80	I AM WOMAN *Polydor WOMTV 1*	11	13 wks
11 Oct	80	COUNTRY ROUND UP *Polydor KOWTV 1*	64	3 wks
18 Oct	80	MONSTERS OF ROCK *Polydor 2488 810*	16	5 wks
6 Dec	80	THE HITMAKERS *Polydor HOPTV 1*	45	10 wks
12 Jan	85	BREAKDANCE 2 – ELECTRIC BOOGALOO		
		Polydor POLD 5168	34	20 wks
1 Nov	86	SIMON BATES – OUR TUNE *Polydor PROLP 10*	58	5 wks

Pye

9 May	59	● CURTAIN UP *Pye Nixa BRTH 0059*	4	13 wks
23 Jun	62	HONEY HIT PARADE		
		Pye Golden Guinea GGL 0129	13	7 wks
30 Nov	62	ALL THE HITS BY ALL THE STARS		
		Pye Golden Guinea GGL 0162	19	2 wks
7 Sep	63	HITSVILLE *Pye Golden Guinea GGL 0202*	11	6 wks
14 Sep	63	THE BEST OF RADIO LUXEMBOURG		
		Pye Golden Guinea GGL 0208	14	2 wks
23 Nov	63	HITSVILLE VOL. 2 *Pye Golden Guinea GGL 0233*	20	1 wk
4 Jan	64	THE BLUES VOL. 1 *Pye NPL 28030*	15	3 wks
22 Feb	64	FOLK FESTIVAL OF THE BLUES (LIVE		
		RECORDING) *Pye NPL 28033*	16	4 wks
30 May	64	THE BLUES VOL. 2 *Pye NPL 28035*	16	3 wks
10 Feb	68	STARS OF '68 *Marble Arch MAL 762*	23	3 wks
16 Oct	71	PYE CHARTBUSTERS *Pye PCB 15000*	36	1 wk
18 Dec	71	PYE CHARTBUSTERS VOL. 2 *Pye PCB 15001*	29	3 wks

Ronco

21 Oct	72	● 20 STAR TRACKS *Ronco PP 2001*	2	13 wks
23 Jun	73	★ THAT'LL BE THE DAY *Ronco MR 2002/3*	1	8 wks
8 Nov	75	BLAZING BULLETS *Ronco RTI 2012*	17	8 wks
6 Dec	75	GREATEST HITS OF WALT DISNEY		
		Ronco RTD 2013	11	12 wks
13 Dec	75	A CHRISTMAS GIFT *Ronco P 12430*	39	5 wks
24 Jan	76	STAR TRACKIN' 76 *Ronco RTL 2014*	9	5 wks
8 Jan	77	CLASSICAL GOLD *Ronco RTD 42020*	24	12 wks
16 Jul	77	SUPERGROUPS *Ronco RTL 2023*	57	1 wk
26 Nov	77	BLACK JOY *Ronco RTL 2025*	26	13 wks
18 Mar	78	BOOGIE NIGHTS *Ronco RTL 2027*	5	7 wks
18 Nov	78	BOOGIE FEVER *Ronco RTL 2034*	15	11 wks
9 Jun	79	ROCK LEGENDS *Ronco RTL 2037*	54	3 wks
3 Nov	79	ROCK 'N' ROLLER DISCO *Ronco RTL 2040*	3	11 wks
8 Dec	79	PEACE IN THE VALLEY *Ronco RTL 2043*	6	18 wks
22 Dec	79	MILITARY GOLD *Ronco RTD 42042*	62	3 wks
25 Oct	80	STREET LEVEL *Ronco RTL 2048*	29	5 wks
8 Nov	80	● COUNTRY LEGENDS *Ronco RTL 2050*	9	12 wks
15 Nov	80	RADIOACTIVE *Ronco RTL 2049*	13	9 wks
29 Nov	80	SPACE INVADERS *Ronco RTL 2051*	47	3 wks
6 Dec	80	THE LEGENDARY BIG BANDS *Ronco RTL 2047*	24	6 wks
9 May	81	★ DISCO DAZE AND DISCO NITES		
		Ronco RTL 2056 A/B	1	23 wks
19 Sep	81	● SUPER HITS 1 & 2 *Ronco RTL 2058 A/B*	2	17 wks
24 Oct	81	COUNTRY SUNRISE/COUNTRY SUNSET		
		Ronco RTL 2059 A/B	27	11 wks

14 Nov	81	ROCK HOUSE *Ronco RTL 2061*	44	4 wks
12 Dec	81	MISTY MORNINGS *Ronco RTL 2066*	44	5 wks
12 Dec	81	MEMORIES ARE MADE OF THIS		
		Ronco RTL 2062	84	4 wks
26 Dec	81	● HITS HITS HITS *Ronco RTL 2063*	2	10 wks
24 Apr	82	● DISCO UK & DISCO USA *Ronco RTL 2073*	7	10 wks
15 May	82	● CHARTBUSTERS *Ronco RTL 2074*	3	10 wks
3 Jul	82	● OVERLOAD *Ronco RTL 2074*	10	8 wks
28 Aug	82	SOUL DAZE/SOUL NITES *Ronco RTL 2080*	25	10 wks
11 Sep	82	● BREAKOUT *Ronco RTL 2081*	4	8 wks
30 Oct	82	MUSIC FOR THE SEASONS *Ronco RTL 2075*	41	8 wks
27 Nov	82	CHART WARS *Ronco RTL 2086*	30	7 wks
27 Nov	82	THE GREAT COUNTRY MUSIC SHOW		
		Ronco RTD 2083	38	7 wks
18 Dec	82	THE BEST OF BEETHOVEN/STRAUSS/		
		TCHAIKOWSKY/MOZART (4 LPs)		
		Ronco RTL 2084	49	10 wks
25 Dec	82	★ RAIDERS OF THE POP CHARTS		
		Ronco RTL 2088	1	17 wks
19 Mar	83	● CHART RUNNERS *Ronco RTL 2090*	4	13 wks
21 May	83	● CHART ENCOUNTERS OF THE HIT KIND		
		Ronco RTL 2091	5	10 wks
4 Jun	83	MUSIC FOR THE SEASONS *Ronco RTL 2075*	74	2 wks
18 Jun	83	LOVERS ONLY *Ronco RTL 2093*	12	13 wks
16 Jul	83	HITS ON FIRE *Ronco RTL 2095*	11	10 wks
17 Sep	83	● THE HIT SQUAD – CHART TRACKING		
		Ronco RON LP 1	4	9 wks
17 Sep	83	THE HIT SQUAD – NIGHT CLUBBING		
		Ronco RON LP 2	28	7 wks
12 Nov	83	HIT SQUAD – HITS OF '83 *Ronco RON LP 4*	12	11 wks
17 Dec	83	● GREEN VELVET *Ronco RON LP 6*	6	17 wks
7 Jan	84	CHART TREK VOLS. 1 & 2 *Ronco RON LP 8*	20	9 wks
21 Jan	84	● SOMETIMES WHEN WE TOUCH		
		Ronco RON LP 9	8	14 wks
24 Mar	84	BABY LOVE *Ronco RON LP 11*	47	6 wks
7 Apr	84	DREAMS AND THEMES *Ronco RON LP 10*	75	2 wks

Green Velvet was re-issued on Telstar STAR 2252.

Serious

7 Jun	86	UPFRONT 1 *Serious UPFT 1*	17	10 wks
23 Aug	86	UPFRONT 2 *Serious UPFT 2*	27	6 wks
1 Nov	86	UPFRONT 3 *Serious UPFT 3*	37	5 wks
31 Jan	87	UPFRONT 4 *Serious UPFT 4*	21	5 wks
28 Mar	87	SERIOUS HIP-HOP 2 *Serious SHOP 2*	95	1 wk
28 Mar	87	UPFRONT 5 *Serious UPFT 5*	21	6 wks
23 May	87	UPFRONT 6 *Serious UPFT 6*	22	6 wks
4 Jul	87	BEST OF HOUSE VOLUME 1 *Serious BEHO 1*	55	12 wks
15 Aug	87	UPFRONT 7 *Serious UPFT 7*	31	4 wks
12 Sep	87	BEST OF HOUSE VOLUME 2 *Serious BEHO 2*	30	7 wks
17 Oct	87	HIP HOP '87 *Serious HHOP 87*	81	1 wk
17 Oct	87	UPFRONT 8 *Serious UPFT 8*	22	6 wks
14 Nov	87	BEST OF HOUSE VOLUME 3 *Serious BEHO 3*	61	3 wks
12 Dec	87	BEST OF HOUSE MEGAMIX *Serious BOIT 1*	96	1 wk
19 Dec	87	UPFRONT 9 *Serious UPFT 9*	92	1 wk

Starblend

12 Nov	83	IN TOUCH *Starblend STD 9*	89	2 wks
23 Jun	84	BROKEN DREAMS *Starblend SLTD 1*	48	7 wks
27 Apr	85	12 X 12 MEGA MIXES *Starblend INCH 1*	77	2 wks
3 Aug	85	AMERICAN DREAMS *Starblend SLTD 12*	43	8 wks
21 Dec	85	CHRISTMAS AT THE COUNTRY STORE		
		Starblend NOEL 1	94	1 wk
12 Jul	86	DISCOVER COUNTRY/DISCOVER NEW		
		COUNTRY *Starblend DNC 1*	60	3 wks
16 Aug	86	HEARTBREAKERS *Starblend BLEND 3*	38	8 wks
20 Sep	86	ABSOLUTE ROCK 'N' ROLL *Starblend SLTD 15*	88	1 wk

Street Sounds

19 Feb	83	STREET SOUNDS EDITION 2		
		Street Sounds STSND 002	35	6 wks
23 Apr	83	STREET SOUNDS EDITION 3		
		Street Sounds STSND 003	21	5 wks
25 Jun	83	STREET SOUNDS EDITION 4		
		Street Sounds STSND 004	14	8 wks
13 Aug	83	STREET SOUNDS EDITION 5		
		Street Sounds STSND 005	16	8 wks

Date	Title	Pos	Weeks
8 Oct 83	**STREET SOUNDS EDITION 6** *Street Sounds STSND 006*	23	5 wks
22 Oct 83	**STREET SOUNDS ELECTRO 1** *Street Sounds ELCST 1*	18	8 wks
17 Dec 83	**STREET SOUNDS EDITION 7** *Street Sounds STSND 007*	48	4 wks
7 Jan 84	**STREET SOUNDS ELECTRO 2** *Street Sounds ELCST 2*	49	7 wks
3 Mar 84	**STREET SOUNDS HI-ENERGY** *Street Sounds HINRG 16*	71	1 wk
10 Mar 84	**STREET SOUNDS CRUCIAL ELECTRO** *Street Sounds Electro ELCST 999*	24	10 wks
10 Mar 84	**STREET SOUNDS EDITION 8** *Street Sounds STSND 008*	22	7 wks
7 Apr 84	**STREET SOUNDS ELECTRO 3** *Street Sounds ELCST 3*	25	9 wks
12 May 84	**STREET SOUNDS EDITION 9** *Street Sounds STSND 009*	22	5 wks
9 Jun 84	**STREET SOUNDS ELECTRO 4** *Street Sounds ELCST 4*	25	9 wks
30 Jun 84	**STREET SOUNDS UK ELECTRO** *Street Sounds ELCST 1984*	60	4 wks
21 Jul 84	**LET THE MUSIC SCRATCH** *Street Sounds MKL 1*	91	3 wks
11 Aug 84	**STREET SOUNDS CRUCIAL ELECTRO 2** *Street Sounds ELCST 1000*	35	6 wks
18 Aug 84	**STREET SOUNDS EDITION 10** *Street Sounds STSND 010*	24	6 wks
6 Oct 84	**STREET SOUNDS ELECTRO 5** *Street Sounds Electro ELCST 5*	17	6 wks
10 Nov 84	**STREET SOUNDS EDITION 11** *Street Sounds STSND 011*	48	4 wks
9 Mar 85	**STREET SOUNDS ELECTRO 6** *Street Sounds ELCST 6*	24	10 wks
9 Mar 85	**THE ARTISTS VOLUME 1** *Street Sounds ARTIS 1*	65	4 wks
18 May 85	**STREET SOUNDS ELECTRO 7** *Street Sounds ELCST 7*	12	7 wks
18 May 85	**STREET SOUNDS EDITION 12** *Street Sounds STSND 12*	23	4 wks
13 Jul 85	**STREET SOUNDS ELECTRO 8** *Street Sounds ELCST 8*	23	5 wks
13 Jul 85	**THE ARTISTS VOLUME 2** *Street Sounds ARTIS 2*	45	4 wks
17 Aug 85	**STREET SOUNDS EDITION 13** *Street Sounds STSND 13*	19	9 wks
17 Aug 85	**STREET SOUNDS N.Y. VS. L.A. BEATS** *Street Sounds ELCST 1001*	65	4 wks
5 Oct 85	**STREET SOUNDS ELECTRO 9** *Street Sounds ELCST 9*	18	6 wks
12 Oct 85	**THE ARTISTS VOLUME 3** *Street Sounds ARTIS 3*	87	2 wks
16 Nov 85	**STREET SOUNDS EDITION 14** *Street Sounds STSND 14*	43	3 wks
21 Dec 85	**STREET SOUNDS ELECTRO 10** *Street Sounds ELCST 10*	72	6 wks
21 Dec 85	**STREET SOUNDS EDITION 15** *Street Sounds STSND 15*	58	8 wks
29 Mar 86	**STREET SOUNDS HIP-HOP ELECTRO 11** *Street Sounds ELCST 11*	19	5 wks
5 Apr 86	**STREET SOUNDS EDITION 16** *Street Sounds STSND 16*	17	7 wks
21 Jun 86	**JAZZ JUICE 2** *Street Sounds SOUND 4*	96	1 wk
28 Jun 86	**STREET SOUNDS HIP-HOP ELECTRO 12** *Street Sounds ELCST 12*	28	4 wks
19 Jul 86	**STREET SOUNDS EDITION 17** *Street Sounds STSND 17*	35	5 wks
6 Sep 86	**STREET SOUNDS HIP-HOP ELECTRO 13** *Street Sounds ELCST 13*	23	5 wks
11 Oct 86	**JAZZ JUICE 3** *Street Sounds SOUND 5*	88	1 wk
11 Oct 86	**STREET SOUNDS EDITION 18** *Street Sounds STSND 18*	20	5 wks
11 Oct 86	**STREET SOUNDS HIP-HOP ELECTRO 14** *Street Sounds ELCST 14*	40	3 wks
15 Nov 86	**STREET SOUNDS HIP-HOP ELECTRO 15** *Street Sounds ELCST 15*	46	2 wks
6 Dec 86	**STREET SOUNDS EDITION 19** *Street Sounds STSND 19*	61	3 wks
24 Jan 87	**STREET SOUNDS CRUCIAL ELECTRO 3** *Street Sounds ELCST 1002*	41	3 wks
7 Feb 87	**STREET SOUNDS ANTHEMS – VOLUME 1** *Street Sounds MUSIC 5*	61	3 wks
14 Feb 87	**STREET SOUNDS EDITION 20** *Street Sounds STSND 20*	25	4 wks
13 Jun 87	**STREET SOUNDS HIP-HOP ELECTRO 16** *Street Sounds ELCST 16*	40	3 wks
4 Jul 87	**STREET SOUNDS DANCE MUSIC '87** *Street Sounds STSND 871*	40	5 wks
15 Aug 87	**JAZZ JUICE 5** *Street Sounds SOUND 8*	97	1 wk
15 Aug 87	**STREET SOUNDS HIP-HOP 17** *Street Sounds ELCST 17*	38	3 wks
12 Sep 87	**STREET SOUNDS '87 VOLUME 2** *Street Sounds STSND 872*	47	3 wks
12 Sep 87	**BEST OF WEST COAST HIP-HOP** *Street Sounds MACA 1*	80	2 wks
24 Oct 87	**STREET SOUNDS HIP-HOP 18** *Street Sounds ELCST 18*	67	1 wk

Stylus

Date	Title	Pos	Weeks
3 Aug 85	**THE MAGIC OF TORVILL AND DEAN** *Stylus SMR 8502*	35	9 wks
17 Aug 85	**NIGHT BEACH** *Stylus SMR 8501*	15	8 wks
24 Aug 85	**DISCO BEACH PARTY** *Stylus SMR 8503*	29	10 wks
23 Nov 85	**TELLYHITS – 16 TOP TV THEMES** *Stylus/BBC BBSR 508*	34	6 wks
14 Dec 85	**VELVET WATERS** *Stylus SMR 8507*	54	4 wks
28 Dec 85	**CHOICES OF THE HEART** *Stylus SMR 8511*	87	2 wks
8 Mar 86	● **NIGHT BEAT II** *Stylus SMR 8613*	7	9 wks
17 May 87	**LET'S HEAR IT FROM THE GIRLS** *Stylus SMR 8614*	17	10 wks
5 Jul 86	**TELLY HITS 2** *Stylus/BBC BBSR 616*	68	2 wks
1 Nov 86	**BLACK MAGIC** *Stylus SMR 619*	26	9 wks
8 Nov 86	● **HIT MIX '86** *Stylus SMR 624*	10	14 wks
22 Nov 86	**CLASSICS BY CANDLELIGHT** *Stylus SMR 620*	74	4 wks
14 Mar 87	**BANDS OF GOLD – THE SWINGING SIXTIES** *Stylus SMR 726*	55	6 wks
21 Mar 87	**BANDS OF GOLD – THE SENSATIONAL SEVENTIES** *Stylus SMR 727*	75	4 wks
28 Mar 87	**BANDS OF GOLD – THE ELECTRIC EIGHTIES** *Stylus SMR 728*	82	1 wk
11 Jul 87	● **SIXTIES MIX** *Stylus SMR 733*	3	25 wks
24 Oct 87	**THE HIT FACTORY** *Stylus SMR 740*	18†	10 wks
21 Nov 87	**HIT MIX – HITS OF THE YEAR** *Stylus SMR 744*	29†	6 wks

Tamla Motown

Date	Title	Pos	Weeks
3 Apr 65	**A COLLECTION OF TAMLA MOTOWN HITS** *Tamla Motown TML 11001*	16	4 wks
4 Mar 67	**16 ORIGINAL BIG HITS – VOL. 4** *Tamla Motown TML 11043*	33	3 wks
17 Jun 67	**TAMLA MOTOWN HITS VOL. 5** *Tamla Motown TML 11050*	11	40 wks
21 Oct 67	● **BRITISH MOTOWN CHARTBUSTERS** *Tamla Motown TML 11055*	2	54 wks
10 Feb 68	**MOTOWN MEMORIES** *Tamla Motown TML 11064*	21	13 wks
24 Aug 68	**TAMLA MOTOWN HITS VOL. 6** *Tamla Motown STML 11074*	32	2 wks
30 Nov 68	● **BRITISH MOTOWN CHARTBUSTERS VOL. 2** *Tamla Motown STML 11082*	8	11 wks
25 Oct 69	★ **BRITISH MOTOWN CHARTBUSTERS VOL. 3** *Tamla Motown STML 11121*	1	93 wks
21 Feb 70	**COLLECTION OF BIG HITS VOL. 8** *Tamla Motown STML 11130*	56	1 wk
24 Oct 70	★ **MOTOWN CHARTBUSTERS VOL. 4** *Tamla Motown STML 11162*	1	40 wks
17 Apr 71	★ **MOTOWN CHARTBUSTERS VOL. 5** *Tamla Motown STML 11181*	1	36 wks
23 Oct 71	● **MOTOWN CHARTBUSTERS VOL. 6** *Tamla Motown STML 11191*	2	36 wks
26 Feb 72	**MOTOWN MEMORIES** *Tamla Motown STML 11200*	22	4 wks
18 Mar 72	**MOTOWN STORY** *Tamla Motown TMSP 1130*	21	8 wks
29 Nov 72	● **MOTOWN CHARTBUSTERS VOL. 7** *Tamla Motown STML 11215*	9	16 wks
3 Nov 73	● **MOTOWN CHARTBUSTERS VOL. 8** *Tamla Motown STML 11246*	9	15 wks
26 Oct 74	**MOTOWN CHARTBUSTERS VOL. 9** *Tamla Motown STML 11270*	14	15 wks

1 Nov 75	● MOTOWN GOLD *Tamla Motown STML 12003*	8	35 wks
5 Nov 77	MOTOWN GOLD VOL. 2 *Motown STML 12070*	28	4 wks
7 Oct 78	● BIG WHEELS OF MOTOWN *Motown EMTV 12*	2	18 wks
2 Feb 80	★ THE LAST DANCE *Motown EMTV 20*	1	23 wks
2 Aug 80	THE 20TH ANNIVERSARY ALBUM *Motown TMSP 6010*	53	2 wks

Telstar

16 Oct 82	● CHART ATTACK *Telstar STAR 2221*	7	6 wks
6 Nov 82	MIDNIGHT IN MOTOWN *Telstar STAR 2222*	34	16 wks
18 Dec 82	DIRECT HITS *Telstar STAR 2224*	41	2 wks
8 Jan 83	DANCIN' – 20 ORIGINAL MOTOWN MOVERS *Telstar STAR 2225*	97	1 wk
5 Feb 83	INSTRUMENTAL MAGIC *Telstar STAR 2227*	68	5 wks
30 Apr 83	20 GREAT ITALIAN LOVE SONGS *Telstar STAR 2230*	28	6 wks
4 Jun 83	IN THE GROOVE – THE 12 INCH DISCO PARTY *Telstar STAR 2228*	20	12 wks
12 Nov 83	ROOTS REGGAE/REGGAE ROCK *Telstar STAR 2233*	34	6 wks
19 Nov 83	SUPERCHART '83 *Telstar STAR 2236*	22	9 wks
4 Feb 84	● THE VERY BEST OF MOTOWN LOVE SONGS *Telstar STAR 2239*	10	22 wks
26 May 84	DON'T STOP DANCING *Telstar STAR 2242*	11	12 wks
13 Oct 84	● HITS HITS HITS – 18 SMASH ORIGINALS *Telstar STAR 2243*	6	9 wks
8 Dec 84	LOVE SONGS – 16 CLASSIC LOVE SONGS *Telstar STAR 2246*	22	12 wks
15 Dec 84	● GREEN VELVET (re-issue) *Telstar STAR 2252*	10	10 wks
7 Sep 85	OPEN TOP CARS AND GIRLS IN T-SHIRTS *Telstar STAR 2257*	13	9 wks
16 Nov 85	● THE LOVE ALBUM *Telstar STAR 2268*	7	18 wks
16 Nov 85	★ GREATEST HITS OF 1985 *Telstar STAR 2269*	1	17 wks
30 Nov 85	THE PRINCE'S TRUST COLLECTION *Telstar STAR 2275*	64	5 wks
7 Dec 85	PERFORMANCE – THE VERY BEST OF TIM RICE AND ANDREW LLOYD WEBBER *Telstar STAR 2262*	33	7 wks
7 Dec 85	MORE GREEN VELVET *Telstar STAR 2267*	42	5 wks
18 Oct 86	● THE CHART *Telstar STAR 2278*	6	12 wks
1 Nov 86	ROCK LEGENDS *Telstar STAR 2290*	54	7 wks
8 Nov 86	LOVERS *Telstar STAR 2279*	14	16 wks
8 Nov 86	● THE GREATEST HITS OF 1986 *Telstar STAR 2286*	8	13 wks
22 Nov 86	SIXTIES MANIA *Telstar STAR 2287*	19	22 wks
6 Dec 86	MOTOWN CHARTBUSTERS *Telstar STAR 2283*	25	12 wks
28 Mar 87	THE DANCE CHART *Telstar STAR 2285*	23	8 wks
3 Oct 87	TRACKS OF MY TEARS *Telstar STAR 2295*	27	7 wks
21 Nov 87	GREATEST HITS OF 1987 *Telstar STAR 2309*	12†	6 wks
28 Nov 87	ALWAYS AND FOREVER *Telstar STAR 2301*	41†	5 wks
28 Nov 87	DANCE MIX '87 *Telstar STAR 2314*	39†	5 wks
28 Nov 87	SIXTIES PARTY MEGAMIX ALBUM *Telstar STAR 2307*	46†	5 wks
26 Dec 87	THE GREATEST LOVE *Telstar STAR 2316*	44†	1 wk
26 Dec 87	LIFE IN THE FAST LANE *Telstar STAR 2315*	73†	1 wk

Green Velvet was a re-issue of Ronco RON LP4.

Towerbell

28 Sep 85	THE TV HITS ALBUM *Towerbell TVLP 3*	26	13 wks
8 Feb 86	● THE DANCE HITS ALBUM *Towerbell TVLP 8* ...	10	11 wks
15 Mar 86	THE CINEMA HITS ALBUM *Towerbell TVLP 9* ..	44	9 wks
12 Apr 86	THE TV HITS ALBUM TWO *Towerbell TVLP 10* ..	19	7 wks
17 May 86	SISTERS ARE DOIN' IT *Towerbell TVLP 11*	27	9 wks
7 Jun 86	TWO'S COMPANY *Towerbell TVLP 12*	51	5 wks
28 Jun 86	DANCE HITS II *Towerbell TVLP 13*	25	8 wks
2 Aug 86	THE ORIGINALS *Towerbell TVDLP 14*	15	3 wks
9 Aug 86	YOU'VE GOT TO LAUGH *Towerbell TVLP 15*	51	3 wks

Warwick

29 Nov 75	ALL-TIME PARTY HITS *Warwick WW 5001*	21	8 wks
17 Apr 76	● INSTRUMENTAL GOLD *Warwick WW 5012*	3	24 wks
29 May 76	HAMILTON'S HOT SHOTS *Warwick WW 5014* ..	15	5 wks
8 Jan 77	SONGS OF PRAISE *Warwick WW 5020*	31	2 wks
29 Jan 77	HIT SCENE *Warwick PR 5023*	19	5 wks
11 Mar 78	● FONZIE'S FAVOURITES *Warwick WW 5037*	8	16 wks
25 Nov 78	LOVE SONGS *Warwick WW 5046*	47	7 wks

2 Dec 78	BLACK VELVET *Warwick WW 5047*	72	3 wks
31 Mar 79	LEMON POPSICLE *Warwick WW 5050*	42	6 wks
7 Apr 79	COUNTRY PORTRAITS *Warwick WW 5057*	14	10 wks
10 Nov 79	20 SMASH DISCO HITS (THE BITCH) *Warwick WW 5061*	42	5 wks
16 Feb 80	COUNTRY GUITAR *Warwick WW 5070*	46	3 wks
14 Nov 81	DISCO EROTICA *Warwick WW 5108*	35	8 wks
10 Apr 82	PS I LOVE YOU *Warwick WW 5121*	68	3 wks
6 Nov 82	HITS OF THE SCREAMING 60'S *Warwick WW 5124*	24	10 wks
22 Dec 84	MERRY CHRISTMAS TO YOU *Warwick WW 5141*	64	2 wks

Other Compilation Albums

10 Mar 62	GREAT MOTION PICTURE THEMES *HMV CLP 1508*	19	1 wk
9 Mar 63	● ALL STAR FESTIVAL *Philips DL 99500*	4	19 wks
24 Aug 63	THE MERSEY BEAT VOL. 1 *Oriole PS 40047*	17	5 wks
11 Sep 66	STARS CHARITY FANTASIA SAVE THE CHILDREN FUND *SCF PL 145*	6	16 wks
8 Apr 67	● HIT THE ROAD STAX *Stax 589–005*	10	16 wks
21 Oct 67	BREAKTHROUGH *Studio Two STWO 1*	2	11 wks
11 May 68	BLUES ANYTIME *Immediate IMLP 014*	40	1 wk
7 Aug 71	TIGHTEN UP VOL. 4 *Trojan TBL 163*	20	7 wks
21 Aug 71	CLUB REGGAE *Trojan TBL 159*	25	4 wks
4 Sep 71	TOTAL SOUND *Studio Two STWO 4*	39	4 wks
30 Oct 71	STUDIO TWO CLASSICS *Studio Two STWO 6*	16	4 wks
4 Dec 71	BREAKTHROUGH *MFP 1334*	49	1 wk
22 Jan 72	★ CONCERT FOR BANGLADESH (recorded live) *Apple STCX 3385*	1	13 wks
2 Jun 73	20 ORIGINAL CHART HITS *Philips TV 1*	9	11 wks
2 Jun 73	NICE 'N' EASY *Philips 6441 076*	36	1 wk
15 Mar 75	SOLID SOUL SENSATIONS *Disco Diamond DDLP 5001*	30	1 wk
16 Aug 75	NEVER TOO YOUNG TO ROCK *GTO GTLP 004*	30	5 wks
6 Dec 75	SUPERSONIC *Stallion SSM 001*	21	6 wks
31 Jan 76	REGGAE CHARTBUSTERS 75 *Cactus CTLP 114*	53	1 wk
22 May 76	● A TOUCH OF COUNTRY *Topaz TOC 1976*	7	7 wks
3 Jul 76	GOLDEN FIDDLE AWARDS 1976 *Mountain TOPC 5002*	45	2 wks
3 Jul 76	A TOUCH OF CLASS *Topaz TOC 1976*	57	1 wk
27 Nov 76	ALL THIS AND WORLD WAR II *Riva RVLP 2* ..	23	7 wks
16 Jul 77	THE ROXY LONDON WC2 *Harvest SHSP 4069* ..	24	5 wks
6 Aug 77	NEW WAVE *Philips 6300 902*	11	12 wks
11 Mar 78	STIFF'S LIVE STIFFS *Stiff GET 1*	28	7 wks
25 Mar 78	HOPE AND ANCHOR FRONT ROW FESTIVAL *Warner Bros. K 66077*	28	3 wks
17 Jun 78	WHITE MANSIONS *A & M AMLX 64691*	51	3 wks
28 Oct 78	ECSTACY *Lotus WH 5003*	24	6 wks
9 Dec 78	STARS ON SUNDAY BY REQUEST *Curzon Sounds CSL 0081*	65	3 wks
19 May 79	BOOGIE BUS *Polystar 9198 174*	23	11 wks
26 May 79	A MONUMENT TO BRITISH ROCK *Harvest EMTV 17*	13	12 wks
9 Jun 79	THAT SUMMER *Arista SPART 1088*	36	8 wks
21 Jul 79	★ THE BEST DISCO ALBUM IN THE WORLD *Warner Bros. K 58062*	1	17 wks
3 Nov 79	MODS MAYDAY 79 *Arista FOUR 1*	75	1 wk
8 Mar 80	THE WANDERERS *Gem GEMLP 103*	48	7 wks
24 May 80	PRECIOUS METAL *MCA MCF 3069*	60	2 wks
22 Nov 80	CASH COWS *Virgin MILK 1*	49	1 wk
14 Mar 81	SOME BIZZARE ALBUM *Some Bizzare BZLP 1* ..	58	1 wk
4 Apr 81	● ROLL ON *Polystar REDTV 1*	3	13 wks
4 Apr 81	REMIXTURE *Champagne CHAMP 1*	32	5 wks
30 May 81	STRENGTH THROUGH OI *SKIN 1*	51	5 wks
8 Aug 81	ROYAL ROMANCE *Windsor WIN 001*	84	1 wk
17 Oct 81	MONSTER TRACKS *Polystar HOPTV 2*	20	8 wks
31 Oct 81	CARRY ON OI *Secret SEC 2*	60	4 wks
21 Nov 81	SLIP STREAM *Beggars Banquet BEGA 31*	72	3 wks
12 Dec 81	LIVE AND HEAVY *Nems NEL 6020*	100	2 wks
19 Dec 81	WE ARE MOST AMUSED *Ronco/Charisma 2067* ..	30	9 wks
27 Mar 82	● JAMES BOND'S GREATEST HITS *Liberty EMTV 007*	4	13 wks
27 Mar 82	PUNK AND DISORDERLY *Abstract AABT 100* ..	48	8 wks
17 Apr 82	MUSIC OF QUALITY AND DISTINCTION VOL. 1 *Virgin V 2219*	25	4 wks
15 May 82	SEX SWEAT AND BLOOD *Beggars Banquet BEGA 34*	88	1 wk

14 Aug 82	SONETO Rough Trade ROUGH 37	66	3 wks
4 Sep 82	PUNK AND DISORDERLY (FURTHER CHARGES) Anagram GRAM 001	91	2 wks
11 Sep 82	THE BEST OF BRITISH JAZZ FUNK VOL. 2 Beggars Banquet BEGA 41	44	4 wks
25 Sep 82	OI OI THAT'S YER LOT Secret SEC 5	54	4 wks
2 Oct 82	MODERN HEROES TV Records TVA 1	24	7 wks
9 Oct 82	ENDLESS LOVE TV Records TVA 2	26	8 wks
23 Oct 82	STREETPOISE VOL. 1 Epic/Streetware STR 32234	51	4 wks
6 Nov 82	FLASH TRACKS Priority PTVL 1	19	7 wks
25 Dec 82	PARTY FEVER/DISCO MANIA TV Records TVA 5	71	3 wks
14 May 83	THE LAUGHTER AND TEARS COLLECTION WEA LTC 1	19	16 wks
28 May 83	GET ON UP RCA BSLP 5001	35	5 wks
18 Jun 83	TEARDROPS Ritz RITZ SP 399	37	6 wks
2 Jul 83	WIRED FOR CLUBS (CLUB TRACKS VOL. 1) Mercury CLUBL 001	58	4 wks
3 Sep 83	COME WITH CLUB (CLUB TRACKS VOL. 2) Club CLUBL 002	55	2 wks
24 Sep 83	CLASSIC THEMES Nouveau Music NML 1001	61	2 wks
15 Oct 83	LOVE THE REASON Respond RRL 501	50	3 wks
26 Nov 83	THIS ARE TWO TONE Two Tone CHR TT 5007	51	9 wks
26 Nov 83	TWELVE INCHES OF PLEASURE Proto PROTO 1	100	1 wk
2 Jun 84	ESSENTIAL DISCO AND DANCE Nouveau Music NML 1010	96	1 wk
16 Jun 84	EMERALD CLASSICS Stoic SRTV 1	35	14 wks
16 Jun 84	20 REGGAE CLASSICS Trojan TRLS 222	89	1 wk
21 Jul 84	ROCKABILLY PSYCHOS AND THE GARAGE DISEASE Big Beat WIK 18	88	3 wks
11 Aug 84	CHUNKS OF FUN Loose End CHUNK 1	46	5 wks
8 Sep 84	RECORD SHACK PRESENTS – VOLUME 1 Record Shack RSTV 1	41	4 wks
8 Dec 84	THE CHRISTMAS CAROL COLLECTION Fame WHS 413000	75	2 wks
16 Feb 85	STARGAZERS Kasino KTV 1	69	3 wks
30 Mar 85	REGGAE HITS VOLUME 1 Jetstar JETLP 1001	32	11 wks
30 Mar 85	DREAM MELODIES Nouveau Music NML 1013	91	1 wk
6 Apr 85	TOMMY BOY GREATEST BEATS Tommy Boy ILPS 9825	44	6 wks
25 May 85	● OUT NOW! Chrysalis/MCA OUTV 1	2	16 wks
1 Jun 85	MASSIVE Virgin V 2346	61	3 wks
24 Aug 85	20 HOLIDAY HITS Creole CTV 1	48	6 wks
19 Oct 85	IQ6:ZANG TUMB TUUM SAMPLED ZTT IQ6	40	4 wks
26 Oct 85	● OUT NOW! 2 Chrysalis/MCA OUTV 2	3	12 wks
26 Oct 85	REGGAE HITS VOLUME 2 Jetstar JELP 1002	86	2 wks
21 Dec 85	THE CHRISTMAS CAROL COLLECTION Fame WHS 41–3000–1	90	1 wk
22 Mar 86	MASTERS OF METAL Powersaw NE 1295	38	4 wks
22 Mar 86	NUMA RECORDS YEAR ONE Numa NUMA 1004	94	1 wk
14 Jun 86	BEAT RUNS WILD Mercury WILD 1	70	2 wks
21 Jun 86	HEAR 'N' AID Vertigo VERH 35	50	2 wks
16 Aug 86	● THE HEAT IS ON Portrait PRT 10051	9	12 wks
16 Aug 86	SUMMER DAYS, BOOGIE NIGHTS Portrait PRT 10052	40	6 wks
20 Sep 86	THE HOUSE SOUND OF CHICAGO DJ International LONLP 22	54	7 wks
18 Oct 86	THE POWER OF LOVE West Five WEF 4	33	7 wks
1 Nov 86	FORMULA THIRTY 2 Mercury PROLP 9	80	3 wks
8 Nov 86	ULTIMATE TRAX VOLUME 1 Champion CHAMP 103	66	2 wks
17 Jan 87	THE HOUSE SOUND OF CHICAGO London LONLP 22	52	5 wks
7 Mar 87	ULTIMATE TRAX VOLUME 2 Champion CHAMP 1005	50	2 wks
28 Mar 87	HEAT OF SOUL VOLUME 1 Mastersound MASL 001	96	1 wk
18 Apr 87	THE HOUSE SOUND OF CHICAGO VOLUME 2 London LONLP 32	38	7 wks
2 May 87	THE PRINCE'S TRUST TENTH ANNIVERSARY BIRTHDAY PARTY A&M AMA 3906	76	2 wks
30 May 87	THE SOLAR SYSTEM Solar MCG 3338	70	1 wk
6 Jun 87	CHICAGO JACKBEAT VOLUME 2 Rhythm King/Mute LEFTLP 2	67	2 wks
4 Jul 87	DANCE MANIA VOLUME 1 Needle DAMA 1	46	4 wks
11 Jul 87	LONELY IS AN EYESORE 4AD CAD 703	53	2 wks
18 Jul 87	ULTIMATE TRAX 3 – BATTLE OF THE DJs Champion CHAMP 1008	69	2 wks
18 Jul 87	JACK TRAX – THE FIRST ALBUM Jack Trax/Indigo JTRAX 1	83	2 wks
1 Aug 87	FIERCE Cooltempo CTLP 4	37	6 wks
8 Aug 87	KICK IT! – THE DEF JAM SAMPLER VOLUME 1 Def Jam KICKIT 1	19	7 wks
22 Aug 87	THE PRINCE'S TRUST CONCERT 1987 A&M PTA 1987	44	3 wks
5 Sep 87	RARE RCA NL 90070	80	1 wk
3 Oct 87	JACK TRAX – THE SECOND ALBUM Jack Trax JTRAX 2	61	2 wks
24 Oct 87	THE WORD Zomba HOP 217	86	1 wk
31 Oct 87	JACKMASTER VOLUME 1 DJ International JACKLP 501	36	4 wks
14 Nov 87	URBAN CLASSICS Urban URBLP 4	96	1 wk
5 Dec 87	SPECIAL OLYMPICS – A VERY SPECIAL CHRISTMAS A&M AMA 3911	40	4 wks

FILM SOUNDTRACKS

8 Nov 58	★ SOUTH PACIFIC RCA RB 16065	1	286 wks
8 Nov 58	● THE KING AND I Capitol LCT 6108	4	103 wks
8 Nov 58	● OKLAHOMA Capitol LCT 6100	4	90 wks
6 Dec 58	● CAROUSEL Capitol LCT 6105	8	15 wks
31 Jan 59	● GIGI MGM C 770	2	88 wks
10 Oct 59	● PORGY AND BESS Philips ABL 3282	7	5 wks
23 Jan 60	● THE FIVE PENNIES London HAU 2189	2	15 wks
7 May 60	● CAN CAN Capitol W 1301	2	31 wks
28 May 60	PAL JOEY Capitol LCT 6148	20	1 wk
23 Jul 60	HIGH SOCIETY Capitol LCT 6116	16	1 wk
5 Nov 60	BEN HUR MGM C 802	15	3 wks
21 Jan 61	NEVER ON SUNDAY London HAT 2309	17	1 wk
18 Feb 61	● SONG WITHOUT END Pye GGL 30169	9	10 wks
29 Apr 61	● SEVEN BRIDES FOR SEVEN BROTHERS MGM C 853	6	22 wks
3 Jun 61	● EXODUS RCA RD 27210	17	1 wk
11 Nov 61	● GLENN MILLER STORY Ace Of Hearts AH 12	12	7 wks
24 Mar 62	★ WEST SIDE STORY Philips BBL 7530	1	175 wks
28 Apr 62	● IT'S TRAD DAD Columbia 33SX 1412	3	21 wks
22 Sep 62	THE MUSIC MAN Warner Bros. WB 4066	14	9 wks
3 Nov 62	PORGY AND BESS RCA APG 60002	14	7 wks
15 Jun 63	JUST FOR FUN Decca LK 4524	20	2 wks
31 Oct 64	● MY FAIR LADY CBS BPG 72237	9	51 wks
31 Oct 64	GOLDFINGER United Artists ULP 1076	14	5 wks
16 Jan 65	● MARY POPPINS HMV CLP 1794	2	82 wks
10 Apr 65	★ SOUND OF MUSIC RCA RB 6616	1	381 wks
30 Apr 66	FUNNY GIRL Capitol W 2059	19	3 wks
11 Sep 66	● DR ZHIVAGO MGM C 8007	3	106 wks
22 Jul 67	CASINO ROYALE RCA Victor SF 7874	35	1 wk
29 Jul 67	A MAN AND A WOMAN United Artists SULP 1155	31	11 wks
28 Oct 67	● THOROUGHLY MODERN MILLIE Brunswick STA 8685	9	19 wks
9 Mar 68	● THE JUNGLE BOOK Disney ST 3948	5	51 wks
21 Sep 68	STAR Stateside SSL 10233	36	1 wk
12 Oct 68	● THE GOOD, THE BAD AND THE UGLY United Artists SULP 1197	2	18 wks
23 Nov 68	● OLIVER RCA Victor SB 6777	4	107 wks
23 Nov 68	CAMELOT Warner Bros. WS 1712	37	1 wk
8 Feb 69	● CHITTY CHITTY BANG BANG United Artists SULP 1200	10	4 wks
10 May 69	FUNNY GIRL CBS 70044	11	22 wks
14 Jun 69	● 2001 – A SPACE ODYSSEY MGM CS 8078	3	67 wks
20 Dec 69	● EASY RIDER Stateside SSL 5018	2	67 wks
24 Jan 70	JUNGLE BOOK (re-issue) Disney BVS 4041	25	26 wks
7 Feb 70	● PAINT YOUR WAGGON Paramount SPFL 257	2	102 wks
14 Mar 70	HELLO DOLLY Stateside SSL 10292	45	2 wks
18 Jul 70	WOODSTOCK Atlantic 2662 001	35	19 wks
24 Apr 71	● LOVE STORY Paramount SPFL 267	10	33 wks
12 Feb 72	● CLOCKWORK ORANGE Warner Bros. K 46127	4	46 wks
8 Apr 72	FIDDLER ON THE ROOF United Artists UAD 60011/2	26	2 wks
13 May 72	2001 – A SPACE ODYSSEY (re-issue) MGM 2315 034	20	2 wks
29 Nov 72	SOUTH PACIFIC (re-issue) RCA Victor SB 2011	25	2 wks

Date	Title	Pos	Wks
31 Mar 73	CABARET *Probe SPB 1052*	13	22 wks
14 Apr 73	LOST HORIZON *Bell SYBEL 8000*	36	3 wks
22 Sep 73	JESUS CHRIST SUPERSTAR *MCA MDKS 8012/3*	23	18 wks
23 Mar 74	● THE STING *MCA MCF 2537*	7	35 wks
27 Apr 74	AMERICAN GRAFFITI *MCA MCSP 253*	37	1 wk
8 Jun 74	A TOUCH OF CLASS *Philips 6612 040*	32	1 wk
5 Oct 74	SUNSHINE *MCA MCF 2566*	47	3 wks
5 Apr 75	TOMMY *Polydor 2657 014*	21	9 wks
31 Jan 76	JAWS *MCA MCF 2716*	55	1 wk
5 Mar 77	MOSES *Pye 28503*	43	2 wks
9 Apr 77	★ A STAR IS BORN *CBS 86021*	1	54 wks
2 Jul 77	THE BEST OF CAR WASH *MCA MCF 2799*	59	1 wk
11 Mar 78	★ SATURDAY NIGHT FEVER *RSO 2658 123*	1	65 wks
22 Apr 78	● THE STUD *Ronco RTD 2029*	2	19 wks
29 Apr 78	CLOSE ENCOUNTERS OF THE THIRD KIND *Arista DLART 2001*	40	6 wks
6 May 78	THE LAST WALTZ *Warner Bros. K 66076*	39	4 wks
20 May 78	THANK GOD IT'S FRIDAY *Casablanca TGIF 100*	40	5 wks
27 May 78	FM *MCA MCSP 284*	37	7 wks
8 Jul 78	★ GREASE *RSO RSD 2001*	1	47 wks
12 Aug 78	SGT PEPPER'S LONELY HEARTS CLUB BAND *A&M AMLZ 66600*	38	2 wks
7 Oct 78	CONVOY *Capitol EST 24590*	52	1 wk
30 Jun 79	THE WORLD IS FULL OF MARRIED MEN *Ronco RTD 2038*	25	9 wks
14 Jul 79	THE WARRIORS *A&M AMLH 64761*	53	7 wks
6 Oct 79	QUADROPHENIA *Polydor 2625 037*	23	16 wks
5 Jan 80	THE SECRET POLICEMAN'S BALL *Island ILPS 9601*	33	6 wks
9 Feb 80	SUNBURN *Warwick RTL 2044*	45	7 wks
16 Feb 80	GOING STEADY *Warwick WW 5078*	25	10 wks
8 Mar 80	THE ROSE *Atlantic K 50681*	68	1 wk
7 Jun 80	THE GREAT ROCK 'N' ROLL SWINDLE *Virgin V 2168*	16	11 wks
19 Jul 80	● XANADU *Jet JET LX 526*	2	17 wks
16 Aug 80	CAN'T STOP THE MUSIC *Mercury 6399 051*	9	8 wks
14 Apr 81	DANCE CRAZE *2-Tone CHRTT 5004*	5	15 wks
12 Dec 81	THE SECRET POLICEMAN'S OTHER BALL *Springtime HAHA 6003*	69	4 wks
6 Sep 80	★ FAME *RSO 2479 253*	1	25 wks
20 Mar 82	THE SECRET POLICEMAN'S OTHER BALL (THE MUSIC) *Springtime HA-HA 6004*	29	5 wks
17 Jul 82	THE SOUND OF MUSIC (re-issue) *RCA Ints 5134*	98	1 wk
4 Sep 82	ROCKY III *Liberty LBG 30351*	42	7 wks
4 Sep 82	ANNIE *CBS 70219*	83	2 wks
11 Sep 82	BRIMSTONE AND TREACLE *A&M AMLH 64915*	67	3 wks
12 Feb 83	AN OFFICER AND A GENTLEMAN *Island ISTA 3*	40	14 wks
25 Jun 83	RETURN OF THE JEDI *RSO RSD 5023*	85	5 wks
2 Jul 83	● FLASHDANCE *Casablanca CANH 5*	9	30 wks
1 Oct 83	STAYING ALIVE *RSO RSBG 3*	14	8 wks
21 Apr 84	FOOTLOOSE *CBS 70246*	7	25 wks
21 Apr 84	AGAINST ALL ODDS *Virgin V 2313*	29	10 wks
16 Jun 84	● BREAKDANCE *Polydor POLD 5147*	6	29 wks
7 Jul 84	BEAT STREET *Atlantic 780154*	30	13 wks
18 Aug 84	ELECTRIC DREAMS *Virgin V 2318*	46	7 wks
29 Sep 84	GHOSTBUSTERS *Arista 206 559*	24	25 wks
16 Feb 85	BEVERLY HILLS COP *MCA MCF 3253*	24	32 wks
22 Jun 85	A VIEW TO A KILL *Parlophone BOND 1*	81	1 wk
11 Jan 86	BACK TO THE FUTURE *MCA MCF 3285*	66	8 wks
1 Feb 86	MISTRAL'S DAUGHTER *Carrere CAL 221*	53	3 wks
1 Feb 86	● ROCKY IV *Scotti Brothers SCT 70272*	3	22 wks
5 Apr 86	ABSOLUTE BEGINNERS *Virgin V 2386*	19	9 wks
26 Apr 86	OUT OF AFRICA *MCA MCF 3310*	81	2 wks
5 Jul 86	LABYRINTH *EMI America AML 3104*	38	2 wks
11 Oct 86	● TOP GUN *CBS 70296*	4	30 wks
11 Apr 87	THE BLUES BROTHERS *Atlantic K 50715*	64	14 wks
2 May 87	PLATOON *WEA WX 95*	90	2 wks
18 Jul 87	BEVERLY HILLS COP 2 *MCA MCF 3383*	71	5 wks
1 Aug 87	THE LIVING DAYLIGHTS *Warner Bros. WX 111*	57	6 wks
1 Aug 87	● WHO'S THAT GIRL *Sire WX 102*	4†	22 wks
22 Aug 87	LA BAMBA *London LONLP 36*	24	15 wks
3 Oct 87	FULL METAL JACKET *Warner Bros. 925 613-1*	60	4 wks
31 Oct 87	DIRTY DANCING *RCA BL 86408*	26†	9 wks

The West Side Story album on Philips BBL 7530 during its chart run changed label and number to CBS BPG 62058.

STAGE CAST RECORDINGS

Date	Title	Pos	Wks
8 Nov 58	● MY FAIR LADY (BROADWAY) *Philips RBL 1000*	2	129 wks
24 Jan 59	● WEST SIDE STORY (BROADWAY) *Philips BBL 7277*	3	27 wks
26 Mar 60	● AT THE DROP OF A HAT (LONDON) *Parlophone PMC 1033*	9	1 wk
26 Mar 60	● FINGS AIN'T WOT THEY USED TO BE (LONDON) *Decca LK 4346*	5	11 wks
2 Apr 60	● FLOWER DRUM SONG (BROADWAY) *Philips ABL 3302*	2	27 wks
7 May 60	● FOLLOW THAT GIRL (LONDON) *HMV CLP 1366*	5	9 wks
21 May 60	● MOST HAPPY FELLA (BROADWAY) *Philips BBL 7374*	6	13 wks
21 May 60	MAKE ME AN OFFER (LONDON) *HMV CLP 1333*	18	1 wk
28 May 60	● FLOWER DRUM SONG (LONDON) *HMV CLP 1359*	10	3 wks
9 Jul 60	MOST HAPPY FELLA (LONDON) *HMV CLP 1365*	19	1 wk
30 Jul 60	WEST SIDE STORY (BROADWAY) *Philips SBBL 504*	14	1 wk
10 Sep 60	● OLIVER (LONDON) *Decca LK 4359*	4	91 wks
11 Mar 61	KING KONG (SOUTH AFRICA) *Decca LK 4392*	12	8 wks
6 May 61	● MUSIC MAN (LONDON) *JMH CLP 1444*	8	13 wks
24 Jun 61	● SOUND OF MUSIC (BROADWAY) *Philips ABL 3370*	4	19 wks
22 Jul 61	BYE-BYE BIRDIE (LONDON) *Philips ABL 3385*	17	3 wks
22 Jul 61	BEYOND THE FRINGE (LONDON) *Parlophone PMC 1145*	13	17 wks
29 Jul 61	● SOUND OF MUSIC (LONDON) *HMV CLP 1453*	4	68 wks
9 Sep 61	● STOP THE WORLD I WANT TO GET OFF (LONDON) *Decca LK 4408*	8	14 wks
14 Jul 62	● BLITZ (LONDON) *HMV CLP 1569*	7	21 wks
18 May 63	HALF A SIXPENCE (LONDON) *Decca LK 4521*	20	2 wks
3 Aug 63	PICKWICK (LONDON) *Philips AL 3431*	12	10 wks
4 Jan 64	MY FAIR LADY (BROADWAY) *CBS BPG 68001*	19	1 wk
22 Feb 64	AT THE DROP OF ANOTHER HAT (LONDON) *Parlophone PMC 1216*	12	11 wks
3 Oct 64	● CAMELOT (BROADWAY) *CBS APG 60001*	10	12 wks
16 Jan 65	CAMELOT (LONDON) *HMV CLP 1756*	19	1 wk
11 Mar 67	● FIDDLER ON THE ROOF (LONDON) *CBS SBPG 70030*	4	50 wks
28 Dec 68	● HAIR (LONDON) *Polydor 583–043*	3	94 wks
30 Aug 69	OLIVER (LONDON) (re-issue) *Decca SPA 30*	23	4 wks
6 Sep 69	HAIR (BROADWAY) *RCA SF 7959*	29	3 wks
19 Feb 72	GODSPELL (LONDON) *Bell BELLS 203*	25	17 wks
18 Nov 78	EVITA (LONDON) *MCA MCF 3257*	24	18 wks
1 Aug 81	● CATS (LONDON) *Polydor CATX 001*	6	26 wks
6 Nov 82	MACK AND MABEL (BROADWAY) *MCA MCL 1728*	38	7 wks
7 Aug 84	STARLIGHT EXPRESS (LONDON) *Starlight/Polydor LNER 1*	21	9 wks
15 Feb 86	LES MISERABLES (LONDON) *First Night ENCORE 1*	72	4 wks
21 Feb 87	★ THE PHANTOM OF THE OPERA (LONDON) *Polydor PODV 9*	1†	45 wks

STUDIO CAST RECORDINGS

Date	Title	Pos	Wks
25 Jun 60	SHOWBOAT *HMV CLP 1310*	12	1 wk
8 Feb 72	● JESUS CHRIST SUPERSTAR *MCA MKPS 2011/2*	6	20 wks
22 Jan 77	● EVITA *MCA MCX 503*	4	35 wks
10 Nov 84	● CHESS *RCA PL 70500*	10	16 wks
18 May 85	WEST SIDE STORY *Deutsche Grammophon 41525*	11	32 wks
2 Nov 85	CHESS PIECES *Telstar STAR 2274*	87	3 wks
10 May 86	WEST SIDE STORY – HIGHLIGHTS *Deutsche Grammophon 45963*	72	6 wks
17 May 86	DAVE CLARK'S 'TIME' *EMI AMPH 1*	21	6 wks
11 Oct 86	● SOUTH PACIFIC *CBS SM 42205*	5	24 wks
27 Jun 87	MATADOR *Epic VIVA 1*	26	5 wks
21 Nov 87	MY FAIR LADY *Decca MFL 1*	60	6 wks

TV and RADIO SOUNDTRACKS and SPIN-OFFS

Date		Title	Pos	Weeks
13 Dec 58	●	**OH BOY!** *Parlophone PMC 1072*	9	14 wks
4 Mar 61	●	**HUCKLEBERRY HOUND** *Pye GGL 004*	10	12 wks
30 Feb 63		**THAT WAS THE WEEK THAT WAS** *Parlophone PMC 1197*	11	9 wks
28 Mar 64		**STARS FROM STARS AND GARTERS** *Pye GGL 0252*	17	2 wks
4 Nov 72		**THE BBC 1922–1972 (TV AND RADIO EXTRACTS)** *BBC 50*	16	7 wks
4 Jan 75		**BBC TV'S BEST OF TOP OF THE POPS** *Super Beeb BELP 001*	21	5 wks
10 Apr 76	★	**ROCK FOLLIES** *Island ILPS 9362*	1	15 wks
22 Oct 77		**10 YEARS OF HITS – RADIO ONE** *Super Beeb BEDP 002*	39	3 wks
8 Apr 78	●	**PENNIES FROM HEAVEN** *World Records SH 266*	10	17 wks
1 Jul 78		**MORE PENNIES FROM HEAVEN** *World Records SH 267*	31	4 wks
15 Dec 79		**FAWLTY TOWERS** *BBC REB 377*	25	10 wks
14 Feb 81		**HITCHHIKERS GUIDE TO THE GALAXY VOL. 2** *Original ORA 54*	47	4 wks
1 Aug 81		**THE MUSIC OF COSMOS** *RCA RCALP 5032*	43	10 wks
21 Nov 81		**BRIDESHEAD REVISITED** *Chrysalis CDL 1367*	50	12 wks
23 Oct 82		**ON THE AIR – 60 YEARS OF BBC THEME MUSIC** *BBC REF 454*	85	3 wks
26 Nov 83		**REILLY ACE OF THEMES** *Red Bus BUSLP 1004*	54	6 wks
4 Feb 84		**AUF WIEDERSEHEN PET** *Towerbell AUF 1*	21	6 wks
18 Feb 84		**THE TUBE** *K-Tel NE 1261*	30	6 wks
8 Sep 84		**SONG AND DANCE** *RCA BL 70480*	46	4 wks
26 Oct 85		**MIAMI VICE** *BBC REMV 584*	11	8 wks
16 Nov 85		**EASTENDERS SING-ALONG** *BBC REB 586*	33	10 wks
15 Feb 86	●	**JONATHAN KING'S ENTERTAINMENT USA** *Stylus SMR 8612*	6	11 wks
18 Oct 86		**THE VERY BEST OF ENTERTAINMENT USA VOLUME 2** *Priority UPTVR 1*	44	4 wks
6 Dec 86	●	**MUSIC FROM THE BBC TV SERIES 'THE SINGING DETECTIVE'** *BBC REN 608*	10	18 wks
27 Jun 87		**THE ROCK 'N' ROLL YEARS 1956–59** *BBC REN 631*	80	2 wks
27 Jun 87		**THE ROCK 'N' ROLL YEARS 1960–63** *BBC REN 632*	84	1 wk
27 Jun 87		**THE ROCK 'N' ROLL YEARS 1964–67** *BBC REN 633*	71	2 wks
27 Jun 87		**THE ROCK 'N' ROLL YEARS 1968–71** *BBC REN 634*	77	1 wk
3 Oct 87		**MOONLIGHTING – THE TV SOUNDTRACK ALBUM** *MCA MCF 3386*	50	6 wks
17 Oct 87		**MIAMI VICE 2 – MUSIC FROM THE TV SERIES** *MCA MCGC 6019*	71	4 wks
28 Nov 87		**THE CHART SHOW DANCE HITS '87** *Chrysalis ADD 1*	39	5 wks

MISCELLANEOUS

Date		Title	Pos	Weeks
12 Sep 70		**EDINBURGH MILITARY TATTOO 1970** *Waverley SZLP 2121*	34	4 wks
18 Sep 71		**EDINBURGH MILITARY TATTOO 1971** *Waverley SZLP 2128*	44	1 wk
11 Dec 71		**ELECTRONIC ORGANS TODAY** *Ad-Rhythm ADBS 1*	48	1 wk
8 Dec 73	●	**MUSIC FOR A ROYAL WEDDING** *BBC REW 163*	7	6 wks
27 Dec 75		**STRINGS OF SCOTLAND** *Philips 6382 108*	50	1 wk
8 Aug 81	★	**THE ROYAL WEDDING** *BBC REP 413*	1	11 wks
18 May 85		**VICTORY IN EUROPE – BROADCASTS AND REPORTS FROM BBC CORRESPONDENTS** *BBC REC 562*	61	1 wk
9 Aug 86		**ROYAL WEDDING** *BBC REP 596*	55	1 wk

HIT ALBUMS
FACTS AND FEATS

CLIFF RICHARD appears on the television programme *Oh Boy*   unaware that at least forty-three hit albums are in store for him.

	Weeks
MIKE OLDFIELD	466
ANDY WILLIAMS	439
LED ZEPPELIN	411
TOM JONES	404
SHADOWS	395
STATUS QUO	392
THE SOUND OF MUSIC (Original Soundtrack)	382
JIM REEVES	381
MICHAEL JACKSON	373

(plus 55 weeks with Jackson Five, 10 weeks with Diana Ross, Gladys Knight and Stevie Wonder, and 9 weeks with Diana Ross)

JAMES LAST	370
GENESIS	363
BARBRA STREISAND	361
DIANA ROSS	358

(plus 45 weeks with Marvin Gaye, 10 weeks with Michael Jackson, Gladys Knight and Stevie Wonder, and 9 weeks with Michael Jackson)

BRUCE SPRINGSTEEN	356
MADONNA	355
ELECTRIC LIGHT ORCHESTRA	345
STEVIE WONDER	325

(plus 10 weeks with Diana Ross, Gladys Knight and Michael Jackson)

THE BEATLES are groomed during filming of *A Hard Day's Night*.

MOST WEEKS ON CHART

The following table lists the 204 recording acts that have spent 100 weeks or more on the British albums chart from the first chart on 8 Nov 1958 up to and including the chart of 26 Dec 1987. It is, of course, possible for an act to be credited with two or more chart weeks in the same week if the act has more than one album on the chart in any one week.

	Weeks
BEATLES	1081
SIMON AND GARFUNKEL	1034
ELVIS PRESLEY	1018
DIRE STRAITS	900
DAVID BOWIE	829
QUEEN	796
PINK FLOYD	702
ROLLING STONES	642
CLIFF RICHARD	638
FRANK SINATRA	613

(plus 23 weeks with Count Basie)

FLEETWOOD MAC	600
ELTON JOHN	597
U2	587
ROD STEWART	557
BOB DYLAN	541
BEACH BOYS	524
MEAT LOAF	521
PHIL COLLINS	519
ABBA	499
CARPENTERS	473
PAUL McCARTNEY/WINGS	467
NEIL DIAMOND	466

Russ Tamblyn (front centre) leads the Jets against the Sharks in *West Side Story*. When you're a Jet, you're number one for thirteen weeks.

The Man Who Sold The World was the lowest placed official studio release of DAVID BOWIE. Lulu had a hit single with the title song.

SADE in action in 1985 shortly before the release of *Promise*.

The Temptations have scored 99 weeks, plus a further 31 weeks with Diana Ross and the Supremes, totalling 130 weeks. John Mayall accumulates 97 chart weeks, plus 17 more with Eric Clapton, altogether 114 weeks. Peter Sellers has clocked up 84 weeks, plus 18 with Sophia Loren, 10 with Anthony Newley and Joan Collins, and 1 more with Harry Secombe and Spike Milligan, a total of 113 weeks. Nat 'King' Cole has been on the charts for 95 weeks as a soloist, 7 weeks with George Shearing and 1 week with Dean Martin, a total of 103 weeks. Marvin Gaye has scored 93 weeks as a solo act, plus 45 weeks with Diana Ross and 4 with Tammi Terrell, totalling 142 weeks. Gladys Knight has scored 94 weeks with the Pips and 10 more with Diana Ross, Michael Jackson and Stevie Wonder, a total of 104 weeks. Mr. Acker Bilk has scored 76 weeks as a soloist and with his Paramount Jazz Band, a further 61 weeks with Chris Barber, and 24 weeks with Kenny Ball and Chris Barber, making a total of 161 weeks. Scott Walker has been on the chart for 44 weeks as a soloist, and 96 more as a Walker Brother, a total of 140 weeks. David Cassidy has scored 94 weeks as a soloist, plus 13 with the Partridge Family, total 107 weeks. Each member of Crosby, Stills and Nash has totalled over 100 weeks on the chart, although as a trio they managed only 14 weeks. David Crosby totals 105 weeks: 7 weeks as a soloist, 5 weeks in his duo with Nash, and 79 weeks with Crosby, Stills, Nash and Young. Graham Nash has had 8 weeks on the chart as a soloist, so totals 106 weeks. Stephen Stills has scored 7 weeks as a soloist, plus 7 as leader of Stephen Stills' Manassas, and 5 with the Stills-Young Band to add to his C, S & N and C, S, N & Y weeks, for a total of 112 weeks. The Royal Philharmonic Orchestra has had label credit on albums occupying chart space for 106 weeks: 90 with Louis Clark wielding the baton, and 16 with the RPO receiving top billing.

217	DIRE STRAITS	1986
198	DAVID BOWIE	1983
182	DAVID BOWIE	1973
177	BRUCE SPRINGSTEEN	1985
168	U2	1985
167	SIMON AND GARFUNKEL	1970
158	DIRE STRAITS	1985
135	TOM JONES	1968
131	PHIL COLLINS	1985
127	MADONNA	1987
126	U2	1987
125	JOHNNY CASH	1970
125	MADONNA	1986
122	BEATLES	1970
121	OTIS REDDING	1968
117	QUEEN	1987
116	BEACH BOYS	1968
116	DIRE STRAITS	1984
116	POLICE	1980
115	MOODY BLUES	1970
115	JIM REEVES	1964
113	PHIL COLLINS	1986
112	ABBA	1978
112	BOB DYLAN	1965
112	ELECTRIC LIGHT ORCHESTRA	1979
111	ANDY WILLIAMS	1971
109	GEORGE MITCHELL MINSTRELS	1962
108	PINK FLOYD	1977
107	DAVID BOWIE	1974
107	DIRE STRAITS	1983
107	MICHAEL JACKSON	1984
107	QUEEN	1986
106	ABBA	1977
106	CARPENTERS	1974
105	DURAN DURAN	1983
105	ELTON JOHN	1975
104	BEATLES	1964
104	BEATLES	1974
104	SIMON AND GARFUNKEL	1973
103	FOUR TOPS	1968
102	LED ZEPPELIN	1970
102	SIMON AND GARFUNKEL	1971
101	HERB ALPERT	1967
101	SIMON AND GARFUNKEL	1974
100	BLONDIE	1979
100	SIMON AND GARFUNKEL	1975
100	U2	1984

Simon and Garfunkel have racked up 100 chart weeks in a year 5 times. Dire Straits have done it 4 times, in consecutive years (1983 to 1986 inclusive). The Beatles, David Bowie and U2 have topped the century in three years, while Abba, Phil Collins, Madonna and Queen have done it twice.

1958	ELVIS PRESLEY	16*
1959	FRANK SINATRA	56*
1960	ELVIS PRESLEY	51
1961	ELVIS PRESLEY	91*
1962	GEORGE MITCHELL MINSTRELS	109*
1963	CLIFF RICHARD	72
1964	JIM REEVES	115*
1965	BOB DYLAN	112
1966	BEACH BOYS	95
1967	HERB ALPERT	101
1968	TOM JONES	135*
1969	SEEKERS	66
1970	SIMON AND GARFUNKEL	167*
1971	ANDY WILLIAMS	111
1972	CAT STEVENS	89
1973	DAVID BOWIE	182*
1974	DAVID BOWIE	107
1975	ELTON JOHN	105
1976	DEMIS ROUSSOS	84
1977	PINK FLOYD	108
1978	ABBA	112
1979	ELECTRIC LIGHT ORCHESTRA	112
1980	POLICE	116
1981	BARRY MANILOW	92
1982	JAPAN	85
1983	DAVID BOWIE	198*
1984	DIRE STRAITS	116
1985	BRUCE SPRINGSTEEN	177
1986	DIRE STRAITS	217*
1987	MADONNA	127

Elvis Presley and David Bowie have each been the year's chart champions three times, and Dire Straits have won twice. No other act has been chart champion more than once.

(* denotes record annual total at the time)

198	David Bowie
107	Dire Straits
105	Duran Duran
97	Michael Jackson *(plus 26 more with Jackson Five)*
87	U2
83	Kids from Fame
78	Phil Collins
76	Meat Loaf
69	Men At Work
66	Richard Clayderman

David Bowie's total of 198 weeks (in other words, the equivalent of four albums on the chart every week) established a new record for most chart weeks in one year. The previous record was set in 1973 – by David Bowie.

116	Dire Straits
107	Michael Jackson *(plus 29 more with Jackson Five)*
100	U2
97	Queen
87	Lionel Richie
69	Duran Duran
	Spandau Ballet
67	Eurythmics
	Barbra Streisand
66	Billy Joel
	Elton John

Phil Collins scored 65 weeks as a solo artist, and a further 35 with Genesis. Dire Straits matched the achievement of David Bowie in 1973 and 1974 by recording two consecutive years with more than 100 chart weeks.

QUEEN return from an Australian tour in 1974, their first chart year.

177	Bruce Springsteen
168	U2
158	Dire Straits
131	Phil Collins
86	Wham!
79	Queen
78	Paul Young
77	Madonna
73	Prince
72	Tears For Fears

1985 was the first year in which four different acts scored over 100 weeks since 1974. It was also the first year in which three acts scored over 150 weeks, the equivalent of at least 3 albums in the chart each week throughout the year. Dire Straits, by clocking up 100 weeks for the third straight year, equalled Simon and Garfunkel's record set in 1973, 74 and 75.

217	Dire Straits
125	Madonna
113	Phil Collins
	(plus 28 more with Genesis)
107	Queen
95	Simple Minds
86	U2
81	Talking Heads
68	Eurythmics
63	A-Ha
62	Five Star
62	ZZ Top

For the first time ever a female vocalist, Madonna, topped the 100 week level. Dire Straits, U2, Phil Collins and Queen all survived from the 1985 lists. Dire Straits' total of 217 weeks on the chart was a new annual best total, and their fourth consecutive annual total of 100 weeks or more – another record.

127	Madonna
	(plus 22 weeks on Who's That Girl soundtrack)
126	U2
117	Queen
91	Luther Vandross
84	Dire Straits
83	Simply Red
81	Fleetwood Mac
76	Pet Shop Boys
75	Whitney Houston
58	Five Star
58	Level 42

Phil Collins scored 56 weeks solo, and 57 more with Genesis. Madonna achieved the distinction of becoming the first female act to become the year's top album act, and her score of 127 weeks was a new distaff record. Five Star created a far more obscure record by being the tenth equal most charted album act of the year for the second year running! For the fourth consecutive year, Queen were among the top ten acts of the year. For U2, it was a fifth straight year among the leaders, and for Dire Straits their ninth year.

MOST HIT ALBUMS

An album is a hit if it spends only one week at number 100. Double, treble and quadruple albums count as only one hit. Re-issues do not count as a new hit.

91	ELVIS PRESLEY
52	JAMES LAST
49	FRANK SINATRA
	(plus 1 with Count Basie)
43	CLIFF RICHARD
34	ROLLING STONES
29	BOB DYLAN
28	SHIRLEY BASSEY
27	ELTON JOHN
26	DAVID BOWIE
26	JIM REEVES
26	DIANA ROSS
	(plus 2 with Marvin Gaye, and 1 with Gladys Knight, Stevie Wonder and Michael Jackson)

DIRE STRAITS: most weeks on chart in 1986.

25	BEACH BOYS
24	NEIL DIAMOND
24	JOHNNY MATHIS

(plus 1 with Natalie Cole, 1 with Deniece Williams and 1 with Henry Mancini)

24	ANDY WILLIAMS
23	BEATLES
21	SHADOWS
21	STATUS QUO
19	JETHRO TULL
19	TOM JONES
18	SANTANA

(Carlos Santana 3 more with various other partners)

18	DEEP PURPLE
18	HAWKWIND

(includes 1 as Hawklords)

18	PAUL McCARTNEY/WINGS
18	WHO
18	NEIL YOUNG

(plus 1 with Stills-Young Band and 3 with Crosby, Stills, Nash and Young)

17	JIMI HENDRIX

(plus 1 with Curtis Knight)

17	GARY NUMAN/TUBEWAY ARMY
17	ROD STEWART

(plus 1 with the Faces)

16	BLACK SABBATH
16	MARC BOLAN/T. REX/ TYRANNOSAURUS REX
16	JOHNNY CASH
16	TANGERINE DREAM
15	HERB ALPERT
15	ERIC CLAPTON

(plus 1 with Cream)

15	GENESIS
15	MIKE OLDFIELD
15	PINK FLOYD
15	QUEEN
15	SLADE
15	YES
14	CARPENTERS
14	ALICE COOPER
14	JOHN DENVER

(plus 1 with Placido Domingo)

14	DAVID ESSEX
14	ROY ORBISON
14	BARBRA STREISAND
14	DON WILLIAMS
14	STEVIE WONDER

(plus 1 with Diana Ross, Gladys Knight and Michael Jackson)

13	VAN MORRISON
13	MOODY BLUES
13	TEMPTATIONS

(plus 3 with Diana Ross and the Supremes)

13	WISHBONE ASH
12	ELVIS COSTELLO

(includes 1 as the Costello Show)

12	FLEETWOOD MAC
12	KISS

ELVIS COSTELLO is shown after attending a Paul Simon concert at the Royal Albert Hall in 1987.

12	MANTOVANI
12	JOHN MAYALL
12	ROXY MUSIC

(plus 1 with Bryan Ferry)

12	STRANGLERS
12	DONNA SUMMER
12	URIAH HEEP
11	ABBA
11	RAY CONNIFF
11	CURE
11	EVERLY BROTHERS

(Phil Everly 1 more solo)

11	HOLLIES
11	BUDDY HOLLY
11	ENGELBERT HUMPERDINCK
11	MICHAEL JACKSON

(plus 1 with Diana Ross, Gladys Knight and Stevie Wonder)

11	BILLY JOEL
11	JOHN LENNON/PLASTIC ONO BAND
11	LONDON SYMPHONY ORCHESTRA
11	BARRY MANILOW
11	BOB MARLEY AND THE WAILERS
11	JONI MITCHELL
11	MOTORHEAD
11	LEO SAYER
11	10 CC

(plus 1 with Godley and Creme)

11	THIN LIZZY

(plus 1 with Phil Lynott)

11	UB 40
11	FRANK ZAPPA
10	BARCLAY JAMES HARVEST
10	BEE GEES
10	MAX BYGRAVES
10	BYRDS
10	BARBARA DICKSON
10	VAL DOONICAN
10	ELECTRIC LIGHT ORCHESTRA
10	EMERSON LAKE AND PALMER

(Emerson, Lake and Powell 1 more)

10	RORY GALLAGHER
10	JACKSONS

(4 as Jackson Five, 6 as Jacksons, plus 1 with Michael Jackson)

10	JUDAS PRIEST
10	BERT KAEMPFERT
10	KING CRIMSON
10	KINKS
10	LED ZEPPELIN
10	GEORGE MITCHELL MINSTRELS
10	OLIVIA NEWTON-JOHN
10	ALAN PARSONS PROJECT
10	RAINBOW
10	SHOWADDYWADDY
10	SIOUXSIE AND THE BANSHEES
10	DIONNE WARWICK
10	BARRY WHITE

George Benson has made 9 hit albums, and 1 more with Earl Klugh. Rick Wakeman has hit the charts 9 times, plus once more with Kevin Peek. Simon and Garfunkel have had 9 hit albums. Paul Simon has 7 more solo hit albums and Art Garfunkel 6.

MOST TOP TEN HIT ALBUMS

The rules for this category are the same as for Most Hit Albums, except that the album must have made the Top 10 for at least one week.

36	ELVIS PRESLEY
27	CLIFF RICHARD
27	FRANK SINATRA

(plus 1 with Count Basie)

26	ROLLING STONES	6	RUSS CONWAY	5	SLADE
23	BOB DYLAN	6	DIRE STRAITS	5	SPANDAU BALLET
18	BEATLES	6	PETER GABRIEL	5	BRUCE SPRINGSTEEN
18	DAVID BOWIE	6	HOLLIES	5	BARBRA STREISAND
16	PAUL McCARTNEY/WINGS	6	ENGELBERT HUMPERDINCK	5	SUPERTRAMP
16	STATUS QUO			5	SUPREMES

26 ROLLING STONES
23 BOB DYLAN
18 BEATLES
18 DAVID BOWIE
16 PAUL McCARTNEY/WINGS
16 STATUS QUO
15 ELTON JOHN
14 QUEEN
14 ROD STEWART
(plus 1 with the Faces)
13 BEACH BOYS
13 PINK FLOYD
13 JIM REEVES
12 GENESIS
12 WHO
11 TOM JONES
10 LED ZEPPELIN
10 SHADOWS
10 ANDY WILLIAMS
9 BLACK SABBATH
9 ELVIS COSTELLO
9 DEEP PURPLE
9 ROXY MUSIC
(plus 1 with Bryan Ferry)
9 YES
8 ABBA
8 JIMI HENDRIX
8 JOHNNY MATHIS
(plus 1 with Deniece Williams)
8 MOODY BLUES
8 STEVIE WONDER
7 BEE GEES
7 CARPENTERS
7 CREAM
(plus 1 with Eric Clapton)
7 DEPECHE MODE
7 ELECTRIC LIGHT ORCHESTRA
7 EMERSON LAKE AND PALMER
7 FLEETWOOD MAC
7 BUDDY HOLLY AND THE CRICKETS
7 JOHN LENNON/PLASTIC ONO BAND
7 DIANA ROSS
(plus 1 with Marvin Gaye)
7 STRANGLERS
7 10 CC
(plus 1 with Godley & Creme)
7 THIN LIZZY
7 UB40
7 ULTRAVOX
6 SHIRLEY BASSEY
6 BLONDIE
6 MARC BOLAN/T. REX/ TYRANNOSAURUS REX
6 KATE BUSH

6 RUSS CONWAY
6 DIRE STRAITS
6 PETER GABRIEL
6 HOLLIES
6 ENGELBERT HUMPERDINCK
6 JAM
6 JETHRO TULL
6 MADNESS
6 BARRY MANILOW
6 MANTOVANI
6 GEORGE MITCHELL MINSTRELS
6 GARY NUMAN/TUBEWAY ARMY
6 POLICE
6 RUSH
6 LEO SAYER
6 SIMON AND GARFUNKEL
(Paul Simon 5 more solo, Art Garfunkel 2 more solo)
6 SMITHS
6 CAT STEVENS
6 WHITESNAKE
5 AC/DC
5 HERB ALPERT
5 JOHNNY CASH
5 ERIC CLAPTON
(plus 1 with Cream)
5 CULTURE CLUB
5 CURE
5 JOHN DENVER
5 NEIL DIAMOND
5 VAL DOONICAN
5 EAGLES
5 ECHO AND THE BUNNYMEN
5 DUANE EDDY
5 EURYTHMICS
5 EVERLY BROTHERS
5 BRYAN FERRY
(plus 1 with Roxy Music)
5 FREE
5 IRON MAIDEN
5 JACK JONES
5 KINKS
5 JAMES LAST
5 MARILLION
5 BOB MARLEY AND THE WAILERS
5 MEAT LOAF
5 MIKE OLDFIELD
5 RAINBOW
5 SANTANA
(plus 1 with Mahavishnu John McLaughlin)
5 SHOWADDYWADDY
5 PAUL SIMON
(plus 6 with Simon and Garfunkel)

5 SLADE
5 SPANDAU BALLET
5 BRUCE SPRINGSTEEN
5 BARBRA STREISAND
5 SUPERTRAMP
5 SUPREMES
(plus 1 with the Four Tops, plus 1 with Diana Ross and the Temptations)

Madonna has had 4 Top Ten albums, plus the major role in the success of the soundtrack album from her film *Who's That Girl?*. The only act to hit the chart 10 times or more and to take every hit into the Top Ten is Led Zeppelin, who scored 10 Top Tens out of 10 tries.

MOST NUMBER ONE ALBUMS

12 Beatles
9 Rolling Stones
8 Abba
8 Led Zeppelin
7 Rod Stewart
6 David Bowie
6 Bob Dylan
6 Elvis Presley
6 Paul McCartney/Wings
5 Police
5 Cliff Richard
4 Genesis
4 Elton John
4 Queen
4 Roxy Music
(1 with Bryan Ferry)
4 Shadows
4 Status Quo
3 Boney M
3 Kate Bush
3 Deep Purple
3 Fleetwood Mac
3 John Lennon
3 George Mitchell Minstrels
3 Moody Blues
3 Gary Numan/Tubeway Army
3 Pink Floyd
3 Simple Minds
3 Slade
3 Barbra Streisand
3 T. Rex
3 U2
3 Andy Williams

Simon and Garfunkel have 2 number one albums, and Paul Simon has scored 2 more solo. Diana Ross and the

Supremes have 2 number ones and 1 more with the Temptations. Phil Collins has hit the top twice as well as 4 times with Genesis (listed above). Bryan Ferry has 1 solo number one to go with the 4 Roxy Music chart-toppers, on all of which he sang lead and on 1 of which he was given equal billing with Roxy Music as it also featured several solo Ferry tracks. Sting has 1 solo number one album as well as 5 as lead singer with Police. Michael Jackson has only 2 number one albums to his name, but he features on 1 more with the Jacksons, which also features solo Michael Jackson tracks. George Michael has 1 solo chart-topping album and 2 more as half of Wham!

MOST WEEKS AT NUMBER ONE

163	Beatles
115	Cast of *South Pacific* (OST)*
70	Cast of *The Sound of Music* (OST)
49	Abba
49	Elvis Presley
48	Simon and Garfunkel *(Paul Simon 9 more solo)*
43	Rolling Stones
27	Cliff Richard
27	Rod Stewart
22	Carpenters
22	Bob Dylan
21	Elton John
21	Shadows
20	David Bowie
19	George Mitchell Minstrels
18	Cast of *Saturday Night Fever* (OST)
18	Dire Straits
16	Paul McCartney/Wings
15	Police
15	Barbra Streisand
14	Led Zeppelin
13	Beach Boys
13	Cast of *Grease* (OST)
13	Cast of *West Side Story* (OST)
13	Michael Jackson *(plus 3 with Jacksons)*
13	Roxy Music
12	Adam and the Ants
12	Kids From Fame
12	Bob Marley and the Wailers
12	Queen
12	T. Rex
10	John Lennon
10	Diana Ross and the Supremes *(plus 4 with the Temptations)*
10	Stylistics
10	Slim Whitman

Phil Collins has spent 8 weeks at number one on his own and 8 weeks as part of Genesis.

* (OST) – Original Soundtrack. List excludes appearances on compilations and soundtracks.

MOST HITS WITHOUT A TOP TEN HIT

Only four acts have had ten or more hit albums without ever reaching the Top 10. They are **Tangerine Dream** (16 hits), **Van Morrison** (13 hits), **Barclay James Harvest** (10 hits) and **Alan Parsons Project** (10 hits). **James Last** has hit the Top 10 only 5 times out of 52 chart entries, which include a run of 31 consecutive hit albums which all missed the Top 10. **Neil Young** has so far clocked up 16 hit albums since his last Top 10 hit. There have been 54 hit compilation albums on the Street Sounds label totalling 262 weeks on the charts, but the highest placing for any of them is 12 by *Street Sounds Electro* 7 in Mar 1985.

MOST HITS WITHOUT A NUMBER ONE HIT

52	JAMES LAST *(who has had one no. 2 hit)*
28	SHIRLEY BASSEY *(who has had one no. 2 hit)*
26	DIANA ROSS *(who has had two no. 2 hits)*
24	NEIL DIAMOND *(who has had one no. 2 hit)*
19	SANTANA *(who have had two no. 6 hits)*
18	HAWKWIND *(who have had one no. 9 hit)*
17	JIMI HENDRIX *(who has had two no. 2 hits)*
16	JOHNNY CASH *(who has had one no. 2 hit)*
16	TANGERINE DREAM *(whose biggest hit reached no. 12)*
15	HERB ALPERT *(who has had one no. 2 hit)*
15	ERIC CLAPTON *(who has had three no. 3 hits)*

LONGEST CLIMB TO NUMBER ONE

3 years 298 days *My People Were Fair And Had Sky In Their Hair, But Now They're Content To Wear Stars On Their Brows*
Tyrannosaurus Rex: from 13 Jul 68 to 6 May 72

2 years 67 days *40 Greatest Hits*
Elvis Presley: from 5 Jul 75 to 10 Sep 77

1 year 321 days *Fame*
Original Soundtrack: from 6 Sep 80 to 24 Jul 82

1 year 83 days *Tubular Bells*
Mike Oldfield: from 14 Jul 73 to 5 Oct 74

Eight other albums have taken 30 weeks or more to reach the top spot, as follows:
Rumours by Fleetwood Mac **49 weeks**
The Freewheelin' Bob Dylan **48 weeks**
Like A Virgin by Madonna **44 weeks**
Black and White Minstrel Show by the George Mitchell Minstrels **36 weeks**
Born In The U.S.A. by Bruce Springsteen **36 weeks**
Andy Williams' *Greatest Hits* **35 weeks**
Band On The Run by Wings **33 weeks**
And I Love You So by Perry Como **30 weeks**

Tyrannosaurus Rex hit number one with the longest titled album ever to hit the top only after it was re-released in 1972 as a double album with *Prophets, Seers, Sages and the Angels Of The Ages*. Presley's album hit the top in the period immediately following his death. *Tubular Bells* spent 11 weeks at number two before climbing to the very top, and *Rumours* remained 32 weeks in the Top 10 before hitting the number one slot. *The Freewheelin' Bob Dylan* climbed to the top in its seventh chart run.

MOST WEEKS ON CHART BY ONE ALBUM

This is a list of all the albums that have spent a total of 100 weeks or more on the chart. Re-releases and re-issues are counted, provided that the re-issue is identical to the original release.

	weeks
RUMOURS *Fleetwood Mac*	402
BAT OUT OF HELL *Meat Loaf*	395
THE SOUND OF MUSIC *Original Soundtrack*	382
GREATEST HITS *Queen*	312
BRIDGE OVER TROUBLED WATER *Simon and Garfunkel*	303
DARK SIDE OF THE MOON *Pink Floyd*	294
SOUTH PACIFIC *Original Soundtrack*	288
GREATEST HITS *Simon and Garfunkel*	283
TUBULAR BELLS *Mike Oldfield*	264
FACE VALUE *Phil Collins*	247
MAKIN' MOVIES *Dire Straits*	247
JEFF WAYNE'S WAR OF THE WORLDS *Various*	226
LOVE OVER GOLD *Dire Straits*	197
LIVE – UNDER A BLOOD RED SKY *U2*	192
WEST SIDE STORY *Original Soundtrack*	175
THE RISE AND FALL OF ZIGGY STARDUST AND THE SPIDERS FROM MARS *David Bowie*	168
SERGEANT PEPPER'S LONELY HEARTS CLUB BAND *Beatles*	164
OFF THE WALL *Michael Jackson*	160
ALCHEMY – DIRE STRAITS LIVE *Dire Straits*	159
THE BUDDY HOLLY STORY *Buddy Holly*	156
CAN'T SLOW DOWN *Lionel Richie*	154
MANILOW MAGIC *Barry Manilow*	151
LIKE A VIRGIN *Madonna*	150
THE BEATLES 1962–1966 *Beatles*	148
PRIVATE DANCER *Tina Turner*	146
WAR *U2*	143
BEST OF THE BEACH BOYS *Beach Boys*	142
THRILLER *Michael Jackson*	139
GOING PLACES *Herb Alpert*	138
LED ZEPPELIN II *Led Zeppelin*	138
NO JACKET REQUIRED *Phil Collins*	137
BROTHERS IN ARMS *Dire Straits*	136
HELLO I MUST BE GOING *Phil Collins*	135
ELIMINATOR *ZZ Top*	135
GREATEST HITS *Abba*	130
DIRE STRAITS *Dire Straits*	129
LOVE SONGS *Barbra Streisand*	129
MY FAIR LADY *Original Broadway Cast*	129
THE BEST OF THE SEEKERS *Seekers*	125
BAND ON THE RUN *Wings*	124
THE FIRST ALBUM/MADONNA *Madonna*	123
THE UNFORGETTABLE FIRE *U2*	123
HUNKY DORY *David Bowie*	120
NO PARLEZ *Paul Young*	119
DURAN DURAN *Duran Duran*	118
BORN IN THE U.S.A. *Bruce Springsteen*	117
THE SINGLES 1969–1973 *Carpenters*	116
FANTASTIC! *Wham!*	116
GREATEST HITS *Andy Williams*	116
JOHNNY CASH AT SAN QUENTIN *Johnny Cash*	114
THE BEATLES 1967–1970 *Beatles*	113
GREATEST HITS *Glen Campbell*	113
AND I LOVE YOU SO *Perry Como*	109
THE JAZZ SINGER *Neil Diamond*	109
RIO *Duran Duran*	109
OUT OF THE BLUE *Electric Light Orchestra*	108
OLIVER *Original Soundtrack*	107
CHARIOTS OF FIRE *Vangelis*	106
LEGEND *Bob Marley and the Wailers*	106
DOCTOR ZHIVAGO *Original Soundtrack*	106
PARALLEL LINES *Blondie*	105

FLEETWOOD MAC's *Rumours* surged forward to become the album that has spent most weeks on chart.

Five of the six Dire Straits albums released to the end of 1987 are in this list. The odd one out is *Communique*. Three albums each by the Beatles, Phil Collins, Simon and Garfunkel and U2 have spent over 100 weeks on the chart, and two each by David Bowie, Duran Duran, Electric Light Orchestra, Michael Jackson and Madonna have hit the three figure mark. In the past two years there have been three title holders for the record of longest stay on the chart – *The Sound Of Music* Soundtrack, *Bat Out Of Hell*, and finally, from 24 Oct 1987, Fleetwood Mac's *Rumours*, which has now enjoyed almost eight years on our albums chart.

The sales of a record are not necessarily reflected in the length of its chart run. *Off The Wall* has had a longer chart run than Michael Jackson's all-time best seller, *Thriller*, while Dire Straits' biggest seller, *Brothers In Arms*, still has some way to go before its chart life overtakes that of *Makin' Movies*, *Love Over Gold* or *Alchemy*.

LEAST SUCCESSFUL CHART ACT

Since 8 Aug 1981, when the chart was extended from a Top 75 to a Top 100, eight acts have achieved the minor distinction of a chart career consisting of only one week at number 100. These acts, in chronological order, are:

17 Oct 81 RONNIE LAWS . . . . Solid Ground
17 Dec 83 SLEIGHRIDERS . . . . A Very Merry Disco
11 Feb 84 EUROPEANS . . . . Live
30 Jun 84 WENDY O. WILLIAMS . . . . . . W.O.W.
30 Mar 85 SECOND IMAGE . . . Strange Reflections
12 Oct 85 ALIEN SEX FIEND . . . Maximum Security
29 Nov 86 SHOP ASSISTANTS . . . . . Shop Assistants
3 Oct 87 BOLSHOI . . . . Lindy's Party

There is also one compilation album which took the number 100 slot for just one week:

26 Nov 83 VARIOUS ARTISTS
       . . . . Twelve Inches Of Pleasure

MOST ALBUMS ON THE CHART IN ONE WEEK

Dire Straits' total of 217 weeks on the chart in one year (1986) is the equivalent of an average of four albums in the Top 100 in every week of the year. Only four artists in the history of the albums chart have charted seven albums in one week, as follows:

14 albums in a chart of 60	Elvis Presley . . 10 Sep 1977
12 albums in a chart of 60	Elvis Presley . . 17 Sep 1977
11 albums in a chart of 60	Elvis Presley . . . 1 Oct 1977
11 albums in a chart of 60	Elvis Presley . . . 8 Oct 1977
10 albums in a chart of 100	David Bowie . . . 16 Jul 1983
9 albums in a chart of 60	Elvis Presley . . 24 Sep 1977
9 albums in a chart of 100	David Bowie . . 11 Jun 1983
9 albums in a chart of 100	David Bowie . . . . 9 Jul 1983
8 albums in a chart of 20	Jim Reeves . . . 26 Sep 1964
8 albums in a chart of 100	David Bowie . . 27 Aug 1983
7 albums in a chart of 20	Jim Reeves . . . 29 Aug 1964
7 albums in a chart of 20	Jim Reeves . . . . 5 Sep 1964
7 albums in a chart of 20	Jim Reeves . . . . 3 Oct 1964
7 albums in a chart of 20	Jim Reeves . . . 10 Oct 1964
7 albums in a chart of 60	Elvis Presley . . 15 Oct 1977
7 albums in a chart of 100	David Bowie . . 14 May 1983
7 albums in a chart of 100	David Bowie . . 21 May 1983
7 albums in a chart of 100	David Bowie . . 28 May 1983
7 albums in a chart of 100	David Bowie . . . 4 Jun 1983
7 albums in a chart of 100	David Bowie . . 18 Jun 1983
7 albums in a chart of 100	David Bowie . . . 30 Jul 1983
7 albums in a chart of 100	David Bowie . . 20 Aug 1983
7 albums in a chart of 100	Bruce Springsteen
	. . . . 15 Jun 1985

(nine consecutive weeks) to 10 Aug 1985

Of all these instances, only Elvis Presley on 10 Sep 1977 and Bruce Springsteen for four weeks from 6 Jul 1985 held the top spot. The most complete chart domination was by Jim Reeves on 26 Sep 1964, when he accounted for 40% of the albums chart. Bruce Springsteen is the only example of an artist charting *all* his albums to date, and getting as many as seven on the chart at once. Only Jim Reeves on 3 Oct 1964 and Elvis Presley on 10 Sep 1977 placed three albums in the Top 10. In 1986, Dire Straits charted all six of their albums (one of which was a double album) for a total of twelve weeks. For seven of those weeks they held the number one spot.

THE TOP TWENTY ALBUM ACTS

A table showing the comparative achievements of the 20 most charted album acts of all time.

ACT	YEAR FIRST CHARTED	TOTAL WEEKS	TOTAL HITS	TOP TEN	NO. ONES	MOST CHARTED ALBUM
BEATLES	1963	1081	23	18	12	*Sgt. Pepper*: 164 wks
SIMON AND GARFUNKEL	1966	1034	9	6	2	*Bridge Over Troubled Water*: 303 wks
ELVIS PRESLEY	1958	1018	91	36	6	*Blue Hawaii*: 65 wks
DIRE STRAITS	1978	900	6	6	2	*Makin' Movies*: 247 wks
DAVID BOWIE	1972	829	26	18	6	*Ziggy Stardust*: 168 wks
QUEEN	1974	796	15	14	4	*Greatest Hits*: 312 wks
PINK FLOYD	1967	702	15	13	3	*Dark Side Of The Moon*: 294 wks
ROLLING STONES	1964	642	34	26	9	*Rolling Stones*: 51 wks
CLIFF RICHARD	1959	638	43	27	5	*Love Songs*: 43 wks
FRANK SINATRA	1958	613	49	27	1	*My Way*: 59 wks
FLEETWOOD MAC	1968	600	12	7	3	*Rumours*: 402 wks
ELTON JOHN	1970	597	27	15	4	*Goodbye Yellow Brick Road and Greatest Hits*: 84 wks
U2	1981	587	7	4	3	*Live – Under A Blood Red Sky*: 192 wks
ROD STEWART	1970	557	17	14	7	*Atlantic Crossing*: 88 wks
BOB DYLAN	1964	541	29	23	6	*Greatest Hits*: 82 wks
BEACH BOYS	1965	524	25	13	2	*Best Of The Beach Boys*: 142 wks
MEAT LOAF	1978	521	5	5	1	*Bat Out Of Hell*: 395 wks
PHIL COLLINS	1981	519	3	3	2	*Face Value*: 247 wks
ABBA	1974	499	11	8	8	*Greatest Hits*: 130 wks
CARPENTERS	1971	473	14	7	2	*The Singles 69–73*: 116 wks

With the exception of the **Rolling Stones**, **Frank Sinatra**, **Bob Dylan**, **Beach Boys**, **Abba** and **Carpenters**, all these acts hit the charts for at least one week during 1987. Both **Elvis Presley** and **Frank Sinatra** featured on the first chart of all. The most recent arrival to the charts of any of the Top 20 acts is by **U2**, whose first week of album chart action was the week ending 29 Aug 1981.

If we look at these top acts on the basis of the average number of weeks each hit album stays on the chart (i.e. Total Weeks divided by Total Hits), the top five rank as follows:

PHIL COLLINS . . . . average chart run per hit . . . . 173.0 weeks
DIRE STRAITS . . . . average chart run per hit . . . . 150.0 weeks
SIMON AND GARFUNKEL . . . . average chart run per hit . . . . 114.9 weeks
MEAT LOAF . . . . average chart run per hit . . . . 104.2 weeks
U2 . . . . average chart run per hit . . . . 83.9 weeks

At the other end of this scale, Elvis Presley averages only 11.2 weeks on chart for each hit, and Frank Sinatra 12.5 weeks. Cliff Richard (14.8), Bob Dylan (18.7) and the Rolling Stones (18.9) also average less than 20 chart weeks per hit album. James Last averages only 7.1 weeks per hit, but he is not yet one of the Top 20 album acts.

CLIFF RICHARD in 1959 with Bruce Welch (left) and Hank B.
Marvin (right) of the Shadows, who featured on all his early
albums and had hits of their own.

Weeks

8 Nov 58   SOUTH PACIFIC Film Soundtrack (RCA) 70

12 Mar 60   THE EXPLOSIVE FREDDY CANNON Freddy Cannon (Top Rank) . . . 1

19 Mar 60   SOUTH PACIFIC Film Soundtrack (RCA) 19

30 Jul 60   ELVIS IS BACK Elvis Presley (RCA) 1

6 Aug 60   SOUTH PACIFIC Film Soundtrack (RCA) 5

10 Sep 60   DOWN DRURY LANE TO MEMORY LANE 101 Strings (Pye) 5

15 Oct 60   SOUTH PACIFIC Film Soundtrack (RCA) 13

14 Jan 61   GI BLUES Elvis Presley (RCA) 7

4 Mar 61   SOUTH PACIFIC Film Soundtrack (RCA) 1

11 Mar 61   GI BLUES Elvis Presley (RCA) 3

1 Apr 61   SOUTH PACIFIC Film Soundtrack (RCA) 1

8 Apr 61   GI BLUES Elvis Presley (RCA) 12

1 Jul 61   SOUTH PACIFIC Film Soundtrack (RCA) 4

29 Jul 61   BLACK AND WHITE MINSTREL SHOW George Mitchell Minstrels (HMV) . 4

26 Aug 61   SOUTH PACIFIC Film Soundtrack (RCA) 1

2 Sep 61   BLACK AND WHITE MINSTREL SHOW George Mitchell Minstrels (HMV) . 1

9 Sep 61   SOUTH PACIFIC Film Soundtrack (RCA) 1

16 Sep 61   BLACK AND WHITE MINSTREL SHOW George Mitchell Minstrels (HMV) . 1

23 Sep 61   THE SHADOWS Shadows (Columbia) . . . 4

21 Oct 61   BLACK AND WHITE MINSTREL SHOW George Mitchell Minstrels (HMV) . 1

28 Oct 61   THE SHADOWS Shadows (Columbia) . . . 1

4 Nov 61   21 TODAY Cliff Richard (Columbia) 1

11 Nov 61   ANOTHER BLACK AND WHITE MINSTREL SHOW George Mitchell Minstrels (HMV) 8

6 Jan 62   BLUE HAWAII Elvis Presley (RCA) 1

13 Jan 62   THE YOUNG ONES Cliff Richard (Columbia) 6

24 Feb 62   BLUE HAWAII Elvis Presley (RCA) 17

23 Jun 62   WEST SIDE STORY Film Soundtrack (Philips/CBS) 5

28 Jul 62   POT LUCK Elvis Presley (RCA) 5

Weeks

1 Sep 62   WEST SIDE STORY Film Soundtrack (CBS) 1

8 Sep 62   POT LUCK Elvis Presley (RCA) 1

15 Sep 62   WEST SIDE STORY Film Soundtrack (CBS) 1

22 Sep 62   THE BEST OF BALL, BARBER AND BILK Kenny Ball, Chris Barber and Acker Bilk (Pye) 1

29 Sep 62   WEST SIDE STORY Film Soundtrack (CBS) 3

20 Oct 62   THE BEST OF BALL, BARBER AND BILK Kenny Ball, Chris Barber and Acker Bilk (Pye) 1

27 Oct 62   OUT OF THE SHADOWS Shadows (Columbia) 3

17 Nov 62   WEST SIDE STORY Film Soundtrack (CBS) 1

24 Nov 62   OUT OF THE SHADOWS Shadows (Columbia) 1

1 Dec 62   ON STAGE WITH THE BLACK AND WHITE MINSTRELS George Mitchell Minstrels (HMV) 2

15 Dec 62   WEST SIDE STORY Film Soundtrack (CBS) 1

22 Dec 62   OUT OF THE SHADOWS Shadows (Columbia) 1

29 Dec 62   BLACK AND WHITE MINSTREL SHOW George Mitchell Minstrels (HMV) . 2

12 Jan 63   WEST SIDE STORY Film Soundtrack (CBS) 1

19 Jan 63   OUT OF THE SHADOWS Shadows (Columbia) 2

2 Feb 63   SUMMER HOLIDAY Cliff Richard and the Shadows (Columbia) 14

11 May 63   PLEASE PLEASE ME Beatles (Parlophone) 30

7 Dec 63   WITH THE BEATLES Beatles (Parlophone) 21

2 May 64   ROLLING STONES Rolling Stones (Decca) 12

25 Jul 64   A HARD DAY'S NIGHT Beatles (Parlophone) 21

19 Dec 64   BEATLES FOR SALE Beatles (Parlophone) 7

6 Feb 65   ROLLING STONES No. 2 Rolling Stones (Decca) 3

27 Feb 65	BEATLES FOR SALE Beatles (Parlophone)	1
6 Mar 65	ROLLING STONES No. 2 Rolling Stones (Decca)	6
17 Apr 65	FREEWHEELIN' BOB DYLAN Bob Dylan (CBS)	1
24 Apr 65	ROLLING STONES No. 2 Rolling Stones (Decca)	1
1 May 65	BEATLES FOR SALE Beatles (Parlophone)	3
22 May 65	FREEWHEELIN' BOB DYLAN Bob Dylan (CBS)	1
29 May 65	BRINGING IT ALL BACK HOME Bob Dylan (CBS)	1
5 Jun 65	SOUND OF MUSIC Soundtrack (RCA)	10
14 Aug 65	HELP Beatles (Parlophone)	9
16 Oct 65	SOUND OF MUSIC Soundtrack (RCA)	10
25 Dec 65	RUBBER SOUL Beatles (Parlophone)	9
19 Feb 66	SOUND OF MUSIC Soundtrack (RCA)	10
30 Apr 66	AFTERMATH Rolling Stones (Decca)	8
25 Jun 66	SOUND OF MUSIC Soundtrack (RCA)	7
13 Aug 66	REVOLVER Beatles (Parlophone)	7
1 Oct 66	SOUND OF MUSIC Soundtrack (RCA)	18
4 Feb 67	MONKEES Monkees (RCA)	7
25 Mar 67	SOUND OF MUSIC Soundtrack (RCA)	7
13 May 67	MORE OF THE MONKEES Monkees (RCA)	1
20 May 67	SOUND OF MUSIC Soundtrack (RCA)	1
27 May 67	MORE OF THE MONKEES Monkees (RCA)	1
3 Jun 67	SOUND OF MUSIC Soundtrack (RCA)	1
10 Jun 67	SERGEANT PEPPER'S LONELY HEARTS CLUB BAND Beatles (Parlophone)	23
18 Nov 67	SOUND OF MUSIC Soundtrack (RCA)	1
25 Nov 67	SERGEANT PEPPER'S LONELY HEARTS CLUB BAND Beatles (Parlophone)	1
2 Dec 67	SOUND OF MUSIC Soundtrack (RCA)	3
23 Dec 67	SERGEANT PEPPER'S LONELY HEARTS CLUB BAND Beatles (Parlophone)	2
6 Jan 68	VAL DOONICAN ROCKS BUT GENTLY Val Doonican (Pye)	3
27 Jan 68	SOUND OF MUSIC Soundtrack (RCA)	1
3 Feb 68	SERGEANT PEPPER'S LONELY HEARTS CLUB BAND Beatles (Parlophone)	1
10 Feb 68	GREATEST HITS Four Tops (Tamla Motown)	1
17 Feb 68	GREATEST HITS Diana Ross and the Supremes (Tamla Motown)	3
9 Mar 68	JOHN WESLEY HARDING Bob Dylan (CBS)	10
18 May 68	SCOTT 2 Scott Walker (Philips)	1
25 May 68	JOHN WESLEY HARDING Bob Dylan (CBS)	3
15 Jun 68	LOVE ANDY Andy Williams (CBS)	1
22 Jun 68	DOCK OF THE BAY Otis Redding (Stax)	1
29 Jun 68	OGDEN'S NUT GONE FLAKE Small Faces (Immediate)	6
10 Aug 68	DELILAH Tom Jones (Decca)	1
17 Aug 68	BOOKENDS Simon and Garfunkel (CBS)	5
21 Sep 68	DELILAH Tom Jones (Decca)	1
28 Sep 68	BOOKENDS Simon and Garfunkel (CBS)	2
12 Oct 68	GREATEST HITS Hollies (Parlophone)	6
23 Nov 68	SOUND OF MUSIC Soundtrack (RCA)	1
30 Nov 68	GREATEST HITS Hollies (Parlophone)	1
7 Dec 68	THE BEATLES Beatles (Apple)	7
25 Jan 69	BEST OF THE SEEKERS Seekers (Columbia)	1
1 Feb 69	THE BEATLES Beatles (Apple)	1
8 Feb 69	BEST OF THE SEEKERS Seekers (Columbia)	1
15 Feb 69	DIANA ROSS AND THE SUPREMES JOIN THE TEMPTATIONS Diana Ross/Supremes/Temptations (Tamla Motown)	4
15 Mar 69	GOODBYE Cream (Polydor)	2
29 Mar 69	BEST OF THE SEEKERS Seekers (Columbia)	2
12 Apr 69	GOODBYE Cream (Polydor)	1
19 Apr 69	BEST OF THE SEEKERS Seekers (Columbia)	1
26 Apr 69	GOODBYE Cream (Polydor)	1
3 May 69	BEST OF THE SEEKERS Seekers (Columbia)	1
10 May 69	ON THE THRESHOLD OF A DREAM Moody Blues (Deram)	2
24 May 69	NASHVILLE SKYLINE Bob Dylan (CBS)	4
21 Jun 69	HIS ORCHESTRA, HIS CHORUS, HIS SINGERS, HIS SOUND Ray Conniff (CBS)	3
12 Jul 69	ACCORDING TO MY HEART Jim Reeves (RCA International)	4
9 Aug 69	STAND UP Jethro Tull (Island)	3
30 Aug 69	FROM ELVIS IN MEMPHIS Elvis Presley (RCA)	1
6 Sep 69	STAND UP Jethro Tull (Island)	2
20 Sep 69	BLIND FAITH Blind Faith (Polydor)	2
4 Oct 69	ABBEY ROAD Beatles (Apple)	11
20 Dec 69	LET IT BLEED Rolling Stones (Decca)	1
27 Dec 69	ABBEY ROAD Beatles (Apple)	6
7 Feb 70	LED ZEPPELIN 2 Led Zeppelin (Atlantic)	1

14 Feb 70	MOTOWN CHARTBUSTERS VOL. 3 Various (Tamla Motown)	1
21 Feb 70	BRIDGE OVER TROUBLED WATER Simon and Garfunkel (CBS)	13
23 May 70	LET IT BE Beatles (Parlophone)	3
13 Jun 70	BRIDGE OVER TROUBLED WATER Simon and Garfunkel (CBS)	4
11 Jul 70	SELF PORTRAIT Bob Dylan (CBS)	1
18 Jul 70	BRIDGE OVER TROUBLED WATER Simon and Garfunkel (CBS)	5
22 Aug 70	QUESTION OF BALANCE Moody Blues (Threshold)	3
12 Sep 70	COSMO'S FACTORY Creedence Clearwater Revival (Liberty)	1
19 Sep 70	GET YOUR YA YAS OUT Rolling Stones (Decca)	2
3 Oct 70	BRIDGE OVER TROUBLED WATER Simon and Garfunkel (CBS)	1
10 Oct 70	PARANOID Black Sabbath (Vertigo)	1
17 Oct 70	BRIDGE OVER TROUBLED WATER Simon and Garfunkel (CBS)	1
24 Oct 70	ATOM HEART MOTHER Pink Floyd (Harvest)	1
31 Oct 70	MOTOWN CHARTBUSTERS VOL. 4 Various (Tamla Motown)	1
7 Nov 70	LED ZEPPELIN 3 Led Zeppelin (Atlantic)	3
28 Nov 70	NEW MORNING Bob Dylan (CBS)	1
5 Dec 70	GREATEST HITS Andy Williams (CBS) . .	1
12 Dec 70	LED ZEPPELIN 3 Led Zeppelin (Atlantic)	1
19 Dec 70	GREATEST HITS Andy Williams (CBS) . .	4
16 Jan 71†	BRIDGE OVER TROUBLED WATER Simon and Garfunkel (CBS)	11
3 Apr 71	HOME LOVING MAN Andy Williams (CBS)	2
17 Apr 71	MOTOWN CHARTBUSTERS VOL. 5 Various (Tamla Motown)	3
8 May 71	STICKY FINGERS Rolling Stones (Rolling Stones)	4
5 Jun 71	RAM Paul and Linda McCartney (Apple) . .	2
19 Jun 71	STICKY FINGERS Rolling Stones (Rolling Stones)	1
26 Jun 71	TARKUS Emerson, Lake and Palmer (Island)	1
3 Jul 71	BRIDGE OVER TROUBLED WATER Simon and Garfunkel (CBS)	5
7 Aug 71	HOT HITS 6 Various (MFP)	1
14 Aug 71	EVERY GOOD BOY DESERVES FAVOUR Moody Blues (Threshold)	1
21 Aug 71	TOP OF THE POPS VOL. 18 Various (Hallmark)	3

† This includes 8 weeks at number one when charts were not published due to a postal strike.

11 Sep 71	BRIDGE OVER TROUBLED WATER Simon and Garfunkel (CBS)	1
18 Sep 71	WHO'S NEXT Who (Track)	1
25 Sep 71	FIREBALL Deep Purple (Harvest)	1
2 Oct 71	EVERY PICTURE TELLS A STORY Rod Stewart (Mercury)	4
30 Oct 71	IMAGINE John Lennon/Plastic Ono Band (Apple)	2
13 Nov 71	EVERY PICTURE TELLS A STORY Rod Stewart (Mercury)	2
27 Nov 71	TOP OF THE POPS VOL. 2 Various (Hallmark)	1
4 Dec 71	FOUR SYMBOLS Led Zeppelin (Atlantic)	2
18 Dec 71	ELECTRIC WARRIOR T. Rex (Fly)	6
29 Jan 72	CONCERT FOR BANGLADESH Various (Apple)	1
5 Feb 72	ELECTRIC WARRIOR T. Rex (Fly)	2
19 Feb 72	NEIL REID Neil Reid (Decca)	3
11 Mar 72	HARVEST Neil Young (Reprise)	1
18 Mar 72	PAUL SIMON Paul Simon (CBS)	1
25 Mar 72	FOG ON THE TYNE Lindisfarne (Charisma)	4
22 Apr 72	MACHINE HEAD Deep Purple (Purple) .	2
6 May 72	PROPHETS, SEERS AND SAGES AND THE ANGELS OF THE AGES/MY PEOPLE WERE FAIR AND HAD SKY IN THEIR HAIR . . . BUT NOW THEY'RE CONTENT TO WEAR STARS ON THEIR BROWS Tyrannosaurus Rex (Fly Double Back)	1
13 May 72	MACHINE HEAD Deep Purple (Purple) .	1
20 May 72	BOLAN BOOGIE T. Rex (Fly)	3
10 Jun 72	EXILE ON MAIN STREET Rolling Stones (Rolling Stones)	1
17 Jun 72	20 DYNAMIC HITS Various (K-Tel)	8
12 Aug 72	20 FANTASTIC HITS Various (Arcade) . .	5
16 Sep 72	NEVER A DULL MOMENT Rod Stewart (Philips)	2
30 Sep 72	20 FANTASTIC HITS Various (Arcade) . .	1
7 Oct 72	20 ALLTIME HITS OF THE FIFTIES Various (K-Tel)	8
2 Dec 72	25 ROCKIN' AND ROLLIN' GREATS Various (K-Tel)	3
23 Dec 72	20 ALLTIME HITS OF THE FIFTIES Various (K-Tel)	3
13 Jan 73	SLAYED Slade (Polydor)	1
20 Jan 73	BACK TO FRONT Gilbert O'Sullivan (MAM)	1
27 Jan 73	SLAYED Slade (Polydor)	2
10 Feb 73	DON'T SHOOT ME, I'M ONLY THE PIANO PLAYER Elton John (DJM)	6

24 Mar 73	BILLION DOLLAR BABIES Alice Cooper (Warner Bros.) 1
31 Mar 73	20 FLASHBACK GREAT HITS OF THE SIXTIES Various (K-Tel) 2
14 Apr 73	HOUSES OF THE HOLY Led Zeppelin (Atlantic) 2
28 Apr 73	OOH LA LA Faces (Warner Bros.) 1
5 May 73	ALADDIN SANE David Bowie (RCA Victor) 5
9 Jun 73	PURE GOLD Various (EMI) 3
30 Jun 73	THAT'LL BE THE DAY Various (Ronco) . 7
18 Aug 73	WE CAN MAKE IT Peters and Lee (Philips) 2
1 Sep 73	SING IT AGAIN Rod Stewart (Mercury) . . 3
22 Sep 73	GOAT'S HEAD SOUP Rolling Stones (Rolling Stones) 2
6 Oct 73	SLADEST Slade (Polydor) 3
27 Oct 73	HELLO Status Quo (Vertigo) 1
3 Nov 73	PIN UPS David Bowie (RCA) 5
8 Dec 73	STRANDED Roxy Music (Island) 1
15 Dec 73	DREAMS ARE NOTHIN' MORE THAN WISHES David Cassidy (Bell) 1
22 Dec 73	GOODBYE YELLOW BRICK ROAD Elton John (DJM) 2
5 Jan 74	TALES FROM TOPOGRAPHIC OCEANS Yes (Atlantic) 2
19 Jan 74	SLADEST Slade (Polydor) 1
26 Jan 74	AND I LOVE YOU SO Perry Como (RCA) 1
2 Feb 74	THE SINGLES 1969–73 Carpenters (A & M) 4
2 Mar 74	OLD, NEW, BORROWED AND BLUE Slade (Polydor) 1
9 Mar 74	THE SINGLES 1969–73 Carpenters (A & M) 11
25 May 74	JOURNEY TO THE CENTRE OF THE EARTH Rick Wakeman (A & M) 1
1 Jun 74	THE SINGLES 1969–73 Carpenters (A & M) 1
8 Jun 74	DIAMOND DOGS David Bowie (RCA) . . 4
6 Jul 74	THE SINGLES 1969–73 Carpenters (A & M) 1
13 Jul 74	CARIBOU Elton John (DJM) 2
27 Jul 74	BAND ON THE RUN Wings (Apple) 7
14 Sep 74	HERGEST RIDGE Mike Oldfield (Virgin) 3
5 Oct 74	TUBULAR BELLS Mike Oldfield (Virgin) . 1
12 Oct 74	ROLLIN' Bay City Rollers (Bell) 1
19 Oct 74	SMILER Rod Stewart (Mercury) 1
26 Oct 74	ROLLIN' Bay City Rollers (Bell) 1
2 Nov 74	SMILER Rod Stewart (Mercury) 1
9 Nov 74	ROLLIN' Bay City Rollers (Bell) 2
23 Nov 74	ELTON JOHN'S GREATEST HITS Elton John (DJM) 11

8 Feb 75	HIS GREATEST HITS Engelbert Humperdinck (Decca) 3
1 Mar 75	ON THE LEVEL Status Quo (Vertigo) 2
15 Mar 75	PHYSICAL GRAFFITI Led Zeppelin (Swansong) 1
22 Mar 75	20 GREATEST HITS Tom Jones (Decca) . . 4
19 Apr 75	THE BEST OF THE STYLISTICS Stylistics (Avco) 2
3 May 75	ONCE UPON A STAR Bay City Rollers (Bell) 3
24 May 75	THE BEST OF THE STYLISTICS Stylistics (Avco) 5
28 Jun 75	VENUS AND MARS Wings (Apple) 1
5 Jul 75	HORIZON Carpenters (A & M) 2
19 Jul 75	VENUS AND MARS Wings (Apple) 1
26 Jul 75	HORIZON Carpenters (A & M) 3
16 Aug 75	THE BEST OF THE STYLISTICS Stylistics (Avco) 2
30 Aug 75	ATLANTIC CROSSING Rod Stewart (Warner Bros.) 5
4 Oct 75	WISH YOU WERE HERE Pink Floyd (Harvest) 1
11 Oct 75	ATLANTIC CROSSING Rod Stewart (Warner Bros.) 2
25 Oct 75	40 GOLDEN GREATS Jim Reeves (Arcade) 3
15 Nov 75	WE ALL HAD DOCTORS' PAPERS Max Boyce (EMI) 1
22 Nov 75	40 GREATEST HITS Perry Como (K-Tel) 5
27 Dec 75	A NIGHT AT THE OPERA Queen (EMI) 2
10 Jan 76	40 GREATEST HITS Perry Como (K-Tel) 1
17 Jan 76	A NIGHT AT THE OPERA Queen (EMI) 2
31 Jan 76	THE BEST OF ROY ORBISON Roy Orbison (Arcade) 1
7 Feb 76	THE VERY BEST OF SLIM WHITMAN Slim Whitman (United Artists) 6
20 Mar 76	BLUE FOR YOU Status Quo (Vertigo) . . . 3
10 Apr 76	ROCK FOLLIES TV Soundtrack (Island) . . 2
24 Apr 76	PRESENCE Led Zeppelin (Swansong) 1
1 May 76	ROCK FOLLIES TV Soundtrack (Island) . . 1
8 May 76	GREATEST HITS Abba (Epic) 9
10 Jul 76	A NIGHT ON THE TOWN Rod Stewart (Riva) 2
24 Jul 76	20 GOLDEN GREATS Beach Boys (Capitol) 10
2 Oct 76	BEST OF THE STYLISTICS VOL. 2 Stylistics (H & L) 1
9 Oct 76	STUPIDITY Dr Feelgood (United Artists) 1
16 Oct 76	GREATEST HITS Abba (Epic) 2

		Weeks
30 Oct 76	SOUL MOTION Various (K-Tel)	2
13 Nov 76	THE SONG REMAINS THE SAME Led Zeppelin (Swansong)	1
20 Nov 76	22 GOLDEN GUITAR GREATS Bert Weedon (Warwick)	1
27 Nov 76	20 GOLDEN GREATS Glen Campbell (Capitol)	6
8 Jan 77	DAY AT THE RACES Queen (EMI)	1
15 Jan 77	ARRIVAL Abba (Epic)	1
22 Jan 77	RED RIVER VALLEY Slim Whitman (United Artists)	4
19 Feb 77	20 GOLDEN GREATS Shadows (EMI)	6
2 Apr 77	PORTRAIT Frank Sinatra (Reprise)	2
16 Apr 77	ARRIVAL Abba (Epic)	9
18 Jun 77	LIVE AT THE HOLLYWOOD BOWL Beatles (Parlophone)	1
25 Jun 77	THE MUPPET SHOW Muppets (Pye)	1
2 Jul 77	A STAR IS BORN Soundtrack (CBS)	2
16 Jul 77	JOHNNY MATHIS COLLECTION Johnny Mathis (CBS)	4
13 Aug 77	GOING FOR THE ONE Yes (Atlantic)	2
27 Aug 77	20 ALL TIME GREATS Connie Francis (Polydor)	2
10 Sep 77	ELVIS PRESLEY'S 40 GREATEST HITS Elvis Presley (Arcade)	1
17 Sep 77	20 GOLDEN GREATS Diana Ross and the Supremes (Tamla Motown)	7
5 Nov 77	40 GOLDEN GREATS Cliff Richard (EMI)	1
12 Nov 77	NEVER MIND THE BOLLOCKS HERE'S THE SEX PISTOLS Sex Pistols (Virgin)	2
26 Nov 77	SOUND OF BREAD Bread (Elektra)	2
10 Dec 77	DISCO FEVER Various (K-Tel)	6
21 Jan 78	THE SOUND OF BREAD Bread (Elektra)	1
28 Jan 78	RUMOURS Fleetwood Mac (Warner Bros.)	1
4 Feb 78	THE ALBUM Abba (Epic)	7
25 Mar 78	20 GOLDEN GREATS Buddy Holly/Crickets (MCA)	3
15 Apr 78	20 GOLDEN GREATS Nat King Cole (Capitol)	3
6 May 78	SATURDAY NIGHT FEVER Various (RSO)	18
9 Sep 78	NIGHT FLIGHT TO VENUS Boney M (Atlantic/Hansa)	4
7 Oct 78	GREASE Soundtrack (RSO)	13
6 Jan 79	GREATEST HITS Showaddywaddy (Arista)	2
26 Jan 79	DON'T WALK – BOOGIE Various (EMI)	3
10 Feb 79	ACTION REPLAY Various (K-Tel)	1
17 Feb 79	PARALLEL LINES Blondie (Chrysalis)	4
17 Mar 79	SPIRITS HAVING FLOWN Bee Gees (RSO)	2

		Weeks
31 Mar 79	GREATEST HITS VOL. 2 Barbra Streisand (CBS)	4
28 Apr 79	THE VERY BEST OF LEO SAYER Leo Sayer (Chrysalis)	3
19 May 79	VOULEZ-VOUS Abba (Epic)	4
16 Jun 79	DISCOVERY Electric Light Orchestra (Jet)	5
21 Jul 79	REPLICAS Tubeway Army (Beggars Banquet)	1
28 Jul 79	THE BEST DISCO ALBUM IN THE WORLD Various (Warner Bros.)	6
8 Sep 79	IN THROUGH THE OUT DOOR Led Zeppelin (Swansong)	2
22 Sep 79	THE PLEASURE PRINCIPLE Gary Numan (Beggars Banquet)	1
29 Sep 79	OCEANS OF FANTASY Boney M (Atlantic/Hansa)	1
6 Oct 79	THE PLEASURE PRINCIPLE Gary Numan (Beggars Banquet)	1
13 Oct 79*	EAT TO THE BEAT Blondie (Chrysalis)	1
13 Oct 79*	REGGATTA DE BLANC Police (A & M)	4
10 Nov 79	TUSK Fleetwood Mac (Warner Bros.)	1
17 Nov 79	GREATEST HITS VOL. 2 Abba (Epic)	3
8 Dec 79	GREATEST HITS Rod Stewart (Riva)	5
12 Jan 80	GREATEST HITS VOL. 2 Abba (Epic)	1
19 Jan 80	PRETENDERS Pretenders (Real)	4
16 Feb 80	THE LAST DANCE Various (Motown)	2
1 Mar 80	STRING OF HITS Shadows (EMI)	3
22 Mar 80	TEARS AND LAUGHTER Johnny Mathis (CBS)	2
5 Apr 80	DUKE Genesis (Charisma)	2
19 Apr 80	GREATEST HITS Rose Royce (Whitfield)	2
3 May 80	SKY 2 Sky (Ariola)	2
17 May 80	THE MAGIC OF BONEY M Boney M (Atlantic/Hansa)	2
31 May 80	McCARTNEY II Paul McCartney (Parlophone)	2
14 Jun 80	PETER GABRIEL Peter Gabriel (Charisma)	2
28 Jun 80	FLESH AND BLOOD Roxy Music (Polydor)	1
5 Jul 80	EMOTIONAL RESCUE Rolling Stones (Rolling Stones)	2
19 Jul 80	THE GAME Queen (EMI)	2
2 Aug 80	DEEPEST PURPLE Deep Purple (Harvest)	1
9 Aug 80	BACK IN BLACK AC/DC (Atlantic)	2
23 Aug 80	FLESH AND BLOOD Roxy Music (Polydor)	3

* Two charts published this week because of a change in chart collation.

Date	Album	Weeks
13 Sep 80	TELEKON Gary Numan (Beggars Banquet)	1
20 Sep 80	NEVER FOR EVER Kate Bush (EMI)	1
27 Sep 80	SCARY MONSTERS AND SUPERCREEPS David Bowie (RCA)	2
11 Oct 80	ZENYATTA MONDATTA Police (A & M)	4
8 Nov 80	GUILTY Barbra Streisand (CBS)	2
22 Nov 80	SUPER TROUPER Abba (Epic)	9
24 Jan 81	KINGS OF THE WILD FRONTIER Adam and the Ants (CBS)	2
7 Feb 81	DOUBLE FANTASY John Lennon (Geffen)	2
21 Feb 81	FACE VALUE Phil Collins (Virgin)	3
14 Mar 81	KINGS OF THE WILD FRONTIER Adam and the Ants (CBS)	10
23 May 81	STARS ON 45 Starsound (CBS)	5
27 Jun 81	NO SLEEP TIL HAMMERSMITH Motorhead (Bronze)	1
4 Jul 81	DISCO DAZE & DISCO NITES Various (Ronco)	1
11 Jul 81	LOVE SONGS Cliff Richard (EMI)	5
15 Aug 81	THE OFFICIAL BBC ALBUM OF THE ROYAL WEDDING Soundtrack (BBC)	2
29 Aug 81	TIME Electric Light Orchestra (Jet)	2
12 Sep 81	DEAD RINGER Meat Loaf (Epic)	2
26 Sep 81	ABACAB Genesis (Charisma)	2
10 Oct 81	GHOST IN THE MACHINE Police (A & M)	3
31 Oct 81	DARE Human League (Virgin)	1
7 Nov 81	SHAKY Shakin' Stevens (Epic)	1
14 Nov 81	GREATEST HITS Queen (EMI)	4
12 Dec 81	CHART HITS '81 Various (K-Tel)	1
19 Dec 81	THE VISITORS Abba (Epic)	3
9 Jan 82	DARE Human League (Virgin)	3
30 Jan 82	LOVE SONGS Barbra Streisand (CBS)	7
20 Mar 82	THE GIFT Jam (Polydor)	1
27 Mar 82	LOVE SONGS Barbra Streisand (CBS)	2
10 Apr 82	THE NUMBER OF THE BEAST Iron Maiden (EMI)	2
24 Apr 82	1982 Status Quo (Vertigo)	1
1 May 82	BARRY LIVE IN BRITAIN Barry Manilow (Arista)	1
8 May 82	TUG OF WAR Paul McCartney (Parlophone)	2
22 May 82	COMPLETE MADNESS Madness (Stiff)	2
5 Jun 82	AVALON Roxy Music (Polydor)	1
12 Jun 82	COMPLETE MADNESS Madness (Stiff)	1
19 Jun 82	AVALON Roxy Music (Polydor)	2
3 Jul 82	THE LEXICON OF LOVE ABC (Neutron)	3
24 Jul 82	=THE LEXICON OF LOVE ABC (Neutron)	1
	=FAME Original Soundtrack (RSO)	1
31 Jul 82	FAME Original Soundtrack (RSO)	1
7 Aug 82	KIDS FROM FAME Kids from Fame (BBC)	8
2 Oct 82	LOVE OVER GOLD Dire Straits (Vertigo)	4
30 Oct 82	KIDS FROM FAME Kids from Fame (BBC)	4
27 Nov 82	THE SINGLES, THE FIRST TEN YEARS Abba (Epic)	1
4 Dec 82	THE JOHN LENNON COLLECTION John Lennon (Parlophone)	6
15 Jan 83	RAIDERS OF THE POP CHARTS Various Artists (Ronco)	2
29 Jan 83	BUSINESS AS USUAL Men At Work (Epic)	5
5 Mar 83	THRILLER Michael Jackson (Epic)	1
12 Mar 83	WAR U2 (Island)	1
19 Mar 83	THRILLER Michael Jackson (Epic)	1
26 Mar 83	THE HURTING Tears For Fears (Mercury)	1
2 Apr 83	THE FINAL CUT Pink Floyd (Harvest)	2
16 Apr 83	FASTER THAN THE SPEED OF NIGHT Bonnie Tyler (CBS)	1
23 Apr 83	LET'S DANCE David Bowie (EMI America)	3
14 May 83	TRUE Spandau Ballet (Reformation)	1
21 May 83	THRILLER Michael Jackson (Epic)	5
25 Jun 83	SYNCHRONICITY Police (A & M)	2
9 Jul 83	FANTASTIC! Wham! (Inner Vision)	2
23 Jul 83	YOU AND ME BOTH Yazoo (Mute)	2
6 Aug 83	THE VERY BEST OF THE BEACH BOYS Beach Boys (Capitol)	2
20 Aug 83	18 GREATEST HITS Michael Jackson plus the Jackson Five (Telstar)	3
10 Sep 83	THE VERY BEST OF THE BEACH BOYS Beach Boys (Capitol)	1
17 Sep 83	NO PARLEZ Paul Young (CBS)	1
24 Sep 83	LABOUR OF LOVE UB 40 (DEP International)	1
1 Oct 83	NO PARLEZ Paul Young (CBS)	2
15 Oct 83	GENESIS Genesis (Charisma/Virgin)	1
22 Oct 83	COLOUR BY NUMBERS Culture Club (Virgin)	3
12 Nov 83	CAN'T SLOW DOWN Lionel Richie (Motown)	1
19 Nov 83	COLOUR BY NUMBERS Culture Club (Virgin)	2
3 Dec 83	SEVEN AND THE RAGGED TIGER Duran Duran (EMI)	1
10 Dec 83	NO PARLEZ Paul Young (CBS)	1
17 Dec 83	NOW THAT'S WHAT I CALL MUSIC Various Artists (EMI/Virgin)	4

14 Jan 84	NO PARLEZ Paul Young (CBS)	1
21 Jan 84	NOW THAT'S WHAT I CALL MUSIC Various Artists (EMI/Virgin)	1
28 Jan 84	THRILLER Michael Jackson (Epic)	1
4 Feb 84	TOUCH Eurythmics (RCA)	2
18 Feb 84	SPARKLE IN THE RAIN Simple Minds (Virgin)	1
25 Feb 84	INTO THE GAP Thompson Twins (Arista)	3
17 Mar 84	HUMAN'S LIB Howard Jones (WEA)	2
31 Mar 84	CAN'T SLOW DOWN Lionel Richie (Motown)	2
14 Apr 84	NOW THAT'S WHAT I CALL MUSIC 2 Various Artists (EMI/Virgin)	5
19 May 84	LEGEND Bob Marley and the Wailers (Island)	12
11 Aug 84	NOW THAT'S WHAT I CALL MUSIC 3 Various Artists (EMI/Virgin)	8
6 Oct 84	TONIGHT David Bowie (EMI America) . .	1
13 Oct 84	THE UNFORGETTABLE FIRE U2 (Island)	2
27 Oct 84	STEELTOWN Big Country (Mercury) . . .	1
3 Nov 84	GIVE MY REGARDS TO BROAD STREET Paul McCartney (Parlophone) . . .	1
10 Nov 84	WELCOME TO THE PLEASURE DOME Frankie Goes To Hollywood (ZTT)	1
17 Nov 84	MAKE IT BIG Wham! (Epic)	2
1 Dec 84	THE HITS ALBUM/THE HITS TAPE Various Artists (CBS/WEA)	7
19 Jan 85	ALF Alison Moyet (CBS)	1
26 Jan 85	AGENT PROVOCATEUR Foreigner (Atlantic)	3
16 Feb 85	BORN IN THE U.S.A. Bruce Springsteen (CBS)	1
23 Feb 85	MEAT IS MURDER Smiths (Rough Trade)	1
2 Mar 85	NO JACKET REQUIRED Phil Collins (Virgin)	5
6 Apr 85	THE SECRET OF ASSOCIATION Paul Young (CBS)	1
13 Apr 85	THE HITS ALBUM 2/THE HITS TAPE 2 Various Artists (CBS/WEA)	6
25 May 85	BROTHERS IN ARMS Dire Straits (Vertigo)	2
8 Jun 85	OUR FAVOURITE SHOP Style Council (Polydor)	1
15 Jun 85	BOYS AND GIRLS Bryan Ferry (EG)	2
29 Jun 85	MISPLACED CHILDHOOD Marillion (EMI)	1
6 Jul 85	BORN IN THE U.S.A. Bruce Springsteen (CBS)	4
3 Aug 85	BROTHERS IN ARMS Dire Straits (Vertigo)	2

17 Aug 85	NOW THAT'S WHAT I CALL MUSIC 5 Various Artists (EMI/Virgin)	5
21 Sep 85	LIKE A VIRGIN Madonna (Sire)	1
28 Sep 85	HOUNDS OF LOVE Kate Bush (EMI) . . .	2
12 Oct 85	LIKE A VIRGIN Madonna (Sire)	1
19 Oct 85	HOUNDS OF LOVE Kate Bush (EMI) . . .	1
26 Oct 85	THE LOVE SONGS George Benson (K-Tel)	1
2 Nov 85	ONCE UPON A TIME Simple Minds (Virgin)	1
9 Nov 85	THE LOVE SONGS George Benson (K-Tel)	1
16 Nov 85	PROMISE Sade (Epic)	2
30 Nov 85	THE GREATEST HITS OF 1985 Various Artists (Telstar)	1
7 Dec 85	NOW THAT'S WHAT I CALL MUSIC 6 Various Artists (EMI/Virgin)	2
21 Dec 85	NOW – THE CHRISTMAS ALBUM Various Artists (EMI/Virgin)	2
4 Jan 86	NOW THAT'S WHAT I CALL MUSIC 6 Various Artists (EMI/Virgin)	2
18 Jan 86	BROTHERS IN ARMS Dire Straits (Vertigo)	10
29 Mar 86	HITS 4 Various Artists (CBS/WEA/RCA Ariola)	4
26 Apr 86	STREET LIFE – 20 GREAT HITS Bryan Ferry/Roxy Music (EG)	5
31 May 86	SO Peter Gabriel (Virgin)	2
14 Jun 86	A KIND OF MAGIC Queen (EMI)	1
21 Jun 86	INVISIBLE TOUCH Genesis (Charisma) .	3
12 Jul 86	TRUE BLUE Madonna (Sire)	6
23 Aug 86	NOW THAT'S WHAT I CALL MUSIC 7 Various Artists (EMI/Virgin)	5
27 Sep 86	SILK AND STEEL Five Star (Tent)	1
4 Oct 86	GRACELAND Paul Simon (Warner Bros.)	5
22 Nov 86	HITS 5 Various Artists (CBS/WEA/RCA Ariola)	2
6 Dec 86	NOW THAT'S WHAT I CALL MUSIC 8 Various Artists (EMI/Virgin)	6
17 Jan 87	THE WHOLE STORY Kate Bush (EMI) . .	2
31 Jan 87	GRACELAND Paul Simon (Warner Bros.)	3
21 Feb 87	PHANTOM OF THE OPERA Original London Cast (Polydor)	3
14 Mar 87	THE VERY BEST OF HOT CHOCOLATE Hot Chocolate (RAK)	1
21 Mar 87	THE JOSHUA TREE U2 (Island)	2
4 Apr 87	NOW THAT'S WHAT I CALL MUSIC 9 Various Artists (EMI/Virgin/Phonogram) .	5
9 May 87	KEEP YOUR DISTANCE Curiosity Killed The Cat (Mercury)	2

	Weeks
23 May 87	IT'S BETTER TO TRAVEL Swing Out Sister (Mercury) 2
6 Jun 87	LIVE IN THE CITY OF LIGHT Simple Minds (Virgin) 1
13 Jun 87	WHITNEY Whitney Houston (Arista) 6
25 Jul 87	INTRODUCING THE HARD LINE ACCORDING TO TERENCE TRENT D'ARBY Terence Trent D'Arby (CBS) . . . 1
1 Aug 87	HITS 6 Various Artists (CBS/WEA/BMG) 4
29 Aug 87	HYSTERIA Def Leppard (Bludgeon Riffola) 1
5 Sep 87	HITS 6 Various Artists (CBS/WEA/BMG) 1
12 Sep 87	BAD Michael Jackson (Epic) 5
17 Oct 87	TUNNEL OF LOVE Bruce Springsteen (CBS) 1
24 Oct 87	NOTHING LIKE THE SUN Sting (A & M) 1
31 Oct 87	TANGO IN THE NIGHT Fleetwood Mac (Warner Bros.) 2
14 Nov 87	FAITH George Michael (Epic) 1
21 Nov 87	BRIDGE OF SPIES T'Pau (Siren) 1
28 Nov 87	WHENEVER YOU NEED SOMEBODY Rick Astley (RCA) 1
5 Dec 87	NOW THAT'S WHAT I CALL MUSIC 10 Various Artists (EMI/Virgin/Polygram) . . 4+

There have been 341 albums which have topped the chart since Nov 1958, compared with 524 number one singles in exactly the same period. This means that the average stay at number one for an album is 4.5 weeks, while for a single it is only 2.9 weeks.

Of the 341 number ones, 46 have been Greatest Hits albums, and 38 have been compilation albums. The first Greatest Hits collection to hit the top was *The Four Tops' Greatest Hits*, on 10 Feb 68, and since then Greatest Hits albums have spent 201 weeks at the head of the lists, about one week in five. Abba have placed three Greatest Hits albums at number one, while the Beach Boys, the Stylistics and Diana Ross and the Supremes have each had two number one *Best Of . . .* albums.

The first compilation album to top the charts was *Motown Chartbusters Vol. 3*, on 14 Feb 70, thus giving Tamla Motown the record of achieving the first chart-topping Compilation and Greatest Hits albums. Since then, a further 37 compilation albums have totalled 154 weeks at the very top. The most successful compilation album in chart terms has been *20 All Time Hits Of The Fifties*, which stayed at number one for a total of 11 weeks at the end of 1972. The *Now That's What I Call Music* series of albums has achieved nine number ones out of the first ten releases, plus a bonus number one for *Now – The Christmas Album*, and a total of 49 weeks at the top since 17 Dec 83, when the first album of the series climbed to the top. This means that for very nearly one week in four for the past four years a *Now* album has headed the lists.

MOST CONSECUTIVE WEEKS AT NUMBER ONE BY ONE ALBUM

70	SOUTH PACIFIC *Film Soundtrack* . . . . from 8 Nov 58
30	PLEASE PLEASE ME *Beatles* . . . . from 11 May 63
23	SERGEANT PEPPER'S LONELY HEARTS CLUB BAND *Beatles* . . . . from 10 Jun 67
21	WITH THE BEATLES *Beatles* . . . . from 7 Dec 63
21	A HARD DAY'S NIGHT *Beatles* . . . . from 25 Jul 64
19	SOUTH PACIFIC *Film Soundtrack* from 19 Mar 60
18	THE SOUND OF MUSIC *Film Soundtrack* . . . . from 1 Oct 66
18	SATURDAY NIGHT FEVER *Film Soundtrack* . . . . from 6 May 78
17	BLUE HAWAII *Elvis Presley* . . . . . . from 24 Feb 62
14	SUMMER HOLIDAY *Cliff Richard and the Shadows* . . . . from 2 Feb 63
13	SOUTH PACIFIC *Film Soundtrack* . . . . from 15 Oct 60
13	BRIDGE OVER TROUBLED WATER *Simon and Garfunkel* . . . from 21 Feb 70
13	GREASE *Film Soundtrack* . . . . from 7 Oct 78
12	GI BLUES *Elvis Presley* . . . . from 8 Apr 61
12	ROLLING STONES *Rolling Stones* . from 2 May 64
12	LEGEND *Bob Marley and the Wailers* . . . . from 19 May 84
11	ABBEY ROAD *Beatles* . . . . from 4 Oct 69
11	BRIDGE OVER TROUBLED WATER *Simon and Garfunkel* . . . . from 16 Jan 71*
11	THE SINGLES 1969–1973 *Carpenters* . . . . from 9 Mar 74
11	ELTON JOHN'S GREATEST HITS *Elton John* . . . . from 23 Nov 74
10	THE SOUND OF MUSIC *Film Soundtrack* . . . . from 5 Jun 65
10	THE SOUND OF MUSIC *Film Soundtrack* . . . . from 16 Oct 65
10	THE SOUND OF MUSIC *Film Soundtrack* . . . . from 19 Feb 66
10	JOHN WESLEY HARDING *Bob Dylan* . . . . from 9 Mar 68
10	20 GOLDEN GREATS *Beach Boys* . . . . from 24 Jul 76
10	KINGS OF THE WILD FRONTIER *Adam and the Ants* . . . . from 14 Mar 81
10	BROTHERS IN ARMS *Dire Straits* . . . . from 18 Jan 86

* Includes 8 weeks at number one when charts were not published because of a postal strike.

115	SOUTH PACIFIC	Film Soundtrack
70	THE SOUND OF MUSIC	Film Soundtrack
41	BRIDGE OVER TROUBLED WATER	Simon and Garfunkel
30	PLEASE PLEASE ME	Beatles
27	SERGEANT PEPPER'S LONELY HEARTS CLUB BAND	Beatles
22	GI BLUES	Elvis Presley (Film Soundtrack)
21	WITH THE BEATLES	Beatles
21	A HARD DAY'S NIGHT	Beatles (Film Soundtrack)
18	BLUE HAWAII	Elvis Presley (Film Soundtrack)
18	SATURDAY NIGHT FEVER	Film Soundtrack
17	ABBEY ROAD	Beatles
17	THE SINGLES 1969–1973	Carpenters
14	SUMMER HOLIDAY	Cliff Richard and the Shadows (Film Soundtrack)
14	BROTHERS IN ARMS	Dire Straits
13	WEST SIDE STORY	Film Soundtrack
13	JOHN WESLEY HARDING	Bob Dylan
13	GREASE	Film Soundtrack
12	THE ROLLING STONES	Rolling Stones
12	KINGS OF THE WILD FRONTIER	Adam and the Ants
12	THE KIDS FROM 'FAME'	The Kids From Fame
12	LEGEND	Bob Marley and the Wailers
11	BEATLES FOR SALE	Beatles
11	20 ALL TIME HITS OF THE FIFTIES	Various Artists
11	ELTON JOHN'S GREATEST HITS	Elton John
11	GREATEST HITS	Abba
10	ROLLING STONES NO. 2	Rolling Stones
10	20 GOLDEN GREATS	Beach Boys
10	ARRIVAL	Abba

A scene from the stage show of SOUTH PACIFIC.

1958 The American inventor Peter Goldmark was inspired to devise the long playing record while listening to classical music at a party. He realized he was always annoyed having to get up and change several 78s just to hear a complete piece. He thought there had to be a market for a single disc that could contain an entire symphony or sonata.

The eighteen albums that hit the chart in the last 8 weeks of 1958, the first weeks of *Melody Maker*'s Top Ten chart, demonstrated that Goldmark's invention had other applications. None of the eighteen best-sellers was a classical orchestral performance! Thirteen were by adult male performers with wide audience appeal and five were of show business origin – that is, stage, screen or television.

The soundtrack to *South Pacific* was number one for each of the 8 weeks, a prelude to its equally total domination of the 1959 lists. The man with the most LPs to chart was Frank Sinatra, who touched the Top Ten four times. Elvis Presley had the most total weeks on chart, that is to say a sum of the runs of each of his hit LPs. Both 'Elvis' Golden Records' and 'King Creole' were on every one of the eight charts.

The other artists who contributed to the all-male domain were Perry Como, Russ Conway, Mario Lanza, the American satirist Tom Lehrer, and Johnny Mathis. Perhaps Lanza was the closest to what Goldmark had in mind: one side of his disc was the soundtrack to the film about the classical tenor Enrico Caruso, *The Great Caruso*.

1959 It can be whispered in reverent awe or shouted from the rooftops, but the achievement is so great that it cannot be conveyed in casual conversation: the original soundtrack to the film *South Pacific* was at number one for the entire year 1959. It led the list for every one of the 52 weeks, a feat which has never been matched. 'Here In My Heart' by Al Martino was on top of the singles scene for every chart in 1952, but the important qualification here is that there were no tables until 14 November.

'South Pacific' truly stands alone as the statistical star of the LP charts, though later discs would surpass it in sales. This family favourite boasted a wide range of memorable music, from the love ballad 'Some Enchanted Evening' (an American number one for Perry Como) to the novelty tune 'Happy Talk' (eventually a UK number one for Captain Sensible).

Film soundtracks were still the leading money-spinners in the LP market of 1959. The form was only a decade old, and soundtracks, Broadway cast performances and classical works were the most logical initial uses of Peter Goldmark's invention, requiring the additional space a long player could provide. The movie versions of *Gigi* and *The King and I* were notable winners in 1959, as was the New York stage production of *West Side Story*.

Rock-and-roll vocalists, previously content with singles, made further inroads into the album field, but Frank Sinatra still scored the most weeks on chart for a solo singer. Elvis Presley was a close second, registering an impressive success with 'Elvis'

Golden Records'. The chart appearance of two LPs by Cliff Richard was the best 1959 showing by a young Briton.

'Curtain Up!', a compilation of stars from the London Palladium hosted by Bruce Forsyth, enjoyed a 13-week run, but the most impressive performance by a show business star was that of Peter Sellers, who spent 32 weeks in the Top Ten with two solo LPs and a further 5 with his colleagues the Goons.

1960

'South Pacific' dominated the album charts one more time in 1960, though not to the extent it had in 1959. It was in the best-sellers for every one of the 53 charts of the year, the only title to achieve that run, but it did occasionally let other discs take the top spot. Number one on the very first *Record Retailer* album chart, that of 10 March, was 'The Explosive Freddy Cannon', which fell in fragments the following week after giving Cannon the distinction of being the first rock-and-roll singer to have a number one LP. The second, Elvis Presley, may be a more predictable choice, but even he only managed 1 week at the summit, scoring with 'Elvis Is Back'. The other disc to interrupt the 'South Pacific' streak was 'Down Drury Lane To Memory Lane', a nostalgic effort by the studio group 101 Strings.

Rock-and-roll made great progress in the long playing market in 1960. The previous year only four rockers had charted in the entire 12 months. This time five of the top six acts were rock stars, though the majority of chart artists were still not of this nature. Presley pipped Peter Sellers as the individual with most weeks on the chart, though Sellers would have ranked above Presley if the computation included his additional appearances with the Goons and Sophia Loren, not, one must add, on the same disc.

American guitarist Duane Eddy's surprisingly strong showing in fourth place should not be overlooked. The Shadows would be the only other rock instrumentalists to do well in a year-end tally.

1961

Commercial success does not guarantee artistic immortality, as the George Mitchell Minstrels have proved. Their *Black and White Minstrel Show* was an enormous success on television, record and stage, but an entire generation has grown up in, shall we say, the dark about their achievements.

'The Black and White Minstrel Show' was the only album to stay in the chart for the whole of 1961. It accumulated 7 weeks at number one in four separate visits, while 'Another Black and White Minstrel Show' had a single mighty 8-week run at the top. Mass audiences loved the old-time performances of The Minstrels, many of whom blacked up to sing vintage popular songs. It was the dated nature of their material, as well as increased sophistication concerning racial matters, which spelled an end to large scale interest in the group in the late sixties.

Elvis Presley was the outstanding artist for the second consecutive year, enjoying 22 weeks at number one with the soundtrack to *GI Blues*. The granddaddy of film favourites, 'South Pacific', put in a final 9 weeks at the peak before retiring. It was a bumper year for original cast recordings of stage musicals, with a strong emphasis on the London stage. 'Oliver', 'Sound of Music' and 'Stop the World I Want to Get Off' all had lengthy runs with British rosters. The year saw hit honours for the well-

remembered 'Beyond the Fringe' and the completely forgotten 'King Kong'. Even the London cast of 'Bye Bye Birdie' flew out of the wings and into the charts.

Frank Sinatra continued his series of fine years, entering the Top Twenty with seven titles on four different labels. Cliff Richard had three new top two successes and one happy hangover from 1960, 'Me and My Shadows'. '21 Today' was his first number one, though his mates beat him to the top by 6 weeks with their debut disc 'The Shadows'.

1962

Elvis Presley and the George Mitchell Minstrels overachieved again in 1962. The King of rock-and-roll notched up 18 weeks at number one with his 'Blue Hawaii' soundtrack, more time at the top than any other long player that year, and he ruled the roost for 6 more weeks with 'Pot Luck'. The Minstrels led the list with their new release, 'On Stage With the George Mitchell Minstrels', and then encored with their 1960 issue, the original 'Black and White Minstrel Show'. Their three albums tallied a total of 109 weeks in the chart, the first time any act had hit the century.

Compared to these two artists the rest of the field failed to flame, though 'South Pacific' again managed to appear in every one of the 52 charts. The new film sensation was 'West Side Story', surpassing its significant stage sales to pace the pack for 12 weeks. Four unusual multi-media successes were the soundtrack to 'It's Trad Dad', the original cast albums of the London production *Blitz*, and two Dorothy Provine sets inspired by her television series *The Roaring 20s*. Further evidence of the taste for trad was the appearance of a budget album at number one for 2 weeks, 'The Best of Kenny Ball, Chris Barber and Acker Bilk'. Barber and Bilk had appeared together on two fast-selling packages in 1961.

The Shadows achieved the fabulous feat of nabbing their second number one with their second effort, 'Out of the Shadows'. They shared credit on Cliff Richard's table-topping 'The Young Ones'. Cliff managed to top the Shads in weeks on chart thanks to his subsequent release, the literally timed and titled '32 Minutes and 17 Seconds'.

1963

Beatlemania spread like a flash fire in 1963, and the album chart showed its effects. The Fab Four's 'Please Please Me' seized the top spot on 11 May and held it for 30 consecutive weeks, to be replaced only by 'With the Beatles', which kept clear for a further 21. The Liverpudlians had come from nowhere to hold the premier position for 1 week shy of a full year. It was nothing short of a musical revolution: from their arrival until 1968, only one non-rock album would have a look at number one. A field that had been the domain of the soundtrack and cast album overnight became ruled by rock. It was hard to believe that 1963 had begun with 'The Black and White Minstrel Show' still in the lead.

With a couple of notable exceptions, the film and stage market dried up overnight. It is not surprising that they died in tandem, since the movie tracks were invariably Broadway shows adapted to the cinema. When the Great White Way stopped producing many memorable musicals, album sales dwindled accordingly. 'West Side Story' was a survivor in 1963, charting through the entire year.

Cliff Richard was the weeks on chart champ this time, his total

fed by three new successes. No one could have predicted that the second highest figures would be achieved equally by Elvis Presley and Buddy Holly. The Pelvis began twitching in anxiety as the soundtracks to three bad films did progressively worse. Holly, dead for four years, had always been a strong album seller, but really surged in 1963 when the poignantly-titled collection 'Reminiscing' joined the list of his other posthumous best-sellers.

Frank Ifield proved a one-year though not a one-hit wonder, reaching number three with two releases. He never came close again. Frank Sinatra rebounded with three top tenners, including a team-up with Count Basie that went to number two.

1964

The Beatles and Rolling Stones monopolized the number one position during 1964, making it the purest year for rock music in terms of holding the top spot. The only 12 weeks John, Paul, George and Ringo were not ahead with either 'With the Beatles', 'A Hard Day's Night' or 'Beatles For Sale', their chief competition was in front with the debut disc 'The Rolling Stones'. The fresh triumphs of 'A Hard Day's Night' and 'Beatles For Sale' gave the Beatles four number ones in four releases, a 100 per cent success ratio they maintained through all of their 11 official outings, though two other issues, a compilation and the 'Yellow Submarine' soundtrack on which they played only a part, fell short of the top. No other act has hit number one every time with as many records.

The Fab Four's quartet of hit LPs gave them 104 weeks on chart, the second time a century had been achieved. But even they were outdistanced in this regard by Jim Reeves. The American country singer had enjoyed two big albums to accompany his two strong singles in the first half of the year. After he died in a plane crash in July, nine further packages made the chart, six in a 4-week period. Gentleman Jim accumulated 115 weeks on chart in all, a record that would stand until 1968.

Third in the weeks on chart category was Roy Orbison, who enjoyed the distinction of seeing his 'In Dreams' set on every chart of the year, a feat attained for the second consecutive year by 'West Side Story'. Cliff Richard had only one new album, below average for his early years, and Elvis Presley definitely slipped as none of his three long players reached the top three.

1965

For the three middle years of the sixties only the Beatles, Rolling Stones, Bob Dylan and 'The Sound of Music' reached number one, trading off in a seemingly endless sequence. The first three were the rock artists who came to represent the spirit of the decade, while the last was a show business phenomenon that came, saw, conquered, and wouldn't go away.

The Beatles began the year on top with 'Beatles For Sale' and ended it there with 'Rubber Soul', having spent much of the summer there as well with 'Help'. Bob Dylan had the second highest total of chart-toppers, two, succeeding 'The Freewheelin' Bob Dylan' with his own 'Bringing It All Back Home', but his most impressive statistic was his 112 weeks on chart. Much of his back catalogue charted in late 1964 and 1965. Though primarily considered an album artist, he also logged five top thirty singles in 1965, his peak year.

Dylan's dear friend Joan Baez shared his success, with three charters to follow her 1964 debut. Infuriatingly for chartists, her winners confusingly included not just 'Joan Baez' but 'Joan Baez No. 5' and 'Farewell Angelina'. She taught Chicago all they knew about titles.

Though Miss Baez was the front-running credited female vocalist, Julie Andrews accounted for the greatest grosses with her soundtracks. 'Mary Poppins' spent the most weeks on chart of any 1965 title, 50, and 'The Sound of Music' began a run to rival that of 'South Pacific', accumulating its first 20 weeks at number one.

Sir Winston Churchill had a posthumous Top Ten LP, 'The Voice of Sir Winston Churchill'.

1966

Cash register tills came alive to 'The Sound of Music' in 1966. If the Beatles or Rolling Stones didn't have a new album, the star soundtrack of the sixties kept the number one position warm. It followed 'Rubber Soul' and preceded 'Aftermath'; it moved back in the aftermath of 'Aftermath' and before 'Revolver'. When the latter Beatles album had shot its shot, Julie Andrews and company skipped back to the top for the last 3 months of the year.

'The Sound of Music' was the only album to spend all of 1966 in the best sellers. It was as big an international phenomenon as a UK success. *Time* reported that it had sold seven million copies by Christmas, outmoving all other stage or screen sets, even the legendary 'South Pacific'.

The musical version of the Von Trapp family story was a timely purchase in any season, not linked to fad or fashion. The Beatles' unprecedented popularity, on the other hand, had made every one of their new discs an immediate must purchase. A short period of colossal concentrated sale would now be followed by a chart decline. Hence 'Revolver', a summer number one, was almost gone by Christmas. Parlophone, wanting a Beatles product for the major marketing month of the year, issued 'A Collection of Beatles Oldies' in December. However, the fans weren't fooled. It peaked at seven, a commercial miscalculation.

The Beach Boys spent more weeks on the chart than anyone in 1966, with five long players accumulating 95 weeks between them. This success reflected their four consecutive top three singles. One album, the classic 'Pet Sounds', did better in Britain than America, reaching number two.

The other album artist of note was Herb Alpert, who garnered 89 weeks, but while his Tijuana Brass LPs loitered on the list they did not reach the highest chart positions.

1967

History remembers 1967 as the year of flower power and psychedelia. The only real evidence of this in the upper echelons of the LP charts was the tremendous success of the Beatles' landmark 'Sergeant Pepper's Lonely Hearts Club Band' and the considerable achievement of 'Are You Experienced?' by the Jimi Hendrix Experience.

'Sergeant Pepper', chosen the best rock album of all time in two international critics' polls, spent exactly half the year at number one. The other 26 weeks were divided between the recurrent 'The Sound of Music' and the first-time sets by the distinctly unpsychedelic Monkees. In a year when they had six hit singles and a cult television show, the 'fabricated four' reached the top with 'The Monkees' and 'More of the Monkees'.

JOAN BAEZ, an artist of note in 1965.

With only those four albums going all the way in 1967, it was a major achievement to get to number two. Hendrix and band did. Cream did respectably but not quite as well, earning Top Ten placings with their first two cartons of 'Fresh Cream' and 'Disraeli Gears'. The Rolling Stones surprisingly peaked at three with 'Between The Buttons'.

It was a fine year for easy listening and soul. In addition to 'Best Of The Beach Boys', records that rode the roster for all 52 weeks included the soundtracks of *The Sound of Music* and *Dr Zhivago* and 'Going Places' by Herb Alpert and the Tijuana Brass. Alpert paced the pack with 101 weeks on chart, though the Beach Boys were a close second with 97. Tom Jones had three Top Ten issues and the Dubliners, Irish singers enjoying a year of British popularity, had two.

This was the best year on record for Geno Washington, an outstanding live soul attraction. Otis Redding and the Four Tops also had strong chart performances, but they would do even better in 1968.

1968

The album chart lost its sense of discipline in 1968. In previous years the number of different artists who had reached number one, not counting performers on film soundtracks, could be counted on the fingers of one hand. This time no fewer than a dozen different acts went all the way, with occasional further appearances by 'The Sound of Music'.

The nature of the chart-toppers changed, too. Recently the number one spot had been the property of the world's outstanding rock talents. In 1968 Val Doonican, Tom Jones and Andy Williams managed to head the hordes. The Small Faces and Scott Walker enjoyed their only number one LPs, and Simon and Garfunkel tallied their first. The Four Tops, Otis Redding, and Diana Ross and the Supremes broke the all-white stranglehold on the top spot. The only black faces to have been there before were the made-up ones of the George Mitchell Minstrels. Sadly, Redding's number one was achieved posthumously. Four albums charted after his death, two studio sets, a compilation, and a live LP.

For the fifth time in six seasons, the Fab Four had the Christmas number one, this year with the double disc 'The Beatles', often referred to as 'The White Album'. The Rolling Stones could reach no higher than three for the second straight year. Bob Dylan, on the other hand, had a marvellous comeback from his motorcycle mishap, spending 13 weeks at number one with 'John Wesley Harding'.

Tom Jones had 135 weeks on the chart, the highest total yet achieved in any calendar year. Otis Redding also broke the previous high, set by another aeroplane casualty, Jim Reeves, by tallying 121 weeks. In the How Great Thou Were department, Elvis Presley only had 1 week on the chart in 1968, as did the George Mitchell Minstrels. The Mothers of Invention did better than both of them put together.

1969

For the third time the Beatles began and ended a year with different albums at number one. Their double LP 'The Beatles' ushered 1969 in and 'Abbey Road' showed it out. The 11 straight weeks the latter disc spent on top just before Christmas was the longest consecutive stint by any record since 'Sergeant Pepper'. 'Abbey Road' returned to the summit in the last week of the year, marking the fifth occasion in 1969 when a former number one

encored at that position. This statistic demonstrates the instability of the chart during these 12 months.

Familiar faces pacing the pack included Bob Dylan, who successfully flirted with country music in 'Nashville Skyline', the Rolling Stones, who managed a week out front with 'Let It Bleed', and Elvis Presley, who scored a glorious comeback with 'From Elvis In Memphis'. Other rock luminaries who led the list included Cream, whose farewell set 'Goodbye' had three separate appearances at number one, the Moody Blues, who scored the first of their three toppers, and Jethro Tull, making their only standout stint with 'Stand Up'.

But one cannot overlook the achievement of the easy listening mogul Ray Conniff, who spent 3 weeks ahead of the herd without the benefit of a hit single. Jim Reeves astonished all by registering the only number one of his career 5 years after his death. It should be noted, however, that his 'According to My Heart' was a budget album.

'Best of the Seekers' bested all competition on five separate occasions. The Australians had the most weeks on chart with a fairly feeble total of 66, three ahead of Simon and Garfunkel, who tallied their total without the benefit of a new release.

One LP most chartologists might not have thought of as a number one which did get there was 'Diana Ross and the Supremes Join the Temptations'. One LP most chartologists might have thought of as a number one which did not get there was the Who's rock opera 'Tommy', which had to settle for the second spot.

1970

Simon and Garfunkel were the mighty men of the new decade's first year. Britain's best-selling album of the seventies, 'Bridge Over Troubled Water', dominated the chart, spending 23 weeks at number one. The closest competitors, 'Abbey Road' and 'Led Zeppelin III', managed 5 weeks each. The S&G catalogue also sold handsomely in the wake of 'Water', giving the duo an astonishing 167 weeks on the chart in a single year, easily smashing Tom Jones' record of 135.

With the exception of the compilations 'Motown Chartbusters Vol 3 & 4' and the Christmas number one, 'Andy Williams' Greatest Hits', every chart-topper was by a rock artist. The Beatles began their break-up year with 'Abbey Road' and parted with their spring smash 'Let It Be'. Fab Four fans obviously didn't want to say goodbye, buying enough various Beatle albums to give the group 122 weeks in the chart, the highest total of any year in their career. In parallel fashion, the greatest American star of the sixties, Bob Dylan, also had his last two number one LPs in 1970, those being 'Self Portrait' and 'New Morning'.

It was a banner year for what was then called progressive music. The Moody Blues had a number one and an admirable 115 weeks on the chart. Led Zeppelin flew over all followers with both 'II' and 'III'. Pink Floyd exploded with a real mother, 'Atom Heart Mother', and Black Sabbath won hosannas for heavy metal with their powerful 'Paranoid'.

The outstanding performance by an artist in a supporting role was by Johnny Cash. Though he did not get to number one, the former Sun star did notch up 125 weeks on the chart as four albums entered on the heels of his phenomenally successful 'Johnny Cash at San Quentin'.

1971

'Bridge Over Troubled Water' was the outstanding album of yet another year, accumulating 17 weeks at number one, more than any other title. It was the only LP to appear on every one of the year's weekly tabulations.

Simon and Garfunkel works spent a total of 102 weeks on the chart during 1971, a sum exceeded only by the product of the prolific Andy Williams. The long-time hitmaker was at the peak of his career courtesy of his popular television series, and two different titles, 'Greatest Hits' and 'Home Loving Man', reached number one for him during the 12-month period. No other artist had more than one chart-topper this year, although three lots of uncredited session singers and instrumentalists did go all the way with budget compilations of cover versions. If anyone was involved with more than one of these productions, they have wisely remained silent.

Two ex-Beatles led the list with solo albums, Paul McCartney with 'Ram' and John Lennon with 'Imagine', though additional credits were given to Linda McCartney and the Plastic Ono Band, respectively. 'Sticky Fingers', the Rolling Stones' first effort on their eponymous label, gave them a one-for-one record. They continued their 100 per cent performance until their 1974 issue, 'It's Only Rock and Roll', only hit number two. The Stones' competitors for the title of the World's Greatest Live Rock and Roll Band, the Who, scored their only chart-topper ever, 'Who's Next', while after a year of dominating the singles scene T. Rex managed an album number one in 'Electric Warrior'. Other acts enjoying outstanding years included Led Zeppelin, Rod Stewart, James Taylor, and the veteran Frank Sinatra. Only the 'My Way' man and Elvis Presley were still going strong from the original crew of 1958.

1972

Marc Bolan and a load of other people dominated the album charts in 1972. The T. Rex phenomenon was merely one aspect of genuine fan fervour. The appearance of five Various Artist LPs at number one was a triumph of marketing.

The year began with 'Electric Warrior' retaining the top spot. In May a double re-issue, 'My People Were Fair'/'Prophets Seers and Sages', grabbed the glory for a week, bearing the original label credit of Tyrannosaurus Rex. That an artist's old material released under an obsolete name could get to number one indicated the frenzied following T. Rex had at the time. The following set, 'Bolan Boogie', also went all the way. T. Rex were the first act to have three number one albums in 1 year.

Bolan's boys were one of four attractions to spend between 80 and 90 weeks on the chart in 1972. Cat Stevens did best with 89 in a year when no one hit the century.

Rod Stewart had his second good year as 'Never a Dull Moment' went to number one and 'Every Picture Tells a Story' continued a long run. These were the first two of six consecutive toppers by the leader of the Faces. That group's 'A Nod's as Good as a Wink' reached the second slot in 1972, narrowly missing an unusual double for Stewart. No artist had ever scored number ones as a soloist and a group member in the same year, though Cliff Richard had made it on his own and with the Shadows backing him. Paul Simon came close, touching the top with his eponymous solo debut in 1972, but 'Bridge Over Troubled Water' had just stopped making occasional appearances at number one.

Outside of the 'Concert for Bangladesh' triple album, the

Various Artists compilations that led the list for 27 weeks, over half the year, were assembled by marketing firms for television advertising. This innovation in merchandising started a packaging trend that lasted for over a decade. Sales of this type of disc generally offered no indication of how popular taste in music was changing, as success was attributable to the impact of the commercial rather than the music itself.

1973

David Bowie and Max Bygraves have never shared the concert stage, but they certainly were together in the 1973 album charts. The innovatory space rocker had six hit LPs that year, the singalong star five. Two of Bowie's efforts, 'Aladdin Sane' and 'Pin Ups', were number ones, while the resuscitated 'Hunky Dory' soared to three. Bygraves scored three Top Ten entries with his everybody-join-in approach to medleys of old favourites. One of his charters boasted perhaps the most ludicrous title of all time, '100 Golden Greats'.

'The Rise and Fall of Ziggy Stardust and the Spiders From Mars' had broken Bowie big in '72. Now he ruled the album chart, accumulating an unprecedented 182 weeks on the list during '73 with the six different titles. This sum shattered the mark of 167 weeks set by Simon and Garfunkel in 1970. Ironically, the defunct duo still managed to total 104 weeks in 1973, three years after their break-up, with the potent pairing of 'Greatest Hits' and 'Bridge Over Troubled Water'.

The siblings from the States, the Carpenters, managed 88 weeks in the list to tie Max Bygraves for third, though the positions reached were less impressive. Elton John and Slade both achieved two number ones, Gilbert O'Sullivan his only one and Roxy Music their first. Rod Stewart nabbed one as a soloist and another as a member of the Faces, completing the odd double that had eluded him in 1972.

Perhaps the most telling statistic of the year is that twenty different albums reached number one. This new high suggested that even the outstanding artists were not dominating the charts as firmly as in the sixties, and that marketing departments had learned how to achieve great sales in a limited time period.

1974

Two artists who were already strong in 1973, the Carpenters and Elton John, surged in 1974. Richard and Karen accumulated 17 weeks at number one in four summit visits with 'The Singles 1969–73', the highest total since 'Bridge Over Troubled Water'. The bespectacled pianist, who had scored two number ones the previous 12 months, bagged another brace this time, reigning with 'Caribou' and the Christmas number one 'Elton John's Greatest Hits'.

Another keyboard wizard did a double. For the second successive year the previously unknown feat of hitting the heights both as a soloist and a group member was achieved. Rick Wakeman's last album with Yes, 'Tales From Topographic Oceans' was the year's first number one. That spring the synthesizer star topped the table again with his own 'Journey to the Centre of the Earth'.

Dramatic evidence that the album and singles charts had grown far apart was offered in September. Mike Oldfield held the first two long player discs with his new release, 'Hergest Ridge', and his 1973 classic, 'Tubular Bells'. The Osmonds were at one and two in the seven-inch stakes with their own 'Love Me For a Reason' and Donny and Marie's 'I'm Leaving It (All) Up To

ELTON JOHN, an ascending star in the seventies.

You'. Oldfield and Osmonds – two more different artists could hardly be imagined.

David Bowie narrowly nudged the Carpenters in the weeks on chart table in 1974, 107 to 106. In the process he picked up his third career number one, 'Diamond Dogs'.

The Beatles were close behind with 104, thanks to the year-long persistence of their 1973 compilations, '1962–66' and '1967–70'. Paul McCartney was doubtless more pleased by the 7-week tenure at the top of Wings' 'Band on the Run'.

1975

The album and singles charts showed greater similarities in 1975 than in the immediate past. The three best-selling singles of the year were by the Bay City Rollers, Rod Stewart and the Stylistics, and all three artists also achieved number one LPs. 'Best of the Stylistics' spent more weeks in the Top Ten than any other disc, a statistic that startles until one recalls it benefited from a mighty marketing campaign that included considerable television advertising.

Other greatest hits albums that went to the summit courtesy of blurbs on the box included anthologies by Perry Como, Engelbert Humperdinck, Tom Jones and Jim Reeves; mass appeal singers logically benefited most from mass advertising. The one collection that went to number one naturally as a result of the artist's current popularity rather than artificial stimulus was 'Elton John's Greatest Hits'. By leading the list for the last 5 weeks of 1974 and the first 5 of 1975, the Pinner prodigy matched the Stylistics' 10 weeks over 2 calendar years. Elton was out front on his own with his total of 105 weeks on the chart, approached only by the slow-to-fade Simon and Garfunkel, whose back catalogue stayed around for one hundred more 7-day spells.

The year ended with Queen's 'A Night at the Opera' pacing the pack. It included the Christmas number one single, 'Bohemian Rhapsody'. Status Quo, Led Zeppelin and Pink Floyd all lent the number one spot a heavier touch during the course of '75. Max Boyce translated his Welsh superstardom into disc sales with the first comedy number one ever.

1976

Beware of Greeks bearing gift tokens. There must have been a lot of them about in 1976, because Demis Roussos came from out of the Aegean blue to spend more weeks in the album chart than any other artist. The man-mountain scaled the survey with two top five entries, 'Happy to Be' and 'Forever and Ever', in reaching his total of 84 weeks, 1 more than Queen, 2 more than John Denver, and 3 more than Pink Floyd. Roussos also topped the singles chart with his 'Roussos Phenomenon' EP, the first time an Extended Play disc triumphed in that table.

The low magnitude of the leading weeks on chart total suggests that no artist dominated the field as David Bowie had only recently. This was indeed the case, as only Led Zeppelin zapped two number ones in 1976, both of which stayed on top for only 1 week. Were there a trend it would appear to have been in greatest hits compilations, with number one packages coming from Perry Como, Roy Orbison, Slim Whitman, Abba, the Beach Boys, and Glen Campbell. The legendary guitar star Bert Weedon actually made it all the way with a set of other people's hits. This information should not suggest that Weedon, Whitman, Como, Campbell or even the Beach Boys were enjoying a renaissance in singles sales, merely that television marketing of

the greatest hits LP had reached the peak of its success. Only the 11 weeks spent at the summit by 'Abba's Greatest Hits', the highest sum of list leading weeks in 1976, reflected fame on forty-five. Indeed, the SuperSwedes were enjoying their best year on the singles chart.

'Rock Follies' and 'Stupidity' (by Dr Feelgood) both reached the top without benefit of a hit single. For 'Rock Follies' the feat was doubly distinctive: the Andy Mackay–Howard Schuman score was the first television soundtrack ever to top the album chart.

1977

Marketing was the main matter when it came to getting to number one in 1977. Clever campaigns, with a heavy emphasis on television advertising, succeeded in helping several artists who had gone cold back to glory.

Slim Whitman, who had registered one hit single in 20 years, was once again brilliantly promoted to the premier long player position by United Artists marketing. The Beatles had their first summit scaler since 'Let It Be' with an extremely after-the-fact live album. Connie Francis and Bread, both of whom had fallen flat lately, had number one compilations. The roll call of artists who vaulted to Valhalla with TV anthologies reads like a Hall of Fame: Johnny Mathis, Elvis Presley, Cliff Richard, Diana Ross and the Supremes, the Shadows, and Frank Sinatra. By its very nature this plethora of platters could only be issued once, so 1977 was the peak of this kind of catalogue culling.

The only number one greatest hits album that was part of the natural flow of an artist's output was Abba's. The SuperSwedes were on top for a total of 10 weeks, more than any other act or compilation. The Sex Pistols made history with their debut disc, 'Never Mind the Bollocks Here's the Sex Pistols', number one for 2 weeks in November despite some retail reluctance to display the provocative title. It was the first New Wave number one.

Pink Floyd bested Abba for most weeks on chart, 108 to 106, on the basis of their new number two, 'Animals', and their still-selling back list. In the year of his death Elvis Presley accumulated 95 weeks with an unprecedented eighteen titles, almost all re-entries.

1978

Two film soundtracks proved it was still possible for albums to achieve lengthy runs at number one, television advertising campaigns and a diverging market notwithstanding. 'Saturday Night Fever' stayed on top for 18 weeks, the longest uninterrupted reign since that of 'Sergeant Pepper's Lonely Hearts Club Band', and indeed there were fewer number one LPs in 1978, eight, than in any year since 1967, the time of the classic Beatles release.

'Grease' was the other movie megahit, spending 13 weeks at the head of the hits. Since John Travolta starred in both films, one might assume he was on the number one for 31 weeks of the year, the most by any artist since the cast of 'The Sound of Music' achieved the same figure in 1966. But though Travolta was shown on the cover of 'Fever', earning a royalty, he did not figure in the music. The Bee Gees, whose tunes dominated the motion picture, did not appear on the screen.

The real winner was the Robert Stigwood Organisation, which issued both films and discs. The phenomenal sales these RSO albums and the singles from them enjoyed encouraged the music business to expand, an inflation of overheads that proved financially ill-advised when no similar sellers followed in the next few years.

Boney M, who shocked the system by scoring a pair of chart topping singles in the same year, also enjoyed their most successful LP, 'Nightflight to Venus'. Abba earned 7 more number one weeks with 'The Album' and managed 112 weeks on chart during the year, clearly outdistancing all competition. Fleetwood Mac's 'Rumours', America's top record of 1977, finally managed 7 days at the summit in Britain.

1979

Nineteen different albums played musical chairs with the number one position in 1979, more than twice the total of toppers the previous year. No piece of product could compete with RSO's 1978 soundtracks in terms of length of stay at the summit. 'The Best Disco Album in the World', a Warner Brothers compilation released at the height of the disco craze and supported by television advertising, managed the longest stint, 6 weeks. Indeed, Warners as a company may have been the sales star of the year, managing to place three consecutive number ones at the top in their first week of release. Certainly the artists involved – Led Zeppelin, Gary Numan and Boney M – could not have been appealing to the same buyers.

The real star performers of 1979 were Abba, Blondie and the Electric Light Orchestra. The first two names each achieved two number ones, spending totals of 7 and 5 weeks ahead respectively. Gary Numan did nab one winner under his own name and another in his group Tubeway Army, but each of those only stayed in the lead for 1 week.

ELO's mark of merit was the 112 weeks spent on the chart by their various albums, including the number one 'Discovery'. The Jeff Lynne-led ensemble had their finest 12 months, enjoying four Top Ten singles as well. The only act to approach ELO in weeks on chart was Blondie with an exact century; Earth Wind and Fire trailed in third with 68.

'Bat Out of Hell' by Meat Loaf and Jeff Wayne's 'War of the Worlds' each spent the entire year on the chart as they headed for two of the longest runs in recent times. Neither album ever reached number one, but both ultimately outsold almost every disc that did in 1979.

1980

Twenty-three different albums led the list at some point during 1980, the most in any single year to date. The number one position was like New England's fabled weather: if you didn't like it, you could stick around for an hour and it might change. Johnny Mathis, Genesis and Rose Royce appeared in quick succession, and if the rapid variation from easy listening to rock to soul wasn't enough for the catholic consumer Sky followed with a kind of classical and pop hybrid that was impossible to categorize.

With more number one albums in a year than David Bowie has had images in a career, staying in front for even a month was an achievement. The Pretenders made it with their eponymous debut disc, and Roxy Music found 4 weeks in two stints with 'Flesh and Blood'. The star performers of the year were Police and Abba. The Bleach Boys had their second number one LP, 'Zenyatta Mondatta', and scored 116 on chart in total, far in front of the 70-week sum of runner-up AC/DC. The SuperSwedes once again had chart-toppers early and late in a year, registering in January with 'Greatest Hits Volume 2' and beginning a 9-week rule in November with 'Super Trouper'.

An extremely odd circumstance characterized the spring. For the entire season, albums had 2-week runs at number one and were then replaced. Seven LPs were in the spring string. The previous record for consecutive 2-week reigns had been a mere two, so this development was certainly curious if ultimately unimportant.

1981

To find the top album artists of 1981 one didn't have to look far beyond the letter 'A' in alphabetical browser bins. Abba began and ended the year at number one with 'Super Trouper' and 'The Visitors', extending their string of chart-topping LPs to 7. Adam and the Ants were the breakout act of the year, accumulating 12 weeks at the summit with 'Kings of the Wild Frontier', the longest leading stint. 'Kings' was also one of five long players to stay the course for the entire year. It was joined by previous Adam material and the end-of-year release 'Prince Charming' to give the Ants 87 weeks on the chart, a total topped only by Barry Manilow. The American balladeer bettered the Ant total by 5 weeks. Personal appearances and heavy promotion gave him a career peak in Britain several years after he had done his best at home.

One had to look hard to find evidence of the growth of technopop, the synthesized sound making great inroads in the singles market. 'Dare' by the Human League was the nation's best-seller for 1 week, but this was before the fourth single from the set, 'Don't You Want Me', became the year's Christmas number one and propelled its parent back up the charts in 1982. Ultravox, important pioneers of technopop, re-entered for another 48 weeks with 'Vienna' on the strength of the single of the same name.

There were oddities, as always. 'The Royal Wedding' of Prince Charles to Lady Diana Spencer was number one for a fortnight, twice as long as Motorhead managed with their equally live 'No Sleep Till Hammersmith', but the Royals never challenged the heavy metal merchants to a battle of the bands.

1982

'Remember my name', Irene Cara advised in the title tune of the film *Fame*, 'I'm gonna live forever.' Well, almost. *Fame* itself proved to be more enduring than any of the young people in it.

When the BBC began broadcasting the American television series *Fame*, a spin-off from the Alan Parker movie, Cara's original version of the song zoomed to the top of the singles chart. The US label for her solo efforts, Network, did not have a UK distribution deal at the time, so the RSO soundtrack was the only LP available containing the hit. 'Fame' went to number one, and it seemed as if a quaint resuscitation of a former American hit had peaked quickly. It was actually only the beginning of a phenomenon.

BBC Records' 'The Kids From Fame' television cast collection, number two while the movie melodies were ahead, proceeded to lead the list itself. Fuelled by two Top Ten singles, this album sold over 850,000 copies by December, surpassing even the previous year's 'Royal Wedding' to become the BBC's best-selling long player.

RCA had leased the album because BBC1 could only plug vinyl with the BBC label, and they needed to establish the singing actors as a recording act. Mission accomplished, they issued a second TV platter, 'The Kids From Fame Again', and this also made the top three.

The sales success of the 'Kids From Fame' was peculiar to Britain. In contrast, the only LP that outsold theirs in the UK in 1982 was by a worldwide star. 'Love Songs' by Barbra Streisand was the year's best seller. That it did so well was mildly surprising, since it was a make-do collection with only two new songs assembled in lieu of new product.

ABC distinguished themselves by spending their first-ever week on the chart at number one with 'The Lexicon of Love'. The debut marked another first, the initial joint number one on the album chart. 'The Lexicon of Love' shared the spotlight with – yes – 'Fame'.

1983

Two of the greatest stars of the early seventies outpaced the pack this year, but whereas one, David Bowie, had already set album chart standards, Michael Jackson had previously been best known as a singles artist. Despite his string of Motown smashes the boy star had never enjoyed a Top Ten long player, either as a soloist or with the Jackson Five. He managed to reach number five in 1979 with 'Off the Wall', his solo start on Epic, but nothing prepared the world for what happened in 1983.

'Thriller' first entered the sweepstakes in December 1982, but by the end of its first month of release had only climbed to fifteen. It was only with the release of the second single from the set, 'Billie Jean', that the platter peaked. It scaled the summit three times for a total of 7 weeks and was the year's best-seller. Michael enjoyed 3 further weeks at number one when Motown's repackaged '18 Greatest Hits' proved popular during the summer. This compilation was credited to Michael Jackson Plus the Jackson Five, a brand-new billing, and gave Motown the LP sales this material had been denied earlier. This set was also one of the year's ten top sellers.

The fan fever which accompanied 'Thriller' pulled 'Off the Wall' back for a long stint, gave 'E. T. The Extra Terrestrial' soundtrack, on which the artist appeared, a brief run, and lifted 'Michael Jackson 9 Single Pack' into the charmed circle, the first time exclusively seven-inch material had been listed as an album. The llama lover totalled 123 weeks on chart, a figure that would have beaten all competitors in all but four previous years.

This year, however, David Bowie achieved a total eclipse of the chart, setting a new mark with 198. This staggering sum beat his old record of 182, established a full decade earlier in 1973. Although the chart had expanded to a top 100 during the interim, giving an artist a greater chance of re-entering the list at lower levels with dated product, Bowie must be credited with having the only real golden oldie in the year-end 100, 'The Rise and Fall of Ziggy Stardust and the Spiders From Mars'. Nearly all his success this year came in the wake of 'Let's Dance', which entered at number one. Thirteen Bowie titles in all appeared in the fifty-three charts of 1983. Ten Bowie albums were in the week of 16 July, the year's greatest monopoly.

Phil Collins racked up 78 weeks on chart on his own and also did very well with Genesis, whose eponymous album went to number one. Meat Loaf followed closely with 76. His long-running 'Bat Out of Hell' was listed for yet another full year, moving up to fourth place on the all-time longevity list. Mighty sales figures were accumulated by Paul Young, whose 'No Parlez'

went to the head of the class on three occasions, and Lionel Richie, whose 'Can't Slow Down' came out late in the autumn but was still one of 1983's Top Twenty.

Richard Clayderman, the French pianist cleverly marketed in both print and television, enjoyed two of the year's Top 100 and amassed 66 weeks on chart. He was far and away 1983's most successful instrumentalist.

The commanding position of the leading male soloists should not obscure the fact that thirteen of the year's twenty top albums were by groups. Culture Club were number one for 5 weeks with 'Colour By Numbers' and Men at Work toiled the same time at the top with 'Business As Usual'. Duran Duran only managed 1 week ahead of the field with 'Seven and the Ragged Tiger' but did stockpile 105 weeks on chart, more than any group save Dire Straits, who garnered 107 without issuing any new material.

Twenty-three different titles reached number one during 1983, more than in any previous calendar year. This was a clear indication that no single act dominated the twelve months. Even Michael Jackson's superlative showing in Britain was modest compared to what he achieved in the United States.

This was another year in which female artists did not come close to the levels of their male counterparts. Bonnie Tyler was the only female artist to spend even a single week ahead of the field, though Alison 'Alf' Moyet was the featured vocalist with two-week champs Yazoo. Barbra Streisand was the woman winner in weeks on chart with 57, but most of these were the final flings of 1982's list leader, 'Love Songs'. Dionne Warwick totalled 44 weeks as her comeback continued.

The most noteworthy variety of female achievement from a chart-watcher's point of view was the faddish popularity of a new form – the workout album. Two of the year's Top 100 were of this sort, 'Jane Fonda's Workout Record' and Felicity Kendal's 'Shape Up and Dance (Volume 1)'. Jackie Genova also charted with an exercise exemplar.

Another ingenious use of the LP form to make money came at Christmas when EMI and Virgin became the first two major companies to team up for a television-marketed compilation. 'Now That's What I Call Music' closed the year at number one and seemed certain to invite imitation in 1984.

1984

The face that dominated music advertising on television in George Orwell's dreaded year turned out not to be Big Brother but a pig. The porker was the meaty mascot of the EMI/Virgin anthologies 'Now That's What I Call Music'. These sets of recent hits were given heavy television exposure to generate short periods of intense sales activity.

The strategy worked. The first 'Now' ended 1983 and began 1984 at number one. The second moved into the penthouse in April and the third checked in during August. The three double albums spent a total of 15 of the year's 52 weeks on top, more than any individual act managed to achieve. 'Now 4' did well enough in its mere month of release to be one of 1984's Top Ten but was kept out of number one by CBS/WEA's even more lucrative imitative compilation 'The Hits Album/The Hits Tape'.

No labels had ever placed three packages of recent hits at number one in the same year. Tamla Motown had reached the top with two of 'Motown Chartbusters' volumes in 1970 and two of the 'Top of the Pops' collections of cover versions led the list a year later. K-Tel managed three chart toppers with programmes of oldies in the company's most visible year, 1972.

The success of the 'Now' formula was of a different nature than these previous collections. Tamla Motown was primarily a singles label and had only managed three number one LPs when it began its 'Chartbuster' series. The K-Tel campaigns recycled dated merchandise. 'Now' and 'Hits' promoted packages of fresh material, some still in the charts, by artists who nearly all had current albums of their own that might be hurt by the outside availability of their choicest cuts. In this auto-cannibalistic fashion leading British labels redirected the profits to be made from compilation albums back from independent marketers to their own coffers.

Television advertising also played a prominent part in the success of the longest-running number one of the year, Bob Marley and the Wailers' 'Legend'. Despite the Rastaman's legendary status the group had only achieved three Top Ten albums in his lifetime, leaving a large potential audience for a quality collection. 'Legend' proved to be that collection, spending 12 consecutive weeks at number one; the longest leading run, the film soundtrack 'Grease', tallied 13 straight in 1978.

The top-selling album of 1984 was 'Can't Slow Down' by Lionel Richie. Though it was only number one for a fortnight it was near the top most of the year, fuelled by a succession of hit singles. The Motown marvel was one of an astonishing seven albums to stay on the chart for the entire year. These 52-week winners were 'Can't Slow Down', Michael Jackson's 'Thriller', Paul Young's 'No Parlez', Meat Loaf's 'Bat Out of Hell', Queen's 'Greatest Hits' and U2's 'Live – Under a Blood Red Sky'. 'Thriller' and 'No Parlez' both returned to number one during 1984 for a total of four visits each. No long-player since 'The Carpenters 1969–1973' had gone to the head of the class on so many occasions. The eight-month gap between 'Thriller's' third and fourth stints at the summit was the longest interval since ten months separated turns by *The Sound of Music* soundtrack in 1968.

Though Lionel Richie had the year's best seller, other male artists also achieved outstanding feats. Billy Joel had the most albums on chart in a single week, six. They surged in sales during June to coincide with a visit to Britain and a televised Wembley Arena concert. Nik Kershaw managed two of the year's Top Fifty, Elton John two of the Top 100. Michael Jackson also had a brace of best-sellers, 'Off the Wall' continuing its revival. Combining the runs of his solo albums and the weeks in residence of Michael Jackson Plus the Jackson Five's '18 Greatest Hits' gave a total of 136. Even crediting Michael with only half a share of the compilation's 29 weeks would put him ahead of the second most ubiquitous act, Dire Straits, who accumulated 116 weeks, still enough to place them in the all-time Top Ten for most in a single year.

Other groups with noteworthy performances included U2, who totalled an even 100 weeks on chart; Queen, who had two of the year's Top Fifty; and Wham!, whose 'Make It Big' was one of the year's Top Five. The Smiths scored two Top Tens on the independent Rough Trade label and 'Welcome to the Pleasuredome' gave ZTT its first week at number one. Unlike Frankie Goes to Hollywood, ZZ Top had to work long and hard for a smash, and 'Eliminator' only reached the Top Ten in its 72nd week on chart.

It was not a great year for female soloists. None reached number one, though women did make the top spot as members of Eurythmics and the Thompson Twins. Sade had the biggest seller by a woman, 'Diamond Life', while Elaine Paige had two of the year's Top 100. Barbra Streisand accumulated 67 weeks on chart to lead the ladies.

Instrumentalists fared poorly. Richard Clayderman was the only non-vocalist in the year's Top 100. The French pianist had most weeks on chart, 30 in all.

A noteworthy development in lower regions of the chart was that the independent compilation company Street Sounds attained fifteen charters during the year. The devotional artist Bryn Yemm had three new albums in, more than any other British act. 1984 was itself a star. It was the first year to have three hit LPs named after it.

1985

The long distance runner wasn't lonely in 1985. Nine albums remained on the chart for the entire fifty-two weeks, and four acts accumulated totals in excess of one hundred weeks on chart. The reason most marathon men and women stayed in stride was that their albums were mined for hit singles. With continued radio exposure, the LPs just kept selling.

Astonishing records were set. After a series of UK stadium dates Bruce Springsteen placed his entire catalogue of seven albums in the Top Fifty. Never before had an artist with that large a body of work got the lot that high. Springsteen finished the year with a total of 177 weeks on chart, the third best figure ever. 'Born in the U.S.A.' was one of the nine discs that saw the year through. It wound up the number four seller of 1985. Competing with The Boss for the title of Male Artist of the Year, Phil Collins finished with fewer weeks on chart, a still spectacular 131, but managed to nab the number two spot of the year-end tabulation with 'No Jacket Required'.

The whole country was talking about the Jones boys. The Welsh chorister with the unbroken voice, Aled, had three of the year's leading hundred hits. Howard, no relation, had one of the most unusual, the first smash LP comprising entirely of 12-inch mixes. Other outstanding male artists included Paul Young, whose two long players both finished in the year-end table. Both his 'No Parlez' and Lionel Richie's 'Can't Slow Down' continued lengthy runs. Meat Loaf's 'Bat Out Of Hell' finally fell from favour when 'Hits Out Of Hell' did well, but still managed to add 31 weeks to equal 'The Sound of Music' as the all-time high.

Madonna was clearly the female artist of 1985; her 'Like a Virgin' (the third best-selling set of the year) and her retitled first album both entered the Top Fifty. As noteworthy as her own success was the extremely strong showing by female artists in general. Seven of the year's top twenty were either by female soloists or outfits with female vocalists. Sade's two albums both finished in the Top Twenty. They were in the company of efforts by Alison Moyet, Kate Bush, Eurythmics and Tina Turner. Barbara Dickson also had a good year, with two of 1985's Top 100.

Dire Straits and U2 vied for Group of Year honours. Mark Knopfler's lot put in a special claim with the year's number one, 'Brothers In Arms'. 1985 was the third successive year in which Dire Straits exceeded 100 weeks on chart, a feat previously performed only by Simon and Garfunkel. During the three-year period 1983–85, Mark's men leapt from 33rd to 8th on the all-

MICHAEL JACKSON changed the face of the album charts with *Thriller*.

time list. Despite their achievements they were slightly pipped in weeks on chart by U2, 168 to 158. Both were among the half-dozen best figures ever achieved. The Irish band were also on a prolonged hot streak, having vaulted from 20 to 375 weeks on chart during the last three years.

Richard Clayderman retained his laurels as leading solo instrumentalist, but James Last bounced back as the top orchestra. It was also a good year for what might be called up-market material, with Andrew Lloyd Webber's 'Requiem', Leonard Bernstein's operatic version of 'West Side Story' and the Anderson/Rice/Ulvaeus 'Chess' all in 1985's Top 100.

The most successful broadcasting and charity event of all time, Live Aid, achieved another distinction as the single happening that has most influenced the album chart. The deaths of Elvis Presley and Jim Reeves had previously brought many of their LPs back to the lists, but the sales effects of Live Aid were unprecedented. In the 27 July chart nine albums by acts in the concert re-entered the Top 100, four after a long absence, and twenty-one previously peaked packages suddenly surged. The act judged the finest by BBC audience research did best in sales, too. Queen's 'The Works' re-entered at thirty, 'Greatest Hits' bounced back fifty-five places, and lead singer Freddy Mercury's 'Mr Bad Guy' regained forty lost positions. U2 did even better than was theoretically possible, not only coming back with their first two albums to place all five of their LPs in the list, but entering with a US import, 'Wide Awake in America'. They now had more chart positions than official releases.

The impact of Live Aid was reflected in the chart through the summer. The craze of 1984, the TV compilations of recent and current hits, abated only slightly, with three EMI/Virgin 'Now' packages in the year-end Top Ten and two CBS/WEA 'Hits' collections in the Top Twenty.

1986

Were there a pinball machine of the album chart it would have tilted this year as Dire Straits amassed an unprecedented 217 listed weeks, an average of over four placings per week. No act had ever reached the double century in a single year. Dire Straits hit and easily surpassed the figure.

That 'Brothers In Arms' was the year's number two in sales, slipping down just one place from 1985's top spot, was remarkable enough. That Mark Knopfler's band was so popular that a substantial part of Dire Straits' back catalogue resided in the best sellers was astounding. 'Love Over Gold' and 'Alchemy', works from 1982 and 1984 respectively, finished in the year's Top 100, a noteworthy distinction in an era when almost everything over eighteen months of age goes to the back of the browser bins.

There was another artist, however, who accounted for three of the Top 100 of 1986. Madonna sold stacks of all three of her releases, and 'True Blue' was the year's number one. All told she spent 125 weeks on chart, by far the highest figure ever achieved by a woman. No female soloist or group had ever gathered in excess of 100 weeks, although there had been women in Abba, Blondie and the Carpenters, acts which hit triple figures. Even so, Madonna's 125 weeks was more impressive than any of their tallies.

In the rich-get-richer category old friends Phil Collins and Queen excelled themselves, Collins moving up to third in the annual weeks on chart listing. Though his total fell from 131 to 113 he made amends by sharing Genesis' 28 weeks. Queen

broke through the century mark for the first time while staying in the Top Ten artists list for the third consecutive year.

One sobering aspect of the year's best-seller lists was the preponderance of greatest hits albums. Wham!, the Police, Kate Bush and Bryan Ferry/Roxy Music all ended the session in the Top Twenty, each with collections of old material. Three of these artists were bowing out permanently, guaranteeing there would be places for new acts in the 1987 table. Consumer preference for the encore performance extended to slightly newer material as the 'Now' and 'Hits' series stayed strong, 'Now' nabbing the year's third and sixth spots and 'Hits' a pair in the twenty.

With 'Graceland' by Paul Simon the year's number four, the most impressive performance by a new artist was that of Whitney Houston, the 1985 debutante whose self-titled album rounded out the Top Five. This set became the best-selling first disc and most successful album by a woman ever.

Madonna and Collins were the only two solo artists in the year-end weeks on chart Top Ten. The LP list seemed the province of the big groups in 1986, with Simple Minds enjoying their biggest year and U2 finishing in the charmed circle for the fourth year in succession even though it had no new issues. Talking Heads put in their finest career outing, while A-Ha and Five Star cut impressive figures in their first full year of activity.

For the best showing by an instrumentalist one had to drop down to number 53 of 1986, 'Rendezvous' by Jean-Michel Jarre. Other distinctions included the all-star studio recording of 'South Pacific' as top classical disc, although this type of popular endeavour was beginning to be called the 'crossover' classical. Luciano Pavarotti had the best-selling album of standard classical repertoire.

A nadir of original titling may have been established by number 100 on the year-end chart, 'The Chart', though 'Hits 3', 'Hits 4' and 'Hits 5' also failed to make deposits in the memory bank.

1987

Whatever you thought of the charts in 1987, you had to agree it was a 'Bad' year. Lightning struck a second time for Michael Jackson as he once again achieved a year-end number one. The main difference was that whereas the champ of 1983, 'Thriller', had started slowly in 1982 and grown gradually, 'Bad' was a massive number one in its first week and retained its edge to finish several lengths in front. The new set was only the second package in history to debut at number one in both the UK and US charts. The first was another of this year's giants, 'Whitney', which wound up at number three for 1987. Ms Houston appeared to be seriously threatening her own record for the world's best-selling album by a woman, 'Whitney Houston'.

'Bad', in contrast, seemed to pose no threat to 'Thriller', far and away the most successful LP ever released. Its global sales at about forty million were well ahead of the immediate runners-up, including 'Rumours' by Fleetwood Mac, but that 1977 phenomenon had its own reason to celebrate ten years later. During the course of 1987 it overtook 'Bat Out of Hell' to become the longest-runner in chart chronicles, accumulating 402 weeks by year's end. Meat Loaf's historic hit had a 395 score and the platter it passed in February 1986, 'The Sound of Music' film track, held at 382.

The reappearance of 'Rumours' can be attributed to three recent developments. It became a budget album and was a more

MADONNA – top female artist of 1985.

attractive buy at a lower price. Secondly, the group's new release 'Tango in the Night' was a 1987 number one and one of the year's Top Ten, drawing attention to back Mac tracks. Finally, the continued growth of the compact disc market gave a new lease of life to many classic albums. Collectors who already had black vinyl copies bought CD versions for their superior sound.

The Beatles benefited most clearly from this. All of their original studio sets were issued on CD in 1987, and all charted. The 20th anniversary of 'Sergeant Pepper's Lonely Hearts Club Band' attracted massive media attention and boosted the classic package back to the Top Three. The Fab Four's sales surge widened their lead over Simon and Garfunkel in the all-time weeks on chart table. At the end of 1985 John, Paul, George and Ringo led Paul and Art 1021–1017. The score two years later stood 1081–1034. Elvis Presley, who a decade after his death was still selling many thousands of albums, moved up to 1018. The Top Three seemed a never-ending race between no longer active artists.

Though Madonna did not have one of the year's Top Ten sellers she was the most charted artist of 1987, her albums making 127 appearances. This tally exceeded the record for a female artist she herself set only the previous year. Madonna closed in on Barbra Streisand and Diana Ross in the race to become the leading woman in the all-time weeks on chart derby.

U2 and Queen followed the champ with 126 and 117 weeks respectively, both continuing their lengthy run of strong showings and improving on their fine 1986 figures. Dire Straits did well, too, their 84 weeks giving them a career total of exactly 900, the top total of acts still recording.

The year's strongest debuts were made by Rick Astley and T'Pau, both of whose first albums were in the year-end Top Ten. Luther Vandross made the highest first impression in the Top Ten artists section, coming in fourth with 91 weeks. In seven previous years this total would have been sufficient to lead the list.

'Now' and 'Hits' continued to sell strongly, both series placing a pair in the top dozen of the twelve months. They were now established as the longest running high volume compilation titles ever, surpassing 'Motown Chartbusters' and collections of anonymous cover versions. 'Now' retained its sales edge over 'Hits'.

'The Phantom of the Opera' made history by becoming the first original cast recording to top the UK chart. In this respect 'My Fair Lady' may have been unlucky. In the very first chart of 1958 and peaking at number two, it may have been a number one had its earlier sales been tabulated.

The best-selling album by an instrumental act came from the Shadows, whose 'Simply Shadows' was the year's 42nd biggest title. It came 26 years after the group's first hit, the chart-topping 'The Shadows'. To show how they have survived, consider that the only other group to get to number one in 1961, the George Mitchell Minstrels, are unknown to the modern generation of record buyers. The top band of 1987, U2, seemed already to be enshrined in legend. 'The Joshua Tree' was the year's number two and a biography of the group reached the top ten of the book charts, even having the audacity briefly to overtake *The Guinness Book of British Hit Singles* in sales.

THE PHANTOM OF THE OPERA made history in 1987.

BONO surges to the front of the Wembley Arena stage in June, 1987, as U2 surged up the all-time weeks on chart list.